Lecture Notes in Computer S

Commenced Publication in 1973
Founding and Former Series Editors:
Gerhard Goos, Juris Hartmanis, and Jan van Leeuwen

Roger Dingledine   Philippe Golle (Eds.)

Financial Cryptography and Data Security

13th International Conference, FC 2009
Accra Beach, Barbados, February 23-26, 2009
Revised Selected Papers

 Springer

Volume Editors

Roger Dingledine
The Tor Project
Dedham, MA, USA
E-mail: arma@mit.edu

Philippe Golle
Palo Alto Research Center
Palo Alto, CA, USA
E-mail: pgolle@parc.com

Library of Congress Control Number: Applied for

CR Subject Classification (1998): E.3, D.4.6, K.6.5, K.4.4, C.2, J.1, F.2.1-2

LNCS Sublibrary: SL 4 – Security and Cryptology

ISSN	0302-9743
ISBN-10	3-642-03548-5 Springer Berlin Heidelberg New York
ISBN-13	978-3-642-03548-7 Springer Berlin Heidelberg New York

springer.com

© Springer-Verlag Berlin Heidelberg 2009
Printed in Germany

Typesetting: Camera-ready by author, data conversion by Scientific Publishing Services, Chennai, India
Printed on acid-free paper   SPIN: 12720385   06/3180   5 4 3 2 1 0

Preface

This volume contains the proceedings of the 13th International Conference on Financial Cryptography and Data Security, held at the Accra Beach Hotel and Resort, Barbados, February 23–26, 2009.

Financial Cryptography and Data Security (FC) is a well-established international forum for research, advanced development, education, exploration and debate regarding information assurance in the context of finance and commerce. The conference covers all aspects of securing transactions and systems.

The goal of FC is to bring security and cryptography researchers and practitioners together with economists, bankers, and policy makers. This year, we assembled a vibrant program featuring 21 peer-reviewed research paper presentations, two panels (on the economics of information security and on authentication), and a keynote address by David Dagon.

Despite a proliferation of security and cryptography venues, FC continues to receive a large number of high-quality submissions. This year, we received 91 submissions (75 full-length papers, 15 short papers and 1 panel). Each submission was reviewed by at least three reviewers. Following a rigorous selection, ranking and discussion process, the Program Committee accepted 20 full-length papers, 1 short paper and 1 panel. The overall acceptance rate was 24%.

Organizing the conference to meet such high standards has been a true team effort. We would like to thank all those who made FC 2009 possible: the directors of the International Financial Cryptography Association, the Program Committee and external reviewers for their thorough reviews, the keynote speaker and panel members, Rafael Hirschfeld for his help in selecting the venue and planning the conference, Betty Gale and the conference staff of the Accra Beach Hotel, and the authors and participants for continuing to make Financial Cryptography and Data Security a thriving forum for disseminating information security research.

Finally, we owe a debt of gratitude to our sponsors—PGP, Google, HP Labs, Nokia and Bibit—whose support during these trying economic times was crucial to the continued success of the conference.

May 2009

Roger Dingledine
Philippe Golle
Tyler Moore

Financial Cryptography and Data Security 2009

The 13th International Conference on Financial Cryptography and Data Security (FC 2009) was organized by the International Financial Cryptography Association (IFCA).

Executive Committee

General Chair	Tyler Moore (Harvard University)
Program Chairs	Roger Dingledine (Tor Project)
	Philippe Golle (Palo Alto Research Center)
Local Arrangements Chair	Rafael Hirschfeld (Unipay)

Program Committee

Alessandro Acquisti	Carnegie Mellon University, USA
Ross Anderson	University of Cambridge, UK
N. Asokan	Nokia Research Center, Finland
Nikita Borisov	University of Illinois Urbana-Champaign, USA
George Danezis	Microsoft Research, UK
Sven Dietrich	Stevens Institute of Technology, USA
Stefan Dziembowski	University of Rome La Sapienza, Italy
Matt Edman	Rensselaer Polytechnic Institute, USA
Nick Hopper	University of Minnesota, USA
Stanislaw Jarecki	University of California Irvine, USA
Aggelos Kiayias	University of Connecticut, USA
Arjen Lenstra	EPFL and Alcatel-Lucent Bell Laboratories, Switzerland and USA
Ninghui Li	Purdue University, USA
Ilya Mironov	Microsoft Research, USA
David Molnar	University of California Berkeley, USA
Steven Myers	Indiana University Bloomington, USA
Bryan Parno	Carnegie Mellon University, USA
Kazue Sako	NEC, Japan
Len Sassaman	K.U. Leuven, Belgium
Radu Sion	Stony Brook University, USA
Jessica Staddon	Palo Alto Research Center, USA
Paul Syverson	Naval Research Lab, USA
Patrick Tsang	Dartmouth College, USA

External Reviewers

Toshinori Araki
Chris Arnold
Man Ho Au
Ali Bagherzandi
Adam Barth
Eric Chan-Tin
Sherman S.M. Chow
Jun Furukawa
Weili Han
Rob Jansen
Ari Juels
Marcelo Kaihara
Ponnurangam Kumaraguru
Jiangtao Li
Zi Lin
Xiaomin Liu
Karsten Loesing
Ziqing Mao
Nick Mathewson

Jon McLachlan
Ian Molloy
Steven Murdoch
Meredith L. Patterson
Serdar Pehlivanoglu
Eleanor Rieffel
Sasha Romanosky
Stuart Schechter
Elaine Shi
Vitaly Shmatikov
Sara 'Scout' Sinclair
Diana Smetters
Sid Stamm
Isamu Teranishi
Carmela Troncoso
Eugene Vasserman
Nicholas Weaver
Hong-Sheng Zhou

Sponsors

PGP (Silver)
Google (Bronze)
HP Labs (Bronze)
Nokia (Bronze)
Bibit (In kind)

Table of Contents

Mitigating Inadvertent Insider Threats with Incentives

Debin Liu, XiaoFeng Wang, and L. Jean Camp

School of Informatics, Indiana University

Abstract. Inadvertent insiders are trusted insiders who do not have malicious intent (as with malicious insiders) but do not responsibly managing security. The result is often enabling a malicious outsider to use the privileges of the inattentive insider to implement an insider attack. This risk is as old as conversion of a weak user password into root access, but the term inadvertent insider is recently coined to identify the link between the behavior and the vulnerability. In this paper, we propose to mitigate this threat using a novel *risk budget* mechanism that offers incentives to an insider to behave according to the risk posture set by the organization. We propose assigning an insider a risk budget, which is a specific allocation of risk points, allowing employees to take a finite number of risk-seeking choice. In this way, the employee can complete her tasks without subverting the security system, as with absolute prohibitions. In the end, the organization penalizes the insider if she fails to accomplish her task within the budget while rewards her in the presence of a surplus. Most importantly. the risk budget requires that the user make conscious visible choices to take electronic risks. We describe the theory behind the system, including specific work on the insider threats. We evaluated this approach using human-subject experiments, which demonstrate the effectiveness of our risk budget mechanism. We also present a game theoretic analysis of the mechanism.

Keywords: Insider Threat, Incentive Engineering, Human Subject, Game Theory.

1   Introduction

Organizations have long been struggling with the dilemma of how to protect themselves from those parties they must trust in the ordinary course of business. These parties, called insiders, include employees, contractors, consultants and others who have access to critical aspects of the organization. An insiders privileged position gives him the opportunity to easily abuse organizational trust for personal gain. This creates a grave risk to the confidentiality, integrity and availability of critical information assets. For example, the National Association of State Chief Information Officers [1] reports 80% of publicized data breaches came from organizational threats instead of outside threats in 2006, and in 2005, more than half were attributed to insider threats. Another report from [2] estimates around half of survey participants experienced an insider incident in 2007.

Generally speaking, there are two types of insider threats based on the insiders' intents. Malicious insiders are individuals with varying degrees of harmful intentions. Inadvertent insiders are the individuals who do not have malicious intent. The E-Crime

R. Dingledine and P. Golle (Eds.): FC 2009, LNCS 5628, pp. 1–16, 2009.

Watch survey investigates insider malicious attacks, but most IT experts agree that most leaks of information and security breaches are not criminal but the result of accidents and human errors [3]. According to the Department of Commerce, U.S. businesses use more than 76 million PCs and laptops. There are 200 million business users of Microsoft Office worldwide. They send over 100 million documents via email daily [4]. And this is only the information shared over email, and does not consider any other electronic means. Undeniably, much of this data is work-related and requires transmission. Yet, for that which is not, the risk to the organization is invisible to the insider making the decision to take an electronic risk.

In this paper we focus on how to mitigate inadvertent insider threats. Inadvertent insiders are usually defined as inattentive, complacent, or untrained people who require authorization and access to an information system in order to perform their jobs. Such people may not realize the risks incumbent to having access to their system resources. For example, they are operating in a network-centric environment, that creates the possibility that a virus downloaded to one computer could infect a myriad of other computers connected to the same network. Some have jobs that are dominated by routine activities. As their tasks become more mundane, the likelihood will increase that a complacent user may not fully appreciate the potential consequences should an error lead to the leaking of sensitive information [5] [6]. Even a person with significant experience in computing may not have an appreciation for security risks. For example, an individual employee may not understand the value of updating anti-virus signatures on a regular basis. For untrained users, it is not a matter of intending to do harm, it is a matter of not having the requisite information to make informed choices about security.

Risk communication has the potential to mitigate the inadvertent insider threats [4]. A properly designed warning message could help an inadvertent insider understand the potential risk of their actions. A reliable informative alert can reduce the possibility that a complacent user makes a mistake when his activity is risky. With the detailed information, an untrained user can receive educational information from the risk communication and make an informed choice. Yet even excellent risk communication is no panacea to the inadvertent insider threats. Previous research has shown that even a well-delivered risk communication message cannot fully educate and inform most common users [7]. To many people, such risk communication messages are annoying rather than thankworthy.

Thus the problem of the inadvertent insider is two fold. First the individual does not know of the risk and may reject or avoid risk communication. Second, the incentives are incorrectly aligned for the individual insider. The insider or employee wants to keep his or her job. The insider wants to finish the tasks assigned without being interrupted to update an application; or even forced to seek entertainment at alternative sites.

Given that the insiders are usually rational and motivated by realizing their personal gains [8], we believe incentive modeling can help us understand an inadvertent insiders motives and strategies. We consider the following scenario. An inadvertent insider is about to download a football sport screensaver to his company computer. There are two websites offering free downloads of such screensavers. One of them is rated as "high risk website containing adware, spyware and viruses download" by security vendors while the other one is rated as low risk. Although some messages may pop up and warn the user to keep away from that risky website, he may still visit the risky website regardless of any risk caused by his download posed to his company computer system. Currently browser-centric warnings would be identical for both websites. As an inadvertent insider, the user is only motivated by his personal gain, in this case the sport screensaver. Thus he decides to ignore the risk-warning message. In other words, the risk communication is not effective.

In our scenario, the cost of downloading from a risky website is born by the company rather than the user, and there is no incentive for the user to take risk communication seriously and worry about any potential risk caused by his actions. In this paper, we propose to shift the cost of risk from the organization to the inadvertent insider. By using incentive engineering, we designed a mechanism to encourage the users to self-manage their risks, discourage the users against their risky activities, and thus mitigate the inadvertent insider threats. Our approach gives each user a bucket of risk points called risk budget, and every move the user takes could cost him some points. If the user runs out of his budget before having his job done, he could be subject to certain penalty from his organization. On the other hand, if he behaves prudently and finishes his task before using up his points, the organization can reward him. The assignment of risk budgets is determined by the natures of individual positions. Our research shows that such a simple approach turns out to be very effective at suppressing irresponsible behaviors, according to our experimental studies. We also analyzed our approach using game theory.

The rest of the paper is organized as follows. Section 2 reviews the related work. In Section 3, we introduce our risk budget mechanism, and move on to describe human-subject experiments that evaluated our approach in Section 4 and Section 5. A game theoretic analysis is presented in Section 6 for better understanding of our mechanism. We conclude the paper and describe the future work in Section 7.

2 Related Work

The apparent irrationality of end users in choosing with whom to share information creates inadvertent insiders. The inadvertent insider can be informed by incentive mechanisms and deterred from making risky choices. The incentives have to be aligned with the interests of the users [9] [10]. For example, security incentives that prevent users from performing critical tasks will be ignored or disabled.

The core research challenge our design addresses is how to engineer incentives so either the risk behaviors incur some cost, or enable the end user to detect the security costs of a misbehaving account. Essentially the research question is how to encourage users not be risk-seeking (e.g., inadvertent insiders) by utilizing incentives.

Solutions to the problem of inadvertent insiders have included insurance that correlates with security practices [11], changing defaults so that security is difficult to avoid [12], more careful accounting of actual costs [13] and improved system usability [14] [15]. It is the core contention of the proposed research agenda that there is a clear and profound need for effective risk communication. While there have been studies of user conceptions of privacy [16] [17] and usable security [18]; these have focused on system design rather than contextual behaviors.

We assert that effective security communication is critical for handling the problem of the inadvertent insider. Changing behavior requires both communicating security information and motivating the appropriate security behaviors. The essential point is that the purpose of security communication is not conveying the perfect truth to the users, but rather to prompt them to take an appropriate action to defend their system against a certain threat [9] [10]. Mitigation of security risks that are behavior-based do not require that the user have knowledge of the risk, but rather a general idea of the nature of that risk.

For the inadvertent insider considering violating security policy, the risks corresponding to the policy-forbidden actions are rarely clearly identified. In no case is there an indicator of risk-averse action that might be taken in order to reduce the risks should the user choose the particular action [19]. For example, if users choose to subvert a policy by using public email providers (e.g. Gmail) to share documents, there is no education about readily available encryption options. Yet a communication about the risks of sending documents and the option of encryption could be included should the employee go to a free email site. The efficacy of incentive technologies is to some degree a function of the assumptions of human risk behaviors in the network [20]. We will design and build our incentive mechanisms upon foundational insights that have emerged from studies on human-computer interaction and game theoretic studies of behavior.

The combination of game theory, incentives, and human interaction is what makes this work unique. In comparison, [21] proposed an access control system that used a market to distribute access tokens where the price may be set by the data owner. In this case, the response is statics and the system does not evaluate the responses in order to identify the nature of user. Nor does the system embed risk communication or risk mitigation. Horizontal Integration [22] proposes the use of risk tokens and risk calculations to manage access control. Tokens are distributed to employees in a hierarchical approach, by the organization. Again, employees trade tokens for access. Similarly the system does not use any game theoretical pricing, does not address user behavioral history, and ignores issues of risk mitigation and communication. [23] describes the mechanisms for distributing risk token to employees for access control. While these proposal use an approach that is conceptually similar to the risk budget concept, none of these approaches offers the employers opportunities for risk mitigation. Nor do the approaches engage the benign employee in risk communication in order to enable a more informed decision by the employee. But the most significant difference between the proposed research and the work described here is that we conceptualize the use of resources as a game, with different types of players. For example, in the systems above, an insider could abuse her the tokens for her personal gains. We add incentives (e.g., punishment and rewards) to regulate insiders and mitigate possible risk budget abuse. We also limit the possible damage, by tracking and responding to insider behaviors in a strategic manner (to the extent that the game theoretic model is solvable).

We will also build on the insights of [24]. FuzzyMLS considers access control as an exercise in risk management. Access control decisions are a function of the risk of action or access, risk tolerance of the individual requesting access, and risk mitigation. FuzzyMLS also computes a quantified estimate of risk associated with a human subject.

FuzzyMLS utilizes risk tokens in that zone of uncertainty, a fuzzy or gray area, between permission and denial and proposes an unspecified market for risk exchanges. Such a risk exchange could prove hazardous to an organization, as an insider could build significant risk rights while remaining invisible to the organization. FuzzyMLS does not address the state of the machine requesting the access. FuzzyMLS uses the organizational level of the individual to determine the risk characteristic associated with the user. The past behaviors or choices of the user (e.g., risk seeking or risk averse) are not considered. While FuzzyMLS uses the language of economics, it is not informed in any way by the economics of security nor does it embed incentives that are understandable by the user. For example, they propose using a ROI (return on investment) model to reward users who avoid risk and market to trade risk, yet no implementation or method of calculation is proposed. In contrast, we have built a proof of concept and seek support to build a more complete prototype. While there were no user tests of FuzzyMLS, the fact that the decisions are opaque to the user indicates that the incentive structure may be ineffective in practice.

3   Risk Budget Mechanism

The problem of inadvertent insider threats is that the cost of risk is born by the organization rather than the users who initiate risky activities. In order to shift the cost back to the users themselves, we propose a risk budget mechanism. The principles of our risk budget mechanism are as follows.

- Every user is assigned a bucket of risk points for his task.
- A users risky activity will cost him some risk points.
- A user will be punished once a users risk budget gets exhausted.
- The more points remain the more rewards a user gets when he complete his task.

The requirement of consuming risk points, together with the punishment and the reward, shift the cost of risk to the users. The risk budget mechanism visualizes the cost to user and produces incentives that motivate the users to avoid risky activities.

3.1   Risk Budget Assignment

We denote the bucket of risk points for a user i by B_i. The size of the bucket is determined by the organization based on the user's task description, and the organizations preference. For example, if a user's job requires exploring the Internet and visiting various websites with a potential high risk, he will have a higher risk budget than someone whose main work is database maintenance. For instance, an employee who visits rating sites and social network sites to manage the companys reputation will have a large risk budget. An employee in human resources who can access the payroll database will have a very small risk budget. A user's security preference may also be considered when assigning him a risk budget. To put it simple, a risk-seeking user will be given a more limited risk budget.

3.2   Points Payment

As we focus on inadvertent insiders, it is reasonable to recognize that all the potentially harmful insiders are not malicious and thus they only take actions based on their privileges and access. Since the organization knows the insiders access, it knows all the possible valid actions a user can take. In addition, we assume the organization is able to associate a risk rating with each action or access right. Each action the user i has the privilege to take, a_j, is associated with a given price in terms of risk points, p_{aj}. Our current research uses web-surfing activities to study the general idea of risk budget. In this case, the point price of visiting a website can be identified from the website's ratings given by various sources [12] [25]. A further study on this direction could lead to risk-aware access control, which we plan to pursue in the follow-up research.

3.3   Punishments

The incentive against risk-seeking behaviors our approach offers is the punishment inflicted on the users once they empty their risk budget. Such punishment refers to some form of cost that is enforced by the organization and triggered by the risk budget exhaustion. It could be an audit or mandatory training program or a loss of access. The budget size implies a risk limit that the organization could bear for a specified task. And the punishment translates the exhausted budget into a cost that directly aligns the companys and users incentives. The risk budget connects the risk suffered by the organization and the posted cost born by the users. As a result, the risk points spent by a user can reflect his willingness to launch a risky action.

3.4   Rewards

The punishment caused by an exhausted risk budget brings an incentive to the user against risky action. However, such a punishment only happens only when the user empties his risk budget, which can be late. Moreover, it is desirable that the user can be encouraged to choose the least risky path for accomplishing his task, which minimizes the risk the organization is exposed to. To this end, we take a measure that rewards the user according to the surplus of his risk budget. Simply speaking, the fewer risk points consumed the more rewards the user will get. Formally, we define a reward as a function $R(p)$ of the remaining risk point p after a task is completed. In practice, the rewards can be paid in the form of welfare. For example, the unspent risk points are accumulated from day to day. Once the points reach some level, the user can then redeem his points in exchange of a vacation or a bonus or a prize. Prior research shows that a combination of penalties and rewards is more effective in employee motivation than penalties alone [26].

3.5   An Example

Within the risk budget mechanism, users can no longer abuse their privileges without bearing any cost. As an example, consider an Internet commerce researcher whose job demands a daily Internet surfing. Suppose the user has a daily risk budget B_i for downloading documents the Internet. He can visit a website w_j that costs him risk points

p_j to perform the downloading, which costs him another p_k. Alternatively, he can visit another website w_j that requires p_j for visit and p_k for document downloading. The prices p_j, p_k, p_j and p_k are set by the organization based on its perception and evaluation of potential risks. Assuming $B_i > (p_j + p_k) > (p_j + p_k)$, we expect user i voluntarily chooses the second website, which incurs lower risks, under our risk budget mechanism.

4   Experiment Design

We conducted two human-subject experiments in order to evaluate our risk budget mechanism. The first experiment was designed for understanding users' risk behaviors, and the second one aimed at studying the change of these behaviors under our incentive mechanism. The outcomes of these experiments are elaborated in Section 5. These experiments were based upon a firefox browser extension we implemented for monitoring a user's web browsing behaviors, adjusting his risk points and enforcing penalty/reward policies.

4.1   Recruitment

We recruited 40 participants for the experiments and divided them randomly into two groups: 20 for the first experiment and the other 20 for the second experiment. All participants were recruited voluntarily from the undergraduates at Indiana University, Bloomington. None of the participants were majored in information security related fields. Most of them were in their freshmen year.

4.2   Ratings

We determined the risk rating of a website using a mechanism proposed in the prior research [25]. The mechanism rates websites as follows.

1. Those websites that have been previously visited are trusted unless otherwise identified;
2. Those websites that have not been previously visited are considered untrusted;
3. The ratings of an untrusted website comes from McAfee SiteAdvisor [27].

Detailed information on the reputation system itself can be found in [25]. However, this mechanism was used for convenience and in fact nearly random ratings could have been used in the experiments without loss of generality of the results. In fact, because of the nature of the reputation system, all negative ratings were a result of McAfee. Note that McAfee SiteAdvisor is a system of automated testers that continually search the Internet via browsing websites with human browsers and honey monkeys. The searchers download files, clicks on adds, and enter information on sign-up forms. The results are documented and supplemented with feedback from users, comments from website owners, and analysis from researchers. In our experiments, a participant was charged with a randomly-generated price ranging from 10 to 20 points whenever he/she was about to visit a risky website. The reason why we ask for a random charge is that we would like to discover the risk payment distribution. Such risk payment distribution will help us determine an effective and reasonable risk price in our future study on risk-aware access control.

4.3 Task Descriptions

There are arguably thousands of websites offering free downloads of screensavers on the Internet. Many of them contain malicious content, yet distinguishing between the dangerous, potentially annoying, and benign websites is difficult. Downloading active or potentially active content can be high-risk activity. Thus it was this risk activity that was chosen as the basis of the experiments.

In the experiments, each participant was asked to locate five screensavers from five different websites respectively. In other words, the experiment consisted of five tasks. Each task was to locate and select a screensaver from any website. All participants were free to choose any website to surf and download the requested screensavers. They had multiple choices to complete their tasks.

Following are the detailed instructions these participants received:

1. Search for the websites offering free screen savers downloads from the web.
2. From the search results, choose five websites: website-1, website-2, website-3, website-4 and website-5.
3. From website-1, please take a screenshot of an animal screensaver.
4. From website-2, please take a screenshot of a nature screensaver.
5. From website-3, please take a screenshot of a sport screensaver.
6. From website-4, please take a screenshot of a space screensaver.
7. From website-5, please take a screenshot of a flower screensaver.
8. Thank you. You have completed the experiment.

The goal was to create a somewhat mundane set of tasks when the completion of the task resulted in immediate payment. Rather than testing the security interaction as if security were the goal, our experimental design was to create a set of tasks that are orthogonal (or even in opposition to) security.

4.4 Experiment One

In the first experiment, the participants were asked to pick five different websites from their previous search results as described above. All websites were rated according to the security vendors websites risk ratings [12] [25]. A website was considered high risk if it were rated as "high risk website containing adware, spyware and viruses download". When a participant clicked on the link of a high risk website, a warning message appeared. Such warning messages communicated with participants about the potential risks of the website and asked for their confirmation. A screenshot of the warning message is shown in Figure 1.

Certainly others have documented the general tendency to swat security boxes out of the way in order to complete tasks. Determining the prevalence of this behavior and ensuring consistency of the wording of the messages were critical reasons for this first experiment.

Fig. 1. The Screenshot of The Warning Message in Experiment One

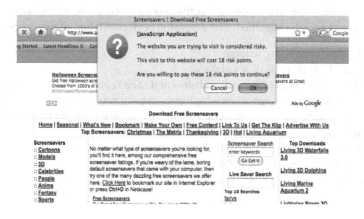

Fig. 2. The Screenshot of The Warning Message in Experiment Two

We recorded the browsing history, the participants responses to the warning messages and the time used for completing the task. The outcomes of the experiment, designated as data set R1, is presented as a baseline of local users' risk behaviors.

4.5 Experiment Two

In the second experiment, every participant was given an identical initial risk budget. If a website was tagged as high risk, it was then associated with a risk price from our rating mechanism. This second set of 20 participants was asked to complete the same task under the additional constraint of their risk budgets. If they successfully accomplished their tasks, they received $10 plus an additional amount based on the risk budget. If any participant exhausted a risk budget, that participant forfeited their compensation. In addition, if any participant failed to complete the experiment, that participant would similarly forfeit compensation.

Participants were also rewarded with risk budget surplus with a bonus, whose amount depended on the amount of points left in his bucket. For instance, a participant who saves 20 points receives $10 for completing his task and an additional $2 for the saving. The formula we used to calculate the bonus is $10 \times (B - P_c)/B$, where B is the budget size and P_c is the points consumed in the experiment. Thus participants could make up to $20 and a little as nothing. When a participant clicked on the URL of a high risk website, a warning message appeared. The warning contained not only the same text as the previous warning but also an indicator of the risk cost for the visit. A screenshot of the warning message is shown in Figure 2.

As with the first experiment we recorded the participants browsing history, their responses to the warning messages, and the total time used for completing the task. In addition we recorded prices (in risk points) paid for web activities, and the risk points remaining when the task was complete. The set of results is denoted as R2.

4.6   Firefox Browser Extension

Both experiments were based upon a Firefox browser extension, which was triggered whenever a browser was launched. The extension performed the following operations:

1. Detect a new page being loaded;
2. Check the domain name of a webpage;
3. Maintain a list of target high risk websites and their reputations according to [25];
4. Pop up a warning message when a high risk website was visited;
5. Ask for confirmation and or rejection of the visit choice from the participant;
6. Record the response;
   (In experiment two, the extension also took the following actions:)
7. Generate a price based on a website's reputation;
8. Track of participants risk budgets.

5   Data Analysis

We recorded the results of Experiment one, R1 and Experiment two,R2, as noted above. These data consists of participants browsing history, their responses to each pop-up warning message and the time they spent to accomplish their tasks. Furthermore, R2 also contains participants' payments for risky websites in terms of risk points and their risk budgets. A snippet of R1 and R2 is shown in Figure 3. At the end of each record is the time that a participant took to complete the experiment. The notation "@Y@" indicates a decision to perform a risky activity, for example, visiting a dangerous website, and "N" points to the action that avoids potential risks, for example, refraining from surfing dangerous sites. In R2, the numbers posterior to these notations is the prices a participant paid in the experiment and his remaining risk points.

5.1   Risk Behaviors

During the first experiment, the first group of participants received 104 pop-up warning messages in total. In the second experiment, there were 106 pop-ups for the other 20

R1

......

www.google.com,www.google.com,images.google.com,www.freesaver.com,coolscreensavers.googlepages.com,www.tnpsc.com,@Y@,www.google.com,ww
w.fabuloussavers.com,@Y@,www.fabuloussavers.com,@Y@,www.google.com,www.space-screensavers.com,@Y@,www.google.com,www.3d-screensaver-
downloads.com,www.3d-screensaver-downloads.com,,www.google.com,www.freesaver.com,Monday, October 13, 2008,7:52:13,5

......

R2

......

www.google.com,www.google.com,www.freesaver.com,www.google.com,www.webshots.com,www.google.com,www.scenicreflections.com,N,
13,188,www.google.com,www.google.com,www.google.com,www.google.com,findarticles.com,fbgdc.com,popularscreensavers.smileycentral.com,ww
w.widgetworld.nl,www.google.com,www.sports-logos-screensavers.com,@Y@,17,83,www.google.com,www.space-screensavers.com,N,
15,83,www.google.com,N,11,83,www.google.com,www.google.com,www.3deepspace.com,www.google.com,www.thegardenhelper.com,83,Sunday,
October 12, 2008,10:33:31,6

......

Fig. 3. The snippet of R1 and R2

participants. In other words, to complete the same task, the participants in both experiments encountered statistically similar numbers of risk warnings. However, their risk behaviors were significantly different. Among 104 warning messages, the participants in Experiment one made 81 risk-seeking decisions (i.e., continuing to visit dangerous websites) and 23 risk-averse decisions (i.e., avoiding risk websites). Under our risk budget mechanism, the participants in Experiment two responded with 11 confirmations of risk-seeking behaviors and 95 responses of risk-averse behaviors. The following figures show their risk behavior distributions.

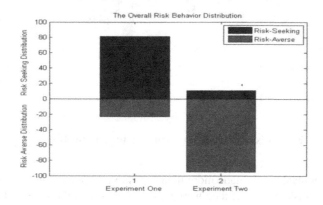

Fig. 4. Differences of Risk Behavior Distributions in two experiments

From these figures, we can observe the significant impact our mechanism can exert on users to suppress their risk-seeking behaviors. Through issuing proper rewards and penalties, the risk budget approach shifted the participants' risk behaviors from a strong preference of risk seeking to a strong preference of risk averse.

5.2   Risk Boundary

There were 11 positive responses from participants that confirmed risk-seeking behaviors in Experiment two. The average payment made by those who chose to bear risks was merely 16 points. This is in a stark contrast to what happened in Experiment one,

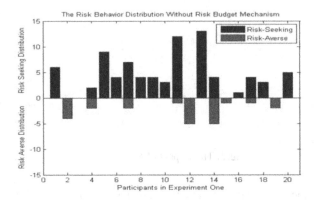

Fig. 5. Risk Behavior Distributions in Experiment One

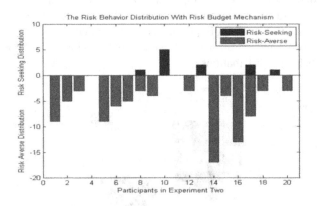

Fig. 6. Risk Behavior Distributions in Experiment Two

where 20% participants each made more than 7 positive responses, which amounts to depletion of their risk budgets if they were assigned ones with the sizes of those used in Experiment two. In Experiment two, we actually did not observe any participants failed the task and exhausted their risk budgets. These experimental results clearly indicate that penalty and rewards based upon risk budgets can effectively motivates users against abuse of their privileges. Meanwhile such an incentive helps establish a boundary for organizations and helps them to manage their risk.

5.3   Regulation Friction

The results of Experiment one show that without any incentive users are not willing to change their behaviors. We consider this is caused by a regulation friction that defines the efforts made by the users to adopt a risk-averse strategy instead of a risk-seeking strategy. In our experiments, we measured this regulation friction using time interval.

The average time interval for completing the task in Experiment one is 5 minuets and 45 seconds. It becomes 6 minuets in Experiment two. Therefore, the regulation friction is only 15 seconds, merely 4.3% of the efforts participants made in Experiment one. Such a small friction can be easily overcome with a penalty/reward mechanism, as demonstrated in Experiment two.

6 Analysis

Our risk budget mechanism offers incentives to users to behave responsibly, shifts the cost of risk to insiders themselves, and encourages them against risk activities. The experiment results demonstrate its positive impacts to users risk behavior. In this section, we first analyze the risk budget mechanism using game theory, and then discuss how to implement our mechanism in practice.

6.1 Risk Budget Mechanism as a Game

Game theory studies the strategic interactions among rational players in which every player chooses its optimal move based upon its counter-speculation of other's optimal moves. A solution of a game is determined by the point of equilibrium, which defines fixed point of players' strategic interactions [26].

Inadvertent insiders are rational and motivated by incentives. Therefore game theory is an ideal tool to model their interactions with their organization. Applications of game theory to the insider problem have the potential to predict the best move an intelligent and knowledgeable insider may take and enable organizations to prepare for that move.

A typical game consists of a set of players, their action spaces, and their payoff functions. We model the risk budget mechanism as a game played between a user and an organization administrator. Both players are rational and their objectives are to maximize their payoffs. A user's payoff is calculated based on the penalty and the rewards he receives. In addition, a cost is incurred by his efforts to choose a path with minimal risk to accomplish his tasks. The administrator's payoff is measured by the cost brought in by risky activities and the rewards provided to the user. In the presence of a reasonable risk budget and penalty for failing a mission, depletion of one's budget before job completion is an unlikely choice. Therefore, we only consider the situation where users choose between whether to take an optimal path to complete a task list, which avoids excessive risks but introduces the costs for planning, and a suboptimal one that will spends the entire risk budget on the task. The administrator's action space contains two actions: "not rewarding the user whose risk budget is not empty" and "rewarding such a user". The first action reflects the organization's strategy in experiment one, while the

Table 1. Structure of User Response Game

	Risk-Seeking	Risk-Averse
No Reward	$(-P_1, 0)$	$(-P_2, -C)$
Reward	$(-P_1 - R_1, R_1)$	$(-P_2 - R_2, R_2 - C)$

other one reflects the organization's strategy in experiment two. The user's action set includes two strategies: the risk-seeking strategy and the risk-averse strategy. The game is presented in the normal form as follows.

The notation is explained below.

- P_1 represents the cost of risk to the organization when the user adopts a risk-seeking strategy.
- P_2 represents the cost of risk to the organization when the user adopts a risk-averse strategy.
- $P_1 > P_2$
- R_1 represents the reward given to the user when a risk-seeking strategy is adopted.
- R_2 represents the reward given to the user when a risk-averse strategy is adopted.
- $R_1 << R_2$
- C represents the friction between the risk-seeking and the risk-averse strategy, namely, the cost for saving risk points while still accomplishing one's task.

The objective of a player in the game is to maximize his payoffs. An optimal strategy for a player is contingent on the strategy of the other player. When both players' strategies are optimal with regards to their counterparts, their interactions are "fixed" in a way that none of them has the incentive to change to another strategy. Such a strategy pair is called a Nash Equilibrium. A Nash Equilibrium offers a credible prediction of the user's moves, as it gives the user the best he can get given the administrator's strategy. It also identifies the system administrator's best countermeasure to the user's strategy.

In our game, when the administrator chooses not to reward the user whose budget is not empty then the user's best response is the "risk-seeking" strategy. This explains the reasoning of the results of Experiment one. When the administrator chooses the "reward" action, the user will choose the "risk-seeking" strategy if $R_1 > R_2 - C$, otherwise he will choose the "risk-averse" strategy. As we explained in the previous section, the friction C is small. Thus $R_1 < R_2 - C$ given then the user's optimal strategy is the "risk-averse".

Interestingly, in this game, the Nash equilibrium is *(No reward, Risk seeking)*. Such an outcome, however, is not in the organization's interest as there is a result *(Reward, Risk averse)* giving it a better payoff $-P_2 - R_2$ when $R_2 < P_1 - P_2$. This situation is similar to the classic prisoner's dilemma game [26], where the equilibrium does not offer players desirable payoffs. This dilemma can be avoided when the game is played repeatedly, which makes *(Reward, Risk averse)* part of an equilibrium strategies: this is because the organization knows if it does not reward the users this round, they will be risk averse in the future.

6.2 Application of Our Mechanism

From the game theoretic analysis, we can see that in order to make the mechanism work the inequality, $R_1 < R_2 - C$, must hold. Therefore it is critical to determine the parameters of the risk budget mechanism before it can be applied to a practical scenario.

As described in previous section, the friction C can be measured in the time interval. In practice, this friction could be estimated from observed time differences between taking different paths to accomplish the same task. Another way to parameterize our mechanism is to adjust the reward functions and monitor the risks brought in by users' activities, until the distribution of risk behaviors becomes acceptable.

7 Conclusion and Future Work

Inadvertent insider poses a grave security threat to the security of organizations. To mitigate this threat, we proposed in this paper a novel risk budget mechanism that encourages insiders to behave responsibly. Our mechanism assigns individual users a risk budget, which represents the amount of risks an organization can tolerate to let its employees accomplish their tasks. Each action of a user will cost him certain risk points. Once the budget is depleted and the user does not finish his work, a big penalty ensues. On the other hand, those who diligently seek the path that reduces the organization's risk, which is manifested from the surplus of their budget, will be rewarded. Our experimental study shows that our approach exerts significantly impacts to rational users' risk attitudes, and evidently shifts their behaviors from risk seeking to risk averse. In the future, we plan to study the effectiveness of our approach beyond the scenario of web browsing, and explore the possibility of combining the idea of risk budgeting with existing access control mechanisms.

References

1. NASCIO. State cios take action now! Technical report, National The Association of State Chief Information Officers (2007)
2. CSO. The 2007 ecrime watch survey. Technical report, the U.S. Secret Service, Carnegie Mellon University Software Engineering Institute's (2007)
3. Homeland defense journal (2007)
4. Report to the nation on occupational fraud and abuse. Technical report, Association of Certified Fraud Examiners, Inc. (2006)
5. Zeckhauser, R.: Behavioral versus rational economics: What you see is what you conquer. Journal of Experimental Psychology 59(4), 435–449 (1986)
6. Gefen, D.: E-commerce: the role of familiarity and trust. The International Journal of Management Science 28, 725–737 (2000)
7. Stolfo, S., Bellovin, S., Hershkop, S., Keromytis, A., Sinclair, S., Smith, S. (eds.): Insider Attack and Cyber Security: Beyond the Hacker. Springer, Heidelberg (2008)
8. Acquisti, A., Gross, R.: Imagined communities: Awareness, information sharing and sharing on facebook. In: Danezis, G., Golle, P. (eds.) PET 2006. LNCS, vol. 4258, pp. 36–58. Springer, Heidelberg (2006)
9. Randazzo, M.R., Cappelli, D.M., Keeney, M.M., Moore, A.P., Kowalski, E.F.: Insider threat study: Illicit cyber activity in the banking and finance sector. Technical report (2004)
10. Asgharpour, F., Liu, D., Camp, L.J.: Mental models of security risks. In: Dietrich, S., Dhamija, R. (eds.) FC 2007 and USEC 2007. LNCS, vol. 4886, pp. 367–377. Springer, Heidelberg (2007)
11. Camp, L.J.: Mental models of computer security. In: FC: International Conference on Financial FC: International Conference on Financial Cryptography. LNCS. Springer, Heidelberg (2007)

12. Camp, L.J.: Net trust: Signaling malicious web sites. I/S A Journal of Law and Policy in the Information Socirty 3(2), 211–235 (2007)
13. Kesan, J., Shah, R.: Establishing software defaults: Perspectives from law, computer science, and behavioral economics. The Notre Dame Law Review 82(2), 583–634 (2006)
14. Adkins, R.: An insurance style model for determining the appropriate investment level. In: Third Workshop on the Economics of Information Security, Minneapolis, MN (2004)
15. Karofsky, E.: Return on security investment: calculating the security investment equation. Secure Business Quarterly 1 (2001)
16. Masone, C., Smith, S.W.: Towards usefully secure email. IEEE Technology and Society (Special Issue on Security and Usability) 26, 25–34 (2007)
17. Good, N., Grossklags, J., Thaw, D., Perzanowski, A., Mulligan, D.K., Konstan, J.: User choices and regret: Understanding users' decision process about consensually acquired spyware. I/S: A Journal of Law and Policy for the Information Society 2(2) (January 2006)
18. Goldberg, I., Hill, A., Shostack, A.: Trust, ethics and privacy. Boston University Law Review 81, 407–422 (2001)
19. Cranor, L.F., Garfinkel, S.: Security and Usability. O'Reilly, Cambridge (2005)
20. Chajewska, U., Koller, D., Parr, R.: Making rational decisions using adaptive utility elicitation. In: Proceedings of the 7th Conference on Artificial Intelligence (AAAI 2000) and of the 12th Conference on Innovative Applications of Artificial Intelligence (IAAI 2000). AAAI Press, Menlo Park (2000)
21. Yemini, A., Dailianas, D., Florissi, Huberman, G.: Marketnet: Market-based protection of information systems. In: The 12th Int. Symp. on Dynamic Games and Applications (2006)
22. MITRE Corporation. Horizontal integration: Broader access models for realizing information dominace. Technical Report JSR-04-132, JASON Defense Advisory Panel Reports (2004)
23. Molloy, I., Cheng, P., Rohatgi, P.: Trading in risk: Using markets to improve access control. In: New Security Paradigms Workshop, Olympic, California, September 2008, Applied Computer Security Associates (2008)
24. Cheng, P.-C., Rohatgi, P., Keser, C., Karger, P.A., Wagner, G.M., Reninger, A.S.: Fuzzy multi-level security: An experiment on quantified risk-adaptive access control. In: IEEE Symposium on Security and Privacy, pp. 222–230 (2007)
25. Tsow, A., Viecco, C., Camp, L.J.: Privacy-aware architecture for sharing web histories. IBM Systems Journal (2007)
26. Osborne, M.J., Rubenstein, A.: A Course in Game Theory. The MIT Press, Cambridge (1994)
27. Mcafee siteadvisor

Deterring Online Advertising Fraud through Optimal Payment in Arrears

Benjamin Edelman

Harvard Business School
bedelman@hbs.edu

Abstract. Online advertisers face substantial difficulty in selecting and supervising small advertising partners: Fraud can be well-hidden, and limited reputation systems reduce accountability. But partners are not paid until after their work is complete, and advertisers can extend this delay both to improve detection of improper partner practices and to punish partners who turn out to be rule-breakers. I capture these relationships in a screening model with delayed payments and probabilistic delayed observation of agents' types. I derive conditions in which an advertising principal can set its payment delay to deter rogue agents and to attract solely or primarily good-type agents. Through the savings from excluding rogue agents, the principal can increase its profits while offering increased payments to good-type agents. I estimate that a leading affiliate network could have invoked an optimal payment delay to eliminate 71% of fraud without decreasing profit.

Keywords: online advertising, screening, signaling, contracts, fraud.

1 Introduction

When buying online advertising, principals often seek to contract with agents of unknown quality – often thousands of sites on which ads are to be shown, or thousands of affiliates who are to be paid for promotional methods they devise themselves. Ex ante, it is difficult to assess agent quality or to predict which agents will perform unfavorably. Moreover, it is often impractical to extract a penalty from agents ultimately deemed to be nonproductive. These constraints challenge advertisers and ad networks that seek to reduce marketing fraud and to control the presentation of their offers.

Advertisers' evaluation of marketing partners generally mirrors the task of an employer screening prospective employees, as in Spence's defining work on signaling in labor markets [26]. In particular, just as *Spence* employers cannot observe employee productivity, so too are advertisers unable to foresee marketing partners' practices. But online advertisers benefit from two important capabilities beyond *Spence* employers: First, an advertising principal pays its agents "in arrears" – that is, at some time after each agent completes its work. Second, in each period a principal has some positive probability of learning that an agent is engaged in impermissible ("rogue") marketing practices (if in fact the agent is engaged in such practices).

R. Dingledine and P. Golle (Eds.): FC 2009, LNCS 5628, pp. 17–31, 2009.

Under conditions derived below, a principal can delay all agents' payments in order to deter rogue agents' participation. Meanwhile, by paying good agents to compensate them for the delay, the principal can make itself and the good agents strictly better off.

In Section 2, I present the relevant characteristics of the online advertising industry. In Section 3, I develop a model of a principal paying agents in arrears, and I derive circumstances in which the principal and good-type agents prefer to delay payments. In Section 4, I apply this model to online advertising markets, and I estimate the benefits a leading affiliate network would have achieved by optimally delaying payment. In Section 5, I compare online advertising to other relevant contexts.

2 Principal-Agent Problems in Internet Advertising

The market for Internet advertising features large advertising principals (ad networks and major advertisers) contracting with a numerous small advertising agents such as web sites, blogs, search syndicators, and other marketing partners. For example, affiliate network LinkShare boasts more than a million affiliates promoting offers from the network's hundreds of merchants [22]. Google contracts with an unknown but large number of independent web sites (at least hundreds of thousands) to include its AdSense ad frames [18].

2.1 Rogue Agents in Internet Advertising

Some Internet advertising agents claim payments they have not truly earned. Consider a search engine that places ads onto a syndicator's web site. The syndicator can increase its revenue by clicking the ads on its own site – *click fraud*, in that the associated clicks come from the syndicator rather than from bona fide users. In principle a search engine might manage to identify telltale signs of click fraud, e.g. many clicks coming from a single PC. But in practice, perpetrators disguise their efforts, *i.e.* through the use of *botnets* or others systems to submit fake clicks from a large number of computers. *See e.g.* [3], [7].

On one view, a necessary condition for click fraud is that a click is easy to fake: A robot can "click" an ad just as easily as a human can. How better to distinguish bona fide visitors from robots and fakes? One possibility is to measure something more fundamental: Rather than measuring clicks, measure users' actual purchases. Indeed, some advertising intermediaries, *affiliate networks*, promise to charge advertising fees only when 1) a participating affiliate presents a user with a special tracking link to a merchant's web site, 2) the user clicks that link, and 3) the user subsequently makes a purchase from the corresponding merchant. LinkShare, a leading affiliate network, touts its service as requiring a merchant to "pay only when a sale ... is completed" [20] – emphasizing reduction in an advertiser's supposed risk.

LinkShare correctly points out that fake clicks (*i.e.* click fraud) do not, in and of themselves, garner payment. But rogue affiliates nonetheless find ways to defraud advertisers. For example, some affiliates perform *cookie-stuffing* to claim commission without a user clicking an affiliate tracking link. Consider a popular merchant from which a large proportion of users make a purchase in a given month – say, Amazon. If a user clicks an affiliate link to Amazon, then makes a purchase from Amazon anytime within the next thirty days, Amazon intends to pay a commission to the corresponding affiliate. But a rogue affiliate could modify a web page, banner advertisement, or email so that merely viewing that page, ad, or email would "click" the affiliate's link to Amazon – thereby crediting the affiliate for any Amazon purchases the user makes within the next thirty days. ([10, 14], [13] - exhibit 70) Through such tactics, an affiliate can trick a merchant into paying a commission when in fact the affiliate did nothing to promote the merchant, and when in fact no commission is due.

In an alternate attack on affiliate marketing tracking systems, an affiliate installs (or pays a partner to use) tracking software on a user's computer – software typically known as spyware (for its intrusive tracking of web site visits) or adware (for its display of pop-up ads). This tracking software monitors what merchant web sites a user visits, then opens affiliate links to the corresponding merchants. For example, if the user browses Dell.com, the software invokes its affiliate link to Dell. If the user then makes a purchase from Dell, Dell would mistakenly conclude the affiliate had referred the transaction, and Dell would pay commission accordingly [9, 11, 15].

2.2 The Practical Unavailability of the Legal System in Typical Disputes between Advertising Principals and Agents

In general, rogue advertising agents breach their contracts with advertising principals when they fake clicks, stuff cookies, or otherwise overcharge advertising principals. Upon uncovering such a breach of contract, a principal could file suit to demand redress and to prevent future violations. But in practice, the legal system is effectively unavailable in many disputes with advertising agents.

For one, transaction costs (including attorney fees and management time) tend to exceed the amount of harm cause by any single agent. Transaction costs are particularly weighty given the technical complexity of the violations, the absence of physical evidence, and the lack of expertise among investigators, attorneys, and arbiters. Furthermore, rogue agents are dispersed around the world, inviting jurisdictional disputes and increasing litigation costs. (*See e.g.* [28], reporting rule-breaking affiliates on four continents.)

Even when agents can be identified cost-effectively, agents often lack the resources to make principals whole. Some agents abscond with their ill-gotten gains. Others conceal their wealth in stores of value that are difficult for investigators to uncover [19]. Furthermore, bankruptcy laws let some rogue agents shelter assets in homesteads or in other assets that principals cannot seize [24].

Institutional factors further deter some advertising principals from pursuing rogue agents. For example, a principal may be embarrassed to admit to the public, in open court and in the public record, that it was defrauded. (*See e.g.* [5], questioning why Google declined to pursue a click fraud perpetrator.) Embarrassment is particularly pronounced in those circumstances that survive transaction cost analysis: There is special reason to be embarrassed when a perpetrator successfully stole a large amount of money. Revealing a fraud, even for purposes of achieving redress, could undermine confidence in a network or advertiser: Consumers might not want to buy from a merchant they learn has been cheated. (Consumers might worry that if rogue advertising partners defrauded the merchant, perhaps credit card information isn't safe either.) Similarly, advertisers might not want to advertise with a network they learn has cheaters. (If the network admits it has some cheaters, maybe it has more it hasn't yet found.) In other instances, a principal may blame itself: A principal typically could have caught the prohibited activity earlier, and it seems principals often worry that their initial failure to act will weaken legal claims or, in any event, reputation.

2.3 Technical Protections against Advertising Fraud

Even if rogue advertising agents escape legal redress, as suggested in the prior section, advertising principals could attempt to use technical systems to protect themselves from agent fraud. Indeed, by all indications, many advertising principals make substantial efforts to uncover fraud. For example, Google reportedly examines patterns in paid click data in an attempt to identify and negate click fraud [27]. ValidClick supplements pay-per-click links with JavaScript that reports indicia of fraud (e.g. ads purportedly clicked without movement of a user's mouse). ValueClick Commission Junction uses a web crawler from Cyveillance to uncover cookie-stuffing, among other practices [23]. I personally designed an automated system that manipulates spyware-infected virtual computers in search of unexpected advertising links claiming fees not properly earned [12].

Despite these various efforts to catch online advertising fraud, by all indications fraud remains widespread. Click fraud monitoring services estimate that 16% of paid search clicks were actually click fraud [25]. In my hands-on and automated testing, I have uncovered literally thousands of affiliates using spyware, adware, or cookie-stuffing to claim commissions not properly earned. Discussion sites [1] and consulting services [2] confirm the breadth of rogue online advertising agents.

2.4 Defending against Agents' Multiple and Sequential Identities

Identity verification further complicates an online advertising principal's supervision of its agents. An advertising principal typically interacts with its agents only through electronic communication systems, making it difficult to prevent an agent from registering under multiple separate identities. Using multiple smaller accounts offers clear benefits to agents who intend to use tactics that principals prohibit: If one account gets caught and cancelled, the agent will retain proceeds associated with its other accounts. ([13] - exhibits 2, 6, 7, 8, and 9)

Furthermore, even if a principal successfully uncovers an agent's improper activities, limited identity verification prevents the principal from reliably severing ties with the agent. The principal may eject the agent from its program, but there is little to stop the agent from reapplying under a new name. Online advertising fraud thus faces the same unavoidable pseudonyms considered in [17].

2.5 Penalizing and Deterring Rogue Affiliates

Because the legal system is largely unavailable to advertising principals, and because limited identity verification hinders principals' efforts even to know who they are dealing with, standard legal remedies offer advertising principals no clear way forward. Yet a principal pays its agents on an ongoing basis, and a principal may structure its contracts as it chooses, subject to agents deciding to focus their efforts elsewhere.

One natural approach would require that each agent post a bond. But advertising agents seem hesitant to pay fees to advertising principals when the entire purpose of the relationship is to facilitate payments flowing in the opposite direction (*i.e.* from the principal to the agent). Furthermore, these fees would tend to penalize newcomers, raising the [17] concerns of hindering growth and flexibility. However, advertising agents may be more inclined to accept delayed payment of their earnings, as suggested in the sections that follow.

3 Delayed Payment: Model

Suppose a principal ordinarily makes payment v when an agent completes (more precisely, appears to have completed) some specified task of gross value V to the principal. I take v to be exogenous, *e.g.* the outside option of agents who could perform similar work elsewhere, in a competitive market beyond this model.

Suppose good-type agents exogenously exist with probability p in the principal's pool of would-be agents. Rogue agents exist with probability $1-p$, and their output is worthless to the principal. Section 3.8 defends the decision to take p to be exogenous.

3.1 Outcome under a Simple Contract

Suppose a principal pays v for each seemingly-completed task. The principal receives proportion p of good agents who produce V and receive v. The principal also receives $1-p$ rogue agents who provide the principal with 0 value but also receive v. The principal then obtains profit:

$$\pi_{simple} = p(V - v) + (1 - p)(0 - v) = pV - v \tag{1}$$

That is, the principal makes payment v to each agent, but the principal only receives value V from proportion p of agents.

3.2 Delaying Payment: Good Agents' Demands and Principal's Costs

Suppose the principal imposes a delay in payment to agents. Agents' payments are set by a competitive outside market: If the principal merely delays payment, without offering any corresponding bonus, all good agents will leave the principal for its competitors. To retain good agents in the face of delayed payment, the principal must compensate agents for the delay, *e.g.* via bonus payments.

The principal and agents differ in their relative time preferences. The principal's deposits yield r, the market risk-free real interest rate. Good-type agents discount their future payments from the principal by a higher discount rate, $r + s$. The difference, $s > 0$, is good agents' relative impatience – because they worry the principal will not pay them as promised, or because they lack access to low-cost capital.

Suppose the principal elects to pay its agents with a delay given by proportion q of a year (*e.g.* $q = 0.5$ signifies a 6-month delay). With such a payment delay, good agents will require a larger payment w to accept the principal's offer:

$$w = v(1 + (r + s)q) \tag{2}$$

Here, $r + s$ is the annual bonus percentage required for good agents to accept the delay.[1]

The principal's gross additional cost in making such payments is:

$$w - v = v(1 + (r + s)q) - v = vq(r + s) \tag{3}$$

But in the interim, the principal could invest the amount v for duration q at rate of return r, yielding revenue vqr. Thus the principal's net additional cost of delayed payments is:

$$w - v - vqr = vqs \tag{4}$$

3.3 Delaying Payment: Probability of Detection

Let $\tilde{T}$, a random variable, be the time until a given rogue agent is revealed as such. Let d be the mean time to detection, *i.e.* $E[\tilde{T}] = d$.

Suppose the principal detects rogue agents with a delay that follows an exponential distribution.[2] Let the principal wait time q before paying a given agent. Then the probability that the principal learns the agent is rogue before the principal pays is given by the cumulative distribution function of the exponential distribution:

$$F_T(q) = 1 - e^{-q/d} \tag{5}$$

3.4 Outcome under the Delayed-Payment Contract: Agents' Profits

Suppose a rogue agent's profit margin in serving the principal is m. (Section 3.7 considers outcomes when rogue agents' margins vary in an interval.) Then the rogue agent incurs cost of $c = (1 - m)v$ in producing one unit for the principal.

Let a rogue agent have outside option 0. Rogue agents are therefore deterred from serving a principal if the expected profit from such service is less than 0.[3] Substituting:

$$[\text{expected revenues}] - [\text{costs}] < 0$$
$$v(1 - F_T(q)) - c < 0$$
$$v(1 - F_T(q)) - v(1 - m) < 0 \tag{6}$$
$$1 - F_T(q) < 1 - m$$
$$F_T(q) > m$$

---

[1] For simplicity, I ignore compounding of interest.

[2] Other distributions of detection time generally yield similar results. However, the exponential distribution is a particularly natural choice due to its uniform hazard rate: The exponential distribution implies that, in each period, a principal catches a constant proportion of those rogue agents not yet revealed to be rogue.

[3] By implication, an agent can serve – and a rogue agent can defraud – many principals simultaneously. That is, accepting a relationship with one principal does not require an agent to forego relationships with others. So an agent will accept any relationship that offers positive profit.

This is the *rogue-type non-participation constraint* – the condition that must be satisfied to prevent rogue agents from participating. The left side gives the probability that a rogue agent is caught by the principal within time q, *i.e.* that the rogue agent does not receive the payment. The right side is the agent's margin (as a proportion of the principal's payment). If the agent gets caught more often (in percent) than its margin (in percent), the agent will lose money in expectation and will be deterred from participating.

If rogue agents are detected with an exponential delay, constraint (6) becomes:

$$e^{-q/d} < 1 - m \qquad (7)$$

Rearranging yields the range of q that deters rogue agents:

$$q > -d \ln(1-m) \qquad (8)$$

3.5 Outcome under the Delayed-Payment Contract: Principal's Profit

Suppose the principal can set a q such that only good-type agents choose to work for the principal. The principal then achieves a profit of:

$$\pi_{good-only} = p\Big(V - v(1 + (r+s)q) + vqr\Big) = p(V - v(1 + sq)) \qquad (9)$$

The principal prefers $\pi_{good-only}$ over π_{simple} from (1) if:

$$\pi_{good-only} > \pi_{simple}$$
$$p\big(V - v(1 + sq)\big) > pV - v \qquad (10)$$
$$q < \frac{1-p}{sp}$$

This is the *principal profit constraint* – the condition allowing a principal to pay good agents the required bonus for the delay, while simultaneously increasing principal profit.

If the principal succeeds in deterring all rogue agents by imposing a payment delay of length q, the principal's profit increases as follows:

$$\Delta\pi = \pi_{good-only} - \pi_{simple} = p(V - v(1 + sq)) - (pV - v)$$
$$= -pv - pvsq + v \qquad (11)$$
$$= v(1 - p - psq)$$

$\Delta\pi$ is decreasing in q: All else equal, the principal prefers a shorter payment delay.

3.6 Incentive-Compatible Choice of Delay

To retain good agents while increasing profit, a principal must satisfy (6) and (10) simultaneously. In particular, a principal needs a delay q that is large enough to deter rogue agents, yet small enough not to increase the principal's costs excessively.

In principle, there need not be a value of q that simultaneously satisfies the requirements of both the principal and the good agents. For example, if the probability of detection were very close to C, rogue agents would know they have little chance of being caught, no matter the payment delay. Conversely, if good agents were overly impatient, it might be too costly for merchants to satisfy good agents while deterring rogue agents.

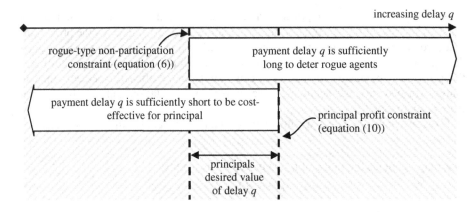

Fig. 1. Incentive-Compatible Choice of Delay

But if the q ranges do overlap, the principal can satisfy both inequalities. Graphically, the principal seeks a q that falls between the dashed lines in Figure 1.

In Section 4.1, I calibrate the model to estimate the permissible ranges of q, yielding estimates that suggest the inequalities do overlap.

3.7 Variations in Rogue Agents' Profit Margins

Suppose a principal faces a variety of rogue agents with varying profit margins m_i, rather than the single m proposed in Section 3.4. The principal then sets q to deter as many rogue agents as possible while satisfying its profit constraint (10) and retaining good agents.

Suppose all profit margins from 0 to 1 are equally likely. (That is, profit margins following the standard uniform distribution.) A given choice of q will then deter all rogue agents whose margin m_i satisfies the rogue-type non-participation constraint:

$$1 - F_T(q) < 1 - m_i \tag{12}$$

Using the cumulative distribution function of the uniform distribution, $F_M(m) = P(M < m) = m$, a given choice of q deters the following proportion of rogue agents:

$$P(1 - F_T(q) < 1 - m_i) = P(m_i > F_T(q)) = F_T(q) \tag{13}$$

Then the principal achieves the following profit:

$$\pi_{some-rogue} = pV - pv(1 + sq) - (1-p)v(1 + sq)(1 - F_T(q)) \tag{14}$$

The final term reflects the principal's loss from paying commissions to those rogue agents whose high profit margins allow them to remain despite payment delay q.

To optimally set q, the principal uses the first-order condition of (14):

$$\frac{d\pi_{some-rogue}}{dq} = -pvs - (1-p)v(s - (1 + sq)f_T(q) - sF_t(q)) = 0 \tag{15}$$

The principal prefers $\pi_{some-rogue}$ from (14) to π_{simple} from (1) if $\pi_{some-rogue} >$ π_{simple} for q selected to satisfy (15). If so, the principal offers the delayed-payment contract specified in Section 3.2. If not, the principal offers only the simple contract of Section 3.1.

If rogue agents are detected with exponential delay, (14) and (15) become

$$\pi_{some-rogue} = pV - pv(1 + sq) - (1-p)v(1 + sq)e^{-\frac{q}{d}} \tag{16}$$

$$\frac{d\pi_{some-rogue}}{dq} = -pvs - (1-p)ve^{-q/d}\left(s - \frac{1 + sq}{d}\right) = 0 \tag{17}$$

With knowledge (or estimates) of detection speed d, good-type prevalence p, and good agents' impatience s, a principal can evaluate (17) to find the payment delay q that maximizes the principal's profit. I present this approach in the following section.

3.8 The Exogeneity of p

Section 3 takes p, the prevalence of good agents, to be exogenous. In principle, p could vary as advertising principals change their anti-fraud tactics. Nonetheless, I view the fixed model of p as appropriate under the circumstances. In particular, experience suggests that few advertising agents shift from fraud to non-fraud, or vice versa. Rather, industry experience indicates that agents are either fraudsters or legitimate, but do not often change back and forth. Thus, the key moral hazard worry, i.e. that an otherwise-good agent would see a principal's compensation scheme and turn to fraud in response, appears less urgent.

My decision to model two types of agents – good and rogue – is also consistent with the literature. For example, [16] similarly presents a mdoel of "good types" and "bad types."

4 Application to Internet Advertising

4.1 Calibrating the Model

To calibrate the model in Section 3, I received data from a major US advertising network. The network specializes in relationships between advertisers and small publishers ("affiliates"), paying publishers in proportion to their sales. Publisher infractions include those described in Section 2, as well as additional infractions such as falsely or deceptively describing the merchants' products or pricing.

The network's 2006-2007 detections of publisher infraction yield an estimate of good-type prevalence $p = 0.86$. Among 2006 active affiliates who were ultimately terminated for cause, the mean time to termination, d, was 0.59 years (217 days). (2006 is the last full year for which such data is available.) (Compare [4], estimating a range of plausible detection rates for other browser-based attacks.)

For a worst-case bound on an affiliate's cost of capital, consider an affiliate whose funds come from a consumer credit card with annual real interest rate of 20%. In contrast, the affiliate network might earn a 2% real return in a low-risk investment. Then $s = 0.18, r = 0.02$.

A typical rogue affiliate might have a profit margin $m = 0.5$. This value reflects that the rogue affiliate's efforts require limited out-of-pocket expenditures, as in the examples in Section 2.1. Substituting into (8):

$$q > -0.59 \, ln(1 - 0.5) = 0.41 \qquad (18)$$

If $q > 0.41$, then rogue affiliates will earn negative profits and will cease to participate.

Meanwhile, from Section 3.5, the principal prefers to pay with delay q if that delay increases profit while retaining good affiliates. Substituting from (10), increasing principal profit requires:

$$q < \frac{1 - 0.86}{(0.18)(0.86)} = 0.90 \qquad (19)$$

For such a principal, the gain from excluding all rogue affiliates is so large that the principal would be willing to pay nearly a year of interest (at a rate given by the difference between the principal's discount rate and the agent's discount rate) in order to exclude all rogue affiliates.

Combining (18) and (19), any q in the range $0.41 < q < 0.90$ will deter rogue affiliates while increasing the principal's profit.

4.2 Variation in Rogue Agents' Profit Margins

Rogue agents incur a variety of costs in attempting to defraud advertising principals. For example, agents typically buy traffic (e.g. from banners, pay-per-click search campaigns, spyware, or adware). Agents also face an imputed cost from the value of their own time in planning and coordinating their tactics.

The preceding section estimates that delayed payments can profitably deter rogue agents if rogue agents all have margin $m = 0.5$. But what if some agents' margins are

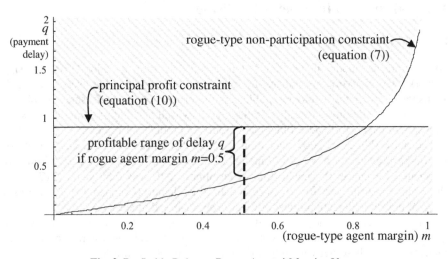

Fig. 2. Profitable Delay as Rogue Agents' Margins Vary

larger or smaller than that value? Figure 2 shows the relationship between payment delay and agent margin. For a variety of agent profit margins m, the plot shows the range of delay q that lets an advertising principal profitably delay payment, consistent with the other parameters estimated in the preceding section. Within the double-hatched area, the principal's profit increases from the use of a delayed-payment contract, and the principal successfully deters rogue agents from participating. If all rogue agents have profit margins below 0.83 (the value of m where (7) and (10) cross), the advertising principal can deter participation of all rogue agents, obtain the increased profit derived in Section 3.5, and pay good-type agents the increased fee described in (2).

If some rogue agents have margins that exceed the value of m where (8) and (10) cross, the advertising principal must turn to the approach presented in Section 3.7. Suppose rogue agents' profit margins follow the distribution posited in 3.7, with all values between 0 and 1 equally likely. Equation (16) reports how the principal's profit varies in its choice of delay. Figure 3 plots the principal's change in profit as payment delay varies.

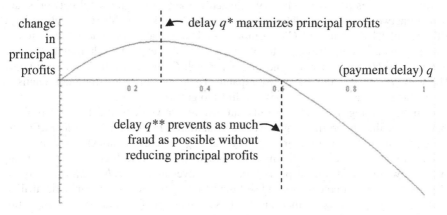

Fig. 3. Effect of Payment Delay on Principal Profits

Consistent with (17), Figure 3 confirms that the principal's maximum profit occurs with delay $q^* = 0.28$ (*i.e.* 15 weeks). At this payment delay, (13) indicates that the principal will deter 44% of rogue agents. Alternatively, the principal could choose a payment delay $q^{**} = 0.61$ (*i.e.* 32 weeks) – foregoing any profit increase from deterring rogue agents, but deterring more rogue agents (namely, 71%).

As the principal further increases its payment delay, it deters participation by additional higher-margin rogue agents. But deterring the highest-margin agents requires that the principal lose good-type agents or accept a reduction in profit (relative to profit under the simple contract in (1)). In particular, if the principal delayed payment long enough to deter the highest-margin rogue agents' participation, the principal would face increasing costs in compensating good-type agents for the delay, and the principal would be unable to pay those costs from the proceeds of excluding rogue agents.

4.3 Implementation in Practice

In general, an advertising principal might not know all the parameter values set out above. But the preceding analysis suggests that a substantial payment delay could be profitable under reasonable market conditions.

Despite the benefits of delaying payment, many advertising industry participants seem to think affiliates should be paid *more* frequently. Consider LinkShare's 2007 move to pay affiliates as often as once per week [11], a move made possible by the transition from printed checks to electronic funds transfers. LinkShare claims to offer "the most publisher-friendly payment plan of the major affiliate networks" – presenting weekly payments as a boon to affiliates. Indeed, both good and rogue affiliates prefer to be paid quickly, all else equal. But by paying its affiliates more often, a network limits its ability to punish affiliates ultimately found to be violating its rules or defrauding merchants. Although good affiliates appreciate being paid quickly, the preceding estimation suggests an interested affiliate network could offer an *increased* payment that good affiliates would value even more than *rapid* payment.

Table 1 reports payment delays of selected marketing programs, ad networks, and affiliate networks. Payment delays range from one week (LinkShare as well as large affiliates of Clickbooth and CPA Empire) to 15 days after the end of each month (ordinary Clickbooth affiliates) to 30 days after the end of each month (Google AdSense) to 60 days after the end of each month (Yahoo's Right Media Network). The web appendix to this paper [8] expands Table 1 to include additional details of applicable rules, as well as citations and links to governing agreements.

In implementing delayed payments, an affiliate network would face the problem that good affiliates' profit margins vary substantially. For example, *content affiliates* place affiliate links within their own material (*e.g.* articles or blogs) – yielding high gross margins because these distribution methods present few direct costs and, in any event, few marginal out-of-pocket costs. Conversely, *search affiliates* buy ad placements from search engines and sell the resulting traffic to merchants via affiliate networks – yielding low net margins due to search engine fees and due to competition from other search affiliates with a similar approach.

A payment delay that satisfies most good-type affiliates might nonetheless prove unworkable for search affiliates due to their lower profit margins. But affiliate networks and merchants could review requests for faster payments on a case-by-case basis – using appropriate indicia of legitimacy (*e.g.* reputation, audit results, *HTTP Referrer* headers showing traffic truly coming from search engines) to confirm the claims of affiliates seeking faster payment. By limiting fast payment to affiliates that survive heightened verification, affiliate networks could reduce fraud while avoiding burdensome investigations of all their affiliates. At present, Table 1 indicates that few marketing systems invoke such subtle analysis: Regnow indicates that fast payment "may" be available to affiliates who meet unspecified additional qualifications, but no other network's public statements report additional substantive requirements for accelerated payment. While some networks (e.g. Clickbooth, CPA Empire, PrimaryAds) offer accelerated payment to large affiliates, substantial earnings in and of themselves are not a clear indicator of trustworthiness.

Table 1. Payment Delays for Selected Marketing Programs

Marketing Program	Payment Frequency & Delay
Amazon Associates	Monthly payment, paid approximately 60 days after the end of each month
Clickbooth	Monthly payment, paid on the 15th day of the next month. Weekly payment, paid 7 days after the end of the week (for affiliates earning >$5000/week)
Commission Junction	Monthly payment, paid on the 20th day of the next month
CPA Empire	Monthly payment, paid 20 days after the end of the month Weekly payments (for affiliates earning >$1000/week)
Google AdSense	Monthly payment, paid approximately 30 days after the end of each month
Hydra Network	Monthly payment, paid within 15 days of the end of the month
LinkShare	Weekly payment
NeverblueAds	Monthly payment, paid within 30 days of the end of each month
PrimaryAds	Monthly payment, paid approximately 30 days after the end of each month. "Aggressive payment terms" ("receive [a] commission check every week") for "high-volume affiliates"
Regnow	Monthly, delay unspecified. Weekly payment "may" be available if an affiliate pays an additional fee and meets an unspecified additional qualification threshold
Right Media Network	Monthly payment, paid within 60 days of the end of each month
Yahoo Publisher Network	Monthly payment, paid 3-4 weeks after the end of the month

Facing the prospect of substantially delayed payments, advertising agents might be concerned about the creditworthiness of their advertising principals. Beginning in 2001, a series of affiliate merchants entered bankruptcy, and in some instances affiliates did not receive the commissions they had earned. But existing institutions can help assure that affiliates are paid as expected. For example, affiliate network Commission Junction now requires that merchants tender prepayments sufficient to cover their anticipated monthly advertising expenses [6], and Commission Junction holds these funds to assure affiliates' subsequent payments. Under a delayed payment regime, merchants would continue to pay networks as usual, on the current schedule – substantially protecting affiliates from lost payments if a merchant became insolvent. Merchants particularly determined to demonstrate their creditworthiness could turn to a formal escrow service or other mechanism to accept and hold affiliates' accrued earnings.

Improving detection technology offers important benefits beyond delayed payment. In particular, improved detections are particularly important if the model in Section 3.3 misstates the probability of detecting a rogue affiliate, *i.e.* if some rogue affiliates have exceptionally effective technologies for avoiding detection no matter how long networks search. But improving enforcement is costly – spiders and crawlers for automated enforcement, human review teams for manual investigations, and managers and attorneys to make final decisions. Delayed payment offer a more expedient alternative – a useful stopgap strategy for use when primary enforcement systems prove inadequate.

5 Other Applications and Future Work

Online advertising markets are one of many markets where agents may be effectively unreachable through the legal system. But in other such contexts, institutions and norms develop to deter misbehavior. For example, apartment tenants generally prepay a security deposit plus first and month's rent. Because tenants have prepaid these fees, landlords are well protected from typical damage – without having to incur litigation costs if damage occurs. Similarly, *neafarios* require payment in advance for their immigration services, protecting them from clients disappearing and failing to pay the promised fee. Conversely, a contingent fee agreement protects a client from the risk of low attorney effort by delaying payment until a better measure of effort (namely, success) becomes available.

Each of these payment rules addresses a market-specific information asymmetry. Although online advertising features similar risk of agent misbehavior, online advertising contracts presently lack any similar institution by which payment structure can enforce good practices. Online advertising would still suffer somewhat from the context-specific unavailability of a bond or other prepayment from the judgment-proof agent. But appropriate selection of a payment delay can achieve the valuable benefits offered by contingent payments in other markets.

I have offered an initial model of agent behavior – with agents moving from one advertising principal to another, but never shifting from rogue to good or vice versa. Future work might appropriately extend my approach to consider agents who respond to changing incentives by modifying their behavior as to a given advertiser, *i.e.* a model in which agents are subject to both moral hazard and adverse selection.

Acknowledgments

I thank George Baker, Eric Budish, Peter Coles, Fuhito Kojima, Jeff Molander, Tyler Moore, David Parkes, Al Roth, and five anonymous referees. I gratefully acknowledge data from an advertising network that prefers not to be referenced by name. This research was supported by the Division of Research and Faculty Development at Harvard Business School.

References

1. ABestWeb, Parasiteware (2008), http://forum.abestweb.com
2. Affiliate Fair Play (2008), http://www.affiliatefairplay.com
3. Barth, A., et al.: Detecting Fraudulent Clicks from BotNets 2.0. Mimeo (2007)
4. Boneh, D., et al.: Crimeware in the Browser. In: Crimeware. Addison-Wesley, Reading (2008)
5. BusinessWeek, Click Fraud: The Business of Cyberstealing (2006), http://www.businessweek.com/technology/content/dec2006/tc20061204_923336.htm
6. Commission Junction, Generate Advertising Order Form (2008), http://help.cj.com/en/ja25)@a/Generate_Advertising_Order_Form_.htm

7. Daswani, N., Stoppelman, M.: The Anatomy of Clickbot. A. In: Proceedings of the First Conference on Hot Topics in Understanding Botnets (2007)
8. Edelman, B.: Delaying Payment to Deter Online Advertising Fraud (2008), http://www.benedelman.org/paymentdelay/
9. Edelman, B.: Auditing Spyware Advertising Fraud: Wasted Spending at VistaPrint (2008), http://www.benedelman.org/news/093008-1.html
10. Edelman, B.: CPA Advertising Fraud: Forced Clicks and Invisible Windows (2008), http://www.benedelman.org/news/100708-1.html
11. Edelman, B.: Spyware Still Cheating Merchants and Legitimate Affiliates (2007), http://www.benedelman.org/news/052107-1.html
12. Edelman, B.: Introducing the Automatic Spyware Advertising Tester (2007), http://www.benedelman.org/news/052107-2.html
13. Edelman, B.: People of the State of New York v. Direct Revenue, LLC – Documents and Analysis (2006), http://www.benedelman.org/spyware/nyag-dr/
14. Edelman, B.: Cookie-Stuffing Targeting Major Affiliate Merchants (2005), http://www.benedelman.org/cookiestuffing/
15. Edelman, B.: The Effect of 180 solutions on Affiliate Commissions and Merchants (2004), http://www.benedelman.org/spyware/180-affiliates/
16. Ely, J., Valimaki, J.: Bad Reputation. NAJ Economics 4, 2 (2002)
17. Friedman, E., Resnick, P.: The Social Cost of Cheap Pseudonyms. Journal of Economics and Management Strategy 10(2), 173–199 (2001)
18. Google, Content Network (2008), https://adwords.google.com/select/afc.html?sourceid=awo&subid=en-us-et-awhp_related
19. Leyden, J.: AOL Seeks Spammer's Buried Gold. Register, August 17 (2006)
20. LinkShare, Affiliate Information (2008), http://www.linkshare.com/affiliates/affiliates.shtml
21. LinkShare. LinkShare Announcements, September 24 (2007), http://www.linkshare.com/rc/announcements.html
22. LinkShare, Industry Leaders Convene to Examine Trends and Share Key Success Strategies at LinkShare Symposium (2002), http://www.linkshare.com/press/convene.html
23. Livingston, B.: Commission Junction Hires Web Detectives. Datamation (2005), http://itmanagement.earthweb.com/columns/executive_tech/article.php/3558911
24. Scanlan, E.: The Fight to Save America's Inbox: State Legislation and Litigation in the Wake of CAN-SPAM. 2 Shidler J. L. Com. & Tech. 12 (2005)
25. Scholz, K.: Industry Click Fraud Rate Hovers at 16 Percent for Third Quarter 2008. ClickForensics, October 23 (2008)
26. Spence, M.: Job Market Signaling. Quarterly Journal of Economics 87(3), 355–374 (1973)
27. Tuzhilin, A.: The Lane's Gifts v. Google Report (2006), http://googleblog.blogspot.com/pdf/Tuzhilin_Report.pdf
28. Zango, 180solutions Sues Former Affiliates for Illegal Software Installations (2005), http://www.zango.com/Destination/Corporate/ReadArticle.aspx?id=29

Privacy-Preserving Information Markets for Computing Statistical Data

Aggelos Kiayias[1,*], Bülent Yener[2,**], and Moti Yung[3]

[1] Computer Science and Engineering,
University of Connecticut, Storrs, CT, USA
[2] Computer Science Department,
RPI, Troy, NY, USA
yener@cs.rpi.edu
[3] Google Inc. and Computer Science, Columbia University
New York, NY, USA
moti@cs.columbia.edu

Abstract. Consider an "information market" where private and potentially sensitive data are collected, treated as commodity and processed
into aggregated information with commercial value. Access and processing privileges of such data can be specified by enforceable "service contracts" and different contract rules can be associated with different data
fields.

Clearly the sources of such data, which may include companies, organizations and individuals, must be protected against loss of privacy
and confidentiality. However, mechanisms for ensuring privacy per data
source or data field do not scale well due to state information that needs
to be maintained. We propose a scalable approach to this problem which
assures data sources that the information will only be revealed as an
aggregate or as part of a large set (akin of k-anonymity constraints).

In particular, this work presents a model and protocols for implementing "privacy preserving data markets" in which privacy relies on
the distribution of the processing servers and the compliance of some
(a quorum) of them with the service contract. We then show how to
compute statistical information important in financial and commercial
information systems, while keeping individual values private (e.g., revealing only statistics that is performed on a large enough sample size). In
detail, we present two novel efficient protocols for privacy-preserving S-
moments computation (for $S = 1, 2, \ldots$) and for computing the Pearson
correlation coefficients.

1 Introduction

Internet users today are often requested to pass personal information to their
health-care providers, to their banks, to insurance companies and other service

---

* Research supported by NSF SGER Award 0751095 and partly by NSF awards
0447808, 0831306.
** Research partly supported by NSF SGER Award 0751069.

R. Dingledine and P. Golle (Eds.): FC 2009, LNCS 5628, pp. 32–50, 2009.
© IFCA/Springer-Verlag Berlin Heidelberg 2009

providers. Similarly, organizations have to disclose private individual data to suppliers and contractors in order to satisfy supply chain requirements. In fact, such information that may be collected by a primary service provider can be sensitive and may be protected by privacy disclosure acts (e.g., HIPAA is such act in the United States) or by business confidentiality agreements. In many cases, appropriately processed data are valuable market assets since they can be used to improve services, increase sales, etc. Therefore it is often important to transfer individual data items from the primary market where they are collected to a "secondary market" where other parties will further process them (e.g., will compute statistics of important parameters) and potentially disclose these secondary processed outcomes as opposed to the original (much more private) data.

We note that the privacy implications in these "data market" settings are dire since the users that provide data have no control on how primary service providers outsource their data. In addition, there is no way to enforce privacy and it is also possible that secondary market entities reside outside the jurisdiction where the data were collected originally (so even a legal procedure can be complicated). Furthermore, collected outsourced data may be stored in datawarehouses such as LexisNexis, can be sold to other parties for data mining, or in the worst case they can be exposed to unauthorized malicious entities who, exploiting a security vulnerability, may access this sensitive information. While these scenarios raise serious privacy concerns, it should be stressed again that there is a clear need for knowledge discovery in the secondary market: First for commercial (e.g., marketing, pricing, improving market efficiencies, service assessment and billing, revising insurance policy estimations), and secondly, for research purposes; and even for safety reasons (e.g., identifying public health hazards, realizing outbreaks such as epidemics or biological warfare instances, market research, etc.). Still in the present situation, "data producers" (i.e., users like all of us, and organizations) have little control over who, how, and what exactly is done with private and sensitive data that are communicated to a secondary market.

The current uncertainty of the way that private information may be taken advantage of, brings forth another important concern: users increasingly use falsification of their personal information when they are filling out Internet forms. Indeed, a number of recent reports [31,44,4,11] show that somewhere from 20% to 50% of online users have provided false data when confronted with an online form with the aim of protecting their privacy. The amount of false information that is collected reduces the usefulness of information databases for legitimate purposes and leads to a waste of resources.

1.1 Our Contributions

Market Trust Infrastructure. We claim that what is needed, given the current situation, is a *trust infrastructure* that will assure users that their personal data is not revealed and that collection is secured at the primary service provider. Further assurance involves the fact that the secondary market aggregation and

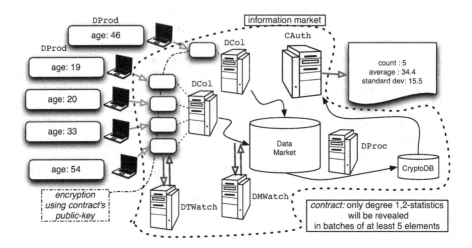

Fig. 1. Privacy Preserving Information Processing. Data producers `DProd` contribute scrambled private information to data collectors `DCol`; scrambled data enter the data-market where they are freely marketed protected by their cryptographic contract. The parties `DTWatch` and `DMWatch` are optional and have the role to ensure that data collected from `DCol` are indeed corresponding to real users. Eventually data are removed by the data market and packed into a crypto-database by the data processor `DProc`. The contract authority `CAuth` verifies the properties of the associated contract and engages in a protocol with `DProc` that reveals the required outcome of the processing. `DProc` should be able to preprocess the cryptodatabase to reduce the computational cost on `CAuth` and the communication complexity.

mining processing has security, integrity and validation built into it. (Note that currently, certificate authority infrastructure is a trust infrastructure for users' credentials but there is no similar entity for information markets).

Privacy Preserving Information Processing. The present work puts forth the notion of "Privacy-Preserving Information Processing" (PIP) to deal with the above basic problem. Central to our scenario is the *privacy-contract*: an agreement between the user and the service provider that will enable the generation of a special record. This is a type of an electronic "smart contract" as the ones advocated in [52]. The framework provides mechanisms for limiting data exposure and manipulation according to the contract, it also provides methods for validating compliance under the contract, in an analogous way to digital signature validation inside a PKI. More specifically: in PIP the data collection operation extends the protocol between the user and the primary service provider where the user (based on local privacy settings) furnishes to the provider, in addition to any other necessary information for primary service, also a contract-enforced-record (CER) which defines rules regarding the encrypted information in the record. In some settings the CER may contain rules contributed by both the service provider and the user (for example the case where a patient interacts with a primary care physician).

To enable secondary data markets that are under control, each CER is based on a template form and contains a sequence of fields that are encrypted according to specialized encryption functions (to be detailed later on). The primary service provider, in turn, has the choice to outsource CERs to a secondary market where they can be processed by following a data processing protocol that will involve the "contract-authority," a distributed entity that is used to safeguard privacy. The contract-authority is implemented in a distributed fashion by various entities possibly including (some of) the users themselves and service providers that wish to be trustees in the privacy-preserving operations. Based on threshold cryptography techniques, access to result decryption will be enforced by quorum control.

Then, PIP is a natural extension of the PKI concept where the data-collector offers a certificate to the data-producer. The certificate in this case has a much broader scope though: not only it provides the authentication of the server identity, but it also includes the following information: (i) the data-structure type of the data that the data-collector is soliciting, (ii) the contract that describes the purpose of the data-collection and its conditions, and possibly (iii) a cryptographic engine that enhances the client's machine with encryption capabilities. All the above information is signed by a *contract authority* (in the same way that the certification authority would sign a server's public-key).

The data producer, after verifying the certificate, supplies its data and is ensured (by the contract authority) that the data it provides will not be used in contract violation. This cryptographic contract binding is achieved by encrypting the data using the included cryptographic engine. *We stress that this means that the data will not be available to the secondary market in cleartext form.* Note that the data-collector will still "own" the submitted data but these will only be identified by descriptive fields (tags) such as "name", "age", "income" while the respective values would be enciphered. At this stage the data-collecting server may store the data or even *trade them freely* as a commodity in a data-market.

It should be stressed at this point that in PIP, nothing changes from the point of view of the user/data-producer: the user software still verifies a certificate (as in a SSL/TLS handshake) and then prompts the human operator to enter the data in an online form that may also be complemented by data produced by the primary service provider (e.g., the user's cat-scan in a medical application).

Naturally, the data also needs to be processed. This requires that the data elements are passed through the authorization of the contract authority who verifies that the submission is compliant with the stated contractual agreements. In particular, data is assembled into a "cryptodatabase", potentially get pre-processed by a data processing entity and is submitted to the contract authority, that verifies the processing request and produces the appropriate aspect of the data processing as described in the contract, to the requesting entity.

PIP Operation	Encoding Size	Communication	Computation
up to S-statistics	$\log N + S \cdot len$	$S(\log N + S \cdot len)$	$\mathsf{dec}(\nu)$
correlation coefficient	$\log N + 2 \cdot len$	$2(\log N + 2 \cdot len)$	$< 3 \cdot \sqrt{\#D_1 \cdot \#D_2} \cdot \mathsf{dec}(\nu)$

Fig. 2. Summary of our results. S is a parameter that specifies the highest moment that is required to be computed; ν is a cryptographic security parameter assumed to satisfy $\nu = \omega(\log N)$ where N is the sample size (i.e., the number of data producers). Data producers are assumed to draw their values from a space D in the first system and from D_1, D_2 for the correlation system; len is the maximum size required to encode any of the numerical elements in D, D_1, D_2; $\mathsf{dec}(\nu)$ is the time required to decrypt a ciphertext corresponding to security parameter ν.

Constructing PIP *schemes.* Next, we identify the major challenge in designing a PIP system which is the following: For a given processing operation, the challenge is to design a *cryptodatabase processing* operation (that is accompanied by an appropriate encryption scheme) so that the contract authority communication and computation complexity becomes a small function of the size of the output of the processing operation (which is the natural lower bound for the complexity for performing the computation over the cleartext data — just from the need to produce all the output).

Based on this, we concentrate on statistics for information processing that is crucial in the context of collecting and processing financial numerical data. Using novel cryptographic constructions together with recently devised existing encryption systems, we present two near optimal PIP systems. These systems enable the evaluation of statistical information from collected numerical data in a private fashion. In particular, we consider the setting where data producers contribute numerical data (e.g., their income, age, revenue, profit etc.) drawn from domains $D_1, D_2, \ldots$ and the data processor wishes to extract the following statistical information:

- S-statistics and S-th moments for $S = 1, \ldots$, that disclose the mean, standard deviation and higher moments (note that with more moments available better approximations of the sample distribution can be made available).
- the correlation coefficient between two samples that enables us to relate two distributions via their corresponding samples.

In particular, if data producers provide the values $v_1, \ldots, v_N$, the data processor can use our first PIP system to extract the r-th sample central moment for $r = 1, \ldots, S$, or more generally can approximate the sample statistical distribution up to the S-th cumulant. Recall that computing cumulants enables one to approximate the Maclaurin expansion of the logarithm of the probability density function of the underlying population distribution. In our second PIP system we show how the data processor can extract the Pearson correlation coefficient from two data columns $v_1, \ldots, v_N, v'_1, \ldots, v'_N$ submitted by the sample of N users.

Our results are summarized in figure 2. Note that the optimal measure (necessary output length) is $S \cdot len$ for the first PIP system and len for the second; it follows that our first scheme almost matches the optimal measure (it is polylog-arithmically related to N and multiplied by the parameter S that specifies the highest moment to be computed — in general S assumed a small constant); our second PIP system has similarly favorable communication; on the other hand, the required computation is proportional to the size of the data space as opposed to proportional to the output of the processing operation which is len; still the size of the data space is always a tractable value in practice.

It should be stressed that our constructions offer absolute privacy (i.e., they reveal nothing but the required output) under the cryptographic conditions and the threshold implementation of the contract authority.

We note though that the inclusion of the same CER to various different PIP operations may result in privacy violations that are unanticipated. For example, a record can be entirely revealed if two different sample mean calculations are performed where the only difference is including and excluding that item — this is a typical problem in statistical database queries. Resolving this issue – to the degree it can be solved – goes beyond the scope of the present work. One possible approach is to restrict subsequent inclusions of a certain CER to a PIP unless it is used in the same context (i.e., with the same CERs that it appeared in the first operation). Such approach would require an ever growing state that keeps track of past PIP operations. Still there are possible alternatives to that end and the basic infrastructure developed herein is consistent with other approaches to ensuring database privacy that can be useful in this respect, in particular adding noise to private data, [17] or using "baits" to catch misbehaving data collectors [29].

1.2   Related Previous Work

We next review a few areas that are related to our notion and explain in what ways our market model is different.

Secure function evaluation. Looking at PIP from a theoretical viewpoint, one can identify it as an instance of a secure multi-party computation with private inputs, a cryptographic primitive that has been studied extensively in the literature, and in fact generic protocols have been constructed that allow arbitrary functionality, see [27]. These protocols are not practical as they require large communication and computation costs; as advocated in [28], it is important to pursue more efficient instantiations of such "secure multi-party computations" and the instantiations that will be described in this proposal characterize an efficient sub-class of such generic protocols. More efficient cryptographic protocol constructions have, in fact, been successful for example a prominent has been electronic voting cf. [14,12,48,49,15,33,30,35,8,6,39,40,41].

Cryptographic database processing for privacy preserving data mining. Knowledge discovery with privacy concerns in terms of Privacy Preserving Data Mining (PPDM) was investigated in the context of secure computation in [43,34,53,2,45,1,22,42,32,54,36,37]. In this setting the focus is on merging or processing data from multiple private datasets that should not be mutually disclosed. The databases are typically owned and operated by entities that may pre-process them and share cryptographically scrambled versions of database aspects. The fundamental difference between this approach and the present work is that the private data are available in a cleartext form to the database owner while in our approach the database owner is not trusted. In other words the previous methods can be used to assist well-to-do data-collectors and processors to adhere to their privacy statements. Nevertheless this approach does little to protect against the problem we are tackling in this work, namely to provide a safeguard mechanism that ensures contract enforcement as well as notification and dispute control at the user level.

Encrypted access control and processing. Enforcing access control through cryptographic means has been utilized numerous times in secure system design (e.g., for file storage cf. [7,26] for hierarchical access control cf. [3,13,50,47]). The PIP setting goes beyond such access control since it focuses on data collection and processing, i.e., access to the data is not only restricted but also requires ciphertext-based processing that should be combined to an aggregation capability as data from many data-producers need to be pulled together prior to processing.

Multi-party communication. A PIP system requires multi-party communication and coordination which is a challenging problem in distributed environments. Dealing with failures and corruptions in multi-party communication systems is the context of Byzantine agreement protocols, a subject that is extensively studied in the literature, e.g. [18,19,25,24]. Byzantine agreement procedures, although they allow multi-party procedures to succeed under typically a threshold assumption on the number of failing parties, they do not constitute a very efficient approach for basing communication in multi-party systems. The approach followed here bases all communication of a multi-party system over a Client-Server communication infrastructure. The potential of the Client-Server communication model for basing security in multi-party computations, has been investigated in [5]. In this work, we employ the client-server architecture as a mechanism for communication, computation assistance and increased trustworthiness (we do not deal with the underlying reliability issues since modern communication is quite reliable and furthermore it is a different layer).

Utilizing Client Interaction. Dealing with privacy in data collection, the encipherment of collected data was also considered in the context of data mining in [56,55,9]. For example in [56], k-anonymity was discussed in the context of a non-trusted database holder; in the suggested approach the data-producers help the database processors produce the k-anonymized version of the database with interaction involving cryptographic operations extending beyond the initial data submission. Compared to the PIP framework we propose here, this approach violates the principle that in a PIP protocol, data producers should not be required to be active in other stages of the system beyond the original data collection stage. Instead in PIP we opt for a logical separation between the roles of contract authorities and data producers where the latter are still given the opportunity to be contract authority shareholders if some of them wish to participate in the trust infrastructure. Moreover the focus of the present work is to provide near optimal solutions to numerical data statistical computation whereas previous work focused on more generic tasks, e.g., [9], that if applied to our setting they would result in protocols that lack privacy (as all numerical values will be revealed as opposed to the final outcome of the computation).

2   The PIP Framework

In PIP there are four basic roles: data-producers (users), data-collectors (primary service providers), data-processors (secondary market entities), and contract-authority servers (that comprise the trust infrastructure). We will refer to these entities as

$$\langle \mathtt{DProd}, \mathtt{DCol}, \mathtt{DProc}, \mathtt{CAserver} \rangle$$

The operation of a privacy-contract-based system will comprise the following four basic operations:

Trust Infrastructure Maintainance. This stage is executed by the "cloud" of CAserver entities. The operation requires two parameters: ν a cryptographic security parameter and ρ a fraction that determines the percentage of CAserver that need to agree for a certain processing operation to take place. The main task of the setup stage is to provide a set of cryptographic keys that will be used in the formation of the CERs. The operation of the system assumes that all CAserver entities may fail or shut-down arbitrarily; moreover, it assumes that at any given moment no bigger than ρ fraction of servers is corrupted by an adversary.

- *Create Initial Key.* An initial group of n CAserver setup a cryptographic key pk so that each each server receives a share sk_i of pk so that any $t = \lceil \rho \cdot n \rceil$ shares can be used to reconstruct the secret but any smaller number reveals no information about the secret in the computational sense.
- *Add* CAserver. This is a protocol between $t = \lceil \rho \cdot n \rceil$ existing servers and a new entity that wish to become a shareholder. It results in the generation of an independent share and the outcome of this operation should be indistinguishable compared to the shares obtained by the $n + 1$ servers (n existing plus the new one) should they have executed the initial key creation step.
- *Remove* CAserver. CAserver entities may arbitrarily shut off and stop participating in the operations of the contract authority server cloud. Depending on the communication model other servers may need to update routing tables.
- *Shares Calibration.* Given that the add/remove server operations modify the number of servers it will be the case that $|t/n - \rho| \geq \epsilon$ where ϵ is a deviation threshold that is a parameter of the system. In such case, a set of t servers execute a protocol that results in a corrected t' threshold equal to $\lceil \rho \cdot n \rceil$.

The above operations can be achieved by employing threshold cryptography techniques: creating the initial key will be based on Shamir's secret-sharing [51] as used in distributed key generation of e.g., [10], while the add-user and share calibration protocols can be based on the poly-to-sum and sum-to-poly protocols of dynamic proactive secret-sharing [20] for example. The communication model that is assumed here is a full-broadcast channel that can be simulated by the cloud of servers using byzantine-agreement in a fully adversarial setting [18,19,25,24]; while in practical settings weaker protocols are still sufficient, say employing a client-server based bulletin-board system.

The public-key is bound to the type of operation and data type of CER records. It is certified by a certification authority and listed in a public directory where users can recover it if needed. For a given privacy-contract $\mathcal{C}$ pertaining to some data type and operation, we will denote by $\mathsf{pk}_{\mathcal{C}}$ the public-key of the contract, by $\mathsf{D}_{\mathcal{C}}$ the data type of the data collected and by and by $f_{\mathcal{C}} : (\mathsf{D}_{\mathcal{C}})^* \rightarrow R_{\mathcal{C}} \cup \{\bot\}$ the type of operation that will be applied after data-collection under the contract $\mathcal{C}$ (note that it may be a class of functions as well but for simplicity we just list a single function for now). Note that we allow $f_{\mathcal{C}}(\boldsymbol{x}) = \bot$, which is to be interpreted that performing the operation $f_{\mathcal{C}}$ on data input $\boldsymbol{x} \in (\mathsf{D}_{\mathcal{C}})^*$ would be in contract violation (this is not a catch-all as a contract violation may be triggered by other conditions as well).

User setup stage. Each user can obtain a signing key; this key is incorporated into the user's software and acts like an authorization token. The primary service provider (say health-care provider) can identify the user using such credential. Moreover, the signing key enables the user to sign CER records so that the following are satisfied:

- *Anonymity of Signatures.* Signatures produced by two distinct users are computationally indistinguishable for any observer, including an entity that corrupted the primary and secondary service providers as well as the contract authority entities.
- *Claiming of Signatures.* Each user can use its signing-key to execute a protocol that will "claim" a posted signature as produced by this user. No user can claim signatures that were not produced by it.

The above operations can be based on the notion of traceable signatures [38] (as they constitute a subset of the requirements put forth there).

Data-collection. In this setting primary service providers will be engaging in communication with the users that will furnish the CERs to the service provider. Each CER will be encrypted under the public-key of the negotiated privacy contract $pk_{\mathcal{C}}$ and signed using the signing-key of the user (note that the anonymity of the signature ensures that no information about the identity of the user is leaked from the signature). In more detail, DCol may present to users/data-producers a form that will facilitate the data-collection operation. The interface will be part of the transaction that the data-producer DProd and DCol are engaged in. The data-collection will include the following steps: first the data-collector and the data-producer will engage in a contract negotiation stage; in simple deployments this will be manual (and as simple as checking that the user read a privacy statement and it accepts it). Still it is possible to build a more elaborate negotiation stage where a client-side sub-system (e.g., a web-browser extension) will negotiate the right contract type out of the ones that the DCol offers based on privacy settings that the user may have selected in advance. At the end of the negotiation stage the DProd will have verified that it is DCol that is collecting the data and that the data will be collected under the conditions of contract $\mathcal{C}$ that DProd accepts. DProd may also obtain a data encapsulation package that will be accompanying the key $pk_{\mathcal{C}}$ (this is a cryptographic engine that will enable the user to scramble the private information). At this stage DProd will be ready to submit the private data that will be encapsulated and submitted to DCol in enciphered form by the client's local host under the public-key $pk_{\mathcal{C}}$.

*CER processing stage.*The CERs can be released by the primary service providers to the secondary market. A data market of CERs can be implemented at this stage that enables the exchange of CER records if this is desired (between secondary market entities). Data processors DProc will eventually form a database of CER records denoted by CDB. At this stage the CDB will be processed according to some prescribed *ciphertext-based* operations and the resulting scrambled outcome will be transmitted to the CAserver entities along with a request to release the appropriate information based on the contract. The contract authorities invoked by the action of DProc will inspect the submitted data for compliance to the contract and subsequently use its private key information to will facilitate the processing of the user data. The privacy safeguard of the system against illicit data usage is exactly at this stage where all data processing requests have to be authorized by the CAserver entities that check whether the contractual agreement is consistent with the intended processing operation that is requested by DProc. In the final step of the data-processing protocol, CAserver entities will return to DProc the value $f_{\mathcal{C}}(x)$ where $x = \langle x_1, \ldots, x_n \rangle \in (D_{\mathcal{C}})^n$ are the data that were collected by n users under the contract $\mathcal{C}$.

In the basic framework as described above, the data processor DProc receives a cryptodatabase CDB that contains the encapsulated data that were submitted by the data-producers. While it is possible to submit the CDB directly to the CAserver entities for processing under the contract function $f_{\mathcal{C}}$, this poses two major shortcomings:

- The communication required to transfer CDB to CAserver's maybe disproportionately large compared to the required output of the data processing protocol.
- The computation cost imposed on CAserver's could be prohibitive as the entities in the worst case would have to decrypt all data and apply the $f_{\mathcal{C}}$ function to them in order to finish the protocol.

To put this into perspective consider the following setting: suppose that the data processor is interested in obtaining the mean salary of all the users in its cryptodatabase under a contract that allows the data-processor to do so provided that the salaries are revealed in batches of at least 1000 individual records. The data-processor may submit to the contract authority 1000 enciphered salary fields and the contract authority will decrypt the data, compute the mean and return it to the data processor. Clearly this solution is sub-optimal: (1) the communication is proportional to 1000 ciphertexts where the outcome of the protocol is a single element. (2) the computation that is imposed on CAserver entities is dependent to the size of all collected data where it would be preferable to be dependent only on the size of the output of the data processing stage.

To resolve the above problem we would like to devise methods that will allow to the data processor DProc to process the cryptodatabase *prior to submitting it* to the CAserver entities so that DProc can recover an object that will encapsulate the value of the mean (in this example) and this value can still be recovered by the contract authority following a protocol that has time and communication complexity proportional to the size of the average itself as opposed to proportional to the size of the cryptodatabase. This puts forth the following formalism:

Definition 1. *A contract function* $f_C : \mathbb{P}^* \to \mathbb{R}$ *is said to support cryptodatabase processing under the encryption scheme* $\langle \mathrm{gen}, \mathrm{enc}, \mathrm{dec} \rangle$ *if the following condition holds: there exist two functions* Combine *and* Reveal *so that for any* $n \in \mathbb{N}$ *and any* $m_1, \ldots, m_n \in D_C$, *if* $\langle pk, sk \rangle \leftarrow \mathrm{gen}(1^n)$, $c_i \leftarrow \mathrm{enc}(pk, m_i)$ *for* $i = 1, \ldots, n$ *and* $c \leftarrow \mathrm{Combine}(c_1, \ldots, c_n)$, *then we have* $\mathrm{Reveal}(sk, c) = f_C(m_1, \ldots, m_n)$.

Note that any function f supports cryptodatabase processing trivially under a public-key encryption scheme $\langle \mathrm{gen}, \mathrm{enc}, \mathrm{dec} \rangle$ by setting Combine to be the identity function and Reveal to simply decrypt each ciphertext individually and then apply the function f_C to the decrypted vector. Given this observation we will be interested in the following problem: given a function f_C find suitable encryption schemes under which the function f_C supports cryptodatabase processing so that (1) the size of the output of Combine is minimal (this will minimize the communication complexity between the data-collector and the data-producer), and (2) the time-complexity of Reveal is minimal (this will minimize the time complexity of the CAserver entities' side of the protocol).

The Data Market. The framework of PIP allows data-collectors to freely trade the encapsulated private data in a data-market. In this section we comment how it is possible to facilitate such data-market operation within our framework.

A challenge of treating (encapsulated) private data as a commodity is the fact that a data-collector is capable of faking data collection from users and accumulate a number of private data fields without actually collecting them from users. Subsequently through free trade he may exchange such corrupt data with actual data in the data-market.

One can tackle this problem as follows: prior to submitting the data the user will receive the direction from the contract specifications to submit the encapsulated data to a data-transfer transaction "watchdog" DTWatch that will validate the transaction. We stress that no data will be revealed to DTWatch; the communication to DTWatch will serve only as a leveraging measure to discourage fake data-creation by the data-producer. DTWatch will receive the encapsulated data and sign them. It may bar data submission from the same IP address and/or maintain a black-list of hosts that are known to be a threat for poison the data market. The data-collector from its point of view will accept only signed encapsulated data.

Each data-collector DCol records the encapsulated data and they become its property but now the private data cannot be modified, get corrupted or manufactured by the data-collector without going through DTWatch. Subsequently, DCol can enter the data into the data-market virtual network where the encapsulated data become a commodity that can be traded. A special entity called the data market watchdog DMWatch will check the validity of the signatures of the DTWatch and will only allow properly signed data to enter the market.

We point at this stage that the DTWatch and DMWatch may communicate in special occasions, and in addition to the above, DMWatch will verify any credentials attached to the encapsulated data as they were attached by the data-transfer-watchdog entity and it may request the revealing of relevant communication transcripts by DMWatch for comparison with the communication transcripts requested from DCol. The data-market-watchdog may also check the identity of DCol against a blacklisting database where previous offenders that have "poisoned" the data-market with illegal data will be entered. In this way DMWatch will protect the encapsulated data as a commodity by isolating misbehaving DCol's (we note nevertheless that always a determined DCol can subvert any data collection system by launching a "distributed data submission" attack if it has the necessary resources, e.g., by utilizing a botnet).

2.1 Homomorphic Encryption Schemes

We will employ two homomorphic encryption schemes that we describe briefly here. The first one is the Paillier encryption scheme [46]; the key generation process selects a large composite $n = pq$, where p, q are two prime numbers that are assumed to be hard to be recovered from n; additionally the Decisional Composite Residuosity assumption holds over $\mathbb{Z}_{n^2}^*$; in particular it is hard to distinguish between the uniform distribution over the whole group and the uniform distribution over the set of n-th residues in $\mathbb{Z}_{n^2}^*$. In this scheme, to encrypt a plaintext $m \in \mathbb{Z}_n$, the sender selects $r \in \mathbb{Z}_n^*$ and transmits the ciphertext $(1 + n)^m r^n \bmod n^2$. In order to recover a plaintext, the receiver first applies the Carmichael value λ that corresponds to n on the ciphertext; this results to the value $(1 + n)^{\lambda m} \bmod n^2$; over the subgroup $\langle (1 + n) \rangle$ in $\mathbb{Z}_{n^2}^*$ the discrete-logarithm problem is easy and as a result the value m is computable. The Paillier encryption is homomorphic with respect to addition over the plaintext group: indeed, given c_1, c_2 and two ciphertexts encrypting m_1, m_2 it is easy to verify that $c_1 \odot c_2 = c_1 \cdot c_2 = (1 + n)^{m_1 + m_2} (r^*)^n \bmod n^2$. The scheme can be turned into a threshold encryption scheme as shown in [16].

The second homomorphic encryption, we will employ is due to Boneh et al. [8]. The key-generation process chooses a bilinear group G that has order $N = pq$; the public-key of the system is set to $\langle G, N, g, g_p \rangle$, where g is a generator of G, and g_p is an element of order p over G. The secret-key is set to the factorization of n. To encrypt a message $m \in \{0, 1, \ldots, t\}$, the value $g^m g_p^r$ is computed where r is selected at random from $\mathbb{Z}_N$. To decrypt a message, the receiver raises the ciphertext c to p something that cancels the random component of the ciphertext and reveals the value g^{mp}. Subsequently, the value m can be computed by solving the discrete-logarithm over $\langle g \rangle$; given that it is not easy to compute discrete-logarithms over that group, the plaintext spaces would have to restricted to logarithmic length. The scheme is homomorphic with respect to addition in the same way that the Paillier encryption, introduced above, is homomorphic. Moreover, the scheme is homomorphic with respect to multiplication for a single operation. This is as follows: using the fact that there exists a bilinear map over G, we have that for two ciphertexts, c_1, c_2, that contain the plaintexts m_1, m_2, it is possible to compute $e(c_1, c_2) = e(g^{m_1} g_p^{r_1}, g^{m_2} g_p^{r_2}) = e(g, g)^{m_1 m_2 + q(r_1 m_2 + r_2 m_1) + q^2 r_1 r_2}$. It follows that processing $e(c_1, c_2) e(g_p, g_p)^s$ would result to a ciphertext encrypting $m_1 \cdot m_2$ (note that the multiplication is thought to be over the integers as long as the domain from which the plaintexts are drawn is selected to be suitably small). The cryptosystem can be ported to the threshold setting using the techniques of [21].

3   Constructing PIP Systems for Statistical Data

In this section we will present two instantiations of the general framework of privacy preserving information processing motivated by statistics extraction from private numerical data.

3.1   PIP for Computing the Moments of a Sample Distribution

In this section we focus on numerical data and in particular how it is possible to extract statistics from the data that the DProd users contribute to draw conclusions about the population probability distribution; we will focus on a univariate analysis and in particular in extracting the central moments of the statistical distribution. Suppose that $x_1, \ldots, x_N$ are the data that are contributed by the data producers. The r-th central moment of the sample statistical distribution is defined as $\frac{1}{N} \sum_{i=1}^{N} (x_i - \mu)^r$ where μ is the first moment that coincides with the sample mean. Computing central moments allows one to calculate k-statistics that are the unique symmetric unbiased estimators of the cumulants of the sample statistical distribution. Sample central moments can be computed easily based on power sums $P_r = \sum_{i=1}^{N} x_i^r$ so in this section we will focus on the computation of such power sums.

We will consider the following description for the contract $\mathcal{C}$ of this section:

> "The data requested entered in this field are numerical and describe the quantity $X \in \mathsf{D}$; they will be used for purpose Y and only statistical information of samples of N elements size will be revealed. The statistical information collected will allow the approximation of the statistical distribution up to degree $S \in \mathbb{N}$."

As an example, consider that $X=$"salary", $\mathsf{Range} = [10K\ldots,500K]$, Y is "market research", and $N = 1000$. The degree S provided in the description of the contract will be the upper bound on the degree of the power sum that can be extracted from the collected data (i.e., only the power sums $P_1,\ldots,P_S$ will be computed by the data processor). This in turn bounds the information about the statistical distribution that is provided by the PIP system (e.g., if $S = 2$ only the mean and the standard deviation will be possible to be extracted). Based on the above we will be interested in the following problem: how is it possible to extract r-power sums for $r \in \{1,\ldots,S\}$ where $S \in \mathbb{N}$ is a parameter from the collected data. The system presented in this section will be based on homomorphic encryption and in particular on Paillier encryption [46] but a specialized encoding will be required. Below let $\langle \mathsf{gen}, \mathsf{enc}, \mathsf{dec}\rangle$ be the Paillier encryption. Note that the homomorphic encryption of the operation suggests that there exist an operation $\odot$ such that $\mathsf{enc}(m) \odot \mathsf{enc}(m') = \mathsf{enc}(m+m')$. The characteristics of our solution are as follows:

• During the data collection stage the data value $v \in \mathsf{D} \subseteq \mathbb{Z}$ will be encrypted as an integer using the $\mathsf{enc}(\cdot)$ Paillier encryption function as follows: $c = \langle c[1],\ldots,c[S]\rangle = \langle \mathsf{enc}(v), \mathsf{enc}(v^2),\ldots,\mathsf{enc}(v^S)\rangle$.

• During the data-processing stage DProc will use the following $\mathtt{Combine}$ function to process the cryptodatabase $c_1,\ldots,c_N$. Recall that each c_i is in fact a vector of the form $\langle c_i[1],\ldots,c_i[S]\rangle$. Using the homomorphic property of the encryption function, DProc calculates the power sum vector ciphertext

$$\langle \bar{c}_1,\ldots,\bar{c}_S\rangle = \langle \odot_{i=1}^N c_i[1],\ldots,\odot_{i=1}^N c_i[S]\rangle$$

Then, it submits the power vector ciphertext for processing and the $\mathtt{CAserver}$ entities will apply its secret-key to recover the power sums $\sum_{i=1}^N v_i^r$ for $r \in \{1,\ldots,S\}$. Note that this requires that the capacity of the Paillier encryption is at least $N \cdot (\max \mathsf{D})^S$ i.e., the capacity of the encryption summation register is of $\log N + S \cdot len$ bits where $len = \log_2 \max \mathsf{D}$ the size required to encode the maximum element of D as an integer.

Efficiency. We observe that the cryptodatabase processing that is performed using $\mathtt{Combine}$ reduces the size of the cryptodatabase from $N \cdot S$ ciphertexts to a vector of S ciphertexts, where each one is of length at least $\log N + S \cdot len$ bits. This makes the communication complexity of the data processing stage only polylog dependent to N (it is only $S \log N + S^2 \cdot len$) and thus very close to the optimal communication that is the output length of the $\mathtt{Reveal}$ function and equals $S \cdot len$ bits. Note that S is only a small constant parameter (e.g., it can be as small as $S = 2$ if one wishes to extract only the mean and the standard deviation of the sample).

Security. Since we use a specialized encoding for the numerical data (a vector of S ciphertexts each one containing consecutive powers of the data input) and it holds that the recovery of the power sums is dependent on conforming to this encoding, the computation relies on the fact that data producers $\mathtt{DProd}$ are following the encoding specifications. This can be ensured by requiring that

DProd proves in zero-knowledge for a ciphertext vector $\langle c[1], \ldots, c[S] \rangle$ that the plaintext of $c[i]$ equals the plaintext of $c[i-1]$ times the plaintext of $c[1]$. This can be done efficiently by employing the proofs of knowledge of [23]. Ensuring that the data collector has submitted the homomorphic aggregation of N ciphertexts can be done by repeating the preprocessing computation at a later stage; for this purpose the aggregated ciphertext submitted to the CAserver entities and the actual crypto database can be stored for post-computation auditing purposes; misbehaving DProc will be caught by comparing the transmitted ciphertext to CAserver entities and the extracted ciphertexts from the data market. Note that data market data are assumed to be assigned in a way that a DProc cannot forge (unless it goes to substantial lengths in introducing a distributed set of data producers, cf. the data market discussion in section 2).

Based on the above we have the following (informally stated):

Theorem 1. *The* PIP *system presented above correctly computes power sums of the inputs of degree up to S and assuming the security of threshold Paillier encryption it preserves the privacy of the data providers.*

3.2   PIP of the Pearson Correlation Coefficient of Two Samples

In this section we show how it is possible to extend the PIP system of the previous section to bivariate correlational statistics focusing on the Pearson correlation coefficient which is used to estimate the the correlation of two random variables x, y. Recall that the correlation coefficient for a sample $\langle x_1, \ldots, x_N \rangle$ equals

$$r_{xy} = \frac{N \sum x_i y_i - \sum x_i \sum y_i}{\sqrt{N \sum x_i^2 - (\sum x_i)^2} \sqrt{N \sum y_i^2 - (\sum y_i)^2}}$$

Evidently, it can be easily computed if one has the power sums P_1, P_2 for the variables x and y as well as the sum of products $\sum x_i y_i$. In order to achieve this type of contract-based computation in this section we employ another type of additive homomorphic encryption that enables the computation of one multiplication as well as unlimited additions that was proposed in [8]. In the encryption scheme of [8] (we refer to it also as BGN encryption) given $c = \mathsf{enc}(m)$ and $c' = \mathsf{enc}(m')$ one can compute a ciphertext of the form $c \odot c' = \mathsf{enc}(m + m)$ but also by changing the representation of ciphertexts to an equivalent one it is possible to compute a ciphertext of the form $\mathsf{enc}(m) \otimes \mathsf{enc}(m) = \overline{\mathsf{enc}}(m \cdot m')$. The disadvantage of the scheme in general is that requires $\mathcal{O}(\sqrt{\#\mathsf{D}})$ steps for decryption where $m \in \mathsf{D}$ using standard time-memory trade-off techniques; while this makes the decryption less efficient than that of Paillier's encryption that was employed in the previous section, the overhead is not substantial for our application domain. The capacity that we will require from the summation register of the encryption would be $\log N + 2 \cdot len$ where len is the size of the maximum element in the integer range the DProd select values.

The contract description that we will employ in this section will be of the following form:

"The data requested entered in these two fields are numerical and describe the quantities $X \in D_1, Y \in D_2$; they will be used for purpose Z and only statistical information of samples of N elements size will be revealed as well as their correlation coefficient. The statistical information collected will allow the approximation of the statistical distribution up to degree 2."

The construction will be built on top of that of section 3.1 with the following modifications:

• During the data collection stage the $x =$ data $\in D_1$ and $y =$ data $\in D_2$ will be encrypted as integers using the enc($\cdot$) encryption function of [8] as follows : $c = \langle c[x], c[y] \rangle = \langle \text{enc}(x), \text{enc}(y) \rangle$.

• During the data-processing stage DProc will use the following Combine function to process the cryptodatabase $c_1, \ldots, c_N$. Each c_i is in fact a vector of the form $\langle c_i[x], c_i[y] \rangle$. Using the homomorphic property of the encryption function, DProc calculates the four power sum ciphertexts $\bar{c}[x] = \odot_{i=1}^{N} c_i[x]$, $\bar{c}[y] = \odot_{i=1}^{N} c_i[y]$, the x-squares and y-squares, $c_i^2[x] = c_i[x] \otimes c_i[x]$, $c_i^2[y] = c_i[y] \otimes c_i[y]$ for all $i = 1, \ldots, n$, and finally all pairwise products, $c_{i,j}[x] = c_i[x] \otimes c_j[x]$, $c_{i,j}[y] = c_i[y] \otimes c_j[y]$, $\tilde{c}_{i,j} = c_i[x] \otimes c_j[y]$. It is evident that with these ciphertexts, the encrypted forms of the three values $N \sum x_i y_i - \sum x_i \sum y_i, N \sum x_i^2 - (\sum x_i)^2, N \sum x_i^2 - (\sum x_i)^2$ can be computed by the data processor by operating entirely over ciphertext. DProc will thus submit to CAserver entities these three ciphertexts.

Using its secret-key CAserver entities will decrypt them in time $\sqrt{\#D_1}, \sqrt{\#D_2}$ and $\sqrt{\#D_1 \cdot \#D_2}$ steps respectively and then return the final outcome by performing the square root and one division operation.

Efficiency. The length of the communication required for the computation of the correlation coefficient is equal to four ciphertexts that each one is of size $\log N + 2 \cdot len$ which is asymptotically optimal given the output size of the Reveal function.

Security. This case can be argued in a similar way to section 3.1 the DProc. Based on the above we have the following (informally stated):

Theorem 2. *The* PIP *system presented above correctly computes the Pearson correlation coefficient of the inputs and assuming the security of threshold BGN encryption it preserves the privacy of the data providers.*

References

1. Aggarwal, G., Mishra, N., Pinkas, B.: Secure computation of the k th-ranked element. In: Cachin, C., Camenisch, J.L. (eds.) EUROCRYPT 2004. LNCS, vol. 3027, pp. 40–55. Springer, Heidelberg (2004)
2. Agrawal, R., Evfimievski, A., Srikant, R.: Information sharing across private databases. In: SIGMOD 2003: Proceedings of the 2003 ACM SIGMOD international conference on Management of data, pp. 86–97. ACM Press, New York (2003)

3. Akl, S.G., Taylor, P.D.: Cryptographic solution to a multilevel security problem. In: CRYPTO, pp. 237–249 (1982)
4. Antecol, M., Bermount, B.: Wired teens aren't naive about online privacy, forrester research, July 24 (2001)
5. Beaver, D.: Commodity-based cryptography. In: Proceedings of the 29th Annual ACM Symposium on the Theory of Computing (STOC 1997), May 1997, pp. 446–455. Association for Computing Machinery, New York (1997)
6. Benaloh, J.C., Yung, M.: Distributing the power of a government to enhance the privacy of voters (extended abstract). In: PODC, pp. 52–62 (1986)
7. Blaze, M.: A cryptographic file system for unix. In: CCS 1993: Proceedings of the 1st ACM conference on Computer and communications security, pp. 9–16. ACM Press, New York (1993)
8. Boneh, D., Goh, E.-J., Nissim, K.: Evaluating 2-dnf formulas on ciphertexts. In: Kilian, J. (ed.) TCC 2005. LNCS, vol. 3378, pp. 325–341. Springer, Heidelberg (2005)
9. Brickell, J., Shmatikov, V.: Efficient anonymity-preserving data collection. In: Eliassi-Rad, T., Ungar, L.H., Craven, M., Gunopulos, D. (eds.) Proceedings of the Twelfth ACM SIGKDD International Conference on Knowledge Discovery and Data Mining, Philadelphia, PA, USA, August 20-23, pp. 76–85. ACM, New York (2006)
10. Canetti, R., Gennaro, R., Jarecki, S., Krawczyk, H., Rabin, T.: Adaptive security for threshold cryptosystems. In: Wiener, M.J. (ed.) CRYPTO 1999. LNCS, vol. 1666, pp. 98–115. Springer, Heidelberg (1999)
11. Cavoukian, A., Hamilton, T.: The privacy payoff. McGraw-Hill, New York (2002)
12. Chaum, D.: Untraceable electronic mail, return addresses, and digital pseudonyms. Communications of the ACM 24, 84–88 (1981)
13. Chick, G.C., Tavares, S.E.: Flexible access control with master keys. In: Brassard, G. (ed.) CRYPTO 1989. LNCS, vol. 435, pp. 316–322. Springer, Heidelberg (1990)
14. Cohen, J.D., Fischer, M.J.: A robust and verifiable cryptographically secure election scheme (extended abstract). In: 26th Annual Symposium on Foundations of Computer Science, Portland, Oregon, October 21–23, pp. 372–382. IEEE, Los Alamitos (1985)
15. Cramer, R., Gennaro, R., Schoenmakers, B.: A secure and optimally efficient multi-authority election scheme. In: Fumy, W. (ed.) EUROCRYPT 1997. LNCS, vol. 1233, pp. 103–118. Springer, Heidelberg (1997)
16. Damgård, I., Jurik, M.: A generalisation, a simplification and some applications of paillier's probabilistic public-key system. In: Kim, K.-c. (ed.) PKC 2001. LNCS, vol. 1992, pp. 119–136. Springer, Heidelberg (2001)
17. Dwork, C.: Differential privacy. In: Bugliesi, M., Preneel, B., Sassone, V., Wegener, I. (eds.) ICALP 2006. LNCS, vol. 4052, pp. 1–12. Springer, Heidelberg (2006)
18. Feldman, P., Micali, S.: Byzantine agreement in constant expected time (and trusting no one). In: 26th Annual Symposium on Foundations of Computer Science (FOCS 1985), Los Angeles, Ca, USA, pp. 267–276. IEEE Computer Society Press, Los Alamitos (1985)
19. Feldman, P., Micali, S.: Optimal algorithms for byzantine agreement. In: Cole, R. (ed.) Proceedings of the 20th Annual ACM Symposium on the Theory of Computing, Chicago, IL, pp. 148–161. ACM Press, New York (1988)
20. Frankel, Y., Gemmell, P., MacKenzie, P.D., Yung, M.: Optimal resilience proactive public-key cryptosystems. In: FOCS, pp. 384–393 (1997)
21. Frankel, Y., MacKenzie, P.D., Yung, M.: Robust efficient distributed rsa-key generation. In: STOC, pp. 663–672 (1998)

22. Freedman, M.J., Nissim, K., Pinkas, B.: Efficient private matching and set intersection. In: Cachin, C., Camenisch, J.L. (eds.) EUROCRYPT 2004. LNCS, vol. 3027, pp. 1–19. Springer, Heidelberg (2004)
23. Fujisaki, E., Okamoto, T.: Statistical zero knowledge protocols to prove modular polynomial relations. In: Kaliski Jr., B.S. (ed.) CRYPTO 1997. LNCS, vol. 1294, pp. 16–30. Springer, Heidelberg (1997)
24. Galil, Z., Mayer, A., Yung, M.: Resolving message complexity of byzantine agreement and beyond. In: Proceedings of the 36th Annual IEEE Symposium on Foundations of Computer Science, FOCS 1995, Milwaukee, WI, October 23-25, 1995, pp. 724–733. IEEE Computer Society Press, Los Alamitos (1995)
25. Garay, J., Moses, Y.: Fully polynomial byzantine agreement in $t + 1$ rounds. In: Aggarwal, A. (ed.) Proceedings of the 25th Annual ACM Symposium on the Theory of Computing, San Diego, CA, USA, pp. 31–41. ACM Press, New York (1993)
26. Goh, E.-J., Shacham, H., Modadugu, N., Boneh, D.: Sirius: Securing remote untrusted storage. In: NDSS. The Internet Society, San Diego (2003)
27. Goldreich, O., Micali, S., Wigderson, A.: How to play any mental game or a completeness theorem for protocols with honest majority. In: STOC, pp. 218–229. ACM, New York (1987)
28. Goldwasser, S.: Multi-party computations: Past and present. In: PODC, pp. 1–6 (1997)
29. Golle, P., McSherry, F., Mironov, I.: Data collection with self-enforcing privacy. ACM Trans. Inf. Syst. Secur. 12(2) (2008)
30. Hirt, M., Sako, K.: Efficient receipt-free voting based on homomorphic encryption. In: Preneel, B. (ed.) EUROCRYPT 2000. LNCS, vol. 1807, pp. 539–556. Springer, Heidelberg (2000)
31. Statistical Research Inc. How people use the internet 2001, study (June 2001)
32. Jagannathan, G., Pillaipakkamnatt, K., Wright, R.N.: A new privacy-preserving distributed k-clustering algorithm. In: Ghosh, J., Lambert, D., Skillicorn, D.B., Srivastava, J. (eds.) SDM. SIAM, Philadelphia (2006)
33. Jakobsson, M.: A practical mix. In: Nyberg, K. (ed.) EUROCRYPT 1998, vol. 1403, pp. 448–461. Springer, Heidelberg (1998)
34. Kantarcioglu, M., Clifton, C.: Privacy-preserving distributed mining of association rules on horizontally partitioned data. IEEE Trans. Knowl. Data Eng. 16, 1026–1037 (2004)
35. Katz, J., Myers, S., Ostrovsky, R.: Cryptographic counters and applications to electronic voting. In: Pfitzmann, B. (ed.) EUROCRYPT 2001. LNCS, vol. 2045, pp. 78–92. Springer, Heidelberg (2001)
36. Kiayias, A., Mitrofanova, A.: Testing disjointness of private datasets. In: S. Patrick, A., Yung, M. (eds.) FC 2005, vol. 3570, pp. 109–124. Springer, Heidelberg (2005)
37. Kiayias, A., Mitrofanova, A.: Syntax-driven private evaluation of quantified membership queries. In: Zhou, J., Yung, M., Bao, F. (eds.) ACNS 2006. LNCS, vol. 3989, pp. 470–485. Springer, Heidelberg (2006)
38. Kiayias, A., Tsiounis, Y., Yung, M.: Traceable signatures. In: Cachin, C., Camenisch, J.L. (eds.) EUROCRYPT 2004. LNCS, vol. 3027, pp. 571–589. Springer, Heidelberg (2004)
39. Kiayias, A., Yung, M.: Self-tallying elections and perfect ballot secrecy. In: Naccache, D., Paillier, P. (eds.) PKC 2002. LNCS, vol. 2274, pp. 141–158. Springer, Heidelberg (2002)
40. Kiayias, A., Yung, M.: Non-interactive zero-sharing with applications to private distributed decision making. In: Wright, R.N. (ed.) FC 2003. LNCS, vol. 2742, pp. 303–320. Springer, Heidelberg (2003)

41. Kiayias, A., Yung, M.: The vector-ballot e-voting approach. In: Juels, A. (ed.) FC 2004. LNCS, vol. 3110, pp. 72–89. Springer, Heidelberg (2004)
42. Kissner, L., Song, D.X.: Privacy-preserving set operations. In: Shoup, V. (ed.) CRYPTO 2005. LNCS, vol. 3621, pp. 241–257. Springer, Heidelberg (2005)
43. Lindell, Y., Pinkas, B.: Privacy preserving data mining. In: Bellare, M. (ed.) CRYPTO 2000. LNCS, vol. 1880, pp. 36–54. Springer, Heidelberg (2000)
44. Nunes, P.F., Kambil, A.: Internet privacy: A look under the covers, accenture institute for strategic change (July 2000), http://www.accenture.com
45. O'Keefe, C.M., Yung, M., Gu, L., Baxter, R.: Privacy-preserving data linkage protocols. In: WPES 2004: Proceedings of the 2004 ACM workshop on Privacy in the electronic society, pp. 94–102. ACM Press, New York (2004)
46. Paillier, P.: Public-key cryptosystems based on composite degree residuosity classes. In: Stern, J. (ed.) EUROCRYPT 1999. LNCS, vol. 1592, pp. 223–238. Springer, Heidelberg (1999)
47. Ray, I., Ray, I., Narasimhamurthi, N.: A cryptographic solution to implement access control in a hierarchy and more. In: SACMAT 2002: Proceedings of the seventh ACM symposium on Access control models and technologies, pp. 65–73. ACM Press, New York (2002)
48. Sako, K., Kilian, J.: Secure voting using partially compatible homomorphisms. In: Desmedt, Y.G. (ed.) CRYPTO 1994. LNCS, vol. 839, pp. 411–424. Springer, Heidelberg (1994)
49. Sako, K., Kilian, J.: Receipt-free mix-type voting scheme: A practical solution to the implementation of a voting booth. In: Guillou, L.C., Quisquater, J.-J. (eds.) EUROCRYPT 1995. LNCS, vol. 921, pp. 393–403. Springer, Heidelberg (1995)
50. Sandhu, R.S.: Cryptographic implementation of a tree hierarchy for access control. Inf. Process. Lett. 27(2), 95–98 (1988)
51. Shamir, A.: How to share a secret. Communications of the ACM 22(11) (1979)
52. Szabo, N.: The idea of smart contracts (1997), http://szabo.best.vwh.net/smart_contracts_idea.html
53. Vaidya, J., Clifton, C.: Privacy preserving association rule mining in vertically partitioned data. In: KDD 2002: Proceedings of the eighth ACM SIGKDD international conference on Knowledge discovery and data mining, pp. 639–644. ACM Press, New York (2002)
54. Yang, Z., Wright, R.N.: Privacy-preserving computation of bayesian networks on vertically partitioned data. IEEE Trans. Knowl. Data Eng. 18(9), 1253–1264 (2006)
55. Yang, Z., Zhong, S., Wright, R.N.: Anonymity-preserving data collection. In: KDD 2005: Proceeding of the eleventh ACM SIGKDD international conference on Knowledge discovery in data mining, pp. 334–343. ACM Press, New York (2005)
56. Zhong, S., Yang, Z., Wright, R.N.: Privacy-enhancing -anonymization of customer data. In: Li, C. (ed.) PODS, pp. 139–147. ACM, New York (2005)

Achieving Privacy in a Federated Identity Management System

Susan Landau[1], Hubert Le Van Gong[1], and Robin Wilton[2]

[1] Sun Microsystems
[2] Future Identity
susan.landau@sun.com, hubert.levangong@sun.com,
futureidentity@fastmail.fm

Abstract. Federated identity management allows a user to efficiently authenticate and use identity information from data distributed across multiple domains. The sharing of data across domains blurs security boundaries and potentially creates privacy risks. We examine privacy risks and fundamental privacy protections of federated identity-management systems. The protections include minimal disclosure and providing PII only on a "need-to-know" basis. We then look at the Liberty Alliance system and analyze previous privacy critiques of that system. We show how law and policy provide privacy protections in federated identity-management systems, and that privacy threats are best handled using a combination of technology **and** law/policy tools.

Keywords: federated identity management, privacy, law, policy.

1 Introduction

In solving one problem, federated identity management raises others. For instance, federated identity management can simplify a user's experience through the use of single sign on (SSO) at multiple websites, thus enabling multiple services to be accessed as a unified whole and simplifying the complex process of managing user accounts after systems merge [16, pp. 16-17]. But by enabling the dynamic use of distributed identity information, federated identity management systems blur the divide between security domains, apparently creating a potential risk to privacy. We believe that separating the different contexts of a user's identity through federation creates *privacy in depth* and can substantially enhance user privacy. In this paper we demonstrate how federated systems can share a user's personally identifiable information (PII)[1] and yet *increase* her privacy.

In this introduction, we provide a brief description of federated identity management, then consider the context in which these protocols operate. In section 2

---

[1] PII is information that can be used to uniquely identify a person. What exactly constitutes PII — e.g., does an IP address do so? — is currently an issue of quite heated public debate.

R. Dingledine and P. Golle (Eds.): FC 2009, LNCS 5628, pp. 51–70, 2009.
© IFCA/Springer-Verlag Berlin Heidelberg 2009

we discuss where the privacy pressure points are in federated identity management and the different roles that policy, contracts, and technology have in protecting privacy within a federated identity management system. There have been various papers showing privacy "threats" against the Liberty Alliance system and proposing solutions. In section 3 we examine these and show that, by and large, the threats arise from a preoccupation with technical solutions where the real problems are social. We also show where the potential breaches presented in earlier papers fail (or fail to matter).

1.1   A Brief Introduction to Federated Identity Management

In federated identity management we have three actors:

- The Principal, or user, who has a particular digital identity;
- The Identity Provider (IdP), whose role is to authenticate the Principal once; the IdP then issues authentication assertions to a:
- Service Provider (SP), which provides services (e.g., access to protected resources) to authenticated Principals.

Sometimes the Principal and user agent (typically a browser) are considered as separate entities; in this paper, we will view them as one.

Authentication can occur in various ways: the SP can initiate an authentication request to the IdP the Principal designates when logged onto an SP, or the Principal can first authenticate at an IdP and then access an SP. In either case, the technology enables SSO, in which the IdP authenticates the Principal, thus allowing her access to protected resources at an SP.

There are currently three major variants of federated identity management — SAML (which underlies the Liberty protocols), InfoCard (which underlies Windows Cardspace), and OpenID — as well as some emergent efforts. The technologies were originally designed for different use cases: SAML and Liberty for business-to-business and business-to-consumer; CardSpace, a .NET component, for consumer-oriented activity; OpenID as a lightweight way to do user authentication (e.g., to reduce spam in blog comments). With time, design principles are converging somewhat. For example, OpenID is now being adapted to compensate for a weak security model. We discuss SAML and Liberty further in §3.1; for a more extensive comparison of SAML, InfoCard, and OpenID, see [16].

1.2   The Role of the Social Contract

A user may disclose information about herself for various reasons: she may give information about various accounts to a financial-services provider in order to do online banking; as a result of employment, she may be compelled by contract to reveal her driver's license number in order to use a company car; she may be required by the state to provide her height, weight, and eye color in order to obtain a driver's license. But while the compulsion in each of these examples is different, each of these systems works only if there is "consent of the governed" — a social contract if you will.

Users benefit from the convenience of single sign-on. They no longer have to remember multiple ways of authenticating at each site. Basic information about a user that she is willing to have at each site in the federation — such as work phone number, work address, company ID number — can just "be there," even while other pieces — marital status, ages and names of dependents, passport number — reside in separate SPs. Authentication at the related sites (e.g., the company online travel provider) is seamless. The user benefits from increased simplicity, while federation allows these distributed facts to be securely asserted.

Personal data, its safe storage and appropriate management, is the subject of legislation in many countries, and achieving compliance with data protection principles is seldom cost neutral. Federated systems enable Identity and Service Providers to benefit from increased efficiency. Some — those that choose to hold less PII — also benefit from decreased risk and compliance cost. A provider can't lose information it doesn't have. All providers benefit from the seamlessness of the networked interactions. IdPs and SPs will also find new business opportunities through these. The providers will also protect themselves through business contracts, technology, and through watching the bottom line. Organizations will only participate in federated identity-management systems if they see the benefit (or the cost in leaving).

If the user feels that her employer, or its delegate, the travel agency or health provider, has inappropriately shared PII, she has recourse to the legal system[2] (in extreme cases, she may choose to leave the company). If the user feels that the government is inappropriately sharing her PII, then, depending on the norms within the state, she may choose not to involve herself in the government identity-management system[3]. If the IdP or SP starts sharing user PII in ways that the user objects to, the contract — implicit or not — must be negotiated.

A social contract is a balance: I give you this, I receive something else in return. If the Principal doesn't find value in the system, if the IdP or SP doesn't realize benefits of efficiency or reduced risk, the social contract fails, the system loses participation, and the identity-management system fails. New Zealand provides a good example. New Zealanders have a strong resistance to "Big Brother," so when their government embarked upon an e-government strategy to provide online delivery of citizen services, the focus was on user privacy and security. The architecture was designed accordingly, with the Identity Verification Service uniquely identifying an individual but forwarding only minimal identity attributes to the Government Logon Service [17, p. 53].

---

[2] Of course, there are instances, such as during law-enforcement investigations, when the question of the Principal's satisfaction is likely to be overridden.

[3] McKenzie et al. observe that social norms vary greatly across the world [17]. New Zealand's identity management system emphasizes user privacy and security, while Scandinavian countries focus on government transparency. The patchwork of U.S. privacy laws can make one wonder if the privacy of video rental data really deserves the same legislative attention as that of banking transactions. In the U.K., a range of public sector policies are being predicated on government data-sharing on a massive scale.

New Zealand's effort points out that all parties must benefit in order for them to participate — and for the system to be viable. Clearly technology is only one part of a complex solution that includes:

- Technology: e.g., mechanisms such as SAML, CardSpace, OpenID
- Business contracts (when applicable, e.g., not always used in OpenID) which, in turn, are part of...
- The legal, regulatory, commercial and technical implementation factors.

What's more, as the legal and regulatory context will change from country to country, a single, uniform technical approach cannot suffice.

Federated ID management systems need the buy-in of all three sets of members: users, identity providers, and service providers. Users are discouraged if participating in the system obviously leads to abuse of their personal data. Identity providers will typically bear liability for the assertions they make, and service providers will seek to reduce their own risk by relying on those assertions. Thus any analysis of the privacy risks of an identity-management system must work by looking at the deployed system holistically.

In fact, the idea of a social contract between the user and other parties reflects a broader principle, namely that each party to a federation must have some sustainable motivation for taking part, and for behaving well in the structure. How that works may well vary from one federation to another — particularly between the public and commercial sectors, where the incentives and penalties can differ enormously. The following table suggests some of the different levels at which there can be an incentive to "behave well" within a federation:

Privacy Driver	Incentive
Best Practices	Improve User Trust
Industry Code of Conduct	Industry Sanctions
Legal and/or regulatory controls	Avoid prosecution and/or liability

2   The Privacy Drivers in Federated Identity Management

When federated identity-management systems were first introduced, there was substantial concern about potential privacy invasiveness. We believe this stemmed from an oversimplified view of the technology. While identity management systems are about sharing information, it is naïve to assume they can succeed if they do so indiscriminately and without regard to context; and this is where user privacy can be enhanced.

As the table illustrates, motivations for good behavior in a federation can be many and varied, and may differ between regulatory contexts. However, there are approaches to the privacy problem that are generally applicable across regulatory contexts; one such is an analysis based on risk. For example, one might identify the following sources of risk in a federated system:

- risk of data disclosure (inappropriate, excessive, without consent);
- risk of metadata disclosure (making it possible to link other pieces of personal data relating to the user, usage patterns, inferred habits and preferences);
- regulatory exposure (if you don't have the data, you don't have to worry about failures of compliance ...).

These can also provide useful input to processes such as Privacy Impact Assessments, e.g., along the lines already established by the Ontario Privacy Commission [18]. Taken together, approaches based on the "privacy drivers" and the sources of risk shown above offer several ways in which the sharing of data can be analysed, classified, segmented, and strategies devised for managing it appropriately in the context in question.

Consider the following example:

- I have an account with American Express. They have whatever PII is required by law. Most importantly, they know I have an account with them.
- I have an account with UPS (and USPS, Fedex, etc.) They have PII (or access to it) that includes my address.
- I have an account at Privatzon, a book seller. They have no PII — other than purchase history.
- I have a Liberty-enabled Discovery Service from my Liberty-enabled Identity Provider.

When I want to buy a book at Privatzon, I login, select the book and request that Privatzon use my preferred payment and shipping services. Privatzon contacts my discovery service requesting my preferred shipper and payment services, and is told they are, say, UPS and American Express. Separating these pieces of data, for which a federated identity-management system is ideally positioned, protects an individual's privacy. Privatzon contacts the two SPs, which respond, one with a one-time credit card[4] and the other with a one-time shipping label — both are just numbers and/or barcodes. PII remains with those SPs that "have a need to know" and isn't otherwise distributed. Thus American Express has no idea UPS was used as a shipping company and inversely UPS does not know about my account at American Express. None of these companies knows about my book-buying habits either. Indeed, a properly designed federated identity-management system can keep these contexts separate, providing individuals with far more privacy protection than they currently have.

While Privatzon wants to know about my preferences for purchases — including what I buy for my sister, my uncle, and myself — so that it can better predict what products to show me as I browse, Privatzon does not need know where I live or what my credit card number is. It only needs to have authorization from my preferred payment service for the charge and to let my preferred shipping service know to whom ("Uncle Tim") the purchase is being sent. Thus Privatzon keeps the information about my purchase preferences, UPS keeps the

---

[4] There are, of course, many solutions using one-time credit numbers, starting with [22].

addresses of my friends and family, while American Express keeps my credit-card information. Both Privatzon and UPS have less information about me that could be inappropriately accessed or disclosed, and thus limit their legal liability and their compliance burden. If I work from home, I can have my work mail — copies of *IEEE Security and Privacy, CACM, Science* — delivered to me without listing my home address in the membership database (and thus publishing my home address). Instead of IEEE, ACM, and AAAS each keeping track of two addresses for me: my home (for delivery of journals) and my work location (for publication of membership lists), the organizations tell the mail provider SP that my journals should go to my_home_address. Meanwhile the organizations print my_work_address in their membership listings. The federated system keeps these separate pieces of my PII separate — and private.

2.1   The Principle of Minimal Disclosure

In the end, if Privatzon is to get paid, if the book is to be shipped, if the pharmacist is to fill a prescription, then the data that is my credit-card number, my uncle's address, and my drug dosage has to reside somewhere. Insiders have always posed the greatest security and privacy threat. Identity-management systems should use the principle of minimal disclosure, and should be able to engage where no PII is exchanged. Federation allows information to be distributed with each SP receiving exactly the information needed for its role — though many service providers may have to adjust to the concept (since they will no longer receive PII). To reduce liability, many organizations will choose to limit the PII they hold (and then protect the PII they hold in various ways: protected databases, strict access rules, careful auditing procedures, as well as some PETs, including those described below). Federated systems allow them to do so, and there have been several approaches to this — both theoretical and within deployed systems.

In 2007 Gevers et al. presented a privacy-preserving method for supplying disparate pieces of information to an SP, e.g., revealing that the user is over eighteen and a citizen of < Belgium, France, etc. > without revealing the user's age or citizenship [4]. Their solution is a "claim evaluator" sitting within an Identity Provider that responds to such queries. Sun built such a system in 2005 to satisfy U.S. government requirements about employee contributions to a political fund. Sun's system checked employee citizenship, employee rank, and stockholder status; based on the information gathered, it returned a yes/no eligibility status for company political (PAC) contributions [25]. This conceptually simple approach is readily understood by the user.

Researchers at IBM Zurich have developed a system, Idemix, that uses zero-knowledge credentials to protect user privacy. A Principal presents an encrypted pseudonym to an SP along with credentials that the Principal uses to prove to the SP that it is the owner of the pseudonym [6]. The unlinkability inherent in Idemix means that the IdP will not be able to cancel unused assertions, something unlikely to be attractive to IdPs or SPs. And if Principal "shares" the pseudonym and credentials with another user, the new user is able to impersonate the Principal *everywhere,* rendering such sharing highly unattractive.

It is important to understand when such minimal disclosure is needed. The IBM researchers present a usage case of a Principal seeking to rent a car online and presenting a credential that shows the Principal possesses a valid credit card and driver's license. But while there is no reason for the rental agency to know more about the user's finances than that she has adequate credit coverage for the car rental, there are numerous reasons why the agency should have information about the driver. If a prior interaction gave rise to a dispute (such as unpaid charges or collision damages), the rental agency wants to know about this before agreeing to lease a car to the Principal. It may be sufficient to be able to link past and present records without necessarily using the Principal's name as the link. Observe that the SP wishes to be able to establish the link even if it is not in the Principal's interests for that to happen. However, when a Principal succeeds in concealing the link between the current interaction and previous detrimental behavior, the ultimate protection (for the Service Provider) may be a legal one, rather than a technical one. In other words, if the Service Provider can subsequently prove — for example, through physical forensics — that the Principal acted deceitfully, the mitigation may be that the SP declines to accept liability for the bad behavior of the Principal.

There are situations in which such "cloaked" interactions between an SP and a Principal as provided by Idemix are appropriate, and situations in which cloaking is inappropriate. Often an identity aware approach is more appropriate and use cases should be carefully analyzed to determine which approach fits the situation best. We should also keep in mind that Idemix' zero-knowledge protocols come at a cost: the running time goes up by a factor of approximately five over "normal" identity-management schemes [6].

2.2 Linkages Only When Appropriate

Where more than two SPs are involved, the question of linkability still arises. Again, the mitigation (this time on the Principal's part), might be technical (such as the use of different identifiers for each SP or the opaque identifiers that Liberty automatically provides) or not (such as a reliance on Data Protection principles restricting "purpose of use" to "purpose of collection").

The canonical use case for preventing the IdP from being able to correlate a Principal with her choice of SPs is one often cited by Dick Hardt [5]: presenting a driver's license to a bartender to prove the Principal is over the legal drinking age without the Motor Vehicle Bureau knowing the particular instance of the use of the credential. This use case governs acceptance of e-government identity-management systems. Citizens are uncomfortable if, in using government-based digital credentials to establish certain aspects of their identity in private-sector authorization, they are exposing private activities.

Various zero-knowledge-based specifications, including Idemix and UProve[24], solve this problem. An alternative solution is provided by Microsoft's InfoCard protocol, which defines a message flow eliminating direct communication between the IdP and the SP; the protocol also offers the option of having the identity selector encrypt the SP's identity so as to prevent the IdP from learning it on receiving a request for a token. Both features together are necessary to ensure that an IdP cannot learn which SPs a Principal visits. The SAML Enhanced Client/Proxy protocol is similar but at present only has the first feature (it could be further profiled to add the second feature).

The question is whether deployers of federated identity systems want such a feature. Although these other identity-management schemes show how to solve the problem of keeping the SP information from the IdP, this may be a problem in search of a solution. The bar-and-driver's-license example is an "off-label" use of the credential — and that aspect is actually the significant aspect of the situation. There is no reason for the Motor Vehicle Bureau to know the Principal has been at a bar, and for this reason we find the IdP's knowing about the "off-label" license usage problematic. On the other hand, the agency has every right to know if a policeman has issued her a ticket for speeding.

Trying to use a non-governmental ID to prove certain properties about the user may not be any better. For example, banks do not underwrite clients' use of bank-based credentials for activities that the banks don't know about[5]. There is a tug-of-war around conflicting needs. A low-trust proof of identity (such as one supplied by OpenID) provides (at risk of coining a truism) a low-quality proof of identity — analogous to a bar accepting hand-written notes that its patrons are over 18. If the user needs a high-quality proof of identity then the identity supplier will likely want some type of control over how that credential is used.

inCommon [7], a federated identity-management program that helps universities share resources, provides an excellent illustration of this type of tradeoff. inCommon uses the SAML-based Shibboleth environment to create a federation whose members are institutions of higher education. Each IdP determines their own authentication mechanism while each SP determines what their access policies are. To obtain resources at an SP, a Principal uses an IdP-issued credential that only says that the Principal is a member of the IdP's institution. Several things make this system work. At the technical level, it is the SAML specifications. At the policy level, Shibboleth depends on trust. At the business level, this is an instance of a low-level access. The Principal doesn't get the keys to the kingdom as a result of their assertion, only access to some online resources at a member institution. Access to more highly valued resources at that institution (e.g., registrar records for cross-registration purposes) would require authorization predicated on attributes other than "is a member of."

2.3   Lowering Exposure

In an analysis of the market failure of P3P, Jane Winn notes that "voluntary, consensus standard-starting processes are more likely to succeed when responding

---

[5] Though the Scandinavian Bank-ID system shows that this divide can be bridged ...under the right conditions. Under the Bank-ID system, bank-issued credentials can be used to authenticate for access to public-sector services. There is an element of technical interoperability, of course, but just as vital is the legal provision for public-sector bodies to rely on credentials issued for a quite unrelated purpose.

to market demand" [26, p. 16]. We believe that the market driver for privacy in federated identity management systems is the liability threat.

If PII is inappropriately released from an identity-management system, then the organization that allowed this to happen will be liable. The privacy pressure point is the organization with the data, giving the organization strong incentives to protect the PII it has — and *to minimize the amount it collects.* In 2003, California enacted breach notification laws requiring notification if unencrypted data has been inappropriately disclosed[6]; many other states have followed suit.

Both IDPs and SPs have to assess whether the personal data they hold exposes them to disproportionate liability or an excessive burden of compliance. However, in such areas as preventing money laundering, working with vulnerable adults and children, etc., for the IDPs or SPs to hold too little personal data can also be a liability.

2.4 Technical versus Legal/Policy Approaches to Privacy

Technological privacy protections are not only necessary to digital identity management, they are fundamental to its existence. Without encryption (symmetric and public-key), digital signatures and other relevant technologies, there would be no digital identity management, federated or otherwise. Yet even where part of the solution to a given privacy problem is technical (e.g.,[22] [23]), legal and policy protections play critical roles.

Take, for instance, the deletion of PII that is no longer needed. There are several technical options here, ranging from destroying the data, or using strong encryption to protect the data and then destroying the keys on a regular schedule, to more complex privacy-enhancing methods. Which solution is most appropriate depends on non-technical factors such as the value of the data, the risk involved in storing it, and in some cases legal requirements.

We do not argue against the technical solutions — indeed, we expect over time to see various of them adopted — but contend that the privacy solutions for identity management should be a combination of technical and non-technical measures, capable of adjusting to different legal, regulatory and liability contexts. We now discuss the Liberty Alliance model, a solution that relies on both.

3   Liberty's Approach

In 2001 issues of online identity and how to simplify it began appearing. The Liberty Alliance, an industry group consisting of technology companies as well as companies concerned with online identity, was formed to develop open specifications for federated identity management. The SAML/Liberty model is now quite mature; it has been deployed in a number of environments, including governments (e.g., New Zealand[17]), healthcare (e.g., Aetna) financial (e.g., Citi) and communication companies (e.g., Deutsche Telekom AG). We continue our

---

[6] SB 1386 covers breaches of financial records, AB 1298, breaches of medical and health information.

discussion of the technology (further detailed in Appendix A), following that
with a discussion of privacy protections in the Liberty system.

3.1   Liberty Protocols: A Brief Overview

Traditionally, users have needed separate accounts with passwords etc. at each
online Service Provider with which they wanted to interact. The *Liberty Identity Federation Framework* (ID-FF) sought to solve that problem by enabling
a Principal to establish pairwise federations with a single account at the Identity Provider (IdP). This made Single Sign-On possible within a *Circle of Trust*
(CoT): a set of Service Providers and one or more Identity Providers.

ID-FF defined protocols for account linking, single sign-on and global logout,
and to accommodate different mechanisms (e.g., browser with redirects, artifacts, etc.). Liberty's ID-FF and OASIS SAML were distinct efforts in developing federated identity management for secure simple sign-on which converged
with OASIS's SAML 2.0 specification, the de-facto standard in federated identity management. SAML 2.0 represents a significant improvement in a number
of aspects including defederation, metadata definition, and authentication levels.

Liberty's Identity Web Services Framework (ID-WSF) uses federated identity
(ID-FF or SAML) as a basis for a web services framework that enables web
service consumers (WSC) to invoke services web service providers (WSP). ID-WSF has three key goals: (i) define safe protocols and practices to protect a user's
online privacy; (ii) leverage the user's identity to enable personalized services;
(iii) allow secure identity-based sharing of resources by a variety of services.

Before a service can be invoked by other web services, it needs to be discoverable and associated with the Principal's Discovery Service (DS). ID-WSF defines
a set of protocols for the entire lifecycle of online services, including support for
3 core operations: (i) registration/association; (ii) discovery; and (iii) invocation.

The main reason for registering a service instance at the DS and associating
it with a Principal is to allow other web services to discover it. This discovery is
the result of a lookup query sent by a requesting WSC to the DS. That request
specifies the Principal's identity as well as search parameters like service type.

In addition to a list of services (WSPs) that matched the lookup request, the
DS also includes security tokens that will allow the WSC to invoke the service
hosted by the WSP(s).

Liberty and SAML use a variety of security technologies: channel security
(server-side certificates for identity providers; TLS1.0, SSL 3.0, or other channel
security protocols, such as IPSec, with appropriately certified keys), security
tokens with a limited lifetime, nonces, and digital signatures for per-transaction
integrity. In addition to those security mechanisms, Liberty identifies specific
elements of its protocol messages that may present privacy risks (due to the
nature of the information they bear) and might need additional security. For
instance, in the most privacy-aware environments, it is recommended to employ
encrypted Name Identifiers. Also an SP can use the NameID Mapping protocol
to add a pseudonym of its choice to an existing federation.

3.2   The Roles of Liberty's Privacy Guardians

The Liberty protocols address only the *exchange* of information. Whatever the parties do to produce or consume the information that was exchanged is outside the scope of these protocols. A Liberty-enabled exchange of information between an IdP and SP starts with a contract specifying partner responsibilities. When engineers discuss the Liberty protocols this step is often omitted; contracts are not omitted in practice. Thus our analysis starts with the *Liberty Privacy and Security Best Practices,* which lays out expectations on handling PII:

> The framework of the Liberty Specifications is built upon the presump-
> tion that PII will be shared ("attribute sharing") only in the context
> of permissions i.e., in line with the Principal's expressed consent and
> preferences. Such attribute sharing should be predicated upon not only
> a prior agreement between the Liberty-enabled providers, but also on
> providing notice to the Principal and obtaining the Principal's consent
> ... Liberty-enabled providers should take reasonable measures to prevent
> unauthorized acquisition of a principal's personal information (e.g., by
> harvesting)[11, p. 9].

Specifically:

- The Identity Provider should safeguard the Principal's credentials and should have some mechanisms in place to require the Authentication Domain to use the credentials in a proper manner.
- Service Providers should inform Principals of their data practices, provide Principals with certain choices regarding secondary uses of the Principal's PII, maintain security of a Principal's PII within their control, and not use or share such information except in accordance with the Service Provider's privacy policy and/or the consent or usage directives of the Principal.
- The Attribute Provider[7] has at least the same responsibilities as Service Providers with respect to clear notice (including notice to the Principal regarding what are the default usage directives and how the Principal can change such usage directives), choice, security, and responsible use and sharing of the Principal's data[11, pp. 9-10].

For PII passing between entities, privacy is achieved through security. Channel security is provided by TLS; protection against replay and main-in-the-middle attacks is provided by digital signing, as is message integrity; correlation of a Principal's PII by multiple SPs is prevented through the use of opaque identifiers (this does not protect against a timing analysis or traffic flow attack).

PII 'at rest' at an entity should be protected through standard mechanisms for data confidentiality and integrity, with audit trails to track data access, etc. Ultimately, though, the protection here is legal. A rogue Service Provider or

---

[7] The Attribute Provider earns its place in the ecosystem purely by serving up attributes on behalf of the user, as opposed to by providing an actual service (such as car rental, payment transactions etc.).

Identity Provider is in a position to violate a Principal's privacy and technical protections can only reduce, not eliminate this risk. One role that a Liberty-enabled system has, however, is in maintaining "contextual integrity."

Disclosures of PII are made in a specific context: shopping history with a particular retailer, health-care data with a family doctor, etc. When the contextual integrity is broken, and disparate pieces of PII — payment details, age, home address, books bought, health records — are combined, we get a remarkably invasive look at an individual's life. Liberty's federated architecture is designed to keep contexts separate.

Closely related to contextual integrity is data aggregation: using information from a variety of sources to determine aspects of a Principal's PII even if that information has not been specifically provided. Liberty guidelines recommend that the IdP — generally more able than the Principal to understand data-aggregation issues — have default policies that limit the release of PII. It may be appropriate for the Principal to be able to override these policies through an opt-in process[8] [10, pp. 22-23].

3.3   Further Steps in Liberty Privacy Protections: The Identity Governance Framework

Although the Liberty protocols protect the privacy of data exchange, there nonetheless remains a gap: explicit mechanisms for exchanging metadata governing data at rest. With the underpinnings provided by the ID-FF and ID-WSF specifications in place, Liberty is preparing an Identity Governance Framework (IGF) [13] that will provide the Principal with a clear framework for assessing whether her privacy is being protected in the way that she wants.

IGF enables the creation of declarative contracts (or policies) between an Attribute Provider and a Service Provider. To achieve this, IGF defines two declarative syntaxes: Attribute Authority Policy Markup Language (AAPML) and client Attribute Requirement Markup Language (CARML).

The Attribute Provider uses AAPML (a profile of OASIS XACML) to create statements pertaining to the access and use of the protected attributes. For instance, it has the ability to express conditions permitting release of the data (e.g., *any authenticated student can read these teaching notes*), obligations for the SP (e.g., *this document shall not be stored for more than two days*), and the need to obtain the Principal's consent. Meanwhile the SP can specify whether the requested attributes will be automatically discarded after usage. Or the SP could request the possibility of modifying the data or forwarding it to another SP. The CARML document created by the SP can either be created and exchanged ahead of time or it can be created and included in the attribute request.

In addition to these declarative syntaxes, IGF also specifies a certain number of basic privacy constraints such as propagation, usage, retention, storage

---

[8] It is interesting to note that some electronic health care projects (e.g., the U.K.'s Summary Health Care Record [21]) have opted for implicit consent to allow access to personal health information. Consent must be expressly revoked by the client.

and display of identity data. Although non-exhaustive, these atomic privacy constraints can be combined using WS-Policy [27]. These are viewed as commitments made by the creator of that request.

3.4 Privacy Leaks in Liberty Protocols

In the years since the Liberty federated model was introduced, there have been a number of papers discussing various privacy concerns in the protocols and model. We now consider these.

Birgit Pfitzmann [19] and Pfitzmann and Waidner [20] found various security and privacy risks in the early Liberty protocols. Pfitzmann pointed out technical ambiguities as well as policy issues that ought to be clarified in the Liberty single signon protocol [19]. Pfitzmann and Waidner demonstrated a man-in-the-middle attack against the Liberty-enabled client and proxy profile: a dishonest service provider could interpose itself between a Principal and an honest service provider (or even simply pretend to be the Principal without an initial request from the Principal) and then request authentication to the SP[9]. This attack is possible because Version 1.0 of the Liberty protocols did not require the SP to sign requests. Pfitzmann and Waidner suggested various ways to protect against the attack. Liberty version 1.1 prevents this by determining the SP's URL from the SP's identity and including the URL in its response.

Alsaleh and Adams' paper describes other consumer privacy issues [2]. On one point we agree: Alsaleh and Adams noted that the lack of standard privacy expression languages could lead to inconsistent interpretation of data privacy directives [2, p.72]. This problem was larger than the Liberty specifications and has recently been addressed in the IGF [13] program. We believe that the other "threats" Alsaleh and Adams posit stem from a fundamental misunderstanding of where the privacy pressure points lie in identity management; we provide detailed responses in Appendix B. But we note that design choices occur in technologies. Sometimes these concern security versus usability. Sometimes they relate to whether to solve a problem technically or via policy or regulation. Almost all of the Alsaleh and Adams' concerns are ones for which legal and policy responses are the most appropriate. Indeed, rather than being a problem for the Liberty specifications, this reinforces the view that the Liberty Alliance was right to complement its technical specification work with guidance on where the boundary lies between the technical and policy aspects of an identity-management system. We see no other comparable group that has paid equivalent attention to this aspect.

Jøsang et al. argue that, "SPs are not able to distinguish between a security assertion that reflects a genuine user service request, or one that represents an SP masquerading as a user" [8, p. 121]. This language could be interpreted either as the man-in-the-middle attack raised by [20] — which was resolved in version 1.1 of the Liberty Identity Federation specifications — or that a dishonest SP could claim to be a Principal at another SP. If the latter is what is meant, the dishonest

---

[9] The problem had been independently discovered by Jonathan Sergent.

SP is not in a position to authenticate as the Principal at the IdP and thus cannot learn anything at the second SP. Jøsang et al. also claim that in a federated model "Different SPs within the same federation domain are technically able to match personal information of the same user because of the mapping between identifiers" [8, p. 1221]. Liberty's use of pairwise, directional opaque identifiers prevents this problem.

Bhargav-Spantzel et al. propose two approaches to protecting the Principal's PII: distribute user identity information amongst several entities and use techniques such as zero-knowledge proofs to prevent identity theft within an IdP or SP [3]. The former is what federated systems do. This paper misunderstands some Liberty protocols. Liberty does not require PKI for Principal authentication [3, p. 25] but rather, allows authentication to be done in a variety of ways [10, p. 10]. Bhargav et al. suggest that a problem with Shibboleth is a single central identity provider. Both Shibboleth and Liberty allow Service Providers to use multiple Identity Providers within a Circle of Trust. The paper correctly observes that Liberty does not account for untrusted SPs or IdPs within the specifications [3, p. 25][10]. The specifications are about data exchanges only; the Liberty Alliance expectation is that individual service and identity providers will develop their own solutions against insider attack.

4   Conclusions

To succeed, digital identity management systems must balance competing sets of needs from users, IDPs, and SPs. Identity-management systems derive both strength and legitimacy from the consent of the individual whose PII is being used. Yet to benefit from the identity and service providers' offerings, the user must disclose PII — and therefore expose it to risk, regardless of the security mechanisms employed. Those organizations that request only minimal PII — and then protect, use and dispose of that PII appropriately — serve the user while minimizing risk and their liability.

Federation allows identity-management systems to be constructed with secure, minimized data exchange and thus to be inherently privacy-protective. The Liberty specifications enable privacy-protecting implementations but cannot mandate them. In the end, implementers must make their risk assessment and decide on the balance between technical and other mitigators.

Laws and policies on the one hand, and technology on the other, form integral parts of effective privacy protection. As the Liberty Alliance observes, "The identity challenge is both technical, business, and policy oriented" [15].

Acknowledgments. Many people have worked on Liberty over the years and developed insights on identity management and its privacy drivers. We have

---

[10] The Liberty ID-WSF Security and Privacy Overview states that, "[T]hese entities may not adhere to their contracts. In that case, the issue is out of scope for Liberty, which is, after all, a set of technical specifications for data exchange. Instead such a situation is appropriately handled by the legal system." [10, p. 15]

greatly benefited from discussions with Jeff Hodges, Paul Madsen, Eve Maler, and Bill Smith. Paul Syverson helped us put the ideas in this paper into a broader context.

References

1. Acquisti, A.: Identity Management, Privacy, and Price Discrimination. IEEE Security and Privacy 6(2), 46–50 (2008)
2. Alsaleh, M., Adams, C.: Enhancing Consumer Privacy in the Liberty Alliance Identity Federation and Web Services Frameworks. In: Danezis, G., Golle, P. (eds.) PET 2006. LNCS, vol. 4258, pp. 59–77. Springer, Heidelberg (2006)
3. Bhargav-Spantzel, A., Squicciarini, A., Bertino, E.: Establishing and Protecting Digital Identity in Federation Systems. CERIAS Tech Report 2007-18
4. Gevers, S., Verslype, K., De Decker, B.: Enhancing Privacy in Identity Management Systems. In: Workshop on Privacy in the Electronic Society, pp. 60–63 (2007)
5. Hardt, D.: Identity 2.0 Keynote, http://youtube.com/watch?v=RrpajcAgR1E
6. idemix for Internet anonymity,
   http://www.zurich.ibm.com/security/idemix/ptext.html (last viewed April 29, 2008)
7. inCommon Federation, http://www.incommonfederation.org/
8. Jøsang, A., AlZomai, M., Suriadi, S.: Usability and Privacy in Identity Managements Systems. In: Australasian Information Security Workshop: Privacy Enhancing Technologies 2007 (2007)
9. Wason, T. (ed.): Liberty Alliance Project, Liberty ID-FF Architecture Overview, Version 1.2 (2005)
10. Landau, S. (ed.): Liberty Alliance Project, Liberty ID-WSF Security and Privacy Overview, Version 1.0 (2003)
11. Varney, C. (ed.): Liberty Alliance Project, Privacy and Security Best Practices, Version 2.0, November 12 (2003)
12. Varney, C., Sheckler, V. (eds.): Liberty Alliance Project, Deployment Guidelines for Policy Decision Makers, Version 2.9, September 21 (2005)
13. Liberty Alliance Project, An Overview of the Id Governance Framework, ed (July 2007),
    http://projectliberty.org/liberty/content/download/3500/23156/
    file/overview-id-governance-framework-v1.0.pdf
14. Hodges, J., Kemp, J., Aarts, R., Whitehead, G., Madsen, P. (eds.): Liberty Alliance Project, Liberty ID-WSF SOAP Binding Specification, Version 2.0 July 7 (2007),
    http://www.projectliberty.org/liberty/content/download/897/6267/file/
    liberty-idwsf-soap-binding-v2.0.pdf
15. Liberty Alliance Papers,
    http://projectliberty.org/liberty/resource_center/papers (last viewed March 27, 2008)
16. Maler, E., Reed, D.: The Venn of Identity: Options and Issues in Federated Identity Management. IEEE Security and Privacy 6(2), 16–23 (2008)
17. McKenzie, R., Crompton, M., Wallis, C.: Use Cases for Identity Management in E-Government. IEEE Security and Privacy 6(2), 51–57 (March/April)
18. Office of the Chief Information and Privacy Officer, Province of Ontario, Privacy Impact Assessment Guidelines (December 1999) (updated June 2001)

19. Pfitzmann, B.: Privacy in Enterprise Identity Federation –Policies for Liberty 2 Single Signon. Elsevier Information Security Technical Report (ISTR), 9/1, pp. 45–58 (2004); preliminary version appeared as Pfitzmann, B.: Privacy in enterprise identity federation. In: Dingledine, R. (ed.) PET 2003, LNCS. vol. 2760, pp. 189–204. Springer, Heidelberg (2003)
20. Pfitzmann, B., Waidner, M.: Analysis of Liberty Single-Sign-on with Enabled Clients. IEEE Internet Computing, 38–44 (November/December 2003)
21. Ranger, S.: NHS e-record opt-out offered. IT Management News, December 19 (2006),
    http://news.zdnet.co.uk/itmanagement/0,1000000308,39285203,00.htm (last viewed January 18, 2009)
22. Shamir, A.: Secureclick: A web payment system with disposable credit card numbers. In: Syverson, P.F. (ed.) FC 2001. LNCS, vol. 2339, pp. 232–242. Springer, Heidelberg (2002)
23. Stubblebine, S.G., Syverson, P.F.: Authentic Attributes with Fine-Grained Anonymity Protection. In: Frankel, Y. (ed.) FC 2000. LNCS, vol. 1962, pp. 276–294. Springer, Heidelberg (2001)
24. U-Prove SDK Overview, April 16 (2007), http://www.credentica.com/ (last viewed May 3, 2008)
25. Wilson, Y.: Personal communication
26. Winn, J.: Information Technology Standards as a Form of Consumer Protection Law. In: Winn, J. (ed.) Consumer Protection in the Age of the Information Economy, Ashgate (2006)
27. Web Services Policy 1.5 Framework (October 2007),
    http://www.w3.org/TR/2004/REC-xmlschema-1-20041028/

A   Liberty Alliance Protocols

We present here an abbreviated discussion of the Liberty Alliance protocols ID-FF, ID-WSF, and Discovery Service. A fuller treatment appears in [9] and [10].

A.1   Federated Identity Frameworks: ID-FF and SAML

Liberty Alliance's ID-FF and OASIS SAML are frameworks that define protocols for (i) Single Sign-On and Account linking (aka. Federation) (ii) Name Registration (iii) Federation Termination and (iv) Single Logout.

Below are steps of a typical SAML2.0 based establishment of a single-sign-on (browser profile).

1. The Principal browses to an SP site and seeks access a protected resource there.
2. The SP responds with a SAML authentication request in an HTML form which after submission turns into either an HTTP Redirect or a POST sent to the IdP.
3. The Principal, if not already authenticated, is prompted with a login form at the IdP.

4. Upon successful authentication, the IdP sends (HTTP POST) to the Principal's browser to the SP with a <Response> message that contains a signed SAML assertion (possibly several). Among other things, the IdP might add information regarding the Principal default Discovery Service to facilitate bootstrapping an ID-WSF sequence as described in the next section.
5. If the SP is satisfied with the content of the assertion it has obtained, the SP grants the Principal access to the protected resource.

Note that pseudonyms are used between the SP and IdP in assertions to prevent account linking, and the NameID mapping protocol allow SPs to change the pseudonym used in federation.

A.2 Identity-Based Web Services Framework: ID-WSF

ID-WSF is a framework for identity-based web services. Its protocols support three core phases: (i) A WSP associating its service with a Principal's identity; a one-time operation for any given web service that enables the Principal to use this service in the future. (ii) A WSC querying a Principal's Discovery Service to look up a resource hosted at another web service provider (WSP). (iii) A WSC accessing a Principal's resource at that WSP, subject to conditions the resource's owner may place on access.

The ID-WSF protocols are based on a Request/Response design pattern. A SOAP binding document describes how such messages are to be created in a SOAP environment.

Service registration and association: ID-WSF defines a sequence of steps to allow a web service provider to become dynamically discoverable:

1. To registers its service instance at the DS, a WSP sends a SOAP message called <SvcMDRegister> at a known endpoint of the DS. This message contains XML metadata that describe its service (web address and type of service, the framework and security mechanisms supported etc.)
2. The DS returns an identifier (called MDID) for future reference.
3. When the Principal browses to WSP's web site, a typical response of the WSP (acting as a regular SP) will be to authenticate the Principal, possibly through single sign on as previously described. This authentication will provide information about the Principal's Discovery Service. The WSP offers to list its service as one of the Principal's known services at the DS.
4. If the Principal consents to this association, the WSP sends a request to the DS including the previously obtained MDID and some additional metadata.
5. Upon success (or failure) DS responds with a message that contains a <Status> element.

Service Discovery and invocation: Once registered and associated to a Principal, a service instance can be discovered and invoked by other web services. Following are the steps involved in this process:

1. To discover services of a certain type that are associated with a particular Principal, a WSC sends a SOAP message called <Query> at the lookup endpoint of the DS. This request contains a RequestedService XML element (possibly several) containing criteria for the lookup request (e.g. service type, etc.). The identity of the Principal is conveyed by the SOAP headers.
2. The DS returns a list of matching services, represented by endpoint references (EPRs). Each EPR contains a security token, crafted by the DS, to allow the WSC to invoke that WSP.
3. WSC can now invoke WSP, presenting the security token it has obtained during the previous step. ID-WSF defines a Create, read, update and delete interface that is designed for data-oriented services. This is the Data Service Templates, which serves as a base for the definition of many specialized interfaces. Liberty supports the definition of service interfaces for various types of services. The current service interfaces defined are personal profile, employee profile, geolocation, contact book and presence.
4. Upon success (or failure) WSP responds with a message that contains a <Status> element.

Additional Protocols: ID-WSF also defines two additional protocols that are important from a privacy perspective:

- The Interaction Service facilitates communication between a WSP and a Principal in cases where consent must be obtained before the WSP grants a WSC access to the Principal's resource it is hosting.
- People Service improves security and privacy in social networks and defines: (i) A service associated to a Principal, (ii) A flexible, privacy-aware framework to manage the people a Principal interacts with (invitations, identity federation), (iii) A SOAP interface for WSPs to query and manipulate information about a Principal's friends and colleagues.
  The People Service also enables further evolution for online transactions by supporting cross-principal interactions based on identity mapping.

B   Detailed Response to Alsaleh and Adams

We have divided the issues raised by Alsaleh and Adams into three categories: those best solved through legal and policy means, those where the Liberty choice was in favor of usability, and those that had already been/are resolved.

1. Privacy Issues Resolved Through Legal/Policy Means:
   (a) Alsaleh and Adams posit a privacy risk during Identity Federation when the IdP introduces the Principal to the CoT [2, pp. 68-69]. That is a policy decision, and is made clear in the Liberty Deployment Guidelines, "The Liberty specifications provide for both access permissions to allow a Principal to specify whether and under what circumstances a Service Provider can obtain given attributes ... Has the Principal consented to all data uses?" [12, p. 8].

(b) Alsaleh and Adams raise concern about user consent for identity federation between IdP and SP; presumably what they mean is account linkage between the Principal's Identity Provider and Service Provider [2, p. 69]. Clearly such account linkage is a Principal's decision[11]; it is not clear why Alsaleh and Adams thought the Liberty framework made it otherwise.

(c) Alsaleh and Adams suggest that if there is a redirect between service providers that have different attribute information about a Principal, then two dishonest service providers could illegally exchange the attribute information, violating the Principal's privacy[2, pp. 70-71]. The key point here is "illegally." Only laws (and contracts, a form of law) can prevent a Service Provider from mishandling Principal information the SP has; technology cannot.

(d) Alsaleh and Adams object to the fact that once the SP has the address of the user attribute resource holder, the SP might retain the address past the current usage [2, pp. 71]. The security token is likely to have expired, but in any case, this is a legal issue; such retention does not conform with the timeliness aspect of the Fair Information Practices [10, p.15].

(e) Alsaleh and Adams state that Interaction Services (IS) hosted by other SPs may have privacy impact on the Principal [2, p. 72]. The IS *must* be trusted by the WSC [10, p. 19]. Vetting is done by the WSC and any liability is at the WSC.

(f) Alsaleh and Adams state that the SP could deny having made a query to the Principal [2, pp. 72-73]. As above, Liberty ID-WSF Security and Privacy Overview observes that such problems are an out-of-band issue, and recommends, "IS providers should make efforts to induce trust in the Principal by offering transaction logs, by employing sufficiently long strong authentication methods, etc." [10, p. 19].

(g) Alsaleh and Adams state that if a Principal deals with two SPs, there is risk of the two sharing PII about the user with each other [2, p. 72]. The opaque handles make such collusion difficult. However, since the SPs each have data about the Principal, such correlation is possible. In this case, the problem is not about the data exchange — the Liberty protocols — but about data at rest.

(h) Alsaleh and Adams observe an SP can amass data about a Principal, thus leading to identification of the Principal [2, p. 72]. This is not about data exchange, but about the fact that once you give data to a provider, they have it. Only law helps here.

(i) Alsaleh and Adams point out that the SP can reuse or share information about the attribute provider that hold the Principal's data [2, p. 72]. This is identical to the issue above.

---

[11] In the enterprise context, the consent is often part of an employment contract. A company might outsource aspects of its core business functions, e.g., human resources, and then the corporation consents — without an explicit request to the Principal — to have these introductions made.

(j) Alsaleh and Adams argue that privacy policies of the Attribute Provider local access policy and the Principal privacy policy might not match [2, p. 72]. Again there needs to be a business/policy/statutory decision on which policy takes precedence.

2. Privacy Issues Resolved in Favor of Usability:

   (a) Alsaleh and Adams believe that the SP knowing the Principal's preferred IdP is a privacy violation [2, p. 69]. The Liberty design decision was to choose usability with a minimum of privacy loss. After all, the IdP may have millions of users; how does the SP knowing that a particular user does so present a privacy disclosure? The reason the SP and IdP have a relationship is precisely because the SP wishes to rely on information the IdP can provide. If the Principal is genuinely concerned about this knowledge, he has the technical option of turning off federation domain cookies, or the procedural one of simply declining to link accounts.

   (b) Alsaleh and Adams claim that there is a risk that an SP could determine which IdP most recently authenticated the Principal from the federation common domain cookie [2, p. 69]. This is as above, with the same minimal privacy loss.

   (c) Alsaleh and Adams express concern that a federated SP can request that an IdP reauthenticate a Principal whenever the SP chooses and that the SP can query the IdP about the type of authentication method [2, p. 71]. All this reveals is information about the IdP's authentication methods that the SP already knows. There is no privacy risk for the Principal; this is feature (not a bug!).

3. Previously Covered Issues:

   (a) Alsaleh and Adams are concerned that a browser redirect can carry Principal PII unencrypted and is thus subject to eavesdropping [2, p. 70]. The Liberty Alliance previously addressed this concern [9, p. 21].

   (b) Alsaleh and Adams claim that an SP can request a resource-holder address for more than one user attribute from an IdP and that creates a privacy breach since the SP may use only one Usage Directive, which might not apply to all the attributes [2, pp. 71-72]. The UsageDirective can be applied to all conveyed attributes as multiple UDs may be employed [14, pp.46-48][12].

   (c) Alsaleh and Adams express concern that an IdP or SP could fabricate user consent and that the Principal has no way to force the SP to sign a request for consent [2, p. 72]. It is true that the Principal trusts the IdP, but that is an out-of-band issue. While it is true that the IS can be co-hosted with the requesting WSC — creating an "obvious" conflict of interest — the question is could this happen in a real deployment? As the *Liberty ID-WSF Security and Privacy Overview* states, it is simply the case that the IS must be trusted by the Principal [10, p. 19].

---

[12] The multiple <UsageDirective> header blocks for a SOAP Header was also true for version 1.2, which appeared in May 2005.

Data Hemorrhages in the Health-Care Sector[*]

M. Eric Johnson

Center for Digital Strategies
Tuck School of Business
Dartmouth College, Hanover NH 03755
{M.Eric.Johnson}@darmouth.edu

Abstract. Confidential data hemorrhaging from health-care providers pose financial risks to firms and medical risks to patients. We examine the consequences of data hemorrhages including privacy violations, medical fraud, financial identity theft, and medical identity theft. We also examine the types and sources of data hemorrhages, focusing on inadvertent disclosures. Through an analysis of leaked files, we examine data hemorrhages stemming from inadvertent disclosures on internet-based file sharing networks. We characterize the security risk for a group of health-care organizations using a direct analysis of leaked files. These files contained highly sensitive medical and personal information that could be maliciously exploited by criminals seeking to commit medical and financial identity theft. We also present evidence of the threat by examining user-issued searches. Our analysis demonstrates both the substantial threat and vulnerability for the health-care sector and the unique complexity exhibited by the US health-care system.

Keywords: Health-care information, identity theft, data leaks, security.

1 Introduction

Data breaches and inadvertent disclosures of customer information have plagued sectors from banking to retail. In many of these cases, lost customer information translates directly into financial losses through fraud and identity theft. The health-care sector also suffers such data hemorrhages, with multiple consequences. In some cases, the losses have translated to privacy violations and embarrassment. In other cases, criminals exploit the information to commit fraud or medical identity theft. Given the highly fragmented US health-care system, data hemorrhages come from

---

[*] Experiments described in this paper were conducted in collaboration with Tiversa who has developed a patent-pending technology that, in real-time, monitors global P2P file sharing networks. The author gratefully acknowledges the assistance of Nicholas Willey and the helpful comments of Lane R. Hatcher. This research was partially supported by the U.S. Department of Homeland Security under Grant Award Number 2006-CS-001-000001, under the auspices of the Institute for Information Infrastructure Protection (I3P). The views and conclusions contained in this document are those of the authors and should not be interpreted as necessarily representing the official policies, either expressed or implied, of the U.S. Department of Homeland Security, the I3P, or Dartmouth College.

R. Dingledine and P. Golle (Eds.): FC 2009, LNCS 5628, pp. 71–89, 2009.

many different sources—ambulatory health-care providers, acute-care hospitals, physician groups, medical laboratories, insurance carriers, back-offices of health maintenance organizations, and outsourced service providers such as billing, collection, and transcription firms.

In this paper we analyze the threats and vulnerabilities to medical data. We first explore the consequences of data hemorrhages, including a look at how criminals exploit medical data, in particular through medical identity theft. Next, we examine types and sources of data hemorrhages through a direct analysis of inadvertent disclosures of medical information on publically available, internet-based file sharing networks. We present an analysis of thousands of files we uncovered. These files were inadvertently published in popular peer-to-peer file sharing networks like Limewire and Bearshare and could be easily downloaded by anyone searching for them. Originating from health-care firms, their suppliers, and patients themselves, the files span everything from sensitive patient correspondence to business documents, spreadsheets, and PowerPoint files. We found multiple files from major health-care firms that contained private employee and patient information for literally tens of thousands of individuals, including addresses, Social Security Numbers, birth dates, and treatment billing information. Disturbingly, we also found private patient information including medical diagnoses and psychiatric evaluations. Finally, we present evidence, from user-issued searches on these networks, that individuals are working to find medical data—likely for malicious exploitation.

The extended enterprises of health-care providers often include many technically unsophisticated partners who are more likely to leak information. As compared with earlier studies we conducted in the banking sector (Johnson 2008), we find that tracking and stopping medical data hemorrhages is more complex and possibly harder to control given the fragmented nature of the US health-care system. We document the risks and call for better control of sensitive health-care information.

2   Consequences of Data Hemorrhages

Data hemorrhages from the health-care sector are diverse, from leaked business information and employee personally identifiable information (PII) to patient protected health information (PHI), which is individually identifiable health information. While some hemorrhages are related to business information, like marketing plans or financial documents, we focus on the more disturbing releases of individually identifiable information and protected health information. In these cases, the consequences range from privacy violations (including violations of both state privacy laws and federal HIPPA standards) to more serious fraud and theft (Figure 1).

On one hand, health-care data hemorrhages fuel financial identity theft. This occurs when leaked patient or employee information is used to commit traditional financial fraud. For example, using social security numbers and other identity information to apply for fraudulent loans, take-over bank accounts, or charge purchases to credit cards. On the other hand, PHI is often used by criminals to commit traditional medical fraud, which typically involves billing payers (e.g., Medicaid/Medicare or private health-care insurance) for treatment never rendered. The US General Accounting

Office estimated that 10% of health expenditure reimbursed by Medicare is paid to fraudsters, including identity thieves and fraudulent health service providers (Bolin and Clark 2004; Lafferty 2007).

PHI can also be very valuable to criminals who are intent on committing medical identity theft. The crime of medical identity theft represents the intersection of medical fraud and identity theft (Figure 1). Like medical fraud, it involves fraudulent charges and like financial identity theft, it involves the theft of identity. It is unique in that it involves a medical identity (patient identification, insurance information, medical histories, prescriptions, test results...) that may be used to obtain medical services or prescription drugs (Ball et al. 2003). Leaked insurance information can be used to fraudulently obtain service, but unlike a credit card the spending limits are much higher—charges can quickly reach tens of thousands or even millions of dollars. And unlike financial credit, there is less monitoring and reporting. Sadly, beyond the financial losses, medical identity theft carries other personal consequences for victims as it often results in erroneous changes to medical records that are difficult and time consuming to correct. Such erroneous information could impact care quality or impede later efforts to obtain medical, life, or disability insurance.

For example, recent medical identity theft cases have involved the sale of health identities to illegal immigrants (Messmer 2008). These forms of theft are a problem impacting payers, patients, and health-care providers. Payers and providers both see financial losses from fraudulent billing. Patients are also harmed when they are billed for services they did not receive, and when erroneous information appears on their medical record.

Between 1998 and 2006, the FTC recorded complaints of over nineteen thousand cases of medical identity theft with rapid growth in the past five years. Many believe these complaints represent the tip of the growing fraud problem, with some estimates showing upwards of a quarter-million cases a year (Dixon 2006, 12-13). Currently, there is no single agency tasked with tracking, investigating, or prosecuting these crimes (Lafferty 2007) so reliable data on the extent of the problem does not exist.

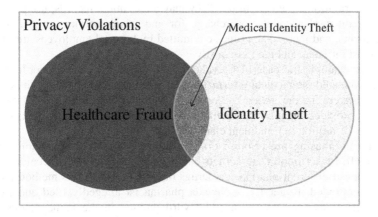

Fig. 1. Consequences of data hemorrhages

The crime of financial identity theft is well understood with clear underlying motives. A recent FTC survey estimated that 3.7% of Americans were victims of some sort of identity theft (FTC 2007). Significant media coverage has alerted the public of the financial dangers that can arise when a thief assumes your identity. However, the dangers and associated costs of medical identity theft are less well understood and largely overlooked. Of course, PHI (including insurance policy information and government identity numbers) can be fraudulently used for financial gain at the expense of firms and individuals. However, when a medical identity is stolen and used to obtain care, it may also result in life-threatening amendments to a medical file. Any consequential inaccuracies in simple entries, such as allergy diagnoses and blood-typing results, can jeopardize patient lives. Furthermore, like financial identity theft, medical identity theft represents a growing financial burden on the private and public sectors.

Individuals from several different groups participate in the crime of medical identity theft: the uninsured, hospital employees, organized crime rings, illegal aliens, wanted criminals, and drug abusers. In many cases the theft is driven by greed, but in other case the underlying motive is simply for the uninsured to receive medical care. Without medical insurance, these individuals are unable to obtain the expensive care that they require, such as complicated surgeries or organ transplants. However, if they assume the identity of a well insured individual, hospitals will provide full-service care. For example, Carol Ann Hutchins of Pennsylvania assumed another woman's identity after finding a lost wallet (Wereschagin 2006). With the insurance identification card inside the wallet, Hutchins was able to obtain care and medication on 40 separate occasions at medical facilities across Pennsylvania and Ohio, accumulating a total bill of $16,000. Had it not been for the victim's careful examination of her monthly billing statement, it is likely that Hutchins would have continued to fraudulently receive care undetected. Hutchins served a 3-month jail sentence for her crime, but because of privacy laws and practices, any resulting damage done to the victim's medical record was difficult and costly to erase.

Hospital employees historically comprise the largest known group of individuals involved in traditional medical fraud. They may alter patient records, use patient data to open credit card accounts, overcharge for and falsify services rendered, create phony patients, and more. The crimes committed by hospital employees are often the largest, most intricate, and the most costly.

Take for example the case of Cleveland Clinic front desk clerk coordinator, Isis Machado who sold the medical information of more than 1,100 patients, to her cousin Fernando Ferrer, Jr., the owner of Advanced Medical Claims Inc. of Florida. Fernando then provided the information to others who used the stolen identities to file an estimated $7.1 million in fraudulent claims (USDC 2006).

Individuals abusing prescription drugs also have a motive to commit medical identity theft. Prescription drug addicts can use stolen identities to receive multiple prescriptions at different pharmacies. Drugs obtained through this method may also be resold or traded. Roger Ly, a Nevada pharmacist allegedly filed and filled 55 false prescriptions for Oxycontin and Hydrocondone in the name of customers. Medicare and insurance paid for the drugs that Ly, allegedly, then resold or used recreationally (USA 2007). The total value of drugs sold in the underground prescription market likely exceeds $1 billion (Peterson 2000). Sometimes, the crimes involving prescription drugs are less serious; a Philadelphia man stole a coworker's insurance identification card to acquire a Viagra prescription, which he filled on 38 separate occasions. The plan finally backfired when the coworker he was posing as attempted to fill his own Viagra prescription and discovered that one had already been filled at another pharmacy. The cost to his company's insurance plan: over $3,000 (PA 2006).

Wanted criminals also have a strong motive to commit medical identity theft. If they check into a hospital under their own name, they might be quickly apprehended by law enforcement. Therefore, career criminals need to design schemes to obtain care. Joe Henslik, a wanted bank robber working as an ad salesman, found it easy to obtain Joe Ryan's Social Security number as part of a routine business transaction (BW 2007). Henslik then went on to receive $41,888 worth of medical care and surgery under Ryan's name. It took Ryan two years to discover that he had been a victim of medical identity theft. Even after discovery, he found it difficult to gain access to his medical records, since his own signature didn't match that of Henslik's forgery.

Anndorie Sachs experienced a similar situation when her medical identity was used to give birth to a drug addicted baby (Reavy 2006). Sachs had lost her purse prior to the incident and had accordingly cancelled her stolen credit cards, but was unaware of the risk of medical ID theft. The baby, which was abandoned at the hospital by the mother, tested positive for illegal drug use, prompting child services to contact Sachs, who had four children of her own. Fortunately, since Sachs did not match the description of the woman who gave birth at the hospital, the problem did not escalate further. If Sachs was not able to prove her identity, she could have lost custody of her children, and been charged with child abuse. Furthermore, before the hospital became aware of the crime, the baby was issued a Social Security number in Sachs name, which could cause complications for the child later in life. Like Sachs, few individuals consider their insurance cards to be as valuable as the other items they carry in their wallet. Moreover, medical transactions appearing on a bill may not be scrutinized as closely as financial transactions with a bank or credit card.

Illegal immigrants also represent a block of individuals with a clear motive to commit medical identity theft. In the case of a severe medical emergency, they will not be refused care in most instances, but if an illegal immigrant requires expensive surgery, costly prescriptions, or other non-emergency care, they have few options. One of the most shocking and well documented cases comes from Southern California, where a Mexican resident fooled the state insurance program, Medi-Cal, into believing that he was a resident and therefore entitled to health care coverage (Hanson 1994). Mr. Hermillo Meave, was transferred to California from a Tijuana, Mexico hospital with heart problems, but told the California hospital that he was from San Diego, and provided the hospital with a Medi-Cal ID card and number. Although the circumstances surrounding Mr. Meave's arrival were suspicious, the hospital went ahead and completed a heart transplant on Mr. Meave. The total cost of the operation was an astounding one million dollars. Only after the surgery did the hospital determine that Mr. Meave actually lived and worked in Tijuana and was therefore not entitled to Medi-Cal coverage.

Perhaps emboldened by the success of Hermillo Meave, a family from Mexico sought a heart transplant for a dying relative just three months later at the very same hospital. This time, fraud investigators were able to discover the plot before the surgery could be completed. While processing the paperwork for the patient who was checked in as Rene Garcia, Medi-Cal authorities found nine other individuals around the state, using the same name and ID number. The hospital had the family arrested and jailed for the attempted fraud, which had cost the hospital $200,000, despite the lack of surgery. The family told investigators that they had paid $75,000 in order to obtain the ID and set up the surgery. The trafficking of identities between Mexico and California is commonplace, but the sale of Medi-Cal identities adds a new dimension to the crime. The disparity in care between California hospitals and Mexican facilities makes the motivation to commit medical identity theft clear: falsified identification is a low-cost ticket to world-class care.

Finally, identity theft criminals often operate in crime rings, sometimes using elaborate ruses to gather the identities of hundreds individuals. In a Houston case, criminals allegedly staged parties in needy areas offering medical deals as well as food and entertainment (USDJ 2007). At the parties, Medicaid numbers of residents were obtained and then used to bill Medicaid for alcohol and substance abuse counseling. The scheme even included fraudulent reports, written by 'certified' counselors. The fraudulent company managed to bill Medicaid for $3.5M worth of services, of which they received $1.8M. In this case, no medical care was actually administered and the medical identity theft was committed purely for financial reasons.

In summary, there are many reasons why individuals engage in medical identity theft, including avoiding law enforcement, obtaining care that they have no way of affording, or simply making themselves rich. Many tactics are used including first hand by physical theft, insiders, and harvesting leaked data. As we saw, PHI can be sold and resold before theft occurs—as in the case of the nine Garcias. The thief may be someone an individual knows well or it could be someone who they've never met.

For health-care providers, the first step in reducing such crime is better protection of PHI by: 1) controlling access within the enterprise to PHI; 2) securing networks and computers from direct intruders; 3) monitoring networks (internal and external) for PII and PHI transmissions and disclosures; 4) avoiding inadvertent disclosures of information. Often loose access and inadvertent disclosures are linked. When access policies allow many individuals to view, move, and store data in portable documents and spreadsheets, the risk of inadvertent disclosure increases.

3 Inadvertent Data Hemorrhages

Despite the much trumpeted enactment of the Health Insurance Portability and Accountability Act (HIPAA), data losses in the health-care sector continue at a dizzying pace. While the original legislation dates back to 1996, the privacy rules regulating the use and disclosure of medical records did not become effective until 2004. Moreover, the related security rules, which mandate computer and building safeguards to secure records, became effective in 2005. While firms and organizations have invested to protect their systems against direct intrusions and hackers, many recent the data hemorrhages have come from inadvertent sources. For example, laptops at diverse health organizations including Kaiser Permanente (Bosworth 2006), Memorial Hospital (South Bend IN) (Tokars 2008), the U.S. Department of Veterans Administration (Levitz and Hechinger 2006), and National Institutes of Health (Nakashima and Weiss 2008) were lost or stolen—in each case inadvertently disclosing personal and business information.

Organizations have mistakenly posted on the web many different types of sensitive information, from legal to medical to financial. For example, Wuesthoff Medical Center in Florida inadvertently posted names, Social Security numbers and personal medical information of more than 500 patients (WFTV 2008). Insurance and health-care information of 71,000 Georgia residents was accidentally posted on Internet for several days by Tampa-based WellCare Health Plans (Hendrick 2008).

The University of Pittsburgh Medical Center inadvertently posted patient informa-tion of nearly 80 individuals including names and medical images. In one case, a pa-tient's radiology image was posted along with his Social Security number, insurance information, medications, and with information on previous medical screenings and procedures (Twedt, 2007). Harvard University and its pharmacy partner, PharmaCare (now part of CVS Caremark), experienced a similar embarrassment when students showed they could easily gain access to lists of prescription drugs bought by Harvard students (Russell 2005). Even technology firms like Google and AOL have suffered the embarrassment of inadvertent web posting of sensitive information (Claburn 2007, Olson 2006)—in their cases, customer information. Still other firms have seen their internal information and intellectual property appear on music file-sharing networks (DeAvila 2007), blogs, YouTube, and MySpace (Totty 2007). In each case, the result was the same: sensitive information inadvertently leaked creating embarrassment, vulnerabilities, and financial losses for the firm, its investors, and customers. In a re-cent data loss, Pfizer faces a class action suit from angry employees who had their personal information inadvertently disclosed on a popular music network (Vijayan 2007). In this paper we examine health-care leaks from a common, but widely misun-derstood source of inadvertent disclosure: peer-to-peer file-sharing networks.

In our past research, we showed that peer-to-peer (P2P) file-sharing networks rep-resented a significant security risk to firms operating within the banking sector (John-son and Dynes, 2007; Johnson 2008). File sharing became popular during the late 1990s with rise of Napster. In just two years before its court-ordered closure in 2001, Napster enabled tens of millions of users to share MP3-formatted song files. Through its demise, it opened the door for many new P2P file-sharing networks such as Gnutella, FastTrack, e-donkey, and Bittorrent, with related software clients such as Limewire, KaZaA, Morpheus, eMule, and BearShare. Today P2P traffic levels are still growing with as many as ten million simultaneous users (Mennecke 2006). P2P clients allow users to place shared files in a particular folder that is open for other users to search. However, there are many ways that other confidential files become exposed to the network (see Johnson et al. 2008 for a detailed discussion). For exam-ple a user: 1) accidentally shares folders containing the information—in some cases confusing client interface designs can facilitate such accidents (Good and Krekelberg (2003)); 2) stores music and other data in the same folder that is shared—this can happen by mistake or because of poor file organization; 3) downloads malware that, when executed, exposes files; or 4) installs sharing client software that has bugs, re-sulting in unintentional sharing of file directories.

While these networks are most popularly used to trade copyrighted material, such as music and video, any material can be exposed and searched for including data-bases, spreadsheets, Microsoft Word documents, and other common corporate file formats. The original exposure of this material over P2P networks is most likely done by accident rather than maliciously, but the impact of a single exposure can quickly balloon. After a sensitive file has been exposed, it can be copied many times by virtually anonymous P2P users, as they copy the file from one another and expose the file to more peers. Criminals are known to engage in the sale and trafficking of valuable information and data. In earlier studies using "honeypot" experiments (experiments that expose data for the purpose of observing how it is stolen), we showed how criminals steal and use both consumer data and corporate information (Johnson et al. 2008). When this leaked information happens to be private customer information, organizations are faced with costly and painful consequences resulting from fraud, customer notification, and consumer backlash.

Ironically, individuals who experience identity theft often never realize how their data was stolen. While there are many ways personal health-care data can be exposed, we will show in the next section how data hemorrhages in P2P networks represent a missing link in the "causality chain." Far worse than losing a laptop or a storage device with patient data (Robenstein 2008), inadvertent disclosures on P2P networks allow many criminals access to the information, each with different levels of sophistication and ability to exploit the information. And unlike an inadvertent web posting, the disclosures are far less likely to be noticed and corrected (since few organizations monitor P2P and the networks are constantly changing making a file intermittently available to a subset of users). Clearly, such hemorrhages violate the privacy and security rules of HIPAA, which call for health-care organizations to ensure implementation of administrative safeguards (in the form of technical safeguards and policies, personnel and physical safeguards) to monitor and control intra and inter-organizational information access.

4   Research Method and Analysis

To explore the vulnerability and threat of medical information leakage, we examined health-care data disclosures and search activity in peer-to-peer file sharing networks. To collect a sample of leaked data, we initially focused on Fortune Magazine's list of the top ten publically traded health-care firms (Fortune Magazine (Useem 2007)). Together those firms represented nearly $70B in US health-care spending (Figure 2).

To gather relevant files, we developed a digital footprint for each health-care institution. A digital footprint represents key terms that are related to the firm—for example names of the affiliated hospitals, clinics, key brands, etc. Searching the internet with Google or P2P networks using those terms will often find files related to those institutions. With the help of Tiversa Inc., we searched P2P networks using our digital signature over a 2-week period (in January, 2008) and randomly gathered a sample of shared files related to health care and these institutions. Tiversa's servers and software allowed us to sample in the four most popular networks (each of which supports the most popular clients) including Gnutella (e.g., Limewire, BearShare), FastTrack (e.g., KaZaA, Grokster), Aries (Aries Galaxy), and e-donkey (e.g., eMule, EDonkey2K). Files containing any one or combination of these terms in our digital footprint were captured. We focused on files from the Microsoft Office Suite (Word, Powerpoint, Excel, and Access). Of course, increasing the number of terms included in the digital

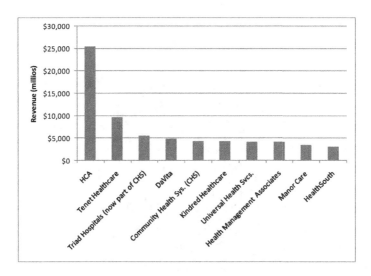

Fig. 2. Revenue of the top ten US health-care firms (Useem 2007)

footprint increases the number file matches found, but also increases false positives—files captured that have nothing to do with the institution in question. Given the large number of hospitals within these ten organizations (more than 500), our goal was to gather a sample of files to characterize the ongoing data hemorrhage. Since users randomly join P2P networks to get and share media (and then depart), the network is constantly changing. By randomly sampling over a 14-day period, we collected 3,328 files for further (manual) analysis.

Of 3,328 documents in our sample, 50.3% could be immediately identified as duplicate copies of the same file (same hash) that had spread or were on multiple IP addresses, leaving us with 1,654 documents to categorize. While duplicate files were not downloaded from the same IP address, duplicate files were collected when a target file had spread to multiple sharing clients. They were also collected from users who joined the network at different IP addresses (what we call an IP shift). Through a manual analysis of the remaining 1,654 files, we found that 71% were not relevant to health care or the organizations under consideration and were downloaded because our search terms overlapped with other subject matter. This was the result of the size and quality of our digital footprint. By casting a large net, we found more files but also many that were not related to the health-care sector. Of the remaining 475 documents, 86 were manually evaluated as duplicate files. With this cross section of data associated with the health-care organizations, we categorized each file evaluating the dangers associated with it. Figure 3 shows a categorization of the 389 unique, relevant files.

The most common type of files found were newspaper and journal articles, followed by documents associated with students studying medicine. This should not come as a surprise as many P2P users are students. Interestingly, we found entire medical texts being shared. We also found many documents dealing directly with medical issues, such as billings, letters to hospitals, and insurance claims. Many of

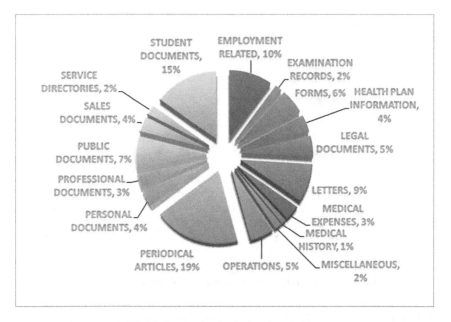

Fig. 3. Summary of unique relevant files

these documents were leaked by patients themselves. For example, we found several patient-generated spreadsheets containing details of medical treatments and costs—likely for tax purposes. Other documents discovered included hospital brochures and flyers, which were intended for public consumption. Finally there were job listings, cover letters, and résumés, all likely saved on computers of job-seekers. The lack interest in sharing these files for a typical P2P user makes it readily apparent that they were likely shared by mistake. However, all of the files weren't so innocuous. After categorizing the files, we found that about 5% of the files recovered by our loosely tuned search were sensitive or could be used to commit medical or financial identity theft.

The set of dangerous documents discovered contained several files that would facilitate medical identity theft. One such document was a government application for employment asking for detailed background information. The document contained the individual's Social Security number, full name, date of birth, place of birth, mother's maiden name, history of residence and acquaintances, schooling history, and employment history (the individual had worked at one of the hospitals under study). Despite the document's three-page forward highlighting the privacy act measures undertaken by the government to protect the information in the document, and the secure Data Hash code stamped at the bottom of every page along with the bolded text 'PRIVACY ACT INFORMATION', this document somehow ended up on to a P2P network.

More disturbing, we found a hospital-generated spreadsheet of personally identifiable information on recently-hired employees including Social Security numbers, contact information, job category etc. Another particularly sensitive document was an

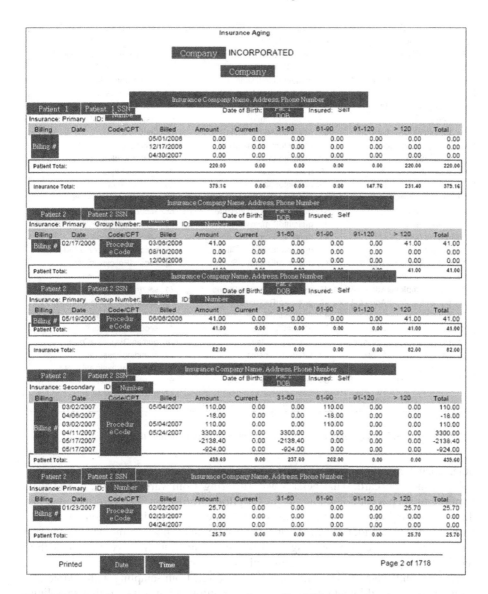

Fig. 4. Excerpt of an insurance againg report. It contains 1718 pages of patient names, social security numbers, dates of birth, insurers, group numbers, and identification numbers (exposing nearly 9000 patients). Personally Identifiable Information has been redacted to protect the identities of the disclosers and patients.

Acrobat form used for creating patient prescriptions. The scanned blank document was signed by a physician and allowed for anyone to fill in the patient's name and prescription information. This document could be used for medical fraud by prescription drug dealers and abusers. Additionally, the doctor's own personal information was included in the document, giving criminals the opportunity to forge

1. FAFA billNumber
2. providerName
3. providerAddressLine1
4. providerCityStateZip
5. providerPhoneNumber
6. providerFederalTaxId
7. patientFirstName
8. patientMiddleInitial
9. patientLastName
10. patientSSN
11. patientPhone
12. patientAddressLine1
13. patientAddressLine2
14. patientCity
15. patientState
16. patientZipCode
17. patientSex
18. patientBirthDate
19. patientEmployerName
20. patientEmployerAddressLine1
21. patientEmployerAddressLine2
22. patientEmployerCity
23. patientEmployerState
24. patientEmployerZipCode
25. patientEmployerPhone
26. caseType
27. admissionDate
28. dischargeDate
29. patientMedRecNo
30. patientMaritalStatus
31. guarantorFirstName
32. guarantorLastName
33. guarantorSSN
34. guarantorPhone
35. guarantorAddressLine1
36. guarantorAddressLine2
37. guarantorCity
38. guarantorState
39. guarantorZipCode
40. guarantorBirthDate
41. guarantorEmployerName
42. guarantorEmployerAddressLine1
43. guarantorEmployerAddressLine2
44. guarantorEmployerCity
45. guarantorEmployerState
46. guarantorEmployerZipCode
47. guarantorEmployerPhone
48. guarantorRelationship
49. totalCharges
50. amountBalance
51. totalPayments
52. totalAdjustments
53. accidentCode
54. accidentDate
55. firstInsuranceName
56. firstInsuranceAddressLine1
57. firstInsuranceCity
58. firstInsuranceState
59. firstInsuranceZipCode
60. firstPolicyNumber
61. firstAuthorizationNumber
62. firstGroupName
63. firstGroupNumber
64. firstInsuredRelationship
65. firstDateEligible
66. firstDateThru
67. secondInsuranceName
68. secondInsuranceAddressLine1
69. secondInsuranceCity
70. secondInsuranceState
71. secondInsuranceZipCode
72. secondPolicyNumber
73. secondGroupName
74. secondGroupNumber
75. secondInsuredRelationship
76. secondDateEligible
77. secondDateThru
78. primaryDiagnosisCode
79. attendingPhysician
80. attendingPhysicianUPIN
81. lastPaymentDate
82. providerShortName

Fig. 5. File contents for over 20,000 patients in one inadvertent disclosure

other documents in his name. Finally, another example we found was a young individual's medical card. This person was suffering from various ailments and was required to keep a card detailing his prescription information. The card included his doctor's name, parent's names, address, and other personal information. A person with a copy of this identification card could potentially pose as the patient and attempt to procure prescription drugs. All of these dangerous files were found with a relatively simple sample of files published for anyone to find.

As a second stage of our analysis, we then moved from sampling with a large net to more specific and intentional searches. Using information from the first sampling, we examined shared files on hosts where we had found other dangerous data. One of the features enabled by Limewire and other sharing clients is the ability to examine all the shared files of a particular user (sometimes called "browse host"). Over the next six months, we periodically examined hosts that appeared promising for shared files.

Using this approach, we uncovered far more disturbing files. For a medical testing laboratory, we found a 1,718-page document containing patient Social Security numbers, insurance information, and treatment codes for thousands of patients. Figure 4 shows a redacted excerpt of just a single page of the insurance aging report

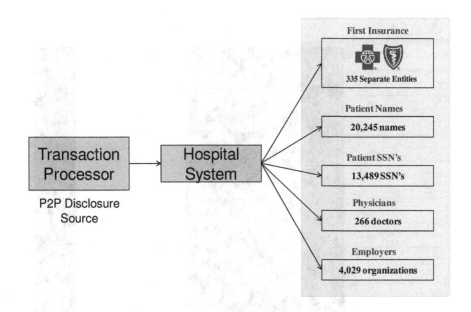

Fig. 6. Hemorrhage exposed a large array of health-care constituents

containing patient name, Social Security number, date of birth, insurer, group number, and identification number. All together, almost 9,000 patient identities were exposed in a single file, easily downloaded from a P2P network.

For a hospital system, we found two spreadsheet databases that contained detailed information on over 20,000 patients including Social Security numbers, contact details, and insurance information. Up to 82 fields of information (see Figure 5) were recorded for each patient—representing the contents of the popular HCFA form. In this case, the hemorrhage came from an outsourced collection agency working for the hospital. However, besides the patients and hospital system, many other organizations were comprised. The data disclosed in this file well-illustrates the complexity of US health care with many different constituencies represented, including 4 major hospitals, 335 different insurance carriers acting on behalf of 4,029 patient employers, and 266 different treating doctors (Figure 6). Each of these constituents was exposed in this disclosure. Of course, the exposure of sensitive patient health-information may be the most alarming to citizens. Figure 7 shows one very small section of the spreadsheet (just three columns of 82) for a few patients (of the nearly 20,000). Note that the diagnosis code (IDC code) is included for each patient. For example, code 34 is streptococcal sore throat; 42 is AIDS; 151.9 is malignant neoplasm of stomach (cancer); 29 is alcohol-induced mental disorders; and 340 is multiple sclerosis. In total the file contained records on 201 patients with different forms of mental illness, 326 with cancers, 4 with AIDS, and thousands with other serious and less serious diagnoses.

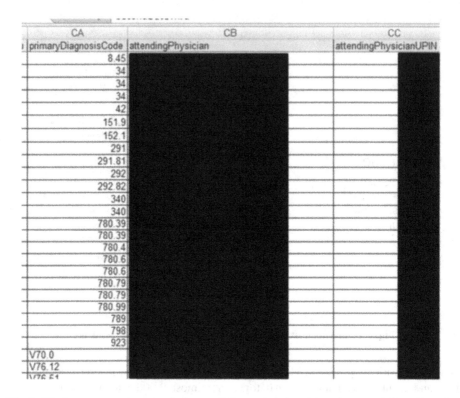

CA	CB	CC
primaryDiagnosisCode	attendingPhysician	attendingPhysicianUPIN
8.45		
34		
34		
34		
42		
151.9		
152.1		
291		
291.81		
292		
292.82		
340		
340		
780.39		
780.39		
780.4		
780.6		
780.6		
780.79		
780.79		
780.99		
789		
798		
923		
V70.0		
V76.12		
V76.51		

Fig. 7. Disclosures expose extreamly personal diagnosis information. A very small section of a spreadsheet for a few (of over 20,000) patients showing IDC diagnosis codes (see http://www.cms.hhs.gov/ICD9ProviderDiagnosticCodes/ or http://www.icd9data.com/). Personally Identifiable Information has not been included in the illustration to protect the identities of the patients and physicians.

For a mental health center, we found patient psychiatric evaluations. All would be considered extremely personal and some were disturbing. We found similar clinical evaluations leaking from Alabama to Nebraska to California.

Of course, these are just few of many files we uncovered. For a group of anesthesiologists, we found over 350MB of data comprising patient billing reports. For a drug and alcohol rehab center, we found similar billing information. From an AIDs clinic we found a spreadsheet with 232 clients including address, Social Security number, and date of birth. And the list goes on. It is important to note that all of these files were found without extraordinary effort and certainly far less effort than criminals might be economically incented to undertake.

With the vulnerability well established, we also investigated the search activity in P2P networks to see if users were looking for health-care data hemorrhages. Again, using our simple digital signature we captured a sample of user-issued searches along with our files. Figure 8 lists a sample of these searches and clearly shows that users are searching for very specific health-care related data in P2P networks.

compudoc medical	computers medical doctors	child medical exam
care office nbc health	billing medical august	child medical release form
hospital records	canada medical test	cigna medical dr
mental hospitals	canadian medical	classified medical records
hospital	caulfield general medical	complete medical exam
hospital letterhead	certficat medical	comprehensive medical
niagara hospital	doctor medical exam	letter for medical bills
american medical	doctors office medical exam	ltr client medical report
connolly medical	doctors orders medical	ltr hjh rosimah medical
dear medical insurance my	doug medical bill	ltr medical body4life
denial of medical insurance	edimis medical software 3.9	ltr medical maternity portland
isilo medical	electronic medical	ltr orange medical head center
medical	electronic medical record	ltr to valley medical
medical claims	electronic medical record.pdf	lytec medical billing
medical exam	electronics & bio medical	medical investigation
medical history	emt medical software	medical journals password
medical passwords	forms medical	medical .txt
medical permission	forms medical liability form	medical abuse records
medical records certification	forms medical office	medical authorization
medical release	ge medical	medical autorization
authorization for medical	ge medical syatems	medical benefits
basic medical forms	medical coding and billing	medical bill
billing medical	medical coding exam	medical billing

Fig. 8. Selection of User-Issued searches related to medical

5 Conclusion

Data hemorrhages from the health-care sector are clearly a significant threat to providers, payers, and patients. The inadvertent disclosers we found and documented in this report point to the larger problem facing the industry. Clearly, such hemorrhages may fuel many types of crime. While medical fraud has long been a significant problem, the crime of medical identity theft is still in its infancy. Today, many of the well-documented crimes appear to be committed out of medical need. However, with the growing opportunity to commit more significant crimes involving large financial rewards, more and more advanced schemes and methods, such as P2P-fueled identity theft, will likely develop. For criminals to profit, they don't need to "steal" an identity, but only to borrow it for a few days, while they bill the insurer carrier thousands of dollars for fabricated medical bills. This combination of medical fraud along with identity theft adds a valuable page to the playbook of thieves looking for easy targets. Stopping the supply of digital identities is one key to halting this type of illegal activity.

The Health Insurance Portability and Accountability Act (HIPAA) was created to protect workers' health insurance coverage when they change or lose employment. It also includes standards for the transfer of healthcare information that are designed to protect the privacy of sensitive patient medical information. The Privacy and Security Rules of HIPAA require covered entities to ensure implementation of administrative safeguards in the form of policies, personnel and physical safeguards to their information infrastructure, and technical safeguards to monitor and control intra and inter-organizational information access (Choi, et al. 2006). Those rules were phased in over time with compliance maturing nearly five years ago (Privacy Rules in April 2003 and Security Rules in April 2005). Unfortunately, recent industry reports suggest low level of HIPAA compliance related to data security and privacy (AHIMA 2006). Variations in provider implementation may also make medical identity theft more difficult to track, identify, and correct. When a patient's medical record has been altered by someone else using their ID, the process used at different providers to correct the record can be confusing for the patient. The erroneous information in the medical file may remain for years. Also people who have been victims of medical identity theft may find it difficult to even know what has been changed or added to their record. Since the thief's medical information is contained within the victim's file, it is given the same privacy protections as anyone under the act. Without the ability to easily remove erroneous information, or figure out the changes contained in a medical record, repairing the damages of medical identity theft can be a very taxing process.

In theory, HHS enforcement of HIPAA is a positive force in the fight against identity theft. It is true that institutions have been fined and required to implement detailed corrective action plans to address inadvertent disclosures of identifiable electronic patient information (HHS 2008). However, many observers note that very few cases have actually resulted in a fine. And while HIPAA could be used to prosecute offending medical professionals, which are historically the largest group of health-care fraud perpetrators, few are ever prosecuted. So it is not clear that this protection of patient identities really discourages inappropriate use of medical information or reduces the chance of hemorrhages. Better compliance with both the security and privacy rules is certainly needed. Of course, HIPAA can do little to stop patients from disclosing their medical identities voluntarily to individuals posing as health care providers, or poorly managing their own computerized documents.

Tighter controls on patient information are a good start, but consumers still need to be educated of the dangers of lost health-care information and how to secure their information on personal computers. Hospitals and others concerned with medical identity theft have begun to undertake measures in order to curb medical identity theft. One of the simplest and most effective measures put in place by hospitals is to request photo identification for admittance to the hospital. In many cases, when a request for photo identification is made, the individual will give up on obtaining care and simply leave the hospital, never to return again. Of course, this measure will likely lose its efficacy in time as criminals become aware of the change in policy. Once a few personal identifiers have been acquired, such as date of birth and Social Security number, a criminal can obtain seemingly valid photo-ID. In the future, insurance companies may need to begin issuing their own tamper-proof photo identification to help stop medical identity theft.

Finally, health-care providers and insurers must enact better monitoring and information controls to detect and stop leaks (Appari and Johnson 2009). Information access within many health-care systems is lax. Coupled with the portability of data, inadvertent disclosures are inevitable. Better control over information access governance (Zhao and Johnson 2008) is an important step in reducing the hemorrhages documented in this report.

References

1. AHIMA – The American Health Information Management Association: The State of HIPAA Privacy and Security Compliance (2006),
   http://www.ahima.org/emerging_issues/
   2006StateofHIPAACompliance.pdf (last accessed on November 2008)
2. Appari, A., Johnson, M.E.: Information Security and Privacy in Healthcare: Current State of Research. Forthcoming in International Journal of Internet and Enterprise Management (2009)
3. Ball, E., Chadwick, D.W., Mundy, D.: Patient Privacy in Electronic Prescription Transfer. IEEE Security & Privacy, 77–80 (March/ April 2003)
4. Bolin, J.N., Clark, L.S.: Avoiding Charges of Fraud and Abuse: Developing and Implementing an Effective Compliance Program. JONA 34(12), 546–550 (2004)
5. Bosworth, M.H.: Kaiser Permanente Laptop Stolen: Personal Data on 38,000 Members Missing. Consumer Affairs, November 29 (2006),
   http://www.consumeraffairs.com/news04/2006/11/
   kaiser_laptop.html
6. BW: Diagnosis: Identity Theft. Business Week, January 8 (2007)
7. Choi, Y.B., Capitan, K.E., Krause, J.S., Streeper, M.M.: Challenges associated with privacy in healthcare industry: Implementation of HIPAA and security rules. Journal of Medical Systems 30(1), 57–64 (2006)
8. Claburn, T.: Minor Google Security Lapse Obscures Ongoing Online Data Risk. Information Week, January 22 (2007)
9. De Avila, J.: The Hidden Risk of File-Sharing. Wall Street Journal, November 7, D1 (2007)
10. Dixon, P.: Medical Identity Theft: The Information Crime that Can Kill You. The World Privacy Forum (2006)
11. FBI: 2006 Financial Crime Report, Federal Bureau of Investigation (Online) 02 28 (2007),
    http://www.fbi.gov/publications/financial/fcs_report2006/
    financial_crime_2006.htm (Cited: 02 04 2008)
12. FTC: 2006 Identity Theft Report, Federal Trade Commission (November 2007),
    http://www.ftc.gov/os/2007/11/
    SynovateFinalReportIDTheft2006.pdf (last accessed on June 18, 2008)
13. Good, N.S., Krekelberg, A.: Usability and privacy: a study of Kazaa P2P file-sharing. In: Proceedings of the SIGCHI Conference on Human Factors in Computing Systems, Ft. Lauderdale, Florida, April 05-10 (2003)
14. Hanson, G.: Illegal Aliens Bilk Sick U.S. system. Insight on the News, April 18 (1994)
15. Hendrick, B.: Insurance records of 71,000 Ga. families made public. Atlanta Journal-Constitution (April 8, 2008),
    http://www.ajc.com/metro/content/metro/stories/2008/04/08/
    breach_0409.html
16. HHS: HHS, Providence Health & Services Agree on Corrective Action Plan to Protect Health Information. U.S. Department of Health & Human Services, News Release (July 17, 2008),
    http://www.hhs.gov/news/press/2008pres/07/20080717a.html
17. Johnson, M.E., Dynes, S.: Inadvertent Disclosure: Information Leaks in the Extended Enterprise. In: Proceedings of the Sixth Workshop on the Economics of Information Security. Carnegie Mellon University, June 7-8 (2007)

18. Johnson, M.E.: Information Risk of Inadvertent Disclosure: An Analysis of File-Sharing Risk in the Financial Supply Chain. Journal of Management Information Systems 25(2), 97–123 (2008)
19. Johnson, M.E., McGuire, D., Willey, N.D.: The Evolution of the Peer-to-Peer File Sharing Industry and the Security Risks for Users. In: Proceedings of HICSS-41, International Conference on System Sciences, January 7-10. IEEE Computer Society, Hawaii (2008)
20. Johnson, M.E., McGuire, D., Willey, N.D.: Why File Sharing Networks Are Dangerous. Communications of the ACM 52(2), 134–138 (2009)
21. Lafferty, L.: Medical Identity Theft: The Future Threat of Health Care Fraud Is Now. Journal of Health Care Compliance 9(1), 11–20 (2007)
22. Levitz, J., Hechinger, J.: Laptops Prove Weakest Link in Data Security. Wall Street Journal (March 26, 2006)
23. Mennecke, T.: Slyck News – P2P Population Continues Climb, June 14 (2006), http://www.slyck.com/news.php?story=1220
24. Messmer, E.: Health Care Organizations See Cyberattacks as Growing Threat. Network World, February 28 (2008)
25. Musco, T.D., Fyffe, K.H.: Health Insurers Anti-fraud Programs, Washington D.C. Health Insurance Association of America (1999)
26. Nakashima, E., Weiss, R.: Patients' Data on Stolen Laptop. Washington Post, March 24, A1 (2008)
27. Olson, P.: AOL Shoots Itself in the Foot. Forbes, August 8 (2006)
28. PA: Pennsylvania Attorney General. Attorney General's Insurance Fraud Section charges former SEPTA employee with using co-worker's ID to obtain Viagra. Harrisburg: s.n., July 6 (2006)
29. Peterson, M.: When Good Drugs Go Gray; Booming Underground Market Raises Safety Concerns, The New York Times, December 14, p. 1 (2000)
30. Reavy, P.: What Baby? ID victim gets a jolt. Deseret News (Salt Lake City). May 2 (2006)
31. Robenstein, S.: Are Your Medical Records at Risk? Wall Street Journal (2008)
32. Russell, J.: Harvard fixing data security breaches: Loophole allowed viewing student prescription orders Boston Globe, January 22 (2005)
33. Tokars, L.: Memorial Hospital loses laptop containing sensitive employee data, WSBT, Febuary 7 (2008), http://www.wsbt.com/news/local/15408791.html
34. Totty, M.: Security: How to Protect Your Private Information, Wall Street Journal, R1 (January 29, 2007)
35. Twedt, S.: UPMC patients' personal data left on Web, Pittsburgh Post-Gazette, April 12 (2007)
36. USDC, United States of America vs. Fernando Ferrer, Jr. and Isis Machado, 06-60261, s.l., United States District Court Southern District of Florida, September 7 (2006)
37. USDJ, US Department of Justice. Six Indicted for Health Care Fraud Scheme in Southeast Texas, Houston, TX: s.n, Press Release (2007)
38. USA: United States Attorney, District of Nevada. Las Vegas Pharmacist Charged with Health Care Fraud and Unlawful Distribution of Controlled Substances, Las Vegas, United States Department of Justice, January 23 (2007)
39. Useem, J.: Fortune 500: The Big Get Bigger. Fortune Magazine, Wall Street Journal 155(8), 81 (2007)
40. Vijayan, J.: Personal data on 17,000 Pfizer employees exposed; P2P app blamed, Computer World. (2007), http://www.computerworld.com/action/article.do?command=viewArticleBasic&articleId=9024491

41. Mike, W.: Medical ID Theft Leads to Lengthy Recovery. Pittsburgh Tribune-Review, 10–24 (2006)
42. WFTV, Medical Center Patient Records Posted On Internet, August 14 (2008), http://www.wftv.com/news/17188045/detail.html?taf=orlc
43. Zhao, X., Johnson, M.E.: Information Governance: Flexibility and Control through Escalation and Incentives. In: Proceedings of the Seventh Workshop on the Economics of Information Security, June 26-27, 2008, Dartmouth College (2008)

Solving Linear Programs Using Multiparty Computation[*]

Tomas Toft[1,2]

[1] CWI Amsterdam, The Netherlands
[2] Dept. of Mathematics and Computer Science, TU/e, The Netherlands

Abstract. Solving linear programming (LP) problems can be used to solve many different types of problems. Immediate examples include certain types of auctions as well as benchmarking. However, the input data may originate from different, mistrusting sources, which implies the need for a privacy preserving solution.

We present a protocol solving this problem using black-box access to secure modulo arithmetic. The solution can be instantiated in various settings: Adversaries may be both active and adaptive, but passive and/or static ones can be employed, e.g. for efficiency reasons. Perfect security can be obtained in the information theoretic setting (up to 1/3 corruptions), while corruption-of-all-but-one is possible in the cryptographic setting. The latter allows a two-party protocol.

The solution is based on the well known simplex method. Letting n denote the number of initial variables and m the number of constraints, each pivot requires only $\mathcal{O}(\text{loglog}(m))$ rounds in which $\mathcal{O}(m(m + n))$ multiplication protocols and $\mathcal{O}(m+n)$ comparison protocols are invoked; this is equivalent to the base-algorithm. A constant-rounds variation is also possible, this increases the number of comparisons to $\mathcal{O}(m^2 + n)$.

Keywords: Multiparty computation, Secure collaboration, Linear programming.

1 Introduction

Multiparty computation (MPC) allows mutually mistrusting parties to jointly perform a computation without revealing their data. It is natural to consider applying such techniques to solving linear programming (LP) problems. The applications are not limited to simply managing resources, though this is of course possible. They span diverse topics, including benchmarking and auctions.

One application of an MPC LP-solver is the relative performance payscheme of Nielsen and Toft [NT07], where employers wish to motivate employees through bonus schemes based on perfomance compared to the competition, i.e. through

[*] Work partially performed at Aarhus University. Supported by the research program Sentinels (http://www.sentinels.nl). Sentinels is being financed by Technology Foundation STW, the Netherlands Organization for Scientific Research (NWO), and the Dutch Ministry of Economic Affairs.

R. Dingledine and P. Golle (Eds.): FC 2009, LNCS 5628, pp. 90–107, 2009.
© IFCA/Springer-Verlag Berlin Heidelberg 2009

benchmarking. But no company is willing to share production costs and other trade secrets with their competitors. This paper provides an efficient instantiation of the primitives needed in [NT07].

Another example is multi-attribute auctions that allow bidding to not only reflect price, but also to take quality into account. In reverse auctions, for instance, one party offers a contract to perform some task, say to construct a road with some minimal specification. Bidders supply their price for doing so, and the cheapest offer is chosen. However, the parties also have private information regarding the cost of, and willingness to pay for, higher quality. Bogetoft and Nielsen have constructed such auctions using LP problems [BN08].

It seems highly likely that economics may provide many other interesting applications. Informally, the *revelation principle* states that for games of incomplete information, there is a revelation mechanism, where it optimal for the players to truthfully supply their preferences (to a "trusted third party" who computes the optimal solution.) With the present work it is simply a question of designing mechanisms as LP problems.

Related Work: There are multiple algorithms for solving LP problems. The ellipsoid and interior point methods due to Khachiyan and Karmarkar respectively [Kha79, Kar84] allow LP problems to be solved in polynomial time. Formulating one of these as a Boolean circuit and applying one of the classic results of MPC, [Yao86, GMW87, BGW88, CCD88], provides a solution. Applying a general solution is expensive, though. The evaluation of every Boolean gate consists of executing some cryptographic primitive, i.e. *every* basic arithmetic operation performed consists of *many* invocations of those primitives. Moreover, constructing a round-efficient solution in the information theoretic setting is not immediate.

Li and Atallah have proposed a solution to solving LP problems [LA06]. They consider two honest-but-curious parties who learn a maximizing assignment to the variables. In addition, they provide ad-hoc checks against malicious behaviour, e.g. verifying that the assignment does not violate any constraints. This may limit the damage possible, but does not rule out malicious behaviour in general.

The solution is based on integer computation (additive sharing and public key cryptography) and simplex, where pivots are performed on a permuted (masked) tableau. Termination is tested publicly implying that the number of iterations is leaked. Complexity is $\mathcal{O}(k(m^2 + mn + \ell(m + n)) + \ell m(n + m))^1$ modular exponentiations, where k is the number of iterations, ℓ the bit-length of the numbers involved, m the number of constraints, and n the number of initial variables. There are, however, a number of problems with Li and Atallah's solution.

The index of the final variable entering the basis is leaked. This is easily fixed by randomizing the tableau at the end. A second problem occurs when the output is determined. Li and Atallah first output the basis, then set the basis variables to their respective values. Seeing only a maximizing solution, however,

---

[1] [LA06] considers n to be the overall number of variables, this is $m + n$ here.

may reveal less information, e.g. it should not be possible to distinguish between basic variables set to zero and co-basic variables. It is highly questionable that this leaks any useful information in practice. Yet, there is no guarantee that this is the case, so the issue must at least be considered before applying the solution.

A more significant problem is that the protocol may provide an incorrect result. The secure computation may also leak information in this case. The problem occurs at the end of the computation. Basis variables are sought out by determining columns with only one non-zero position – doing this blindly does not work. Consider maximizing $f(x_1, x_2) = x_1 + x_2$ under the constraints that $x_1, x_2 \geq 0$ and $c_1 x_1 + c_2 x_2 + x_S = 1$, where x_S is a slack-variable (larger examples are easily constructed.) If $c = c_1 = c_2$, then the final state is

$$
\begin{array}{cccc}
c & c & 1 & 1 \\
0 & 0 & c & 1
\end{array}
$$

which assigns $1/c$ to both x_1 and x_2, which violates the constraint. With some work it should be possible to determine a maximizing assignment, which doesn't violate constraints. However, leakage is a problem: in the above example both parties learn that $c_1 = c_2$.

A final issue is that it is infeasible to perform more than a few pivots. Each pivot potentially doubles the bit-lengths needed to represent the values of the tableau. As the computation is secure, we must not learn the actual bit-lengths, implying that we must always work with full-size numbers. Starting with 32-bit values, after ten iterations these have grown to 32 thousand bits. After twenty they have increased to 32 million. Thus, even for small inputs their basic operations soon become modular exponentiations with a million-bit modulus.

Two related problems are those of Distributed Constraint Satisfaction Problems (DisCSP) and Distributed Constraint Optimization Problems (DCOP). Multiple parties wish to find some optimizing assignment to variables but have private constraints/priorities regarding the solution space. Though seemingly similar, these problems are quite different. First, we consider arbitrarily distributed data. Second and more importantly, their constraints are not linear. Moreover, though DisCSP and DCOP literature state privacy as important, most work focuses solely on efficiency. Full scale MPC solutions for DisCSPs and DCOPs has been considered, e.g. by Silaghi et al. [Sil04, SFP06]. The basic idea in that work is to test the entire search space (with improvements for certain types of problems) and pick a random solution. This exhaustive approach *could* be applied to LP problems, however, with large, rational-valued search spaces this is clearly infeasible.

Contribution: A solution for solving LP problems is constructed based on black-box, secure modular arithmetic along with additional sub-protocols, e.g. for comparison. The notion can be formalized, e.g. using the arithmetic black-box of Damgård and Nielsen [DN03]. Using abstract primitives allows different instantiations. Information theoretic security is possible, e.g. based on Shamir sharing and the protocols of Ben-Or et al. [Sha79, BGW88]. So is computational security, say through threshold Paillier encryption [Pai99, DJ01, CDN01]. Both provide solutions in the multiparty setting and ensure security against active adversaries. The cryptographic solution also allows a two-party version.[2]

As with [LA06], the solution is based on simplex, however, rather than masking the tableau (which is difficult in the present setting), the pivots are performed obliviously. A second difference is that the possibility of cycling – never terminating – is considered here. Though it is rarely encountered in practice, it ensures that termination can be guaranteed. Cryptographic protocols may be applied as building blocks in many settings, and it should not be assumed that the input is "real-world data." Similar to Li and Atallah, information on the number of pivots performed is leaked. Means for reducing the leak (hiding the actual number of pivots) are considered, but as simplex may require an exponential number of pivots, without exponential work there can be no 100% guarantees.

The problems of the protocol of Li and Atallah do not occur in this work. Moreover, the solutions presented in this paper may also be applied there. Finally, the present protocol has slightly better complexity – $\mathcal{O}(m(n+m))$ secure multiplications and $\mathcal{O}(n+m)$ secure comparisons are needed per pivot. With a Paillier based solution, one multiplication is comparable to a constant number of exponentiations, while comparisons are equivalent to $\mathcal{O}(\ell)$ exponentiations; the $\ell m(n+m)$ term is eliminated. With secret sharing, computational complexity improves further, as we are working directly on (shares of) the actual values rather than encryptions – secure multiplications are implemented using modular multiplication rather than exponentiation.

Round complexity takes a hit in the present solution, though. Where [LA06] provides a constant-rounds pivot, here $\mathcal{O}(\log\log(m))$ rounds are needed. A constant round version is possible, but this increases complexity to $\mathcal{O}(n+m^2)$ secure comparisons.

Finally, rather than providing the output, here the result is shared in the end, implying that it may be used in further computation. Moreover, in difference to Li and Atallah, the present solution provides full precision, i.e. it is guaranteed that there are no rounding errors. Note that computing an approximation rather than the exact result may also introduce security problems as demonstrated by Feigenbaum et al., [FIM+06]. It seems unlikely, that this will pose a problem for "real-world input," though.

Overview: Section 2 of this paper describes the cryptographic primitives and introduces notation. Section 3 gives a brief overview of the simplex method. Section 4 introduces notation and primitives for shared arrays. In the remaining sections, the details of the simplex protocol are presented. Section 5 specifies the overall task and contains general remarks. Following this, Sect. 6 describes the implementation of the body of the simplex algorithm using MPC primitives. Sections 7 and 8 considers iteration, termination, and obtaining the result in the end. Finally Sect. 9 considers the required size of the modulus, while Sect. 10 provides concluding remarks.

---

[2] [CDN01] can be modified to provide security against malicious behaviour from all but one parties, though naturally termination cannot be guaranteed in this case.

2   Cryptographic Preliminaries and Notation

Integer arithmetic can be simulated with arithmetic modulo some M, as long as M is chosen sufficiently large, i.e. such that no overflow occurs. Secure integer computation can therefore be simulated using linear, cryptographic primitives also allowing multiplication (through a protocol). This can be instantiated with secret sharing (e.g. Shamir sharing over $\mathbb{Z}_q$) or (threshold) homomorphic public key cryptography (e.g. Paillier encryption.) Both examples imply that M only has large prime-factors, which is required below.

Negative values such as $-a$ will be represented in the natural way, i.e. as $M - a \in \mathbb{Z}_M$. This ensures that both addition and multiplication involving negative values work as desired. We specify no further details regarding the scheme, though we do require that the multiplication protocol is constant-rounds[3] as well as a some form of composition theorem allowing both sequential and parallel execution. This implies that information leaks do not occur in sub-protocols – it can only occur when information is intentionally revealed.

We use terminology from secret sharing, writing secret values in square brackets, $[a]$. Secure computation will be described using an infix notation with

$$[c] \leftarrow [a] \cdot [b]$$

denoting a run of the multiplication protocol on shared inputs a and b; the resulting shares are stored in c. This eases readability and is easily translated to protocol executions and local computation.

The basic measure for communication complexity will be the number of secure multiplications performed. As the underlying primitives are linear, additions and multiplications by public values do not require interaction, and are considered costless. The number of rounds refer to the number of messages transmitted during the entire protocol. This can only be specified through invocations of primitives. However, by assuming that sharing, multiplication, and reconstruction is constant-rounds, the difference will only be off by a constant.

In order to present the protocol a few additional primitives are needed; these can be constructed from the above. First off, shared bits, $[b] \in \{0, 1\}$, are needed. Such values will be used repeatedly, e.g. for conditional selection.

$$[b] \; ? \; [a] : [a']$$

selects either $[a]$ (if $[b]$ is one) or $[a']$ (if $[b]$ is zero) and is a shorthand of

$$[b] \cdot ([a] - [a']) + [a'].$$

Protocols for comparison of shared values are required, with $[a] \overset{?}{<} [a']$ denoting a protocol run resulting in a shared bit, $[a < a']$. This can be realised in constant-rounds, [DFK+06, NO07].[4] An equality test is defined analogously; in both cases the number of multiplications is linear in the bit-lengths of the inputs.

---

[3] This restriction is for complexity analysis alone.

[4] [DFK+06, NO07] are easily modified to consider negative inputs.

3   Simplex

The simplex method is a well-known strategy for solving linear programs. Despite an exponential worst-case complexity, it is efficient in practice and used in a large range of applications. This section will contain a brief overview of (the steps of) the algorithm. For a full description as well as explanation of the details, the reader is referred to [Chv83]. As the basic primitives described in the previous section involve only integer computation, a variation of simplex using integer pivoting is considered. This technique, generally attributed to Edmonds, is described in detail by Rosenberg in [Ros05].

A linear program consists of n variables, $x_1, \ldots, x_n \geq 0$, and m constraints:

$$\sum_{i=1}^{n} c_{j,i} \cdot x_i \leq b_j \text{ for } j \in \{1, \ldots, m\}.$$

The goal is to maximise an objective function, f:

$$f(x_1, \ldots, x_n) = \sum_{i=1}^{n} f_i \cdot x_i,$$

where the $c_{j,i}$ and f_i are integers in this work. In order to maximize f, slack-variables, $x_{n+1}, \ldots x_{n+m} \geq 0$ are introduced, resulting in equalities in the constraints:

$$x_{n+j} + \sum_{i=1}^{n} c_{j,i} x_i = b_j \text{ for } j \in \{1, \ldots, m\}.$$

A solution will be an assignment to the x_i such that the constraints hold. In simplex, solutions allowing only m variables to be positive are constructed, this is known as the basis. Each of these variables are associated with a constraint. All other variables (the co-basis) take the value 0. The execution of the algorithm starts by considering an initial solution with the basis consisting of the slack-variables (taking the values b_j).[5] By repeatedly moving variables in and out of the basis, the problem is rephrased and the solution improved (the value obtained when evaluating f increased) with every iteration until one maximising f is found.

Consider the tableau form of a linear programming problem:

$$
\begin{array}{ccc|cccccc|c}
c_{1,1} & \cdots & c_{1,n} & 1 & 0 & 0 & \cdots & 0 & 0 & b_1 \\
c_{2,1} & \cdots & c_{2,n} & 0 & 1 & 0 & \cdots & 0 & 0 & b_2 \\
& \cdots & & & & & \cdots & & & \cdots \\
c_{m,1} & \cdots & c_{m,n} & 0 & 0 & 0 & \cdots & 0 & 1 & b_m \\
\hline
-f_1 & \cdots & -f_n & 0 & 0 & 0 & \cdots & 0 & 0 & z = 0
\end{array}
$$

where column i, $1 \leq i \leq m + n$, is associated with variable x_i, and row j, $1 \leq j \leq m$ is associated with constraint j.

---

[5] It is assumed that the linear program is origin-feasible, i.e. setting $x_i = 0$ for all i does not violate any constraint. This can be avoided with standard techniques.

For the tableau, the right-most column (except the bottom row), will be known as the b-vector, similarly the bottom row (except the right-most element), will be called the f-vector; note $f_{n+1}, \ldots, f_{n+m}$ initially set to zero. The sub-matrix of the constraints consisting of the columns of the slack-variables is initialised to the identity matrix. The columns of the tableau associated with the basis variables will always be the columns of I multiplied by a positive integer, p' (the previous pivot element, initially 1, see below). The basis variable of the current solution associated with the j'th constraint (row) takes the value b_j/p' in the solution. The value z in the bottom right-hand corner is the objective function, f, evaluated at the current solution and multiplied by p', initially $f(0, \ldots, 0) = 0$.

The integer pivoting variation of the simplex algorithm repeatedly updates the tableau through the following steps:

I. Determine a column, C, with a negative value in the f-vector. The (guaranteed co-basic) variable associated with C is chosen to enter the basis. C will be referred to as the *pivot column*.

II. Determine a row, R, such that its intersection with C, C_R, is positive (constraining) and b_R/C_R is minimal. This row is called the *pivot row*, the element C_R is called the *pivot element*. The basic variable associated with R is the one selected for leaving the basis; after the current iteration the basic variable associated with row R will be the one associated with C.

III. Multiply all entries in the non-pivot rows by the pivot element.

IV. Subtract a multiple of the pivot row from all non-pivot rows such that the updated pivot column will consist entirely of zeros except for the pivot row.

V. Divide all non-pivot rows by the *previous* pivot element (which is initialised to 1).

VI. If one or more negative values in the f-vector exist, go to step I.

One problem with simplex is that it may cycle indefinitely. Though rarely encountered in practice, the issue must be considered. Fortunately it is easily handled using Bland's rule: when confronted with a choice of entering or leaving variable, pick the one with the lowest index, see e.g. [Chv83]. This implies that the index of the variable associated with a row (constraint) must be stored along with it and updated once the entering and leaving variables have been determined.

4   Secret Shared Arrays

Secret shared arrays will be referred to using boldface and capital letters,

$$[\mathbf{A}] = \big([a_1], [a_2], \ldots, [a_k]\big),$$

this is convenient for denoting multiple related, sharings. Indexing is written $[\mathbf{A}](i)$ meaning $[a_i]$. Finally, the length of a shared array will be written $[\mathbf{A}].\mathrm{len}$.

Expressions of the form $[\mathbf{A}]([i])$ are needed. Shared indexes will be stored as unary counters, arrays consisting of all 0's except for the i'th position, which is 1. These will be written in boldface to denote that in essence, they are arrays. Indexing is now simply the computation of a dot product:

$$[\mathbf{A}]\,([\mathbf{i}]) = \sum_{j=1}^{[\mathbf{A}].\mathrm{len}} [\mathbf{A}]\,(j) \cdot [\mathbf{i}]\,(j),$$

with assignments, $[\mathbf{A}]\,([\mathbf{i}]) \leftarrow [x]$, translating to updating *every* entry of $[\mathbf{A}]$,

$$[\mathbf{A}]\,(j) \leftarrow [\mathbf{i}]\,(j)\,?\,[x]:[\mathbf{A}]\,(j).$$

Both require $[\mathbf{A}]$.len secure multiplications, which may be performed in parallel.

The integer value of an index, val($[\mathbf{i}]$), may be computed as $\sum_{j=1}^{[\mathbf{i}].\mathrm{len}} [\mathbf{i}]\,(j) \cdot j$. General indexing – computing $[\mathbf{A}]\,([i])$ where $[i]$ is a field element – is possible by transforming $[i]$ to $[\mathbf{i}]$, [RT07]. Complexity remains linear and constant-rounds.

The notation introduced for arrays will also be used for *shared matrices*. Simplex continuously updates a matrix, $[\mathbf{T}]$, representing the tableau-form of the problem. Indexing is done using two variables; $[\mathbf{T}]\,(r,c)$ denotes the entry in the r'th row, c'th column. The r'th row (c'th column) of $[\mathbf{T}]$ is written $[\mathbf{T}]\,(r,\cdot)$ ($[\mathbf{T}]\,(\cdot,c)$). Viewing columns (rows) as separate arrays allows shared indexes.

Two high-level protocols are also required, first a prefix-or computation on arrays of shared bits, $[\mathbf{B}]$. The goal is $[\mathbf{B}']$, with $[\mathbf{B}']\,(j) = \vee_{i=1}^{j}[\mathbf{B}]\,(i)$ for $1 \le j \le [\mathbf{B}]$.len. A constant-rounds solution using $\mathcal{O}([\mathbf{B}].\mathrm{len})$ multiplications is described in [DFK+06], this is denoted $\mathrm{pre}_{\vee}(\cdot)$. The second requirement is a computation of the minimal element of an array of length k, along with its index. This is possible using $\mathcal{O}(k)$ comparisons in $\mathcal{O}(\mathrm{loglog}(k))$ rounds, as well as $\mathcal{O}(k^2)$ comparisons in $\mathcal{O}(1)$ rounds. Details are available in Appendix A. Note that the result is valid for *any* comparison operator on *any* data.

5   Privacy Preserving Simplex

Assume that a LP problem with n variables $x_1, \ldots, x_n \ge 0$, m constraints $\sum_{i=1}^{n} c_{j,i} \cdot x_i \le b_j$, and objective function $f(x_1, \ldots, x_n) = \sum_{i=1}^{n} f_i \cdot x_i$ is provided in the form of sharings of the values of the constraints and terms of f,

$$[c_{1,1}], \ldots, [c_{m,n}], [b_1], \ldots, [b_m], [f_1], \ldots, [f_n].$$

The problem is assumed to be bounded, i.e. there exists an optimal solution. If this is not the case, it can be detected underway. The goal is an assignment to the x_i maximizing f without violating any constraint. This information can be extracted from the b-vector of the final tableau and the final pivot element.

In the following, m will always denote the number of constraints with n signifying the number of initial variables; overall there are $m + n$ variables. The tableau matrix, $[\mathbf{T}]$, has $m + 1$ rows and $m + n + 1$ columns. The f-vector and b-vector will be denoted $[\mathbf{F}]$ and $[\mathbf{B}]$ respectively, while $[\mathbf{S}]$ of length m stores the indexes of variables associated with the constraints, i.e. the basis. In the current solution $x_{[\mathbf{S}](j)}$ takes the value $\frac{[\mathbf{B}](j)}{[p']}$, where $[p']$ is the most recent pivot element.

6   Translating the Body of Simplex

Translation of the simplex-iteration will be done by considering each of the five steps individually. It is assumed that output from previous steps is available.

Step I, Determining the variable to enter the basis. This step consists of determining the pivot column by computing the minimal index, $[\mathbf{c}]$, such that $[\mathbf{F}]([\mathbf{c}])$ is negative. This is clearly a candidate selected using Bland's rule. The required computation is seen as Protocol 1.

Protocol 1. Selecting the pivot column

Input: The tableau, $[\mathbf{T}]$ (including $[\mathbf{F}]$ by definition).
Output: $[\mathbf{c}]$ and $[\mathbf{C}]$, such that $[\mathbf{F}]([\mathbf{c}])$ is negative, $[\mathbf{c}]$ is minimal, and $[\mathbf{C}]$ is a copy of the $[\mathbf{c}]$'th column of $[\mathbf{T}]$.

    for $i \leftarrow 1, \ldots, n+m$ **do**

        $[\mathbf{D}](i) \leftarrow [\mathbf{F}](i) \overset{?}{<} 0$

    end for

    $[\mathbf{D}'] \leftarrow \mathrm{pre}_\vee([\mathbf{D}])$

5: $[\mathbf{c}](1) \leftarrow [\mathbf{D}'](1)$

    for $i \leftarrow 2, \ldots, n+m$ **do**

        $[\mathbf{c}](i) \leftarrow [\mathbf{D}'](i) - [\mathbf{D}'](i-1)$

    end for

    $[\mathbf{C}] \leftarrow [\mathbf{T}](\cdot, [\mathbf{c}])$

For correctness, note that $[\mathbf{D}](i)$ is 1 if x_i associated with the i'th column is a candidate for entering the basis, otherwise it is 0. $[\mathbf{D}'](i)$ is 1 iff $[\mathbf{D}](i') = 1$ for some $i' \leq i$. Hence, $[\mathbf{c}](i) = 1$ exactly for the smallest i with $[\mathbf{D}](i) = 1$ and 0 otherwise, i.e. of the form required. $[\mathbf{C}]$ is correct by construction.

Regarding complexity, the initial loop performs $n + m$ comparisons. This is followed by a prefix-or of length $m + n$ and a costless loop. The indexing needed to compute $[\mathbf{C}]$ is equivalent to $m + 1$ indexings into arrays of length $n + m$; overall this is $\mathcal{O}(m \cdot (n+m))$ multiplications. For round complexity, note that the body of the initial loop does not depend on previous iterations, thus they may be executed concurrently. This implies $\mathcal{O}(1)$ rounds overall.

Step II, Determining the variable to leave the basis. The goal is to determine the tightest constraint on the variable, $x_{[\mathbf{c}]}$, i.e. find $[\mathbf{r}] \in \{1, 2, \ldots, m\}$ such that

$$[\mathbf{C}]([\mathbf{r}]) \cdot x_{[\mathbf{c}]} = [\mathbf{B}]([\mathbf{r}])$$

implies the smallest, non-negative value of $x_{[\mathbf{c}]}$. In addition to this, (copies of) the pivot row and the pivot element, $[\mathbf{R}]$ and $[p] = [\mathbf{C}]([\mathbf{r}])$, must also be obtained.

$[\mathbf{C}](j) \leq 0$ implies that constraint j does not limit $x_{[\mathbf{c}]}$, thus, only constraints with $[\mathbf{C}](j) > 0$ are relevant; these will be called *applicable*, the rest *non-applicable*. The primary goal is the index, $[\mathbf{r}]$, of an applicable constraint with the *rational* value $\frac{[\mathbf{B}]([\mathbf{r}])}{[\mathbf{C}]([\mathbf{r}])}$ minimal; ties are broken using Bland's rule.

Overall, this step consists of defining a comparison operator on constraints. The protocol for computing a minimal entry of an array noted in Sect. 4 does the rest. Three values of each constraint are needed: For the j'th constraint $[\mathbf{B}](j)$ and $[\mathbf{C}](j)$ define the constraint and whether it is applicable, while $[\mathbf{S}](j)$ must be used when Bland's rule is applied.

In order to simplify the construction of the comparison operator, the problem is transformed such that all non-applicable constraints become applicable. The fractional values of non-applicable constraints is simply replaced by one which is larger than the maximal possible, $\frac{\infty}{1}$. Here ∞ simply represents some value larger than the largest possible value of the $[\mathbf{B}](j)$'s, e.g. $\infty = 2^k$ if these values are k-bit. The updated arrays $[\mathbf{C}']$ and $[\mathbf{B}']$ are computed as

$$([\mathbf{C}'](j), [\mathbf{B}'](j)) \leftarrow \left([\mathbf{C}](j) \overset{?}{>} 0 \, ? \, [\mathbf{C}](j) : 1; \quad [\mathbf{C}](j) \overset{?}{>} 0 \, ? \, [\mathbf{B}](j) : \infty \right)$$

for $1 \leq j \leq m$. This ensures that all constraints are applicable, using only $\mathcal{O}(m)$ comparisons and multiplications in $\mathcal{O}(1)$ rounds. The solution is unchanged as the LP was assumed bounded, i.e. some initial constraint was applicable.

The next task is to define the comparison operator, $\overset{?}{\sqsubset}$, for constraints – triples $([\mathbf{C}'](j), [\mathbf{B}'](j), [\mathbf{S}](j))$. It is in essence just a comparison of non-negative fractions, $\frac{B'}{C'}$, except that in the case of equality, the S values must be compared. Noting that for non-negative integers a_n and b_n, and positive integers a_d and b_d,

$$\frac{a_n}{a_d} < \frac{b_n}{b_d} \Leftrightarrow a_n \cdot b_d < b_n \cdot a_d$$

the desired output may be computed using integer comparison. An analogous equation holds for equality, thus, Bland's rule applies exactly when the two products are equal. Details are seen in Protocol 2. Correctness follows by the above, while complexity is equivalent to the standard comparison under big-$\mathcal{O}$.

Protocol 2. Constraint comparison, $\overset{?}{\sqsubset}$

Input: Triples $([C_i], [B_i], [S_i])$ and $([C_j], [B_j], [S_j])$ representing applicable constraints to be compared – $[C_i]$ and $[C_j]$ represent the relevant entries of the pivot column while $[B_i]$ and $[B_j]$ represent the values of the b-vector. Finally $[S_i]$ and $[S_j]$ are the index-values of the current basis variables associated with the two constraints, i.e. the candidates to leave the basis.

Output: $[b] \in \{0, 1\}$ – one if the left argument, $([C_i], [B_i], [S_i])$, constrains less than the right, $([C_j], [B_j], [S_j])$, with ties broken using Bland's rule.

$[l] \leftarrow [B_i] \cdot [C_j]$

$[r] \leftarrow [B_j] \cdot [C_i]$

$[b] \leftarrow ([l] \overset{?}{=} [r]) \, ? \, ([S_i] \overset{?}{<} [S_j]) : ([l] \overset{?}{<} [r])$

$[r]$ is determined by applying one of the protocols of Appendix A on the array

$$\big(([\mathbf{C}'](1), [\mathbf{B}'](1), [\mathbf{S}](1)), \ldots, ([\mathbf{C}'](m), [\mathbf{B}'](m), [\mathbf{S}](m)) \big)$$

using Protocol 2 as comparison operator. This determines the desired index, $[\mathbf{r}]$, along with the triple, $([C_r'], [B_r'], [S_r])$.[6] Obtaining a copy of the pivot row, $[\mathbf{R}]$, is simply an indexing operation, $[\mathbf{R}] \leftarrow [\mathbf{T}]([\mathbf{r}], \cdot)$. Note that $[C_r'] = [\mathbf{C}']([\mathbf{r}]) = [\mathbf{C}]([\mathbf{r}])$ is the pivot element. Finally, $[\mathbf{S}]$ must reflect the updated basis, i.e. $[\mathbf{S}]([\mathbf{r}])$ must be set to val($[\mathbf{c}]$).

The initial transformation and computing the minimal using Protocol 2 requires $\mathcal{O}(m)$ comparisons and multiplications. Determining $[\mathbf{R}]$ requires $m+n+1$ indexing operations in arrays of length m, and the update of $[\mathbf{S}]$ a single indexing operation of size m. Overall this amounts to $\mathcal{O}(m \cdot (m + n))$ multiplications and $\mathcal{O}(m)$ comparisons in $\mathcal{O}(\log\log(m))$ rounds.

Step III, Multiply all non-pivot rows by the pivot element. The previous steps determined the variables to enter and leave the basis in the form of indexes, $[\mathbf{c}]$ and $[\mathbf{r}]$, as well as the pivot element, $[p]$. The third step consists of multiplying all entries of the tableau – *except* the ones in the pivot row – by the latter. This is accomplished by Protocol 3. For correctness, note that after step 4, all entries in $[\mathbf{M}]$ are $[p]$ except the $[\mathbf{r}]$'th, which is $[1]$. Thus, step 7 multiplies the entries of non-pivot rows by the pivot element, while leaving the pivot row implicitly untouched. Only the indexing with $[\mathbf{r}]$ and the updating of the tableau require multiplication, implying $\mathcal{O}(m \cdot (n + m))$ multiplications in all. Round complexity is constant as all entries of the tableau may be updated concurrently.

Protocol 3. Multiplication of all non-pivot rows by the pivot element

---

Input: The tableau, $[\mathbf{T}]$, the index of the pivot row, $[\mathbf{r}]$, and the pivot element, $[p]$.
Output: The updated tableau, $[\mathbf{T}']$, with all non-pivot rows multiplied by $[p]$.

    for $j \leftarrow 1, \ldots, m + 1$ **do**
        $[\mathbf{M}](j) \leftarrow [p]$
    end for
    $[\mathbf{M}]([\mathbf{r}]) \leftarrow 1$
5: **for** $j \leftarrow 1, \ldots, m + 1$ **do**
        for $i \leftarrow 1, \ldots, n + m + 1$ **do**
            $[\mathbf{T}'](j, i) \leftarrow [\mathbf{M}](j) \cdot [\mathbf{T}](j, i)$
        end for
    end for

Step IV, Subtract a multiple of the pivot row from all non-pivot rows. Note first that as all non-pivot rows have been multiplied by the pivot element, the multiple to subtract from non-pivot row j is the j'th entry of the original pivot column, $[\mathbf{C}]$. The computation is analogous to that of step III; set the multiple to be subtracted from the pivot row to zero and subtract the relevant multiple for each entry in the tableau, Protocol 4. Correctness is equivalent to step III, as is the complexity obtained: $\mathcal{O}(m \cdot (m + n))$ multiplications in $\mathcal{O}(1)$ rounds.

---

[6] An unbounded LP implies that $[B_r'] = \infty$ will occur, allowing this to be detected.

Protocol 4. Subtraction of a multiple of the pivot row from all non-pivot rows

---

Input: The tableau, $[\mathbf{T}]$, the index of the pivot row, $[\mathbf{r}]$, the pivot row, $[\mathbf{R}]$, and the original pivot column, $[\mathbf{C}]$.

Output: The updated tableau, $[\mathbf{T'}]$, such that all non-pivot rows are zero in the pivot column.

$\quad [\mathbf{C}]\,([\mathbf{r}]) \leftarrow 0$
$\quad \textbf{for } j \leftarrow 1, \ldots, m+1 \textbf{ do}$
$\quad\quad \textbf{for } i \leftarrow 1, \ldots, n+m+1 \textbf{ do}$
$\quad\quad\quad [\mathbf{T'}]\,(j,i) \leftarrow [\mathbf{T}]\,(j,i) - [\mathbf{C}]\,(j) \cdot [\mathbf{R}]\,(i)$
5:$\quad\quad \textbf{end for}$
$\quad \textbf{end for}$

Step V, Divide non-pivot rows by the previous pivot element. The final step requires an integer division for all non-pivot row entries. General constant-rounds integer division is possible but expensive. However, this is not a general case: $[p']$ divides $[\mathbf{T}]\,(j,i)$ for all entries not in the pivot row (see [Ros05] for a proof). This simplifies the problem, as division can be implemented as multiplication by the multiplicative inverse (in the field) of the divisor.[7] Element inversion is possible using the well-known protocol of Bar-Ilan and Beaver, [BB89].

Having obtained $\left[(p')^{-1}\right]$, this must be multiplied onto all non-pivot rows. This problem is equivalent to step III; the tableau may be updated with an invocation of Protocol 3. Inversion is efficient, implying that complexity is dominated by Protocol 3, $\mathcal{O}(m \cdot (n+m))$ multiplications in $\mathcal{O}(1)$ rounds.

Overall complexity. Combining the above analyses, the overall complexity of steps I through V is found to be $\mathcal{O}(m \cdot (m+n))$ multiplications and $\mathcal{O}(m+n)$ comparisons. Each step performs at most a constant number of multiplications per entry in the tableau – sometimes hidden in indexing operations – in addition to the comparisons in the first two steps. Round complexity is dominated by step II, $\mathcal{O}(\mathrm{loglog}(m))$. Reducing round complexity to $\mathcal{O}(1)$ increases the number of comparisons to $\mathcal{O}(n+m^2)$.

7   Iteration and Termination

Evaluating the termination condition – determining whether to continue – is costless except for the final (failing) test. Consider an optimistic approach where step I is performed with no knowledge of whether or not $[\mathbf{F}]$ contains a negative entry. If no such entry exists, then the array of test results – and therefore also the "index" determined – will contain all 0's. The sum of entries of the index is therefore 0 in this case, while a proper index sums to 1.

Simple reconstruction at every iteration allows the parties to determine if they are done; this leaks the number of pivots but no more. If this is not acceptable,

---

[7] For Paillier encryption, a negligible number of elements are not invertible; this does not pose a problem.

the point of termination can be hidden using dummy pivots. The termination condition remains secret and computation continues. After each iteration, conditional selections are used to ensure that the final tableau is not changed by choosing the previous one if termination had already occured. This does not alter the big-$\mathcal{O}$ compexity.

Unless exponentially many iterations are performed Some information will be leaked. Needing exponentially many pivots is unlikely, though. It is sometimes stated that in practice, runtime is linear in the number of constraints and logarithmic in the number of variables. Performing U pivots, where U is a *likely* upper bound, reveals only that – as expected – fewer than U pivots were performed.

Other compromises and variations are also possible. Public testing of the termination condition can be restricted to every k'th pivot. The exact number of iterations remains secret, but roughly the right amount are performed. Alternatively, given multiple LP problems of the same size, it is possible to only reveal the overall number of pivots performed. Conditional selection can be used to obliviously replace the "working-tableau" by a fresh problem upon termination, it will not be known what tableau a given pivot considered. The drawback is that every LP problem is touched at every iteration resulting in worse complexity. Naturally, it is also possible to construct hybrids between all these variations.

8   Determining the Solution from the Table

Recall that the goal of securely solving an LP is sharings of the assignments to the variables as well as a sharing of the evaluation of the objective function at that point. By explicitly obtaining sharings, the protocol can be used not only for solving the LP and providing (parts of) the solution directly to parties, it is also possible to use the output as input for additional MPC, allowing the present work to be used as a building block.

The solution consists of rational values given as the b-vector and the final pivot element, $[p']$. These values must be assigned to the basis variables represented by $[\mathbf{S}]$: the j'th basis variable, $x_{[\mathbf{S}](j)}$, takes the value $\frac{[\mathbf{B}](j)}{[p']}$; co-basic variables are simply 0. The result is stored uniquely as $[\mathbf{S}]$, $[\mathbf{B}]$, and $[p']$, but seeing these reveals information. Examples include which slack-variables are in the basis and which basis variable is associated with which constraint.

Computing an array containing the values assigned to the numerator of each x_i in the solution eliminates this problem; this is accomplished by Protocol 5. All variables are initialised to 0, after which the values of $[\mathbf{S}]$ are used to index. m indexing operations on an array of length n[8] provides the desired result.

Naïvely, the updates of the $[\mathbf{X}]\,(i)$ must occur sequentially implying $\mathcal{O}(m)$ rounds. However, no entry of $[\mathbf{X}]$ is updated more than once, as the basis variables are distinct. It is therefore possible to parallelize the conditional selections. "Non-triggering" selections result in a 0 which is to be added to the original value; performing all these in parallel first and *then* performing the additions provides a constant-rounds solution with the same complexity, $\mathcal{O}(n \cdot m)$.

---

[8] Slack-variables are ignored, for $[\mathbf{S}]\,(j) \geq n$ the update does implicitly nothing.

The rational value $[\mathbf{X}](i)/[p']$ is assigned to x_i and can be provided to any party or used in subsequent computation. The same is true for $f(x_1, \ldots, x_n) = [z]/[p']$. However, seeing one of these values leaks the final pivot element. Values must be represented in a canonical way to prevent leakage, i.e. the fractions must be reduced.

Protocol 5. Assigning the solution to the variables, x_i

Input: The solution stored as the b-vector, $[\mathbf{B}]$ and the list of basis variables, $[\mathbf{S}]$.
Output: An array $[\mathbf{X}]$, such that $[\mathbf{X}](i)$ takes the value of the numerator of the value assigned to x_i.

    for $i \leftarrow 1, \ldots, n$ **do**
       $[\mathbf{X}](i) \leftarrow 0$
    end for
    for $i \leftarrow 1, \ldots, m$ **do**
5:    $[\mathbf{X}]([\mathbf{S}](j)) \leftarrow [\mathbf{B}](j)$
    end for

This can be done using the technique of Fouque et al. [FSW02]: rational values may be encoded as numerator times inverse of denominator in the prime field.[9] The conversion is efficient and this provides a canonical representation. Naturally the technique only works for values of a bounded size. However, this issue was already encountered when simulating integer computation; it is merely a question of selecting an appropriate modulus initially.

9 Choosing a Modulus

A final point to consider is the choice of modulus, q. How large numbers must be representable? [Goe94] provides upper bounds on the maximal bit-length of the values of the tableau through Hadamard's inequality. At most

$$L = \log(det_{max}) + B + F + m + n + 1$$

bits are required per value, where B and F are the bit-lengths of the original b_i's and f_i's respectively, while det_{max} is the maximal determinant of an $m \times m$ sub-matrix of constraint-rows. Letting C denote the bit-length of the $c_{j,i}$, by Hadamard's inequality,

$$\log(det_{max}) \leq (m \cdot (2C + \log(m)))/2.$$

Note that q must be of twice this bit-length: comparing fractions require double precision and so does the reduction of fractions at the very end.

As an example, consider the case of 32-bit inputs, 32 variables, and 16 constraints. Approximately 650-bits are required for tableau-values implying that a 1300-bit prime must be used. While relatively large, this cannot be avoided – at least not with perfect precission – as there are LP problems, which require this.

---

[9] This also works Paillier encryption, though not all elements are invertible.

10   Concluding Remarks

The privacy-preserving LP-solver presented is a good solution in the sense that the most used operations – the arithmetic – are cheap. The $\mathcal{O}(m(m \cdot n))$ secure multiplications are simply invocations of a basic primitive. Though this makes the $\mathcal{O}(m + n)$ secure comparisons slightly more difficult, performing bit-wise addition or multiplication is very costly and a lot more difficult.

Regarding privacy, how can we be certain that there are no unintentional information leaks? As noted above, information is only disclosed when a value is *intentionally* revealed; privacy follows from the privacy of the primitives. This only occurs for the termination condition and the output, and neither carry any additional information. The former is either 0 or 1, while the latter is stored in a canonical way.

Note that considering an abstract comparison protocol implies that if a new and improved protocol is constructed, overall complexity of this work immediately improves. Moreover, for an actual implementation of the LP-solver, it could be preferable to use a non-constant-rounds solution. This approach can reduce actual runtime, as expensive tricks to obtain constant-rounds can be avoided. Big-$\mathcal{O}$-complexity remains the same – at least with the present knowledge – but the hidden constants are reduced. Moreover, as those constants are small, the actual number of rounds may increase only slightly if indeed at all.

Acknowledgements

This work could not have been performed without the help of others. Troels Bjerre Sørensen is thanked for introducing me to integer pivoting as well as explaining linear programming and the simplex method. Peter Bro Miltersen is thanked for discussions of the simplex method. Ivan Bjerre Damgård, Jesper Buus Nielsen, and Berry Schoenmakers are thanked for the many discussions, suggestions and comments. Finally, Otto Johnston is thanked for commenting on presentation.

References

[BB89]   Bar-Ilan, J., Beaver, D.: Non-cryptographic fault-tolerant computing in a constant number of rounds of interaction. In: Rudnicki, P. (ed.) Proceedings of the eighth annual ACM Symposium on Principles of distributed computing, pp. 201–209. ACM Press, New York (1989)

[BGW88]   Ben-Or, M., Goldwasser, S., Wigderson, A.: Completeness theorems for noncryptographic fault-tolerant distributed computations. In: 20th Annual ACM Symposium on Theory of Computing, pp. 1–10. ACM Press, New York (1988)

[BN08]   Bogetoft, P., Nielsen, K.: Dea based auctions. European Journal of Operational Research 184(2), 685–700 (2008)

[CCD88]   Chaum, D., Crépeau, C., Damgård, I.: Multiparty unconditionally secure protocols. In: 20th Annual ACM Symposium on Theory of Computing, pp. 11–19. ACM Press, New York (1988)

[CDN01]   Cramer, R., Damgård, I., Nielsen, J.: Multiparty computation from thresh-
           old homomorphic encryption. In: Pfitzmann, B. (ed.) EUROCRYPT 2001.
           LNCS, vol. 2045, pp. 280–300. Springer, Heidelberg (2001)
[Chv83]   Chvátal, V.: Linear Programming. W.H. Freeman, New York (1983)
[DFK⁺06]   Damgård, I., Fitzi, M., Kiltz, E., Nielsen, J., Toft, T.: Unconditionally
           secure constant-rounds multi-party computation for equality, comparison,
           bits and exponentiation. In: Halevi, S., Rabin, T. (eds.) TCC 2006. LNCS,
           vol. 3876, pp. 285–304. Springer, Heidelberg (2006)
[DJ01]   Damgård, I., Jurik, M.: A generalization, a simplification and some ap-
           plications of Paillier's probabilistic public-key system. In: Kim, K.-c. (ed.)
           PKC 2001. LNCS, vol. 1992, pp. 110–136. Springer, Heidelberg (2001)
[DN03]   Damgård, I., Nielsen, J.: Universally composable efficient multiparty com-
           putation from threshold homomorphic encryption. In: Boneh, D. (ed.)
           CRYPTO 2003. LNCS, vol. 2729, pp. 247–264. Springer, Heidelberg (2003)
[FIM⁺06]   Feigenbaum, J., Ishai, Y., Malkin, T., Nissim, K., Strauss, M., Wright, R.:
           Secure multiparty computation of approximations. ACM Transactions on
           Algorithms 2(3), 435–472 (2006)
[FSW02]   Fouque, P., Stern, J., Wackers, G.: CryptoComputing with rationals. In:
           Financial Cryptography 2002. LNCS. Springer, Berlin (2002)
[GMW87]   Goldreich, O., Micali, S., Wigderson, A.: How to play any mental game.
           In: STOC 1987: Proceedings of the nineteenth annual ACM conference on
           Theory of computing, pp. 218–229. ACM Press, New York (1987)
[Goe94]   Goemans, M.: Linear programming. Course notes (October 1994),
           http://www-math.mit.edu/~goemans/notes-lp.ps
[Jáj92]   Jájá, J.: An Introduction to Parallel Algorithms. Addison-Wesley, Reading
           (1992)
[Kar84]   Karmarkar, N.: A new polynomial-time algorithm for linear programming.
           Combinatorica 4(4), 373–395 (1984)
[Kha79]   Khachiyan, L.: A polynomial algorithm in linear programming. Soviet
           Mathematics Doklady 20 (1979)
[LA06]   Li, J., Atallah, M.: Secure and private collaborative linear programming.
           In: Collaborative Computing: Networking, Applications and Worksharing,
           2006. CollaborateCom (2006)
[NO07]   Nishide, T., Ohta, K.: Multiparty computation for interval, equality, and
           comparison without bit-decomposition protocol. In: Okamoto, T., Wang,
           X. (eds.) PKC 2007. LNCS, vol. 4450, pp. 343–360. Springer, Heidelberg
           (2007)
[NT07]   Nielsen, K., Toft, T.: Secure relative performance scheme. In: Deng, X.,
           Graham, F.C. (eds.) WINE 2007. LNCS, vol. 4858, pp. 396–403. Springer,
           Heidelberg (2007)
[Pai99]   Paillier, P.: Public-key cryptosystems based on composite degree resid-
           uosity classes. In: Stern, J. (ed.) EUROCRYPT 1999. LNCS, vol. 1592,
           pp. 223–238. Springer, Heidelberg (1999)
[Ros05]   Rosenberg, G.: Enumeration of all extreme equlibria of bimatrix games with
           integer pivoting and improved degeneracy check, CDAM Research Report
           LSE-CDAM-2005-18 (2005),
           http://www.cdam.lse.ac.uk/Reports/Abstracts/cdam-2005-18.html
[RT07]   Reistad, T., Toft, T.: Secret sharing comparison by transformation and
           rotation. In: Proceedings of the International Conference on Informa-
           tion Theoretic Security (ICITS) 2007. LNCS. Springer, Heidelberg (2007)
           (to appear)

[SFP06]   Silaghi, M., Faltings, B., Petcu, A.: Secure combinatorial optimization sim-
          ulating dfs tree-based variable elimination. In: AI and Math 2006 Proceed-
          ings (2006), http://anytime.cs.umass.edu/aimath06/proceedings.html
[Sha79]   Shamir, A.: How to share a secret. Communications of the ACM 22(11),
          612–613 (1979)
[Sil04]   Silaghi, M.: A suite of secure multi-party computation algorithms for solv-
          ing distributed constraint satisfaction and optimization problems. Techni-
          cal Report CS-2004-04, Florida Institute of Technology (2004)
[Yao86]   Yao, A.: How to generate and exchange secrets. In: Proceedings of the 27th
          IEEE Symposium on Foundations of Computer Science, pp. 162–167 (1986)

A   Computing the Minimal of Multiple Values

An efficient means of obtaining the minimal of multiple shared values is required
in simplex. Formalising the problem, let an array $[\mathbf{A}]$ of length k be given, the
goal will be to compute a sharing of the minimal value, $[min] = \min_{1 \leq i \leq k} [\mathbf{A}](i)$,
along with an sharing of its index, $[\mathbf{i}]$. All of what is described in this appendix
is simple adaptation of results from parallel algorithms, see any text-book e.g.
[Jáj92].

For simplicity assume that k is a power of two. The obvious solution is to
construct a binary tree, Protocol 6. It is easily verified that $\mathcal{O}(k)$ comparisons and
multiplications are used. Moreover, as all computation in the loops parallelize,
the overall round complexity is $\mathcal{O}(\log(k))$. Correctness is immediate.

It is possible to improve on the round complexity of the above. Let $\wedge(\cdot)$ denote
a protocol taking an array of shared bits as input and returning their logical AND
and consider Protocol 7. Each column in the $[\mathbf{B}]$-matrix is associated with an
entry of $[\mathbf{A}]$. For the minimal entry, the column will contain all ones, however, for
a non-minimal entry, at least one zero will exist. Thus, computing the AND of the
bits of every column results in an index for the minimal element. Note that the
protocol provides the correct result even when the minimal entry is not unique,
in this case the minimal index of the minimal value is returned. Concerning
complexity, $\mathcal{O}(k^2)$ comparisons and $\mathcal{O}(k)$ multiplications are required, however,
everything parallelizes and can therefore be performed in $\mathcal{O}(1)$ rounds. The only
non-trivial detail is unbounded fan-in AND. Assuming that $k < q$, where q is
defines the field, this can be done by adding all bits, and computing whether the
sum equals the number of input-bits, i.e. using an equality.

Protocol 7 can be used to construct an $\mathcal{O}(\log\log(k))$ rounds protocol using
only $\mathcal{O}(k)$ comparisons and multiplications. This is done in two steps, first an
$\mathcal{O}(\log\log(k))$ rounds solution using $\mathcal{O}(k \cdot \log\log(k))$ comparisons and multiplications is constructed, this is then used in conjunction with Protocol 6 to construct
a protocol requiring only $\mathcal{O}(k)$. For the full details see [Jáj92] Sect. 2.6.2 and
2.6.3.

Divide $[\mathbf{A}]$ into $\sqrt{k}$ sub-arrays of length $\sqrt{k}$ each, apply recursion, and use
Protocol 7 to compute the minimal from the $\sqrt{k}$ candidates returned. The index
is obtained similar to Protocol 6; this protocol has the stated complexity. The
linear version is obtained through *accelerated cascading*: Perform $\lceil \log\log\log k \rceil$

Protocol 6. $\min_{\mathcal{O}(\log(k))}(\cdot)$ – Computing the minimal element in $\mathcal{O}(\log(k))$ rounds.

Input: $[\mathbf{A}]$, such that $k = [\mathbf{A}].\mathrm{len}$ is a two-power.
Output: $[i]$ and $[min]$, such that $[min] = [\mathbf{A}]([i])$ is minimal.

    if $[\mathbf{A}].\mathrm{len} = 1$ **then**
        $[min] \leftarrow [\mathbf{A}](1)$
        $[i] \leftarrow (1)$
    else
5:      **for** $j \leftarrow 1, \ldots, k/2$ **do**
          $[\mathbf{B}](j) \leftarrow [\mathbf{A}](2 \cdot j - 1) \overset{?}{<} [\mathbf{A}](2 \cdot j)$
          $[\mathbf{A}'](j) \leftarrow [\mathbf{B}](j) ? [\mathbf{A}](2 \cdot j - 1) : [\mathbf{A}](2 \cdot j)$
      end for
      $([i'], [min]) \leftarrow \min_{\mathcal{O}(\log(k))}([\mathbf{A}'])$
10:     **for** $j \leftarrow 1, \ldots, k/2$ **do**
          $[i](2 \cdot j - 1) \leftarrow [\mathbf{B}](j) \cdot [i'](j)$
          $[i](2 \cdot j) \leftarrow (1 - [\mathbf{B}](j)) \cdot [i'](j)$
      end for
    end if

Protocol 7. $\min_{\mathcal{O}(1)}(\cdot)$ – Computing the minimal element in $\mathcal{O}(1)$ rounds.

Input: $[\mathbf{A}]$ with $[\mathbf{A}].\mathrm{len} = k$.
Output: $[i]$ and $[min]$, such that $[min] = [\mathbf{A}]([i])$ is minimal.

    for $j \leftarrow 1, \ldots, k$ **do**
        $[\mathbf{B}](j, j) \leftarrow 1$
    end for
    for $j \leftarrow 1, \ldots, k$ **do**
5:      **for** $j' \leftarrow j + 1, \ldots, k$ **do**
          $[\mathbf{B}](j, j') \leftarrow [\mathbf{A}](j) \overset{?}{>} [\mathbf{A}](j')$
          $[\mathbf{B}](j', j) \leftarrow 1 - [\mathbf{B}](j, j')$
      end for
    end for
10: **for** $j \leftarrow 1, \ldots, k$ **do**
        $[i](j) \leftarrow \wedge([\mathbf{B}](\cdot, j))$
    end for
    $[min] \leftarrow [\mathbf{A}]([i])$

---

iterations of Protocol 6 reducing the problem by a factor of $\log\log(k)$. From there the $\mathcal{O}(k \cdot \log\log(k))$ protocol is applied, the overall result is the desired $\mathcal{O}(\log\log(k))$ rounds, $\mathcal{O}(k)$ comparisons and multiplications.

A final observation is that the protocols above can be used with *any* multiparty comparison on *arbitrary* data, as long as there exists some notion of "minimal." Naturally, the overall complexity depends on the complexity of the comparison operator.

Private Intersection of Certified Sets

Jan Camenisch[1],* and Gregory M. Zaverucha[2],**

[1] IBM Research
Zürich Research Laboratory
CH-8803 Rüschlikon
jca@zurich.ibm.com
[2] Cheriton School of Computer Science
University of Waterloo
Waterloo ON, N2L 3G1, Canada
gzaveruc@cs.uwaterloo.ca

Abstract. This paper introduces certified sets to the private set intersection problem. A private set intersection protocol allows Alice and Bob to jointly compute the set intersection function without revealing their input sets. Since the inputs are private, malicious participants may choose their sets arbitrarily and may use this flexibility to affect the result or learn more about the input of an honest participant. With certified sets, a trusted party ensures the inputs are valid and binds them to each participant. The strength of the malicious model with certified inputs increases the applicability of private set intersection to real world problems. With respect to efficiency the new certified set intersection protocol improves existing malicious model private set intersection protocols by a constant factor.

Keywords: private set intersection, secure two-party computation, certified sets.

1 Introduction

The problem of private set intersection is the following. Alice and Bob hold sets S_A and S_B, respectively. They would like to jointly compute the intersection, in such a way that reveals as little as possible about S_A to Bob and S_B to Alice. In other words, both Alice and Bob should learn $S_A \cap S_B$ but nothing more.

While this task could be completed with general secure multiparty techniques, it is far more efficient to have a dedicated protocol, especially since the number of communication rounds will be constant. A number of such protocols exist in the literature. A problem common to all previous protocols is that the inputs S_A and S_B can be chosen arbitrarily by Alice and Bob. Our protocols allow Alice and Bob to use only certified sets, that is, sets which have been approved by

* Work funded by the European Community's Seventh Framework Programme (FP7/2007-2013) under grant agreement no. 216483.
** Work done while visiting IBM Research. Supported by an NSERC PGS scholarship. Travel supported by MITACS.

a trusted party. The trusted party authorizes the set once for each party, then does not participate in the protocol.

We also consider a variant of private intersection, when Alice and Bob wish to compute the cardinality of the set intersection. This is referred to as the *private intersection cardinality* problem.

Private set intersection protocols may find applications in online recommendation services, medical databases, and many data related operations between companies, which may even be competitors. An example from the law enforcement field is given by Kissner and Song [21]; suppose a law enforcement official has a list of suspects and would like to know if any of them are customers of a particular business. To protect the privacy of the other customers, and keep the list of suspects private, the business and the law use a private set intersection protocol to learn only those names appearing on both lists.

Motivation for certified private sets. The goal of certifying the sets of participants is to restrict their inputs to "sensible" or "appropriate" inputs. This reduces the strength of a malicious participant.

Suppose Bob is malicious in the following sense; he follows the protocol, but wishes to learn as much about S_A as possible. Bob's strategy is to populate a set S'_B with all of his best guesses for S_A and to have $|S'_B|$ be as large as Alice will allow. This maximizes the amount of information Bob learns about S_A.

In the extreme case, Bob may claim S_B contains all possible elements, which will always reveal S_A. He may also vary his set over multiple runs of the protocol, in order to learn more information over time. These attacks are even more powerful when the protocol can be executed anonymously. Note that all this behaviour is permitted in any model which allows the participants to choose their inputs arbitrarily.

The weakness of models which allow arbitrary inputs reduces the practicality of private set operations. The following examples are made possible by the use of certified sets. A certification authority (CA) is a trusted party who certifies that each participant's set is valid. Once the sets are certified, the CA need not be online. For example, suppose companies want to perform set operations on their financial data. Each company uses a different, but trusted, accounting firm who certifies the data. The companies can then perform as many operations with as many other companies with their certified data.

Since our approach to certifying sets shares a lot with anonymous credentials, this area may also benefit from our work. Credential holders may treat values in their certificates as sets, and intersect them. For example, two pseudonymous or anonymous users may intersect their credentials to determine they live in the same city and were born in the same year. As another example, they may determine whether their ages are within y years by intersecting sets of integers $\{age - y, \ldots, age, \ldots, age + y\}$, where age is the certified value from the credential. This facilitates privacy-enhanced social networking.

Credential holders may also prove things such as "I satisfy at least two of the following five conditions". This is effected by privately intersecting the credential with a list of the conditions. The two satisfied conditions may be revealed (by using set intersection) or kept private (by using intersection cardinality).

This work may also find applications in revocation strategies for anonymous services. The revocation list is private and certified to maintain the privacy of revoked users. When an anonymous user authenticates, their singleton set (their certified ID) is intersected with the revocation list. If the user has been revoked, the intersection contains their ID, otherwise the service provider is assured they are not on the revocation list. Using an intersection cardinality protocol would keep the ID hidden and only reveal whether the user was on the list or not. Since the revocation list is certified, the user is assured that the server does not populate it arbitrarily, to de-anonymize users.

Certified sets are also useful in the suspect-list example of Kissner and Song. Privacy conscious businesses will only reveal information about customers when law enforcement has a warrant for such information (signed by a judge). In this case, the judge digitally signs the list of suspect names for the law enforcement agent. This convinces the business owner that information is only being revealed in accordance with a warrant. On the other hand, the business may also get their customer list certified by a credit card company, bank or tax authority to convince the law enforcement agency that the list is complete and contains valid names.

Related Problems. A number of previously studied problems in the literature are similar to private set intersection. We list them to point out how they differ from the current problem.

A *secret handshake* protocol allows Alice and Bob to confirm that they are both members of the same group (a spy agency, for example). At the end of the protocol, both Alice and Bob learn that either they are both members of the group, or nothing at all. This problem can be viewed as private set intersection (or intersection cardinality) with sets of size one.

The *socialist millionaires' problem* is very similar; two parties would like to determine whether they have the same amount of money, or no information if they have different amounts of money [4]. This problem can also be solved by private intersection of singleton sets, and benefits from certification. The bank of each party may certify the balance, ensuring that one may only run the protocol with their true amount of money.

Private information retrieval (PIR) allows Alice to query a database held by Bob, without revealing her query. Alice may make queries for any item of the database and learn arbitrary blocks of it, independent of the set she holds. In a weak model where Alice is trusted to only query for items which belong to her set, PIR could implement private set intersection. As we have argued, many applications of set intersection require security in the presence of malicious adversaries.

Oblivious transfer (OT) is a protocol which allows Alice to transfer one of two items to Bob, such that Bob can choose which item he wants, keep his choice hidden from Alice, and learn nothing about the other item. OT can be used to construct private set intersection protocols (see [14]), however these are less efficient than specialized protocols, and efficiency decreases when elements are chosen from larger domains.

Finally, *password-based key exchange* allows two users who share a low-entropy password to establish a strong shared key. This protocol should fail if the passwords are different, and therefore bears similarity to the private intersection problem with sets of size one. However, the security requirements and definitions are quite different due to the differing goals of the two protocols.

Contributions and Outline. Our new protocol boasts the following features. The protocol (described in Section 6) may output the intersection or the intersection cardinality, and in either case both parties learn the output. Certified sets, which are the inputs to the protocol, are presented in Section 5. Participants can use different certifying authorities, provided both parties trust the CAs. We prove security in the strongest model in the literature: malicious participants with certified inputs. The model is described in Section 2, and the security proof appears in Section 6.3. A strategy for adding fairness in the presence of participants which may abort the protocol prematurely is given in Section 6.4. With respect to computational complexity, the number of arithmetic operations is comparable to existing non-certified methods, however the dominant operations occur in a group with a significantly faster operation. The amount of communication is comparable to previous approaches as well, but again, each communicated element is smaller due to the choice of group. Efficiency is discussed in Section 7. Section 3 will provide background related to the protocol, and Section 4 reviews related protocols from the literature. An explicit description of the zero knowledge protocols used is given in Appendix A.

2   Model and Definition

We work in a stronger version of what is generally called the malicious model, and we focus on the two-party case. The malicious model is formally defined in the book of Goldreich [16, §7.2]. Our model will have the participants, who hold sets they wish to intersect, and the certification authorities (CAs). We assume the CAs will be honest.

In the malicious model, either participant may behave arbitrarily, while privacy is maintained for the honest participant. Limitations of this model are (i) security is only guaranteed when one participant is assumed honest, (ii) we cannot prevent parties from aborting the protocol, and (iii) inputs to the protocol may be arbitrary. We will lift limitation (iii) by allowing only certified sets as inputs. We discuss ways to mitigate unfairness due to aborts in Section 7.4 by applying optimistic fair-exchange protocols [1]. Using these techniques, if one party aborts prematurely, we are guaranteed that both parties learn the same amount of information.

The Ideal Functionality. In the ideal functionality for the private intersection of certified sets a trusted party U will perform the intersection. Essentially, certification authorities will inform U of a participant's certified set, then two parties signal U that they wish to compute the intersection of their sets. We now describe these steps in greater detail.

Certify: Upon receiving a message $(\mathsf{Certify}, S_{P_i}, P_i, \mathrm{CA}_j)$ from CA_j, U records
   that CA_j has certified the set S_{P_i} for use in the protocol by participant P_i.

IdealProtocol: The message $N = (\mathsf{IdealProtocol},\ P_i,\ P_j)$ from P_i, indicates that
   P_i would like to run the protocol with P_j. Upon receiving N from P_i, if U
   has received $(\mathsf{IdealProtocol},\ P_j,\ P_i)$ the IdealProtocol begins, otherwise N is
   stored and U waits. If U has not received $(\mathsf{Certify}, S_{P_i}, P_i, *)$, CA_{P_i} is set to
   null and S_{P_i} is set to $\emptyset$ before IdealProtocol begins. U behaves analogously
   if it has not received $(\mathsf{Certify},\ S_{P_j},\ P_j,\ *)$.

   At each step, after receiving output from U each party must respond with
   either "ok" to continue the protocol, or "abort" to end the protocol at
   this point. This is required to model limitation (ii) above, and to allow
   participants to abort if they do not trust the CA of the other participant.
   Here we describe the IdealProtocol between participants A and B.

1. (a) U sends $\mathrm{CA}_A, |S_A|$ to B.
   (b) B responds ok or abort.
2. (a) U sends $\mathrm{CA}_B, |S_B|, |S_A \cap S_B|$ to A.
   (b) A responds ok or abort.
3. (a) U sends $S_A \cap S_B$ to B.
   (b) B responds ok or abort.
4. (a) U sends $S_A \cap S_B$ to A.
   (b) A responds ok or abort.

Simulation and trusted CAs. In order to simulate the protocol against malicious adversaries, the simulator must know which CAs the honest participant trusts. Without this information the malicious party may distinguish interaction with the simulator from interaction with the honest party since the simulator would not be able to consistently reject the same CAs as the honest participant. Since the list of CAs trusted by a participant is not considered private information, we assume that honest participants make the list public.

Remark 1. A and B should agree to use authorities they both trust before approaching U, since B may learn $|S_A|$ before A can decide that CA_B is untrustworthy (if B is malicious he may learn $|S_A|$ and abort). Since the "role" of the participant in the protocol is not specified, we simply assume that the first person to send the IdealProtocol message will play the role of A in the description of IdealProtocol. If a participant has multiple sets (and/or multiple certifying authorities) these are handled by a associating a different identity to each set, for example $A\|\mathsf{set1}$, $A\|\mathsf{set2}$, etc.

The real world model. In the real world there is no trusted party U, and participants are polynomial time algorithms, initialized with public keys of the CAs as required. A malicious participant may follow any polynomial time strategy.

Remark 2. An honest participant will abort if any deviation from the protocol is detected. Adversarial behaviour can thus serve to accomplish three outcomes.

1. Learning more about the other party's set than what is allowed in the ideal model.
2. Preventing the other party's output from being correct.
3. Using uncertified set elements in a protocol run.

With the definitions of the real and ideal models in place, we can now give a precise definition of a secure certified private intersection protocol.

Definition 1. *Let A and B^* be parties holding sets S_A and S_{B^*} from a domain D, certified by CA_A, CA_{B^*} respectively. Without loss of generality, B^* may behave arbitrarily (real-world adversary). Let Π be a private set intersection protocol, and D be the joint distribution of the outputs of A and B^* from Π when CA_A and CA_{B^*} are honest. Π is a secure certified private intersection protocol if a there exists a simulator (ideal-world adversary) which is given black-box access to B^* such that D is computationally indistinguishable from the joint output distribution of the simulator and A in the ideal world.*

Models for computing the intersection cardinality. A slightly modified ideal model applies to private computation of the intersection cardinality with certified sets. In the description above, Steps 3 and 4 are replaced by the single step "U sends $|S_A \cap S_B|$ to B". The real world model is unchanged.

3   Background

In this section we give the building blocks and notation we will use. The notation $x \in_R X$ denotes that x is chosen uniformly at random from the set X. We use $\{0,1\}^\ell$ to represent the set of all binary strings of length ℓ, as well as the set $[0, 2^\ell - 1]$ of integers. The notation $\pm\{0,1\}^\ell$ is used for the set $[-2^\ell + 1, 2^\ell - 1]$.

3.1   Zero Knowledge Proofs

When presenting protocols we express zero knowledge (ZK) proofs using the notation introduced by Camenisch and Stadler [5]:

$$PK\,\{(x, y, \ldots) : statements \text{ involving } x, y, \ldots\}$$

means the prover is proving knowledge of $(x, y, \ldots)$ such that these values satisfy *statements*. The notation is a short-hand for the various Schnorr-like proof of knowledge of a discrete logarithm protocols which exist for types of statements such as knowledge of, relations between, and the length of discrete logarithms. We sometimes use the notation to describe *any* protocol that implements a proof for the given statement, in this case we write $PK^*\,\{\ldots\}$.

The realization of the proofs of knowledge described above may be done in a variety of ways, each requiring different amounts of interaction and security assumptions. For the security of our protocol, we require that all ZK proofs be efficiently simulated. A protocol for concurrent ZK which may be simulated is given by Damgård [9]. The protocol uses the public key of a third party as the auxiliary string. In the protocols we present, since the CAs public key must be known by both A and B, it may be used as the auxiliary string. Replacing the verifier in a three-move ZK proof by a hash function gives a non-interactive ZK proof of knowledge [12]. Since it is non-interactive, there are no concurrency issues, and simulation is possible in the random oracle model.

3.2   Camenisch-Lysyanskaya Signatures

The Camenisch-Lysyanskaya (CL) signature scheme [7] signs L-tuples of strings from $\{0,1\}^{\ell_m}$. Given a signature on a tuple of elements, we may efficiently prove possession of a signature on some or all elements in the tuple. Further, this proof may be completed without revealing the signature itself.

We now describe a basic version of the scheme, where the signer learns all of the messages. In Section 5 we discuss possible applications of the signer's ability to sign tuples where some of the messages are hidden. A number of length related security parameters are used in the CL-signature scheme. For details on how they are chosen, see [7].

Key generation. For a security parameter ℓ_n, choose an ℓ_n-bit RSA modulus $n = pq$, where $p = 2p'+1$, $q = 2q'+1$, p' and q' are prime. Choose uniformly at random $R_1, \ldots, R_L, S, Z$ from the group of quadratic residues mod n. The public key is $(n, R_1, \ldots, R_L, S, Z)$ and the secret key is (p, q).

Signing algorithm. On input $m_1, \ldots, m_L$, the signer chooses at random a prime e of length $\ell_e > \ell_m + 2$, and a random number v of length $\ell_v = \ell_n + \ell_m + \ell_\emptyset$, where $\ell_\emptyset$ is a security parameter. Compute

$$A = \left(\frac{Z}{R_1^{m_1} \cdots R_L^{m_L} S^v} \right)^{1/e} \pmod{n} .$$

The signature is (A, e, v).

Verification algorithm. (A, e, v) is a valid signature on the message $(m_1, \ldots, m_L)$ if

$$Z \equiv A^e R_1^{m_1} \cdots R_L^{m_L} \pmod{n} ,$$

$m_i \in \pm\{0,1\}^{\ell_m}$, and $2^{\ell_e - 1} < e < 2^{\ell_e}$.

Proof of possession. This proof assumes the prover wishes to keep all messages hidden. Let ℓ_H be a security parameter. Choose $r \in_R \{0,1\}^{\ell_n + \ell_\emptyset}$, and randomize the signature (A, e, v) as $(A' = AS^{-r} \pmod{n}, e, v' = v + er)$. The randomized signature is communicated to the verifier and the prover asserts:

$$PK\{(e, v', m_1, \ldots, m_L) : \frac{Z}{A'^{2^{\ell_e - 1}} R_1^{m_1} \cdots R_L^{m_L}} \equiv \pm A'^e S^{v'} \pmod{n}$$

$$\wedge \quad m_i \in \{0,1\}^{\ell_m + \ell_\emptyset + \ell_H + 2} \text{ for } i = 1 \ldots L$$

$$\wedge \quad e - 2^{\ell_e - 1} \in \pm\{0,1\}^{\ell'_e + \ell_\emptyset + \ell_H + 1}\} .$$

The first predicate convinces the verifier that the signature is in fact valid, while the second and third prove that it is well formed with respect to the system parameters. For details of how the interval checks on e and the m_i are realized, see [7] (this proof is also given in more detail as the part of the protocol in Appendix A). Security of the CL-signature scheme relies on the strong RSA (SRSA) assumption, see [7] for details of this assumption and a security proof.

The proof of possession as stated is of limited utility, it merely asserts that the holder has a signature on some tuple of correctly formed messages. However, we will compose this proof with one to show that certain computations were done using the signed values. This will allow A and B to prove that only signed values are used in the intersection protocol.

3.3 Homomorphic Encryption

We also review two homomorphic encryption schemes used for private set intersection. Both are *additively homomorphic*, i.e. for two encryptions $E(m_1), E(m_2)$ of messages m_1, m_2, $E(m_1) \star E(m_2) = E(m_1 + m_2)$, where $\star$ is a group operation on ciphertexts. It follows by repeated addition that $E(m_1)^c = E(cm_1)$ for an integer c.

The Paillier Cryptosystem. The Paillier cryptosystem [24] encrypts plaintexts from $\mathbb{Z}_n^*$ as ciphertexts in $\mathbb{Z}_{n^2}^*$. Security relies on the decisional composite residuosity assumption, which requires (as a minimum) that n be difficult to factor. For encryption, decryption and to operate on encrypted values requires arithmetic mod n^2.

The cryptosystem is probabilistic, IND-CPA secure, and allows efficient proofs of plaintext knowledge, as well as multiplicative relationships on plaintexts [10]. We will largely treat Paillier encryption as a generic homomorphic encryption scheme with these properties, and do not describe the details of the system here.

A homomorphic Elgamal variant. Our new protocols will use a standard variant of Elgamal encryption [11]. Setup consists of choosing a cyclic group G of prime order q, such that the discrete log problem is difficult in G. The parameter ℓ_q is the bitlength of q. Next choose a generator $g \in G$ and the secret key $x \in_R \mathbb{Z}_q^*$. The public key is $(g, h = g^x)$. To encrypt $m \in \mathbb{Z}_q^*$, choose $r \in_R \mathbb{Z}_q^*$, and compute $E(m) = (g^r, g^m h^r)$. The additive homomorphic property is easily verified. Efficient decryption is not possible; but to recognize an encryption of zero, given x, compute $(g^r)^{-x}(g^m h^r) = g^{-rx} g^{m+rx} = g^m$, which is one precisely when $m = 0$. This test will be sufficient for our protocols, decryption will not be necessary.

As with Paillier, the scheme is probabilistic and IND-CPA secure. ZK proofs of plaintext knowledge are simply proofs of knowledge of discrete logs. It is worth noting that arithmetic in G will be significantly faster than in $\mathbb{Z}_{n^2}^*$ for comparable levels of security and the ciphertexts will be smaller.

3.4 Verifiable Shuffles

A sub-protocol we use in our intersection cardinality protocol is a verifiable shuffle decryption. A *verifiable shuffle* of ciphertexts takes a list of ciphertexts

$e_1, \ldots, e_k$ as input, and outputs a second list of ciphertexts $E_1, \ldots, E_k$, which contain the *same* plaintexts in a permuted order. The public key of the e_i and E_i is the same. In a *verifiable decryption*, the decryptor proves that the decrypted values correspond to the ciphertexts without revealing the private key. A *verifiable shuffle decryption* is the combination: first the ciphertexts are shuffled, then decrypted and proof is given that the plaintexts correspond to input ciphertexts. The result of the operation is that the verifier does not learn which input ciphertexts correspond to which plaintexts, the permutation is kept secret.

One can simply combine a shuffle protocol (such the one of Groth and Ishai [17]), with a proof of correct decryption, or one may use a combined protocol (such as the one of Furukawa [15]). The combined method of Furukawa, which is specialized to Elgamal ciphertexts, requires $14k$ exponentiations and communication of approximately k group elements.

4   Existing Private Intersection Protocols

In this section we describe previously known protocols to solve the private set intersection problem (and variants such as intersection cardinality).

The work of Freedman, Nissim and Pinkas (FNP) was the first to present the private set intersection problem, and protocols to solve it [14]. We will describe their design strategy in some detail, since it underlies most of the subsequent work on this topic (including our own). *Throughout this paper, we assume that* $|S_A| = |S_B| = k$ to simplify presentation, however all of the protocols presented also work when $|S_A| \neq |S_B|$.

Suppose pk_A is the public key of A for the Paillier cryptosystem (or a scheme providing similar features). Let R be a ring, $R[t]$ be the polynomials with coefficients from R, and D be the domain to which S_A and S_B belong. We will require that $|D|/|R|$ is negligible. First, A represents $S_A = (a_1, \ldots, a_k)$ as the roots of a degree k polynomial, $f = \prod_{i=1}^{k}(t - a_i) = \sum_{i=0}^{k} \alpha_i t^i$, then encrypts the coefficients with pk_A. These are then sent to B, who evaluates f at each $b_i \in S_B$ homomorphically. The key observation is that $f(b_i) = 0$ if and only if $b_i \in S_A \cap S_B$. B returns $w_i = E(s_i f(b_i) + b_i)$ to A, for a randomly chosen value s_i. If $b_i \in S_A \cap S_B$ then A leans b_i upon decrypting. If $b_i \notin S_A \cap S_B$ then w_i decrypts to a random value.

This version of the protocol is secure in the semi-honest model. To cope with malicious parties, FNP give protocols to deal with the cases when A may be malicious, or when B may be malicious. They also sketch a strategy for combining the two to handle either A or B behaving maliciously. The protocol uses a cut-and-choose technique, which quickly becomes inefficient in both computation and communication as k grows.

Kissner and Song (KS) [21,22] present improved protocols for more general set operations, as well as protocols for set operations in the multiparty case. We review the crux of their approach. Let s and t be randomly chosen polynomials in $R[t]$ and f, g be polynomials representing sets S_A, S_B respectively, and $\deg s, t, f, g = k$. The authors prove that $sf + tg = \gcd(f, g) \cdot u$, where u

is a uniformly random element of $R[t]$. Combined with the condition that the domain D of S_A and S_B is very small compared to R, the chance that u contains an element from D as a root is low. Therefore the only elements of D which are roots of $sf + tg$ are those in $\gcd(f, g) = S_A \cap S_B$. The parties jointly compute encryptions of $sf + tg$, then decrypt to learn the intersection. The advantage of this representation of $S_A \cap S_B$ is that it composes well with other operations, and handles more than two parties easily.

Their solution for two-party private set intersection, secure in the malicious model, has computation and communication complexity $O(k^2)$. They do not present a protocol for the two party private intersection cardinality problem secure in the malicious model. We also note that their malicious model protocols require the use of Paillier encryption (or a homomorphic scheme with equivalent properties).

Hohenberger and Weis [19] provide protocols for a private disjointness test where A is semi-honest and B may be malicious, and a private intersection cardinality protocol in the semi-honest model. Their protocols are also based on the paradigm of FNP, but use the homomorphic Elgamal variant presented in §3, and rely on the ability to recognize encryptions of zero.

Hazay and Lindell [18] give protocols for two party private set intersection using a novel approach based on oblivious pseudorandom function evaluation (instead of oblivious polynomial evaluation). The protocol is more efficient than previous solutions, however security is proven in a relaxed version of the malicious model. A further difference of this protocol with the one presented here is that the output is only learnt by one participant.

Finally, Kiayias and Mitrofanova [20], and Ye et al. [26] provide protocols for a restricted version of private set intersection, the case when a single bit is output, indicating whether the intersection is non-empty. We omit details of these papers, since solutions to this problem are much less efficient than intersection and cardinality, and differ significantly from the present work.

5   Certified Sets

Here we describe the process a CA uses to certify a set for a participant. Once certified, the set may be used in the private set intersection protocol of Section 6. A discussion of the possibility of using certified sets with existing private set intersection protocols is available in [27].

Certification will be done by the CA, who issues a CL-signature to the set holder A for the set $S_A = (a_1, \ldots, a_k)$. Given this signature (or certificate) A must be able to prove the following.

1. That encrypted coefficients correspond to the polynomial representation of a certified set.
2. That the set used in a computation is certified.
3. The size of the set.

Let S_A be represented by the polynomial $f(t) = \sum_{i=0}^{k} \alpha_i t^i$. The message space of the CL signature scheme used by the CA must have length $k + 1$.

To certify S_A, the CA first signs the coefficients and the degree of the polynomial. Signing coefficients allows requirement 1 to be easily proven. During certification, the user sends $S_A, \alpha_0, \ldots, \alpha_k$ to the CA. The CA checks whether α_i are the coefficients of $f(t) = \prod_{a \in S_A}(t - a)$ and that S_A is valid for the user. Then the CA issues two signatures, one on $(k, \alpha_1, \ldots, \alpha_k)$ and one on $(k, a_1, \ldots, a_k)$.

Proof that the homomorphic Elgamal ciphertexts $E_i = (g^{r_i}, g^{\alpha_i} h^{r_i})$ contain encryptions of certified coefficients is:

$$\text{PK}^*\{(\alpha_0, \ldots, \alpha_{k-1}, r_0, \ldots, r_{k-1}) : \alpha_i \text{ are CL-signed}$$
$$\wedge \, E_i = (g^{r_i}, g^{\alpha_i} h^{r_i}) \text{ for } i = 1, \ldots, k - 1\},$$

where the proof that "α_i are CL-signed" is done as described in §3.2 (and $\text{PK}\{(\alpha_0, \ldots, \alpha_{k-1}, r_0, \ldots, r_{k-1}) : E_i = (g^{r_i}, g^{\alpha_i} h^{r_i}) \text{ for } i = 1, \ldots, k - 1\}$ is a Schnorr-like proof protocol. Proving that elements used in a computation are certified is easy; one simply proves that they are CL-signed. The size of the set $|S_A| = k$ is the first attribute in the signature and should be revealed and checked during proof.

In the case when the CA's public key has $L > k + 1$ bases, the elements corresponding to the additional bases are set to zero and ignored during the protocol.

Extensions. The authentication of set holders may also be included in the certification process, by including an identifier or pseudonym as the first value signed by the CA. During the first proof involving the signature, the holder may reveal or prove something about their identity. Preventing users from sharing their sets and signatures is not possible, but this problem has been studied in the context of anonymous credentials, see [6,8] for some deterrents. Note that shared sets may not be combined to participate in the protocol with a larger set as the CL signature scheme prevents this.

Another possible extension is to allow users to keep some set elements hidden from the CA since this feature is provided by the CL-signature scheme. Some elements may remain completely private, while still preventing the user from changing their set, and limiting the size of the set.

6   New Certified Private Intersection Protocol

We now describe our new protocol for privately computing the intersection and intersection cardinality of certified sets. We begin with an overview before giving complete details.

6.1   Overview

Suppose A has $S_A = (a_1, \ldots, a_k)$ and B has $S_B = (b_1, \ldots, b_k)$. We first sketch a private intersection cardinality protocol where both S_A and S_B are certified. This protocol will be extended below to compute the actual intersection as well. Suppose $f(t) = \sum_{i=0}^{\ell} \alpha_i t^i = \prod_{j=1}^{\ell}(t - a_j)$ represents S_A. G will be the group used for Elgamal homomorphic encryption.

- The CA certifies S_A and S_B using the method from Section 5.

- A encrypts α_i using Elgamal homomorphic encryption (denoted $E(\cdot)$) under his public key, and proves that this was done correctly. In this same proof A proves holdership of a CL-signature on α_i for $i = 1, \ldots, k$, and the cardinality of S_A.

- B first verifies the proof that the encryptions of α_i were formed correctly and checks the cardinality of S_A. B computes $w_i = E(s_i f(b_i))$ where $s_i \in_R \mathbb{Z}_q^*$, for each $b_i \in S_B$ using the homomorphic properties of E. A proof is included that w_i are computed correctly, that b_i are signed and that the cardinality of S_B is correct.

- A decrypts w_i to get $g^{s_i f(b_i)}$, and counts how often $g^{s_i f(b_i)} = 1$; this total is the intersection cardinality.

- A outputs the cardinality to B, and proves it is correct using a verifiable shuffle decryption, as described in §3.4.

Extension to compute $S_A \cap S_B$. The following steps can be added to the protocol to provide the intersection, not just its cardinality.

- When B computes w_i for all $b_i \in S_B$, he stores a lookup table mapping $w_i \leftrightarrow (s_i, b_i)$.

- A decrypts; whenever $w_i = 1$, he proves this to B, who looks up the value
  · (s_i, b_i). In this way B learns $S_A \cap S_B$. A must also prove $f(b_i) \neq 0$ (when this is the case) to convince B that the entire intersection is output.

- B reports $S_A \cap S_B$ to A as pairs (s_i, b_i), who checks it for consistency by checking $w_i \overset{?}{=} E(s_i f(b_i))$ and by checking $|S_A \cap S_B| = |\{i : D(w_i) = 1\}|$.

6.2   Detailed Description

We now describe the complete protocol, with non-interactive ZK proofs, the details of which are given in Appendix A. Recall that Elgamal ciphertexts have the form $E_i = (g^r, g^m h^r)$. In this section we will refer to the first element of the ciphertext E_i as $E_{i,1}$ and to the second as $E_{i,2}$.

Setup:

> A has the set S_A, represented by $f(t) = \sum_{i=0}^k \alpha_i t^i$, certified as in §5.
> B has the set S_B, also certified with the method of §5.
> A generates the homomorphic Elgamal parameters G and $pk_A = (g, h)$ which are made public, and $x = \log_g h$ is kept secret.

Protocol:

1. A computes $E_i = E(\alpha_i) = (g^{r_i}, g^{\alpha_i} h^{r_i})$ using pk_A, $r_i \in_R \mathbb{Z}_q$ for $i = 1, \ldots, k$.

2. A creates

$$P_1 = \text{PK}^*\{(\alpha_0, \ldots, \alpha_k, r_0, \ldots, r_k):$$
$$E_{i,1} = g^{r_i} \wedge E_{i,2} = g^{\alpha_i} h^{r_i} \text{ for } i = 1, \ldots, k$$
$$\wedge k \text{ and } \alpha_i \text{ are CL-signed}\}$$

3. A sends $(E_0, \ldots, E_k, P_1)$ to B.
4. B verifies P_1, and aborts if verification fails.
5. B homomorphically evaluates f at elements in S_B by computing

$$v_i = \left(\prod_{j=0}^{k} E_{j,1}^{(b_i)^j}, \prod_{j=0}^{k} E_{j,2}^{(b_i)^j} \right)$$

for each $b \in S_B$ in random order, then computes $w_i = (v_{i,1}^{s_i}, v_{i,2}^{s_i})$ for $s_i \in_R G$. Note that $w_i = E(s_i f(b_i))$. B stores a table mapping $w_i \leftrightarrow (b_i, s_i)$ (this may be omitted if only the intersection cardinality is desired).

6. B creates the proof

$$P_2 = \text{PK}^*\{(b_0, \ldots, b_k, s_0, \ldots, s_k):$$
$$w_i = \left(\prod_{j=0}^{k} E_{j,1}^{(b_i)^j s_i}, \prod_{j=0}^{k} E_{j,2}^{(b_i)^j s_i} \right), \quad \text{for } i = 1, \ldots, k \qquad \bullet$$
$$\wedge k, b_i \text{ are CL-signed}\} \ .$$

Here we abuse the PK notation somewhat: the proof protocol for P_2 cannot be directly derived from the above description; we explain in the appendix how a protocol proving this statement can be realized.

7. B sends $(w_1, \ldots, w_k, P_2)$ to A.
8. A verifies P_2, and aborts if this fails. A must also check that $s_i \neq 0$ by ensuring that $w_{i,1} \neq 1$ for $i = 1, \ldots, k$.
9. If the intersection cardinality is desired: (if not, skip to Step 10)

   (a) A initializes a counter $c = 0$, decrypts w_i to get $g^{s_i f(b)}$ and increments c if $g^{s_i f(b)} = 1$.
   (b) A outputs c, the size of the intersection. Using a verifiable shuffle decryption protocol, A proves that c of the ciphertexts w_i decrypt to 1, without revealing which ones. (See Section 3.4.)
   (c) B verifies the shuffle decryption proof.
   (d) The protocol terminates.

10. A decrypts w_i for $i = 1, \ldots, k$, and creates the following partition of $\{w_1, \ldots, w_k\}$:

$$C_1 = \{w_i : D(w_i) = 1\} \ ,$$
$$C_y = \{w_i : D(w_i) = y_i \neq 1\} \ .$$

11. A proves that the decryptions of w_i are (or are not) equal to zero with the following proof:

$$P_3 = \text{PK}\{(x) : w_{i,1}{}^x = w_{i,2} \ \vee \ \{i : w_i \in C_1\}$$
$$\wedge \quad w_{i,1}{}^x = w_{i,2}/y_i \ \vee \ \{i : w_i \in C_y\}$$
$$\wedge \quad g^x = h\} \ .$$

The verifier further checks that $y_i \neq 1 \ \vee \ \{i : w_i \in C_y\}$.

12. A sends C_1, C_y, P_3 to B.
13. B verifies P_3. (Note also that B must check that P_3 contains the correct number of statements, i.e. that all w_i appear in one of C_1, C_y).
14. For each i such that $w_i \in C_1$, B recovers (s_i, b_i) from the lookup table, and adds it to a set X.
15. B sends X to A, which contains $S_A \cap S_B$, and A checks that
    (a) $|X| = |C_1|$, and
    (b) $w_i = E(s_i f(b_i))$ (recomputed using the revealed values (s_i, b_i)).
    If either check fails, A learns that B has output $S_A \cap S_B$ incorrectly.

Remark 3. In both steps 11 and 9b when A proves to B that w_i does not contain an encryption of zero, it is important that the decrypted value, $g^{s_i f(b_i)}$, is not revealed since B knows s_i. A must therefore blind the ciphertexts in C_y (which are not encryptions of zero) as $w_i^{u_i}$ where $u_i \in_R \mathbb{Z}_q^*$. Since $s_i, u_i \neq 0$, $g^{s_i u_i f(b_i)} = 1$ if and only if $f(b_i) = 0$, as required.

6.3 Security and Privacy

The following theorem shows that the new protocol securely implements the ideal functionality described in Section 2.

Theorem 1. *The protocol of Section 6.2, when constructed with a secure ZK protocol, and an IND-CPA secure homomorphic encryption scheme, is a secure certified private intersection protocol (by Definition 1) assuming the the SRSA assumption holds.*

Proof. We consider three cases. First, when both A and B are honest we show the protocol output is the same as in the ideal-world (the correct output). Then, in the cases when A or B is malicious, we describe a simulator which satisfies Definition 1.

Suppose Y is the intersection output by the protocol when A and B are honest (for input sets S_A and S_B). If the following two claims hold, then the protocol is correct.

Claim 1: For every $y \in Y$, $y \in S_A$ and $y \in S_B$. Since $y \in Y$, it must therefore be that the decryption of some w_i, which is $g^{s_i f(y)}$ is equal to one (in the notation of Section 6). It must be that $f(y) = 0$, since $s_i \neq 0$ and G has prime order. We are assured that $f(t) = \prod_{a_i \in S_A}(t - a_i)$ by the validity of the CL-signature, therefore the only points at which f is zero are elements of S_A, therefore $y \in S_A$. Since S proves that w_i are computed using nonzero s_i and $b_i \in S_B$, we also have that $y \in S_B$.

Claim 2: For every y such that $y \in S_A$ and $y \in S_B$, we also have $y \in Y$. Similarly, since we are assured by the CL-signature that f is created with elements of S_A and $E(s_i f(b))$ is computed for all $b \in S_B$, it is not possible that some $y \in S_A \cap S_B$ has $f(y) \neq 0$ and as a result, will always be included in Y.

We prove privacy for A, i.e., we describe a simulator SIM_{B^*}, which is given black-box access to B^* in the ideal model such that the output distributions of A and B^* in the real world are indistinguishable from the ones of A and SIM_{B^*} in the ideal world. (Here, B^* may or may not follow the protocol.) The simulator's output is computationally indistinguishable from the view of B^* in a real protocol execution. Intuitively, SIM_{B^*} sits between U (the trusted party) and B^*, and interacts with both in such a way that B^* is unable to distinguish protocol runs with SIM_{B^*} from real-world protocol runs with A.

SIM_{B^*} is the following polynomial time algorithm. First SIM_{B^*} sends (IdealProtocol, B^*, A) to U. IdealProtocol begins and SIM_{B^*} receives $CA_A, |S_A|$. SIM_{B^*} then creates $E_i = E(\alpha_i) = (g^{r_i}, g^{\alpha_i} h^{r_i})$ for randomly chosen (r_i, α_i), and forges the proof P_1. SIM_{B^*} sends P_1 and E_i, to B^* (protocol Step 3), and responds ok to U. Now SIM_{B^*} receives $(w_1, \ldots, w_k, P_2)$ from B^* (protocol Step 7), or if B^* aborts, SIM_{B^*} returns abort to U and stops. Recall that SIM_{B^*} knows the CAs which A trusts, and may therefore reject CA_B (used in P_2) if A does not trust CA_B. If P_2 is invalid, SIM_{B^*} also returns abort to U and stops. From P_2, SIM_{B^*} extracts b_j, $j = 1, \ldots, k$ and the mapping $w_i \leftrightarrow b_j$, i.e., knowledge of which w_i corresponds to an encryption of $f(b_j)$. SIM_{B^*} now receives $S_A \cap S_{B^*}$ from U, which gives SIM_{B^*} enough information to create the sets C_y, C_1 consistent with $w_i \leftrightarrow b_j$ and $S_A \cap S_B$. C_1 and C_y along with forged proofs of decryption P_3 are sent to B^* (protocol Step 12), and SIM_{B^*} responds ok to U. A receives the intersection and the protocol is complete. Finally SIM_{B^*} outputs whatever B^* outputs.

Let us argue that the output distributions in the real and the ideal world are (computationally) indistinguishable. First note that due to the security of the CL signature scheme, B^* in the real world cannot obtain a certificate on a set different from what it can obtain in the ideal world, hence the output of A will be identical in both worlds. We next explain why the view of B^*, as output by SIM_{B^*} is computationally indistinguishable from B^*'s view in real protocol runs with A. The encryptions E_i of random values are indistinguishable from the honest encryptions because the encryption scheme is IND-CPA secure. The forged proofs are also indistinguishable, by the zero-knowledge property. In the last step, the sets C_1, C_y are created exactly as A would in the real world, since at this point SIM_{B^*} has $w_i \leftrightarrow b_j$ and $S_A \cap S_B$. This means that B^* cannot distinguish whether or not it runs with the real world A or with SIM_{B^*}, i.e., any difference in the B^* views would imply one of our assumptions is false.

We now prove privacy for B in a similar manner, by describing an efficient simulator SIM_{A^*}. SIM_{A^*} sends (IdealProtocol, A^*, B) to U, and waits to receive

CA_B, $|S_B|$, $|S_A \cap S_B|$ from U (recall that B is honest and will not abort). SIM_{A^*} receives $E_0, \ldots, E_k$ from from A^* and proof P_1 (protocol Step 3). If P_1 is invalid or if CA_A is untrusted by B or if A^* has aborted, SIM_{A^*} stops and returns abort to U. Otherwise SIM_{A^*} extracts $\alpha_0, \ldots, \alpha_k$ from P_1, recovers S_A and responds ok to U.

Now SIM_{A^*} must perform Step 5. First choose a set Z of $|S_A \cap S_B|$ indices randomly from $\{1, \ldots, k\}$. For every $i \in Z$, compute $w_i = (g^{s_i}, h^{s_i})$ where $s_i \in_R \mathbb{Z}_q^*$. For the remaining indices $j \in \{1, \ldots, k\} - Z$, compute w_j as the homomorphic encryption of random values from $\mathbb{Z}_q^*$. SIM_{A^*} forges the proof that this was done correctly, then receives $S_A \cap S_B$ from U. If A^* does not abort, SIM_{A^*} receives, then verifies P_3. If P_3 is invalid SIM_{A^*} returns abort to U and stops. Otherwise SIM_{A^*} responds with (s_i, b_i) for $b_i \in S_A \cap S_B$ and s_i as chosen above (protocol Step 15).

The indistinguishability in this case comes from the IND-CPA security of the encryption; A^* cannot distinguish w_i for $i \notin Z$ from encryptions created during a real run of the protocol. The check in Step 15 passes since decryption of $w_i = g^{-s_i x} h^{s_i} = 1$, only when $i \in Z$, and therefore only $|S_A \cap S_B|$ times. Note that the mapping $b_i \leftrightarrow s_i$ is unimportant, since $f(b_i) = 0$ and w_i is an encryption of zero when $i \in Z$. Since the forged proof is also indistinguishable, the views of A^* during a real protocol run and the simulation are indistinguishable. Furthermore, due to the security of the CL signatures, the outputs of B in both worlds will be the same. $\qquad\square$

When the homomorphic Elgamal variant is used for encryption, security of the protocol relies on: the SRSA assumption in $\mathbb{Z}_n^*$, the difficulty of the discrete logarithm problem in G, and any additional assumptions required for the security of the zero knowledge proofs.

6.4 Adding Fairness

Until this point we have not addressed the question "What if B aborts the protocol after learning $S_A \cap S_B$, but before A does?". The possibility for such an unfair outcome is undesirable in a situation where either A or B may be malicious. In this section we sketch the incorporation of optimistic fair exchange (OFE) protocols to the private set intersection protocol of §6.2. An OFE scheme allows A and B to swap two values "simultaneously", i.e. both are guaranteed to receive the value held by the other. A trusted third party is present, but only participates when one party does not complete the protocol (hence the term *optimistic*). Example OFE schemes are given in the work of Asokan et al. [1].

To add OFE to our set intersection protocol, we weave two instances of the protocol together, where A and B have opposite roles in each instance. The new protocol is now symmetric, i.e. A and B must perform equivalent operations and communicate equivalent values at the same steps, which are exchanged fairly. Any abort thus results in a fair outcome, where both parties finish with equal knowledge about the other's input set. Using an OFE protocol in such a generic way may yield a protocol with room for improvement; we leave such improvements to future work.

7   Efficiency

A detailed analysis of the computational and communication costs of our new protocol is given in the extended version of this paper [27]. The dominating computations, evaluating the polynomial, all occur in G. A detailed comparison of our new protocol to a certified version of the FNP protocol and/or the malicious, two-party, non-certified protocol of Kissner and Song [21, Figure 8] would be beyond the scope of this work. Communication and computation costs are asymptotically equal, each being $O(k^2)$.

The constants however, will be significantly smaller since Elgamal parameters are smaller than Paillier parameters providing equivalent security. For 80-bits of security, Paillier with a 1024-bit modulus, yields ciphertexts of 2048 bits. In the Elgamal case we may use the elliptic curve group given by NIST curve P-192 (a curve over $\mathbb{F}_p$, where p is a 192-bit prime) [13]. The Elgamal ciphertexts are thus 384 bits, 5.3 times smaller than the equivalent Paillier ciphertext.

In addition to providing faster arithmetic, operating primarily in G allows the protocol to scale to higher security levels. The size of parameters required for Paillier grow quadratically as a function of the security level, while parameters for elliptic curve systems grow linearly (see Lenstra and Verheul [23]).

Since the ZK proofs are relatively simple, they are good candidates for the batch verification techniques of Bellare, Garay and Rabin [2]. Fast exponentiation and multi-exponentiation techniques (see [3] for a survey) are also applicable, and will improve performance significantly.

Finally, if the certification aspects of the protocol are omitted, the result is a fast protocol for private set intersection, or intersection cardinality with malicious model security.

8   Conclusion

We have presented certified sets, and applied them to the private set intersection problem. This approach solves a well-known problem of multiparty computations, namely, how to guarantee that the parties do not lie about their inputs. Future work might consider the natural generalization to certified inputs for general multiparty computation.

References

1. Asokan, N., Shoup, V., Waidner, M.: Optimistic fair exchange of digital signatures. IEEE Journal on Selected Areas in Communications 18, 593–610 (2000)
2. Bellare, M., Garay, J., Rabin, T.: Fast batch verification for modular exponentiation and digital signatures. In: Nyberg, K. (ed.) EUROCRYPT 1998. LNCS, vol. 1403, pp. 236–250. Springer, Heidelberg (1998)
3. Bernstein, D.J.: Pippenger's exponentiation algorithm. Manuscript, http://cr.yp.to/papers.html#pippenger
4. Boudot, F., Schoenmakers, B., Traoré, J.: A fair and efficient solution to the socialist millionaires' problem. Discrete and Applied Math. 111, 23–36 (2001)

5. Camenisch, J., Stadler, M.: Proof systems for general statements about discrete logarithms. Technical Report TR 260, Institute for Theoretical Computer Science, ETH Zürich (1997)
6. Camenisch, J., Lysyanskaya, A.: An efficient system for non-transferable anonymous credentials with optional anonymity revocation. In: Pfitzmann, B. (ed.) EUROCRYPT 2001. LNCS, vol. 2045, pp. 93–118. Springer, Heidelberg (2001)
7. Camenisch, J., Lysyanskaya, A.: A signature scheme with efficient protocols. In: Cimato, S., Galdi, C., Persiano, G. (eds.) SCN 2002. LNCS, vol. 2576, pp. 268–289. Springer, Heidelberg (2003)
8. Camenisch, J., Hohenberger, S., Kohlweiss, M., Lysyanskaya, A., Meyerovich, M.: How to win the clone wars: efficient periodic n-times anonymous authentication. In: Proceedings of CCS 2006, pp. 201–210. ACM Press, New York (2006)
9. Damgård, I.: Efficient concurrent zero-knowledge in the auxiliary string model. In: Preneel, B. (ed.) EUROCRYPT 2000. LNCS, vol. 1807, pp. 418–430. Springer, Heidelberg (2000)
10. Damgård, I., Jurik, M.: A generalisation, a simplification and some applications of Paillier's probabilistic public-key system. In: Kim, K. C. (ed.) PKC 2001. LNCS, vol. 1992, pp. 119–136. Springer, Heidelberg (2001)
11. Elgamal, T.: A public-key cryptosystem and a signature scheme based on discrete logarithms. IEEE Transactions on Information Theory 31, 469–472 (1986)
12. Fiat, A., Shamir, A.: How to prove yourself: practical solutions to identification and signature problems. In: Odlyzko, A.M. (ed.) CRYPTO 1986. LNCS, vol. 263, pp. 186–194. Springer, Heidelberg (1987)
13. National Institute of Standards and Technology. Digital signature standard (DSS). FIPS PUB 186-2 (2000)
14. Freedman, M.J., Nissim, K., Pinkas, B.: Efficient private matching and set intersection. In: Cachin, C., Camenisch, J.L. (eds.) EUROCRYPT 2004. LNCS, vol. 3027, pp. 1–19. Springer, Heidelberg (2004)
15. Furukawa, J.: Efficient verifiable shuffle decryption and its requirement of unlinkability. In: Bao, F., Deng, R., Zhou, J. (eds.) PKC 2004. LNCS, vol. 2947, pp. 319–332. Springer, Heidelberg (2004)
16. Goldreich, O.: The Foundations of Cryptography – Volume 2 Basic Applications. Cambridge University Press, New York (2004)
17. Groth, J., Ishai, Y.: Sub-linear zero-knowledge argument for correctness of a shuffle. In: Smart, N.P. (ed.) EUROCRYPT 2008. LNCS, vol. 4965, pp. 379–396. Springer, Heidelberg (2008)
18. Hazay, C., Lindell, Y.: Efficient protocols for set intersection and pattern matching with security against malicious and covert adversaries. In: Canetti, R. (ed.) TCC 2008. LNCS, vol. 4948, pp. 155–175. Springer, Heidelberg (2008)
19. Hohenberger, S., Weis, S.: Honest-verifier private disjointness testing without random oracles. In: Danezis, G., Golle, P. (eds.) PET 2006. LNCS, vol. 4258, pp. 277–294. Springer, Heidelberg (2006)
20. Kiayias, A., Mitrofanova, A.: Testing disjointness of private datasets. In: S. Patrick, A., Yung, M. (eds.) FC 2005. LNCS, vol. 3570, pp. 109–124. Springer, Heidelberg (2005)
21. Kissner, L., Song, D.: Private and threshold set intersection. Technical report CMU-CS-04-182, School of Computer Science, Carnegie Mellon University (2004)
22. Kissner, L., Song, D.: Privacy preserving set operations. In: Shoup, V. (ed.) CRYPTO 2005. LNCS, vol. 3621, pp. 241–257. Springer, Heidelberg (2005)

23. Lenstra, A.K., Verheul, E.R.: Selecting cryptographic key sizes. Journal of Cryptology 14, 255–293 (2001)
24. Paillier, P.: Public-key cryptosystems based on composite residuosity classes. In: Stern, J. (ed.) EUROCRYPT 1999. LNCS, vol. 1592, pp. 223–239. Springer, Heidelberg (1999)
25. Pass, R.: On deniability in the common reference and random oracle model. In: Boneh, D. (ed.) CRYPTO 2003. LNCS, vol. 2729, pp. 316–337. Springer, Heidelberg (2003)
26. Ye, Q., Wang, H., Pieprzyk, J., Zhang, X.-M.: Efficient disjointness test for private datasets. To appear at ACISP (2009)
27. Extended technical report version of this paper

A   Detailed Description of ZK Proofs

In this section we explicitly state the operations required to realize the ZK proofs and verifications of our new protocol (§6.2), using non-interactive ZK based on the Fiat-Shamir heuristic. Let $H : \{0,1\}^* \to \{0,1\}^{\ell_H}$ be a cryptographic hash function.

Creating P_1 (Step 2)

1. (*Randomize Signature*) Choose $r' \in \{0,1\}^{\ell_n+\ell_\emptyset}$, compute $\tilde{A} = AS^{r'}$ (mod n), compute $\tilde{v} = v + er'$, and compute $e' = e - 2^{\ell_e-1}$.
2. Compute

$$U = \tilde{A}^{r_e} S^{r_{\tilde{v}}} \left(\prod_{i=0}^{k} R_i^{r_{\alpha_i}} \right) \quad (\text{mod } n)$$

   where $r_e \in_R \{0,1\}^{\ell'_e+\ell_\emptyset+\ell_H}, r_{\tilde{v}} \in_R \{0,1\}^{\ell_v+\ell_\emptyset+\ell_H}$. and $r_{\alpha_i} \in_R \{0,1\}^{\ell_m+\ell_\emptyset+\ell_H}$.
3. For $i = 0,\ldots,k$, compute $T_i = g^{r_{r_i}},\ g^{r_{\alpha_i}} h^{r_{r_i}}$, where $r_{r_i} \in_R \{0,1\}^{\ell_q+\ell_\emptyset+\ell_H}$.
4. (*Challenge.*) Compute $c = H(\tilde{A}||U||T_1||\ldots||T_k)$.
5. Compute, in $\mathbb{Z}$: $s_{e'} = r_e - ce'$, $s_{\tilde{v}} = r_{\tilde{v}} - c\tilde{v}$, $s_{\alpha_i} = r_{\alpha_i} - c\alpha_i$ for $i = 0,\ldots,k$, and $s_{r_i} = r_{r_i} - cr_i$ for $i = 0,\ldots,k$.
6. Output $P_1 = (c, s\text{-values from Step 5})$.
7. Send $(P_1, \tilde{A})$ to the verifier.

Verifying P_1 (Step 4)

1. Compute

$$\hat{U} = \left(\frac{Z}{\tilde{A}^{2^{\ell_e-1}}} \right)^c \left(\tilde{A}^{s_{e'}} S^{s_{\tilde{v}}} \right) \left(\prod_{i=0}^{k} R_i^{s_{\alpha_i}} \right)$$

2. Let $E_i = (x_i, y_i)$. For $i = 0,\ldots,k$, compute $\hat{T}_i = x_i^c g^{s_{r_i}},\ y_i^c g^{s_{\alpha_i}} h^{s_{r_i}}$.
3. Compute $\hat{c} = H(\tilde{A}||\hat{U}||\hat{T}_1||\ldots||\hat{T}_k)$. If $\hat{c} \neq c$, reject the proof.
4. Check that $s_{e'} \in \pm\{0,1\}^{\ell'_e+\ell_\emptyset+\ell_H+2}$ and $s_{\alpha_i} \in \pm\{0,1\}^{\ell_m+\ell_\emptyset+\ell_H+3}$.

Creating and verifying P_2 (Steps 6, 8). Due to limited space we sketch the steps required to create and verify P_2. The main statements to be proven in P_2 are: (i) that the b_i values, which are shuffled when used in Step 5, are CL-signed, (ii) that the powers of b_i are computed correctly in the evaluation, and (iii) that the w_i values are computed correctly.

1. Compute the vector C', where $C'_i = g^{b_i} h^{r'_i}$, using the ordering in the CL signature ($r'_i \in_R \mathbb{Z}_q^*$). Prove that all values in C' are signed.
2. Compute the $k \times k$ matrix C, where $C_{i,1} = g^{b_i} h^{r_i}$, $r_i \in_R \mathbb{Z}_q^*$, and $C_{i,j} = (C_{i,j-1})^{b_i}$, where the b_i values are in shuffled order; consistent with Step 5 of the protocol.
3. Prove that the column $C_{i,1}$ is a shuffle of C'. This implies that $C_{i,1}$ is signed.
4. Prove that C is well formed, by showing recursively for each row that $C_{i,j+1} = (C_{i,j})^{b_i} h^{r_{i,j}}$, $r_{i,j} \in_R \mathbb{Z}_q^*$. This proves that powers of b_i are computed correctly, i.e., that the $C_{i,j+1}$ are commitments to b_i^{j+1}.
5. Prove that w_i is computed correctly using row i of C. By using the values from C, we are assured that the w_i are computed using signed b_i values and that the powers have been computed correctly.

Creating P_3 (Step 11). Let $\mathcal{C}_1 = \{w_i : D(w_i) = 1\}$, $\mathcal{C}_y = \{w_i : D(w_i) \neq 1\}$. As noted in Remark 3, to prove that w_i is contained in $\mathcal{C}_y$, we need to reveal a blinded decryption of w_i; therefore we compute the the set $\mathcal{D}_y$ as follows: for each $w_i = (c_1, c_2) \in \mathcal{C}_y$, compute $d_i = c_1^{-xu_i} c_2^{u_i}$ where $u_i \in_R \mathbb{Z}_q^*$, and add d_i to $\mathcal{D}_y$. The proof will then show that $d_i = c_1^{a_i} c_2^{u_i} = c_1^{-xu_i} c_2^{u_i}$, where a_i is an element such that $1 = h^{u_i} g^{a_i}$, i.e., $a_i = -xu_i$ as $h = g^x$. Now, the proof that $c_1^{-x} c_2 = 1$ cannot be done directly, therefore the prover will assert that $c_2 = c_1^x$ (which is equivalent).

1. Compute $t_x = g^{r_x}$ for $r_x \in_R \mathbb{Z}_q^*$.
2. Initialize a set T_1. For each $(c_1, c_2) \in \mathcal{C}_1$ compute $c_1^{r_x}$ and add the result to T_1.
3. Initialize a set T_C. For each i such that $w_i \in \mathcal{C}_y$, choose r_{a_i} and r_{u_i} at random from $\mathbb{Z}_q^*$. Compute $h^{r_{u_i}} g^{r_{a_i}}$ and add it to T_C.
4. Initialize a set T_y. For each $d_i \in \mathcal{D}_y$ compute $c_1^{r_{a_i}} c_2^{r_{u_i}}$, and add the result to T_y.
5. Compute $c = H(\mathcal{C}_1 || \mathcal{C}_y || \mathcal{D}_y || t_x || T_1 || T_C || T_y)$.
6. Compute (in $\mathbb{Z}_q$): $s_x = r_x - cx$, $s_{u_i} = r_{u_i} - cu_i$, and $s_{a_i} = r_{a_i} - ca_i$ for all i such that $d_i \in \mathcal{D}_y$.
7. Output the proof $P_3 = (c, s_x, s_{u_i}, s_{a_i})$.
8. Send P_3, the indices of $\mathcal{C}_1$, $\mathcal{C}_y$, the set $\mathcal{D}_y$ to the verifier.

Verifying P_3 (Step 13). Partition the ciphertexts into sets $\mathcal{C}_1$, $\mathcal{C}_y$, based on index information from the prover. Also ensure $1 \notin \mathcal{D}_y$.

1. Compute $\hat{t}_x = h^c g^{s_x}$.
2. Initialize a set $\hat{T}_1$. For each $(c_1, c_2) \in \mathcal{C}_1$ compute $c_2^c c_1^{s_x}$, and add this value to $\hat{T}_1$.
3. Initialize a set $\hat{T}_C$. For each i such that $w_i \in \mathcal{C}_y$, compute $h^{s_{u_i}} g^{s_{a_i}}$ and add it to $\hat{T}_C$.
4. Initialize a set $\hat{T}_y$. For each $(c_1, c_2) \in \mathcal{C}_y$ and the corresponding $d_i \in \mathcal{D}_y$, compute $d_i^c(c_1^{s_{a_i}} c_2^{s_{u_i}})$, and add the result to $\hat{T}_y$.
5. Compute $\hat{c} = H(\mathcal{C}_1 || \mathcal{C}_y || \mathcal{D}_y || \hat{t}_x || \hat{T}_1 || \hat{T}_C || \hat{T}_y)$. Reject the proof if $\hat{c} \neq c$.

Privacy-Preserving Classifier Learning

Justin Brickell and Vitaly Shmatikov

The University of Texas at Austin, Austin TX 78712, USA

Abstract. We present an efficient protocol for the privacy-preserving, distributed learning of decision-tree classifiers. Our protocol allows a user to construct a classifier on a database held by a remote server without learning any additional information about the records held in the database. The server does not learn anything about the constructed classifier, not even the user's choice of feature and class attributes.

Our protocol uses several novel techniques to enable oblivious classifier construction. We evaluate a prototype implementation, and demonstrate that its performance is efficient for practical scenarios.

Keywords: Privacy, Secure Multiparty Computation, Data Mining.

1 Introduction

Privacy-preserving data analysis is one of the most important applications of secure multi-party computation. In this paper, we develop a privacy-preserving version of a fundamental data-analysis primitive: an algorithm for constructing or learning a *classifier*. Classifiers, such as decision trees, are a mainstay of data mining and decision support [24]. Given a database with multiple attributes (an attribute can be thought of as a column in a database schema), a classifier *predicts* the value of a "target" or "class" attribute from the values of "feature" attributes. One can also think of a classifier as assigning records to certain classes (defined by the value of the class attribute) on the basis of their feature attributes. A popular machine-learning task is to automatically learn a classifier given a training set of records labelled with class attributes. Classifiers built in this way are used for marketing and customer relationship management, development of better recommendation algorithms and services, clinical studies, and many other applications.

We focus on the problem of securely constructing a classifier in a two-party setting where one party provides a database, while the other party provides the parameters of the classifier that it wants to construct from the records in the database. This is a common situation in law-enforcement, regulatory, and national-security settings, where the entity performing the analysis (for example, an agency investigating irregular financial transactions) does not want to reveal which patterns it is mining the database for (for example, to prevent the target of investigation from structuring their transactions so as to avoid scrutiny). Confidentiality of the resulting classifier is also important in scenarios where both the data-analysis techniques and the output of the analysis process constitute

R. Dingledine and P. Golle (Eds.): FC 2009, LNCS 5628, pp. 128–147, 2009.

potentially valuable intellectual property, *e.g.*, when mining patient databases in clinical studies, constructing expert systems and diagnostic frameworks, and so on.

The key privacy properties that the protocol for privacy-preserving classifier learning must guarantee are, informally, as follows. First, the records from which the classifier is constructed should remain confidential from the party who obtains the classifier (except for the information which is inevitably revealed by the classifier tree itself). Second, the data owner should not learn anything about the classifier which has been constructed. While the algorithm for constructing the classifier is standard (*e.g.*, ID3), its parameters—(i) which attributes are used as features?, (ii) which attributes are used as class attributes?, (iii) if the classifier is being constructed only on a subset of database records, what is the record selection criterion?—should remain hidden from the data owner. Note that the latter requirement precludes the data owner from simply computing the classifier on his own.

Previous work on privacy-preserving classifier learning [16,28,29] focused on a very different problem in which the resulting classifier is revealed to *both* parties. This greatly simplifies the protocol because the classifier can be constructed using the standard recursive algorithm—since both parties learn the resulting classification tree, revealing each node of the tree to both parties as it is being constructed does not violate the privacy property. This is no longer true in our setting, which presents a non-trivial technical challenge.

Existing protocols cannot be used in practical scenarios where confidentiality of the classifier is essential. For example, a national-security agency may want to mine records of financial transactions without revealing the classified patterns that it is looking for (defined by its choice of feature and class attributes and of a certain subset of individuals in the database). Other scenarios include construction of a recommendation algorithm from transactional data without revealing it prematurely (*e.g.*, the Netflix Prize competition [22]); clinical studies involving competing medical institutions, each of which is fiercely protective both of their patient data *and* their analysis techniques (which subset of patients to look at, which symptoms to focus on, and so on), because the latter can lead to patentable and potentially lucrative diagnostic methods; expert systems, where the classifier constitutes valuable intellectual property; remote software fault diagnostics [6]; and many others.

In this paper, we use the same basic framework of secure multi-party computation (SMC) as the original paper on privacy-preserving data mining by Lindell and Pinkas [16] and aim to provide the same level of cryptographic security guarantees. We emphasize, however, that (i) our desired privacy properties (in particular, confidentiality of the resulting classifier) are very different and more challenging because the techniques of [16] no longer work; (ii) we allow, but do not assume or require that the data are partitioned between the two parties; and (iii) unlike [16], we provide a prototype implementation and performance measurements in order to evaluate the scalability of the SMC-based approach to privacy-preserving data classification.

Our contributions. We present a cryptographically secure protocol for privacy-preserving construction of classification trees. The protocol takes place between a user and a server. The user's input consists of the parameters of the classifier that he wishes to construct: which data attributes (columns) to use as feature attributes, which as the class attribute, and, optionally, which predicate on records (rows) to use in order to select only a subset of the database records for the classifier construction. The server's input is a relational database. We assume that the schema of the database (*i.e.*, names of attributes and the values they can take) is public, but that the actual records are private.

The user's protocol output is a classification tree constructed from the server's data. The server learns nothing from the protocol; in particular, he does not learn the parameters of the classification algorithm, not even which attributes have been used when constructing the classifier. We re-iterate that the latter requirement precludes the server from computing the classifier on his own, and also makes existing protocols inapplicable.

Our protocol exploits the structure of the classifier-construction algorithm in a fundamental way. In each node of the classification tree, the records are "split" based on the value of some attribute. In order to pick the best attribute for this purpose, the tree-construction algorithm must, in each node of the tree, count the number of records that fall into several categories. In contrast to [16], the database owner should not learn how many of his own records fall into each category, so we must perform this computation in a privacy-preserving manner. If done naïvely, using generic techniques, the computational cost of the resulting protocol would be prohibitive.

Our key technical innovation is to build the tree "one tier at a time" by simultaneously counting the categories for an entire tier of nodes rather than for a single node. By partitioning the categories into mutually exclusive groups, we are able to compute the counts for a whole tier of nodes using the same number of secure circuit evaluations as we would have needed for a single node. This enables a substantial performance gain which bridges the gap between theoretical and practical efficiency.

Our final contribution is to measure the scalability of our prototype implementation and evaluate its performance on realistic datasets. While theoretical protocol designs in the SMC framework abound, actual implementations have been very rare. This makes it difficult to determine whether these (theoretically sound) techniques can actually be applied, even given modern computing power, to anything other than toy examples. Our performance measurements show the limits of SMC-based privacy-preserving data analysis.

2   Related Work

Classifier learning is one of the most fundamental tasks in data mining and machine learning [20, 24]. The privacy-preserving version of the problem was addressed by Lindell and Pinkas [16]. We use the same framework of secure multi-party computation as [16] and provide the same level of cryptographic security. Note, however, that [16] solves a different problem, where the database is *horizontally partitioned* between the parties, and both participants learn the resulting decision tree. By contrast, we consider an (arguably, much more common) problem where one party may hold all of the data, and a second party wishes to construct a classifier which is not revealed to the first party. Our protocol allows the data to be arbitrarily partitioned between the parties, while still maintaining the property that only one party learns the resulting decision tree.

This distinction is not superficial and has important technical ramifications. The fact that *both* parties learn the classifier is used in an essential way in [16] to implement recursive tree construction: because all nodes of the tree are revealed to all parties as part of the final classifier, the algorithm is allowed to reveal the nodes in intermediate steps. Our problem, where the classifier is *not* revealed to the data owner, cannot be solved using the techniques of [16] and requires more sophisticated algorithms.

Other techniques for privacy-preserving classifier construction [8,28,9,30] also assume that both parties learn the classifier. Therefore, they cannot be applied to our problem setting. Unlike [8,28], our solution is accompanied by a practical implementation and does not require a third-party server.

In *randomized* databases, statistical noise is added to individual data entries in order to hide their values. Agrawal and Srikant considered the problem of privacy-preserving classifier construction in this setting [3], but their privacy definition as well as several subsequent definitions were very weak [2,10]. The SuLQ (Sub-Linear Queries) framework enables construction of ID3 classifiers from perturbed data with adequate privacy guarantees [4]. Our approach is different in that our trees are constructed on the original, unperturbed data, and are thus more precise. It can also be applied even to relatively small databases where the sublinearity constraint would restrict the approach of [4] to a very small number of queries. Furthermore, queries are made in the clear in the SuLQ framework, so only the privacy of the server is guaranteed. In contrast, our approach guarantees the privacy of the user's input.

Another class of techniques for privacy-preserving data publishing is based on k-anonymity [7, 26, 27]. In this approach, some of the attributes (so-called "quasi-identifiers") are transformed so that each attribute tuple occurs at least k times in the anonymized database, while other attributes are released untouched. k-anonymous databases can be used for classifier construction [14]. Limitations of k-anonymity include the fact that it cannot be applied to high-dimensional data [1], k-anonymous databases can reveal individuals' sensitive attributes [15,18] and/or whether a given individual has an entry in the database [21,25], and anonymity is not guaranteed against adversaries with background knowledge [18, 19] or even adversaries who simply know the k-anonymization algorithm [32]. This paper provides an alternative way of constructing classifiers that does not involve releasing the data to untrusted users.

An orthogonal problem to *learning* decision trees is that of *evaluating* decision trees so that the data owner does not learn the tree which is being evaluated (*i.e.*, evaluation is oblivious). Recent solutions include [6,11]. We use a (substantially modified) oblivious tree evaluation protocol of [6] as a building block. It provides better efficiency in our setting than [11], where each decision node can only examine a single bit.

3   Cryptographic Tools

Our construction employs several standard cryptographic tools, including secure circuit evaluation (SCE) and homomorphic encryption. We only utilize them for the lowest-level computations in our protocol, and, furthermore, we use SCE in a non-black-box fashion. For the standard secure circuit evaluation, we use a compiler [13] which, given a circuit description, generates a corresponding "garbled circuit" following Yao's method [31,17]. Where an additively homomorphic encryption scheme is needed, we use the Paillier cryptosystem [23].

Our protocol also requires a subprotocol for privacy-preserving *evaluation* of decision trees, described in Appendix A. To achieve practical efficiency, we carefully design circuit logic to allow the same set of inputs to be used across multiple garbled-circuit evaluations, which reduces the number of costly oblivious transfers.

4   Problem Formulation

4.1   Decision-Tree Learning

A *classifier* takes as input a *record* (or transaction) consisting of several attribute values, and outputs a classification label which categorizes the record. *Decision trees* are a common type of classifier. Each internal node in a decision tree examines a single attribute and redirects evaluation to one of several child nodes based on the value of that attribute. Once a leaf node is reached, the classification label contained therein is outputted as the result of classification. Fig. 1 shows an example decision tree that could be used by a marketing department to determine whether a consumer is likely to buy a company's product.

Decision-tree classifiers can be constructed manually by a human expert with domain knowledge, but algorithms for *decision-tree learning* are increasingly popular (*e.g.*, see Algorithm 1). Given a database of records tagged with

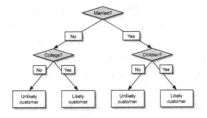

Fig. 1. Example decision tree

Input:
$\mathcal{R}$, the set of feature attributes.
C, the class attribute.
T, the set of records.
d, the current depth.
D, the desired maximum depth.
DECISIONTREE($\mathcal{R}, C, T, d, D$)

1: **if** $d = D$ or $\mathcal{R}$ is empty **then**
2:     return a leaf node with the most frequent class label among the records in T.
3: **else**
4:     Determine the attribute that best classifies the records in T, let it be A.
5:     Let $a_1, ..., a_m$ be the values of attribute A and let $T(a_1), ..., T(a_m)$ be a partition
       of T such that every record in $T(a_i)$ has the attribute value a_i.
6:     Return a tree whose root is labeled A (this is the splitting attribute) and which
       has edges labeled $a_1, ..., a_m$ such that for every i, the edge a_i goes to the tree
       DECISIONTREE($\mathcal{R} - \{A\}, C, T(a_i), d + 1, D$).
7: **end if**

Algorithm 1. The (non-private) recursive decision-tree learning algorithm

classification labels, the algorithm constructs the decision tree recursively from the top down. At the root node, the algorithm considers every attribute and measures the quality of the split that this attribute will provide (see below). The algorithm chooses the "best" attribute and partitions all records by the value of this attribute, creating a child node for each partition. The algorithm is then executed recursively on each partition.

Two popular measures of the "quality" of a split are information gain and the Gini index. Information gain is used in the ID3 and C4.5 algorithms [24], while the Gini index is used in the CART algorithm [5]. Information gain can be computed privately using the $x \log x$ protocol from [16]. Our privacy-preserving protocol for decision-tree learning can use either, but the private computation of the Gini index is more efficient, so we will focus on it.

In the following, suppose that the class attribute (*i.e.*, the target of classification) can assume k different values $c_1, ..., c_k$ and that the candidate splitting attribute A can assume m different values $a_1, ..., a_m$. Denote by $p(c_i)$ the portion of the records whose attribute $C = c_i$, by $p(a_i)$ the portion of the records whose attribute $A = a_i$, and by $p(c_i|a_j)$ the portion of the records that have both attribute $C = c_i$ and attribute $A = a_i$.

The Gini index GINI(A) is computed as:

$$1 - \sum_{i=1}^{k} (p(c_i))^2 - \sum_{j=1}^{m} p(a_j) \sum_{i=1}^{k} p(c_i|a_j)(1 - p(c_i|a_j)) \tag{1}$$

If we use the notation $n(c_i)$ for the *number* of records with attribute $C = c_i$, then we can rewrite (1) as:

$$1 - \sum_{i=1}^{k} \left(\frac{n(c_i)}{|T|} \right)^2 - \sum_{j=1}^{m} \frac{n(a_j)}{|T|} \sum_{i=1}^{k} \frac{n(c_i|a_j)}{|T|} \left(1 - \frac{n(c_i|a_j)}{|T|} \right) \qquad (2)$$

Multiplying this equation by $|T|^3$ gives:

$$|T|^3 - \sum_{i=1}^{k} (n(c_i))^2 |T| - \sum_{j=1}^{m} n(a_j) \sum_{i=1}^{k} n(c_i|a_j) (|T| - (c_i|a_j)) \qquad (3)$$

Since the number of records $|T|$ is fixed, we can compare the Gini index of different attributes using only multiplication and addition. These operations can be easily computed in a privacy-preserving manner using Yao's garbled-circuits method.

4.2 Distributed Decision-Tree Learning

Conventional decision-tree learning is performed by a single user. The user has access to some database T and chooses the set of feature attributes $\mathcal{R}$, the class attribute C, and the number of tiers D. In this paper, we focus on a *distributed* setting, where the database T resides on a server and a remote user chooses $\mathcal{R}$, C, and D. We emphasize that for real-world databases, where the total number of attributes is fairly large, $\mathcal{R}$ may be only a small subset of attributes. For example, attributes of T may include hundreds of demographic features, and the user may be interested only in a handful of them for classification purposes.

In the distributed setting, both parties may have privacy concerns. The server wishes to reveal no more about T than is necessarily revealed by a decision tree based on T. The user, on the other hand, may not wish to reveal which feature attributes $\mathcal{R}$ and class attribute C he selected for the purposes of constructing a classifier.

We assume that several parameters are known to both parties: $|T|$, the number of records in the database; $\mathcal{A}$, the set of all attributes in the database; the set $a_1, ..., a_m$ of possible values for each attribute $A \in \mathcal{A}$; $|\mathcal{R}|$, the number of feature attributes selected by the user; and D, the depth of the decision tree to be constructed.

Branching factor. In the general case, the record database T may contain nominal attributes whose domains have different sizes. For instance, a consumer database may have 2 possible values for the "sex" attribute, and 50 possible values for the "state of residence" attribute. We refer to the number of different values that an attribute can assume as its *branching factor*, because it determines the number of children for each internal node corresponding to that attribute.

When the decision tree is computed in a privacy-preserving manner, all internal nodes must have the same number of children in order to prevent the server from learning any information about which attribute is considered in a given node. Therefore, all attributes must have the same branching factor m. As a pre-processing step, attributes can be padded with unused values so that all attributes have the same branching factor. For simplicity, we assume that each attribute value is encoded as an integer between 0 and $m - 1$, and can thus be represented using $\log_2 m$ bits.

5   Privacy-Preserving Decision-Tree Learning

Our protocol takes place between a server in possession of a database T and a user who wishes to build a classifier for class attribute C based on a set $\mathcal{R}$ of feature attributes. The tree is constructed from the root down, as in the conventional algorithm shown in Fig. 1. Unlike the conventional algorithm, ours is non-recursive. Instead, the tree is constructed one tier at a time. When processing tier i, m^i pending nodes are considered. In the final tier, the pending nodes are transformed into leaf nodes with classification labels in them; in all intermediate tiers, they become internal decision nodes, where the attribute for making the decision is chosen based on the data in T. We now describe the protocol, which is divided into four phases.

5.1   Phase 1: Sharing the Attribute Values

The set of attributes $\mathcal{A}$ found in the database T may be far larger than the set $\mathcal{R} \cup \{C\}$ of attributes that are relevant to tree construction. For an attribute $R_i \in \mathcal{R} \cup \{C\}$ and a record $t \in T$, $t[R_i]$ refers to the attribute value for attribute R_i in record t. For each record $t \in T$ and for each relevant attribute $R_i \in \mathcal{R} \cup \{C\}$, Phase 1 enables the user and the server to learn shares $t[R_i]_U$ and $t[R_i]_S$ such that $t[R_i]_U + t[R_i]_S \pmod{m} = t[R_i]$. This is done using the oblivious attribute selection technique from [6], which is outlined below:

1. For all $A_i \in \mathcal{A}$, the server encrypts $t[A_i]$ using an additively homomorphic encryption scheme, and sends $E[t[A_i]]$ to the user.
2. User creates a blinding value b_i for each relevant attribute R_i, and uses the homomorphic property to add b_i and $t[R_i]$ under encryption. User sends $E[b_i + t[R_i]]$ to the server. User's random share is $t[R_i]_U = -b_i \mod m$.
3. Server decrypts to obtain $b_i + t[R_i]$ and stores $t[R_i]_S = b_i + t[R_i] \mod m$.

We use a blinding value b_i at least 80 bits longer than the $(\log_2 m)$-bit value $t[R_i]$ so that it statistically hides $t[R_i]$. The shares $t[R_i]_U$ and $t[R_i]_S$ will be used in later phases as inputs to small Yao circuits that are generated by the user and evaluated by the server. Therefore, the server needs to learn the random wire keys representing his input shares $t[R_i]_S$ in the circuit. As usual, this is done via a 1-out-of-2 oblivious transfer for each of the $\log_2 m$ bits in the $t[R_i]_S$ values, where the server's input is the jth bit of $t[R_i]_S$, and the user's input is the pair of wire keys representing, respectively, 0 and 1 on the input wire corresponding to this bit.

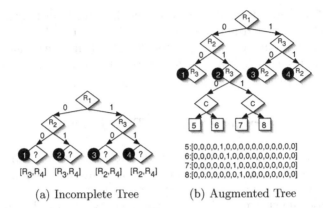

5:[0,0,0,0,1,0,0,0,0,0,0,0,0,0,0,0]
6:[0,0,0,0,0,1,0,0,0,0,0,0,0,0,0,0]
7:[0,0,0,0,0,0,1,0,0,0,0,0,0,0,0,0]
8:[0,0,0,0,0,0,0,1,0,0,0,0,0,0,0,0]

(a) Incomplete Tree   (b) Augmented Tree

Fig. 2. An incomplete decision tree with 4 pending nodes, and the same tree augmented with a feature attribute and class attribute

Unlike the standard Yao protocol, the same input-wire keys are used for multiple circuits. The oblivious transfers can thus be done only once per protocol execution instead of once per circuit evaluation. This results in a substantial performance improvement, since the bulk of computation in secure circuit evaluation is spent on the oblivious transfers.

After performing these preliminary steps, the user participates in the PRIVATEDECISIONTREE($\mathcal{R}, C, D, T$) protocol with the server, which starts Phase 2.

We also observe that our protocol can be applied not only in the case where the server holds the entire database, but also for any vertical or horizontal partitioning of the database between the user and the server. If the database is partitioned, the steps described above are carried out only for the attribute values held by the server. For each value held by the user, the user simply splits it into two random shares and sends one of them to the server. Regardless of the database partitioning, after Phase 1 every attribute value of every record is shared between the user and the server.

5.2   Phase 2: Computing Category Counts

Phase 2 is shown in Algorithm 2 as lines 3–6.

Let d be the depth of the current tier. Within this tier there are m^d pending nodes, and of the original $|\mathcal{R}|$ feature attributes, only $|\mathcal{R}| - d$ remain as candidates to be chosen as the splitting attribute for each pending node because d attributes have already been used. The set of candidate attributes for splitting at a pending node n depends on which attributes were already encountered on the path from the root node to n, and may thus be different for each pending node. For example, Fig. 2(a) shows a tree entering Phase 2 on tier 2. The path to the 3rd pending node consists of the edges $R_1 = 1$ and $R_3 = 0$, so attributes R_1 and R_3 are no longer available as candidates for this node. The candidates for the 3rd pending node are $[R_2, R_4]$, while the candidates for the 2nd pending node are $[R_3, R_4]$,

Let $T(n)$ be the set of records that satisfy the preconditions of node n (for the 3rd pending node in Fig. 2(a), these are records with $R_1 = 1$ and $R_3 = 0$). Let $\{R_{n_1}, ..., R_{n_{|\mathcal{R}|-d}}\}$ be the set of candidate attributes for node n. Finally, let $T_k(n : i, j)$ be the set of records in $T(n)$ that have $R_{n_k} = i$ and $C = j$. To determine the quality of the split that would be provided by choosing R_{n_k} as the splitting attribute for this node, it is necessary to compute $|T_k(n : i, j)|$ for all possible values of i and j ($0 \le i, j \le m$).

For any choice of n, i, and j, the user can build a decision tree to determine whether a given record is in $T_k(n : i, j)$. Using oblivious decision-tree evaluation, the user and the server can then learn shares of $|T_k(n : i, j)|$ without either revealing his private inputs. The problem with this naïve approach is that determining the quality of splitting on a single attribute R_{n_k} requires $m^d \cdot m^2$ oblivious decision-tree evaluations on each record in T (one for each choice of n, i, and j).

Our construction is significantly more efficient because it iterates over the database only *once* by counting $m^d \cdot m^2$ different mutually exclusive categories simultaneously. The key observation is that for each record $t \in T$, there is a unique pending node n such that $t \in T(n)$. Furthermore, for each $t \in T(n)$ and $0 \le k \le |\mathcal{R}| - d$, there are unique i, j such that $t \in T_k(n : i, j)$. Therefore, our construction builds a classifier to determine for which values of n, i, and j the record t belongs to $T_k(n : i, j)$.

To do this, we augment the partially constructed tree P by replacing each pending node with a depth-two subtree that considers attributes C and R_{n_k}. Fig. 2(b) shows the result of augmenting the tree from Fig. 2(a) when $k = 1$. (To avoid clutter, the augmented portion is only shown for the 2nd pending node.) The $m^d \cdot m^2$ leaves of the tree contain vectors of length $m^d \cdot m^2$ as their labels. Each leaf is reachable by records in $T_k(n : i, j)$ for a unique choice of n, i, and j, and the vector used as its label has a single "1" in the position corresponding to $T_k(n : i, j)$ and "0" elsewhere.

Once the augmented tree $P' = P.\text{AUGMENTWITHATTANDCLASS}(k, C)$ has been constructed, the user and server engage in a privacy-preserving decision-tree evaluation protocol for each record $t \in T$. To support oblivious evaluation, the tree must be transformed as follows (see [6] and Appendix A for details). Each node other than the root is encrypted with a random key. Each internal node is replaced by a small Yao circuit that takes as its input the user's and server's shares $t[R_i]_U$ and $t[R_i]_S$ of the relevant attribute values $t[R_i]$ for each $R \in \mathcal{R}$, and outputs the index and decryption key for the appropriate child node. Each leaf node has as its label a vector of $m^d \cdot m^2$ values, encrypted using a user-created instance of an additively homomorphic encryption scheme. As described above, the vector has "1" in the position corresponding to its category, and "0" in all other positions. Note that although the same tree is applied to every record, it must be freshly transformed into a secure tree for each oblivious evaluation.

As the result of oblivious evaluation of augmented trees, the server learns a vector of $m^d \cdot m^2$ ciphertexts. All but one are encryptions of "0." The sole

---

User's Input:
$\mathcal{R}$, the set of feature attributes ($|\mathcal{R}| > D$)
C, the class attribute
D, the desired maximum depth
Server's Input: T, the set of records converted into random wire values.
User's Output: P, a decision tree to classify C from $\mathcal{R}$
PROT:PRIVATEDECISIONTREE(user: $\mathcal{R}, C, D$ server: T)

1: $P =$ new tree
2: **for** $d=0$ to $D-1$ **do**
3:   **for** $k=1$ to $|\mathcal{R}| - d$ **do**
4:     $P'=P.$AUGMENTWITHATTANDCLASS(k, C)
5:     $(|T_k(...)|_U, |T_k(...)|_S) =$ PROT:ENCRYPTEDCOUNTS(user: P' server: T)
6:   **end for**
7:   **for** $n=1$ to m^d **do**
8:     **for** $k=1$ to $|\mathcal{R}| - d$ **do**
9:       $(Q_U^k, Q_S^k) =$ PROT:COMPUTEQUALITY$(|T_k(n:...)|_U, |T_k(n:...)|_S)$
10:     **end for**
11:     bestatt = PROT:ARGMAX (user: $Q_U^1, ..., Q_U^{|\mathcal{R}|-d}$ server: $Q_S^1, ..., Q_S^{|\mathcal{R}|-d}$)
12:     In P, make node n an internal node splitting on attribute $R_{n_{bestatt}}$
13:   **end for**
14: **end for**
15: $P' = P.$AUGMENTWITHCLASS(C)
16: $(|T(...)|_U, |T(...)|_S) =$ PROT:ENCRYPTEDCOUNTS(user: P' server: T)
17: **for** $n=1$ to m^D **do**
18:   bestclass = PROT:ARGMAX(user: $|T(n:*,1)|_U, ..., |T(n:*,m)|_U$
                server: $|T(n:*,1)|_S, ..., |T(n:*,m)|_S$)
19:   In P, make node n a leaf node with label bestclass
20: **end for**
21: **return** p

Algorithm 2. The private "one-tier-at-a-time" decision-tree learning protocol

ciphertext encrypting "1" occurs in the position corresponding to the category of the record (of course, the server cannot tell which ciphertext this is). By summing up these vectors under encryption, the server obtains ciphertexts encrypting the counts $|T_k(n:i,j)|$. The server must then transform these encrypted counts into additive random shares (mod $|T|$), using the same technique as in Sect. 5.1.

The following subroutines are used during Phase 2:

- $P.$AUGMENTWITHATTANDCLASS. This method is executed by the user, and adds two tiers to the tree P: one for the attribute R_{n_k} (different for each pending node) and one for the class attribute C.
- PROT:ENCRYPTEDCOUNTS. This protocol between the user and the server results in the user and server holding shares for the counts $|T_k(n:i,j)|$ for $n=1$ to m^d, $i=1$ to m, and $j=1$ to m. Pseudocode is given in Algorithm 3.

User's Input: A decision tree P with k leaf-nodes. The label of leaf i is a k-length vector with $E[1]$ in position i and $E[0]$ in all other positions.
Server's Input: A record set T for which each bit of each attribute value has been converted into a random wire value.
Output: Let $K = \sum_{t \in T} P(t)$ be the k-length vector whose ith entry is the number of records in T landing in leaf node i. The user's and server's outputs are shares K_U and K_S of K.
ENCRYPTEDCOUNTS(P, T)

  1: $K \leftarrow$ length k vector with each entry set to $E[0]$
  2: **for each** $t \in T$ **do**
  3:      $J \leftarrow$ PRIVATETREEEVAL(P, t)
  4:      $K \leftarrow K + J$ under encryption
  5: **end for**
  6: Split each component of K into shares (mod $|T|$); user decrypts his share

---

Algorithm 3. Protocol to determine how many records fall into each of k categories

5.3 Phase 3: Selecting the Highest-Quality Split

Phase 3 is shown in Algorithm 2 as lines 7–13.

After Phase 2, the user and the server share counts $|T_k(n : i, j)|$ for all pending nodes n in the tier, and for all values of k, i, and j. This enables them to compute $Gini(R_{n_k})$ for each node n using (3), but over $T(n)$ rather then the entire record set T. The user and server must compute

$$|T(n)|^3 - \sum_{j=1}^{m} |T(n)| \, |T_k(n : *, j)|^2 -$$
$$\sum_{i=1}^{m} |T_k(n : i, *)| \sum_{j=1}^{m} |T_k(n : i, j)| \, (|T(n)| - |T_k(n : i, j)|) \ \ .$$

Where $|T(n : *, j)|$ is the number of nodes in $T(n)$ with class attribute $C = j$, and $|T_k(n : i, *)|$ is the number of nodes in $T(n)$ with attribute $R_{n_k} = i$. These values, along with $|T(n)|$, can be computed from the shares $|T_k(n : i, *)|_{\{U,S\}}$ which the user and server hold.

Given the shares (mod $|T|$) of all inputs, a simple circuit produces shares (mod $|T|^3$) of $Gini(R_{n_k})$ for each node n and for each k, using only addition and multiplication. For each pending node n, these shares are then fed into another garbled circuit. This circuit determines which attribute R_{n_k} provides the best split quality. The user updates the tree P with this information, by replacing the pending node n with an internal node that splits on the attribute R_{n_k}.

The following subroutines are used during Phase 3:

– PROT:COMPUTEQUALITY. This protocol uses a garbled circuit to compute the Gini index for node n and attribute R_{n_k}. This protocol takes as input shares (mod $|T|$) of the m^2 counts $|T_k(n : i, j)|$, and returns shares (mod $|T|^3$) of the Gini index.

– PROT:ARGMAX. This protocol takes as input shares of values $v_1, ..., v_n$ and provides the user with an index m such that v_m is greater than or equal to all other values. The server learns nothing.

5.4   Phase 4: Constructing the Bottom Tier

Phase 4 is shown in Algorithm 2 as lines 17–20.

Phase 4 completes the decision tree P by adding the correct labels to its leaf nodes. Each leaf node n should have as its label the most common classification value among the records in $T(n)$. Similar to Phase 2, we can find the most popular classification value for all leaf nodes at once. The incomplete tree P is augmented with a single extra tier which examines the classification node C. Then ENCRYPTEDCOUNTS provides the user and server with the shares of the the counts $|T(n : *, j)|$ for $n=1$ to m^D and $j=1$ to m. Next, a garbled circuit finds the value c such that $|T(n : *, c)|$ is maximal, and makes it the label for node n.

The following subroutines are used during Phase 4:

– P.AUGMENTWITHCLASS. This is executed by the user and adds one additional tier to the tree P for the class attribute C.
– PROT:ENCRYPTEDCOUNTS. Same as in Phase 2, and provides the user and server with shares (mod $|T|$) of $|T(n : *, j)|$.
– PROT:ARGMAX. Same as in Phase 3.

5.5   Security Properties

Due to space constraints, we omit the detailed security argument. We use the same secure multi-party computation framework as the original protocol by Lindell and Pinkas [16] (which applied to a different decision-tree learning problem, as explained above). Just like [16], our basic protocol is secure against a passive attacker. Note that the decision tree resulting from protocol execution has a rich structure and may reveal a substantial amount of information about the database to the user. As is standard in the SMC framework, we do not prevent privacy violations that occur as a result of the protocol output; instead, we guarantee that no *additional* information is revealed.

If the underlying oblivious transfer protocol (used by the data owner to obtain wire-key representations of the records in his database) is secure against an actively malicious chooser, and the server's homomorphic encryption scheme (an instance of which is used during the the oblivious attribute selection protocol) can be verified as well-formed by the user, then our protocol is also secure against an actively malicious data owner. Recall that the data owner plays the role of an (oblivious) circuit evaluator in our protocol.

To obtain security against an actively malicious user, it is necessary to ensure that (a) the oblivious transfer protocol is secure against an actively malicious sender, (b) the user's instance of the homomorphic encryption scheme (used when obliviously counting the sizes of record categories) can be verified as well-formed by the server, and (c) the server can verify that the garbled circuits created by the user are well-formed. Note that the latter can be achieved at a constant additional cost under certain number-theoretic assumptions (*e.g.*, see [12]).

6 Performance

Recall that there are $|\mathcal{A}|$ attributes, each of which has a branching factor of m; $|\mathcal{R}|$ feature attributes; $|T|$ transactions, and depth D. In evaluating the performance of our protocol, we distinguish between online and offline computations. Offline computations include generating m^{d+2} homomorphic encryptions of "0" for each of the $|T|(|\mathcal{R}| - d)$ augmented decision trees used at tier d (user); generating homomorphic encryptions of $|T||\mathcal{A}|$ attributes for oblivious attribute selection (server); garbling of circuits to compute the Gini index and ArgMax (server), and garbling of circuits to compute attribute selection (user). Note that the number of gates in these circuits depends on $|\mathcal{A}|$ and $|T|$ (Gini), $|T|$ and m (ArgMax), and $|\mathcal{A}|$ and m (attribute selection).

The following cryptographic operations must be performed online once per protocol execution: $|T||\mathcal{R}|$ homomorphic additions for oblivious attribute selection (user); $|T||\mathcal{R}|$ homomorphic decryptions (server); and $|T|(|\mathcal{R}| + 1) \log m$ 1-out-of-2 oblivious transfers so that the server can learn wire values for his attribute shares. In addition, the following are performed online to construct tier d (with m^d nodes): symmetric encryption of $(\sum_{h=1}^{d+2} m^h)$ garbled nodes for each of $|T|(|\mathcal{R}| - d)$ augmented decision trees (user); $d + 2$ symmetric decryptions

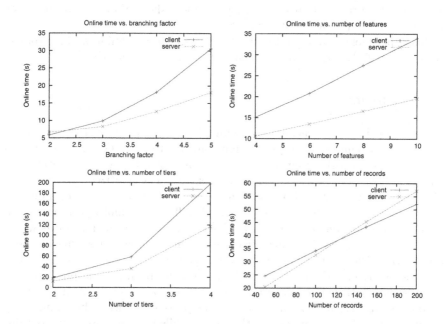

Fig. 3. Online performance of the prototype implementation

Table 1. Runtime for the "cars" dataset from the UC Irvine repository

	sym. enc	sym. dec	homo. dec	homo. add	OTs	eval
user	114s	0s	7.1s	0.07s	185.2s	4.2s
server	0s	171s	8.0s	41.9s		12.7s

and evaluations of garbled attribute selection circuits for each of $|T|(|\mathcal{R}| - d)$ augmented decision trees (server); $|T|(m^{d+2})$ homomorphic additions (server); m^{d+2} homomorphic decryptions (user); evaluation of $m^d(|\mathcal{R}| - d)$ garbled circuits to compute the Gini index at tier d (user); and evaluation of m^d garbled circuits for ArgMax at tier d (user).

Because performance is often a concern when using secure multi-party computation techniques, we evaluated a prototype Java implementation of our protocol. Fig. 3 shows how the online time required by our protocol depends on several parameters of the decision-tree learning problem: the branching factor, the number of feature attributes, the number of tiers, and the number of records. Online time is *independent* of the number of attributes. This makes our protocol especially well-suited to scenarios where the set of feature attributes is a relatively small subset drawn from a very large set of total attributes. Note that this is the common case for databases with demographic information.

To evaluate performance on real-world data, we applied our protocol to the "cars" dataset from the UC Irvine machine-learning repository. This dataset has 1728 records and 7 attributes with a branching factor of 4. We chose to build a tree with 5 feature attributes and 2 tiers. Table 1 shows the time consumed by different online components of our protocol.

This experiment demonstrates that, unlike generic techniques, our protocol can be successfully applied to problem instances of realistic size.

7   Conclusions

The field of privacy-preserving data mining has two approaches to the problem of executing machine-learning algorithms on private data. One approach sanitizes the data through suppression and generalization of identifying attributes and/or addition of noise to individual data entries. The sanitized version is then published so that interested parties can run any data-mining algorithm on it.

The other approach is to use cryptographically secure multi-party computation techniques to construct protocols that compute the same answer as would have been obtained in the non-private case. This approach has typically been applied when the relationship between the parties is symmetric: for example, the database is partitioned between them and the result of the protocol execution is that both parties learn the same output based on the joint database. By contrast, in the sanitization approach, the parties executing the data-mining algorithms do not have any data of their own, while the database owner obtains no output at all.

Even if the data-mining algorithms are the same (*e.g.*, classifier learning), the privacy-preserving versions for the two settings are substantially different. We argue that settings where data are asymmetrically distributed and only one party learns the output are very natural in real-world scenarios. In this paper, we show that it is possible to apply secure multi-party computation techniques to these scenarios. Our protocol requires several technical innovations (such as the ability to obliviously compute the sizes of several record categories in a single pass over the database). Unlike most designs in the literature, our protocol has been implemented, and we demonstrated that it can be efficiently applied even to problem instances of realistic size.

Acknowledgements. This paper is based upon work supported by the NSF grants IIS-0534198 and CNS-0615104, and the ARO grant W911NF-06-1-0316.

References

1. Aggarwal, C.: On k-anonymity and the curse of dimensionality. In: VLDB (2005)
2. Agrawal, D., Aggarwal, C.: On the design and quantification of privacy-preserving data mining algorithms. In: PODS (2001)
3. Agrawal, R., Srikant, R.: Privacy-preserving data mining. In: SIGMOD (2000)
4. Blum, A., Dwork, C., McSherry, F., Nissim, K.: Practical privacy: the SuLQ framework. In: PODS (2005)
5. Breiman, L., Friedman, J.H., Olshen, R.A., Stone, C.J.: Classification and Regression Trees. Wadsworth, Belmont (1984)
6. Brickell, J., Porter, D.E., Shmatikov, V., Witchel, E.: Privacy-preserving remote diagnostics. In: CCS (2007)
7. Ciriani, V., De Capitani di Vimercati, S., Foresti, S., Samarati, P.: k-anonymity. Secure Data Management in Decentralized Systems (2007)
8. Du, W., Zhan, Z.: Building decision tree classifier on private data. In: ICDM (2002)
9. Dwork, C., Nissim, K.: Privacy-preserving data mining on vertically partitioned databases. In: Franklin, M. (ed.) CRYPTO 2004. LNCS, vol. 3152, pp. 528–544. Springer, Heidelberg (2004)
10. Evfimievski, A., Gehrke, J., Srikant, R.: Limiting privacy breaches in privacy-preserving data mining. In: PODS (2003)
11. Ishai, Y., Paskin, A.: Evaluating branching programs on encrypted data. In: Vadhan, S.P. (ed.) TCC 2007. LNCS, vol. 4392, pp. 575–594. Springer, Heidelberg (2007)
12. Jarecki, S., Shmatikov, V.: Efficient two-party secure computation on committed inputs. In: Naor, M. (ed.) EUROCRYPT 2007. LNCS, vol. 4515, pp. 97–114. Springer, Heidelberg (2007)
13. Kruger, L.: Sfe-tools (2008), http://pages.cs.wisc.edu/~lpkruger/sfe/
14. LeFevre, K., DeWitt, D., Ramakrishnan, R.: Workload-aware anonymization. In: KDD (2006)
15. Li, N., Li, T., Venkatasubramanian, S.: t-closeness: Privacy beyond k-anonymity and ℓ-diversity. In: ICDE (2007)
16. Lindell, Y., Pinkas, B.: Privacy preserving data mining. J. Cryptology 15(3), 177–206 (2002)
17. Lindell, Y., Pinkas, B.: A proof of Yao's protocol for secure two-party computation (2004), http://eprint.iacr.org/2004/175

18. Machanavajjhala, A., Kifer, D., Gehrke, J., Venkitasubramaniam, M.: ℓ-diversity: Privacy beyond k-anonymity. In: ICDE (2006)
19. Martin, D., Kifer, D., Machanavajjhala, A., Gehrke, J., Halpern, J.: Worst-case background knowledge for privacy-preserving data publishing. In: ICDE (2007)
20. Mitchell, T.M.: Machine Learning. McGraw-Hill, New York (1997)
21. Nergiz, M., Atzori, M., Clifton, C.: Hiding the presence of individuals from shared database. In: SIGMOD (2007)
22. Netflix. Netflix Prize (2006), http://www.netflixprize.com/
23. Paillier, P.: Public-key cryptosystems based on composite degree residuosity classes. In: Stern, J. (ed.) EUROCRYPT 1999. LNCS, vol. 1592, p. 223. Springer, Heidelberg (1999)
24. Quinlan, J.R.: Induction of decision trees. Mach. Learn. 1(1), 81–106 (1986)
25. Rastogi, V., Suciu, D., Hong, S.: The boundary between privacy and utility in data publishing. In: VLDB (2007)
26. Samarati, P.: Protecting respondents' identities in microdata release. IEEE Trans. on Knowledge and Data Engineering 13(6) (2001)
27. Sweeney, L.: Int. J. Uncertain. Fuzziness Knowl.-Based Syst. Int. J. Uncertain. Fuzziness Knowl.-Based Syst. 10(5), 557–570 (2002)
28. Vaidya, J., Clifton, C.: Privacy-preserving decision trees over vertically partitioned data. In: DBSec (2005)
29. Vaidya, J., Kantarcioglu, M., Clifton, C.: Privacy-preserving Naive Bayes classification. The VLDB Journal 17(4) (2008)
30. Yang, Z., Zhong, S., Wright, R.: Privacy-preserving classification of customer data without loss of accuracy. In: SDM (2005)
31. Yao, A.: How to generate and exchange secrets. In: FOCS (1986)
32. Zhang, L., Jajodia, S., Brodsky, A.: Information disclosure under realistic assumptions: Privacy versus optimality. In: CCS (2007)

A   Privacy-Preserving Evaluation of Decision Trees

Our subprotocol for privacy-preserving evaluation of decision trees is inspired by [6], with several substantial modifications. In [6], attributes can take one of a large number of different values, and each internal node selects one of two children based on a threshold comparison. In this paper's setting, each attribute takes one of m values (m is relatively small), and internal nodes have m children—one for each attribute value.

The privacy requirement is that this evaluation should be oblivious: the evaluator should not learn anything about the structure of the tree except the total number of nodes and the length of the evaluation path, nor *which* of his attributes were considered during evaluation. To achieve the former, the tree is represented as a set of encrypted nodes; decrypting each node reveals the index of the next node (which depends on the value of the attribute considered in the parent node) and the corresponding decryption key. To hide which attribute is considered in each node, the "oblivious attribute selection" protocol [6] splits each of the attributes that will be used during evaluation into two random shares. The circuit creator receives one share and the evaluator receives the other, without learning to which of his attributes this share corresponds.

Each oblivious evaluation of an internal node results in moving control to one of the m child nodes. Unlike in [6], where each node has only two children, we are no longer able to encode the indices and decryption keys for all possible child nodes in the garbled values corresonding to a single output wire. Instead, we use $\log_2$ output wires for every internal node. Each such node is implemented as a circuit which reassembles the two shares of the attribute a considered in this node ($a^E + a^C = a \mod m$, where a^E is the circuit evaluator's share, and a^C is the circuit creator's) and outputs the value of a using $\log_2 m$ output wires. As in the standard Yao's construction, each wire has two random keys associated with it, representing, respectively, 0 and 1. These random keys are used to encrypt a table with m randomly permuted rows (observe that there is a 1:1 correspondence between the rows, all possible values of a, and all possible combinations of bit values on the $\log_2 m$ output wires). For each value of a, the encrypted row contains the index of and the decryption key for the appropriate next node in the evaluation, encrypted under the output-wire keys corresponding to the bit representation of a.

For instance, suppose that $m = 4$, so that each attribute takes values from 0 to 3, and thus each internal node in the tree has 4 children. We represent each node by a gate with two output wires, w_0, w_1. Let w_i^0 and w_i^1 be the random keys representing, respectively, 0 and 1 values for wire i. If the bit representation of a is $\alpha\beta$, then evaluating this gate reveals to the evaluator w_0^α and w_1^β. Note that the evaluator does not learn a.

Let h_a be the string containing the index and the decryption key for the child node corresponding to the attribute value a. The gate is accompanied by a random permutation of the following 4 ciphertexts: $\{\{h_0\}_{w_0^0}\}_{w_1^0}$, $\{\{h_1\}_{w_0^1}\}_{w_1^0}$, $\{\{h_2\}_{w_0^0}\}_{w_1^1}$, $\{\{h_3\}_{w_1^1}\}_{w_1^1}$. Observe that the keys w_0^α and w_1^β decrypt exactly one row of this table, namely, the row corresponding to a. By decrypting it, the evaluator can proceed to the correct child node.

We need another technical trick so that the decision-tree evaluation protocol can be efficiently invoked multiple times on the same set of attributes. Recall that as the result of oblivious attribute selection, the evaluator has a random share for each of his attributes that will be used in some internal decision node. For internal nodes, we have the evaluator provide as input shares $a_1^E, ..., a_r^E$ of all attribute values, while the creator's input is the index i of the attribute considered by the node, and the creator's share a_i^C of this attribute value. The output of the circuit is $a_i^E + a_i^C \pmod{m}$.

With this circuit logic, the evaluator's input is the same for all nodes of all trees created during our protocol. This enables a substantial efficiency gain. Instead of generating random wire keys for each bit of the evaluator's input into each circuit (as in the standard Yao's method), we generate them once, and then re-use this representation for the evaluator's input wires in all circuits. This allows us to perform only a single set of oblivious transfers to provide the evaluator with the the wire keys corresponding to his input bits. These wire keys are then used in all of the garbled circuits.

B   Horizontal Selection

In many applications of decision-tree learning, the user wants to construct a classifier using the records defined by a certain predicate, *i.e.*, from a *horizontal* subset of the database. In other words, the user selects not only a subset of columns to use as features, but also a subset of records (rows), and the protocol should construct a classifier using the data in the selected records only.

This is motivated by real-world scenarios. For example, a proprietary database may contains records for diverse individuals living throughout a nation, while the user is interested in building a marketing classifier only for consumers from a particular region or those belonging to a particular demographic. In this scenario, the user may wish to keep his record selection criterion private so as to avoid revealing his marketing strategy to competitors. Previous protocols for privacy-preserving decision-tree learning cannot solve this problem because, by their design, they reveal the resulting classifier to all protocol participants.

In this scenario, we assume that the user does not have a vertical partition of the database, and, since he does not have access to the database, cannot explicitly specify the indices of the records which satisfy his selection criterion. Instead, he must choose them *implicitly* by providing a selection predicate to be evaluated on all records in the database. The user wants to keep this predicate private from the server. Depending on the scenario, the number of records which satisfy the predicate may need to be revealed to the user, to the server, to both, or to neither.

We will outline an extension to our protocol for the variant in which the number of satisfying records is revealed to the user but not to the server. This variant has some useful properties: the user may not believe that the classifier is of high quality if it is based on too few records (thus it is helpful for the user to know how many records were used in constructing the tree), while the server learns a significant amount of information about the user's predicate if he learns the number of records which satisfy the predicate (thus the user may prefer to have this number hidden from the server). This particular variant does present some privacy risks to the server: if the predicate, which is hidden from the server, selects a very small subset of records, then the resulting decision tree will leak a lot of information about the records in the selected subset.

The extension involves two components: (1) an additional phase of the protocol, in which the user learns the indices of all records in the database that satisfy his selection predicate, and (2) a slight change to the category-counting phase to ensure that the records *not* selected by the user's predicate are not counted as belonging to any category, and thus do not participate in determining the best attributes for each internal decision node of the classifier.

To determine the indices of the records that satisfy the predicate, the user and the server engage in an instance of the oblivious decision-tree evaluation protocol described in Appendix A. The user's predicate is represented as a decision tree which evaluates a record and labels it with true if it satisfies the predicate and false otherwise. This decision tree is then obliviously evaluated for each record in the database T. The protocol of Appendix A guarantees that the results are revealed only to the user, and not to the data owner.

The records *not* satisfying the predicate (*i.e.*, those which the user's predicate evaluated to false) should not be used when constructing the classifier. Recall from Sect. 5.2 that in order to determine the best splitting attribute for each internal node of the classifier, the user builds decision trees whose labels are vectors of ciphertexts that all encrypt "0," except for a single ciphertext—in the position corresponding to the record's category—that encrypts "1." For the records that he wants to "turn off," the user simply constructs the tree where the labels contain encryptions of "0" only. This effectively means that the corresponding record is not included in any of the $T_k(n : i, j)$ categories, and thus has no influence on the Gini index computation which is used to find the best splitting attribute.

Investments and Trade-offs in the Economics of Information Security

Christos Ioannidis[1], David Pym[2,*], and Julian Williams[3]

[1] School of Management, University of Bath
Bath BA2 7AY
England, U.K
c.ioannidis@bath.ac.uk
[2] Hewlett-Packard Laboratories
Bristol BS34 8QZ
England, U.K
david.pym@hp.com
[3] University of Aberdeen Business School
Aberdeen AB24 3QY
Scotland, U.K
julian.williams@abdn.ac.uk

Abstract. We develop and simulate a dynamic model of investment in information security. The model is based on the recognition that both IT managers and users appreciate the trade-off between two of the fundamental characteristics of information security, namely confidentiality and availability. The model's parameters can be clustered in a manner that allows us to categorize and compare the responses to shocks of various types of organizations. We derive the system's stability conditions and find that they admit a wide choice of parameters. We examine the system's responses to the same shock in confidentiality under different parameter constellations that correspond to various types of organizations. Our analysis illustrates that the response to investments in information security will be uniform in neither size nor time evolution.

1 Introduction

Information security and network integrity are issues of the utmost importance to both users and managers. The cost of security breaches and fraud is considerable and Anderson et al (2007) [1] provide a comprehensive review of the issues both technical and legal and offer a set of very useful recommendations. Such issues constitute growing concerns for policy makers, in addition to the legitimate concerns of the specialist technological community of experts. As the importance of networks increases for all individuals who act as both providers and consumers of information, the integrity of such systems is crucial to their welfare. In the presence of threats to the system, agents must decide the amount of resources required to maintain the system at acceptable operational states.

---

* Also: University of Bath, Bath BA2 7AY, England, U.K.; d.j.pym@bath.ac.uk

R. Dingledine and P. Golle (Eds.): FC 2009, LNCS 5628, pp. 148–166, 2009.
© IFCA/Springer-Verlag Berlin Heidelberg 2009

Finding solutions to this resource allocation problem is therefore an important part of the work of IT managers. As with all such decisions, expenditure in protecting a system has an opportunity cost because resources can be deployed for other useful purposes, a situation that requires the manager to demonstrate the desirability of such expenditure given an objective that takes into account that such protection costs are fully justified in the light of a well-specified objective.

The calculation of the optimal investment in information security given the system's configuration is a subject that is relatively recent as the research literature has and focused almost exclusively on technological solutions without recourse to the associated financial costs and the behavioural changes required to implement such purely technological solutions. The economics of information security within the context of an optimizing framework has been addressed relatively recently by Gordon and Loeb (2002) [4], who provide an extensive list of references that address technological issues in information security and point out the distinct lack of rigorous economic analysis of the problem of resource allocation in information security. Gordon and Loeb adopt a static optimization model where IT managers calculate the optimal ratio of investment in information security to the value of the expected loss under different assumptions regarding the stochastic process that generates the security threats. Within the framework of the model, we conclude that a risk-neutral firm should spend on information security just below 37% of the value of the expected loss that will occur in the event of breach.

The model relies on rather restrictive assumptions and has prompted lively debate regarding the 'optimal' ratio of investment in information security. What is of interest is that the relationhip between investment in information security and vulnerability is not always a monotonic function. Hausken (2006) [6] by postulating an alternative functional form of vulnerability shows that the ratio cannot be supported. In similar vein, Willemson (2007) [9] introduces the notion of the existence of a level of expenditure of information security that removes all threats, as an additional parameter, thus completely securing the information. Under this specification the 'optimal' ratio can vary according to the value of this parameter. The author constructs examples where optimal investment ranges between 50% and 100% of the value of information that is protected.

All such models share a number of characteristics such as the knowledge of the 'monetary' value of information that is safeguarded and in addition the very metric of infromation security as such is not defined. It is simply stated in its 'negative' appearance as the value of the loss. Gordon and Loeb concede that the constituent components of the composite 'service' of information security may not be mutually consistent but given the requirements of their model and the assumption that all information can be valued by such decomposition is not necessary for the analysis undertaken.

In this paper, we develop a dynamic model that acknowledges the existence of trade-offs between the fundamental characteristics of information security, namely confidentiality, integrity, and availability (for simplicity here, we restrict to confidentiality and availability; cf. Beautement et al. (2008) [2]). Our inspiration, and justification, for this analysis is derived from an empirical study Beautement et al. (2008) [2]. Specially, two of us (with others), studied and analyzed the costs and benefits of USB memory stick encryption in the context of the use of USB memory sticks by the staff of an investment bank.

The analysis of the paper Beautement et al. (2008) [2] can be summarized conveniently as follows:

- We observe that, for very well-motivated business reasons, the staff of an investment bank use USB memory sticks to store and transfer information at and between a variety of different locations with differing threat and security profiles;
- We observe, and collect supporting empirical data to the effect, that there are availability-driven incentives not to deploy technologies that promote confidentiality — essentially, it is highly inconvenient, and embarrassing, for the bankers to be unable to remember the necessary password in the presence of the client, and may lead to loss of business;
- We build executable mathematical models of the lifecycle of a USB stick which allow the exploration of the influences of various forms of investment — in training, IT support, and monitoring — on the use of encryption for USB memory sticks;
- We observe that the behaviour of these models does indeed support the existence of a trade-off between confidentiality and availability in this context.

Of course, technological solutions, such as biometric access control, may largely solve this particular problem, but we suggest that the methods and models that we are developing will be of use in a wide variety of situations.

Note that, for the purposes both of the study described above and of the model prsented in this paper, we are concerned with the following notions of confidentiality and availability:

- We consider the confidentiality of the system as represented by the extent to which the system is protected against unintended exposures of information. To this extent, to do not consider the confidentiality of information exposed by given breach; rather, we are concerned with the extent to which is protected against further breaches;
- For simplification, we neglect integrity in the model presented herein. In the context of the study of Beautement et al. (2008) [2], corruption of data as a consequence of the use of USB memory is a relatively minor issue, and the model we present herein should be considered to be potentially applicable only in situations in which such a simplification is justifiable. Clearly, other simplifcations are possible and may be supported by different circumstances and examples. We defer a more comprehensive discussion of the variety of models supported by the general framework introduced in § 2, within which integrity can be incorporated, to another occasion;
- Again, as a simplification, we adopt a simple proxy for availability: the degree of inter-connectedness of the system's components, which may be thought of as a measure of the size of the 'attack surface'.

Managers optimize well-defined objective functions in terms of such elements and recognize that investment is costly. The system's state equations determine the system's operational efficacy and the managers' optimal responses when under 'attack' are defined by altering the system's inter-connectness and by the acquiring new investment in information security. All the parameters have explicit behavioural and technical interpretations and allow for the classification of managers' behaviour and the system's architecture.

In § 2, we begin with a summary of the simplifying assumptions, motivated by the study presented in Beautement et al. (2008) [2], employed in this paper. We also provide, following Gianni and Woodford (2002) [3], a brief summary of the general linear stabilization problem and its solutions, and discuss briefly its use, by Nobay and Peel (2003) [8], in monetary policy with asymmetric preferences. In § 3, we describe our model in detail, providing the necessary system of differential and integral equations, together with their interpretation in terms of the concepts of information security. In § 4, we provide a range of examples of constellations of the model's parameters, corresponding to organizations with contrasting information security preferences and management policies, and provide graphs of simulations illustrating the impulse–response of these organizations to a single (exogenous) unit-shock to confidentiality. Finally, in § 5, we provide a range of observations, variations, and extensions about our modelling framework. We provide also two appendices: the first explains the discretization of our models used to generate our simulations; the second explains how our quadratic form of loss functions derives from basic concepts of utility theory.

2   CIA, Investments, and Trade-offs

Organizations deploy systems technologies in order to achieve their business objectives. Typically, it will be necessary for an organization to invest in deploying information security policies, processes, and technologies in order to protect the confidentiality, C, integrity, I, and availability, A, of its business processes. Defences deployed against each of C, I, and A may compromize the other. For now, we neglect integrity, focussing on trade-offs between confidentiality and availability. This simplification is justifiable: in many — though by no means all — situations, corruption of data is not a major issue, and we can be concerned just with the availability of uncorrupted data. In particular, this assumption is reasonable in the context of the empirical study by Beatement et al. (2008) [2] of the use of USB memory sticks, which is discussed at length above and which provides a partial motivation for the model described herein. Of course, there are many situations in which such an assumption is quite unsustainable: Different instantiations of our modelling framework can, as discussed above, capture such situations.

So, in order to formulate its security policy, an organization must determine its security preferences. That is, for each of its business processes, determine the extent to which it prefers to protect each of C, I, and A. For one example, an online bookstore may prefer to defend the availability of its website in order to protect revenue. To do so, it may increase the number and geographical distribution of its servers, thereby greatly increasing the attack surface of the system, and so potentially compromising the confidentiality of data held by the system. For another example, a government intelligence service may be prepared to sacrifice system availability in order to protect the confidentiality of its secrets.

In earlier work with other co-authors Beautement et al. (2008) [2], described above, two of us have established some experimental evidence for the existence of a trade-off between availability and confidentiality — integrity was indeed neglected in this context, in which corruption of data is a relatively minor issue — in the use of USB memory sticks by the employees of a large financial services organization.

In the presence of trade-offs between the constituent components of information security, we adopt a well-established analytical methodology employed in macroeconomics to model optimal instrument setting by the monetary authorities (e.g., central banks) when faced with trade-offs between the economic magnitudes that they wish to control, such as inflation and unemployment.

Following Giannoni and Woodford (2002) [3], the general linear stabilization policy problem can be expressed as a solution to the following control problem, in which the economic interaction structure of the state variables is given in terms of a linear system of the form

$$G \begin{bmatrix} Z_{t+1} \\ E_t z_{t+1} \end{bmatrix} = A_1 \begin{bmatrix} Z_t \\ z_t \end{bmatrix} + A_2 r_t + A_3 u_t \tag{1}$$

where z denotes a vector of endogenous variables and the vector of pre-determined variables is given by Z. The instrument available to the authorities is given by r and the system is disturbed from its original equilibrium position due to the existence of shocks u_t. The objective of the policy is to minimize the quadratic objective function in terms of squared deviations of the variables of interest Π from some a-priori specified target values Π^* by choosing the appropriate value of r given the structure of the system, the loss function,

$$\Lambda = E_t \left\{ \sum_{t=0}^{T} \frac{\delta^{-t}}{2} (\Pi - \Pi^*)^{\mathsf{T}} \, \Omega \, (\Pi - \Pi^*) \right\} \tag{2}$$

where the vector of variables denoted by Π includes values of both z and r. The matrix Ω denotes the variance covariance matrix of the system and δ is the authorities' discount factor. The conditional (on all available information) expectations operator is E_t.

The equilibrium characterization of the system consists of a set of time invariant equations:

$$z_t = \beta_0 + \beta_1 \bar{Z}_t + \beta_2 \bar{u}_t \tag{3}$$

where $^-$ indicates that the structure of the relevant vectors can differ from the one denoted in Equation 1. The imposition of rational expectations requires that the model's predictions of the endogenous variables are equal to the agents' forecasts.

Nobay and Peel (2003) [8] accommodate the absence of symmetric loss in the presence of deviations by employing, in Λ, the linex function whose asymmetry depends upon the choice of the parameter a:

$$g(x_t) = \{\exp(ax_t) - ax_t - 1\}/a^2.$$

In our case, we restrict our analysis to quadratic loss functions but we allow for unequal weights to be applied to its different arguments.

The analysis given by Giannoni and Woodford (2002) [3], together with refinements of the kind suggested by the work of Nobay and Peel (2003) [8], provides a very general framework for capturing the dynamics of investments and trade-offs in information security within which the choices of security and investment properties to be modelled appropriate for a given context, along with associated organizational preferences, can be captured.

In the next section, we develop a model of this type in the context of information security that is inspired by the study presented in Beautement et al. (2008) [2] and briefly discussed above. For simplicity of analysis, we begin with a continuous time model — a conceptually convenient approximation often employed in many mathematical modelling contexts — which we later discretize. We work with a utility, or loss, function that is quadratic in each of its components.

We then examine the system's response to temporary (one-time) shocks (or perturbations, or disturbances) and map the time evolution of the both the control and state variables. Within this framework we are able to gauge the responses to shocks in terms of magnitude and duration. The stability of the system guarantees the eventual return to a stable path. Such methodology for the examination of the responses of a multivariate linear/non-linear system is well-established in the econometric literature, in the context of linear and non-linear vector autoregressive systems, where the impulse–response function (IRF) is calculated (see Hamilton (1994) [5]). An impulse–response function traces out the response of a state-variable of interest to an exogenous shock (this is normally unobserved). Usually the response is portrayed graphically, with the time horizon on the horizontal axis and the magnitude of difference between the undisturbed system and its response to the shock on the vertical axis. Monte Carlo methods are then used for statistical inference to establish whether the calculated responses are statistically significant. In this study, we develop a dynamic system that is subject to a single stochastic disturbance (to confidentiality) and we study the IRF of such system under alternative sets of structural parameters.

3   The Model and Its Meaning

We have explained, in § 2, how we understand confidentiality, integrity, and availability to trade-off against one another. Simplifying, we can neglect integrity — we assume that our storage and processing technologies do not corrupt data — and study the trade-off between confidentiality and availability. This situation is intuitively appealing: disks, DVDs, and memory sticks are quite rarely corrupted, at least in contexts similar to that studied in Beautement et al. (2008)

[2]: increasing a system's availability — for example, by increasing the number and distribution of a system's web-servers — may be thought of as increasing the attack surface of the system, and so reducing the confidentiality of (the information contained within) the system.

The starting point is the utility function, more naturally thought of here as a loss function, expressing the system operators confidentiality and availability preferences. In the given definition, C refers to the aggregate level of confidentiality of information in the system, and $\bar{C}$ is its target, A refers to the aggregate level of availability of information in the system; K denotes the capital stock in information security (i.e., the aggregate value of investments in information security to-date).

We postulate a system whose optimal operational state $(\bar{C}, \bar{A})$ is below its maximal capacity. If the system exceeds such levels the system's reliability becomes problematic and consequently the system's manager attempts to restore it at the predetermined optimal levels. The same happens when the system underperforms because of an 'attack' or any other security breach. The control mechanism in both cases is

$$R = \frac{1}{1 - \xi}, \text{for } \xi \in [0, 1)$$

which may be thought of as capturing the complexity of the system via the extent to which the system is inter-connected: if the proportion of of the system that is inter-connected is zero (i.e., $\xi = 0$), then the system's complexity is trivial (i.e., 1); as ξ tends to 1, however, the complexity of the system tends to infinity. Such a response aims to alter the system's availability. This may be seen as controlling access to the system.

In addition, we postulate that investment in information security that helps managers to restore the system is expensive, as large deviations from its pre-announced target levels undermine the 'credibility' of the managers and may not be authorized by the CFO. The important element here is the presence of the three elements of deviations form pre-agreed targets in the loss function. Further developments can allow for more sophisticated functional forms that restrict the solutions to one-sided deviations from targets. Notice that, as we measure all metrics in the $(0, 1)$ (or $[0, 1)$) interval, that is as proportions, the size of the system is assumed constant. This is an area that we may wish to develop in future models by adopting a metric such as capital stock in information security 'per machine' in the network.

The equations below represent the decision-makers' optimal control problem

$$L(C, A, \dot{K}) = E\left(w_1(C - \bar{C})^2 + w_2(A - \bar{A})^2 + w_3(\dot{K} - \bar{\dot{K}})^2\right), \qquad (4)$$

the loss function, whose solution will be of the form

$$L(R) \triangleq \min_x L(C, A, \dot{K}) \qquad (5)$$

where x is a control variable. In this case, the optimal control issue is based on convex preferences relative to a given set of targets, $\bar{C}$, $\bar{A}$ and $\bar{\dot{K}}$. These are as follows, the target confidentiality, C, availability, A, and target change in investment in information security, $\dot{K}$.

The weights (w_1, w_2, w_3) represent the type of organization, expressing, as discussed in § 4, the organization's security profile preferences. The time evolution of confidentiality and availability are described in Equations 6 and 7. C_0 is an initial value.

$$C = -\alpha(P) \left(\int_{t_0}^{t} \dot{A} \, dt \left(\beta \int_{t_0}^{t'} \dot{K} \, dt' \right)^{-1} \right) + C_0 \tag{6}$$

$$A = \gamma \left(\int_{t_0}^{t'} \dot{R} \, dt' \right) + \delta \left(\int_{t_0}^{t'} \dot{K} \, dt' \right) - \epsilon \left(\int_{t_0}^{t'} \dot{C} \, dt' \right) \tag{7}$$

where $t' < t$.

Investment in information security is triggered by fluctuations in availability and the time dynamics of this are expressed in Equation 8

$$\dot{K} = -\eta \dot{A} \tag{8}$$

The system responds to deviations in confidentiality, as given by Equation 9:

$$\dot{R} = x \left(C - \bar{C} \right) \tag{9}$$

Note that, as $t' \to \infty$, the system stabilizes.

As formulated here, our model shocks only confidentiality. A richer model might, for example, also shock availability. Such a model would need to be formulated with an additional control instrument, so that there would be an instrument corresponding to each shocked dimension.

The weights in the loss function (4) characterize the type of the organization; for example, military and deep-state organizations might put a great deal of weight on C compared to A, whilst a retailer or welfare distributor might place greater value on A compared to C. Finally, the weight on $(\dot{K} - \bar{K})^2$ reflects the system's loss when managers are forced to compromize budgets. Public organizations may be more restricted, compared to private sector firms, and therefore be more reluctant to miss $\bar{K}$, implying a higher weight associated with this deviation in the loss function. The term $w_3(\dot{K} - \bar{K})^2$ deserves more discussion: this is the credibility of the decision maker: if the investment needs to be increased (or decreased) by a large amount, given a conditional set-up, then the initial guesses of the decision maker in setting the equilibrium change in investment were faulty and this results in a subsequent loss of credibility. For example, if a government sets a level of growth in spending of $\bar{K}$, then a sudden requirement to increase the level of spending, from time t to $t + \Delta t$ results in ΔK: if $\frac{\Delta K}{\Delta t} \gg \bar{K}$, then the decision makers' credibility is decreased (based on convex credibility preferences) with subsequent loss of welfare.

Equation 4 is the objective function, which we seek to minimize, and Equation 5 denotes the solution from the optimization of the control variable x from 9.

See Appendix B for an explanation — in terms of basic utility theory — of the justification of loss functions of this form.

Breaches in confidentiality are denoted by P, the stochastic process that generates such events. Their impact is measured by α, and such breaches will be referred to as shocks to the dynamic system represented in equation 6. The system's attack surface is modelled by the availability

$$\int_{t_0}^{t} \dot{A}\, dt,$$

and amplifies the influence of breaches, whilst increases in the capital stock of information security[1],

$$\frac{1}{\int_{t_0}^{t} \dot{K}\, dt},$$

mitigates against the severity of the shock. The effectiveness of this mitigation is measured by the value of the positive parameter β. The availability of the system depends positively of the system's inter-connectedness, $\int_{t_0}^{t} \dot{R}\, dt$ and the capital stock of information security. Increases in confidentiality are expected to exert a negative influence on the system's availability. The positive parameters γ, δ, and ϵ measure the impact of these factors on the system's availability.

IT managers will respond to decreases in availability by increasing investment in information security (8). The managers' response is measured by the parameter, η. In the presence of deviations of confidentiality from its target, IT managers respond by manipulating the system's inter-connectedness. Such response is calculated optimally given the architecture of the system, as captured by the parameters α, β, γ, δ, and ϵ, and the managers' preferences and behaviour as captured by w_1, w_2, w_3, and η, given the choice of targets $\bar{C}, \bar{A}$, and $\bar{K}$.

This set-up offers the opportunity to characterize systems according to their architecture and combine them to the preferences of managers. For example, systems with very effective information security capital and managers valuing availability above confidentiality, $w_2 > w_1$, will adjust differently to the same shock in confidentiality if $w_1 < w_2$. In addition to these distinctions differences in behavioural characteristics, η, will determine the relative rate of adjustment. The multi-variate structure of this model, with its general system parameters, is sufficiently expressive to be able to capture a wide range of system profiles of interest, such as the deep-state and commercial systems previously mentioned.

Table 1 illustrates a proposed set of parameter values for three classes of organization: military, financial, and retail. Each organization has varying requirements for its system's robustness to shocks. For example, military-type organizations require confidentiality to be maintained in preference to availability. As such, the α parameter would be expected to be very large, matching the sensitivity of this type of organization to loss of confidentiality. This cost is determined by the ϵ parameter, which is also very high for this class. Also, military

---

[1] For simplicity of exposition of the initial properties of the model, we do not allow for depreciation in the capital stock of information security.

organizations would be expected to have a high β parameter, given the level of control required relative to the level of expenditure, K. In contrast, financial- and retail-type organizations need to operate on a day to day basis and as such have much higher γ parameters. The cost of loss of reputation to retail is higher and, as such, the main difference between retail organizations and military organizations should be characterized via the ϵ parameter (small for military and very large for retail). Finally, the feedback between change in investment, $\dot{K}$, and change in availability, $\dot{A}$, characterized by the η parameter is also very different for retail and financials, but very similar for military and retail, illustrating financial organizations' ease of redistributing resources for security purposes.

Table 1. Organizational Preferences

Organization Type	System Parameters	Managers' Preference Parameters
Military	$\alpha \gg 0$ $\beta > 0$ $\gamma \to 0$ $\delta < \gamma$ $\epsilon > 0$ $\eta \to 0$	$w_1 \gg w_2 > w_3$
Financial	$\alpha \to 0$ $\beta \to 0$ $\gamma \gg 0$ $\delta \to 0$ $\epsilon \gg 0$ $\eta \gg 0$	$w_1 \simeq w_2 > w_3$
Retail	$\alpha \to 0$ $\beta \to 0$ $\gamma \gg 0$ $\delta \to 0$ $\epsilon \gg 0$ $\eta \to 0$	$w_2 \simeq w_3 \gg w_1$

Having postulated a model — justified by elementary considerations of the nature of investments in information security, including how systems incorporate such investments — we now proceed to examine the system's response to perturbations under alternative parameter constellations that characterize systems and managers with different preferences and behaviours. Table 1 provides examples of the preference of different types of organization.

4   Numerical Examples and Simulations

We select parameter constellations to characterize some systems of interest. We apply the same shock to confidentiality to each of these these systems, and discuss the comparative responses. To proceed with this task, we use the following discretization scheme for the model, with full details given in Appendix A:

$$C_{t+\Delta t} = -\alpha \left(E\left(P_{t+\Delta t}\right)\right) \left(\sum_{t=0}^{t} \Delta A_t + A_0\right) \left(\beta \sum_{t=0}^{t} \Delta K_t + K_0\right)^{-1} + C_0 \quad (10)$$

$$A_{t+\Delta t} = \gamma \left(\sum_{t=0}^{t} \Delta R_t + R_0\right) + \delta \left(\sum_{t=0}^{t} \Delta K_t + K_0\right) - \epsilon \left(\sum_{t=0}^{t} \Delta C_t + C_0\right) \quad (11)$$

$$\Delta K_t = -\eta A_t \quad (12)$$

$$\Delta R_t = x \left(C_t - \bar{C}\right) \quad (13)$$

$$K_{t+\Delta t} = K_t + \Delta K_t \quad (14)$$

$$R_{t+\Delta t} = R_t + \Delta R_t \quad (15)$$

The evolution of the model will be non-explosive provided that the roots of the following polynomial lie within the unit circle:

$$\begin{aligned}
\varsigma = & Z^5 - Z^4 + \left(-\ln\left(\epsilon\right)\ln\left(\alpha\right) + \ln\left(\delta\right)\ln\left(\eta\right)\right) Z^3 \\
& + \left(\ln\left(\epsilon\right)\ln\left(\alpha\right) - \ln\left(\theta\right)\ln\left(\alpha\right)\ln\left(\gamma\right) + \ln\left(\epsilon\right)\ln\left(\beta\right)\ln\left(\eta\right)\right) Z^2 \\
& + \left(\ln\left(\theta\right)\ln\left(\beta\right)\ln\left(\gamma\right)\ln\left(\eta\right) - \ln\left(\delta\right)\ln\left(\eta\right)\right) Z \\
& + \ln\left(\theta\right)\ln\left(\beta\right)\ln\left(\gamma\right)\ln\left(\eta\right) - \ln\left(\epsilon\right)\ln\left(\beta\right)\ln\left(\eta\right)
\end{aligned} \quad (16)$$

The full derivation of this stability condition is given Appendix A.

To elucidate the impact of a single non-persistent shock to confidentiality, C_t, the impulse–response of C_t to a shock to P_t at $t = 0$ is derived numerically. For tractability and exposition, the system responses are illustrated as a percentage deviation from equilibrium of the system following a single unit-shock to confidentiality (i.e., we assume that $P_{t=0} = 1$).

We now illustrate the applicability of our model by exploring, in the subsections below, constellations of parameters that characterize contrasting types of organizations (Organization 1, Organization 2). We denote the contrasting choices of parameters by subscripting with 1 and 2: e.g., w_{11}, w_{12}, etc.. It should be noted that, in all cases, the system returns to equilibrium in finite time.

Example 1: Confidentiality versus Availability

$w_{11} \gg w_{12}, w_{22} \gg w_{21}$

We compare the behaviour of Organization 1, such as a deep-state or intelligence agency, which weighs confidentiality more highly than availability, with Organization 2, such as an online retailer, which weighs availability more highly than confidentiality. These preferences are expressed by the relative values of w_{11} and w_{12}. We assume, for simplicity, that the organizations are similar in all respects.

Example 2: Impact of Confidentiality Deviations

$\gamma_1 \gg \gamma_2,\ \eta_1 > \eta_2$

We compare two otherwise similar organizations for which the impact of the degree of their network inter-connectedness, and hence of deviations of confidentiality from target, is very different. In Organization 1, the parameter γ_1 is relatively large, so that the impact of deviations of confidentiality from the target is large. Organizations with this characteristic might include banks or health agencies. In contrast, Organization 2, which might be a public information service or a social networking site, γ_2 relatively small, so that deviations of confidentiality below target have a relatively small impact on availability. Since $\eta_1 > \eta_2$, Organization 1's investment response is greater than Organization 2's.

Example 3: Level of Vulnerability and Response

$\alpha_1 < \alpha_2,\ \beta_1 < \beta_2,\ \eta_1 > \eta_2$

We compare to otherwise similar organizations which have different levels of vulnerability. Organization 2 is more vulnerable, as $\alpha_1 < \alpha_2$, which is mitigated by greater investment, $\beta_2 > \beta_1$. However, since $\eta_1 > \eta_2$, Organization 1's investment response is greater than Organization 2's.

The three examples above have been chosen to illustrate the effects of changes in essentially one dimension. Clearly, more realistic comparisons would require more delicate analyses with more variation in the various parameters.

In the three sections that follow below, corresponding to the three examples described above, we plot the impulse–response of the system to a unit shock. In each case, we plot for each comparative pair, the following:

- Deviation from equilibrium of each of C, A, and K;
- The evolution of the control variable, x (recall Equation 9).

Organization 1 is plotted on the left, Organization 2 on the right.

Example 1: Confidentiality versus Availability, Figure 1

The recovery of confidentiality and availability to their pre-shock levels is consistent with the managers' preferences. Measures are taken to restore the system's degree of confidentiality rapidly by enforcing prolonged periods of reduced inter-connectedness.

In Organization 1, capital in information security increases almost immediately and then declines monotonically whilst for Orgainzation 2, both confidentiality and availability are restored at almost the same rate whilst capital in information security is of relatively smaller size and it achieves it maximum few periods after shock, exhibiting a somewhat slower rate of return to 'equilibrium'.

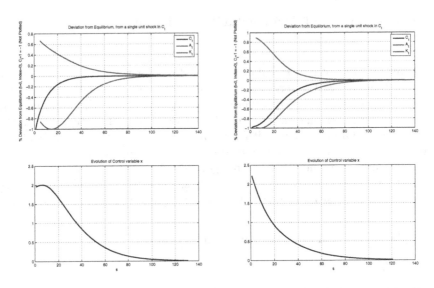

Fig. 1. Confidentiality (w_1) versus Availability (w_2)

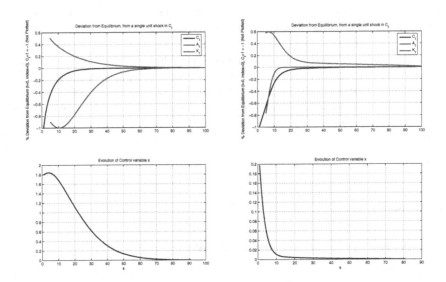

Fig. 2. Impact of Confidentiality Deviations

Example 2: Impact of Confidentiality Deviations, Figure 2

In Organization 1, confidentiality is restored rapidly, and availability lags behind. In Organization 2, confidentiality is restored less rapidly, and availability is the priority. System inter-connectedness is restored less rapidly in the first organization. The evolution of the capital stock is radically different in the two cases. For Organization 1, the initial increase is followed by monotonic reversion to equilibrium, its maximum size not exceeding 0.5. Under the same shock, Organization 2 increases rapidly its capital stock over the subsequent period achieving a maximum value of about 0.75. Having achieved this level, the capital stock is restored to its initial level.

Example 3: Level of Vulnerability and Response, Figure 3

Here confidentiality is restored more rapidly in the Organization 2, but availability lags behind. This greater emphasis on security is also reflected by the longer time taken for the second organization to restore system inter-connectedness.

In both cases, the response of capital stock in information security to the shock is not monotonic: they achieve their maxima after approximately 20 periods with Organization 1 exhibiting a modest initial increase followed by subsequent rapid changes bringing the stock of capital well-above the level achieved by Organization 2.

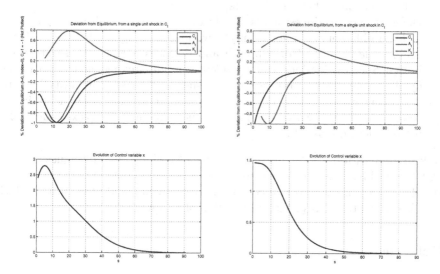

Fig. 3. Level of Vulnerability and Response

The responses of confidentiality and availability show very different patterns of recovery. The managers' response to the perturbation (the value of x) differs both in terms of size (in Organization 1 the response to the deviation is far more aggressive) and time evolution, their sensitivity declines fairly rapidly, albeit from a higher base whilst the managers of the second firm maintain for longer periods low levels of system.

5   Conclusions and Directions

We have presented a framework for evaluating the (relative) consequences of C(I)A preferences based on quadratic loss functions.

The following observations, variations, and extensions are suggested:

- A more careful, empirical examination of the assumptions about the systems and management aspects of information security upon which our modelling framework is based;
- More sophisticated forms of loss functions, including asymmetries within and between the confidentiality, availability and investment terms in the loss function — see, for example, the use of linex functions by Nobay and Peel (2003) [8];
- Consideration of the additional dimension of integrity, thus completing the application of our models to the CIA view of information security;
- The model presented here is about a single stochastic threat to confidentiality. Considering multiple threats — with control instruments corresponding to each dimension to which shocks are applied — would strengthen the applicability of the model. Such an extension would require an understanding of the co-variance between threats;
- Different types of investments in information security mitigate against attacks in different ways: for example, we might ditinguish between defences against the likelihood of a breach and defences against the severity of a breach. Such distinctions would, evidently, require refinements to our model;
- Qualitatively different types of threat, such as threats to integrity by data-destroying viruses which might be expected to trigger investments in, for example, patching, would require a significantly more complex model utilizing the ideas discussed above.

Acknowledgements. We are grateful to several of our colleagues, and to Matthew Collinson in particular, for their comments on this work. We are also grateful to the anonymous referees for many comments and observations which have helped us to improve the presentation of this work.

References

1. Anderson, R., Böhme, R., Clayton, R., Moore, T.: Security economics and the internal market. Report to the European Network and Information Security Agency, ENISA (2007),
   http://www.enisa.europa.eu/doc/pdf/report_sec_econ_&_int_mark_20080131.pdf
2. Beautement, A., Coles, R., Griffin, J., Ioannidis, C., Monahan, B., Pym, D., Sasse, A., Wonham, M.: Modelling the Human and Technological Costs and Benefits of USB Memory Stick Security. In: Eric Johnson, M. (ed.) Managing Information Risk and the Economics of Security, Proc. WEIS 2008. Springer, Heidelberg (2008) (preliminary version), http://weis2008.econinfosec.org/papers/Pym.pdf
3. Giannoni, M.P., Woodford, M.: Optimal Interest-Rate Rules I: General Theory. Working Paper Series 9419, National Bureau of Economic Research, ISSU 9419, ISSN 0898-2937 (2002)
4. Gordon, L.A., Loeb, M.P.: The Economics of Information Security Investment. ACM Transactions on Information and Systems Security 5(4), 438–457 (2002)

5. Hamilton, J.D.: Time Series Analysis. Princeton University Press, New Jersey (1994)
6. Hausken, K.: Returns to information security investment: The effect of alternative information security breach functions on optimal investment and sensitivity to vulnerability. Information Systems Frontiers 8(5), 338–349 (2006)
7. Loistl, O.: The Erroneous Approximation of Expected Utility by Means of Taylor's Series Expansion: Analytic and Computational Results. American Economic Review 66(5), 904–910 (1976)
8. Nobay, R.A., Peel, D.A.: Optimal Discretionary Monetary Policy in a Model of Asymmetric Bank Preferences. Economic Journal 113(489), 657–665 (2003)
9. Willemson, J.: On the Gordon & Loeb Model for Information Security Investment. In: Proc. WEIS (2006), http://weis2006.econinfosec.org/docs/12.pdf

A   Discrete Time Representation and Stability of the Model

Given the model's system representation,

$$C = -\alpha(P) \left(\int_{t_0}^{t} \dot{A} \, dt \left(\beta \int_{t_0}^{t'} \dot{K} \, dt' \right)^{-1} \right) + C_0 \tag{17}$$

$$A = \gamma \left(\int_{t_0}^{t'} \dot{R} \, dt' \right) + \delta \left(\int_{t_0}^{t'} \dot{K} \, dt' \right) - \epsilon \left(\int_{t_0}^{t'} \dot{C} \, dt' \right) \tag{18}$$

$$\dot{K} = -\eta \dot{A} \tag{19}$$

$$\dot{R} = \theta \left(C - \bar{C} \right), \tag{20}$$

assuming simple fixed period time indexing, the discrete time analogues are as follows:

$$C_{t+\Delta t} = -\alpha \left(E \left(P_{t+\Delta t} \right) \right) \left(\sum_{t=0}^{t} \Delta A_t + A_0 \right) \left(\beta \sum_{t=0}^{t} \Delta K_t + K_0 \right)^{-1} + C_0 \tag{21}$$

$$A_{t+\Delta t} = \gamma \left(\sum_{t=0}^{t} \Delta R_t + R_0 \right) + \delta \left(\sum_{t=0}^{t} \Delta K_t + K_0 \right)$$
$$- \epsilon \left(\sum_{t=0}^{t} \Delta C_t + C_0 \right) \tag{22}$$

$$\Delta K_t = -\eta A_t \tag{23}$$

$$\Delta R_t = x \left(C_t - \bar{C} \right) \tag{24}$$

$$K_{t+\Delta t} = K_t + \Delta K_t \tag{25}$$

$$R_{t+\Delta t} = R_t + \Delta R_t \tag{26}$$

For structural stability,

$$\sum_{t=0}^{T>t, T\neq\infty} e' y_t < \infty \tag{27}$$

where e is a unit vector and y_t is the vector evolution of the system equations, C_t, A_t, K_t, and R_t.

Setting the system as a vector problem, and taking logs for linearity and simplifying, the system maybe represented as follows:

$$
\begin{bmatrix} \log C_{n+1} \\ \log A_{n+1} \\ \log K_{n+1} \\ \log R_{n+1} \end{bmatrix} = \begin{bmatrix} 0 & \log \alpha & -\log \beta & 0 \\ \log \varepsilon & 0 & \log \delta & \log \gamma \\ 0 & -\log \eta & 0 & 0 \\ \log \theta & 0 & 0 & 1 \end{bmatrix}' \begin{bmatrix} \log C_n \\ \log A_n \\ \log K_n \\ \log R_n \end{bmatrix}
\tag{28}
$$

$$
+ \begin{bmatrix} 0 & 0 & 0 & 0 \\ 0 & 0 & 0 & 0 \\ 0 & -\log \eta & 0 & 0 \\ 0 & 0 & 0 & 0 \end{bmatrix} \begin{bmatrix} \log C_{n-1} \\ \log A_{n-1} \\ \log K_{n-1} \\ \log R_{n-1} \end{bmatrix}
$$

$$
+ \begin{bmatrix} \log C_0 \\ 0 \\ -\log \theta + \log C_0 \\ 0 \end{bmatrix} + \begin{bmatrix} u_n \\ 0 \\ 0 \\ 0 \end{bmatrix}
$$

$$
\Pi_1 = \begin{bmatrix} 0 & \log \alpha & \log \beta & 0 \\ \log \varepsilon & 0 & \log \delta & \log \gamma \\ 0 & -\log \eta & 0 & 0 \\ \log \theta & 0 & 0 & 1 \end{bmatrix} \quad \Pi_2 = \begin{bmatrix} 0 & 0 & 0 & 0 \\ 0 & 0 & 0 & 0 \\ 0 & -\log \eta & 0 & 0 \\ 0 & 0 & 0 & 0 \end{bmatrix}
\tag{29}
$$

Setting the parameter matrices as a square matrix over the recursion length of the system, the system matrix, $\mathbf{F}$, is

$$
\mathbf{F} = \begin{bmatrix} \Pi_1 & \Pi_2 \\ \mathbf{I} & \mathbf{0} \end{bmatrix}
\tag{30}
$$

where $\mathbf{I}$ is a 4×4 identity matrix and $\mathbf{0}$ is a 4×4 matrix of zeros.

Taking the matrix polynomial roots of the system matrix $\mathbf{F}$ has the following simplified representation:

$$
\begin{bmatrix} 0 \\ 0 \\ 0 \\ \varsigma(Z) = 0 \end{bmatrix}
\tag{31}
$$

where the largest eigenvalue is

$$
\begin{aligned}
\varsigma = {}& Z^5 - Z^4 + \left(-\ln(\epsilon)\ln(\alpha) + \ln(\delta)\ln(\eta) \right) Z^3 \\
& + \left(\ln(\epsilon)\ln(\alpha) - \ln(\theta)\ln(\alpha)\ln(\gamma) + \ln(\epsilon)\ln(\beta)\ln(\eta) \right) Z^2 \\
& + \left(\ln(\theta)\ln(\beta)\ln(\gamma)\ln(\eta) - \ln(\delta)\ln(\eta) \right) Z \\
& + \ln(\theta)\ln(\beta)\ln(\gamma)\ln(\eta) - \ln(\epsilon)\ln(\beta)\ln(\eta)
\end{aligned}
\tag{32}
$$

Therefore the stability of the system will be dependent on the roots of the polynomial from (32) being within the unit circle. For simulation purposes, we transform all parameter values by a fixed constant λ to ensure this stability condition is met.

B   Concave Utility and Convex Preferences

For a given representation of preferences, $U = f(x)$, with $x \in \mathbb{R}$, for the domain of the function in the interval, $[a, b]$, where $a > b$, then if, for all possible points characterized by the ordering $a < x_1 < x_2 < x_3 < b$, if $f(x_2) \geqslant L(x_2)$, where $L(x)$ is a straight line running through, $(x_1, f(x_1))$ and $(x_3, f(x_3))$, the function is said to be concave in the domain $[a, b]$. This also implies that

$$f'(x_1) > f'(x_2) > f'(x_2) \tag{33}$$
$$f''(x_1) < 0 \tag{34}$$

Consider the second-order Taylor expansion of U,

$$\Im(U) = f(\bar{x}) + \frac{f'(\bar{x})}{1!}(x - \bar{x}) + \frac{f''(\bar{x})}{2!}(x - \bar{x})^2 + r \tag{35}$$

Loistl (1976) [7] determines that for standard maximization problems the remainder term is zero, if x is a random variable $x \in \mathbb{R}$, and the moments of x are uniquely determined by its first non-centralized $E(x)$ and second centralized moment $E(x - \bar{x})^2$. For a general target problem, if we consider the expected value of x to be the target value $\bar{x}$, then the following conditions are assumed in equilibrium,

$$r = 0 \tag{36}$$
$$E(x - \bar{x}) = 0 \tag{37}$$
$$E(x - \bar{x})^2 > 0 \tag{38}$$
$$f''(x_1) < 0 \tag{39}$$

For a given set of control variables Ω, whereby $E(x - \bar{x})^2 | \Omega$, maximum welfare is obtained when

$$\Im(U) \triangleq \max_{\Theta} \Im(U | \Theta) \tag{40}$$

Given that, for all x, $f''(x)$ is negative and monotone decreasing to 0 with increasing x_0, the maximization problem inverts to a loss minimization problem by setting $\frac{1}{2} f''(x) = -w$. Utility maximization occurs when

$$\max_{\Theta} \Im(U | \Theta) \equiv \min_{\Theta}\left(w(x - \bar{x})^2 | \Theta\right) \tag{41}$$

B.1   Addition Rules

Consider the variables x, y and z and a representative individual with concave utility $U = f(x, y, z)$, where $(x, y, z) \in \mathbb{R}^3$ for any set of 3-tuple points bounded by $a_{x,y,z} < b_{x,y,z}$; that is,

$$\mathcal{X} = \left\{ \begin{array}{l} a_x < x_1 < x_2 < x_3 < b_x \\ a_y < y_1 < y_2 < y_3 < b_y \\ a_z < z_1 < z_2 < z_3 < b_z \end{array} \right\} \tag{42}$$

The function is concave iff $f(x_2, y_2, z_2) \leq L(x_2, y_2, z_2)$, for all feasible points,

$$(f(a_x, a_y, a_z), a_x, a_y, a_z) \tag{43}$$
$$(f(b_x, b_y, b_z), b_x, b_y, b_z) \tag{44}$$
$$(f(x_1, y_1, z_1), x_1, y_1, z_1) \tag{45}$$
$$(f(x_2, y_2, z_2), x_2, y_2, z_2) \tag{46}$$
$$(f(x_3, y_3, z_3), x_3, y_3, z_3) \tag{47}$$

where $L(.)$ is the hyperplane that passes through $(f(x_1, y_1, z_1), x_1, y_1, z_1)$ and $(f(x_3, y_3, z_3), x_3, y_3, z_3)$. Again this implies that each partial second-order derivative of U is negative:

$$\frac{\partial^2 f(x, y, z)}{\partial x^2} < 0 \qquad \frac{\partial^2 f(x, y, z)}{\partial y^2} < 0 \qquad \frac{\partial^2 f(x, y, z)}{\partial y^2} < 0 \tag{48}$$

Again given a vector Taylor expansion around a set of target points $(\bar{x}, \bar{y}, \bar{z})$,

$$\Im(U) = \sum_{j=0}^{\infty} \left(\frac{1}{j!} (\mathbf{a}.\nabla_{\mathbf{r'}})^j f(\mathbf{r'}) \right)_{\mathbf{r'}=\mathbf{r}} \tag{49}$$

and eliminating cross products and setting

$$\frac{\partial^2 f(x, y, z)}{\partial x^2} = -w_x \qquad \frac{\partial^2 f(x, y, z)}{\partial y^2} = -w_y \qquad \frac{\partial^2 f(x, y, z)}{\partial y^2} = -w_z \tag{50}$$

and given x, y, and z are independent randomly distributed random variables, uniquely defined by their first two moments, the utility maximization problem inverts to the following loss minimization function

$$\max_{\Theta}(\Im(U)) \equiv \min_{\Theta} \left(w_x(x - \bar{x})^2 + w_y(y - \bar{y})^2 + w_z(z - \bar{z})^2 \right) \tag{51}$$

Blue versus Red: Towards a Model of Distributed Security Attacks

Neal Fultz* and Jens Grossklags

School of Information, University of California, Berkeley
102 South Hall, 94720 Berkeley, CA
{nfultz,jensg}@ischool.berkeley.edu

Abstract. We develop a two-sided multiplayer model of security in which attackers aim to deny service and defenders strategize to secure their assets. Attackers benefit from the successful compromise of target systems, however, may suffer penalties for increased attack activities. Defenders weigh the force of an attack against the cost of security. We consider security decision-making in tightly and loosely coupled networks and allow defense expenditures in protection and self-insurance technologies.

Keywords: Game Theory, Economics of Security, Tightly and loosely coupled networks, Protection, Self-insurance.

1 Introduction

If you encounter an aggressive lion, stare him down. But not a leopard; avoid his gaze at all costs. In both cases, back away slowly; don't run (Bruce Schneier, 2007 [37]).

The focus of this paper is a better understanding of attacker motives and strategies when faced with diverse defense patterns (i.e., different protection interdependencies). In particular, we want to provide a mathematical framework with enough nuanced structure to enable more intuitive statements about characteristics of cyber-attack equilibria [14]. We add to the literature on game-theoretic models that have often exclusively focused on the strategic aspects of offensive [15,36] or defensive [22,26,30] actions, respectively.[1]

---

* We thank Alvaro Cárdenas, Nicolas Christin, John Chuang, Roger Dingledine, Paul Laskowski, Adam Shostack, Doug Tygar and the anonymous reviewers for their helpful comments to an earlier version of this paper. All remaining errors are our own. This work is supported in part by the National Science Foundation under ITR award ANI-0331659 (100x100) and with a University of California MICRO project grant in collaboration with DoCoMo USA Labs.

[1] Several research papers explore the optimal strategies of defenders and attackers in graph-theoretic network inoculation games [4,31]. We explore economic security incentives in different models capturing public goods characteristics and the trade-off between protection and self-insurance.

R. Dingledine and P. Golle (Eds.): FC 2009, LNCS 5628, pp. 167–183, 2009.
© IFCA/Springer-Verlag Berlin Heidelberg 2009

The prevalence of widely spread, propagated and correlated threats such as distributed denial of service attacks (DDoS), worms and spam has brought attention to interdependencies existing in computer networks. For an attacker this might create strong economies but sometimes also diseconomies of scale. For example, a single breach of a corporate perimeter may allow an attacker to harvest resources from all machines located within its borders. In other scenarios an attacker may have to shut down every single computer or network connection to achieve an attack goal and thereby incur large costs potentially proportional to network size. More generally, there is an interaction between the structure of the defenders' network, the attack goal and threat model. In Grossklags et al. [22] we analyze a set of canonical games that capture some of these interdependencies.

We distinguish between tightly and loosely coupled networks [33]. In a tightly coupled network all defenders will face a loss if the condition of a security breach is fulfilled. This may be a suitable description, for example, of a network perimeter breach that causes the spread of malicious code to all machines, but also applies to independently acting defenders that try to preserve a common secret or resist censorship. In a loosely coupled network consequences may differ for network participants. For example, an attacker might be interested to gain control over a limited set of compromised machines ("zombies" or "bots") and to organize them into a logical network ("botnet") with the goal of executing a DDoS attack against third parties [28] or sending unsolicited information to and from the bots (i.e., popup advertisements and spam). At other times, an attacker might target a specific set of users (e.g., wealthy users in spearphishing scams). Other users would stay unharmed and are never targeted.

With our work we hope to provide a more complete framework to understand defenders' and attackers' incentives and expected security actions and outcomes for a variety of decision-making situations. In the current paper, we are able to discuss which defense actions are plausible given a motivated and strategically acting attacker. We can comment on several important facets of computer security warfare, such as when deterrence will be successful, or when defenders prefer to abstain from any protective action. With our modeling work we expect to provide the foundations for experimental and empirical research, but we are also interested to evolve the model so that it captures more facets of fully distributed attacks.

The rest of the paper is organized as follows. We briefly review related work on models involving strategic attackers and defenders in Section 2. In Section 3 we introduce our game-theoretic model and its relationship to our prior work. We present our analysis in Section 4 and conclude in Section 5.

2   Related Work

In our prior work, we have provided a broader overview of the literature on security economics [22,23]. Our current interest is centered on the incentives of attackers and game-theoretic models with strategically acting defenders and malefactors.

A number of papers provide practical discussions of economic factors related to computer security. Anderson highlights the oftentimes mismatched security incentives between consumers and commercial institutions that host sensitive data or mediate transactions [3]. Franklin *et al.* collect and analyze activity and pricing data from underground marketplaces [18]. Kshetri [29] and Chung *et al.* [12] explore international aspects of cybercrime. Some researchers have conducted survey or interview studies with hackers and cyber-criminals providing rare insights about their motivations and incentives [10,19].

More formally, Schechter and Smith [36] draw upon the economics of crime literature to construct a model of attackers in the computer security context [5]. They derive the penalties and probabilities of enforcement that will deter an attacker who acts as an utility optimizer evaluating the risks and rewards of committing an offense [8]. Similarly, we consider an attacker utility function that allows offensive players to select the force of attacks while they consider potential penalties from enforcement.

Cavusoglu *et al.* [9] analyze the decision-making problem of a firm when attack probabilities are externally given compared to a scenario when the attacker is explicitly modeled as a strategic player in a game-theoretic framework. Their model shows that if the firm assumes that the attacker responds strategically then in most considered cases the firm will be able to select a more adequate response leading to higher profits. In contrast to Cavusoglu *et al.*, we consider different types of interdependencies and games with multiple attackers and defenders.

Clark and Konrad present a game-theoretic model with one defender and one attacker. The defending player has to successfully protect multiple nodes while the attacker must merely compromise a single point [13]. Their model captures the incentives of a weakest-link game [25], however, with a strategic attacker. We consider multiple individually-rational defenders and allow them to also invest in self-insurance adding an additional perspective to this scenario. Similarly, following Varian's exposition, who also considers strategic attackers, we analyze three canonical contribution functions that determine a common protection level for all defenders [41]. We expand on his analysis of the attacker-defender interaction by considering self-insurance investments as well as security incentives in loosely coupled games.

3   Model

In previous work, we analyzed protection and self-insurance incentives for defenders facing an exogenous attacker [22]. We improve on our *security games* framework by modeling attackers as active and strategic economic actors. In the following, we present the basic framework for the case of N defenders and one attacker. We extend our model to the case of M attackers in Section 4.3.

3.1   Red: Attacker Incentives

The attacker has two actions at her disposal. First, she may choose whether to engage in any attacks at all, and how many defenders k she targets ($0 \leq k \leq N$).

Second, the attacker may choose the force of attacks, a ($0 \leq a \leq 1$), with $a = 1$ representing the attack with the highest impact. In contrast, $a = 0$ denotes an entirely ineffective and harmless attack strategy. The attacker will receive a benefit that is proportional to the force of her attacks, aL, for each not sufficiently protected defender she is able to compromise.

The attacker has to consider H_e, the group security contribution function of the defenders, which has the decisive impact on whether a targeted defender will be compromised. If $H_e = 1$ the defense efforts will always thwart an attack irrespective of a. A value of $H_e = 0$ leaves the defenders completely vulnerable. We present five different variations of H_e in the section on defender incentives.

Additionally, there is a chance that the attacker is caught and fined F, $F > 0$. The probability of being caught for *each* attack made, p_c, is independent of whether the attack was successful or not. Therefore, the expected utility of attacker i is:

$$Red = \begin{cases} \sum_1^k aL(1 - H_e) - (1 - (1 - p_c)^k)F & \text{if Red attacks } (k > 0), \\ 0 & \text{otherwise.} \end{cases} \quad (1)$$

In the current model, we assume that the likelihood of being penalized is related to the number of targeted defenders, k, however, independent of the force of the attack, a. In practice, this likelihood may depend on both parameters since defenders will more frequently involve law enforcement or react vigilantly if attacks are more severe. However, end users and members of small networks are often powerless in their attempts to punish perpetrators of cybercrime. On the one hand, limited and sometimes immaterial damages are an obstacle when users attempt to encourage law enforcement to follow up on their complaints [20]. On the other hand, the cost of identifying an attacker and enforcing a penalty is usually well-beyond the effort needed for a reasonable defense (e.g., cost of forensics, honeypots, maintenance of law enforcement contacts). Users may not want to incur these significant expenses (and we do not consider them in our model). In effect, we assume that a more engaged attacker will face, at least in the aggregate, a higher likelihood of being caught. Of course, there are also obstacles when trying to approximate overall attack activity. For example, enforcement is negatively impacted if multiple jurisdictions are involved [38]. Taken together, we argue that our formulation is a reasonable description for home users and small entities. In contrast, large companies are more likely to mandate thorough investigations and seek involvement of enforcement units after security breaches as a part of their overall security strategy. We defer the analysis of different alternatives for the attacker utility to future work.

3.2   Blue: Defender Incentives

Each of $N \in \mathbb{N}$ defenders receives an endowment W. If she is attacked and compromised successfully, she faces a loss L that is impacted by the force of the attack, a.[2] Defensive players have two security actions at their disposition. Player i can select between a private self-insurance investment, $0 \leq s_i \leq 1$, and a protection level, $0 \leq e_i \leq 1$, that will contribute to a common protection effort. For example, self-insurance includes expenditures in backup technologies, whereas firewalls, patching, and intrusion detections systems are protective efforts [22].[3] Finally, $b \geq 0$ and $c \geq 0$ denote the unit cost of protection and self-insurance, respectively. The generic utility function for a *targeted* defender has the following structure:

$$Blue_i = E(U_i) = W - aL(1 - s_i)(1 - H(e_i, e_{-i})) - be_i - cs_i \qquad (2)$$

where following usual game-theoretic notation, e_{-i} denotes the set of protection levels chosen by players other than i. If the defender is not targeted (for example, if $k = 0$) then the defender will only incur the cost of protection and self-insurance:

$$Blue_i = E(U_i) = W - be_i - cs_i \qquad (3)$$

$H_e = H(e_i, e_{-i})$ is the group "security contribution" function that characterizes the effect of e_i on U_i, subject to the protection levels chosen (contributed) by *all* other players.[4] We will discuss five variations of H_e in the next section.

From Eqs. (2 and 3), the magnitude of a loss depends on three factors: i) whether the defender was targeted by the attacker and with what force of attack (a), ii) whether the individual invested in self-insurance (s_i), and iii) the magnitude of the joint protection level (H_e). Self-insurance always lowers the loss that an individual incurs when compromised by an attack. Protection probabilistically determines whether an attack is successful. Eqn. (2) yields an expected utility.

3.3 Canonical Security Contribution Functions

In prior work [22], we analyzed security games with five different canonical security contribution functions that we will briefly describe in the following. The first three specifications for H_e represent important baseline cases recognized in the public goods literature: total effort, weakest-link and best shot. The attack consequences in these games are tightly coupled; that is, all defenders will face a loss if the level of the security contribution function is not sufficient to block an attack. With two variations of the weakest target contribution function we

---

[2] For simplicity, we analyze the case where attacker gain and defender loss are identical (if the defender is not self-insured). In practice, we would frequently expect that there is a disparity between the two *subjective* values [2].

[3] We also complement work on market insurance for security and privacy. Cyberinsurance can fulfill several critical functions. For example, audit requirements for cyberinsurance can motivate investments in security, and might contribute to a better understanding of the economic value of the protected resources [27]. Several researchers have investigated the impact of correlation of risks and interdependency of agents in networks on the viability of insurance [6,7,35].

[4] We require that H_e be defined for all values over $(0, 1)^N$. However, we do not place, for now, any further restrictions on the contribution function (e.g., continuity).

analyze security scenarios with loosely coupled attack outcomes. In a loosely coupled network consequences may differ for network participants.[5]

Total/average effort security game (*tightly coupled*): The global protection level of the network depends on the sum of contributions normalized over the number of all participants. That is, we define $H(e_i, e_{-i}) = \frac{1}{N} \sum_i e_i$, so that Eqn. (2) becomes

$$E(U_i) = W - aL(1 - s_i)(1 - \frac{1}{N} \sum_k e_k) - be_i - cs_i \ . \tag{4}$$

With the total effort game we consider, for example, the scenario where an attacker wants to slow down distributed transfer of a file on a P2P network. With fewer users protecting their network connectivity the total efficiency of the data communication will be reduced.

Weakest-link security game (*tightly coupled*): The overall protection level depends on the minimum contribution offered over all entities. That is, we have $H(e_i, e_{-i}) = \min(e_i, e_{-i})$, and Eqn. (2) takes the form:

$$E(U_i) = W - aL(1 - s_i)(1 - \min(e_i, e_{-i})) - be_i - cs_i \ . \tag{5}$$

In the weakest-link scenario an attacker wants to breach the perimeter of a closed network (e.g., a virtual private network) by locating a hidden vulnerability such as a weak password. Similarly, the perpetrator might want to learn the identities of members of a filesharing darknet, or some other secret that is shared between multiple users [14].

Best shot security game (*tightly coupled*): In this game, the overall protection level depends on the maximum contribution offered over all entities. Hence, we have $H(e_i, e_{-i}) = \max(e_i, e_{-i})$, so that Eqn. (2) becomes

$$E(U_i) = W - aL(1 - s_i)(1 - \max(e_i, e_{-i})) - be_i - cs_i \ . \tag{6}$$

Sometimes attackers want to remove from circulation or censor a particular piece of information. In this case, they are participating in a best shot scenario. As long as a single copy remains available to the public domain the attack goal is not achieved [17].

k-Weakest-target security game without mitigation (*loosely coupled*): Here, an attacker will *always* be able to compromise the entities with the k lowest protection levels, but will leave other entities unharmed. This game derives from the security game presented in [11]. Formally, we can describe the game as follows:

$$H(e_i, e_{-i}) = \begin{cases} 0 \text{ if } e_i \leq e_{(k)} \\ 1 \text{ otherwise,} \end{cases} \tag{7}$$

---

[5] Please refer to our relevant prior work for detailed interpretations of all sub-games [22,23]. Varian [41] and Hirshleifer [25] discuss also applications outside of the security context such as maintenance of dikes on an island.

which leads to

$$E(U_i) = \begin{cases} W - aL(1 - s_i) - be_i - cs_i & \text{if } e_i \leq e_{(k)}, \\ W - be_i - cs_i & \text{otherwise.} \end{cases} \tag{8}$$

An attacker might be interested in such a strategy if the return on attack effort is relatively low, e.g., when distributing spam. It is also relevant to an attacker with limited skills, a case getting more and more frequent with the availability of automated attack toolboxes [39]; or, when the attacker's goal is to commandeer the largest number of machines using the smallest investment possible [18].

k-Weakest-target security game with mitigation (*loosely coupled*): This game is a variation on the above weakest target game. Whether an attack on the weakest protected players is successful is now dependent on each target's security level. Here, an attacker is not necessarily assured of success. In fact, if all individuals invest in full protection, not a single machine will be compromised. H_e is defined as:

$$H(e_i, e_{-i}) = \begin{cases} 1 - e_i & \text{if } e_i \leq e_{(k)} \\ 1 & \text{otherwise,} \end{cases} \tag{9}$$

so that

$$E(U_i) = \begin{cases} W - aL(1 - s_i)(1 - e_i) - be_i - cs_i & \text{if } e_i \leq e_{(k)}, \\ W - be_i - cs_i & \text{otherwise.} \end{cases} \tag{10}$$

This variation of the weakest target contribution function allows us to capture scenarios where, for instance, an attacker targets a specific vulnerability, for which an easily deployable countermeasure exists.

4   Nash Equilibrium Analysis

4.1   One Attacker, One Defender

Let us consider a general defender security function $H_e = H(e)$. For $N = 1, M = 1$, the utility functions are:

$$Blue = \begin{cases} W - aL(1 - H_e)(1 - s) - be - cs & \text{if Red attacks } (k = 1), \\ W - be - cs & \text{otherwise.} \end{cases} \tag{11}$$

$$Red = \begin{cases} aL(1 - H_e) - p_c F & \text{if Red attacks } (k = 1), \\ 0 & \text{otherwise.} \end{cases} \tag{12}$$

We observe that if $p_c F > L$ then the attacker has no incentive to be active ($a = 0, k = 0$) regardless of the defender's protection decision. On the other hand, if the expected loot (which is subject to the defender's strategy) is greater than the expected fine, a full attack ($a = 1, k = 1$) dominates other offensive strategies.

If protection is more expensive than self-insurance ($b \geq c$) then the defender has no incentive to protect. Then, self-insurance will be purchased as long as the associated cost is lower than the expected loss ($e = 0$, $s = 1$, if $L > c$ given that $a = 1$).

For an arbitrary contribution function (and $b < c$), interior equilibria may exist and are of the form:

$$H_e = 1 - \frac{p_c F}{L} \tag{13}$$

$$a = \frac{b}{L} \tag{14}$$

These conditions represent an interior solution ($0 \leq (H_e, a) \leq 1; k = 1$) as long as the expected fine for the attacker is not larger than the cost of protection ($p_c F \leq b$), and the loss from a security compromise is at least as large as protection costs ($L \geq b$).

If *only* the first condition delivers a non-permissible value (i.e., $p_c F > L$, but $L \geq b$) then there does not exist a *pure* strategy so that the attacker prefers to be active. That is, when choosing a low attack strength she would evade protection efforts by the defender, however, could not gain enough from the attack to pay for the expected fine. A highly virulent attack would immediately motivate the defender to fully protect. We defer the analysis of mixed strategies for this case to future work.

When the second condition (Eq. 14) does not bind ($L < b$), whether or not Eq. 13 holds, then the defender will remain passive ($e = 0$ and $s = 0$) and he will enable the attacker to successfully compromise his resources ($k = 1$ and $a = 1$ if $p_c F \leq L$).

For the simple contribution function, $H_e = e$, there is no interior solution. However, depending on parameter values there are three simple Nash equilibria: *Passivity*, where the defender does not protect and is attacked; *Full self-insurance* where the defender is attacked but is self-insured; and *Deterrence*, where the attacker does not attack and the defender does not protect.

Result 1: If an interior solution exists, the cost-benefit ratio, b/L, imposes limits on Red's willingness to attack. Therefore, reducing b would lead to less intense attacks and a higher expected utility for Blue. Increasing L would serve to reduce the force of attack, and to increase the willingness to protect.

4.2   One Attacker, N Defenders

Considering Eqs. (1 and 2), then the value of H_e is the same for all defenders in a tightly coupled network. In this case, $Red = akL(1 - H_e) - (1 - (1 - p_c)^k)F$. With respect to k, incentives to increase the force of attack are linear and enforcement is asymptotic. The second derivative is strictly positive; maxima can only occur on the endpoints, $k \in \{0, N\}$. Intuitively, an attacker who does not want to leave "cash on the table" will either attack all defenders (rather than a subgroup) or will remain passive.

Internal equilibria, if they exist, are of the general form (with H_0 being the contribution function if the defender defects to passivity or self-insurance unilaterally):

$$H_e = 1 - \frac{(1 - (1 - p_c)^N)F}{aNL} \qquad (15)$$

$$a = \frac{b}{L}(H_e - H_0)^{-1} \qquad (16)$$

In the following we investigate the five different canonical contribution functions to identify Nash equilibria. Note that buying both protection and self-insurance at the same time is strictly dominated for nonzero b and c in all scenarios. If not indicated otherwise all defender strategies are symmetric (i.e., all Blue will select the same strategy).

Total Effort: In a total effort game, $H_e = \frac{1}{N}\sum_{i=1}^{N} e_i$. The second derivative test indicates that the optimal strategies must be corner cases. The conditions to select between the three strategies are as follows:

Full Protection If $Nb = \min(aL, Nb, c)$, then Blue plays (e,s)=(1,0).

Full self-insurance If $c = \min(aL, Nb, c)$, then Blue plays (0,1).

Passivity If $aL = \min(aL, Nb, c)$, then Blue plays (0,0).

Result 2: In a multiple defender total effort game, the relative importance of the cost of protection for the deterrence equilibrium decreases as N increases. Red's utility grows with N in equilibria where she is active.

Weakest-Link: In a weakest-link game, $H_e = \min(e_i)$. The second derivative test indicates that self-insurance is monotone, but protection may have an internal maximum. Therefore, the pure strategies are of the form $(e_i, s_i) \in \{(0,0), (0,1), (\hat{e}_0, 0), (\hat{e}_0, 1)\}$ with $\hat{e}_0$ being a uniformly chosen protection effort of all players. Since $(\hat{e}_0, 1)$ is dominated the conditions for Nash equilibria are as follows:

Protection. If $aL > b$ and $\hat{e}_0 > \frac{aL-c}{aL-b}$, then Blue may coordinate on $(\hat{e}_0, 0)$ for any $\hat{e}_0$ between $\frac{aL-c}{aL-b}$ and an upper boundary value. For an exogenous non-strategic attacker the upper boundary is 1 [22]. Considering a strategic attacker we find that interior solutions with $(0 \le \hat{e}_0 \le 1)$ and $(0 \le a \le 1; k = N)$ may exist. Further, when the upper boundary is less than 1 (conditions can be determined from Eqs. 15 and 16) the threat of high protection may discourage the attacker but also lower the incentives for defenders to invest in protection.

Full Self-insurance. If $c = \min(aL, aL(1 - \hat{e}_0) - b\hat{e}_0, c)$, then Blue plays (0,1).

Passivity. If $aL = \min(aL, b, c)$, then Blue plays (0,0).

Result 3: In the case that full self-insurance costs more than the expected losses with protection, Red's decisions are identical to her choices in the one-on-one game and she attacks all possible targets. On the other hand, if there is a chance that the defenders would have to settle for a low $\hat{e}_0$ and full self-insurance costs less than the expected losses with this protection level then Blue can profitably defect to a self-insurance strategy. Therefore, the ability to coordinate on a high $\hat{e}_0$ is extremely important to defenders.

Protection equilibria become increasingly unlikely with increasing N if we assume that there is at least a small chance that each individual fails to coordinate successfully on a common protection level [22,40]. As Varian suggests "weakest link technology confers an advantage to small [defender] teams" [41]. Red benefits from such coordination failures.

Best Shot: In a best shot game, $H_e = \max(e_i)$. As shown in [22], there is no case in a best shot game with homogeneous defenders in which all defenders choose protection. This is easy to show with an indirect proof: If we assume there is a protection equilibrium for non-trivial parameters, then any single Blue player could profitably deviate by free-riding on his teammates [41]. Because of this, there is no symmetric pure protection equilibrium. Increasing the number of players has no effect on this finding.

Result 4: Due to an inability to coordinate on protection, defenders will prefer to shirk on protection and are vulnerable to a motivated attacker. With $b > c$ defenders will select full self-insurance. If both costs are larger than the expected loss defenders will remain passive.

k-Weakest-Target Game without mitigation: In the following we consider games for loosely coupled contribution functions. Let $\hat{e} = $ the k-th smallest e chosen by any defender i. Any Blue player choosing $e > \hat{e}$ would switch to $\hat{e} + \eta$, where $\eta \to 0$. In that case every player choosing $e < \hat{e}$ would choose $\hat{e} + 2\eta$, thus destabilizing any pure protection strategy attempts with a non-strategic attacker [22]. In Appendix A we include the detailed derivations for a mixed strategy equilibrium. Below we summarize the results.

We can derive the probability distribution function of self-protection in a mixed Nash equilibrium:

$$f = \frac{f_{e*}}{(1 + 2(2k - N)f_{e*}(e - e*))} \tag{17}$$

$$\text{where } f_{e*} = \frac{b}{aL(N - k)\binom{N-1}{j}} \tag{18}$$

This allows us to compute how often strategy $(e, s) = (0, 1)$ is played:

$$q = .5 + (\sum_{j=0}^{k-1} \binom{N-1}{j} - \frac{c}{aL}2^{N-1})/\binom{N-1}{k-1}(N - k) \tag{19}$$

Result 5: If k is not limited, Red will always play (1,N). A mixed strategy for defenders exists. The defensive strategy is given by Eqs. (17 - 19).

k-Weakest-Target Game with Mitigation: A more nuanced version of the above game allows players a degree of individual protection in a loosely coupled scenario. In this case, a pure full protection equilibrium exists as long as protection is less expensive than self-insurance. Furthermore, to find additional mixed strategies an analysis quite similar to the above can find a probability distribution of strategies for Blue. Please refer to Appendix A for the general approach to derive the results. The probability distribution function f of self-protection in a mixed Nash equilibrium is:

$$f = \frac{\frac{b}{aL} - .5^{N-1}\sum_{j=0}^{k-1}\binom{N-1}{j} + \binom{N-1}{k-1}(N-k).5^{N-2}f_{e*}(e - e^*)}{(1-e)\binom{N-1}{k-1}(N-k).5^{N-2}[1 + 2(2k - N)f_{e*}(e - e^*)]}$$

$$\text{where } f_{e*} \approx [\frac{b}{aL} - .5^{N-1}\sum_{j=0}^{k-1}\binom{N-1}{j}]/(1 - e^*)\binom{N-1}{k-1}(N-k).5^{N-2}$$

This distribution is asymptotic at $e = 1$, indicating the benefit of mitigation. Interestingly, the probability of self-insurance is identical to the unmitigated case (see Eq. 19).

From Red's point of view, k is no longer necessarily increasing after its second root. Increasing k too high will force Blue to protect. In this case, because Red is monotone in a, she can first maximize this parameter. She will then choose k such that the cumulative binomial distribution is smaller than the cost benefit ratio, $(k, N, e^*) < b/L$. Blue then backs down into the mixed strategy, leading to a Nash equilibrium.

Result 6: In the weakest target game with mitigation we find that Red actually attacks fewer targets (but with more force) compared to the other games, and Blue players protect and self-insure according to their mixed strategy. Furthermore, as N increases, so does the number of targets that Red attacks.

4.3   M Attackers, N Defenders

Now that the various forms of contribution functions have been analyzed we can generalize from one attacker to $M \in \mathbb{N}$ attackers. We denote with m ($0 \leq m \leq M$) the number of players who decide to engage in offensive actions. Assuming that Blue does not suffer multiple losses from being compromised by one attacker or many, we find Red's new attack force, a_j, by substitution.

Let a be the total strength of all attackers, and a_j the strength of an individual, we can substitute $(1 - (1 - a_j)^m) = a$ into Eq. 11. That is, we assume that defenders suffer from an increased attack force when multiple malefactors engage in offensive actions. Rearranging we find the new strategy, $a_j = 1 - (1 - \frac{b}{L})^{1/m}$. As the number of attackers, m, increases (given a fixed number of defenders, N), each Red will attack with proportionally less force in every game where Red plays an interior strategy. Given a sufficiently large increase in the number of attackers, the resulting decrease in attack force necessary for an interior outcome creates disincentives for attackers to be active considering the expected fine. At this tipping point the group of attackers is deterred from attacking simultaneously. However, if all the Red quit attacking at once, then it becomes profitable for an individual malefactor to restart her offensive efforts, resulting in an unstable outcome. As the number of attackers grows large, they begin to suffer coordination problems (similar to defenders in the best shot game).

Result 7: For tightly coupled games, we can derive the tipping point as m increases (with a being the total aggregate strength of all attackers):

$$(1 - (1 - a)^{1/m})NL > p_c F \tag{20}$$

$$m > \frac{ln(1 - a)}{ln(1 - \frac{p_c F}{NL})} \tag{21}$$

This finding could explain several practices observable with modern malware. For example, security researchers have recorded special cases where worms are coded to attack and replace other worms (e.g., the Netsky email virus removed Mydoom infections), or to strengthen the defenses of a compromised machine to prevent the infiltration by other malicious code (e.g., by downloading patches). Some malware authors utilize command-and-control infrastructures that allow them to throttle attacks, limit damages to compromised machine that might get users' attention (e.g., popups) and, more generally, avoid saturation effects.

5   Conclusions

There are several key findings from this research:

Nash Equilibria: Although the boundaries vary, these games all share common classes of Nash Equilibria:

- Full Attack: In the case that either the cost of self-insurance or the maximum loss is strictly less than the cost of protection, Red attacks with full force, and Blue suffers that cost or self-insures as appropriate.
- Deterrence: If the fine is so high that attacking with any force is not profitable, Red will not attack at all, and Blue need not protect or self-insure.
- Interior Equilibria: There are certain games (as in the weakest-link) where the attacker is active, and the defender protects, but not fully.

Non-equilibrium states: There are several states where pure equilibria do not exist. First, the weakest target game without mitigation and the best shot game do not offer pure symmetric protection strategies. Second, if the number of attackers increases, the network might reach a state of saturation creating coordination problems for the attackers.

Attackers: Including attackers in the game-theoretic model has several important implications. For example, expanding to the multiplayer case, there is an asymmetry between attackers and defenders. Because attackers can attack multiple targets, they can attack fewer defenders and still be profitable. This pushes defenders into undesirable states of protecting when attackers do not attack or not protecting when they do. Taking into account strategic attackers, full protection equilibria become increasingly unlikely.

Loosely and Tightly Coupled Contribution Functions: The attacker's strategy depends on the nature of the contribution function just as much as this is the case for defenders. On the one hand, in the case of a tightly coupled contribution function, attacking all defenders strictly dominates attacking a subset. On the other hand, this is not necessarily true in a loosely coupled game. Instead, it may be more profitable to target fewer defenders, but with more force.

Deterrence: Attackers may be deterred from attacking if the expected fine outweighs the expected earnings from an attack. This occurs when the attacker's break even point is greater than N. In other words, there are not enough targets to be profitable. This does imply that a government could attempt to set enforcement levels and fines such that attackers will be deterred.

Asymmetry: The fact that Red can attack many targets leads to an asymmetrical game where Red has more ability to control the state of the game than Blue.

Attacker Coordination: Bounded attacks become less likely as the number of attackers increases. If the attackers are not coordinated, they will eventually attack with too much force causing the defenders to protect. Compared to a deterrence equilibrium, this is costly for both the defenders and the attackers. This implies that sophisticated attackers will rely on command-and-control infrastructures rather than autonomous agents to manage the spread of their code. These findings also suggest that malware authors will attempt to make their code appear sufficiently benign, so that defenders are not incentivized to protect against it.

Another way that attackers may solve the coordination problem is through the open market. Phishers started to develop a market economy in which also botnet herders participate [1,16]. Botnets can now be rented for spam campaigns and distributed denial of service (DDoS) attacks [42]. This kind of marketplace could have several effects: by leasing time on their bots attackers get additional utility; by utilizing a market it may become harder to track who really launched an attack, decreasing the likelihood of being caught; and this process also significantly reduces the barrier to entry for launching distributed attacks.

Limitations and future work: We have made several assumptions, for example, the homogeneity of the players. In prior work, we have shown that heterogeneity can have a significant impact on defenders' strategies [23]. Other assumptions include the perfect attack and defense assumptions. In reality, there is often no such thing as either. As Anderson points out [3], there is often an asymmetry in finding exploits that favors the attacker.

We have not explicitly accounted for research and reconnaissance costs. These would serve as a barrier to entry for potential attackers. Furthermore, we have assumed that attackers are not directly turning against each other. In reality, rival botnets may be more tempting targets than 'civilians,' and botnet hijacking has been observed 'in the wild' [24].

Another limitation is the assumption of symmetry between the loss for defender and the gain for attackers. We can consider divergent subjective utilities: a) the defense loss is higher (then we would expect deterrence equilibria to be more common), or b) the offense gain is higher (then we would expect internal equilibria to be most common). Similarly, it may not be always the case that an attacker will benefit from a security compromise if the defender is self-insured. For example, installing spyware to gather personal information is of reduced utility if the defender has implemented a credit alert or freeze.

Possible extensions include a model of defensive hacking and activities of vigilante defenders [32]. There are significant economic and ethical questions when defenders can counterattack. If a vigilante defender compromises a botnet, and damages an infected machine, it may be for the greater good, but there is a personal risk of legal liability. This is further complicated by the fact that computer security has become highly industrialized [34]. Firms providing security services and research may be in the best position to actually implement vigilante hacking. But simply eliminating attackers would reduce the need for their products.

The present analysis relies on game theory and, in particular, Nash equilibrium analysis. We plan to expand the analysis to different behavioral assumptions to narrow the gap between formal analysis and empirical observations in the field and the laboratory [21].[6] Notwithstanding, we expect that the results provided in this paper will be of interest to security practitioners and researchers alike.

References

1. Abad, C.: The economics of phishing: A survey of the operations of the phishing market. First Monday 10(9) (2005)
2. Acquisti, A., Grossklags, J.: Privacy and rationality in individual decision making. IEEE Security & Privacy 3(1), 26–33 (2005)
3. Anderson, R.: Why information security is hard - an economic perspective. In: Proceedings of the 17th Annual Computer Security Applications Conference (ACSAC 2001), New Orleans, LA (December 2001)
4. Aspnes, J., Chang, K., Yampolskiy, A.: Inoculation strategies for victims of viruses and the sum-of-squares partition problem. Journal of Computer and System Sciences 72(6), 1077–1093 (2006)
5. Becker, G.: Crime and punishment: An economic approach. Journal of Political Economy 76(2), 169–217 (1968)
6. Böhme, R., Kataria, G.: Models and measures for correlation in cyber-insurance. In: Proceedings of the Fifth Annual Workshop on Economics and Information Security (WEIS 2006), Cambridge, UK (June 2006)

---

[6] See, for example, the application of near rationality to different network games [11].

7. Bolot, J., Lelarge, M.: A new perspective on internet security using insurance. In: Proceedings of the 27th Conference on Computer Communications (INFOCOM 2008), Phoenix, AZ, April 2008, pp. 1948–1956 (2008)
8. Cameron, S.: The economics of crime deterrence: A survey of theory and evidence. Kyklos 41(2), 301–323 (1988)
9. Cavusoglu, H., Raghunathan, S., Yue, W.: Decision-theoretic and game-theoretic approaches to IT security investment. Journal of Management Information Systems 25(2), 281–304 (Fall 2008)
10. Chantler, N.: Profile of a Computer Hacker. Interpact Press, Seminole (1997)
11. Christin, N., Grossklags, J., Chuang, J.: Near rationality and competitive equilibria in networked systems. In: Proceedings of ACM SIGCOMM 2004 Workshop on Practice and Theory of Incentives in Networked Systems (PINS), Portland, OR, August 2004, pp. 213–219 (2004)
12. Chung, W., Chen, H., Chang, W., Chou, S.: Fighting cybercrime: a review and the taiwan experience. Decision Support Systems 41(3), 669–682 (2006)
13. Clark, D., Konrad, K.: Asymmetric conflict: Weakest link against best shot. Journal of Conflict Resolution 51(3), 457–469 (2007)
14. Cornes, R., Sandler, T.: The theory of externalities, public goods, and club goods, 2nd edn. Cambridge University Press, Cambridge (1996)
15. Cremonini, M., Nizovtsev, D.: Understanding and influencing attackers decisions: Implications for security investment strategies. In: Proceedings of the Fifth Annual Workshop on Economics and Information Security (WEIS 2006), Cambridge, UK (June 2006)
16. Cymru, T.: The underground economy: Priceless. ;login: The USENIX Magazine 31(6) (2006)
17. Danezis, G., Anderson, R.: The economics of resisting censorship. IEEE Security & Privacy 3(1), 45–50 (2005)
18. Franklin, J., Paxson, V., Perrig, A., Savage, S.: An inquiry into the nature and causes of the wealth of internet miscreants. In: Proceedings of the 14th ACM Conference on Computer and Communications Security (CCS 2007), Alexandria, VA, October/November 2007, pp. 375–388 (2007)
19. Gordon, S.: The generic virus writer. In: Proceedings of the International Virus Bulletin Conference, Jersey, Channel Islands, September 1994, pp. 121–138 (1994)
20. Granick, J.: Faking it: Calculating loss in computer crime sentencing. I/S: A Journal of Law and Policy for the Information Society 2(2), 207–228 (Spring/Summer 2006)
21. Grossklags, J., Christin, N., Chuang, J.: Predicted and observed behavior in the weakest-link security game. In: Proceedings of the USENIX Workshop on Usability, Privacy and Security (UPSEC 2008), San Francisco, CA (April 2008)
22. Grossklags, J., Christin, N., Chuang, J.: Secure or insure? A game-theoretic analysis of information security games. In: Proceedings of the 2008 World Wide Web Conference (WWW 2008), Beijing, China, April 2008, pp. 209–218 (2008)
23. Grossklags, J., Christin, N., Chuang, J.: Security and insurance management in networks with heterogeneous agents. In: Proceedings of the Ninth ACM Conference on Electronic Commerce (EC 2008), Chicago, IL, July 2008, pp. 160–169 (2008)
24. Higgens, K.J.: Dark Reading (April 2007)
25. Hirshleifer, J.: From weakest-link to best-shot: the voluntary provision of public goods. Public Choice 41(3), 371–386 (1983)

26. Jiang, L., Anantharam, V., Walrand, J.: Efficiency of selfish investments in network security. In: Proceedings of the 2008 Workshop on the Economics of Networks, Systems, and Computation (NetEcon 2008), Seattle, WA, August 2008, pp. 31–36 (2008)
27. Kesan, J., Majuca, R., Yurcik, W.: Three economic arguments for cyberinsurance. In: Chander, A., Gelman, L., Radin, M. (eds.) Securing Privacy in the Internet Age, pp. 345–366. Stanford University Press, Stanford (2008)
28. Kessler, G.: Defenses against distributed denial of service attacks (2000)
29. Kshetri, N.: The simple economics of cybercrimes. IEEE Security & Privacy 4(1), 33–39 (2006)
30. Kunreuther, H., Heal, G.: Interdependent security. Journal of Risk and Uncertainty 26(2–3), 231–249 (2003)
31. Moscibroda, T., Schmid, S., Wattenhofer, R.: When selfish meets evil: Byzantine players in a virus inoculation game. In: Proceedings of the 25th Annual ACM Symposium on Principles of Distributed Computing (PODC 2006), Denver, CO, July 2006, pp. 35–44 (2006)
32. Naraine, R.: Kraken botnet infiltration triggers ethics debate. eWeek.com (May 2008)
33. Pautasso, C., Wilde, E.: Why is the web loosely coupled? A multi-faceted metric for service design. In: Proceedings of the 2009 World Wide Web Conference (WWW 2009), Madrid, Spain, April 2009, pp. 911–920 (2009)
34. Potter, B.: Dirty secrets of the security industry. Defcon XV, Las Vegas (2007)
35. Radosavac, S., Kempf, J., Kozat, U.: Using insurance to increase internet security. In: Proceedings of the 2008 Workshop on the Economics of Networks, Systems, and Computation (NetEcon 2008), Seattle, WA, August 2008, pp. 43–48 (2008)
36. Schechter, S., Smith, M.: How much security is enough to stop a thief? In: Wright, R.N. (ed.) FC 2003. LNCS, vol. 2742, pp. 122–137. Springer, Heidelberg (2003)
37. Schneier, B.: Tactics, targets, and objectives. Wired.com (May 2007)
38. Swire, P.: No Cop on the Beat: Underenforcement in E-Commerce and Cybercrime. Journal on Telecommunications and High Technology Law, forthcoming (2008)
39. The Honeynet Project. Know your enemy: the tools and methodologies of the script-kiddie (July 2000), http://project.honeynet.org/papers/enemy/
40. Van Huyck, J., Battallio, R., Beil, R.: Tacit coordination games, strategic uncertainty, and coordination failure. American Economic Review 80(1), 234–248 (1990)
41. Varian, H.: System reliability and free riding. In: Camp, L., Lewis, S. (eds.) Economics of Information Security. Advances in Information Security, vol. 12, pp. 1–15. Kluwer Academic Publishers, Dordrecht (2004)
42. Weinberg, N.: Botnet economy runs wild. Network World (April 2008)

A   Mixed Strategy for Weakest Target Game Without Mitigation

We investigate whether a mixed strategy can be derived. Assume there is a cumulative distribution of protection strategies F. We can use the cumulative distribution of the binomial distribution to represent the chance that a player will be compromised given a fixed e. The expected utility of Blue is:

$$Blue = aL \sum_{j=0}^{k-1} \binom{N-1}{j} F_e^j (1 - F_e)^{N-1-j} - be_i - cs_i \qquad (22)$$

In Nash equilibria, the first order condition must hold:

$$0 = aL(N - k)\binom{N-1}{j}F_e^{k-1}(1 - F_e)^{N-1-k}(f) - b$$

$$\frac{b}{aL(N - k)\binom{N-1}{j}} = F_e^{k-1}(1 - F_e)^{N-1-k}(f)$$

$$\frac{b}{aL(N - k)\binom{N-1}{j}} = exp\{(k - 1)lnF_e + (N - 1 - k)ln(1 - F_e)\}(f)$$

$$f = \frac{b}{aL(N - k)\binom{N-1}{j}exp\{(k - 1)lnF_e + (N - 1 - k)ln(1 - F_e)\}}$$

Then we can expand the exponentiated part about $e^* =$ the median of f using a Taylor expansion. Thus,

$$f = \frac{b}{aL(N - k)\binom{N-1}{j}(\frac{1}{2})^{N-2}(1 + 2(2k - N)f_{e^*}(e - e*))} \tag{23}$$

$$\text{where } f_{e^*} = \frac{b}{aL(N - k)\binom{N-1}{j}} \tag{24}$$

$$\text{thus } f = \frac{f_{e^*}}{(1 + 2(2k - N)f_{e^*}(e - e*))} \tag{25}$$

The approximation of f about e^* is asymptotic as $e \to e*$. Knowing that Blue will never play $e > aL/b$ because of dominance, we estimate $e^* = aL/b$.

If insurance is not overpriced, then we know $F(0) = q; Blue(0,0) = c$:

$$pl\sum_{j=0}^{k-1}\binom{N-1}{j}q^j(1 - q)^{N-1-j} = c \tag{26}$$

Using a Taylor expansion again, we find:

$$\frac{1}{2}^{N-1}\sum_{j=0}^{k-1}\binom{N-1}{j} - (\frac{1}{2})^{N-1}\binom{N-1}{k-1}(N - k)(q - .5) = c/aL \tag{27}$$

$$-\binom{N-1}{k-1}(N - k)(q - .5) = \frac{c}{aL}2^{N-1} - \sum_{j=0}^{k-1}\binom{N-1}{j} \tag{28}$$

$$q = .5 + (\sum_{j=0}^{k-1}\binom{N-1}{j} - \frac{c}{aL}2^{N-1})/\binom{N-1}{k-1}(N - k) \tag{29}$$

Optimised to Fail:
Card Readers for Online Banking

Saar Drimer, Steven J. Murdoch, and Ross Anderson

Computer Laboratory, University of Cambridge, UK
http://www.cl.cam.ac.uk/users/{sd410,sjm217,rja14}

Abstract. The Chip Authentication Programme (CAP) has been introduced by banks in Europe to deal with the soaring losses due to online
banking fraud. A handheld reader is used together with the customer's
debit card to generate one-time codes for both login and transaction authentication. The CAP protocol is not public, and was rolled out without any public scrutiny. We reverse engineered the UK variant of card
readers and smart cards and here provide the first public description of
the protocol. We found numerous weaknesses that are due to design errors such as reusing authentication tokens, overloading data semantics,
and failing to ensure freshness of responses. The overall strategic error
was excessive optimisation. There are also policy implications. The move
from signature to PIN for authorising point-of-sale transactions shifted
liability from banks to customers; CAP introduces the same problem for
online banking. It may also expose customers to physical harm.

Keywords: banking security, reverse engineering, authentication, liability, chip and PIN.

1   Introduction

The late Roger Needham once remarked that 'optimisation is the process of
taking something that works and replacing it with something that almost works,
but is cheaper'. The history of cryptographic protocols – both in the research
literature and in the field – is littered with examples of optimisation; of protocols
that failed because designers had left out some contextual or other information
that, on casual inspection, had seemed unimportant but whose absence led to
catastrophic failure. Anderson and Needham thus argued that in the protocol
world, robustness is closely tied to explicitness [1]. This paper presents a new
and disturbing real-world example of an actually deployed banking protocol that
fails because it has been excessively optimised.

Online banking is growing almost everywhere; in the UK, for example, there
has been a 174% increase in the number of users between 2001 and 2007 [2].
This is easy enough to explain: online banking is convenient for customers, and
lets bankers cut their staff costs. But, as banking has moved online, fraud has
followed. Losses in the UK from online banking fraud were £21.4m in the period

R. Dingledine and P. Golle (Eds.): FC 2009, LNCS 5628, pp. 184–200, 2009.

Fig. 1. NatWest and Barclays issued CAP readers on the left and right, respectively. An opened NatWest CAP is shown in the centre. These readers are given to bank customers for free.

of January to June 2008, an increase of 185% when compared to the same period of the previous year [3].

One of the most common forms of attack is "phishing". Here, criminals send emails impersonating banks, asking customers to click on a link under some false pretence; if they do, a malicious copy of their bank's website asks for their authentication data. Another common attack involves malware; authentication details are stolen by a software keylogger on the customer's PC.

To resist these attacks, some bank websites only ask for some characters from the customer's password, or ask for them to be entered in drop-down boxes rather than at the keyboard; some banks have switched to one-time passwords such as the printed "iTAN" codes used by German banks [4], or electronic one-time-password generators such as the RSA SecurID.

However, one-time passwords are still vulnerable to a real-time man-in-the-middle attack. Here, the malware or phishing website initiates a fraudulent transaction with the customer's bank at the same time as it prompts the customer for their password or one-time code. The process may even be triggered when the customer attempts a transaction, rather than prompting them to do one. In any event, as the fraudulent transaction is being performed at the same time as the customer is trying to do a real one, a time-dependent or one-time password will still be valid.

This class of attack can be resisted by cryptographically binding the one-time code to the data of the transaction being attempted – *transaction authentication*. A robust way to do this is to provide the customer with an electronic signature device with a trustworthy display on which she could verify the transaction data, a trusted path to authorise a digital signature, and a tamper-resistant store for the signing key.

Such devices were foreseen by the EU Electronic Signature Directive which provided for signatures thus created to be admissible as evidence in legal

Fig. 2. We used FPGA boards to snoop on CAP transactions (left) and emulate a card (right). Using a USB card reader we emulated a CAP reader (centre).

proceedings. However such devices typically cost $100 or more. The Chip Authentication Programme (CAP)[1] is a lower-cost implementation of this general approach.

Individual countries have adopted different variants of CAP based on the original specification. In this paper we examine the UK version. It uses the deployed "Chip & PIN" smart card infrastructure. Participating banks have sent out handheld smart card readers, shown in Figure 1, with keypads and displays which, with a customer's card and PIN, generate one-time passwords.

Even though Chip & PIN is based on the public EMV standard (named after its initiators – Europay, MasterCard, and Visa), the CAP standard is secret and so not subject to scrutiny, despite being a critical security component the public must rely on for banking transactions. Therefore, in Section 2 we describe the results of successfully reverse engineering the system. In Section 3 we describe how CAP is used in online banking, and in Section 4 a number of security vulnerabilities we discovered in the underlying protocol and its implementation by two British banks. Finally, we propose some improvements to the system in Section 5 and discuss policy implications of the failures in Section 6.

2   Protocol Description

We used three different techniques to reverse engineer the protocol. First, we monitored communications between legitimate cards and readers (Figure 2 left), using an FPGA based protocol analyser we designed. Second, we emulated a reader and challenged the card (Figure 2 centre). Finally, we constructed an FPGA based card emulator in order to interrogate the reader (Figure 2 right). In all three cases we fully controlled the input, at either the electrical interface or keypad, so our approach was in effect an adaptive chosen text attack. We did not attempt to extract or study the code running on either the smart card or CAP reader, so we cannot be certain that we have a full implementation of the

---

[1] CAP is the MasterCard brand; Visa's version is called Dynamic Passcode Authentication (DPA).

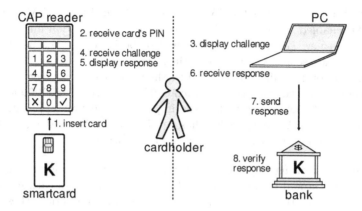

Fig. 3. In *respond* mode, after initiating an online banking session, the user inserts the card into the reader (1), keys in the PIN (2), and then enters the challenge given by the web page (3,4). When the CAP reader's response is displayed (5), the user enters it into the appropriate field on the web page (6). Since the card and bank share a cryptographic key, the bank can verify that the response is correct given what it knows about the state of the card's transaction counter (7,8).

protocol. However, based on our analysis, we have been able to generate CAP response codes and use them successfully on real bank websites. An example protocol run, collected by our protocol analyser, can be found in Appendix A.

CAP operates in three modes – *identify*, *respond*, and *sign*. These differ in the information a user is asked to enter before a response code is generated. For all three modes a PIN is required first. Thereafter, *identify* just returns a one-time code; for *respond* a numerical challenge is required; and for *sign* an account number and a value are needed. The numerical response code is a compressed version of a MAC computed by the card under its key; it is calculated over the information entered by the customer, a transaction counter, and a flag showing whether the PIN matches the one stored on the card. A *respond* transaction is shown in Figure 3.

The implementation of the CAP system is heavily based on the EMV smart card protocol being introduced throughout Europe for credit and debit card point-of-sale transactions. In the UK, EMV is known under the "Chip & PIN" brand. Using EMV as the basis for CAP reduced development and deployment costs; using the existing debit card base meant that the CAP devices themselves did not need to be personalised.

An overview of the CAP protocol flow is given below, with emphasis on how it deviates from EMV. For more information we refer the reader to the EMV specification [5].

Select application. EMV cards may be multi-application, so the reader must select the right one. The reader tests if the card is CAP enabled by searching a list of application identifiers stored on the card, and selects the first one available.

As the application identifiers for CAP are distinct from those for EMV, if a card is not CAP enabled the reader will fail to select an application and reject the card. Hence, a new generation of cards had to be issued by the participating banks before they sent CAP readers to their customers.

The application identifiers attempted by the CAP readers we have examined, in the order in which they are tried, are 0xA0000000048002, 0xA0000000038002, and 0xA0000002040000. NatWest cards implement the first application, and Barclays the second. Although HBOS has not deployed CAP readers, their cards are CAP enabled and implement the second application.

Read records. Following application selection, the reader requests a list of all the data records stored by a card. These form a hierarchy, with each node being prefixed by a one or two byte *tag*. In a standard EMV transaction, these would include account number, public key certificates, signatures, and so on. With CAP, only three entries are of interest – the card data object lists (CDOL1 and CDOL2), identified by tags 0x8C and 0x8D respectively, and the CAP bit filter[2], identified by the tag 0x9F56. Tag 0x9F55 is also present on cards, with value 0xA0, but its purpose is unclear.

PIN verification. Once the reader has successfully read all available records, it prompts the customer for a 4-digit PIN. This is sent to the card as the payload to the EMV standard VERIFY command. If three consecutive PIN verifications fail, the card will lock itself until taken to an ATM and reset with the correct PIN. While the EMV standard allows for a transaction to continue if the PIN verification fails or is omitted, the CAP reader requires that the card accept the PIN before continuing. Surprisingly, this is a serious bug; we'll discuss the reason in Section 4.1.

Cryptogram generation. Next, the reader requests an application cryptogram from the card, using the GENERATE AC command. The reader first requests an Authorization Request Cryptogram (ARQC), indicating that it wishes to perform an online EMV transaction. The card then responds with an ARQC, indicating that the card is willing to do so. If this was an EMV transaction, the reader would send the ARQC to the bank for verification, but it cannot do so because it is offline. So the reader then requests an Application Authentication Cryptogram (AAC), indicating that it wishes to cancel the transaction.

A similar transaction flow might be seen during a point-of-sale transaction if a shop is only willing to accept online transactions but fails to connect to the bank (e.g. if the phone line is engaged). This protocol may have been designed so that CAP maintains maximum compatibility with EMV smart card applications. While EMV supports offline transactions by requesting a Transaction Certificate (TC) instead of an ARQC, some card risk-management algorithms may lock up if there are too many consecutive offline attempts. Cancelling the transaction should reset the smart card's risk-management parameters.

---

[2] The CDOL name and tag are defined in the EMV specification, but the CAP bit filter is not. We therefore had to coin our own term for it.

Table 1. Relevant CAP fields and their values

Field	Tag (hex)	Value (hex)
Terminal Country Code	9F1A	0000
Terminal Verification Results	95	8000000000
Transaction Currency Code	5F2A	0000
Transaction Date	9A	010101 for app. 0xA0000000038002, 000000 for app. 0xA0000000048002
Authorisation Response Code	8A	5A33
Other Amount	9F03	000000000000
Transaction Type	9C	00

The first and second GENERATE AC call is controlled by the CDOL1 and CDOL2 respectively. Each CDOL lists a series of tags, specifying which data items must be included in the command payload. The two fields used for CAP are Authorized Amount (AA – 0x9F02), and Unpredictable Number (UN – 0x9F37). Normally, the former would store the value of the transaction, and the latter would be a terminal supplied nonce. For CAP *identify*, both are zero; for *respond*, AA is zero and UN is the challenge; and for *sign*, AA is the transaction value and UN is the destination account number.

Other tags in the CDOL have hard-coded default values provided by the CAP reader. The values we have observed being produced by the NatWest and Barclays CAP readers are shown in Table 1.

Reader response formatting. The response to a GENERATE AC call includes a 16-bit application transaction counter (ATC), a Cryptogram Identification Data (CID) type code, Issuer Application Data (IAD) which includes the result of the PIN verification, and an Application Cryptogram (AC) which is a MAC over all this data. The MAC method used to calculate the cryptogram, and the structure of the IAD, are not specified by the EMV standard, as they are proprietary to the card issuer. In practice, a common choice is 3DES CBC MAC, under a session key. This session key is derived from a card master key shared between the issuing bank and the card, and the ATC. One example session key derivation algorithm, designed to resist power analysis, is described in the optional part (Common Core Definitions) of the EMV specifications [5, Book 2, Annex 1.3].

The data from the first GENERATE AC call and the CAP bit filter (from the read records stage) are used to generate the response code. Going through each bit of the bit filter from left to right, if the bit is a '1' the corresponding bit from the GENERATE AC response is kept; otherwise it is discarded. The result is a number with the same number of bits as the bit filter has '1's. Finally, this number is converted from binary to decimal with leading zeros are removed; the result is then displayed on the reader's screen. An example of this process is shown in Table 2.

Table 2. An example of a NatWest card CAP computation. The fields of the GENERATE AC response are the Cryptogram Identification Data (CID, 1 byte), Application Transaction Counter (ATC, 2 bytes), Application Cryptogram (AC, 8 bytes), and the Issuer Application Data (IAD, variable length).

	CID	ATC	AC	IAD
Card output	80	A52D	AD452EF6BA769E4A	06770A03A48000
Bitmask	00	001F	0000000000FFFFF	00000000008000
Filter	..	..0D	...........69E4A	...........8...
Filter (binary)	0	1|101 0|110 1|001 1|110 0|100 1|010 1		
Filter (hex)		1AD3C95		
Decimal response		28130453		

We have seen the following bit filters:

NatWest 00 001F 0000000000FFFFF 00000000008000
Barclays 80 00FF 000000000001FFFF 00000000000000
HBOS   80 007F E00000000003FFF 00000000008000

The NatWest Bank uses a bit filter that selects the five least significant bits of the ATC, the 20 least significant bits of the MAC, and one bit from the proprietary issuer application data field. Barclays uses a bit filter that selects the top bit of the cryptogram type, the least significant eight bits of the ATC, and the least significant 17 bits of the MAC. HBOS uses a bit filter that selects the top bit of the cryptogram type, the least significant seven bits of the ATC, 17 non-contiguous MAC bits, and one bit from the proprietary issuer application data field. The CID type field should always be 0x80 for an ARQC – perhaps it is selected because an AAC may be generated, or simply to ensure a leading-one and so a fixed-length response.

Response verification. Since the bank knows the input to the GENERATE AC call, and can reconstruct the ATC provided it knows the most significant bits not included in the response, it can repeat the MAC and check if the response entered by the customer matches the expected value.

3   Use in Online Banking

CAP provides an authentication token, but does not specify how it should be used. Each bank has made its own decision on which of the three modes to use, and the semantics of the data fields. This is problematic from a usability perspective, since the inconsistent user experience will make it easier for phishing attacks to manipulate user behaviour.

NatWest only uses the *respond* mode, with an 8-digit challenge. For money transfers, the first four digits of the challenge are random and the last four are the last four digits of the destination account number. Where there is no account number, such as transactions to change personal details, the last four digits are '4444'. Logging into online banking does not require the CAP code, and the value of a transaction is not authenticated.

In contrast, Barclays does require an *identify* response for login. For performing a transaction, a *sign* response is required, with destination account number and transaction value entered. A significant weakness is that there is no bank-provided freshness in the transaction. While the ATC does ensure that a response cannot be replayed, the bank has no assurance that the CAP's response was generated recently.

4   Vulnerabilities

4.1   Card Theft

A serious problem is that CAP readers may be used during mugging. Since the roll-out of Chip & PIN, a criminal who has stolen a card needs to know its PIN to use it in card-present transactions. In July 2008 two French students were tortured to death in their London residence six days after it was broken into and a computer stolen. Days after the murders the police revealed that the attackers were after the students' card PINs [6]. In February 2007, two Manchester men murdered a 62 year old security guard after he refused to reveal his card's PIN [7].

Previously, muggers marched a victim to an ATM to ensure he gave them the right PIN. Now, with CAP, criminals have a portable device that will tell them if their victim is lying. While the EMV protocol always permitted such a device to be built, that requires technical skill, and wasn't in practice done. CAP has made the capability ubiquitous. It reduces the risk to muggers, as now they can keep their victims in a quiet place, and not risk being caught or seen by CCTV by going near an ATM. It would have been easy enough for the banks to design CAP without revealing the result of the PIN verification, but they failed to foresee the risk.

In our view, this was negligent: authentication tokens designed by other firms, such as the Racal Watchword (also known as Sytek PFX Passport [8]), would generate an erroneous response if the wrong PIN was entered but would not indicate this to the user, and so are not vulnerable. Worse, the two banks that have flooded the UK with CAP readers have thereby placed not only their own customers in harm's way, but have also endangered the customers of other banks who have enabled their debit cards for CAP. It remains to be seen whether customers will be able to demand cards that are not CAP-enabled and thus do not put them at needless physical risk.

There are other issues related to card theft. For example, if a customer is issued with an ATM card, the same card and PIN will be used for CAP, and so the PIN digits on the reader will wear down. Because customers are encouraged to carry their CAP readers around with them, it may be stolen along with their cards, perhaps telling the thief which digits to try. If the PIN has 4 distinct digits this leaves 24 different orderings, this increases the chance of an attacker guessing the correct PIN in three attempts from 1 in 3333 to 1 in 8. If a customer has multiple cards with the same PIN, the attacker has even better odds.

4.2 Software Implementation

CAP was intended to offer a trustworthy user device to defeat the malware that infests ever more PCs. However, it is inconvenient for users, and prevents integration between home/office banking software and online accounts. Therefore, there is demand for a software implementation of CAP, which sends commands to a smart card connected to a PC. With some reverse-engineering effort, and access to the public EMV specifications, it is straightforward to implement this system, because the CAP readers contain no secret. We may therefore expect this demand to be met by software vendors, leading to malware-infected PCs having unfettered access to smart cards and PINs, not only opening up online banking fraud, but also allowing cloned ATM magnetic strip cards to be made and relay attacks [9] to be implemented[3].

4.3 Middleperson Attacks

A fundamental problem with smart card payment at the point of sale is that the customer has no trustworthy display to show what transaction the card is authorising. Drimer and Murdoch [9] demonstrated how this weakness could be exploited by a criminal who sets up a tampered Chip & PIN terminal, which displays one transaction, but actually is relaying the smart card communications to a counterfeit card being used for a much higher value transaction. Also, since the same card and PIN are used for ATM withdrawals, a criminal could also withdraw cash. Since CAP introduces yet another role for the smart card, a criminal with a tampered Chip & PIN terminal could generate CAP responses as well.

In current online banking, both static identifiers (i.e. username and password) and a CAP response are typically required. The risk of wide-scale attacks is limited so long as these static identifiers are not stored on the card. However, targeted attacks against high net-worth individuals – whale phishing, or whaling – are becoming a problem. One example is an attack against the Novalis Ubuntu Institute in South Africa [10]. Here, a phishing or malware attack collected the CFO's account credentials. In themselves, these are not sufficient to place a transaction, because an authorisation code is also sent to the registered account holder's mobile phone. So one criminal went to the mobile phone shop impersonating her driver, offered a counterfeit ID and the phone number of a female accomplice who impersonated the CFO herself, and requested a new SIM for the CFO's account. He used this, along with the account credentials, to empty the institute's account of R90 460 (approximately £6 000). We understand that the bank and phone company are disputing liability for this fraud.

---

[3] We are aware of at least one C implementation of CAP, although it has the Barclays bit filter hard-coded – http://aa.gg/free/barclays-pinsentry.c

A similar attack could be performed with CAP. The customer, using a tampered Chip & PIN terminal, would insert their card and enter their PIN as usual. The terminal would then generate the necessary CAP responses, and optionally also carry out the legitimate transaction. Shortly after, the customer would receive a personalised phone call or email, stating that a suspicious transaction had been noticed (stating the shop name they just used), asking for their online banking credentials. Since Barclays only uses *identify* and *sign* mode, there is no server-provided freshness or a timestamp, so the previously collected responses can be used, provided the customer had not logged into online banking in the meantime. With NatWest, which uses *respond*, there is a server-provided nonce, so the fraudulent transaction has to be in near real-time, and account credentials would need to be collected before the CAP responses were generated. The banks could resist this problem by offering separate CAP-only cards, but NatWest refused to do so for one of us.

CAP has also been proposed for authenticating online purchases, through the "Verified by Visa" and "MasterCard SecureCode" schemes. Here the problem might be even worse, as most if not all the details needed for an online purchase are stored or printed on the card. CAP is also being rolled out for authenticating citizens to the "Government Gateway", a single sign-on system for accessing UK government services [11]. Currently the government are believed to be issuing cards specifically for this purpose, so the relay attack above would be resisted, but if they try to optimise by sharing the existing card base then attacks could be expected.

4.4 Supply-Chain Infiltration

CAP was unpopular when introduced [12], as customers did not want to have a reader for each bank, or have to carry them around to use online banking both at home, work, or while travelling. Customers were reassured that other banks' readers are compatible, and they can use another person's reader if they do not have their own. This behaviour makes it easy to infiltrate the CAP supply chain. For example, CAP readers are available for sale on eBay – a criminal could tamper with them so that they copy the chip details (which on many cards includes a copy of the magnetic strip) and record the PIN.

Later, the CAP reader could disable itself, so the owner will send it back to the seller for a refund. The criminal could then make fraudulent ATM withdrawals abroad where magnetic strip transactions are accepted. The CAP reader could also prompt for other details, such as the printed CVV code or online banking credentials, for use in the attack described in Section 4.3. An enhancement to the attack would be to send a CD with the CAP reader, which auto-installs malware to collect online banking credentials. Criminals could even install a compact GSM module into the CAP for sending back information in real-time. The police have already found Chip & PIN terminals that have been tampered with during or soon after manufacture and contain GSM mobile phones to send card and PIN data to criminals [13].

4.5   Social Engineering

The security of CAP depends on users properly understanding the semantics of the data they are being asked to enter into the reader. That is, for Barclays, the customer must verify the destination account number from a trustworthy source before entering it. For NatWest, the customer must verify that the last four digits of the challenge provided to them by the website match the last four digits of their desired destination bank account number. These instructions are complicated, unintuitive, and not made clear to customers. It is therefore likely that a phishing website could induce a customer to enter fraudulent details into the CAP reader, and send the response to the attacker. This exploit is made even more likely by the vague prompts for each data item. Rather than asking for the destination account number for a payment, the Barclays CAP reader simply displays 'REF:'.

4.6   Protocol Weaknesses

The CAP protocol has been highly optimised to reduce the amount of information customers need to enter and to maximise backwards compatibility – this has introduced vulnerabilities. For example, the lack of server freshness allows CAP responses to be requested long before they are needed, as described in Section 4.3. Another flaw is the overloading of the Unpredictable Number field of the input to GENERATE AC command: in *respond* mode it is the challenge, but in *sign* mode it is the destination account number. This means that a CAP response in *sign* mode for a zero transaction is a valid *respond* mode response.

An attacker could use this property in a social engineering attack, to defeat customers who are trained to be suspicious about *respond* mode. By asking the victim to perform a 'test transaction' to a dummy account, and assuring them the value is £0 so they are safe, the attacker can get a valid response and use it for fraudulent purposes. Currently, the risk of this attack is low, because only the Barclays CAP reader accepts a £0 transaction, and Barclays do not currently use *respond* mode – it is unclear whether this is by design or fortuitous accident. However it does illustrate the fragility of the protocol, and the failure to follow accepted design principles such as type explicitness [1].

Another example of excessive optimisation is in the NatWest protocol variant, of including a nonce as the first four digits of the *respond* mode challenge. Initially, the server provided nonce appears to defeat the attack in Section 4.3, because the nonce cannot be discovered without getting the online banking credentials first. However, there is a time-space tradeoff – if the shop's malicious Chip & PIN terminal requests a large number of responses from the card (with random nonces), and then later requests a sufficient number of challenges from the online banking site, there will be a nonce collision and so he would know a valid response. With 100 challenges and responses, the probability of success is approximately 63%.

The bank website could check for excessive transaction counter gaps, or limit the number of challenges generated. However, the card's transaction counter is incremented merely by inserting it into a reader, so fairly large gaps will be common and locking accounts on this basis would increase support call costs. In fact, after deploying CAP, banks have removed other protections – Barclays lifted their transaction limit from £1 000 to £10 000. Even if this attack is currently detected, the small nonce creates a fragile protocol and a minor website update may open the vulnerability again.

5   Fixing the Vulnerabilities

The basic principle behind CAP – a trusted user interface and secure cryptographic microprocessor – is sound. However the system has been optimised literally to death. Re-using ATM cards for point of sale and CAP saved money but created a vulnerability to relay attack, and increased the risk of violent mugging and murder. Omitting a server-provided nonce removed assurance that responses are freshly generated. Overloading fields introduce a social engineering vulnerability, as it makes the system model too complex for the average user to be expected to visualize.

The type confusion between *respond* and *sign* could be fixed on the CAP reader by including a response-type flag in the GENERATE AC input. Also, the time-memory attack against nonce guessing could be mitigated by a narrower window for acceptable values of the ATC. However, the other flaws require a more substantial re-design. The mugging vulnerability is a side-effect of the EMV design – a PIN can be checked by the card itself, with no authentication. Adopting the Racal Watchword approach, of returning an erroneous response if the wrong PIN is entered, would fix this problem, but harm usability.

The German CAP variant, TAN generator (HHD 1.3) [14], incorporates defences against a number of the attacks we discuss in the paper. The challenge displayed by the bank website includes a prefix which customises the user prompts. This reduces the risk of social engineering because the field descriptions are more specific (e.g. 'account number' or 'IBAN', rather than 'REF'). The prefix is also incorporated in the response calculation, fixing the type confusion vulnerability. All types of challenges may include a random nonce (up to 7 digits), providing an assurance of freshness. Finally, PIN verification by the card is optional, reducing the risk from mugging.

One error in CAP appears to have been trying too hard to reduce the number of characters the user has to type. This is the root cause of several vulnerabilities. Only including the last four digits of the account number in the NatWest system increases the risk of a fraudster having a matching or similar account. This, and the inadequate or missing nonce, could be resolved by having a higher bandwidth channel between the computer and CAP reader, so not requiring the customer to re-type the transaction, allow full account details to be displayed, and permit a large nonce to be incorporated in the response.

One example of a high-bandwidth channel is the USB-connected FinTS (Financial Transaction Services) class 3 smart card reader, incorporating a keypad and display [15]. This would be problematic for use in Internet cafés, inconvenient to carry, and may require complicated driver installation. The Cronto transaction authentication system [16] uses the visual channel, generating a specialised barcode, read by a camera phone or a dedicated client device. As with a class 3 smart card reader, full transaction details are displayed without the inconvenience and security implications of manual input, but it requires no physical connection to the PC. A PIN may optionally be used, and as with Racal Watchword, it does not provide confirmation to a mugger if the entered PIN is incorrect. In addition, customers could be given a duress PIN [17] (as offered with RSA SecurID) which permits access to the system but that triggers an alarm at the bank.

Making it harder to implement CAP in software would also have been desirable for security. Making the specification secret was insufficient as it could be reverse engineered, so following Kerckhoffs' principles [18], a key should be embedded in the CAP reader, which is used to HMAC the response. If the key is global across all readers, there is a risk of compromise, even if stored in tamper-resistant memory, so a key revocation procedure would be needed. Switching to a per-device key would be more secure. It would prevent customers from sharing CAP readers, between banks or customers, or buying them off eBay but this may in fact be beneficial, as discussed in Section 4.4.

6   Policy Implications

In many respects, CAP is an improvement over the existing static password scheme. However, it may not be beneficial to customers because while banks are liable for fraud due to forged signatures, there is no statutory protection for the victims of electronic fraud [19]. UK banks have also recently changed the voluntary code of practice – the Banking Code – to make customers liable for fraud if they do not have up-to-date anti-virus and firewall software [20]. Having deployed a new security system, even with weaknesses, the banks have further reduced customer protection.

While the Banking Code does state that the bank must show that the customer is liable, it does not say what evidence the bank must record, what evidence is sufficient to prove liability, and who the proof must be presented to. In practice, where the case is heard by the Financial Ombudsman Service, the bank merely has to claim that a chip was read and a PIN was used [21], and the evidence used to reach this conclusion will be kept secret from the customer. We may expect a similar position to be taken when PINs are used for online banking too.

This shift in liability is particularly problematic because the specification of CAP is secret, and it is not subject to any public certification procedure. In contrast, the EU Digital Signature Directive requires Common Criteria certification, which implies a public certification report. It also requires the full transaction be authenticated, through a dedicated trusted display. This would however have cost maybe $100 per device. Instead, the banks have optimised the design, and this reminded us of the late Roger Needham's description of optimisation which we quoted in the introduction.

Recent events in financial markets have highlighted shortcomings in banking regulation in Europe and elsewhere. Here then is another shortcoming: the regulators should not have believed the banks' security models any more than their models of asset pricing and risk. In particular, regulators should not have simultaneously allowed banks to transfer liability to their customers and optimise the security engineering.

Acknowledgements

We thank the anonymous reviewers, Nicholas Bohm, Mike Bond, Joseph Bonneau, Richard Clayton, and Boris Hemkemeier for valuable comments and suggestions. Markus Kuhn and Xilinx have contributed hardware for our experiments. Saar Drimer's research is funded by Xilinx, Inc. Steven Murdoch is funded by the Tor Project and employed part-time by Cronto Ltd.

References

1. Anderson, R.J., Needham, R.M.: Robustness principles for public key protocols. In: Coppersmith, D. (ed.) CRYPTO 1995. LNCS, vol. 963, pp. 236–247. Springer, Heidelberg (1995)
2. APACS: Online banking usage amongst over 55s up fourfold in five years (August 2007), http://www.apacs.org.uk/media_centre/press/08_24_07.html
3. APACS: APACS announces latest fraud figures (September 2008), http://www.apacs.org.uk/APACSannounceslatestfraudfigures.htm
4. RedTeam: iTAN online-banking security system. CAN-2005-2779 (August 2005), http://www.redteam-pentesting.de/advisories/rt-sa-2005-014.txt
5. EMVCo, LLC: EMV 4.1. (June 2004), http://www.emvco.com/
6. Taylor, M.: Police think French pair tortured for pin details. The Guardian (July 2008), http://www.guardian.co.uk/uk/2008/jul/05/knifecrime.ukcrime
7. Jenkins, R.: 'brainless thugs' get life term. The Times (May 2008), http://www.timesonline.co.uk/tol/news/uk/crime/article3850647.ece
8. Wong, R.M., Berson, T.A., Feiertag, R.J.: Polonium: an identity authentication system. In: IEEE Symposium on Security and Privacy, p. 101 (1985)
9. Drimer, S., Murdoch, S.J.: Keep your enemies close: Distance bounding against smartcard relay attacks. In: USENIX Security Symposium (August 2007)
10. Finn, C.: MTN not budging on fraud issue. IOL technology (May 2008), http://www.ioltechnology.co.za/article_page.php?iSectionId=2885&iArticl%eId=4402087
11. Lomas, N.: Government gateway 2.0 looks to fatter future. silicon.com (October 2007), http://www.silicon.com/publicsector/0,3800010403,39168629,00.htm
12. Make Card Readers Optional (2008), http://www.stopthecardreaders.org/
13. Samuel, H.: Chip and pin scam 'has netted millions from British shoppers'. Telegraph (October 2008), http://www.telegraph.co.uk/news/newstopics/politics/lawandorder/3173346%/Chip-and-pin-scam-has-netted-millions-from-British-shoppers.html

14. ZKA: ZKA-TAN-Generator: Belegungsrichtlinien für die Dynamisierung der TAN (January 2008),
http://www.hbcizka.de/dokumente/spezifikation_deutsch/
Belegungsrichtli%nien%20TANGenerator%20ve1.3%20final%20version.pdf
15. Rütten, C., Bachfeld, D.: Ausweispflicht: Sicheres home-banking mit der chipkarte. c't (17), 98–103 (2008),
http://www.heise.de/kiosk/archiv/ct/08/17/098_Ausweispflicht
16. Cronto: Products datasheet,
http://www.cronto.com/download/Cronto_Products_Datasheet.pdf
17. Davida, G., Frankel, Y., Tsiounis, Y., Yung, M.: Anonymity control in E-cash systems. In: Luby, M., Rolim, J.D.P., Serna, M. (eds.) FC 1997. LNCS, vol. 1318, pp. 1–16. Springer, Heidelberg (1997)
18. Kerckhoffs, A.: La cryptographie militaire. Journal des sciences militaires 9, 5–38 (1883)
19. Bohm, N., Brown, I., Gladman, B.: Electronic commerce: Who carries the risk of fraud? The Journal of Information, Law and Technology (3) (October 2000),
http://www2.warwick.ac.uk/fac/soc/law/elj/jilt/2000_3/bohm/
20. Banking Code Standards Board: The banking code (March 2008),
http://www.bankingcode.org.uk/
21. Drimer, S., Murdoch, S.J., Anderson, R.: Thinking inside the box: system-level failures of tamper proofing. In: IEEE Symposium on Security and Privacy, Oakland, May 2008, pp. 281–295 (2008)

A   Annotated Protocol Log

Collected from a NatWest reader and card performing a *respond* computation (ISO 7816, T=0 protocol). Personal details have been redacted.

```
Command: 00a4040007 (select application)
Proc:    a4
Data:    a0000000048002
Proc:    61
Status:  6112 (more data available)

Command: 00c0000012 (application selected)
Proc:    c0
Data:    6f108407a0000000048002a5055f2d02656e
Proc:    90
Status:  9000 (OK)

Command: 80a8000002 (initiate transaction)
Proc:    a8
Data:    8300
Proc:    61
Status:  6108 (more data available)

Command: 00c0000008 (transaction initiated)
```

```
Proc:     c0
Data:     8006100008010100
Proc:     90
Status:   9000 (OK)
```

```
Command: 00b2010c00 (get static data length)
Proc:     6c
Status:   6c57 (wrong length)
```

```
Command: 00b2010c57 (read static data)
Proc:     b2
Data:     7055
            8e0a 00000000000000000100 (CVM list)
        9f5501 a0 (unknown)
        9f5612 00001f00000000000fffff00000000008000 (bit filter)
        8c15 9f02069f03069f1a0295055f2a029a039c019f3704 (CDOL1)
        8d17 8a029f02069f03069f1a0295055f2a029a039c019f3704 (CDOL2)
Proc:     90
Status:   9000 (OK)
```

```
Command: 80ca9f1700 (get PIN try counter length)
Proc:     6c
Status:   6c04 (wrong length)
```

```
Command: 80ca9f1704 (get PIN try counter)
Proc:     ca
Data:     9f170103 (3 remaining tries)
Proc:     90
Status:   9000 (OK)
```

PIN entered

```
Command: 0020008008 (verify PIN)
Proc:     20
Data:     24xxxxffffffffff
Proc:     90
Status:   9000 (OK)
```

Challenge entered: 12345678

```
Command: 80ae80001d (generate AC)
Proc:     ae
Data:     00000000000000000000000000008000000000000000000000012345678
Proc:     61
Status:   6114 (more data available)
```

```
Command: 00c0000014 (return ARQC)
Proc:    c0
Data:    8012800042b7f9a572da74caff06770a03a48000
Proc:    90
Status:  9000 (OK)

Command: 80ae00001f (generate AC)
Proc:    ae
Data:    5a3300000000000000000000000000000080000000000000000000000012345678
Proc:    61
Status:  6114 (more data available)

Command: 00c0000014 (return AAC)
Proc:    c0
Data:    80120000424f1c597723c97d7806770a03258000
Proc:    90
Status:  9000 (OK)
```

Response returned: 4822527

Expecting the Unexpected: Towards Robust Credential Infrastructure

Shouhuai Xu[1] and Moti Yung[2]

[1] Department of Computer Science, University of Texas at San Antonio
shxu@cs.utsa.edu
[2] Google Inc. and Department of Computer Science, Columbia University
moti@cs.columbia.edu

Abstract. Cryptographic credential infrastructures, such as Public key infrastructure (PKI), allow the building of trust relationships in electronic society and electronic commerce. At the center of credential infrastructures is the methodology of digital signatures. However, methods that assure that credentials and signed messages possess *trustworthiness* and *longevity* are not well understood, nor are they adequately addressed in both literature and practice. We believe that, as a basic engineering principle, these properties have to be built into the credential infrastructure rather than be treated as an after-thought since they are crucial to the long term success of this notion. In this paper we present a step in the direction of dealing with these issues. Specifically, we present the basic engineering reasoning as well as a model that helps understand (somewhat formally) the trustworthiness and longevity of digital signatures, and then we give basic mechanisms that help improve these notions.

Keywords: Credential infrastructures, PKI, digital signatures, key compromise, hit-and-run attack, hit-and-stick attack, insider attack.

1 Introduction

The celebrated notion of digital signing was put forth as modern cryptography started. Its security definition [10], and the security of many of its derived notions (like that of group signature [5]), does not capture the fact that the signature lives in a system and does not assure the *trustworthiness* and *longevity* of digital signatures over time within a system context, due to the following reasons.

First, trustworthiness of digital signatures is questionable when a verifier does not have other means to determine that a digital signature was indeed issued or activated by the alleged signer (as was mentioned in [8]). To see this, observe that private signing keys can be compromised in real computer systems (cf., for example, [13,24] for practical attacks). Such attacks can, in fact, defeat even advanced digital signature techniques (e.g., forward-secure signing [1,3], key-insulated signing [7], intrusion-resilient signing [17], threshold signing [6], proactive signing [23]), although the damage may be mitigated. Moreover, even if a private signing key is stored in a tamper-resistant hardware (e.g., cryptographic

R. Dingledine and P. Golle (Eds.): FC 2009, LNCS 5628, pp. 201–221, 2009.

co-processor [30] or Trusted Platform Module [27]) that may also frustrate side-channel attacks [19], the private signing function could still be compromised because an attacker, who has compromised the computer of a signer, can request the hardware to sign messages [21]. Note that compromises like the above (i.e., access to the signing function) were assumed also in the digital signature security definition of [10] as well as in the relevant variants (e.g., threshold and proactive signatures [14], group signing [2]).

Second, longevity of digital signatures becomes questionable because a dishonest signer can later "plausibly" repudiate some (past) signatures. To see this, it has been observed early on that a dishonest signer could abuse her private signing key or function to commit unlawful activities, while blaming them to the attacker who has compromised the private signing key. As an extreme example, a dishonest signer can launch attacks against her own computer so as to fool the machine forensics mechanisms and commit fraud without being held accountable. Note that such threats were not accommodated in the cryptographic model of digital signatures [10] as well as its variants (e.g., [14,2]), because it always treats the signers as the target of attacks.

The above two threats to trustworthiness and longevity of (non-anonymous and anonymous) digital signatures are **inevitable** due to the imperfection of forensics analysis mechanisms. Moreover, there is an **unexpected** threat to the trustworthiness and longevity of digital signatures — many or all of the cryptographic keys in use may be compromised — either due to a fundamental progress in cryptanalysis (e.g., a polynomial-time factorization algorithm) or due to the more likely Trojan Horses in operating systems and/or hardware devices. A specific attack of this kind is the recent incident of rogue CA [26].

Our contributions. We propose a novel model (Section 2) for helping understand the trustworthiness and longevity of digital signatures based on various realistic threats. Our model has the following features. First, it accommodates a participant we call "liability-holder" (e.g., an employer, an insurance vendor or the signer herself), which is responsible for the consequences of digital signatures. This allows us to capture insider threats (i.e., malicious signers). Second, it reflects the strength of the relevant security mechanisms: (1) *compromise-resistant* mechanisms that may be deployed to prevent attacks from compromising the private signing keys or functions, or from compromising the signers; (2) *compromise-detection* mechanisms that may be deployed to detect the compromise of private signing keys or functions; (3) *history-preservation* mechanisms that may be deployed to ensure the integrity of the system history state information; and (4) *forensics-like analysis* mechanisms that may be deployed to determine when an attack actually occurred. Third, it brings a useful concept of "grey period," during which there may be some signatures for which we do not know for sure who should be held accountable: the private signing key owners, or the attacker that has compromised the private signing keys or functions.

Our model suggests as an ultimate goal to eliminate the grey periods (i.e., uncertainties) which capture the afore-mentioned **inevitable** threats against trustworthiness and longevity of digital signatures. Although we are unable to accomplish this, we present a solution (Section 3) reducing the length of grey periods. Our solution is based on a digital signature anchoring service, whereby digital signatures can be deposited at some servers that are operated by agents we call anchors. The anchors and servers are only *semi-trusted* because they cannot frame the honest users, and any misbehaving anchors/servers can be immediately detected by any honest participant.

Finally, we extend (in Section 7) our solution to deal with the **unexpected** threats that many or all of the employed cryptosystems may be broken.

Related works. We are not aware of works similar to the model we put forth here. Nevertheless, our model can serve as a building-block in a higher-level risk management (e.g., the cost and risk analysis of operating a PKI [25]). On the other hand, regarding our concrete solution to dealing with the *inevitable*, namely for reducing the length of grey periods, there are three related prior works. These three important works represent the state of uneasiness regarding the actual trust and robustness of credential mechanisms. First among them is digital timestamping, due to Haber and Stornetta [12], which aimed at improving the trustworthiness of digital signatures. However, the similarity between times-tamping and our solution is limited to the fact that both of them use collision-resistant hash functions to build data structures that are variants of Merkle trees [22]. Whereas, the important differences between them are the following. (i) Dig-ital timestamping only asserts when a signature was issued, and does not offer any extra assurance that a signature was indeed issued by the alleged signer. That is, timestamping cannot deal with what we will call hit-and-run and in-sider attacks, which are alleviated by our solution. (ii) Our data structure adopts a "signature verification keys"-oriented organization, which leads to convenient queries and signature verifications even if the past signatures are truncated (so as to avoid monotonic increase of the tree size). This has no counterpart in [12].

Second, Just and van Oorschot [18] investigated the problem of undetected key compromises, and proposed an architecture-centric solution by introducing a third party. Although their solution bears some similarity to ours, there are important differences. (i) They assumed that each user has two cryptographic keys — one private signing key and one symmetric message authentication key — such that compromise of one does not mean compromise of the other. In their suggested scenario, one key may be stored on a user's local computer whereas the other is stored on a hardware token. In contrast, we assume that a user may keep her keys on a single computer, which may be compromised. (ii) The third party in their model is assumed to be *fully-trusted*; otherwise, their constructions would allow the third party, who may be colluding with an attacker that may have compromised the private signing key of an honest user, to frame the honest user without being held accountable. In contrast, the third party in our solution is only *semi-trusted* because it has no power to frame any user and its misbehavior can be detected by any honest user.

Third, Itkis [15] investigated a primitive-centric method, which requires the use of absolutely random bits (i.e., even pseudorandom bits are not sufficient) due to a subtle technical reason. This is very restrictive, and our architecture-centric method does not suffer from this (i.e., pseudorandomness is sufficient in our approach). Moreover, Itkis [15] did not consider the important issue of managing digital signatures, whereas we do.

Outline. Section 2 presents our model of digital signature trustworthiness and longevity. Section 3 presents a solution framework for reducing the length of grey periods. Before presenting an instantiation of the framework in Section 6, we present two building-blocks in Section 4 and Section 5, respectively. In Section 7 we discuss how to deal with the unexpected situation where cryptosystems in use are broken. Section 8 concludes this paper with some open problems. Due to space limitation, we leave the review of cryptographic primitives to Appendix A and analyses of the schemes to the full version of the present paper [29].

2   Modeling Signature Trustworthiness and Longevity

Participants. We consider a *liability-holder* in addition to the signer, verifier and attacker in the cryptographic model of digital signatures [10]. The signer or user u has a pair of public and private keys $(\mathsf{pk}_u, \mathsf{sk}_u)$ with respect to some secure signature scheme (in the sense of [10]). We assume that pk_u is published via some reliable means (e.g., certified by a certificate authority). Since the private key sk_u is often stored on u's computer, it can get compromised (e.g., when u's computer is compromised). Moreover, u can become dishonest or malicious at some point in time. We assume that all the participants are PPT algorithms.

Adversary. In addition to the traditional attacker based on pure cryptanalysis, we consider three attacks against the trustworthiness and longevity of digital signatures. Among the three attacks, which we call *hit-and-run*, *hit-and-stick* and *insider*, we are only able to deal with the hit-and-run attack and the insider attack (dealing with the hit-and-stick attack is a challenging open problem).

- Hit-and-run attack: Such an adversary compromises u's computer, steals the private key sk_u, and then leaves the computer (i.e., does not reside on the computer or tamper with it). The adversary may abuse the compromised sk_u to produce digital signatures that can be verified using pk_u.
- Hit-and-stick attack: Such an adversary resides on the victim computer after compromising it (e.g., by embedding Trojan Horses or tampering with the system). In this case, the victim computer is virtually controlled by the adversary until the compromise is detected. This is a very powerful attack that dismisses many countermeasures. For example, deploying a mechanism to tell a computer program and a human being apart (in hope of ensuring that every signing request is issued by a human being) does not necessarily defeat the attack, as long as the mechanism is implemented on the same victim computer. Defeating such an adversary is left open, and seems to require independent replication (in different machines and so on).
- Insider attack: Such an attack is launched by u herself. In the case that some third party (e.g., employer of u or some insurance provider) is the liability-holder for signatures generated using sk_u, the attack is clearly possible. Even

if u is the liability-holder, the attack is still possible because u may have the incentive to deny some (past) signatures by blaming them on the attacker who compromised sk_u. Moreover, u can launch an attack against sk_u so that she can attribute signatures to the compromise of sk_u.

Private signing key lifecycle. As depicted in Figure 1, a private signing key sk_u becomes effective (e.g., via the certification of pk_u) at time T_0, ceases functioning (e.g., via the immediate revocation of pk_u) at time T_4 because its compromise has become evident. At time T_4, forensics-like analysis may be in-

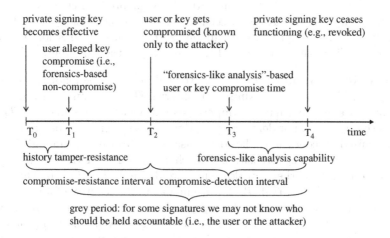

Fig. 1. A scenario of private signing key lifecycle

voked to help determine the time interval $[T_0, T_1]$ during which neither the user u nor the private key sk_u was compromised, and the time interval $[T_3, T_4]$ such that the user u or the private key sk_u was compromised at time no later than T_3. The interval $[T_1, T_3]$ can be seen as the approximation of T_2, which is the actual time at which u or sk_u gets compromised but may be known only to the attacker (i.e., the defender may never discover the time T_2 for certain).

Applying the model to analyze the hit-and-run and hit-and-stick attacks. The following observations (see the lower-half of Figure 1) apply to both attacks, no matter if u is the liability-holder or not. First, the time interval $[T_3, T_4]$ captures the capability of the forensics-like mechanisms in after-the-fact investigation of attacks. A better capability means a longer $[T_3, T_4]$ or smaller T_3. Second, the time interval $[T_0, T_2]$ captures the security strength of u's computer system in tolerating attacks. A better security means a longer $[T_0, T_2]$. Third, the time interval $[T_2, T_4]$ captures the capability of the mechanisms for detecting compromises. Fourth, the time interval $[T_1, T_4]$ is called the "grey period" because there may exist some signatures that were issued during this time interval, but cannot be attributed to the actual producer (i.e., u or the adversary who has compromised sk_u) with certainty.

Applying the model to analyze the insider attacks. The following observations apply, again, regardless of whether u is the liability-holder or not. First, the time interval $[T_0, T_1]$ captures strength of u's computer in tolerating tampering attacks. This is important because u may be honest at time T_0, becomes dishonest at time T_2, and may have the incentive to tamper the system history information. A better history tamper-resistance means a longer $[T_0, T_1]$. Second, the time interval $[T_3, T_4]$ captures the capability of the forensics-like mechanisms for after-the-fact investigation of attacks. A better capability means a longer $[T_3, T_4]$. Third, the time interval $[T_0, T_2]$ captures the security strength of u's computer system in tolerating attacks (e.g., preventing or deterring u from being compromised). A better security means a longer $[T_0, T_2]$. Fourth, the time interval $[T_2, T_4]$ captures the capability of the mechanisms for detecting compromises. Fifth, the time interval $[T_1, T_4]$ is again the "grey period."

Properties of ideal solutions. The above analyses offer the following insights. First, it is an ideal case to maximize the interval $[T_0, T_1]$. Namely, to make u's system history state information tamper-resistant, which means that $T_2 - T_1 = 0$ and thus the signer cannot deny any past signatures it generated before u or sk_u is compromised. Second, it is the ideal case to maximize the interval $[T_3, T_4]$, namely to deploy perfect forensics-like mechanisms for after-the-fact investigation of compromise of either u or sk_u, which would imply $T_3 - T_2 = 0$. Third, it is ideal to maximize the interval $[T_0, T_2]$ by enhancing the security of a user's computer and/or private signing key sk_u. Fourth, it is ideal to minimize the interval $[T_2, T_4]$. Since it may not be possible to absolutely prevent the compromise of keys or computers, we do need mechanisms that can detect their compromise as soon as possible. We require that the compromise-detection mechanism have *no false positives*, although this may imply that it can return an answer like "I don't know." This is crucial because in many cases the disputes can lead to lawsuits that require reliable evidence. Fifth, it is ideal to minimize the "grey period" interval $[T_1, T_4]$. Given that private signing keys can eventually get compromised and that the attackers may not always get held accountable, insurance would become a very useful mechanism for enhancing the trustworthiness of digital signatures (e.g., a signature assured either by an employer or by a third party would be more trustworthy). It is thus important to shorten the "grey period" so as to protect the liability-holder.

3   DSAS: A Framework for Reducing Grey Periods

Our solution framework, as depicted in Figure 2, is called Digital Signature Anchoring Service (DSAS). In this framework, we consider a set of users or signers, verifiers, and anchors that can be the liability-holders or some economically-motivated third parties. Note that some participants may play the roles of both verifiers and signers. Suppose that each signer has a pair of public and private keys with respect to a digital signature scheme that is secure in the sense of Goldwasser et al. [10]. The anchors are assumed to be highly secure — their systems cannot be compromised by average attackers (nevertheless, in Section 7 we

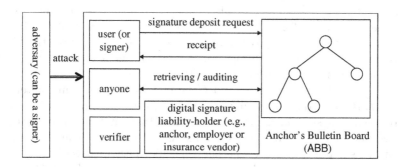

Fig. 2. DSAS framework

will discuss what if the anchors' cryptosystems may be compromised). However, the anchors are assumed to be only *semi-trusted*, meaning that they may launch attacks against some honest signers as long as such attacks cannot be traced back to them. An anchor maintains an Anchor's Bulletin Board (ABB), which is used to publish the digital signatures deposited at it.

Definition 1. (DSAS) *A DSAS scheme consists of the following protocols.*

DSAS.Initialization: *Given a primary security parameter* κ, *each participant generates the cryptographic keys. The signature verification keys are appropriately published. Moreover, a data structure called Anchor's Bulletin Board (ABB) is initialized as* ABB_0 *at time* t_0.

DSAS.Deposit: *Suppose the current content of ABB is* ABB_{i-1}, *which was updated at time* t_{i-1}. *When a signer,* u, *deposits a signature,* sig, *the anchor authenticates* u *as well as* sig. *If both authentications succeed (i.e.,* TRUE $\leftarrow$ DSAS.Deposit$(1^\kappa, u, sig)$), *the anchor returns a receipt (e.g., the anchor signs the message that "sig will appear in* ABB_i *at time* t_i*"). Note, as mentioned above, that the upper-layer application of the DSAS service is orthogonal to the focus of the present paper.*

DSAS.Update: *Denote by* Δ_i *the signatures deposited after time* t_{i-1}. *At time* t_i, *the anchor updates* ABB_{i-1} *as* $\text{ABB}_i \leftarrow$ DSAS.Update$(1^\kappa, \text{ABB}_{i-1}, \Delta_i)$. *The anchor may send back to every user, who deposited a signature after* t_{i-1}, *an "attestation" indicating how the user may verify that her signature is appropriately published in* ABB_i.

DSAS.Retrieve: *Kinds of queries can be issued with respect to* ABB_i, *dependent upon the applications. The first example is for a signer to check that her deposited signature appropriately appeared in* ABB_i. *The second example is for anyone to check that, given* ABB_{i-1} *and* Δ_i, ABB_i *was appropriately updated. The third example is for anyone to retrieve the signatures deposited during a time period.*

To define security of DSAS, let adversary $\mathcal{A}$ have access to the following oracles: $Init(1^\kappa)$, which executes DSAS.Initialization(1^κ); $Deposit(1^\kappa, u, sig)$, which executes DSAS.Deposit$(1^\kappa, u, sig)$ that returns TRUE; $Update(1^\kappa, \text{ABB}_{i-1}, \Delta_i)$, which executes DSAS.Update(1^κ, ABB$_{i-1}$, Δ_i); $Retrieve(1^\kappa, \ldots)$, which executes DSAS.Retrieve($1^\kappa, \ldots$); $Corr$, which captures that the anchor becomes dishonest and returns all the secrets of the anchor; $HaR(u)$, which captures the hit-and-run attack and returns the cryptographic secrets of signer u; $Insider(u)$, which turns an honest signer u into an insider attacker.

Note that $HaR(\cdot)$, $Insider(\cdot)$, and $Corr$ may be queried immediately after querying $Init$ so as to accommodate the situations where some participants are compromised at system initialization. Note also that multiple $Init$ queries may be made, but we only need to consider one in which the attacker may succeed. The notations $\exists$ and $\not\exists$ indicate whether a specific query was ever made. In order to capture the successful attack events, we allow $\mathcal{A}$ to invoke DSAS.Deposit and DSAS.Update. Such executions are different from the $Deposit$ and $Update$ oracle queries, which lead to executions on behalf of the signers or the anchor. Formally,

Definition 2. (properties of DSAS) *A DSAS scheme should possess:*
DSAS.correctness: *If the signers and the anchor are honest, the anchor's ABB is always appropriately updated with respect to the deposits and, for any i, anyone can verify* ABB$_i$ = DSAS.Update(1^κ, ABB$_{i-1}$, Δ_i).
DSAS.no-impersonation: *The probability that an attacker successfully impersonates an honest signer, whose cryptographic secrets are not compromised, to the anchor is negligible in κ. Formally,*

$$\Pr\left[\begin{array}{l} \sigma \leftarrow \mathcal{A}^{Init(1^\kappa),Deposit(1^\kappa,\cdot,\cdot),Update(1^\kappa,\cdot,\cdot),Retrieve(1^\kappa,\ldots),HaR(\cdot),Insider(\cdot)}(1^\kappa): \\ \not\exists Insider(u) \wedge \not\exists HaR(u) \wedge \text{TRUE} \leftarrow \text{DSAS.Deposit}(1^\kappa, u, sig) \end{array} \right] = \epsilon(\kappa),$$

DSAS.uniqueness: *The probability for anyone to provide* ABB$'_{i-1} \neq$ ABB$_{i-1}$ *or* $\Delta_i \neq \Delta'_i$ *but* DSAS.Update(1^κ, ABB$_{i-1}$, Δ_i) = DSAS.Update(1^κ, ABB$'_{i-1}$, Δ'_i) *is negligible in κ.*

$$\Pr\left[\begin{array}{l} (i, \text{ABB}_{i-1}, \text{ABB}'_{i-1}, \Delta_i, \Delta'_i) \leftarrow \\ \mathcal{A}^{Init(1^\kappa),Deposit(1^\kappa,\cdot,\cdot),Update(1^\kappa,\cdot,\cdot),Retrieve(1^\kappa,\ldots),HaR(\cdot),Insider(\cdot),Corr}(1^\kappa): \\ \text{DSAS.Update}(1^\kappa, \text{ABB}_{i-1}, \Delta_i) = \text{DSAS.Update}(1^\kappa, \text{ABB}'_{i-1}, \Delta'_i) \\ \wedge(\text{ABB}_{i-1} \neq \text{ABB}'_{i-1} \vee \Delta_i \neq \Delta'_i) \end{array} \right] = \epsilon(\kappa),$$

DSAS.attack-evidence: *Suppose the private key of an honest signer was compromised at time t and the attacker deposited a signature using the compromised key at time $t' > t$. Then this compromise can be detected when the victim user deposits her first signature at time $t^* > t' > t$. Moreover, given two conflicting signatures, it is possible to infer when the signer's computer compromised by a hit-and-run attack or the signer became an insider.*

4   Building-Block I: Anchor's Bulletin Board (**ABB**)

Definition 3. (ABB) *An ABB scheme consists of the following algorithms.*
ABB.Initialization: *Initialization of the data structure* ABB$_0$ *at time t_0.*
ABB.Update: *Denote by Δ_i the signatures deposited by the honest users after time t_{i-1}. At time t_i, the anchor updates* ABB$_{i-1}$ *to* ABB$_i$*, where* ABB$_i$ $\leftarrow$ Update(1^κ, ABB$_{i-1}$, Δ_i).
ABB.Retrieve: *Kinds of queries can be issued with respect to* ABB$_i$*, dependent on the applications.*

To define security of ABB, let adversary $\mathcal{A}$ have access to the following oracles: $Init(1^\kappa)$, which executes ABB.Initialization(1^κ); $Update(1^\kappa, \text{ABB}_{i-1}, \Delta_i)$, which executes ABB.Update($1^\kappa, \text{ABB}_{i-1}, \Delta_i$); $Retrieve(1^\kappa, \ldots)$, which executes ABB.Retrieve($1^\kappa, \ldots$); $Corr$, which captures that an anchor becomes dishonest and returns all the secrets of the anchor. Note also that multiple $Init(1^\kappa)$ queries may be made, but we only need to consider one in which the attacker may succeed. To capture the successful attack events, we allow the attacker to explicitly execute ABB.Update, which is different from the oracle query of $Update(1^\kappa, \cdot, \cdot)$.

Definition 4. (properties of ABB) *An* ABB *scheme should have:*
ABB.correctness*: ABB is always appropriately updated, meaning that anyone can always verify that* $\text{ABB}_i = \text{ABB.Update}(1^\kappa, \text{ABB}_{i-1}, \Delta_i)$ *for any i.*
ABB.uniqueness*: The probability for anyone to provide* $\text{ABB}_{i-1} \neq \text{ABB}'_{i-1}$ *or* $\Delta_i \neq \Delta'_i$ *but* $\text{ABB.Update}(1^\kappa, \text{ABB}_{i-1}, \Delta_i) = \text{ABB.Update}(1^\kappa, \text{ABB}'_{i-1}, \Delta'_i)$ *is negligible in* κ*. Formally,*

$$\Pr \left[\begin{array}{l} (i, \text{ABB}_{i-1}, \text{ABB}'_{i-1}, \Delta_i, \Delta'_i) \leftarrow \mathcal{A}^{Init(1^\kappa), Update(1^\kappa, \cdot, \cdot), Retrieve(1^\kappa, \ldots), Corr}(1^\kappa) : \\ \text{ABB.Update}(1^\kappa, \text{ABB}_{i-1}, \Delta_i) = \text{ABB.Update}(1^\kappa, \text{ABB}'_{i-1}, \Delta'_i) \\ \wedge (\text{ABB}_{i-1} \neq \text{ABB}'_{i-1} \vee \Delta_i \neq \Delta'_i) \end{array} \right] = \epsilon(\kappa),$$

Construction. We design ABB as a three-level, binary Merkle hash tree. At the bottom there are many Level 3 hash trees, each of which represents the signatures with respect to a signature verification key. At the middle there is a single Level 2 hash tree, each leaf of which corresponds to the root of a Level 3 hash tree. At the top there is a single Level 1 hash tree, the right-most child of which corresponds to the root of the Level 2 hash tree. The ABB is "signature verification keys"-oriented. This is to allow efficient queries about (some) digital signatures with respect to a public verification key deposited during a time interval. This is fulfilled by retrieving only one leave of the Level 2 hash tree.

Given ABB published at time t_i, we denote by $M_j(t_i)$ the root of the jth Level 3 hash tree in ABB_i, by $N(t_i)$ the root of the Level 2 hash tree in ABB_i, and by $R(t_i)$ the root of the Level 1 hash tree in ABB_i.

An ABB may be *signatures-preserved*, meaning that all the signatures that have been deposited so far appear in the ABB (i.e., the size of the ABB is monotonically increasing), or *signatures-compressed*, meaning that only the most recently deposited signatures explicitly appear in the ABB whereas previously deposited signatures are "compressed" in a certain way. We will mention their differences in our ABB construction, which is given below and analyzed in [29]. An illustrative example is given in Appendix B.

ABB.Initialization: ABB_0 is initiated at time t_0 as a Level 2 hash tree, whose root $N(t_0) = R(t_0)$ is the Level 1 hash tree (i.e., a single node tree at this point), and leaves $M_1(t_0), M_2(t_0), \ldots$ correspond to the individual-wise or group-wise signature verification keys.

ABB.Update: Denote by $\Delta_{j,i}$ an ordered set (or list) of the signatures that have been deposited with respect to the jth Level 3 hash tree since time t_{i-1}. At time t_i, the anchor executes the following to update ABB_{i-1} to ABB_i.

1. Update the Level 3 hash trees: There are two cases.

   Signatures-preserved case: For each j, the jth Level 3 hash tree with root $M_j(t_{i-1})$ in ABB_{i-1} becomes the left-most leaf node in the new jth Level 3 hash tree, and the signatures in $\Delta_{j,i}$ appear as the other leaf nodes, whose left-to-right order corresponds to the order at which they were deposited.

   Signatures-compressed case: For each j, the root $M_j(t_{i-1})$ of the jth Level 3 hash tree in ABB_{i-1} (i.e., every node other than the root is "pruned") becomes the left-most leaf node in the new Level 3 hash tree, and the signatures in $\Delta_{j,i}$ appear as the other leaf nodes, whose left-to-right order corresponds to the order at which they were deposited.

   The values of the roots of the new Level 3 hash trees in ABB_i are computed as usual. In the ideal case, the new Level 3 hash trees are perfect binary trees.

2. Update the Level 2 hash tree: After updating the roots of the new Level 3 hash trees, the value of the root of the new Level 2 hash tree is also updated as $N(t_i)$.

3. Update the Level 1 hash tree: The root of the Level 1 hash tree in ABB_{i-1}, namely $R(t_{i-1})$, becomes the left child of the new Level 1 hash tree in ABB_i. The root of the new Level 2 hash tree, namely $N(t_i)$, becomes the right child of, the new Level 1 hash tree in ABB_i. The value of the root of the new Level 1 hash tree, namely $R(t_i)$, is computed as usual. The resulting signature as well as the new Level 1, 2, and 3 trees are published as ABB_i.

ABB.Retrieve: Kinds of queries can be issued with respect to ABB_i, dependent upon the applications. Examples are: *First*, given a signature verification key corresponding to the jth Level 3 hash tree and a time interval $[t, t']$, one can immediately find all the signatures deposited during that time period in the signatures-preserved case. This can be done by, for example, computing the difference between the corresponding two Level 3 trees updated at time t and t', respectively. In the case only one copy of the tree is preserved (although this is unlikely because storage is getting cheaper and cheaper), the same task can be done by extending the root of Level 3 trees to include the time at which the ABB, and thus the Level 3 trees, are updated. Similarly, given a time interval $[t, t']$, one can find all the signatures deposited during that time period in the signatures-preserved case (e.g., by combining the signatures deposited during that period of time). *Second*, given a signature deposit receipt, one can immediate check whether the signature in question does appear in the Level 3 tree corresponding to the signature verification key. *Third*, given the "attestation" of a deposited signature — the values of the siblings of the nodes on the path from the signature in question to the root, one can immediately check whether the attestation ends at a leaf or the root of the Level 1 hash tree. If there is anything wrong, a complaint is issued against the anchor. The validity of the complaint can be checked by any honest party (e.g., judge) or in a distributed fashion, and the dishonest participant may be appropriately punished.

5   Building-Block II: Stateful Authentications (**AUTH**)

Definition 5. (stateful authentication method) *A stateful authentication method* AUTH *consists of the following (interactive) algorithms.*
AUTH.Initialization: *Given a primary security parameter* κ, *this (interactive) algorithm bootstraps some cryptographic contexts. Moreover, the user u maintains some state information* $\mathsf{state}_{u,v}$ *and the verifier v maintains some state information* $\mathsf{state}_{v,u}$.
AUTH.Authentication: *This is an interactive algorithm run by u and v.*

1. *The user u presents the verifier v a bitstring* η, *a function of* $\mathsf{state}_{u,v}$.
2. *Upon receiving from u a bitstring* η, *v executes an algorithm to decide whether to accept the bitstring. The decision is based on, among other things, the state information* $\mathsf{state}_{v,u}$. *If the authentication is successful, denote it by* TRUE $\leftarrow$ AUTH.Authentication(1^κ, $\langle\eta, \mathsf{state}_{u,v}\rangle$, $\mathsf{state}_{v,u}$).
3. *If v accepts, v updates* $\mathsf{state}_{v,u}$ *and u updates* $\mathsf{state}_{u,v}$ *appropriately.*

To define security of AUTH, let $\mathcal{A}$ have access to the following oracles: $Init(1^\kappa)$, which executes AUTH.Initialization(1^κ); $Authentication(1^\kappa, u, v)$, which executes AUTH.Authentication(1^κ, $\langle\eta, \mathsf{state}_{u,v}\rangle$, $\mathsf{state}_{v,u}$) that returns TRUE; $HaR(u)$, which captures the hit-and-run attack and returns the cryptographic secrets of signer u; $Insider(u)$, which turns an honest signer u into an insider attacker. Note that $HaR(\cdot)$ and $Insider(\cdot)$ may be queried immediately after querying $Init(1^\kappa)$ so as to accommodate the situations where some participants are compromised at system initialization. Note also that multiple $Init(1^\kappa)$ queries may be made, but we only need to consider one in which the attacker may succeed. The notation $\exists$ and $\not\exists$ indicate whether a specific query was ever made. To capture the successful attack events, we allow the attacker to explicitly execute AUTH.Authentication. Such executions are different from the *Authentication* oracle queries, which lead to executions on behalf of the authenticators.

Definition 6. (properties of stateful authentication methods) *A stateful authentication method should have the following properties:*
AUTH.correctness: *For any execution of* AUTH.Authentication *between an honest user u and an honest verifier v, v always accepts.*
AUTH.no-impersonation: *An adversary, who does not compromise the cryptographic key of an honest user u, can impersonate u with only a probability negligible in* κ. *Formally,*

$$\Pr\begin{bmatrix} (\sigma, \mathsf{state}_\mathcal{A}) \leftarrow \mathcal{A}^{Init(1^\kappa), Authentication(1^\kappa,\cdot,\cdot), HaR(\cdot), Insider(\cdot)}(1^\kappa) : \\ \not\exists Insider(u) \wedge \not\exists HaR(u) \wedge \\ \text{TRUE} \leftarrow \text{AUTH.Authentication}(1^\kappa, \langle\cdot, \mathsf{state}_\mathcal{A}\rangle, \mathsf{state}_{v,u}) \end{bmatrix} = \epsilon(\kappa),$$

AUTH.attack-evidence: *Suppose the cryptographic key of an honest user was compromised at time t and the attacker authenticated at least once using the compromised key to the verifier at time* $t' > t$. *Then this compromise can be detected when the victim user authenticates herself to the verifier the first time at time* $t^* > t' > t$.

Construction. The design rationale behind our construction is given in Appendix C. The construction is based on the afore-discussed "twisted" use of forward-secure signatures, where the signer plays the role of a user in the AUTH scheme. It can be based on any concrete forward-secure signature scheme (e.g., [1,3,16]), as long as it satisfies the properties reviewed in Section A. Let δ_T be the allowed maximal time interval before a forced key update, and θ is the allowed number of authentications before a forced key update. Denote by T the system time corresponding to the most recent execution of the *key update algorithm*, by T' the current system time, by α the index of the periods that have elapsed, by β the accumulated number of authentications since system initialization, by γ the the number of new authentications since time T. Selections of these parameters are dependent upon the system policies. The construction is presented below, analysis of which is given in [29].

AUTH.Initialization: A user u, who plays the role of the signer in a forward-secure signature scheme, generates its public and private key pair $(pk_u, sk_{u,0})$. The user u sends pk_u to the verifier v and sets $\mathsf{state}_{u,v} \leftarrow \langle T, \delta_T, \theta, \alpha = 0, \beta = 0, \gamma = 0, pk_u, sk_{u,\alpha}\rangle$, whereas v sets $\mathsf{state}_{v,u} \leftarrow \langle T, \delta_T, \theta, \alpha = 0, \beta = 0, \gamma = 0, pk_u, pk_{u,\alpha}\rangle$ where $pk_{u,\alpha}$ can be derived from pk_u.

AUTH.Authentication: Suppose u holds $\mathsf{state}_{u,v} = \langle T, \delta_T, \theta, \alpha, \beta, \gamma, pk_u, sk_{u,\alpha}\rangle$ and v holds $\mathsf{state}_{v,u} = \langle T, \delta_T, \theta, \alpha, \beta, \gamma, pk_u, pk_{u,\alpha}\rangle$.

- The *key update algorithm* is executed when one of the following three conditions is satisfied: (1) the system is just initialized; (2) the user has conducted θ authentications; (3) $T' - T \geq \delta_T$. In any case, u sets $\alpha \leftarrow \alpha + 1$ and $\gamma \leftarrow 0$, derives $sk_{u,\alpha}$ from $sk_{u,\alpha-1}$, and sets $\mathsf{state}_{u,v} \leftarrow \langle T, \delta_T, \theta, \alpha, \beta, \gamma, pk_u, sk_{u,\alpha}\rangle$; whereas v sets $\alpha \leftarrow \alpha + 1$ and $\gamma \leftarrow 0$, possibly derives $pk_{u,\alpha}$ from pk_u, and sets $\mathsf{state}_{v,u} \leftarrow \langle T, \delta_T, \theta, \alpha, \beta, \gamma, pk_u, pk_{u,\alpha}\rangle$.
- The following authentication protocol is executed whenever one of the following two conditions is satisfied: (1) the key has just been updated and thus a dummy authentication is executed; (2) the user needs to authenticate herself to the verifier. The protocol has the following steps:

  1. User u generates a forward-secure signature σ on the concatenation of T, α, β, γ as well as possibly a (dummy) message using private key $sk_{u,\alpha}$. Then, it sends σ as well as the relevant information to the verifier v.
  2. If σ is valid with respect to $pk_{u,\alpha}$, v accepts and sets $\mathsf{state}_{v,u} \leftarrow \langle T, \delta_T, \theta, \alpha, \beta + 1, \gamma + 1, pk_u, pk_{u,\alpha}\rangle$.
  3. If v accepts, u sets $\mathsf{state}_{u,v} \leftarrow \langle T', \delta_T, \theta, \alpha, \beta + 1, \gamma + 1, pk_u, sk_{u,\alpha}\rangle$.

6   Putting the Pieces Together to Instantiate DSAS

Having explored the building-blocks, now we present our DSAS main construction, which is an integration of the above **Constructions I** and **II**. Its security and extensions are described in [29].

DSAS.Initialization: Given a primary security parameter κ, the anchor SA generates a pair of public and private keys $(pk_{\mathsf{SA}}, sk_{\mathsf{SA}})$ for signing receipts and possibly the roots of the Level 1 hash trees. A user u initiates its own cryptosystem

$(\mathsf{pk}_u, \mathsf{sk}_u)$ for generating digital signatures that need be deposited. Moreover, the following two procedures are executed. (i) Execute AUTH.Initialization to initialize a stateful authentication method (as in **Construction II**). Especially, $(pk_u, sk_{u,0})$ is generated. (ii) Execute ABB.Initialization to initialize ABB_0.

DSAS.Deposit: A user u executes AUTH.Authentication to authenticate herself to the anchor using $sk_{u,i}$ (as in **Construction II**) on either a dummy message M' or a signature sig with respect to pk_u, where sig is to be deposited. The anchor SA verifies the validity of the request as in AUTH.Authentication using $pk_{u,i}$, and in the case of depositing a digital signature, the validity of sig using pk_u. The anchor may return a receipt signed with sk_{SA} (e.g., its signature on the message that "this signature, sig, will appear in ABB_i at time t_i"). The receipt may be forwarded by the signer to the signature verifier.

DSAS.Update: The anchor SA executes ABB.Update, and may send back to the users the "attestations" of their newly deposited signatures. An attestation includes (1) the time t_i at which ABB_i is published, and (2) the siblings of all the nodes on the path from the node that is being attested to the root $R(t_i)$.

DSAS.Retrieve: This is the same as ABB.Retrieve.

7   Dealing with the Unexpected

Recall that we assumed that the hash functions are collision resistant, the digital signature schemes and the forward-secure digital signature schemes are secure with respect to the respective well-accepted definitions. What if some or even all of these assumptions are broken by a powerful attacker? Note that our model already accommodated that the private signing keys may be compromised by whatever means, which subsumes that the private keys are cryptanalyzed, which in turn breaks the security of the digital signature schemes. Moreover, if the private signing keys are compromised by whatever means, it would be possible that the forward-secure signing keys are compromised. Since the forward-secure signing scheme is employed to provide another layer of protection, it would be without loss of generality to focus on the situation where the hash functions may be broken [28] and the private signing keys may be compromised. For example, the very recent incident — digital signatures based on MD5 hash function allow the attacker to obtain a rogue CA certificate [26] — can be adequately dealt with using our solution by depositing the certificate signatures.

Given such a powerful attacker, it is possible that the attacker can present faked signatures that can be verified with respect to the ABB. As we now discuss, there are a range of methods for alleviating the damage of such an attacker.

We start with the scenario that the hash function h may be broken (i.e., it turns out not to be collision-resistant). To deal with this, we can append each node (both leaf and internal) of the ABB tree with a value computed using a "newly-available", supposed-to-be-more-secure hash function, denoted by h. For example, in the case of Figure 3(c), the leaf node annotated with $h(pk_4)$ now becomes a pair $(h(pk_4), \mathsf{h}(h(pk_4)))$, and the leaf node annotated with $h(sig_1)$ now becomes a pair $(h(sig_1), \mathsf{h}(h(sig_1)))$. Then, the internal node annotated as $a = h(h(pk_4), h(sig_1))$ now becomes a pair $(a, h(h(h(pk_4)), h(h(sig_1))))$. The same procedure is applied throughout the tree in a bottom-up fashion. Note that it should be clear that we cannot simply replace, for example, the root $R(t_2)$ with $(R(t_2), h(R(t_2))$. Note also that the above method was inspired by Haber [11], who deals a similar problem but in a simpler situation. This way, compromising hash function h and all the digital signing keys — except the anchor's private key sk_{SA} for signing the root of ABB— *after* the employment of h does not allow the attacker to breach security of DSAS. In what follows we deal with the two exceptions: (1) the anchor's private signing key sk_{SA} may be compromised; (2) no such h is available.

Q1: What if the signing key sk_{SA} of the anchor is compromised? Recall that the anchor may use sk_{SA} to issue deposit receipts and/or sign the root of the ABB trees. In the case sk_{SA} is compromised, the attacker could abuse it to impersonate the anchor to issue cryptographically-legitimate receipts. However, such an attack can be detected when the anchor updates the ABB because the signature verifiers cannot validate the receipts, which are forwarded by the signer to the verifiers. In response to such an emergence, the anchor needs to identify which signatures are truly deposited at its ABB via the DSAS service, and which signatures are not. For this purpose, we can let the anchor commit another pair of public and private keys, say (pk'_{SA}, sk'_{SA}), when pk_{SA} is first published or certified (by a higher-level CA). To further enhance security, the commitment scheme could be "information-theoretically hiding and computationally binding" such that even a computationally unbounded attacker cannot figure out pk'_{SA} before the anchor decommits it, except for a negligible probability. Moreover, the cryptosystem corresponds to pk'_{SA} may be different from the cryptosystem corresponds to pk_{SA} (e.g., "discrete logarithm"-based vs. factorization-based) and may use a larger security parameter. Then, the anchor could use sk'_{SA} to sign the receipts of the signatures that were deposited at the anchor itself, where the receipts were previously signed using sk_{SA}. Of course, if sk_{SA} is compromised by the attacker who breaks into the anchor's computer or device, it is natural that sk'_{SA} is stored on a device different from the one that stores sk_{SA}, which is always a prudent practice anyway.

Note that the above method of introducing a new pair of public and private keys (pk'_{SA}, sk'_{SA}) can be extended to introduce a set of such cryptosystems, which exhibit increasing strength of security (e.g., using increasingly larger security parameters). Note also that the above method has the consequence that we must put a stronger trust, than in the basic scheme, in the anchor because the anchor has the potential to dispute signatures it endorsed before (e.g., when the anchor realized the risk of endorsing certain signatures may be too high at a later point in time). Fortunately, this may be tolerable because the anchor has a short period of time (i.e., between two updates of ABB) to decide whether to cheat or not. Thus, there is still a "grey period" as indicated in the model discussed in Section 2, which is however short.

Q2: What if there is no hash function such as h that is available, or such h is available only after the attacker compromises the cryptographic signing keys (either by cryptanalysis of by breaking into the anchor's computer or device) as well as h? This scenario is similar to the case that the private key of the anchor, namely sk_{SA}, may be compromised. Thus, we can adopt a similar countermeasure, namely by including an "information-theoretically hiding and computationally-binding" commitment of public key pk'_u in the certificate of the public key pk_u. This way, when sk_u is compromised, which can be detected after at most a single period of time (i.e., between two updates of ABB), user u can use sk'_u to certify the signatures generated using sk_u in the past periods of time. Of course, we must assume that sk'_u is stored at a secure place different from the place where sk_u was stored, at least in the case that sk_u could be compromised by breaking into u's computer or device (rather than cryptanalysis). Note that this mechanism can alleviate the problem when the signing algorithms of the users used some hash functions that may be later broken — a scenario not accommodate in the afore-discussed h being broken later. Note also that user u could abuse this method to dispute some signatures she issued before, but arguably within the last period of time (i.e., between two updates of ABB). That is, there is still a "grey period" as indicated in the model discussed in Section 2, but it is short.

8   Conclusion and Future Work

We presented a model for understanding trustworthiness and longevity of digital signatures in the presence of compromised private signing keys/functions, or malicious signers. The model offers hints for designing solutions to alleviate the problem of grey periods, during which there are signatures for which we are not certain who should be held accountable. The hints guided us to design a solution to deal with the inevitable threats. We also showed how to extend our solution to deal with the unexpected threats that all of the deployed cryptosystems are broken.

Our investigation inspires several interesting open problems. First, how can we defeat the hit-and-stick attack? Second, is it possible to eliminate grey periods? Third, the compromise-detection mechanism we investigated is passive. How can we design a proactive one (e.g., is it possible to exploit some HoneyKeys — the cryptographic analogy of techniques known as Honeynet — to help detect compromises of computers)? Fourth, how should we deal with the case of some "non-traditional" use of digital signatures. For example, abuse-free contract signing [9] is a kind of signatures useful in contract signing. It is not clear how can we adapt the present solution to accommodate them *without* jeopardizing the abuse-freeness property to some extent.

Acknowledgement. We thank the anonymous reviewers for their useful comments, and Jean Camp for bringing [25] to our attention.

Shouhuai Xu was supported in part by AFOSR, NSF, and UTSA.

References

1. Anderson, R.: On the forward security of digital signatures. Technical report (1997)
2. Bellare, M., Micciancio, D., Warinschi, B.: Foundations of group signatures: Formal definitions, simplified requirements, and a construction based on general assumptions. In: Biham, E. (ed.) EUROCRYPT 2003. LNCS, vol. 2656. Springer, Heidelberg (2003)
3. Bellare, M., Miner, S.: A forward-secure digital signature scheme. In: Wiener, M. (ed.) CRYPTO 1999. LNCS, vol. 1666, p. 431. Springer, Heidelberg (1999)
4. Bellare, M., Yee, B.: Forward-security in private-key cryptography. In: Joye, M. (ed.) CT-RSA 2003. LNCS, vol. 2612, pp. 1–18. Springer, Heidelberg (2003)
5. Chaum, D., van Heyst, E.: Group signatures. In: Davies, D.W. (ed.) EUROCRYPT 1991. LNCS, vol. 547, pp. 257–265. Springer, Heidelberg (1991)
6. Desmedt, Y., Frankel, Y.: Threshold cryptosystems. In: Brassard, G. (ed.) CRYPTO 1989. LNCS, vol. 435, pp. 307–315. Springer, Heidelberg (1990)
7. Dodis, Y., Katz, J., Xu, S., Yung, M.: Strong key-insulated signature schemes. In: Desmedt, Y.G. (ed.) PKC 2003. LNCS, vol. 2567, pp. 130–144. Springer, Heidelberg (2002)
8. Ellison, C., Schneier, B.: Ten risks of pki: What you?re not being told about public key infrastructure. Computer Security Journal XVI(1) (2000)
9. Garay, J., Jakobsson, M., MacKenzie, P.: Abuse-free optimistic contract signing. In: Wiener, M. (ed.) CRYPTO 1999. LNCS, vol. 1666, p. 449. Springer, Heidelberg (1999)
10. Goldwasser, S., Micali, S., Rivest, R.: A digital signature scheme secure against adaptive chosen-message attacks. SIAM J. Computing 17(2), 281–308 (1988)
11. Haber, S.: Long-lived digital integrity using short-lived hash functions. Cryptology ePrint Archive, Report 2007/238 (2007), http://eprint.iacr.org/
12. Haber, S., Stornetta, W.: How to time-stamp a digital document. In: Menezes, A., Vanstone, S.A. (eds.) CRYPTO 1990. LNCS, vol. 537, pp. 437–455. Springer, Heidelberg (1991)
13. Harrison, K., Xu, S.: Protecting cryptographic keys from memory disclosures. In: IEEE DSN 2007 (2007)
14. Herzberg, A., Jakobsson, M., Jarecki, S., Krawczyk, H., Yung, M.: Proactive public key and signature schemes. In: ACM CCS 1997 (1997)
15. Itkis, G.: Cryptographic tamper evidence. In: ACM CCS 2003 (2003)
16. Itkis, G., Reyzin, L.: Forward-secure signatures with optimal signing and verifying. In: Kilian, J. (ed.) CRYPTO 2001. LNCS, vol. 2139, p. 332. Springer, Heidelberg (2001)
17. Itkis, G., Reyzin, L.: Sibir: Signer-base intrusion-resilient signatures. In: Yung, M. (ed.) CRYPTO 2002. LNCS, vol. 2442, p. 499. Springer, Heidelberg (2002)
18. Just, M., van Oorschot, P.: Addressing the problem of undetected signature key compromise. In: NDSS 1999 (1999)
19. Kocher, P.: Timing attacks on implementations of Diffie-Hellman, RSA, DSS, and other systems. In: Koblitz, N. (ed.) CRYPTO 1996. LNCS, vol. 1109, pp. 104–113. Springer, Heidelberg (1996)
20. Lamport, L.: Password authentication with insecure communication. Comm. of ACM 24(11), 770–771 (1981)
21. Loscocco, P., Smalley, S., Muckelbauer, P., Taylor, R., Turner, S., Farrell, J.: The inevitability of failure: The flawed assumption of security in modern computing environments. In: NISSC 1998 (1998)

22. Merkle, R.: Secrecy, Authentication, and Public Key Systems. PhD thesis (June 1979)
23. Ostrovsky, R., Yung, M.: How to withstand mobile virus attacks (extended abstract). In: PODC 1991 (1991)
24. Shamir, A., van Someren, N.: Playing 'hide and seek' with stored keys. In: Franklin, M.K. (ed.) FC 1999. LNCS, vol. 1648, p. 118. Springer, Heidelberg (1999)
25. Simpson, I.: Modeling the Risks and Costs of Digitally Signed Certificates in Electronic Commerce. In: Proceedings of the Second USENIX Workshop on Electronic Commerce
26. Sotirov, A., Stevens, M., Appelbaum, J., Lenstra, A., Molnar, D., Osvik, D., de Weger, B.: Md5 considered harmful today: Creating a rogue ca certificate (2009), http://www.win.tue.nl/hashclash/rogue-ca/
27. TCG, https://www.trustedcomputinggroup.org/
28. Wang, X., Yin, Y., Yu, H.: Finding collisions in the full sha-1. In: Shoup, V. (ed.) CRYPTO 2005. LNCS, vol. 3621, pp. 17–36. Springer, Heidelberg (2005)
29. Xu, S., Yung, M.: Expecting the Unexpected: Towards Robust Credential Infrastructure. Full version of the present paper, www.cs.utsa.edu/~shxu
30. Yee, B.: Using secure coprocessors. PhD thesis, Carnegie Mellon University

A   Cryptographic Preliminaries

Let κ be a security parameter. We often prove the security of a cryptographic scheme by showing that the probability an adversary breaks the scheme, $\epsilon(\kappa)$, is negligible. A function $\epsilon : \mathbb{N} \to \mathbb{R}^+$ is negligible if for any c there exists κ_c such that $\forall \kappa > \kappa_c$ we have $\epsilon(\kappa) < 1/\kappa^c$. We say a family of hash functions $h : \{0,1\}^k \times \{0,1\}^* \to \{0,1\}^\kappa$ is collision-resistant if, for any $K \in \{0,1\}^k$, the probability for any probabilistic polynomial-time (PPT) algorithm to find x_1 and x_2, such that $x_1 \neq x_2$ but $h_K(x_1) = h_K(x_2)$, is negligible in κ. Given that $h_K(\cdot)$ is determined once K is chosen, we will write it as $h(\cdot)$ for short. We will use Merkle hash trees [22], in which the value of an internal node is the hash of its children's values.

Digital signatures. A signature scheme consists of: a *key generation algorithm* that takes as input a security parameter κ and outputs a pair of public and private keys (pk, sk); a *signing algorithm* that takes as input a message m and a private key sk, and outputs a signature σ; a *verification algorithm* that takes as input a message m, a public key pk and a candidate signature σ, and decides whether to accept the signature. Security of digital signatures is traditionally captured by the existential unforgeability under adaptive chosen-message attack, meaning that the probability for an attacker, who may have access to many message-signature pairs, to generate a new signature is negligible in κ [10].

Forward-secure signatures. In a forward-secure signature scheme [1,3], the system time is divided into periods (e.g., days) such that the private key of a signer is changed periodically (i.e., daily), but the public key remains unchanged. Such a scheme consists of: a *key generation algorithm* for generating a pair of public and private keys (pk, sk_0); a *key update algorithm* for the signer to periodically update its period private key as sk_i at the beginning of the ith period, and perhaps also for a verifier to derive the corresponding period public key pk_i (from pk) at the beginning of the ith period; a *signing algorithm* for the signer to sign messages using the period private key sk_i; and a *verification algorithm* for a verifier to check the validity of a signature using the period public key pk_i. Basically, the `forward-security` property means that an adversary, who may have compromised period private key sk_i (possibly $i = \infty$), can generate a valid signature with respect to any pk_j with only a negligible probability, where $j < i$. The intuition is that compromise of a current private key does not allow the adversary to compromise any past private key.

B   An Illustrative Example

Figure 3 shows some illustrative snapshots of an ABB. The trees framed by double solid lines are the Level 1 hash trees, the trees framed by single solid

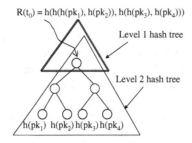

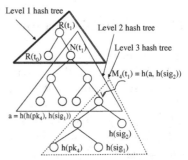

(a) ABB_0 at time t_0 (signatures-preserved case and signatures-compressed case): initialization with four user public keys

(b) ABB_1 at time t_1 (signatures-preserved case and signatures-compressed case): user pk_4 deposited two signatures

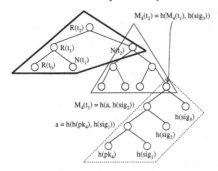

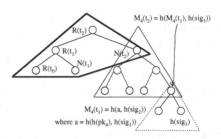

(c) ABB_2 at time t_2 (signatures-preserved case): user pk_4 deposited one new signature

(d) ABB_2 at time t_2 (signatures-compressed case): user pk_4 deposited one new signature

Fig. 3. An illustration of an example ABB snapshots

lines are the Level 2 hash trees, and the trees framed by single dashed lines are the Level 3 hash trees.

Suppose there are four users (or groups of users in the case of depositing anonymous signatures). Figure 3(a) depicts ABB_0, which was initialized at time t_0. Specifically, the leaves of the Level 2 hash tree correspond to the four public keys. The root value is $R(t_0) = N(t_0) = h(h(h(pk_1), h(pk_2)), h(h(pk_3), h(pk_4)))$, where h is a collision-resistant hash function. Note that the Level 1 hash tree consists of a single node, namely the root of the Level 2 hash tree. Moreover, each leaf of the Level 2 hash tree can be seen as the root of the corresponding Level 3 hash tree, which consists of a single node though.

Suppose during the time interval between t_0 and t_1 the owner of pk_4 deposited two signatures, sig_1 and sig_2. ABB_1 is depicted in Figure 3(b). Note that the signatures-preserved case and the signatures-compressed case are the same, because there are no signatures to compress at this point. Note that the root of the updated Level 3 hash tree corresponding to pk_4 is $M_4(t_1) = h(h(h(pk_4), h(sig_1)), h(sig_2))$, the root of the updated Level 2 hash tree is $N(t_1)$, and the root of the updated Level 1 hash tree is $R(t_1) = h(R(t_0), N(t_1))$. The attestation for signature sig_1 is $(t_1; h(pk_4), h(sig_2), \ldots, R(t_0), R(t_1))$, and so on.

Suppose during the time interval between t_1 and t_2, the owner of pk_4 deposited one signature, sig_3. There are two cases:

- Figure 3(c) depicts ABB_2 in the signatures-preserved case. The root of the updated Level 3 hash tree becomes $M_4(t_2) = h(M_4(t_1), sig_3)$, the root of the updated Level 2 hash tree becomes $N(t_2)$, and the root of the updated Level 1 hash tree becomes $R(t_2) = h(R(t_1), N(t_2))$. Moreover, the updated Level 3 hash tree has all previously deposited signatures, as well as $h(pk_4)$, as its leaves.
- Figure 3(d) depicts ABB_2 in the signatures-compressed case. The updated Level 1 and 2 hash trees are the same as in the signatures-preserved case, but the updated Level 3 hash tree does not have all previously deposited signatures as its leaves. Indeed, the new root $M_4(t_2)$ only has the "compression" of the signatures, denoted by $M_4(t_1)$, as its left child.

C   Design Rationale

As mentioned before, our framework aims at detecting the compromise of a private signing key as soon as possible. This can be fulfilled via a stateful authentication method coupled with a "twisted" use of forward-secure signatures; this is done in a fashion independent of the digital signatures that are being deposited. The twist is due to the following. First, a user updates her private key with respect to the adopted forward-secure signature scheme either after signing a pre-determined number of messages, or after a pre-determined period of time (this is particularly relevant when a user does not issue digital signatures often). Second, whenever a user updates her private key in the adopted forward-secure signature scheme, the user should use the updated private key to authenticate herself to the anchor for a dummy message (this can be automatically done by the user's software for a better deployment convenience). The design can be justified by answering the following two questions.

Q1: Why forward-secure signatures, but not others? We examined other seemingly plausible designs, which however do not fulfill the desired assurance. First, we notice that a *symmetric* key authentication system, traditional message authentication scheme and forward-secure message authentication scheme [4] alike, does not fulfill the desired assurance. This is because the anchor is only semi-trusted, and thus can leak an honest signer's symmetric authentication key to an attacker without being held accountable. If the attacker compromises an honest signer's private key, which is used to generate digital signatures that need be deposited, the attacker can generate valid signatures with respect to some past time. These signatures can make (some of) the honest signer's past signatures questionable, because the signed messages may be contradictory to each other. Perhaps more importantly, a dishonest signer can plausibly repudiate some previously deposited signatures by claiming that they were generated by an attacker, which causes a longer grey period $[T_1, T_4]$ because the virtual interval $[T_1, T_2]$ becomes longer. For a similar reason, it does not work to let a signer and the anchor maintain a common state information such as an incremental counter, or the time at which the last signature was deposited. Second, the above vulnerability suggests to adopt an *asymmetric* design. A concrete example is to let a user set up a one-way hash chain (cf. Lamport [20]) such that the user selects s_0 and sends $s_\ell = H^\ell(s_0)$ to the anchor. Then the ith deposit request is associated with $s_{\ell-i} = H^{\ell-i}(s_0)$, where H is a member of a one-way hash function family. However, this design still has the afore-mentioned vulnerability that can cause a longer grey period $[T_1, T_4]$. This is because when the user is compromised, s_0 is compromised and thus the attacker can derive any s_i (even without colluding with the anchor).

By utilizing forward-secure signatures, the above vulnerabilities are dismissed and $[T_1, T_2]$ is reduced, even if T_2 is not known to the defender. It is possible to replace forward-secure signatures with, for example, signatures corresponding to independent period public keys. However, this would require the users to frequently generate fresh public and private key pairs.

Q2: Why the twisted, but not the standard, use of forward-secure signatures for authentication? A standard use of forward-secure signatures, while providing the desired "asymmetry," has the following vulnerability. Suppose a signer is honest at system initialization time T_0, but becomes dishonest at time T_2. Suppose $T^* > T_2$ is the time at which the private key with respect to the adopted forward-secure signature scheme should be updated, but the now dishonest user does not follow the protocol. When the compromise becomes evident at time T_4, the dishonest signer can blame all the signatures generated during the time interval $[T_2, T_4]$ to the attacker who has compromised its private key. That is, the standard use of forward-secure signatures does not provide any means to deal with such a malicious behavior. The problem is caused by the fact that the periodical key update operations are done at the signer end and at the anchor end in an independent fashion. Our "twist" alleviates this problem, by forcing a signer to authenticate herself to the anchor whenever there is a private key update. Moreover, the signer is forced to update her period private key whenever (1) she has authenticated a pre-determined number of times since the last key update, or (2) a pre-determined length of time has elapsed since the last key update. This means that the resulting periods are not necessarily of the same length, but the longest time interval between two authentications conducted by a signer is upper bounded by a pre-determined parameter. Putting this into the context of the above example, the signer is thus forced to authenticate herself to the verifier at time T^*, where $T_2 < T^* < T_4$. This leads to a shorter grey period $[T^*, T_4]$.

Optical DNA

Deepak Vijaywargi[1], Dave Lewis[2], and Darko Kirovski[3]

[1] Dept. of Electrical Engineering, University of Washington, Seattle, WA 98195, USA
[2] Microsoft Corp., One Microsoft Way, Redmond, WA 98052, USA
[3] Microsoft Research, One Microsoft Way, Redmond, WA 98052, USA

Abstract. A certificate of authenticity (COA) is an inexpensive physical object with a random and unique structure S which is hard to near-exactly replicate. An inexpensive device should be able to scan object's physical "fingerprint," a set of features that represents S. In this paper, we explore one set of requirements that optical media such as DVDs should satisfy, to be considered as COAs. As manufacturing of such media produces inevitable errors, we use the locations and count of these errors as a "fingerprint" for each optical disc: its optical DNA. The "fingerprint" is signed using publisher's private-key and the resulting signature is stored onto the optical medium using a post-production process. Standard DVD players with altered firmware that includes publisher's public-key, should be able to verify the authenticity of DVDs protected with optical DNA. Our key finding is that for the proposed protocol, only DVDs with exceptional wear-and-tear characteristics would result in an inexpensive and viable anti-counterfeiting technology.

1 Introduction

COUNTERFEITING is regarded as a form of illegal trade where the seller fools the buyer into believing that the merchandise is authentic and collects the full "legal-market" price on the product. The counterfeiter usually earns profit margins that are higher than that of the original manufacturer due to lack of development and marketing costs. The software industry has suffered from this problem since the inception. To date, a few tools have been efficient in attenuating counterfeiting.

Since the early work out of Sandia National Labs by Bauder and Simmons [1], certificates of authenticity have attracted attention as a possible remedy. A *certificate of authenticity* (COA) is a digitally signed physical object with a random unique structure such that: **R1** – the cost of creating and signing original COAs is small, **R2** – the cost of manufacturing a COA instance is substantially lower than the cost of its near-exact replication, **R3** – the cost of verifying the authenticity of a signed COA is small, and **R4** – a COA must be robust to ordinary wear and tear. In essence, COAs connect the physical and digital world into a unifying concept that could be applied to a variety of security applications, ranging from anti-skimming for credit cards to tamper-evident seals [2].

In this paper, we propose COAs built based upon the fact that optical media, even when freshly imprinted, still have numerous errors due to the nature of

R. Dingledine and P. Golle (Eds.): FC 2009, LNCS 5628, pp. 222–229, 2009.
© IFCA/Springer-Verlag Berlin Heidelberg 2009

their manufacturing process. There are four sets of detectable errors that occur: (e1) – for each disc imprinted using the same "negative," (e2) – uniquely per disc and their detection is nearly deterministic, (e3) – uniquely per disc however the likelihood that they are detected is ∼0.5, and (e4) – due to wear and tear. Sets e1–3 occur at manufacturing, while the set e4 increases throughout the lifetime of the disc. Although production errors can be controlled as the adversary would stamp discs using a "negative" that already has desired errors imprinted, the adversary cannot control the rate of additional inevitable errors (e1–3) using a low-cost manufacturing process and materials. Thus, the expectation is that "counterfeit" DVDs would always have at least twice as many errors as "authentic" ones for comparable printing technologies. We denote "fingerprints" constructed based upon such errors: *optical DNA* (o-DNA). For widely accepted o-DNA, costs related to **R1** and **R3** would be negligible.

Using o-DNA within the cryptographic realm is simple. When creating an o-DNA instance, i.e., optical disc, the publisher digitally signs the positions of manufacturing errors on this disc using a traditional PKCS [3] as follows. First, the "fingerprint" is scanned using a standard DVD player modified to output the low-level errors, then compressed into a fixed-length string f. Arbitrary text t associated with the disc is then concatenated to f, $w = f\|t$, hashed, and signed using the private key of the issuer. Next, the resulting signature s, w, and optionally, publisher's certificate, are encoded onto the o-DNA instance using a post-production mechanism. SONY, for example, offers a technology that allows for several hundred bytes to be imprinted onto a disc post molding and bonding.[1]

Verification of o-DNA instances is straightforward provided that the verifier is in possession of publisher's public key. We assume that a malicious party cannot tamper with a specific verifier used in-field, however, verifier's full design spec is considered public knowledge. The verifier does not need to store any secrets to fulfill its basic task. The key component of the verifier is a function, $d(f, f')$, that computes the proximity of the signed and in-field scanned "fingerprint." If s is valid and $d(f, f') < \delta$ then the instance would be deemed authentic (δ is a relatively small constant). The system should tolerate a relatively high rate of false negatives because publishers can choose to react only if they receive uncharacteristically high ratio of "false negatives" from a specific source. Figure 1 details the issuing and verification of o-DNA instances using a block diagram.

Finally, we refer the Reader to review a short survey of related work on COAs in [2]. We also mention that there exist several technologies for copy protection of DVDs[2], all with a common problem: all bits that contribute to the protection and are readable by a standard DVD player are easy to circumvent in software. A rare instance of relative success is Microsoft's XBOX which uses a distinct obfuscated low-level data/track format substantially different from DVD and a custom DVD player that can read such optical discs.

---

[1] Unfortunately, we are not aware of any technical references to this technology, hence we refer to it as personal communication with SONY.

[2] See informal survey at Wikipedia:
http://en.wikipedia.org/wiki/CD_copying_software

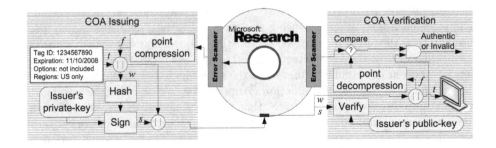

Fig. 1. Diagram of actions taken while signing and verifying an o-DNA instance

2 Optical DNA

Here, we describe how o-DNA is constructed and review its security features. The 120mm DVD standard is detailed in [4]. Impression-based manufacturing of DVDs is a well understood process with low variance of output produced within the same manufacturing facility; however, with possibly strong variance of output across different facilities – in particular for low-quality manufacturing.

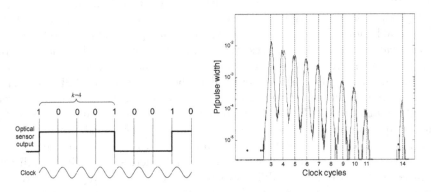

Fig. 2. (left) An example of encoding 100010010 using an NRZI encoder. (right) Distribution of pulse-widths for t_i over the 24th millimeter of a high-quality DVD with the installation data for Microsoft Visual Studio 5.0.

The sensor readout of the physical specification from a DVD consists of an NRZI-encoded signal clocked at 26.1MHz [4]. The signal is "high" or "low" depending on whether there is a pit or a land on the optical disc. The NRZI encoding is such that between two "ones" (i.e., signal floor changes) the signal stays at the same level for integer $k \in \mathbb{C}, \mathbb{C} \equiv \{3, 4, 5, 6, 7, 8, 9, 10, 11, 14\}$ number of clock cycles. The encoding is illustrated in Figure 2(left). Due to manufacturing inefficiencies, in general the distance between two signal floor changes is not an exact multiple of the master clock cycle – it is rather a random variable t that can be represented as: $t_i \equiv k_i + \mathcal{N}(0, \sigma_M), k_i \in \mathbb{C}$, where $\mathcal{N}(0, \sigma_M)$ denotes a random zero-mean Gaussian variable with standard deviation equal to σ_M. Generally we recognize that high-quality manufacturing should have relatively low σ_M. We assume in o-DNA that the legal publisher of protected DVDs is using state-of-the-art manufacturing, i.e., that it is hard to achieve significantly better error rates by an adversarial manufacturing process. Although the error model is likely to be smooth over $|t_i - k_i|$, for a small ε, we postulate:

(i)   Probability that a signal with $\frac{1}{2} - \varepsilon < |t_i - k_i| < \frac{1}{2} + \varepsilon$ is incorrect, is 0.5.
(ii) Probability that a signal with $\frac{1}{2} - \varepsilon \geq |t_i - k_i|$ is incorrect, is 0.
(iii) Probability that a signal with $\frac{1}{2} + \varepsilon \leq |t_i - k_i|$ is incorrect, is 1.

Figure 2(right) presents the distribution of pulse-widths t_i over the 24th millimeter of a single high-quality DVD with the installation data for Microsoft Visual Studio 5.0. The probability that t_i is close to an integer value is relatively high and conversely the probability that t_i is half-way between two integers, is around two orders of magnitude lower. To estimate the error rate, in Figure 3(left) we plot the distribution of $\varepsilon = ||t_i - k_i| - 0.5|$ over the same disc instance used to plot the distribution in Figure 2(right). The data was collected using a reference DVD player by AudioDev with an analog TTL-output representing the NRZI encoded signal recorded at the output of the optical sensor in the DVD player [5]. The TTL-output was sampled at a rate of 10Gsamples/sec to produce accurate statistics. Figure 3(left) illustrates that the likely error rate on the disc used in the experiment, assuming an error threshold $\varepsilon \in [0.05, 0.1]$ and that $\Pr[\frac{1}{2} + \varepsilon \leq |t_i - k|] = 0$, is roughly on the order of 10^{-3}.

The DVD standard uses an efficient codec for converting an alphabet $\mathcal{A}$ that consists of 16-bit symbols encoded using NRZI, into an alphabet $\mathcal{L}$ of 256 8-bit words [4]. Not all 16-bit symbols belong to $\mathcal{A}$, hence we distinguish between legal (that belong to $\mathcal{A}$) and illegal 16-bit symbols. Figure 3(right) illustrates

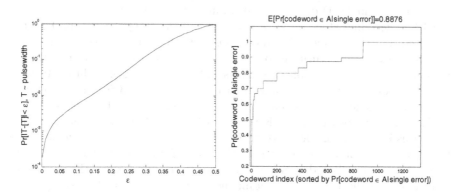

Fig. 3. (left) Distribution of $\varepsilon = ||t_i - k_i| - 0.5|$ over the 24th mm of a DVD with the installation data for MS Visual Studio 5.0. (right) Probability of illegal symbol after an occurrence of a single-position error on a legal 16-bit symbol from $\mathcal{A}$. Symbols from $\mathcal{A}$ are sorted based upon the resulting probability, i.e., $\sim 30\%$ of all symbols in $\mathcal{A}$ never produce an error detectable during NRZI decoding.

the probability that a legal 16-bit keyword remains legal after the event of an arbitrary single position error. Since the probability of an error is relatively low, we consider only the case when a symbol from $\mathcal{A}$ is affected by only one error. The overall probability that a 16-bit erroneous symbol cannot be found in the look-up table $\mathcal{A} \rightarrow \mathcal{L}$, is roughly $p = 10^{-1}$. That means that although there exists an error on the optical disc, the likelihood p that it will be detected during NRZI decoding is low. Such errors are detected accurately in higher levels of decoding.

The main synchronization primitive for low-level encoding in the DVD standard is a cluster of 26 data fields. Each field consists of a specific synchronization pattern (32 NRZI-bits long) and a payload of 91 symbols from $\mathcal{A}$ (1456 NRZI-bits payload). The synchronization pattern is a 32-bit synchronization symbol selected from a specific 32-symbol alphabet $\mathcal{S}$ [4]. The 38688-bit clusters represent the main storage unit on a DVD. We classify all error cases as:

a) **illegal codeword** – (32%) a payload symbol is altered due to an error; the resulting codeword cannot be found in the set of legal words $\mathcal{A}$.

b) **codeword still in $\mathcal{A}$ after error** – (not detected) a payload symbol is altered due to an error; the new symbol exists in $\mathcal{A}$.

c) **shift required to correct a synchronizing symbol** – (63%) errors commonly shift the synch symbols with respect to their correct position within a cluster. Typically, adjustment shifts for one or two positions are sufficient to realign the synch symbols.

d) **illegal synch codeword** – ($< 1\%$) a synch symbol is altered due to an error; the new codeword is not found in the set of legal synch codewords $\mathcal{S}$.

e) **all zeroes codeword** – (4%) – all bits of a symbol equal zero. Such a symbol is not legal both in $\mathcal{A}$ and $\mathcal{S}$; it deserves special attention because it corresponds to a specific manufacturing error.

Percentages presented immediately after the item title in the previous list, specify the occurrence rate for each error type that we detected on the 24th millimeter of our DVD disc under test. Since we did not soft-decode data past the EFM decoding step, we were not able to identify errors of type **b)**. It is expected that the number of such errors is ~10x greater than errors of type **a)**.

Since many manufacturing errors manifest as signals with pulsewidths far from integer clock values, some of these errors will be read differently during distinct DVD read-outs. For example, assume a pulsewidth $d_i = 3.501$ clock cycles. A DVD player could read this pulsewidth as 2 or 3 zeroes in different read-outs. Clearly only one of the values is correct, whereas the other one is erroneous. Since this is a probabilistic effort, while both issuing and verifying the errors of the o-DNA, the player needs to read the same track several times in order to detect most errors. Based upon our error model, reading L times the desired set of tracks from the DVD that contain the "fingerprint," would be sufficient to detect at least $1 - 2^{-L}$ of **e3** errors in that region.

Verification of the o-DNA consists of two steps:

I **verifying that the in-field disc is the same as the issued one** – when scanning, it is trivial for the publisher to identify errors of type **e1** – by comparison with media printed from the same "negative," **e2** and **e3** – by the likelihood of detection in multiple readouts. Dr. Holger Hoffman from Technicolor Inc. has estimated that for a specific sample of DVDs manufactured at their facilities, the ratio of error sets **e1**:**e2**:**e3** is 65:17:28. The o-DNA issuer would sign all of them including their types. During verification, the in-field multi-scan (L times) of errors should identify all errors of type **e2** and most errors of type **e1** and **e3**. Thus, we use the following detector in this step: $||\mathbf{e1} \cap \mathbf{et}|| \geq \alpha_1||\mathbf{e1}||$, $||\mathbf{e2} \cap \mathbf{et}|| \geq \alpha_2||\mathbf{e2}||$, and $||\mathbf{e3} \cap \mathbf{et}|| \geq \alpha_3||\mathbf{e3}||$, where constants $\alpha_1 = \alpha_2 \approx 1$ and α_3 is relatively close to 1 but proportional to L. Operator $||\cdot||$ returns the cardinality of the argument. Set **et** represents all the errors extracted during an in-field test of an o-DNA instance.

II **verifying that the in-field test does not yield too many errors**; the adversary can imprint error sets **e1**, **e2**, and **e3** during an adversarial effort and thus, create a match in step I. However, she cannot control the manufacturing process to the extent to prevent additional expected manufacturing errors. Therefore, the expectation is that she will produce approx. $||\mathbf{e1} \cup \mathbf{e2} \cup \mathbf{e3}||$ additional errors on the counterfeit disc using a printing technology similar to the publisher's. Therefore, the verifier must check whether $||\mathbf{et}|| \leq ||\mathbf{e1} \cup \mathbf{e2} \cup \mathbf{e3}||(1+\beta)$, where β is a real positive scalar smaller than but relatively close to 1 (e.g., $\beta = 0.8$).

Assuming that there is no adversarial attack, the probability of a false positive is practically equal to zero even for relatively small $||\mathbf{e1} \cup \mathbf{e2} \cup \mathbf{e3}||$. The probability of a false negative is proportional to the α parameters and can be tuned to be relatively low. It is rather important that the cardinality of the set of additional errors due to wear and tear $||\mathbf{e4}||$ is not greater than $\beta||\mathbf{e1} \cup \mathbf{e2} \cup \mathbf{e3}||$ – in the opposite case, the verifier would report false negatives. This is a crucial issue with the proposed technology as current wear and tear characteristics of DVDs are far from acceptable [6]. Thus, our key conclusion is that o-DNA, as defined, would be applicable only to DVDs with superior wear and tear characteristics – clearly, scratch resistant materials and more sophisticated sensors would have to be used to enable o-DNA. Another critical comment is the fact that algorithms for symbol decoding are not mandated by the ECMA standard – thus, different manufacturers may use different multiword, usually Viterbi, decoders that could impact error detection. To enable o-DNA, the word decoders in a DVD player would need to be standardized. However, once the standardization is established, o-DNA would represent an exceptionally inexpensive way to identify authentic DVDs, a tool that could be essential in fighting counterfeiting. As expected, the converse part of the grey market where the buyer willingly purchases an obviously pirated DVD copy cannot be addressed by any anti-counterfeiting technology.

Finally, we consider an implementation of o-DNA, where at an error rate of 10^{-3}, an error read-out from the 24th millimeter (approx. 10^3 revolutions) of a standard DVD disc, is sufficient to produce $||\mathbf{e1} \cup \mathbf{e2} \cup \mathbf{e3}||$ on the order of 10^2. The resulting o-DNA message stored back onto the DVD would be approx. 1Kb long. Since the disc encounters 24 revolutions per second at 1x playback speed, one can observe that the verification of an o-DNA could be done in approx. L seconds at 32x playback speed.

3   The DVD Manufacturing Process

DVD media is created using a high-speed automated replication process. Initial glass master of data to be used for disc creation is created via a photolithography process using a laser beam recorder to expose a photo resist coated blank glass master. For DVD5 a single glass master is required as data is wholly contained on one layer of the disc. The glass master is "developed" after exposure resulting in a pattern of bumps in the remaining photo resist. The glass master is nickel metal plated to create a "father," a mirror image negative of the data created by the laser beam recording process on the glass master. The "father" is separated from the glass master and plated with nickel again to create a "mother" positive (same as the original glass master). One "father" can create 5 to 20 "mothers." Each "mother" is again nickel plated to create a stamper; a single "mother" can create up to 50 stampers, the stamper is again a negative image of the original data created by the laser beam glass mastering, each stamper can create up to 10^5 discs. The stampers are separated from the "mother" after plating, and then "punched" to correct outside diameter and correct hub hole inner diameter as required for the specific molding equipment.

The punched stamper is mounted inside the molding chamber of the manufacturing line. Molten polycarbonate is injected under pressure, heat and humidity into the mold chamber. The pattern of pits and lands on the stamper are impressed into the clear polycarbonate under several tons of pressure. The polycarbonate is rapidly cooled via chilled water flowing through the mold chamber housing and separated from the stamper and ejected from the mold chamber. This is considered a DVD half disc, as it is one layer of the final DVD. At this point the disc would not reflect a laser beam in the DVD player. For DVD5 the following steps are then executed. The ejected clear polycarbonate is plated with a layer of reflective material such as aluminum using a sputtering process in order to reflect the laser beam in the DVD player. A clear half disc is bonded onto the aluminum coated half disc creating a final disc 1.2mm thick, with the data in the middle of the disc at ~0.6mm from the bottom surface.

In each of the steps above mechanical tolerances will be present. The degree of jitter and degree of run out in the original glass master will set a baseline for the final finished discs as to the number of errors present. As each plating process to create the "father," "mothers" and stampers is executed additional mechanical tolerances and microscopic differences will be introduced again resulting in varying levels of intrinsic errors. Each stamper will have its own unique set of errors as a result of the tolerance of punching the stamper and mechanically mounting that stamper into a molding chamber.

Once the molding process begins sources of error are mechanical wear on the stamper (a single stamper can create up to 10^5 impressions), as each disc is stamped the stamper wears, resulting in disc #1 of that stamper being different than disc #10^5 from that stamper. However, if the line is run less than 10^5 discs and the stamper is removed and subsequently placed back into a mold chamber the process of dismounting the stamper, handling, storing, and reinstalling the stamper will introduce mechanical tolerance changes.

Each disc created by the molding process is subject to the feed temperature of the polycarbonate, the heat, humidity and pressure in the mold chamber, the quality of the polycarbonate, and how rapidly the polycarbonate is cooled. The mechanical handling of the separation from the stamper and transfer into the remaining processes can all introduce mechanical stresses and changes that will impact the final error signature of the disc. For example, the speed at which the polycarbonate cools and how rapidly the polycarbonate is pulled from the stamper will create changes in the shapes of the pits and lands, these changes can result in errors. The sputtering processes to apply either the semi reflective material or the fully reflective aluminum also have mechanical tolerances that will impact the thickness of the reflective material as well as the amount of reflectivity across the surface of the disc. Changes in reflectivity of the disc as it is scanned by the laser in the DVD player will impact the error rate of the disc. Bonding the two half discs together introduces potential differences in the run out of the two half discs. Finally the finishing of the label on the top surface of the disc can introduce mechanical stresses that create errors. All of these sources of mechanically induced differences in the finished disc will impact its error rates.

4   Summary

Storing one bit on an optical disc costs $\sim 10^{-13}$ dollars, far less than on most other storage media. In this paper, we propose o-DNA, a cryptographically secure low-cost system for counterfeit deterrence of optical media. We recognize robustness to wear-and-tear as the only design criterion for optical discs that implicates o-DNA's efficiency.

Acknowledgements

We would like to thank Vencil Wells from AudioDev, Dr. Paul Liao from Panasonic Research, Jared Feldner from LeCroy, Dr. Holger Hoffman from Technicolor, Hiroo Umeno and June Dorris from Microsoft XBOX, and Dr. David Heckerman from Microsoft Research for discussions that improved this article.

References

1. Simmons, G.J.: Identification of data, devices, documents and individuals. In: IEEE International Carnahan Conference on Security Technology, pp. 197–218 (1991)
2. DeJean, G., Kirovski, D.: RF-DNA: Radio-Frequency Certificates of Authenticity. In: Paillier, P., Verbauwhede, I. (eds.) CHES 2007. LNCS, vol. 4727, pp. 346–363. Springer, Heidelberg (2007)
3. IEEE 1363-2000: Standard Specifications For Public Key Cryptography (2000)
4. Standardizing Information and Communication Systems. 120 mm DVD - Read-Only disc. Standard ECMA-267. 3rd edn. (2001)
5. Audiodev CAT300 DVD Reference Player, http://www.audiodev.com/?id=2088
6. Slattery, O., et al.: Stability Comparison of Recordable Optical Discs – A Study of Error Rates in Harsh Conditions. Journal of Research of the NIST 109(5), 517–524 (2004)

Passwords: If We're So Smart, Why Are We Still Using Them?*

Cormac Herley[1], P.C. van Oorschot[2], and Andrew S. Patrick[3]

[1] Microsoft Research, Redmond, U.S.A
[2] School of Computer Science, Carleton University, Canada
[3] National Research Council, Ottawa, Canada

Abstract. While a lot has changed in Internet security in the last 10 years, a lot has stayed the same – such as the use of alphanumeric passwords. Passwords remain the dominant means of authentication on the Internet, even in the face of significant problems related to password forgetting and theft. In fact, despite large numbers of proposed alternatives, we must remember more passwords than ever before. Why is this? Will alphanumeric passwords still be ubiquitous in 2019, or will adoption of alternative proposals be commonplace? What must happen in order to move beyond passwords? This note pursues these questions, following a panel discussion at Financial Cryptography and Data Security 2009.

1 Introduction

Passwords have served us well for many years, but they suffer from a number of problems that suggest their reign should be coming to an end. Users often choose weak passwords, making guessing and brute-force dictionary and exhaustive attacks feasible. Users also frequently forget passwords, necessitating expensive customer support calls or automated backup authentication schemes (often involving challenge questions, which may be even weaker forms of authentication). Because of these cognitive challenges, users frequently store copies of their passwords (in places vulnerable to attackers), and use the same password for multiple systems. Users also can have their passwords stolen through phishing, social engineering, man-in-the-middle, and keylogging attacks. The static nature of passwords then allows repeated unauthorized access by attackers.

Even with all of these problems, passwords remain the dominant method for access control. There are reasons to be optimistic about change, however. The popular press has frequent stories about identity theft and fraud, and there appears to be increasing awareness, even among unsophisticated users, about password issues. Few consumer security problems get more attention than banking passwords. Many banks have altered their authentication mechanisms, suggesting a willingness to adapt and go beyond traditional passwords. There has also been a surge of activity in proposing alternatives to password authentication, both in the academic research literature and the startup scene. As economic

---

* Version: April 3, 2009.

R. Dingledine and P. Golle (Eds.): FC 2009, LNCS 5628, pp. 230–237, 2009.

gain has emerged as a primary motivation for computer security exploits, there should be increased motivation to move beyond simple passwords. On the other hand, despite these signs of real need and a desire for change, adoption of authentication alternatives has been very slow.

In this note we consider possible reasons why we are moving so slowly in replacing problematic password systems, how we might accelerate the progress, and where we might be in ten years. Rather than focus on the specifics of particular technologies, we prefer to consider forces that drive or retard progress, including technology, economics, and usability.

2   Some Proposed Alternatives to Basic Passwords

Numerous authentication alternatives and enhancements to basic passwords have been proposed, each with its own advocates. Two-factor authentication schemes, where the user demonstrates possession of a physical token, reduce or eliminate a number of problems associated with passwords. These schemes have seen relatively limited use, other than for very high value accounts, because of usability issues, cost of tokens and support (including replacement), the need for server changes, and the expanding key-chain problem (where users require a separate token for each account). Cell phones and various types of trusted mobile devices have been suggested as a means of achieving a two-factor scheme using a device that users already carry. Public-key infrastructure with client-side certificates offers significantly stronger authentication than passwords, but it has achieved very limited deployment. Biometrics, for example in the form of fingerprints or iris scans, are used in some secure settings, but there are unresolved issues around deployment, privacy, and authentication from untrusted hardware.

Alternatives that claim to preserve the usability and convenience of passwords while overcoming their most serious shortcomings are frequently proposed. For example, graphical passwords (e.g., see Chiasson [5, Chapter 2] for a recent survey) offer the possibility of improved strength, memorability, and usability. Combinations of text and graphical passwords [15] may also offer advantages.

In addition to proposals to replace passwords, researchers and developers have explored techniques to alleviate some of the threats associated with password use. On-screen keyboards, for example, attempt to evade password-stealing keyloggers by having the user enter the password using a graphically displayed keyboard. While this helps against malware that logs keystrokes, it is vulnerable to more sophisticated logging malware and browser plug-ins. Phishing toolbars [13] attempt to alert users before they enter credentials on low reputation web-sites.

Techniques such as SiteKey [2] have been deployed by a number of major financial institutions; these attempt to have the user authenticate the site only after verifying that a personalized image is present. Another recent innovation, EV SSL (extended validation SSL) certificates [4], require that the grantee (i.e., the web-site) undergo greater vetting from the Certifying Authority. The real benefit of these new technologies remains questionable. Studies have shown that users largely ignore the absence of a SiteKey image and EV SSL indicators

[18,20]. The need for automated password reset mechanisms has sparked interest in systematic analysis of challenge questions and backup authentication [17].

3   Barriers to Moving beyond Passwords

There are many barriers to moving beyond ubiquitous alphanumeric passwords.

Diversity of requirements. Passwords are used to protect a wide range of services, from financial transactions to free webmail and social networking sites. No authentication alternative proposed to date is suitable for all of these services, splintering the target markets and weakening the case for adoption of any one new technology. The best solution often depends heavily on specific use cases.

Competing technical proposals. As noted above, there is no shortage of proposed alternatives to basic password authentication. Each has different advantages, disadvantages, and costs, all competing for mindshare.

Competing goals among stakeholders. Different views of costs and benefits are held by web sites, browser manufacturers, vendors of anti-virus software and security technologies, industry standards bodies, governments, and end-users. In some cases, an organization mandating "stronger" authentication may risk customer defection to competitors who continue with "more usable" authentication technologies (such as basic passwords).

Scarcity of loss data. There is a scarcity of data on the scale, frequency, nature and financial impact of password loss incidents, as well as on the number and nature of adversaries. For example there are orders of magnitude difference between various estimates of phishing losses [11]. When password loss does occur, we seldom have good data on whether phishing, social engineering, man-in-the-middle or keylogging was responsible. It is difficult to "fix" security without reliable measurements of what is broken, especially when the solutions are not cheap or easy. Even with relevant loss-related data, it may be difficult for an organization to make trade-off decisions about known loss incidents caused by weak password authentication versus the unknown costs of possible customer defection and increased support.

User reluctance and usability. Stronger authentication often requires additional user effort and buy-in. It is notoriously hard to motivate users about "better security." Solutions that concentrate on making passwords non-guessable risk increasing the forgetting problem, while solutions that concentrate on the forgetting problem can increase the risk of guess-ability. Solutions that concentrate on lost and stolen passwords risk introducing additional costs and complexity.

Individual control of end-user platforms. Online merchants as well as service providers largely rely on leveraging existing software and platforms (e.g., browser and operating system) which end-users have individually obtained at their own expense and preference. This limits alternatives which require specific platforms or software deployments. For example, in the U.S., banks apparently cannot force users to secure their own end-systems, leaving a big technical challenge.

No single organization can impose a solution. The combination of the above factors, plus a decentralized and global Internet that no one organization owns or controls, has resulted in a lack of consensus on what we need to do to move beyond alphanumeric passwords. Anderson et al. [1] discuss related issues in their report on the broader topic of barriers, incentives, and failures in the market for network and information security within the European Union.

4 Moving beyond Passwords

Having reviewed barriers to making changes, we next consider, through a series of questions, what it will take to move beyond passwords.

Q1: Are any of the problems with current passwords true show-stoppers?

One viewpoint is that the problem is not as large as imagined. End-users are comfortable using weak passwords and asking for password resets when they forget them. It is unclear how much password strength helps if phishing and key-logging are the main threats [9]. Parties who do suffer pain from the present use of passwords, as direct financial losses, management cost, or usability, apparently are either: (1) not suffering enough to trigger a switch to alternatives, or (2) not in a position to evoke change. Some service providers may believe that to keep costs down it is better to minimize direct contact with customers (e.g., avoiding support calls) than to deploy stronger authentication.

A different viewpoint is that there are big problems, which are either hidden, unknown, or knowingly under-stated. Surprisingly little is actually known about large-scale usage of passwords on the Internet. For example, despite conditions in banking user agreements (e.g., in Canada) which stipulate that users must not re-use passwords across applications [14], a study of the Internet password habits of half a million browser toolbar users [8] indicates that cross-site password re-use is very common. A related problem, largely unstudied to date, is the impact on memorability and usability when end-users must remember many different passwords.

While passwords and credit card numbers are largely transported over SSL today, the roll-out of EV SSL certificates [12,20] apparently complicates the task for end-users already struggling with interpreting the previous browser security cues (e.g., lock icon, https indicator). This may be viewed as negative progress in the usability of certificate interfaces over the past fifteen years.

One emerging use of passwords in Europe and Canada is PINs related to chip-cards (smartcards) – cards with embedded micro-processors. In the U.K. "chip and PIN" intiative [7], signatures authorizing financial transactions are replaced by consumer entry of a 4-digit PIN. The vendor motivation for adopting the new system is an off-loading of liability. Users become responsible for all approved transactions where authorization relied on a correct PIN, whereas for traditional magnetic-stripe technology with signatures, users are liable for losses in disputed transactions only if they are shown to be negligent or involved in fraud. (From a legal perspective in countries like the U.K., liability related to signature forgery falls on the relying party. PIN-authorized transactions apparently fall outside the scope of such statutory protection, and banks assert that use of a PIN implies cardholder negligence.) Consumers may be particularly unhappy to learn this detail of the new technology in light of prior demonstrations [6] that chip and PIN readers can leak user PINs.

Q2: What major security improvements have been adopted in the past 15 years by banks, related to online banking security and passwords?

In an attempt to reduce password theft (i.e., phishing attacks), online banks are starting to employ site verification schemes. For example, SiteKey [2] asks users to assign a unique image to their login credentials, and to only proceed with a login if their image is displayed back to them. An empirical study [18] suggests, however, that users will still enter their banking passwords when presented with fraudulent messages claiming that the image authentication server is down (although these results may be problematic [16]). SiteKey may be more effective as marketing effort (users feel more secure) than as a security enhancement.

SSL continues to be used for protecting passwords for countless online banking sites, and for protecting credit card numbers during online transactions. For the latter, security "enhancements" such as the third party verifier services Verified By Visa and Mastercard SecureCode have emerged. During a registration phase, a user must enter the 3-digit sequence printed on the back of their credit card along with other personal information, and choose a (new) password. On subsequent online card usage, the verifier service requests this password, but not the 3-digit code. (Oddly, some vendor sites request the 3-digit sequence be re-entered, before transferring the user on to the verifier service.) Of course, once such a 3-digit number is input to the Internet, its security value erodes. Users trained to do so make easy prey for phishers; and, this approach gives end-users the privilege of remembering yet another password. Some banks in Canada similarly now require or recommend a second (extra) password be used for higher risk financial transactions. Whether to consider these as "improvements" is unclear.

Banks are starting to deploy dynamic challenge questions and two-factor authentication. Orthogonal to these is a move towards authentication of specific transactions. Bank of America's optional SafePass, for example, requires that customers register a mobile phone that can receive text messages that contain one-time authentication codes [3]. It will be interesting to monitor the success of this program, its support costs, and how often people lose or change cell phone numbers, or claim they don't have their cell phone handy. Software implementations of one-time passcodes generators are receiving renewed interest – e.g., a new iPhone application [10] supports one-time passwords for AOL, eBay, and PayPal. Ideally, transaction authorization or transaction integrity systems will cryptographically bind one-time authorization codes with specific transaction details.

Several proposals have been made for one-time passwords for credit cards (e.g., [19]). Deployment examples include the American Express Private Payments scheme and Discover Card's Secure Online Account Numbers. Similar schemes allow end-users to dynamically generate one-time card numbers for on-line purchases (e.g., Citicards). While a promising direction, adoption has been limited, perhaps due to lack of promotion or low consumer motivation due to loss limits on credit cards. The main development for improving credit card transaction security appears to be in transaction authentication and back-end (system side) profiling. One might conclude that no password alternative yet proposed has better cost-benefit attributes, or that banks' existing back-end mechanisms are cheaper than anything involving customers more directly.

Q3: If we have made little progress on password authentication – perhaps the simplest Internet security problem – are researchers and security vendors fooling themselves if we think that our technologies solve real-world problems?

While passwords seem to be a simple technology, it seems unfair to suggest that authentication is the simplest Internet security problem. Indeed, many of the most difficult problems in Internet security can be reduced to authentication, and when we say authentication we often mean authorization.

No doubt, some researchers fail to do proper research into discovering the true real-world requirements, and fail to understand that in practice, complete solutions are needed. No doubt, some security vendors fail to build products that ideally meet needs, and under-estimate deployment and inter-operability issues with products. The economic barriers and incentives involved in security solutions are only recently receiving attention. Evidently, the solutions proposed so far would cost more than the problem, and good back-end transaction monitoring may mean that this state will remain for some period of time.

In addition, academics and researchers often have personal biases and over-position their own proposals as full solutions, in part due to a competitive process which often requires marketing in order for papers to be accepted for publication. Given the investment in passwords, both in infrastructure and in user acceptance and understanding, it is very difficult to see partial solutions displacing the incumbent technology. For example, it is hard to justify investment in a proposal that addresses phishing, but not key-logging, or one that helps when the user logs in from a particular machine, but not when roaming on other machines. This means that many proposals that have great merit and solve real problems do not achieve traction because they don't solve all the problems, or fail to solve a sufficient fraction of the problems relative to the extra costs.

Q4: Why have North America and Europe chosen different paths in online banking password authentication to date?

Many European banks use one-time password lists for authentication in online banking, while simple passwords (with presumably more back-end profiling) are more common in the U.S. and Canada. It is not clear to us which of the two is the better path. One possible reason for the difference is perhaps Europeans are more familiar/comfortable with real-world authentication and tolerate extra effort as required for security; passports are more common in Europe, for historical reasons.

It may also be that the differences are largely due to regulations related to liability for losses. In North America, banks have been largely responsible for covering losses unless there is evidence of fraud by the customer. This reduces the motivation for users to invest time and energy in better authentication. There may also be less customer loyalty in the U.S., with banking customers more likely to switch banks for competitive reasons; this might make banks reluctant to implement any changes that increase the costs or complexity for the customer.

5   Accelerating Progress and Predictions for 2019

Perhaps significant progress cannot be made without a major economic event or catastrophe that creates a tipping point – that is, only when the direct losses related to the use of simple passwords are large enough will there be a ground-swell of adoption of more efficient solutions or advanced technologies. On the other hand, an innovative, cost-effective solution may emerge and trigger widespread adoption, like the relatively inexpensive, conceptually simple, SSL in browsers.

More government regulation may be required, with serious penalties when use of weak technologies results in losses. The players with power (e.g., financial institutions) prefer to shift liability and responsibility for losses onto those without power (e.g., the customers). This is a significant problem if powerless customers are experiencing real hardships in the form of indirect costs, such as time lost and mental stress, when security breaches occur. If the direct losses, suffered by banks, are far smaller than these indirect costs, endured by customers, there will be little impetus for banks to drive change. It may be that only government regulations will address such a difference in power. Anderson et al. [1] suggest numerous policy changes involving additional regulations.

Where will we be in ten years? Will passwords be completely replaced by other authentication methods, or will we still be struggling with the same issues? Likely any adoption of stronger authentication technologies will be gradual and that decisions to deploy new schemes will be based on economic factors such as the value of transactions and the nature of the risks. Low-value, casual transactions may well still use ordinary passwords in ten years or even twenty.

We expect that economics and usability are far more likely than technological developments to be the primary drivers of authentication changes. As mentioned earlier, until the direct economic losses become large enough, there may be little incentive to make changes that could lead to problems in support costs or usability. Also, in the absence of tools to measure the economic losses and the effectiveness of new technological proposals, we expect the adoption of password alternatives to continue to be difficult to justify.

Acknowledgements. We would like to thank Bob Blakley and Fabian Monrose for ideas during planning of the panel; participants of FC '09 for a lively and productive discussion; and M. Mannan, Steven Murdoch, and Susan Landau (who also graciously moderated the panel) for helpful comments. The second author acknowledges NSERC funding of his Canada Research Chair in Network and Software Security, an NSERC Discovery Grant, and NSERC ISSNet.

References

1. Anderson, R., Bohme, R., Clayton, R., Moore, T.: Security Economics and the Internal Market. ENISA (European Network and Information Security Agency). Shortened version: Security Economics and European Policy (March 2008)
2. Bank of America – Online Banking. SiteKey at Bank of America, http://www.bankofamerica.com/privacy/sitekey/
3. Bank of America. SafePass: Online Banking Security Enhancements, http://www.bankofamerica.com/privacy/index.cfm?template=learn_about_safepass
4. CA/Browser Forum, http://www.cabforum.org/
5. Chiasson, S.: Usable Authentication and Click-Based Graphical Passwords. PhD thesis, Carleton University, Ottawa, Canada (January 2009)
6. Drimer, S., Murdoch, S.J., Anderson, R.: Thinking Inside the Box: System-level Failures of Tamper Proofing. In: Proc. 2008 IEEE Symposium on Security and Privacy (2008)
7. Drimer, S., Murdoch, S.J., Anderson, R.: Optimised To Fail: Card Readers for Online Banking. In: Financial Cryptography and Data Security (2009)
8. Florêncio, D., Herley, C.: A Large-scale Study of Web Password Habits. In: Proc. of World Wide Web Conference (2007)
9. Florêncio, D., Herley, C., Coskun, B.: Do Strong Web Passwords Accomplish Anything? In: Proc. of Usenix HotSec (2007)
10. Hansell, S.: What's the Password? Only Your iPhone Knows. Bits Blog (Business, Innovation, Technology, Society), The New York Times, March 31 (2009)
11. Herley, C., Florêncio, D.: A Profitless Endeavor: Phishing as Tragedy of the Commons. In: New Security Paradigms Workshop (NSPW) (2008)
12. Jackson, C., Simon, D.R., Tan, D.S., Barth, A.: An Evaluation of Extended Validation and Picture-in-Picture Phishing Attacks. In: Dietrich, S., Dhamija, R. (eds.) FC 2007 and USEC 2007. LNCS, vol. 4886, pp. 281–293. Springer, Heidelberg (2007)
13. Jakobsson, M., Myers, S. (eds.): Phishing and Countermeasures: Understanding the Increasing Problem of Electronic Identity Theft. John Wiley and Sons, Chichester (2007)
14. Mannan, M., van Oorschot, P.C.: Security and Usability: The Gap in Real-World Online Banking. In: New Security Paradigms Workshop 2007 (NSPW) (2007)
15. van Oorschot, P.C., Wan, T.: TwoStep: An Authentication Method Combining Text and Graphical Passwords. In: 4th MCETECH Conference on eTechnologies. LNBIP, vol. 26, pp. 233–239. Springer, Heidelberg (2009)
16. Patrick, A.S.: Commentary on research on new security indicators (2007), http://www.andrewpatrick.ca/essays/commentary-on-new-security-indicators/ (retrieved March 3, 2009)
17. Rabkin, A.: Personal Knowledge Questions for Fallback Authentication. In: SOUPS (2008)
18. Schechter, S.E., Dhamija, R., Ozment, A., Fischer, I.: The Emperor's New Security Indicators. In: Proc. 2007 IEEE Symposium on Security and Privacy (2007)
19. Shamir, A.: SecureClick: A Web Payment System with Disposable Credit Card Numbers. In: Financial Cryptography (2001)
20. Sobey, J., Biddle, R., van Oorschot, P.C., Patrick, A.S.: Exporing User Reactions to Browser Cues for Extended Valiation Certificates. In: Jajodia, S., Lopez, J. (eds.) ESORICS 2008. LNCS, vol. 5283, pp. 411–427. Springer, Heidelberg (2008)

Defeating Cross-Site Request Forgery Attacks with Browser-Enforced Authenticity Protection

Ziqing Mao, Ninghui Li, and Ian Molloy

Department of Computer Science, Purdue University
305 N. University Street, West lafayette, IN 47906
{zmao,ninghui,imolloy}@cs.purdue.edu

Abstract. A cross site request forgery (CSRF) attack occurs when a user's web browser is instructed by a malicious webpage to send a request to a vulnerable web site, resulting in the vulnerable web site performing actions not intended by the user. CSRF vulnerabilities are very common, and consequences of such attacks are most serious with financial websites. We recognize that CSRF attacks are an example of the confused deputy problem, in which the browser is viewed by websites as the deputy of the user, but may be tricked into sending requests that violate the user's intention. We propose Browser-Enforced Authenticity Protection (BEAP), a browser-based mechanism to defend against CSRF attacks. BEAP infers whether a request reflects the user's intention and whether an authentication token is sensitive, and strips sensitive authentication tokens from any request that may not reflect the user's intention. The inference is based on the information about the request (e.g., how the request is triggered and crafted) and heuristics derived from analyzing real-world web applications. We have implemented BEAP as a Firefox browser extension, and show that BEAP can effectively defend against the CSRF attacks and does not break the existing web applications.

Keywords: Cross-Site Request Forgery, Web Security, Browser Security.

1 Introduction

Cross-site request forgery, also known as one-click attack or session riding and abbreviated as CSRF or XSRF, is an attack against web applications [18,19,25]. In a CSRF attack, a malicious web page instructs a victim user's browser to send a request to a target website. If the victim user is currently logged into the target website, the browser will append authentication tokens such as cookies to the request, authenticating the malicious request as if it is issued by the user. Consequences of CSRF attacks are most serious with financial websites, as an attacker can use CSRF attacks to perform financial transactions with the victim user's account, such as sending a check to the attacker, purchasing a stock, purchasing products and shipping to the attacker.

A CSRF attack does not exploit any browser vulnerability. As long as a user is logged into the vulnerable web site, simply browsing a malicious web page can lead to unintended operations performed on the vulnerable web site. Launching

R. Dingledine and P. Golle (Eds.): FC 2009, LNCS 5628, pp. 238–255, 2009.

such CSRF attacks is possible in practice because many users browse multiple sites in parallel, and users often do not explicitly log out when they finish using a web site. A CSRF attack can also be carried out without a user visiting a malicious webpage. In a recent CSRF attack against residential ADSL routers in Mexico, an e-mail with a malicious IMG tag was sent to victims. By viewing the email message, the user initiated an HTTP request, which sent a router command to change the DNS entry of a leading Mexican bank, making any subsequent access by a user to the bank go through the attacker's server [2].

CSRF appeared in the Open Web Application Security Project (OWASP) top 10 web application threats in 2007 (ranked at 5) [16]. Several CSRF vulnerabilities against real-world web applications have been discovered [24,20,21]. In 2007, a serious CSRF vulnerability in Gmail was reported [22]. It allowed a malicious website to surreptitiously add a filter to a victim user's Gmail account that forwards emails to a third party address. CSRF vulnerabilities are very common. The potential damage of CSRF attacks, however, has not been fully realized yet. We quote the following from an online article [8],

> Security researchers say it's only a matter of time before someone awakens the "sleeping giant" and does some major damage with it – like wiping out a user's bank account or booking a flight on behalf of a user without his knowledge.
> "There are simply too many [CSRF-vulnerable Websites] to count," says rsnake, founder of ha.ckers.org. "The sites that are more likely to be attacked are community websites or sites that have high dollar value accounts associated with them – banks, bill pay services, etc."

Several defense mechanisms have been proposed and used for CSRF attacks. However, they suffer from various limitations (see Section 2.3).

In this paper, we study browser-based defense against CSRF attacks, which is orthogonal to server-side defenses. The websites should follow the best practice to defend against the CSRF attacks before browser-side defenses are universally adopted. One crucial advantage of a browser-based solution compared with a server-side solution is that a user who started using the protected browser will immediately have all his web browsing protected, even when visiting websites that have CSRF vulnerabilities. Furthermore, because the number of major browsers is small, deploying protection at the browser end can be achieved more easily, compared with deploying server-side defenses at all websites.

We recognize that CSRF attacks are an example of the confused deputy problem. The current web design assumes that the browser is the deputy of the user and that any HTTP request sent by the browser reflects the user's intention. This assumption is not true as many HTTP requests are under the control of the web pages and do not necessarily reflect the user's intention. This becomes a security concern for HTTP requests that have sensitive consequences (such as financial consequences).

Our solution to this problem is to enhance web browsers with a mechanism ensuring that *all sensitive requests sent by the browser should reflect the user's intention*. We achieve that by inferring whether an HTTP request reflects the intention of the user and whether an authentication token is sensitive, and stripping all sensitive authentication tokens from the HTTP requests that may not reflect the user's intention. We call it *Browser-Enforced Authenticity Protection*.

We have implemented a prototype of BEAP as a Firefox browser extension. The implementation consists of about 800 lines of Javascript. An extension without modifying the browser core enables easy initial deployment. The full benefit of BEAP will be achieved if it is implemented in major web browsers. We use theoretical analysis and experiments to show that BEAP can effectively defend against the CSRF attacks and it does not break the existing web applications.

In Section 2, we describe the background, the related work, and the CSRF vulnerabilities we found in real-world web applications. We describe our proposal and the prototype implementation in Section 3. In Section 4, we analyze the effectiveness and compatibility of our proposal. Finally, we conclude in Section 5.

2   Understanding CSRF Attacks and Existing Defenses

CSRF attacks exploit existing authenticated sessions. Two common approaches for maintaining authenticated web sessions are cookies and HTTP authentication credentials, which we call *authentication tokens*.

Cookies [13] are pieces of text data sent by the web server to the browser. The browser stores the cookies locally and sends them along with every further request to the original web site who sets them. After a web site has authenticated a user, for example, by validating the user name and password entered by the user, the web site can send back a cookie containing a "session ID" that uniquely identifies the session, which is referred to as *authentication cookie*. If the web server relies only on cookies for user authentication, every request that has a valid authentication cookie is interpreted as an intended request issued by the authenticated user who owns the session. When sending a cookie to a browser, the website can specify an optional attribute expires among other three attributes. The expires field takes the value of a date that indicates how long the cookie is valid. After the date passes, the browser deletes the cookie. If the expires field is omitted, then the cookie is called a *session cookie* and should be deleted when user closes the web browser. Cookies with an expires field are called *persistent cookies*. Most financial websites and sensitive services specify the authentication cookie as a session cookie, because the session cookies are removed when the browser is closed and won't be abused by others who may share the same computer and browser.

HTTP authentication [4], an authentication mechanism defined in the HTTP protocol [6], is widely used within Intranet environments. In the mechanism, when accessing a webpage that requires authentication, the browser will popup a dialog asking for the username and password. After entering the information, the credential is encoded and sent to the web server via the Authorization request header. The browser remembers the credential until the browser is closed. When later the user visiting the webpages in the same authentication realm, the browser automatically includes the credential in the request via the Authorization header.

CSRF attacks use HTTP requests that have lasting observable effects at the web site. Two request methods are used in real-world HTTP requests: GET and POST. According to the HTTP/1.1 RFC document [6], the GET method, which is known as a "safe" method, is used to retrieve objects. The GET requests should not have any lasting observable effect (e.g., modification of a database). The operations that have lasting observable effects should be requested using the method POST. The POST requests have a request body and are typically used to submit forms. However, there exist web applications that do not follow the standard and use GET for requests that have lasting side effects.

Visiting web pages in one site may result in HTTP requests to another site; these are called cross-site requests. More precisely, in a cross-site request, the link of the request is provided by a website that is different from the destination website of the request. Cross-site requests are common. For example, a webpage may include images, scripts, style files and sub-frames from a third-party website. When the user clicks a hyper-link or a button contained in a webpage, the linked URL may be addressing a third-party website.

2.1 The CSRF Attack

The general class of cross site request forgery (CSRF) attacks was first introduced in a posting to the BugTraq mailing list [25], and has been discussed by web application developers [18,19]. CSFR attacks use cross-site requests for malicious purposes. For example, suppose that the online banking application of bank.com provides a "pay bills" service using an HTML form. The user asks the bank to send a check to a payee by completing the form and clicking the "Sumbit" button. Upon the user clicking the button, a POST request is sent to the server, together with the authentication cookie. When the web server receives this HTTP request, it processes the request and sends a check to the payee identified in the request.

A CSRF attack works as follows. While accessing the bank account, the user simultaneously browses some other web sites. One of these sites, evil.org, contains a hidden form and a piece of JavaScript. As soon as the user visits the web page, the browser silently submit the hidden form to bank.com. The format and content of the request is exactly the same as the request triggered by the user clicking the submit button in the "pay bill" form provided by the bank. On sending the request, the user's browser automatically attaches the authentication cookies to the request. Since the session is still active in the server, the request will be processed by the server as issued by user. As illustrated in this example, POST requests can be forged by a hidden form. If the bank uses GET request for the pay bill service, the request can be easily forged by using various HTML elements, such as ⟨img⟩, ⟨script⟩, ⟨iframe⟩, ⟨a⟩ (hyper-link) and so on.

We note that as long as a user is logged in to a vulnerable web site, a single mouse click or just browsing a page under the attacker's control can easily lead to unintended operations performed on the vulnerable web site.

CSRF vs. XSS. CSRF vulnerabilities should not be confused with XSS vulnerabilities. In XSS exploits, an attacker injects malicious scripts into an HTML document hosted by the victim web site, typically through submitting text embedded with code which is to be displayed on the page, such as a blog post. Most XSS attacks are due to vulnerabilities in web applications which fail in sanitizing untrustworthy inputs which might in turn be displayed to users. CSRF attacks do not rely on the execution and injection of malicious JavaScript code. CSRF vulnerabilities are due to the use of cookies or HTTP authentication as the authentication mechanism. A web site that does not have XSS vulnerabilities may contain CSRF vulnerabilities.

2.2   Real-World CSRF Vulnerabilities

In order to understand how commonly the CSRF vulnerability exists in the real-world web applications, one of the authors of the paper examined about a dozen web sites for which he has an account and usually visits. As a result, we found four of them are vulnerable to CSRF attacks as shown in Table 1. We verified all the attacks with Firefox 2.0.

Table 1. The CSRF vulnerabilities discovered in real world websites

Vulnerable web site	Targeted sensitive operation
A university credit union site	Money transfer between accounts; adding a new account
A university web mail	Deleting all emails in the Inbox
An online forum for HTML development	Posting a message; updating user profile
Department portal site	Editing biography information

The university credit union site relies on session cookies for authentication. Some services provided in the online banking are vulnerable to the CSRF attack. In particular, adding new accounts and transferring money between accounts are vulnerable. In the experiment, we conducted a benign attack that transfers $0.01 from the victim's checking account to the saving account. We also successfully launch an attack to add an external account. Combining these two enables the adversary to transfer money from the victim's account to an arbitrary external account. Fortunately, the bank requires contacting the help-desk personally to confirm the operation of adding an external account. And also the bill paying service is not vulnerable.

The university web mail uses session cookies for authentication. Most sensitive operations (e.g., sending an email, changing the password) are protected against the CSRF attacks using secret token validation (see Section 2.3). However, the feature of "managing folders" is vulnerable, and a CSRF attack can be launched to remove all emails in the victim's Inbox.

In an online forum for HTML development, all operations are vulnerable to the CSRF attack. The attacker is able to impersonate the victim user to send a posting, update the user profile, and so on. The vulnerable forum is created using phpBB [17], which is the most widely used open source forum solution. All forums created using phpBB 2.0.21 or earlier are vulnerable to the CSRF attack [23]. This is a well-known vulnerability and there are CSRF attack generators for phpBB forums available online. Many public forums have upgraded to phpBB 2.0.22 or later, but there are still many forums using the vulnerable versions.

In the departmental portal site, a CSRF attack is able to edit the biography information of the victim shown on the webpage.

We have reported the vulnerabilities to the websites of the university credit union and the university web mail; we did not expose the name of those websites here because they have not fixed the vulnerabilities yet. These examples of vulnerabilities demonstrate that there exist a considerable amount of web services vulnerable to the CSRF attacks and the potential damage could be severe.

2.3   Existing CSRF Defenses

Several defense mechanisms have been proposed for CSFR attacks, we now discuss their limitations.

Filtering authentication tokens from cross-site requests. Johns et al. [10] proposed a client-side proxy solution, which strips all authentication tokens from a cross-site request. The proxy intercepts web pages before they reach the browser and appends a secret random value to all URLs in the web page. Then the proxy removes the authentication tokens from the requests that do not have a correct random value. The solution breaks the auto-login feature and content sharing websites (such as Digg, Facebook, etc.) because it does not distinguish legitimate cross-site requests from malicious cross-site requests. In addition, it does not support HTML dynamically created in the browser and cannot work with SSL connections.

Authenticating web forms. The most popular CSRF defense is to authenticate the web form from which an HTTP request is generated. This is achieved by having a shared random secret, called a as a *secret validation token*, between the web form and the web server. If a web form provides a sensitive service, the web server embeds a secret validation token in an invisible field or the POST action URL of the form. Whenever form data is submitted, the request is processed only if it contains the correct secret value. Not knowing the secret, the adversary cannot forge a valid request. One drawback of this approach is it requires nontrivial changes to the web applications. Moreover, as pointed out by Barth et al. [3], although there exist several variants of this technique they are generally complicated to implement correctly. Many frameworks accidentally leak the secret token to other websites. For example, NoForge proposed in [11] leaks the token to other websites through the URL and the HTTP Referer header.

Referer-checking. In many cases, when the browser issues an HTTP request, it includes a Referer header that indicates which URL initiated the request. A web application can defend itself against CSRF attacks by rejecting the sensitive requests with a Referer of a different website. A major limitation with this approach is that some requests do not have a Referer header. There does not exist a standard specification on when to and when not to send the Referer header. Different browser vendors behave differently. Johns and Winter [10] give a summary on when browsers do not send the Referer header in major browsers. As a result, both a legitimate request and a malicious request may lack the Referer header. The adversary can easily construct a request lacking the Referer header. Moreover, because the Referer header may contains sensitive information that impinges on the privacy of web users, some users prohibit their browsers to send Referer header and some network proxies and routers suppress the Referer headers. As a result, simply rejecting the requests lacking a Referer header incurs a compatibility penalty. Barth et al. [3] suggested a new Origin header that includes only the hostname part of the Referer header, to alleviate the privacy concern. It remains to be seen whether this will be adopted. In conclusion, using a server-side referer-checking to defeat the CSRF attacks has a dilemma in handling the requests that lack a Referer header.

Restricting cross-domain requests based on server-provided policies. Terri et al. [15] proposed a new policy model named Same Origin Mutual Approval (SOMA), which enhanced the existing same-origin policy model by requiring mutual approval for sending cross-domain HTTP requests. The SOMA model requires changes to both web applications and browsers; in their model a web application specifies the approved peers and the browsers must enforce the policy. The SOMA model is able to prevent cross-site request forgery attacks launched only from unapproved websites. If the web application must accept requests from sites that are not trustworthy, in order to prevent CSRF attacks, the web application must be partitioned across sub-domains; pages that perform sensitive actions must be placed in sub-domains that only approve requests from trusted domains. This requires the application developer to identify sensitive pages, make potentially significant changes to both the application and their domain structure, and identify trusted domains, all of which are nontrivial.

While some applications, such as web based banking, are a natural fit for SOMA where cross-site requests have little benefit to either the application developer or the user, many web based applications are not. For example, consider the Web 2.0 model for building web applications. It would be impractical and impossible for web developers of social-networking, social-bookmarking, video-sharing, wikis, etc. implement a SOMA approved domain list. The very philosophy behind the Web 2.0 movement is in fact contradictory to the SOMA model.

2.4   A Variant of CSRF Attack

All existing CSRF defenses fail when facing a variant of CSRF attacks mentioned in [7] and [3]. We use the Facebook as an example to illustrate the attack. Facebook allows the users to post an article or a video from any website to the user's own profile. For example, the user can post a video from Youtube.com to his Facebook profile by clicking "Share – Facebook" under the video. When clicking the link, the following GET request is sent to the Facebook: `http://www.facebook.com/sharer.php?u=http://www.youtube.com/ watch?v=VIDEO_ID&t=VIDEO_TITLE`. This request loads a confirmation page (Fig. 1(A)) which asks the user the click a "Post" button to complete the transaction. After the user clicking the "Post" button, a POST request is sent to `http://www.facebook.com/ajax/share.php` to confirm the posting operation.

An attacker is able to launch a CSRF attack that posts anything to the victim user's profile. On the malicious webpage, the attacker includes an iframe linking to the posting confirmation page (Fig. 1(A)). In addition, the attacker is able to auto-scroll the iframe to the "Post" button and hide other parts of the page by using two nested iframes and manipulating the sizes of the iframes. The sample code of the attack with Firefox 2.0 is given in Appendix A. As a result, what is shown in the browser looks like Fig. 1(B). The user can be easily tricked to click the "Post" button without knowing that he is posting something to his own Facebook profile.

Facebook.com uses secret validation token to defend against CSRF attacks. However, because the request is sent by user clicking the "Post" button in the confirmation page provided by Facebook the request will include a correct validation token. Using a referer-checking would also fail because the final posting request has a Referer header of Facebook.com.

This attack is traditionally defended using "frame busting", in which the target webpage includes a piece of JavaScript to force itself to be displayed in a top-level frame [12]. However, this defense can be defeated if the attacker disables the JavaScript in the sub-frame that links to the target webpage [9].

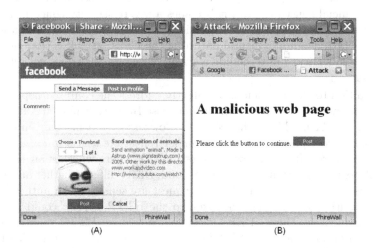

Fig. 1. (A): The confirmation page that posts a video from Youtube.com to the Facebook profile; (B): A malicious page that includes (A) as an iframe and tries to trick the user click the button without seeing other parts of (A)

3   Browser-Enforced Authenticity Protection (BEAP)

CSRF attacks are particularly difficult to defend because cross-site requests are a feature of the web. Many web sites use legitimate cross-site requests, and some of these usages require the attachment of cookies to cross-site requests to work properly (e.g., posting a video from Youtube to Facebook in the above example). To effectively defend against CSRF attacks, one needs as much information about an HTTP request as possible, in particular, how the request is triggered and crafted. Such information is available only within the browser. Existing defenses suffer from the fact that they do not have enough information about HTTP requests. They either have to change the web application to enhance the information they have or to use unreliable source of information (such as Referer header). Even when such information is available, it is still insufficient. For example, they cannot defend against the attack in Section 2.4 because while they can tell the request is coming from their web form, they do not know that the web form is actually embedded in a page controlled by the attacker.

We focus on browser-based defense against CSRF attacks. It is well known that CSRF is a confused deputy attack against the browser. The current web design assumes that the browser is *always* the deputy of the user and that any HTTP request sent by the browser reflects the user's intention. This assumption is not true as many HTTP requests are under the control of the web pages and do not necessarily reflect the user's intention. This confusion causes no harm when these requests have no sensitive consequences, and merely retrieve web pages from the web server. However, when these requests have sensitive consequences (such as financial consequences), it becomes a severe security concern. Because such requests occur in authenticated sessions, these requests have authentication tokens attached. The fundamental nature of the CSRF attack is that the user's browser is easily tricked into sending a sensitive request that does not reflect the user's intention.

Our solution to this problem is to directly address the confused deputy problem of the browser. More specifically, we propose Browser-Enforced Authenticity Protection (BEAP), which enhances web browsers with a mechanism ensuring that *all sensitive requests sent by the browser reflect the user's intention*. BEAP achieves this through the following. First, BEAP infers whether an HTTP request reflects the intention of the user. Second, BEAP infers whether authentication tokens associated with the HTTP request are sensitive. An authentication token is sensitive if attaching the token to the HTTP request could have sensitive consequences. Third, if BEAP concludes that an HTTP request reflects the user's intention, the request is allowed to be sent with authentication tokens attached. If BEAP concludes that an HTTP request may not reflects the user's intention, it strips all sensitive authentication tokens from the HTTP request. In this rest of this section, we describe BEAP in details.

3.1   Inferring the User's Intention

In inferring whether an HTTP request reflects the user's intention, we classify the requests into two types depending on the source of the request. Type-1 requests are caused by the webpages hosted in the browser. When displaying a webpage, the browser may send additional requests to retrieve the resources included in the web page, such as images, scripts and so on. These resources may come from the same website or a third-party website. Similarly, when the user clicks a hyper-link or a button contained in a webpage, requests are sent by the browser. In addition, the Javascripts contained in the webpages may send requests as well. In all these cases, the URLs and contents of the requests are determined by the source webpage. Whether such a request reflects the user's intention is inferred by *browser-enforced Source-set checking*, which we will explain soon.

Type-2 requests are not associated with a source webpage. For example, when the user clicks an URL embedded in an email, the URL is passed to the browser as a startup argument, resulting in an HTTP request that is not associated with any webpage already hosted in the browser. We use the following *user-interface intention heuristics* to infer whether a type-2 request reflects the user's intention.

1. *Address-bar-entering.* When the user types in a URL in the address bar and hits enter, the request sent by the browser is considered as intended, because we can assure that the user intends to visit the URL she typed in.

   Note that we distinguish between typing in by keyboard and pasting from the clipboard. The adversary may send the victim an email, which contains a URL that links to a CSRF attack. Instead of providing a hyper-link for the user to click, the email can ask the user to copy and paste the URL to the browser's address-bar. To defeat this trick, only when the URL is typed in to the address-bar by the keyboard, the request is intended. If the URL is pasted from the clipboard, the request is not considered to be intended.

2. *Bookmark-clicking.* When the user selects a link from the bookmarks, the request is considered as intended, because users are usually careful in maintaining the bookmarks.

3. *Default-homepage.* When the browser displays the default home page either when it starts or when user clicks the "homepage" button, the request is considered intended, because the configuration of default homepage is set by the user and cannot be easily modified by malicious web sites.

All other type-2 requests are not considered to be intended. For example, when the user clicks a link from the history, or when the user clicks a link outside the browser (e.g., in an email or a word document), the requests are not considered as intended. When performing those actions, users normally do not have a clear idea about which web site they are going to. The history and the links outside the browser may contain malicious contents that could launch CSRF attacks. Note that these requests are still allowed to proceed, we will only strip sensitive authentication tokens from them.

Browser-enforced *Source-set* Checking. To determine whether a type-1 request reflects the user's intention, we borrow the idea from the server-side referer-checking technique. Our approach has two significant differences. First, the enforcement is done by the browser rather than the web application. In this way, the Referer header does not need to be sent to the web server. This addresses the privacy concerns caused by sending out the Referer header, and it is compatible to the browsers and network devices that block the Referer header. In addition, the browser is able to check the Referer for all requests whose links are provided by a webpage (type-1 requests); so it avoids the dilemma in the server-side referer-checking with the requests that lack a Referer header. Second, we extend the notion of Referer to *Source-set* by taking into account the visual relationships among webpages in the browser. As a result, we can defeat the CSRF attack against Facebook mentioned in Section 2.4. *Source-set* checking can only be done in the browser.

Intuitively, the *Source-set* of a request includes all web pages that can potentially affect the request. We define the *Source-set* as follows.

Definition 1. *The* referer *of a request is the webpage that provides the link to the request. The* Source-set *of a request includes its referer and all webpages hosted in ancestor frames of the referer.*

For example, in Fig. 1, when the user clicks the "Post" button in the last tab, a request is sent to Facebook.com. The referer of the request is the innermost iframe that links to `http://www.facebook.com/sharer.php`. The *Source-set* includes the referer and its two ancestor webpages that are from the malicious website (In the attack, the malicious webpage includes an iframe linking to another malicious webpage, which further includes an iframe linking to Facebook. See Appendix A for the sample code of the attack).

The rationale for including all ancestors of the referer page in the *Source-set* of a request is because all ancestor webpages can potentially affect the request. Users are typically unaware of the existence of the frame hierarchy, and they assume they are visiting the website hosted in the top-level frame with the URL shown in the address-bar. The parent frame is able to manipulate the URL, size, position and scrolling of child frame, to fool the user. As a result, when the user performs some actions in the child frame, those actions may not reflect the user's intention. Therefore, the referer and all its ancestor webpages are considered to be in the *Source-set* of a request.

Given a type-1 request, we consider it reflect the user's intention if all webpages in the *Source-set* are from the same website as the destination of the request. This is based on the following assumption: a request sent by a website to itself reflects the user's intention. In other words, a website won't launch a CSRF attack against itself.

3.2   Inferring the Sensitive Authentication Tokens

We have introduced a mechanism to infer whether an HTTP request reflects the user's intention. A simple way to defend against the CSRF attacks is to strip all cookies and other authentication tokens from all requests that may not reflect the user's intention. However, such a policy would break some existing web applications. In particular, it would disable the legitimate cross-site requests that need to carry authentication tokens. An important observation is that although legitimate cross-site requests may need to carry an authentication token, legitimate cross-site requests typically do not lead to sensitive consequence, because sensitive operations typically require an explicit confirmation that is done in the target website. Based on this observation, we further infer whether an authentication token is sensitive or not for a request, and strip only sensitive authentication tokens from requests that may not reflect the user's intension.

We use heuristics derived from analyzing the real-world web applications to determine whether an authentication token is sensitive or not for a request, based on the following information: (1) Whether the request is GET or POST. (2) Whether the token is a session cookie, a persistent cookie or an HTTP authorization header. (3) Whether the communication channel is HTTP or HTTPS. Our heuristics are summarized in Table 2 and are explained below.

Table 2. The default policy enforced by the browser

	GET		POST
	HTTP	HTTPS	
Session Cookies	Not Sensitive	Sensitive	Sensitive
Persistent Cookies	Not Sensitive		
HTTP Authorization Header	Sensitive		

The HTTP authorization headers are always sensitive. The HTTP authorization headers are typically used in the home/enterprise network. The services using the authorization headers for authentication are typically sensitive, e.g., home router administration, enterprise network services. In addition, it would be severe if a malicious website in the Internet is able to launch a CSRF attack against a service inside the Intranet.

For cookies we distinguish between the two request methods. All cookies that are attached to the POST requests are sensitive for two reasons. First, according to the HTTP/1.1 RFC document, all the operations that have lasting observable effects should be requested using the method POST. Second, the POST requests are used to submit forms and forms are mostly submitted to the same website as that provides the form. So to strip authentication tokens from the cross-site POST requests will protect all web applications that follow the RFC standard, and won't affect the existing web applications.

However, there exist some web applications that do not follow the standard and use GET requests for sensitive operations. We would like to protect those web applications against the CSRF attacks as well. For the cookies with GET requests, the policy further distinguishes between the session cookies and persistent cookies. The persistent cookies (those that have an expiration date) with GET requests are not sensitive. The persistent cookies are commonly used by the websites to provide personalized services without asking the user to explicitly log in. For example, `Amazon.com` displays recommendations based on the user's

Fig. 2. Youtube provides links to various content sharing websites under the video

history activities. This is achieved by storing the user's identity and related information in persistent cookies. If the user links to Amazon.com from a third party website (e.g., a search engine), the request should carry the persistent cookies so that Amazon.com is able to recognize the user and provides a personalized service. Therefore, there exists legitimate cross-site GET requests that need to carry persistent cookies. On the other hand, most sensitive web applications (especially financial websites such as banks) use session cookies (those that does not have an expiration date and will be deleted when the browser is closed) as the authentication token for sensitive operations. For example, the persistent cookies are not enough for a user to place an order in Amazon.com, he needs to type in his password to obtain a session cookie to place an order. Some financial websites provide a "Remember me" option with the login form, but typically that is used to remember the user's username, the user still needs to type in the password to obtain a session cookie in order to access his account. Furthermore, using persistent cookies for sensitive operations is a bad practice, because the users may access their accounts from public computers (e.g., in an Internet Cafe). Using persistent cookies for authenticating sensitive operations would allow the persons who use the same computer following the user to impersonate the user.

It is a bit complicated for the session cookies with GET requests. We observe some websites issue legitimate cross-site GET requests that need to carry session cookies. In particular, the content sharing websites, such as Digg, Facebook, etc., allow people to discover and share contents from anywhere on the Internet, by submitting links and stories. Many webpages include links to the submission pages of those websites, so that the users can easily post the current article or video to their accounts. For example, as shown in Figure 2, Youtube.com provides links to various content sharing websites under each video. When clicking the Facebook link, a GET request is sent from Youtube.com to Facebook.com. If the user already logs in to Facebook.com, the request will carry the session cookie and the user can be directly linked to the submission page (Fig. 1(A)) without logging in again. To preserve this functionality of the content sharing websites, the policy treats the session cookies with GET requests using the HTTP protocol as not sensitive. In contract, the session cookies with GET requests using the HTTPS protocol are sensitive, because the sensitive services are typically served over HTTPS.

In conclusion, we infer whether an authentication token is sensitive as summarized in Table 2. To defend against the CSRF attack, we strip the sensitive authentication tokens from the requests that may not reflect the user's intention.

3.3   Implementation

We have implemented a prototype of our proposal as a Firefox browser extension. It consists of about 800 lines of Javascript code. The prototype supports Firefox 2.0-3.0 and is available for download from Mozilla.org[1]. The extension intercepts each request when it is going to be sent, and removes the cookies and HTTP authorization headers that are not allowed to be attached according to the policy. The user interface in Firefox is implemented using XUL (XML User Interface Language), which is an XML user interface markup language. The XUL is flexible and extensible. To implement the user intention heuristics for type-1 requests, the extension hooks onto the events corresponding to those actions and overloads the event-handlers. To compute the *Source-set* of each request, the extension first identified the referer of the request, and then computes the source-set based on the frame hierarchy. The overhead introduced by our implementation is minimal. See Appendix B for details.

4   Evaluation and Discussions

Effectiveness of BEAP. How effective is BEAP for defending against CSRF attacks? In other words, how effective dose BEAP achieves "all sensitive requests sent by the browser reflect the user's intention"? We now answer these questions by analyzing under what assumptions the two inferences work correctly.

We observe that, under three assumptions, a CSRF attack always results in a request that BEAP considers to not reflect the user's intention. First, the browser has not been compromised. BEAP is not designed to defend against attacks that exploit vulnerabilities in browsers to take over the browser or the operating system. BEAP defends against CSRF attacks, which exploit web browsers' design feature of allowing cross-site requests. Defending against browser exploitation is orthogonal to our work. Second, a user will not type in a CSRF attack URL in the address bar, or include a CSRF attack page in the bookmark, or use it as the default homepage. Under these two assumptions, type-2 requests that are considered as intended are not CSRF attacks. Third, a website does not include CSRF attacks against itself. This ensures that any CSRF attack via type-1 requests will be correctly classified. The third assumption means that we cannot defend against CSRF attacks that are injected into the target website. For example, the attacker may be able to inject a CSRF attack into a forum via a posting, which sends a posting on the victim's behalf. In this case, the malicious request is actually not a cross-site request, and will be treated as intended. Such an attack cannot be defeated by a pure client-side defense, because the browser

---

[1] https://addons.mozilla.org/en-US/firefox/addon/9416

cannot tell which requests in a webpage are legitimately added by the web site and which ones are maliciously added by user postings. The problem should be addressed by having the web application sanitize the user input to be displayed in the website, similar to defending against XSS attacks.

Second, BEAP allows non-sensitive cookies to be sent with requests that are not intended. This causes no harm when these requests do not have sensitive consequences. This is true assuming that websites do not contain sensitive operations that (1) use GET requests and rely on persistent cookies for authentication, or (2) use GET requests over HTTP and rely on session cookies for authentication. We would like to point out that these are all bad practices and are vulnerable to attacks other than CSRF attacks. First, using GET for requests that have sensitive consequence violates the HTTP/1.1 standard [6]. Second, when using persistent cookies for authenticating sensitive services, the accounts can be easily stolen if the user access the account in a public computer. Third, serving sensitive service over HTTP enables the network attacker to launch session injection attack. In particular, we did not observe any financial websites violate these assumptions; they are all hosted over HTTPS and relying on session cookies for authentication.

We have also experimentally evaluated our implementation, by verifying that it successfully defends against all attacks we have found in Section 2.2.

Compatibility of BEAP. BEAP will strip cookies and HTTP authentication headers from some requests. Would this affect the existing web applications and change the user's browsing experiences? We now show that the answer is no.

First, we point out that cookie blocking has already been used for other purposes. Cookies, such as those set by `doubleclick.com`, can be used to track users' browsing behavior and violate user' privacy. Because of this, Internet Explorer 6 and later versions protect the user's privacy with respect to cookies [14]. In particular, IE requires web sites to deploy policies as defined by P3P (Platform for Privacy Preferences) [1]. When a website does not provide a P3P policy or the policy does not satisfy the user's preference, IE performs cookie filtering against the website. The approach applied by IE's cookie filtering has similarities with our defense against the CSRF attacks, but it aims at protecting privacy while we aim at protecting authenticity. The cookie filtering infers whether a cookie may violate the user privacy based on the type of the cookie and the heuristics derived from real-world web applications. When the focus is privacy rather than authenticity, persistent cookies are considered more sensitive than session cookies, and a persistent cookie with no associated P3P policy is "leashed", and will not be attached to requests downloading third-party content. And also a third-party cookie with no associated P3P policy is denied.

We tested the compatibility of our implementation against 19 popular websites ranging 6 categories as shown in Table 3. On each website, we logged in the account and tried the major functionalities provided by the website and the operations that normal users would perform. For some of them, we created a new user account. Everything worked well, and all the browsing experiences remained unchanged. We did not use a crawler or an automatic tool to perform a large-scale

Table 3. The web applications used for compatibility evaluation

Categories	Web sites	Operations
Email	Gmail, Hotmail	Check emails, send emails, change settings
Social network	MySpace, Facebook	create accounts, add friends, modify the profiles
Online shopping	Amazon, ebay	place bids, buy items, update the profiles
Financial sites	PayPal, Chase, Citi Cards, American Express, Fidelity, Discover Cards, PEFCU	add a bank account, money transfer, pay bills
Personal desktop	iGoogle, Windows Live	Setup a personal desktop
Internet portal	Yahoo!	Check emails, write a movie review

compatibility testing, because testing the compatibility is possible only when we have an account on a website and log into the account to perform authenticated operations. In particular, creating web accounts on financial websites typically require having physical accounts.

Finally, we note that while we have not encountered web sites that use cross-site requests in a way affected by BEAP's policy, it is certainly plausible for such sites to exist. However, we note that the functionalities provided by these web sites are not disabled. When cookies are stripped, the worst case is that the user needs to re-enter the password in order to perform certain operations.

5   Conclusions

CSRF vulnerabilities are common in real-world web applications, and the consequences of such attacks are most severe with financial websites. We have proposed a browser-based mechanism called BEAP to defend against the CSRF attacks. It infers whether a request sent by the browser is sensitive and whether an authentication token is sensitive, and strips sensitive authentication tokens from any request that may not reflect the user's intention. We have implemented BEAP as a browser extension for Firefox, and have shown that BEAP can effectively defend against the CSRF attacks, and does not break the existing web applications.

Acknowledgement

This work is supported by NSF CNS-0448204 (CAREER: Access Control Policy Verification Through Security Analysis And Insider Threat Assessment), and by sponsors of CERIAS.

References

1. The platform for privacy preferences project (p3p), http://www.w3.org/TR/P3P
2. The web hacking incidents database (2008),
   http://www.webappsec.org/projects/whid/byid_id_2008-05.shtml

3. Barth, A., Jackson, C., Mitchell, J.C.: Robust defenses for cross-site request forgery. In: Proc. ACM Conference on Computer and Communications Security (CCS) (October 2008)
4. Franks, J., Hallam-Baker, P., Hostetler, J., Lawrence, S., Leach, P., Luotonen, A., Stewart, L.: HTTP authentication: Basic and digest access authentication. RFC 2617 (June 1999), http://www.ietf.org/rfc/rfc2617.txt
5. Google. Load time analyzer 1.5, firefox add-on (March 2007), https://addons.mozilla.org/en-US/firefox/addon/3371
6. Group, N.W.: Hypertext transfer protocol – HTTP/1.1. RFC 2616 (June 1999), http://www.ietf.org/rfc/rfc2616.txt
7. Hansen, R., Stracener, T.: Xploiting google gadgets: Gmalware and beyond (August 2008)
8. Higgins, K.J.: CSRF vulnerability: A 'sleeping giant' (2006)
9. Jackson, C.: Defeating frame busting techniques (2005), http://www.crypto.stanford.edu/framebust/
10. Johns, M., Winter, J.: RequestRodeo: Client side protetion against session riding. In: Proceedings of the OWASP Europe 2006 Conference (2006)
11. Jovanvoic, N., Kirda, E., Kruegel, C.: Preventing cross site request forgery attacks. In: Proceedings of the Second IEEE Conference on Security and Privacy in Communication Networks (September 2006)
12. Koch, P.: Frame busting, http://www.quirksmode.org/js/framebust.html
13. Kristol, D., Montulli, L.: HTTP state management mechanism. RFC 2965 (October 2000), http://www.ietf.org/rfc/rfc2965.txt
14. MSDN. Privacy in internet explorer 6, http://msdn.microsoft.com/en-us/library/ms537343VS.85.aspx
15. Oda, T., Wurster, G., van Oorschot, P., Somayaji, A.: Soma: Mutual approval for included content in web pages. In: Proc. ACM Conference on Computer and Communications Security (CCS) (October 2008)
16. OWASP. Top ten most critical web application security vulnerabilties. Whitepaper (2007), http://www.owasp.org/index.php/Top_10_2007
17. phpBB. Create communities worldwide, http://www.phpbb.com
18. Shiflett, C.: Foiling cross-site attacks (October 2001), http://shiflett.org/articles/foiling-cross-site-attacks
19. Shiflett, C.: Security corner: Cross-site request forgeries (December 2004), http://shiflett.org/articles/cross-site-request-forgeries
20. US-CERT. Cross-site request forgery (CSRF) vulnerability in @mail webmail 4.51. CVE-2006-6701 (December 2006), http://nvd.nist.gov/nvd.cfm?cvename=CVE-2006-6701
21. US-CERT. Multiple cross-site request forgery (CSRF) vulnerabilities in phpmyadmin before 2.9.1. CVE-2006-5116 (October 2006), http://nvd.nist.gov/nvd.cfm?cvename=CVE-2006-5116
22. US-CERT. Google gmail cross-site request forgery vulnerability. Vulnerability Note 571584 (October 2007), http://www.kb.cert.org/vuls/id/571584
23. US-CERT. Cross-site request forgery (CSRF) vulnerability in privmsg.php in phpbb 2.0.22. CVE-2008-0471 (January 2008), http://nvd.nist.gov/nvd.cfm?cvename=CVE-2008-0471
24. US-CERT. Cross-site request forgery (CSRF) vulnerability in the Linksys wrt54gl wireless-g broadband router. CVE-2008-0228 (January 2008), http://nvd.nist.gov/nvd.cfm?cvename=CVE-2008-0228
25. P. W. Cross-site request forgery (2001), http://www.tux.org/~peterw/csrf.txt

Appendix

A   The Attack Code of the Facebook Example

The following code is constructed for Firefox 2.0.

1. The top-level frame of the malicious webpage.

```
<html>
    <head>
        <title>Attack</title>
    </head>
    <body>
        <br><h1>A malicious web page</h1></br>
        Please click the button to continue.
        <iframe src ="inner.html" width=70 marginwidth="25%" height=20
        scrolling="no" frameborder="0" class="iframe"></iframe>

    </body>
</html>
```

2. The mid-level frame "inner.html".

```
<html>
    <body onload="window.scrollTo(1440, 980);">
        <iframe src="http://www.facebook.com/sharer.php?u=
        http%3A//www.youtube.com/watch%3Fv%3DnQSZOri6PjO&
        t=Sand%20animation%20of%20animals."
        width=3000 height=1000 frameborder=0></iframe>
    </body>
</html>
```

B   Performance Evaluation

We evaluated the performance overhead introduced by the browser extension. The experiment was carried out on a 2.19GHz Intel Core 2 Duo with 2GB of memory , running the Windows operating system. We used Firefox 2.0.0.13 as a base for performance comparison. We compared the page loading times for account login on a few common web sites. The page loading times are measured using the Load Time Analyzer extension [5]. Each page is loaded 5 times, and the loading times are averaged. The results is shown in Table 4. The performance overhead is less than 8%, with an average of 2%.

Table 4. The comparison of the page loading times for login

Web sites	MySpace	iGoogle	Paypal	Yahoo!	eBay
Page loading times for login (base)	2629	1352	6422	1094	1387
Page loading times for login (upgraded)	2733	1464	6484	1125	1399

Evil Searching: Compromise and Recompromise of Internet Hosts for Phishing

Tyler Moore[1] and Richard Clayton[2]

[1] Harvard University, Center for Research on Computation and Society, USA
`tmoore@seas.harvard.edu`
[2] Computer Laboratory, University of Cambridge, UK
`richard.clayton@cl.cam.ac.uk`

Abstract. Attackers compromise web servers in order to host fraudulent content, such as malware and phishing websites. While the techniques used to compromise websites are widely discussed and categorized, analysis of the methods used by attackers to identify targets has remained anecdotal. In this paper, we study the use of search engines to locate potentially vulnerable hosts. We present empirical evidence from the logs of websites used for phishing to demonstrate attackers' widespread use of search terms which seek out susceptible web servers. We establish that at least 18% of website compromises are triggered by these searches. Many websites are repeatedly compromised whenever the root cause of the vulnerability is not addressed. We find that 19% of phishing websites are recompromised within six months, and the rate of recompromise is much higher if they have been identified through web search. By contrast, other public sources of information about phishing websites are not currently raising recompromise rates; we find that phishing websites placed onto a public blacklist are recompromised no more frequently than websites only known within closed communities.

1 Introduction

Criminals use web servers to host phishing websites that impersonate financial institutions, to send out email spam, to distribute malware, and for many other illegal activities. To reduce costs, and to avoid being traced, the criminals often compromise legitimate systems to host their sites. Extra files – web pages or applications – are simply uploaded onto a server, exploiting insecurities in its software. Typical techniques involve the exploitation of flaws in the software of web-based forums, photo galleries, shopping cart systems, and blogs. The security 'holes' that are taken advantage of are usually widely known, with corrective patches available, but the website owner has failed to bother to apply them.

The criminals use a number of techniques for finding websites to attack. The most commonly described is the use of scanners – probes from machines controlled by the criminals – that check if a remote site has a particular security vulnerability. Once an insecure machine is located, the criminals upload 'rootkits' to ensure that they can recompromise the machine at will [26], and then

R. Dingledine and P. Golle (Eds.): FC 2009, LNCS 5628, pp. 256–272, 2009.
© IFCA/Springer-Verlag Berlin Heidelberg 2009

exploit the machine for their own purposes – or perhaps sell the access rights on the black market [10]. If the access obtained is insufficient to deploy a rootkit, or the criminal does not have the skills for this, the website may just have a few extra pages added, which is quite sufficient for a phishing attack.

An alternative approach to scanners, that will also locate vulnerable websites, is to ask an Internet search engine to perform carefully crafted searches. This leverages the scanning which the search engine has already performed, a technique that was dubbed 'Google hacking' by Long [16]. He was interested not only in how compromisable systems might be located, but also in broader issues such as the discovery of information that was intended to be kept private. Long called the actual searches 'googledorks', since many of them rely upon extended features of the Google search language, such as 'inurl' or 'intitle'.

In this paper we examine the evidence for the use of 'evil searches': googledorks explicitly intended to locate machines that can be used in phishing attacks.[1] In Section 2 we explain our methodology and give details of our datasets. Although it is widely accepted that criminals use these techniques, to our knowledge, this is the first study to document their prevalence 'in the wild'.

We make a number of contributions. In Section 3 we clearly establish 'cause and effect' between the use of evil searches and the compromise of web servers and estimate the extent of evil searching. In Section 4 we study website *re*-compromise, showing that over 19% of compromised servers host a phishing website on at least one more occasion. In Section 4.3 we demonstrate a clear linkage between evil search and these recompromises. However, 'findability' is not necessarily bad; in Section 5 we consider the subset of websites that appear in PhishTank's publicly available list of compromised sites and find evidence that being listed in PhishTank slightly decreases the rate of recompromise, demonstrating the positive value of this data to defenders. Our final contribution, in Section 6, is to discuss the difficulties in mitigating the damage done by evil searching, and the limitations on using the same searches for doing good.

2   Data Collection Methodology

We receive a number of disparate 'feeds' of phishing website URLs. We take a feed from a major brand owner, which consists almost exclusively of URLs for the very large number of websites attacking their company, and another feed that is collated from numerous sources by the Anti-Phishing Working Group (APWG) [3]. We fetch data from two volunteer organizations: 'PhishTank' [21], which specializes in the URLs of phishing websites, and 'Artists Against 419' [4], which mainly deals with sites designed to facilitate auction scams or complex advanced fee fraud conspiracies. We also receive feeds from two 'brand protection' companies who offer specialist phishing website take-down services. These companies amalgamate feeds from numerous other sources, and combine them with data from proprietary phishing email monitoring systems.

---

[1] While we focus on websites used for phishing, once a site is found it could be used for any malevolent purpose (e.g., malware hosting).

Table 1. Categorization of phishing website hosting, October 2007–March 2008

Type of phishing attack	Count	%
Compromised web servers	88 102	75.8
Free web hosting	20 164	17.4
Rock-phish domains	4 680	4.0
Fast-flux domains	1 672	1.4
'Ark' domains	1 575	1.4
Total	116 193	100

Although by their nature these feeds have substantial overlaps with each other, in practice each contains a number of URLs that we do not receive from any other source. The result is that we believe that our database of URLs is one of the most comprehensive available, and the overwhelming majority of phishing websites will come to our attention. In principle, we could use capture-recapture analysis to estimate what proportion of sites we were unaware of, as attempted by Weaver and Collins [27]. However, the lack of independence between the various feeds makes a robust estimate of coverage impractical to achieve.

2.1 Phishing-Website Demographics

In this paper we consider the phishing websites that first appeared in our feeds during the six month period from October 2007 through March 2008. We can split these into a number of different categories according to the hosting method used. Table 1 summarizes their prevalence.

By far the most common way to host a phishing website is to compromise a web server and load the fraudulent HTML into a directory under the attacker's control. This method accounts for 75.8% of phishing. It is these sites, and the extent to which they can be located by evil searches, that this paper considers.

A simpler, though less popular approach, is to load the phishing web page onto a 'free' web host, where anyone can register and upload pages. Approximately 17.4% of phishing web pages are hosted on free web space, but since there is no 'compromise' here, merely the signing up for a service, we do not consider these sites any further.

We can also distinguish 'rock-phish' and 'fast-flux' attacks, where the attackers use malware infected machines as proxies to hide the location of their web servers [19]. A further group, we dub 'Ark', appears to use commercial web hosting systems for their sites. All of these attackers use lengthy URLs containing randomly chosen characters. Since the URLs are treated canonically by the use of 'wildcard' DNS entries, we ignore the specious variations and just record canonical domain names. Collectively, these three methods of attack comprise 6.8% of phishing websites. Once again, because the exploitation does not involve the compromise of legitimate web servers, and hence no evil searching is required, we do not consider these attacks any further.

Table 2. Evil search terms found in Webalizer logs, June 2007–March 2008

Search type	Websites	Phrases	Visits
Any evil search	204	456	1 207
Vulnerability search	126	206	582
Compromise search	56	99	265
Shell search	47	151	360

2.2 Website-Usage Summaries

Many websites make use of The Webalizer [24], a program for summarizing web server log files. It creates reports of how many visitors looked at the website, what times of day they came, the most popular pages on the website, and so forth. It is not uncommon to leave these reports 'world-readable' in a standard location on the server, which means that anyone can inspect their contents.

From June 2007 through March 2008, we made a daily check for Webalizer reports on each website appearing in our phishing URL feeds. We recorded the available data – which usually covered activity up to and including the previous day. We continued to collect the reports on a daily basis thereafter, allowing us to build up a picture of the usage of sites that had been compromised and used for hosting phishing websites.

In particular, one of the individual sub-reports that Webalizer creates is a list of search terms that have been used to locate the site. It can learn these if a visitor has visited a search engine, typed in particular search terms and then clicked on one of the search results. The first request made to the site that has been searched for will contain a 'Referrer' header in the HTTP request, and this will contain the terms that were originally searched for.

2.3 Types of Evil Search

In total, over our ten month study, we obtained web usage logs from 2 486 unique websites where phishing pages had been hosted (2.8% of all compromised websites). Of these usage logs, 1 320 (53%) recorded one or more search terms.

We have split these search terms into groups, using a manual process to determine the reason that the search had been made. Many of the search terms were entirely innocuous and referred to the legitimate content of the site. We also found that many advanced searches were attempts to locate MP3 audio files or pornography – we took no further interest in these searches.

However, 204 of the 1 320 websites had been located one or more times using 'evil' search terms, viz: the searches had no obvious innocent purpose, but were attempts to find machines that might be compromised for some sort of criminal activity. We distinguish three distinct types of evil search and summarize their prevalence in Table 2.

Vulnerability searches are intended to pick out a particular program, or version of a program, which the attacker can subvert. Examples of searches in this group include 'phpizabi v0.848b c1 hfp1' (CVE-2008-0805 is an unrestricted file upload vulnerability) and 'inurl: com_juser' (CVE-2007-6038 concerns the ability of remote attackers to execute arbitrary PHP code on a server).

Compromise searches are intended to locate existing phishing websites, perhaps particular phishing 'kits' with known weaknesses, or just sites that someone else is able to compromise. Examples include 'allintitle: welcome paypal' and 'inurl:www.paypal.com' which both locate PayPal phishing sites.

Shell searches are intended to locate PHP 'shells'. When attackers compromise a machine they often upload a PHP file that permits them to perform further uploads, or to search the machine for credentials – the file is termed a shell since it permits access to the underlying command interpreter (bash, csh etc.). The shell is often placed in directories where it becomes visible to search engine crawlers, so we see searches such as 'intitle: "index of" r57.php' which looks for a directory listing that includes the r57 shell, or 'c99shell drwxrwx' which looks for a c99 shell that the search engine has caused to run, resulting in the current directory being indexed – the drwxrwx string being present when directories have global access permissions.

3   Evidence for Evil Searching

So far, we have observed that some phishing websites are located by the use of dubious search terms. We now provide evidence of evil searches leading directly to website compromise. While difficult to attain absolute certainty, we can show that there is a consistent pattern of the evil searches appearing in the web logs at or before the time of reported compromise.

3.1   Linking Evil Search to Website Compromise

Figure 1 presents an example timeline of compromises, as reconstructed from our collections of phishing URLs and Webalizer logs. On 30 November 2007, a phishing page was reported on the http://chat2me247.com website with the path /stat/q-mono/pro/www.lloydstsb.co.uk/lloyds_tsb/logon.ibc.html.

We began collecting daily reports of chat2me247.com's Webalizer logs. Initially, no evil search terms were recorded, but two days later, the website received a visit triggered by the search string 'phpizabi v0.415b r3'. Less than 48 hours after that, *another* phishing page was reported, with the quite different location of /seasalter/www.usbank.com/online_banking/index.html.

Given the short period between search and re-compromise, it is very likely that the second compromise was triggered by the search. Also, the use of a completely different part of the directory tree suggests that the second attacker was unaware of the first. Figure 1 shows a screenshot from a web search in April 2008 using the same evil search term: chat2me247.com is the 13th result out of 696 returned by Google, suggesting a high position on any attacker's target list.

We have observed similar patterns on a number of other websites where evil search terms have been used. In 25 cases where the website is compromised

1: 2007-11-30 10:31:33 phishing URL reported: `http://chat2me247.com`
`/stat/q-mono/pro/www.lloydstsb.co.uk/lloyds_tsb/logon.ibc.html`
2: 2007-11-30 no evil search term   0 hits
3: 2007-12-01 no evil search term   0 hits
4: 2007-12-02 phpizabi v0.415b r3   1 hit
5: 2007-12-03 phpizabi v0.415b r3   1 hit
6: 2007-12-04 21:14:06 phishing URL reported: `http://chat2me247.com`
`/seasalter/www.usbank.com/online_banking/index.html`
7: 2007-12-04 phpizabi v0.415b r3   1 hit

Fig. 1. Screenshot and timeline of a phishing website compromise using an evil search

multiple times (as with `chat2me247.com`), we have fetched Webalizer logs in
the days immediately preceding the recompromise (because we were studying
the effects of the initial compromise). For these sites we are able to ascertain
whether the evil search term appears before compromise, on the same day as
the compromise, or sometime after the compromise.

Figure 2 (top) shows a timeline for the 25 websites with Webalizer data before
and after a second compromise. For 4 of these websites, the evil search term
appeared before the recompromise. For the vast majority (20), the evil search
term appeared on the day of the recompromise. In only one case did the evil
search term appear only after recompromise. Since most evil terms appear at
or before the time of recompromise, this strongly suggests that evil searching is
triggering the second compromise. If the evil searches had only occurred after
website compromise, then there would have been no connection.

We also examined the Webalizer logs for an additional 177 websites with evil
search terms but where the logs only started on, or after, the day of the compromise (see Figure 2 (bottom)). Again, in most cases (157) the evil search term
appeared from the time of compromise. Taken together, evil search terms were

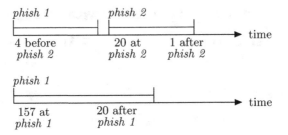

Fig. 2. Timeline of evil web search terms appearing in Webalizer logs

used at or before website compromise 90% of the time. This is further evidence that evil searching is a precursor to the compromise of many web servers.

3.2   Estimating the Extent of Evil Search

We can use the incidence of phishing websites that have Webalizer logs as a sample to estimate the overall prevalence of evil search when servers are compromised and used to host phishing websites.

Recall that we have obtained search logs for 1 320 phishing websites, and that 204 of these websites include one or more evil search terms in these logs. Frequently, the record shows one visit per evil search.

Unfortunately, Webalizer only keeps a record of the top 20 referring search terms. Hence, if a site receives many visitors, any rarely occurring search term will fall outside the top 20. We therefore restrict ourselves to considering just the 1 085 of Webalizer-equipped hosts that have low enough traffic so that even search terms with one visit are recorded. Of these hosts, 189 include evil search terms, or approximately 17.6% of the hosts in the sample. Viewed as a sample of all compromised phishing websites, the 95% confidence interval for the true rate of evil searching is (15.3%, 19.8%).

This estimate is only valid if the hosts with Webalizer logs represent a truly random sample. A number of factors may affect its suitability:

– Running Webalizer (or programs that it may be bundled with) may affect the likelihood of compromise. We have no evidence for any such effect.
– Sites running Webalizer are not representative of the web server population as a whole. Webalizer typically runs on Unix-like operating systems. Since many compromised servers run on Windows hosts, we cannot directly translate the prevalence of evil web search terms to these other types.
– Evil searches are only recorded in the website logs if the attacker clicks on a search result to visit the site. Using automated tools such as Goolag [6], or simple cut & paste operations, hides the search terms. This leads us to underestimate the frequency of evil searches.

On balance, we feel sites with Webalizer logs are a fair sample of all websites.

3.3   Other Evidence for Evil Searches

There is a substantial amount of circumstantial evidence for the use of evil searches by criminals seeking machines to compromise. Hacker forums regularly contain articles giving 'googledorks', sometimes with further details of how to compromise any sites that are located. However, published evidence of the extent to which this approach has replaced older methods of scanning is hard to find, although the topic is already on the curriculum at one university [15].

LaCour examined a quarter of the URLs in the MarkMonitor phishing URL feed, and was reported [13] as finding that, "75% had been created by using some 750 evil search terms, and the related PHP vulnerabilities". Unfortunately, he was misquoted [14]. LaCour did collect 750 evil searches from hacker forums, but he did not establish the extent to which these were connected to actual machine compromises, whether for phishing or any other purpose.

What LaCour was able to establish from his URL data was that for the October to December 2007 period, 75% of attacks involved machine compromise, 5% were located on free web-hosting and 20% were the categories we have called rock-phish, fast-flux and Ark. These figures are roughly in line with our results in Table 1 above. He then observed, from the paths within the URLs, a strong link with PHP vulnerabilities, particularly 'Remote File Inclusion' (RFI) [8]. This is what led him to speculate that evil searches and subsequent RFI attacks are a key element in the creation of 75% of all phishing websites.

4   Phishing Website Recompromise

Removing phishing websites can be a frustrating task for the banks and other organizations involved in defending against phishing attacks. Not only do new phishing pages appear as fast as old ones are cleared, but the new sites often appear on the web servers that were previously compromised and cleaned up. This occurs whenever the sysadmin removing the offending content only treats the symptoms, without addressing the root problem that enabled the system to be compromised in the first place.

We now provide the first robust data on the *rate* of phishing-website recompromise. We show how the recompromise rate varies over time, and then provide evidence of how evil search raises the likelihood of recompromise.

4.1   Identifying When a Website Is Recompromised

Websites may be recompromised because the same attacker returns to a machine that they know to be vulnerable. Alternatively, the recompromise may occur because a different attacker finds the machine and independently exploits it using the same vulnerability, or even a second security flaw. We think it unlikely that a single attacker would use multiple security flaws to compromise a machine when just one will do the trick.

The general nature of the security flaw that has been exploited is often quite obvious because the phishing pages have been added within particular parts of the directory structure. For example, when a particular user account is compromised the phishing pages are placed within their filespace; when a file upload vulnerability is exploited, the pages are put in sub-directories of the upload repository. However, since it is not always possible to guess what exploit has been used, we instead consider how much time elapses between phishing reports to infer distinct compromises.

If two phishing websites are detected on the same server within a day of each other, it is more likely that the same attacker is involved. If, instead, the attacks are months apart, then we believe that is far more likely that the website has been rediscovered by a different attacker. We believe that attackers usually have a relatively small number of machines to exploit at any given moment and are unlikely to keep compromised machines 'for a rainy day' – this is consistent with the short delay that we generally see between detection (evil search logged) and use (phishing website report received).

Our equating of long delays with different attackers is also based on the distribution of recompromises over time. If we treat every phishing site on a particular server as a different attack, whatever the time delay, then we observe a recompromise rate of 20% after 5 weeks, rising to 30% after 24 weeks. If we insist that there is a delay of at least 3 weeks between attacks to consider the event to be a recompromise, then the rates change to 2% after 5 weeks and 15% after 24 weeks. The long term rates of recompromise vary substantially for cut-off points of small numbers of days, which we believe reflects the same attackers coming back to the machine. However, the long term rates of recompromise hardly change for cut-off times measured in weeks, which is consistent with all recompromises being new attackers.

An appropriate cut-off point, where there is only a small variation in the results from choosing slightly different values, is to use a gap of one week. We therefore classify a phishing host as recompromised after receiving two reports for the same website that are at least 7 days apart. Using a 7-day window strikes a reasonable balance between ensuring that the compromises are independent without excluding too many potential recompromises from the calculations.

As a further sanity check, we note that for 83% of website recompromises occurring after a week or longer, the phishing page is placed in a different directory than previously used. This strongly suggests that different exploits are being applied, and therefore, different attackers are involved.

4.2   Measuring Website Recompromise Rates

The rate of website recompromise should only be considered as a function of time. Simply computing the recompromise rate for all phishing websites in the October to March sample would skew the results: websites first compromised on October 1st would have six months to be recompromised, while websites first compromised in late March would have far less time. For this reason, we consider website recompromise in four-week intervals. For instance, we test whether a website compromised on October 1st has been recompromised by October 29th, November 26th, and so on. Similarly, we can only check whether a website compromised on March 1st 2008 has been recompromised by March 29th.

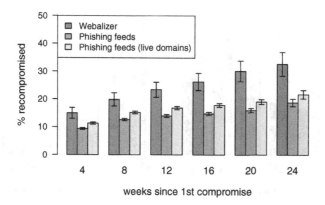

Fig. 3. Recompromise rates for phishing websites over time. The error bars show the 95% confidence interval for the true value of the recompromise rate.

Figure 3 plots phishing website recompromise over time. The graph includes recompromise rates for the 1 320 Webalizer hosts, along with the 36 514 other hosts we recorded between October 2007 and March 2008. In both cases, the recompromise rate increases over time: 15% of hosts with Webalizer logs are recompromised within 4 weeks, rising steadily to 33% within 24 weeks. The recompromise rate for the other hosts is somewhat lower, but follows the same pattern: 9% are recompromised within 4 weeks, rising to 19% within 24 weeks.

What might explain the discrepancy in the recompromise rates for the Webalizer sample? One factor is that the sites with Webalizer logs, by definition, were accessible at least once shortly after being reported. This is not the case for all hosts – some phishing websites are completely removed before we are able to access them.[2]

Sites that quickly disappear are far less likely to be recompromised in the future. Hence, Figure 3 also plots the recompromise rates for the 29 986 websites that responded at least once. The recompromise rate for these websites is slightly higher than that for all phishing websites.

In any event, the results from this graph offer a strong indication that phishing website recompromise happens frequently. Many website administrators are not taking adequate steps to prevent recompromise following an intrusion.

4.3   Evil Searching and Recompromise

Section 3.1 established that evil searches can precede website compromise. We now show that the evil searches are linked to much higher rates of recompromise.

Figure 4 (left) compares the recompromise rates for hosts in the Webalizer sample. Sites with evil search terms in the logs are far more likely to be

---

[2] Many sites that are compromised are long-abandoned blogs and image galleries. It is not surprising that a number of these are removed altogether, rather than being cleaned up and left publicly available.

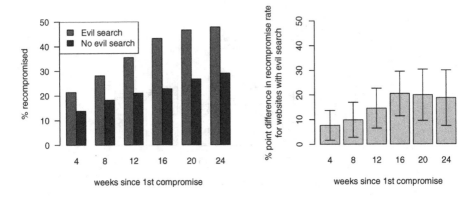

Fig. 4. Recompromise rates for phishing websites with and without evil search responses found in the Webalizer logs (left). The right graph shows the percentage point difference along with 95% confidence intervals.

recompromised than sites without such terms. Hosts reached by evil search face a 21% chance of recompromise after 4 weeks, compared to 14% otherwise. Within 24 weeks these numbers rise to 48% and 29% respectively.

Moreover, these differences are statistically significant. Figure 4 (right) plots the percentage point difference between recompromise rates when evil and non-evil searches are present, along with 95% confidence intervals. For instance, there is a 20.4 percentage point difference in recompromise rates after 16 weeks (43.2% recompromise for evil searches compared to 22.8% for the rest). The evil search recompromise rate is nearly twice that of ordinary phishing websites for the period. What does this mean? Vulnerable websites that can be found through web search are likely to be repeatedly rediscovered and recompromised until they are finally cleaned up.

5   PhishTank and Recompromise

We have shown that attackers use web search to find websites to compromise. We now consider whether they are using public phishing website blacklists as an alternative way to find sites to compromise. These blacklists provide valuable data for 'phishing toolbars' that block visits to fraudulent websites. Most blacklists are kept hidden: Google's SafeBrowsing API [12] only allows users to verify suspected URLs, while the APWG's blacklist [3] is only available to members.

In contrast, 'PhishTank' [21] provides an open source blacklist which is generated and maintained through web-based participation. Users are invited to submit URLs of suspected phishing websites and verify each other's entries. Consequently, PhishTank provides a permanent record of phishing websites dating back to its inception in late 2006. They also publish a more dynamic list of recently active phishing websites. We now test whether appearing in PhishTank's public blacklist makes website recompromise more likely.

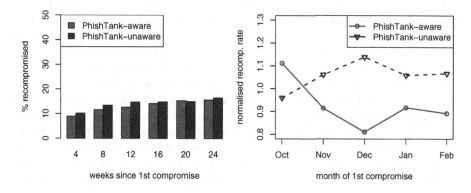

Fig. 5. Recompromise rate for phishing websites appearing on the public website Phish-Tank (left); normalized 4-week recompromise rates based upon the month of first compromise (right)

It is unfair to simply compare recompromise rates for sites PhishTank knows about with those of which it is unaware. While aiming to be comprehensive, in practice PhishTank fails in this aim, and is aware of only 48% of the phishing websites in our collection. Since some of our other URL feeds get some of their data from PhishTank, it is more accurate to view PhishTank as a subset of the phishing URLs we record. So although PhishTank has a roughly even chance of recording a particular phishing incident, there will be further chances to record the host if it is recompromised. This biases PhishTank's record to include a disproportionate number of hosts where multiple compromises occur.

Consequently, we apply a fairer test to determine whether a host's appearance in PhishTank makes it more likely to be recompromised. We compare the recompromise rates of new hosts following their first compromise. 9 283 hosts detected by PhishTank during their first reported compromise are compared against 15 398 hosts missed by PhishTank during the first compromise. Since we are only considering URLs reported from October 2007 to March 2008, we ignore URLs first appearing in PhishTank prior to October 2007.

The results are presented in Figure 5 (left) and show that new websites appearing in PhishTank are no more likely to be recompromised than new websites that do not appear. Website recompromise over the short term (up to 12 weeks) is less for websites publicized in PhishTank compared to those hidden from it. Within 4 weeks, PhishTank-aware phishing websites are recompromised 8.9% of the time, compared to 10.2% for sites not reported to PhishTank. A similar trend holds for recompromised websites within 8 and 12 weeks, with recompromise rates around two percentage points lower for websites known to PhishTank. These differences are maintained with 95% confidence. However, over the longer term (16 to 24 weeks), the recompromise rates become indistinguishable.

Why might sites appearing in PhishTank be recompromised less often? It appears that defenders are paying more attention to PhishTank's lists than attackers are. By making its blacklist available free of charge, more support staff at ISPs and sysadmins are informed of compromised websites in need of cleanup. Other companies sell phishing feeds to aid ISPs in this manner, but PhishTank's free service may be more widely adopted. As more defenders become aware of PhishTank (and consequently aware of more phishing websites), we might expect PhishTank's recompromise rate to diminish further over time. To test this hypothesis in our data, Figure 5 (right) plots recompromise rates after 4 weeks for phishing websites based on the month the site is reported. The data is normalized with respect to the overall phishing activity in the relevant month. In October, the recompromise rate for websites reported to PhishTank is higher than in the set of websites of which PhishTank is unaware. However, this situation turns around thereafter, with the recompromise rates for sites in PhishTank reducing and becoming *lower* than the rising recompromise rate for the sites which PhishTank missed.[3]

Based on our data analysis, we conclude that the good offered by PhishTank (better information for defenders) currently outweighs the bad (exploitation of compromised websites by attackers). However, the use of PhishTank by both attackers and defenders might change dynamically over time. Consequently, we believe that continued monitoring is necessary in case attackers begin to leverage PhishTank's public blacklist.

6   Mitigation Strategies

Thus far we have demonstrated clear evidence that evil searches are actively used to locate web servers for hosting phishing websites. We have also shown that server re-compromise is often triggered by evil search. Therefore, we now consider how evil searches might be thwarted, in order to make the criminals' task harder. We set out and review a number of mitigation strategies, the first two of which can be implemented locally, whereas the others require action by outside parties. Unfortunately each has drawbacks.

Strategy 1: Obfuscating targeted details. Evil searches could be made less effective if identifying information such as version numbers were removed from web server applications. While this might make it a bit harder for attackers to discover vulnerable websites, it does nothing to secure them.

Damron [7] argued for obfuscation by noting that removing the version numbers from applications is easy for the defender, while adding a significant burden for the attacker. However, defenders also stand to gain from detailed application information, as the presence of a version number can assist sysadmins in keeping track of which of their users continues to run out of date software.

We note that very few of the evil search terms we examined contained explicit version numbers, but merely sought to identify particular programs. The final

---

[3] In October 2007 PhishTank added highly-publicized features to its website, which permit searches for phishing sites based on ASNs, and RSS feeds of new entries within an ASN; exactly meeting the requirements of an ISP that wished to keep track of any compromised customers.

objection to this strategy is that obscuring version numbers still leaves users exposed to 'shotgun' attackers who run all of their exploits against every candidate site without worrying whether or not it is running a vulnerable version.

Strategy 2: Evil search penetration testing. Motivated defenders could run evil searches to locate sites that might be compromised and then warn their owners of the risk they were running. For many evil searches, which only return a handful of exploitable sites amongst many thousands of results, this is unlikely to be an effective scheme. Furthermore, the search results are usually just hints that only indicate the potential for compromise. Confirming suspicions normally requires an active attack, which would be illegal in most jurisdictions.

Strategy 3: Blocking evil search queries. An alternative approach is for the search engines to detect evil searches and suppress the results, or only provide links to law enforcement sites. Given their inherent specificity, constructing a comprehensive and up-to-date blacklist of evil searches is likely to be difficult and costly. Blocking some of the more obvious terms (e.g., those found in Long's popular database [11]) is unlikely to be effective if the terms used by the criminals rapidly evolve. In any event, the search engines are unlikely to have any meaningful incentive to develop and deploy such a list.

Strategy 4: Removing known phishing sites from search results. The low-cost option of removing currently active phishing sites from the search results has almost nothing to recommend it. Search engines suppress results for known child-pornography sites, and Google prevents users from clicking through to sites that are hosting malware [9] until they are cleaned up [17]. However, phishing presents different circumstances. Malware is placed on high traffic sites where removal from search results is a powerful incentive towards getting it removed, but phishing sites are often on semi-abandoned low traffic sites where the incentive to remove will be limited. Although the evil search will not work while the phishing site is active, the site will be findable again as soon as the fraudulent pages are removed. This approach would also prevent any use of searches by defenders, which means that it does some harm as well as doing little good.

Strategy 5: Lower the reputation of previously phished hosts discoverable by evil search terms. In addition to flagging active phishing URLs, website reputation services such as SiteAdvisor [18] already give a warning for websites that consistently host malicious content. Since we have shown that a substantial proportion of systems that host a phishing website are later recompromised, such services might mark previously compromised hosts as risky. Furthermore, it would be entirely prudent to proactively flag as a much higher risk any hosts used for phishing which can also be found by evil search terms. The magnitude of the risk should reflect our finding that about half of these sites will be recompromised within 24 weeks.

7   Related Work

As indicated earlier, very little academic research has examined the use of search engines to compromise websites. However, researchers have recently begun to recognize the importance of empirically studying electronic crime. Thomas and Martin [25] and Franklin *et al.* [10] have characterized the underground economy by monitoring the advertisements of criminals on IRC chatrooms. Provos *et al.* [22] tracked malicious URLs advertising malware, finding that 1.3% of incoming Google search queries returned links to malware-distributing URLs. Moore and Clayton [19] studied the effectiveness of phishing-website removal by recording site lifetimes. Collins *et al.* [5] used NetFlow data on scanning, spamming and botnet activity to classify unsafe IP address ranges. The current work contributes to this literature by measuring the prevalence of evil search terms for compromising websites and the impact on site recompromise.

Another related area of literature is the economics of information security [2]. One key economic challenge identified by this literature is overcoming asymmetric information. Better measurement of security is needed, from the prevalence of vulnerabilities in competing software to the responsiveness of ISPs in cleaning up infected hosts. Publishing accurate data on website recompromise can identify serial underperformers and highlight opportunities for improvement. Google and StopBadware [23] publicly disclose infected websites, and it has been claimed that this disclosure encourages prompt cleanup [9]. At a policy level, Anderson *et al.* [1] have recommended that regulators collect better data on system compromise and use it to punish unresponsive ISPs.

8   Conclusion

In this paper, we have presented clear evidence that the criminals who are compromising web servers to host phishing websites are using Internet search engines to locate vulnerable machines. We have found direct evidence of these 'evil searches' in 18% of our collection of Webalizer logs from phishing sites, and believe the true prevalence to be even higher.

We have also shown a clear linkage with the recompromise of servers. The general population of phishing websites exhibits a recompromise rate of 19% after 24 weeks, but where evil searches are found in the logs, the rate reaches 48%. Although the use of evil searches has been known about anecdotally, this is the first paper to show how prevalent the technique has become, and to report upon the substantial rates of recompromise that currently occur.

In contrast, phishing website URLs that are made public by the PhishTank database currently enjoy a slight, but statistically significant, reduction in their recompromise rates. This suggests that defenders are able to use the database in order to reduce criminal attacks, and that the sometimes touted benefits of keeping attack data hidden from public view may be minimal.

Other strategies for mitigating evil search that work by limiting attackers' access to information – obfuscating version numbers, filtering search results, blocking evil search queries – we also consider to be flawed. The most promising countermeasure we discuss is to incorporate a website's likelihood of recompromise into the calculation of its reputation.

References

1. Anderson, R., Böhme, R., Clayton, R., Moore, T.: Security economics and the internal market. European Network and Information Security Agency (ENISA) (2008), http://enisa.europa.eu/doc/pdf/report_sec_econ_&_int_mark_20080131.pdf
2. Anderson, R., Moore, T.: The economics of information security. Science 314(5799), 610–613 (2006)
3. Anti-Phishing Working Group, http://www.apwg.org/
4. Artists Against 419, http://www.aa419.org/
5. Collins, M.P., Shimeall, T.J., Faber, S., Janies, J., Weaver, R., De Shon, M., Kadane, J.: Using uncleanliness to predict future botnet addresses. In: Proceedings of the ACM SIGCOMM Conference on Internet Measurement (IMC), pp. 93–104. ACM Press, New York (2007)
6. Cult of the Dead Cow. Goolag Scanner Specifications (January 2008), http://goolag.org/specifications.html
7. Damron, J.: Identifiable fingerprints in network applications. USENIX ;login 28(6), 16–20 (2003)
8. Dausin, M.: PHP File Include Attacks. Tipping Point (February 2008), http://dvlabs.tippingpoint.com/blog/2008/02
9. Day, O., Palmen, B., Greenstadt, R.: Reinterpreting the disclosure debate for web infections. In: 7th Workshop on the Economics of Information Security (WEIS) (2008)
10. Franklin, J., Paxson, V., Perrig, A., Savage, S.: An inquiry into the nature and causes of the wealth of Internet miscreants. In: Proceedings of the 14th ACM Conference on Computer and Communications Security (CCS), pp. 375–388 (2007)
11. Google Hacking Database, http://johnny.ihackstuff.com/ghdb.php
12. Google Safe Browsing API, http://code.google.com/apis/safebrowsing/
13. Higgins, K.J.: Phishers Enlist Google 'Dorks'. DarkReading (March 2008), http://www.darkreading.com/document.asp?doc_id=149324
14. LaCour, J.: Personal communication, March 28 (2008)
15. Lancor, L., Workman, R.: Using Google hacking to enhance defense strategies. In: Proceedings of the 38th SIGCSE Technical Symposium on Computer Science Education, pp. 491–495 (2007)
16. Long, J.: Google Hacking Mini-Guide. informIT (May 2004), http://www.informit.com/articles/article.aspx?p=170880
17. Mavrommatis, P.: Malware Reviews via Webmaster Tools (August 2007), http://googlewebmastercentral.blogspot.com/2007/08/malware-reviews-via-webmaster-tools.html
18. McAfee Inc. SiteAdvisor, http://www.siteadvisor.com
19. Moore, T., Clayton, R.: Examining the impact of website take-down on phishing. In: Anti-Phishing Working Group eCrime Researcher's Summit (APWG eCrime), pp. 1–13. ACM Press, New York (2007)
20. Netcraft Inc. March 2008 Web Server Survey (2008), http://news.netcraft.com/archives/web_server_survey.html
21. PhishTank, http://www.phishtank.com/

22. Provos, N., Mavrommatis, P., Rajab, M., Monrose, F.: All your iFrames point to us. In: 17th USENIX Security Symposium, pp. 1–15 (2008)
23. Stop Badware, http://www.stopbadware.org/
24. The Webalizer, http://www.mrunix.net/webalizer/
25. Thomas, R., Martin, J.: The underground economy: priceless. USENIX ;login 31(6), 7–16 (2006)
26. Watson, D., Holz, T., Mueller, S.: Know your Enemy: Phishing. The Honeynet Project & Research Alliance (May 2005),
    http://www.honeynet.org/papers/phishing/
27. Weaver, R., Collins, M.P.: Fishing for phishes: applying capture-recapture methods to estimate phishing populations. In: Anti-Phishing Working Group eCrime Researcher's Summit (APWG eCrime), pp. 14–25. ACM Press, New York (2007)
28. Yahoo! Inc. Yahoo! Search Web Services, http://developer.yahoo.com/search/

Detecting Denial of Service Attacks in Tor

Norman Danner, Danny Krizanc, and Marc Liberatore

Department of Mathematics and Computer Science
Wesleyan University
Middletown, CT 06459 USA

Abstract. Tor is currently one of the more popular systems for anonymizing near real-time communications on the Internet. Recently, Borisov et al. proposed a denial of service based attack on Tor (and related systems) that significantly increases the probability of compromising the anonymity provided. In this paper, we propose an algorithm for detecting such attacks and examine the effectiveness of the obvious approach to evading such detection. We implement a simplified version of the detection algorithm and study whether the attack may be in progress on the current Tor network. Our preliminary measurements indicate that the attack was probably not implemented during the period we observed the network.

Keywords: Anonymity, reliability, denial of service, attack, detection.

1 Introduction

A low-latency anonymous communication system attempts to allow near-real-time communication between hosts while hiding the identity of these hosts from various types of observers. Such a system is useful whenever communication privacy is desirable — personal, medical, legal, governmental, or financial applications all may require some degree of privacy. Financial applications that might benefit from such privacy include e-cash or credit systems, contract proposal and acceptance, or retrieval of financial data.

Dingledine et al. developed the Tor [3] system for such communication. Tor (and other related systems) anonymizes communication by sending it along paths of anonymizing proxies. Syverson et al. [6] showed that such systems are vulnerable to a passive adversary who controls the first and last proxies along such a path. More recently, Borisov et al. [2] showed that an adversary willing to engage in denial of service (DoS) could increase their probability of compromising anonymity. When a path is reconstructed after a denial of service, new proxies are chosen, and thus the adversary has another chance to be on the endpoints of the path.

Our contributions are as follows. We prove that an adversary engaging in the DoS attack in an idealized Tor-like system can be detected by probing at most $3n$ paths in the system, where n is the number of proxies in the system. Through simulation, we show that an adversary attempting to avoid detection by

R. Dingledine and P. Golle (Eds.): FC 2009, LNCS 5628, pp. 273–284, 2009.

engaging in DoS probabilistically can still be detected, and that the attempt to avoid detection radically degrades the effectiveness of the attack. Finally, using measurements of connection drop rates across Tor nodes, we implement a version of the detection algorithm and conclude it is unlikely that such an attack was in progress during the time period the network was observed.

We introduce related work and present the attack in more detail in Section 2. Section 3 describes the algorithm to detect attacker-controlled nodes, and Section 4 describes one possible attacker strategy to avoid detection, along with an evaluation of its effectiveness. This is followed by our measurements of Tor node drop rates (Section 5) and the results of a practical implementation of our detection algorithm (Section 6). We conclude in Section 7.

2 The Denial of Service Attack

We model the Tor network with a fully connected undirected graph[1]. The set N of vertices of the graph represent the Tor nodes (or routers), and the edges represent network connections between nodes. We define n to be $|N|$.

Tor sets up circuits (also referred to as tunnels) consisting of three nodes; in our model, this equates to a path containing three vertices (in order) and the corresponding edges between them. To simplify the analysis, we allow the same node to appear on the path more than once – that is, nodes are chosen uniformly at random with replacement. Application level communications between an initiator and a responder is then passed through the circuit. We assume that a timing cross-correlation attack works perfectly, i.e., the adversary can break the system's anonymity properties if it controls the first and last node along the path by observing the timing of communications between an initiator and responder.

In any attack we assume some subset C of N are compromised, that is, they are collaborators under the control of an adversary that will attempt to break the anonymity of users in the system. As with N, we define c to be $|C|$. Here we limit our attention to the nodes within the Tor network, under the assumption that an adversary will compromise some of these nodes in an attempt to link initiators and responders.

In actual deployments of Tor, not all nodes can appear in all locations on the path. In particular, only certain nodes can be the final node on the path; in all other ways, they are identical to other nodes. These nodes are referred to as exit nodes. Let $E \subseteq N$ be the set of exit nodes where $e = |E|$.

Syverson et al. [6] observed that a passive adversary controls both the first and last node of a path with probability $\frac{c^2}{n^2}$ if all nodes may act as exit nodes. In the case where exit nodes are selectively compromised this may be improved to $\frac{c^2}{ne}$. (Currently approximately one third of Tor nodes act as exit nodes at any one time.)

---

[1] Some individual Tor nodes may disable connections on specific ports or to specific IP addresses. We have not determined if these significantly limit the graph.

Levine et al. [4] observe that if long-lived connections between an initiator and responder are reset at a reasonable rate then such an attack will be able to compromise anonymity with high probability within $O(\frac{n^2}{c^2}\ln n)$ resets.

In order to further improve the chances of compromise of communications over a Tor circuit a number of researchers [5,1,2] have suggested that compromised nodes that occur on paths in which they are not the first or last node artificially create a reset event by dropping the connection. Borisov et al. [2] analyze the following version of this attack on Tor:

> If the adversary acts as a first or last router on a tunnel, the tunnel is observed for a brief period of time and matched against all other tunnels where a colluding router is the last or first router, respectively. If there is a match, the tunnel is compromised; otherwise, the adversary kills the tunnel by no longer forwarding traffic on it. The adversary also kills all tunnels where it is the middle node, unless both the previous and next nodes are also colluding.

In this case, the adversary controls the endpoints of a randomly generated path with probability

$$\frac{c^3 + c^2(n-c)}{c^3 + c^2(n-c) + (n-c)^3} = \frac{\alpha^3 + \alpha^2(1-\alpha)}{\alpha^3 + \alpha^2(1-\alpha) + (1-\alpha)^3}$$

where $\alpha = c/n$ is the fraction of compromised nodes,

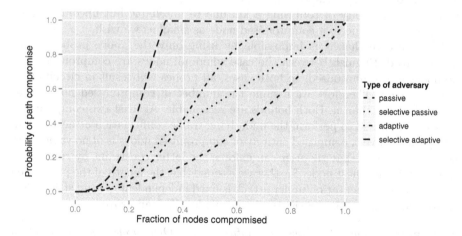

Fig. 1. A comparison of the probability of an circuit being compromised, given either the passive or adaptive (Borisov) adversary. The selective adversary, in either case, compromises only exit nodes.

Assuming that not all nodes are exit nodes and $C \subseteq E$ the endpoints of the path are compromised with probability:

$$\frac{c^3 + c^2(n - c)}{c^3 + c^2(n - c) + (n - c)^2(e - c)} = \frac{\alpha^3 + \alpha^2(1 - \alpha)}{\alpha^3 + \alpha^2(1 - \alpha) + (1 - \alpha)^2(\frac{e}{n} - \alpha)}$$

The conclusion by Borisov et al. is that their optimization brings significant gains to the attacker. As shown in Figure 1, it is strongly in the attacker's interest to kill circuits that can't be compromised. The gain from this attack is even more pronounced when exit nodes are selected for compromise before other nodes.

3 Detecting the Attack

In this section we show how to detect such a DoS attack using $O(n)$ probes of the network where a probe consists of setting up a circuit using a given path through the network and passing data through it. We assume a naive attacker that follows the procedure precisely as formulated above. Further we assume that the time taken for an attacker to detect a match is negligible when compared to the expected time between circuit kills due to unreliable but uncompromised nodes. I.e., we assume that if a probe results in a circuit being killed inside of a short period of time after being created, this is due to the fact that there is at least one compromised node on the circuit and that it is not the case that both endpoints of the corresponding path are compromised. Note that by sending traffic with a predictable pattern through the circuit we can make the time taken for detection very low. As we discuss below, by repeating the experiment we can make the probability of confusing a kill due to unreliable but uncompromised nodes and a kill due to a compromised node as small as we wish.

First observe that it is impossible by using only the above probes of the network to distinguish between the case where all nodes are compromised and no nodes are compromised. In both cases, all probes will result in circuits that are not killed. Therefore we assume the number of compromised nodes is at least 2 but less than n. Both bounds are reasonable: At least two compromised nodes are required to perform the underlying traffic confirmation attack, and an anonymity network composed entirely of compromised nodes is of no value to an honest user. Note that the user can enforce the latter constraint by running or sponsoring one honest node. Further we assume that the length of the paths used by the Tor implementation under attack is fixed independent of (and strictly less than) n and that paths consist of distinct nodes. We can prove:

Theorem 1. *Under the above assumptions, using $O(n)$ probes we can detect all of the compromised nodes of the Tor network. For the case of paths of length 3 the number of probes required is at most $3n$.*

Proof. Let k be the length of the paths used by the Tor implementation under consideration. We denote the probe consisting of the path of length k starting with u_1 and ending with u_k with edges between u_i and u_{i+1} for $i = 1, \ldots, u_{k-1}$ by $(u_1, \ldots, u_k)$. We say a probe *succeeds* if the circuit is not killed, otherwise it *fails*.

Choose a set $X = \{x_1, \ldots, x_{k-1}\}$ of $k-1$ (distinct) nodes, arbitrarily. Perform the following set of probes: $(x_1, y, x_2, \ldots, x_{k-1})$ for each y not in X. One of three cases results.

Case 1: All $n - k + 1$ probes succeed. In this case both x_1 and x_{k-1} are compromised. For any other node y, we can determine if it is compromised by using the probe $(x_1, \ldots, x_{k-1}, y)$. If it succeeds then y is compromised, if not, y is uncompromised. (To test nodes in X, replace them in the above probe set with an arbitrary node not in X and try a probe with the given node in the last position.)

Case 2: Among the $n - k + 1$ probes, at least one succeeds and at least one fails. If either endpoint were compromised, then either all probes would succeed (if the other endpoint were compromised) or all probes would fail (if the other endpoint were uncompromised). Thus neither endpoint is compromised. But then if any of $x_2, \ldots, x_{k-2}$ were compromised every probe would fail. Thus in this case all of the nodes in X are uncompromised, any y for which the probe failed is compromised, and any y for which the probe succeeded is uncompromised.

Case 3: All $n - k + 1$ probes fail. In this case we can conclude that either all nodes in X are uncompromised and all nodes not in X are compromised, or at least one of the nodes in X is compromised. For each pair of nodes $x_i, x_j \in X$ consider probes of length k of the form $(x_i, y, \ldots, x_j)$, where positions 3 through $k - 1$ consist of $X \setminus \{x_i, x_j\}$ in an arbitrary fixed order and y ranges over nodes not in X. Suppose that for some pair $x_i, x_j \in X$ all probes succeed. It is easy to see that at least one node in X must be compromised, from which it follows that x_i and x_j are compromised; we proceed as in Case 1 to determine the status of the remaining nodes. Otherwise, for each pair $x_i, x_j \in X$ there is $y \notin X$ such that the probe $(x_i, y, \ldots, x_j)$ fails. Notice that in this case, if there is at least one uncompromised node in X, then there is exactly one uncompromised node in X. Now we consider probes of length k of the form $(x, \ldots, y)$, where $x \in X$, positions 2 through $k - 1$ consist of $X \setminus \{x\}$ in an arbitrary fixed order, and y ranges over nodes not in X. Suppose every probe of the form $(x, \ldots, y)$ fails. If there were exactly one compromised node in X, then necessarily every node not in X is uncompromised, which means that there is exactly one compromised node in the entire network, violating our assumption that there are at least two such nodes[2]. Thus we conclude that no nodes in X are compromised and all nodes not in X are compromised. Otherwise there are $x \in X$ and $y \notin X$ such that $(x, \ldots, y)$ succeeds. Suppose x were not compromised. Then there would be a compromised node in $X \setminus \{x\}$ or y would be compromised; in either case the

---

[2] The full attack is impossible with a single compromised node, though an adversary could still perform an occasional denial of service with one such node. A single compromised node could be detected in a number of probes linear in n, though we omit the details here.

probe $(x, \ldots, y)$ would fail, a contradiction. So x is compromised and hence x is the only compromised node in X. Furthermore, the compromised nodes not in X are precisely those y such that the probe $(x, \ldots, y)$ succeeds.

The worst case number of probes occurs in Case 3 in which we do at most $(\binom{k-1}{2} + k - 1)(n - k + 1)$ probes beyond the initial $n - k + 1$ probes that define the cases[3]. As k is assumed to be fixed independent of n this is clearly $O(n)$. For the case $k = 3$ (the default for Tor), we notice that the initial set of probes and the first set of probes in Case 3 are the same, so in fact we conclude that the total number of probes is $\leq 3n$. $\square$

Above we state that (under the perhaps unrealistic assumption that the results of probes are independent) repeated probes can be used to distinguish the cases of an attacker killing a circuit and that of a circuit consisting of honest nodes failing. To do this, for any given probe of the above algorithm we repeat the probe l times where l (determined below) depends upon on the probability of error in the algorithm we find acceptable. If all l of the trials fail we report that the path contains at least one compromised node and that at least one end point that is honest. Otherwise we conclude the path contains all honest nodes or both end points are compromised.

Assume that an attacker always successfully kills a circuit it is on that it does not control. Then a probe consisting of l independent trials can be wrong only if (a) an honest circuit fails l times in a row or (b) a circuit with both end points compromised fails l times in a row. Assume that any given circuit fails due to unreliable nodes or edges with probability f. Then, under the independence assumption, (a) or (b) occur with probability at most f^l, i.e., the probability that a probe consisting of l independent trials is correct is at least $1 - f^l$. If the algorithm performs m such probes the probability they are all correct is greater than $(1 - f^l)^m$. Assume we require that our algorithm correctly identifies all nodes as either honest or compromised with probability at least $1 - \epsilon$. Then it is easy to see (using standard approximations) that choosing

$$l > \frac{\ln \ln(\frac{1}{1-\epsilon}) - \ln m}{\ln f}$$

is sufficient. If we take $m = 3000$ (the worst case number of probes for a 1000 node Tor network), $f = .2$ (an approximate bound the observed probability of path failures on Tor — see Section 5) and $\epsilon = .001$ (so that we expect less than one misidentification) we see that $l = 10$ is more than sufficient.

Of course, we require that the above repeated probes be independent which is highly unlikely to be the case. But by spreading the repetitions out over time we can increase our confidence that observed failures are not random.

4   Attacker Strategy

An intelligent attacker will be aware that killing circuits at a rate higher than the background rate can, in theory, be detected. Here, we consider the case of an

---

[3] Since some probes will be repeated, the actual number can be made a bit smaller.

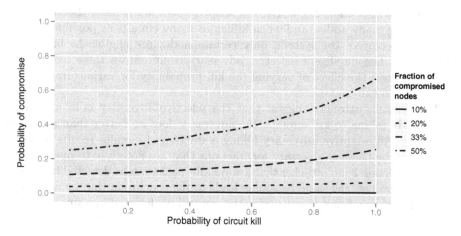

Fig. 2. Probability of an circuit formation being compromised, given the adaptive adversary. We assume that $e = \frac{1}{3}$ of nodes are exit nodes, but that the adversary is not selective targeting such nodes.

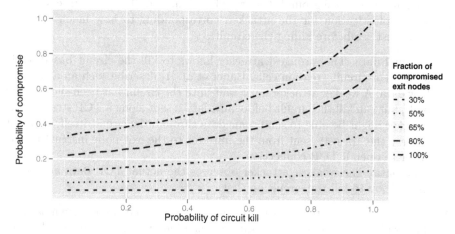

Fig. 3. Probability of an circuit formation being compromised, given the selective adaptive adversary. We assume that $e = \frac{1}{3}$ and that assume that the background kill rate is zero, but the general shape of the graph remains when changing these assumptions.

attacker that kills some fraction of the circuits through nodes under its control. In particular, circuits that contain compromised nodes, but where both endpoints are not compromised, are killed. The attacker can choose to kill any fraction of such circuits, from all (which is Borisov's description of the DoS attack) to none (equivalent to the passive adversary).

Figure 2 shows the effect of varying the kill probability for various fractions of compromised nodes, obtained through simulations conforming to the assumptions in Section 2. Clearly, the adaptive attacker is most effective when in control of many nodes, and when killing as many circuits as possible.

In the deployed Tor system, only certain nodes are eligible to be last in the circuit. The intelligent selective adversary compromises these exit nodes. Figure 3 shows the effect of varying the kill probability for various fractions of compromised exit nodes.

These results strongly suggest that the selective adversary is in a difficult position. In failing to kill circuits, the adversary does no better than a passive adversary. An adaptive adversary killing a fraction of circuits results in small gains over the passive adversary for fractions that are not close to one. As discussed in Section 3, an attacker that always kills paths can be detected in a small number of probes; the same reasoning leads to the conclusion that an adversary that kills any significant fraction of paths can still be detected in a small number of probes.

5   Measuring Failure Rates in Tor

As already mentioned, implementation of our detection algorithm is dependent upon knowing the background drop-rate for circuits in Tor. We can consider a range of sophistication for the attacker, corresponding to how much data the attacker must see before killing the circuit:

1. Minimal data. The strongest attacker knows to kill the circuit based solely on the Tor circuit creation cells. Bauer et al. [1] describe such an attacker.
2. Low data. A weaker attacker must wait until the circuit has been successfully built, but can kill the circuit before any data is sent along a TCP stream. The attacker might be able to send some data through the circuit itself, or might observe the Tor cells sent from the initiator to the exit node instructing the latter to open a TCP connection.
3. High data. The weakest attacker observes the actual TCP data and bases its decision to kill the circuit on that.

Accordingly, we conducted an experiment in which we repeatedly downloaded a file through Tor and measured the rates of the different failure modes. The controlling process launches a `curl` process to download the file. The Tor proxy is responsible for circuit creation; the controlling process ignores circuits with exit policies that do not allow the download, but otherwise attaches one `curl` process to one circuit. We then monitor the various failure rates. Kills by the minimal-data attacker correspond to circuit creation failures. Kills by the low-data attacker correspond to attempting to attach a `curl` process to a successfully-built circuit, but the process then receiving either no reply from the server or timing out[4]. Kills by the high-data attacker correspond to a `curl` process failing to completely download the file.

---

[4] We also used the Tor Control protocol to measure the failure rate of the instruction to the exit node to open a TCP connection to the recipient; the results are comparable to those reported here.

Circuits launched	4995		
Circuit failure at hop 1	106	(2.1%)	
Circuit failure at hop 2	258	(5.2%)	
Circuit failure at hop 3	640	(12.8%)	
Total circuit construction failures	1004	(20.1%)	(minimal-data)
curl processes launched	3010		
No reply or timeout	537	(17.8%)	(low-data)
Partial file	6	(0.2%)	(high-data)

Fig. 4. Observed Tor drop-rates corresponding to different-strength attackers

We present our findings in Figure 4[5]. We can treat these failure rates as upper bounds on the corresponding background rates in Tor. An immediate conclusion that we can draw from these measurements is that detecting a minimal-, low-, or high-data attacker using l-times repeated probe version of our detection algorithm requires taking $l = 10, 9$, and 3, respectively. Since it is possible that some version of the DoS attack was in progress when we performed our measurements, the failure rates among honest nodes may in fact be lower; additional measurements along the lines of those described in Section 6 are in order to identity potentially suspicious nodes and determine whether the failure rates decrease significantly when those nodes are removed from the experiment.

6   Detection in Practice

The detection algorithm described in Section 3 along with the measurements made above provide a reasonably practical method for detecting the DoS attack in progress, and serves as a theoretical upper bound on the amount of work necessary to discover such an attack. A number of simplifications are possible if we assume the existence of a single, presumably honest, onion router under our control. In essence, this single honest router is a trustworthy guard node [8]. This trust is important: Borisov et al. note that the use of guard nodes in general may make the selective adversary more powerful when performing the predecessor attack [7]. The assumption of a trusted guard node avoids this problem entirely. We note that this assumption is not strong—by "trusted" here we mean that the node itself is not under the control of an attacker. This can be arranged by installing one's own onion router and using it as the guard node. We further note that this assumption hinges upon the trusted node being indistinguishable from other nodes and that it be unknown to the adversary. If these conditions do not hold, then the adversary can choose to not attack connections from the trusted node and remain hidden. In this sense, the simplified detection algorithm is easier for the attacker to game.

---

[5] These rather high failure rates are consistent with those reported by Mike Perry at BlackHat USA 2007, available at
http://www.blackhat.com/html/bh-media-archives/bh-archives-2007.html

Regardless, what are the advantages of this approach? First, observe that we need only probe nodes that are advertised as exit nodes, as there is a clear reason for an attacker to control exit nodes over non-exit nodes. Second, circuits in Tor are configurable by the initiator. In particular, paths of length two can be created, where the first node is known to be honest and the second, exit node's behavior can be observed. These simplifications allow for a practical, simplified algorithm for detecting the attack. We describe this algorithm in the following text. We then describe our implementation of the algorithm as well as the limitations and assumptions of the algorithm. Finally, we present the results of several runs of the algorithm on the Tor network.

First, query the Tor directory servers for a list of all public nodes. Filter this list based upon the nodes that are flagged as *valid, running, stable, exit* nodes, as these should be most advantageous for the adversary to compromise. Call this list of nodes the *candidates*. Then, repeat the following steps l times, where larger values of l increase certainty as described in Section 3: For each candidate node, create a circuit where the first node is known to be honest, and the second is a candidate. Retrieve a file through this circuit, and log the results. Each such test either succeeds completely, or fails at some point, either during circuit creation or other initialization, or during the retrieval itself. Either failure mode could be the result of a natural failure (e.g., network outages, overloaded nodes), or an attacker implementing the DoS attack. A candidate node with a high failure rate is a *suspect*; this failure rate can be tuned with the usual trade-off between false positives and negatives.

Once the list of suspect nodes is generated, the following steps are repeated l' times for an appropriately chosen l'. Each possible pairing of suspect nodes is used to create a circuit of length two. As above, the circuits thus created are used to perform a retrieval, and the successes and failures are logged. In this set of trials, we are looking for paths with low failure rates over the l' trials. Nodes on such paths could be under control of an adaptive adversary, and are termed *guilty*.

Also, consider a graph, where vertices are nodes, and edges exist between guilty nodes. If such paths form a clique, there are a limited number of explanations: One is that the guilty nodes are actually malicious; another is that all have good connectivity with one another, but bad connectivity with the honest node used to form the list of suspects. We suspect that larger cliques are less likely to be due to the latter, particularly if the nodes appear to be running on disparate networks. We have not verified this conjecture.

We implemented this algorithm on the Tor network, using a Tor node we had been running for several months prior as our honest node. We formed suspect lists with $l = 20$, looking for a failure rate of greater than 0.5 when retrieving a 100 kB file. We then attempted to find cliques of guilty nodes, using $l' = 10$ and a failure rate of less than 0.2.

Our results were mixed. Over the course of five days, we created and tested candidate lists once per day, tested suspects, and identified cliques of guilty nodes. Our observations are as follows. The set of candidates for any particular trial contained around two hundred nodes, although the union of all such sets contained nearly two hundred fifty nodes. Any given trial typically discovered about twenty suspect nodes, though the union of all such sets contained about fifty nodes. Two of the trials revealed cliques of size five, though the membership sets of these two cliques were disjoint.

Do these results indicate the presence of an attacker? Naively, if we were to assume all tests were independent, the likelihood of such cliques arising by chance alone is infinitesimal. However, the tests are not independent. For example, a node that is overloaded will refuse connections, or perhaps will be so congested that TCP timeouts will be reached, resulting in a failure of the stream being carried by the circuit. Such an overload will persist over time, reducing the independence between each of the l probes sent to a given node. We attempted to control for this effect by temporally spacing the probes by at least half an hour, but there is no way for a given Tor node to be sure of the reason for a failure elsewhere in a circuit.

We performed a modified version of this test. After creating the suspect list, we interleaved probes of the suspect, again as exits, through our honest node, as in the candidate probes. The purpose of these probes were to determine if the suspect nodes' performance had changed in the time since the suspect list was generated. Again, results were mixed: some suspects remained suspicious, while others had improved performance. Without exception, those whose performance improved did not appear to be guilty when examining the probes of suspect-paths.

We also performed a third version of test, where pairs of suspects were the entry and exit nodes on a path of length three. The third node was our trusted node. In this test, we saw the overall average failure rate rise back to the level observed when searching for suspect nodes. No suspicious cliques emerged.

More measurements should be performed to make more definitive statements about the presence of the denial of service attack in the Tor network. We plan to validate the simplified and general detection algorithms in simulation. We further plan to perform more systematic measurements on the Tor network, depending upon the results of our validation and feedback from the Tor community.

7 Conclusion

The denial of service attack on Tor-like networks is potentially quite powerful, allowing an adversary attempting to break the anonymity of users at a rate much higher than when passively listening. Fortunately, this power comes at a price: We have shown that an attacker performing the denial of service is easily detected. We have presented an algorithm that deterministically detects such attackers with a number of probes into the network linear in the number of nodes in the network. Further, we have shown that while an attacker may choose to deny service probabilistically in an attempt to avoid detection, such an attempt is self-defeating: Most of the attacker's gain occurs as the probability of denial approaches one — lower values do not gain much over a passive approach, but are still detectable in a linear number of probes. Finally, we have presented preliminary evidence that no such attack is currently being executed within the deployed Tor network, on the basis of the background connection drop rate within Tor and on an practical version of our detection algorithm.

Acknowledgments. We would like to thank George Bissias for noting an error in an earlier version of the proof in Theorem 1.

References

1. Bauer, K., McCoy, D., Grunwald, D., Kohno, T., Sicker, D.: Low-resource routing attacks against tor. In: WPES '07: Proceedings of the 2007 ACM Workshop on Privacy in Electronic Society, pp. 11–20. ACM Press, New York (2007)
2. Borisov, N., Danezis, G., Mittal, P., Tabriz, P.: Denial of service or denial of security? How attacks on reliability can compromise anonymity. In: CCS 2007: Proceedings of the 14th ACM Conference on Computer and Communications Security, pp. 92–102. ACM Press, New York (2007)
3. Dingledine, R., Mathewson, N., Syverson, P.: Tor: The second-generation onion router. In: Proceedings of the 13th USENIX Security Symposium, August 2004, pp. 303–320 (2004)
4. Levine, B.N., Reiter, M.K., Wang, C., Wright, M.K.: Timing attacks in low-latency mix-based systems. In: Juels, A. (ed.) FC 2004. LNCS, vol. 3110, pp. 251–265. Springer, Heidelberg (2004)
5. Overlier, L., Syverson, P.: Locating hidden servers. In: 2006 IEEE Symposium on Security and Privacy, pp. 100–114. IEEE Computer Society Press, Los Alamitos (2006)
6. Syverson, P., Tsudik, G., Reed, M., Landwehr, C.: Towards an analysis of onion routing security. In: Federrath, H. (ed.) Designing Privacy Enhancing Technologies. LNCS, vol. 2009, pp. 96–114. Springer, Heidelberg (2001)
7. Wright, M., Adler, M., Levine, B.N., Shields, C.: An analysis of the degradation of anonymous protocols. In: Proceedings of the Network and Distributed System Security Symposium (NDSS 2002), pp. 38–50. Internet Society (February 2002)
8. Wright, M., Adler, M., Levine, B.N., Shields, C.: Defending anonymous communication against passive logging attacks. In: Proceedings of the 2003 Symposium on Security and Privacy, pp. 28–41. IEEE Computer Society Press, Los Alamitos (2003)

Cryptographic Combinatorial Securities Exchanges

Christopher Thorpe and David C. Parkes

Harvard University School of Engineering and Applied Sciences
cat@seas.harvard.edu, parkes@seas.harvard.edu

Abstract. We present a useful new mechanism that facilitates the atomic exchange of many large baskets of securities in a combinatorial exchange. Cryptography prevents information about the securities in the baskets from being exploited, enhancing trust. Our exchange offers institutions who wish to trade large positions a new alternative to existing methods of block trading: they can reduce transaction costs by taking advantage of other institutions' available liquidity, while third party liquidity providers guarantee execution—preserving their desired portfolio composition at all times. In our exchange, institutions submit encrypted orders which are crossed, leaving a "remainder". The exchange proves facts about the portfolio risk of this remainder to third party liquidity providers without revealing the securities in the remainder, the knowledge of which could also be exploited. The third parties learn either (depending on the setting) the portfolio risk parameters of the remainder itself, or how their own portfolio risk would change if they were to incorporate the remainder into a portfolio they submit. In one setting, these third parties submit bids on the commission, and the winner supplies necessary liquidity for the entire exchange to clear. This guaranteed clearing, coupled with external price discovery from the primary markets for the securities, sidesteps difficult combinatorial optimization problems. This latter method of proving how taking on the remainder would *change* risk parameters of one's own portfolio, without revealing the remainder's contents or its own risk parameters, is a useful protocol of independent interest.

1 Introduction

In [21] we introduced the idea of a cryptographic securities exchange for individual equities, motivated by the unfavorable price impact and possible exploitation of information associated with block trades.[1] In that paper, we consider an exchange of single securities, and, typically, securities are traded as single asset types in most alternative trading systems.

We now introduce the *cryptographic combinatorial securities exchange,* where entire *baskets* of securities may be bought or sold, rather than single positions. This has important applications for portfolios of securities where entering various positions piecemeal would subject the investor to portfolio risk. Specifically, if a large portfolio is optimized to have certain correlations among its assets, and it takes hours or days to find a counterparty to fill each of various positions in a basket trade that liquidates a percentage of or rebalances that portfolio, the correlations no longer hold whenever one order is

---

[1] Exchanges of very large positions of securities.

R. Dingledine and P. Golle (Eds.): FC 2009, LNCS 5628, pp. 285–304, 2009.
© IFCA/Springer-Verlag Berlin Heidelberg 2009

filled before another order. Our exchange, which provides for atomic trades that are guaranteed to clear, eliminates this execution risk on portfolio balance.

Another benefit of the cryptographic combinatorial exchange is that cryptography hides valuable information about intended trades that can be exploited. As described in detail in our previous work [21], knowledge of investors' upcoming trades is often exploited – and has a measurable price impact. It would likely be impossible to operate a combinatorial securities exchange without cryptography, because few institutions would trust any third party with the details of their intended trades "in the clear". Our solution employs cryptography as well as hardware and network security to build an exchange that protects the secrecy of institutions' trades before and after the exchange takes place.

We complete our introduction with a discussion of existing commercial protocols and related work from the finance and cryptography literature. In Section 2 we define the cryptographic combinatorial securities exchange. Section 3 describes our proofs of portfolio risk on an encrypted basket of securities that represents the net holdings after multiple baskets are combined in a transaction. In Sections 4, 5 and 6 we discuss real-world requirements our exchange might have in determining reasonable exchange fees, protecting the exchange from exploitative trading practices, and securing data after a round of the exchange is over. An appendix includes efficiency calculations showing that a Paillier-based cryptosystem permits a practical implementation of our protocol, and further discussion on calculating optimal fees and commissions for participants in the exchange.

1.1   Existing Commercial Protocols

While many existing alternative trading systems (ATS's) exist for block trades, no existing ATS protects traders' information and guarantees atomic execution of baskets of securities. Institutions still fear that knowledge of their liquidity can be exploited in various ways, and rely on information broker ATS's like Liquidnet who strictly limit membership to the trading network to parties who are only trading for liquidity reasons. A second problem with many ATS's is that there is typically no guarantee of execution.

We work to ameliorate all of these concerns: our proposal enhances trust by not only keeping trades secret until the market is to clear but also proving the results correct; it also improves liquidity by giving the exchange an efficient mechanism to guarantee execution for all of the trades submitted to it— while still keeping the particular equities in the incoming institutions' baskets secret; and it provides an atomic basket trading paradigm.

Currently for large basket trades (involving more than one security), the transactions are too complex for the pairwise trade matching that existing ATS's like Liquidnet and Pipeline offer. Institutions who need to trade a basket of securities atomically to maintain the integrity of a diversified portfolio may not wish to undertake the risk of executing the trades one security at a time. Thus, institutional investors who wish to trade several large positions at once in a *basket order* often hire an investment bank. They describe the basket to a small number of trusted investment banks who agree to provide liquidity, without disclosing the exact securities that comprise the basket in advance— information that could be exploited. When deciding how much to charge for liquidating a basket, the banks learn only certain risk parameters, such as index membership, daily trading volume, and market correlation; these enable them to estimate their risk and costs in the absence of complete data. This process takes some time: typically institutions will send information about a basket to a liquidity provider in the morning, who then analyzes the information and replies within hours.

Our new cryptographic combinatorial exchange provides the improved efficiency of institution-to-institution trading with the reduced portfolio risk from guaranteed execution of atomic basket trades. Cryptography makes such an exchange feasible by providing necessary trust: exploitable data remain secret, and every action and result can be proven correct.

In our combinatorial exchange, institutions submit baskets of buy and sell orders which are filled by other institutions' sell and buy orders (respectively). The unfilled orders comprise a remainder basket, which clears the exchange when filled by a cooperating third party (assumed to be an investment bank). Prices for each security can be determined by the primary markets, so that the exchange need only discover trading interest.

We believe this to be the first characterization of a cryptographic combinatorial exchange: a number of participants submit bundles to buy and sell goods (in our example, securities), and the market finds an optimal allocation of trades to maximize the benefit of all participants. While such combinatorial exchanges typically require significant computation to find optimal allocations,[2] our exchange makes two important simplifications that eliminate the hard combinatorial problem. First, prices are defined externally by the primary markets, and second, our clearing of the remainder via a third party means that all bundles are filled and the market clears at equilibrium.

1.2 Related Work

Bossaerts et al. [1] describe a "combined-value trading mechanism" similar to our approach and survey related work from the finance literature. We argue that one important reason that such mechanisms have still not been adopted is because institutions are unwilling to divulge the composition of their baskets. Cryptography solves this problem, and may well hold the answer to implementing more expressive trading mechanisms in practice.

Szydlo [20] first proposed the application of zero-knowledge proofs to disclosing facts about equities portfolios. In his highly relevant and pioneering work, a hedge fund proves that its portfolio complies with its published risk guidelines without revealing the contents of its portfolio. Szydlo's proofs are not situated in a transactional context, but rather in the context of a hedge fund reporting portfolio risk characteristics that are based on the claimed securities in its portfolio. In our case, we are interested in proving portfolio risk on a portfolio derived from combining baskets of securities, for example, in order to liquidate a newly derived remainder basket computed from a combination of many incoming baskets.

Another difference in our work is the use of encryption over commitments. Encryptions allow the exchange to issue proofs about combinations of the institutions' baskets

---

[2] Indeed, even defining "optimal" in such an exchange is challenging!

without requiring their continued involvement. Were we to employ commitments, we would require institutions to decommit their baskets before computing the remainder; this provides an opportunity for repudiation. While the homomorphic Pedersen commitments Szydlo employs are more efficient than homomorphic encryptions, we desire nonrepudiation: once a basket is committed to in a transaction, the institution may not later refuse to reveal that basket. Since any non-repudiatable commitment is equivalent to an encryption,[3] we elect to employ encryptions directly. This may also mitigate so-called protocol completion incentive problems (see [3] for a related discussion in the context of auctions), because institutions who lose their incentive to participate cannot benefit from refusing to complete the protocol.

While surprisingly little academic research has been published on applications of cryptography in securities trading (see [21] for a discussion), more work has been done on combinatorial exchanges (CE's). In a CE, buyers and sellers come together in a common exchange to trade bundles of various goods (where bundles may have instructions to buy or sell, or both.) In the general case, solving the price and winner determination problems in a combinatorial exchange is extremely difficult; in our cryptographic combinatorial securities exchange, we get around these by taking all prices from the fair prices already established by the primary markets (price determination), and employing "liquidity providers" who guarantee enough liquidity for the entire exchange to clear (winner determination). See Parkes et al. [13], and Smith et al. [19] for a formal treatment of combinatorial exchanges and related work.

2   Cryptographic Combinatorial Securities Exchanges

Our cryptographic combinatorial securities exchange offers basket traders guaranteed execution and efficient liquidity discovery. It keeps information completely secret until it is necessary, eliminating opportunities for fraud, and proves every result correct without revealing unnecessary information.

Our protocol is simple: institutions submit encrypted baskets; the exchange closes; the exchange creates an encrypted remainder and proves risk characteristics to third party liquidity providers; these liquidity providers bid on their commission; and the winning provider clears the market by liquidating the remainder. Prices clear at prices determined by the primary markets.

Any basic cryptographic protocols supporting provably correct, secrecy-preserving computation over private inputs, such as those described in [15,16,21], are sufficient to construct our exchange. As our protocol does not depend on specific features, such as a particular homomorphism, we do not burden our exposition with specific implementation details. Rather, we assume implementors of our protocol will select an underlying cryptosystem appropriate to their specific needs at the time.

Moreover, these protocols are practically efficient and support the calculations of risk and interval proofs essential to our protocol. To verify this claim, we implemented the cryptographic operations necessary to conduct our protocol and report results in

---

[3] To enjoy nonrepudiation, a commitment must be deterministically invertible. A function that is binding, hiding, and invertible (presumably via some secret) is clearly equivalent to an encryption.

Appendix A. We discuss the implications of the partial trust in our third party required by these protocols and mechanisms for mitigating such trust in Section 6.

2.1 Preliminaries

We employ the following primitive operations necessary to reveal the portfolio risk profile:

- Prove that a ciphertext is the encrypted result of a polynomial function over multiple encrypted values and/or constants x, y. We write $E(x) \oplus E(y)$ to signify the computation yielding $E(x+y)$; $E(x) \otimes E(y)$ yields $E(x \times y)$. $E(X) \odot E(Y)$ signifies the "dot product" of vectors X and Y of encrypted values. In addition, $\bigoplus_i E(x_i)$ yields $E(\sum_i x_i)$.
- Prove whether one encrypted value is greater than another. We write $E(x) \trianglelefteq E(y)$ to signify the computation proving that $x \leq y$ given the two encryptions; we use analogous notation for the other inequality operators.
- Prove whether one encrypted value is (not) equal to another.

If a homomorphic cryptosystem is used for the computations, such as the system described by Paillier [11] and elaborated in [5] and [15], then additional preparation is required to prove results of computations employing both additions and multiplications. Since no known cryptosystem is doubly homomorphic,[4] we require instead that whatever underlying cryptosystem is employed support proofs of correct computation of both addition and multiplication. In a homomorphic cryptosystem, a verifier would check one operation by direct computation over ciphertexts, and the other by receiving information from the prover. For example, using Paillier encryption, a verifier could check addition by simply multiplying ciphertexts; she would only be able to check multiplication with the help of a prover using (non-interactive) protocols such as those described in [5,15].

We assume that interactive interval proofs (see, for example, [2,9,15]) can also be performed efficiently in a non-interactive setting using the Fiat-Shamir heuristic [7]; a strong cryptographic hash of input data simulates the verifier's actions during an interactive proof. Since the encrypted inputs are probabilistic encryptions generated by independent parties, the output of a suitable cryptographic hash on those values should yield data with sufficient (apparent) randomness.

2.2 Problem Definition

We construct a protocol to operate a cryptographic combinatorial securities exchange in which multiple parties may exchange baskets of securities while limiting exploitation of any information submitted to the exchange. The participants in the protocol include the "exchange" itself, "institutions" who submit basket orders to the exchange, and "liquidity providers" who clear unfilled orders. The institutions, liquidity providers, and external auditors also, as "verifiers", verify the accuracy of any information promulgated

---

[4] That is, there exist two distinct operations over the space of ciphertexts that correspond directly to addition *and* multiplication over the space of plaintexts.

by the exchange. When describing a protocol to communicate the risk of accepting a basket of securities, we refer to the "institutions" who send the basket to a "recipient" counterparty. We employ these functional terms throughout our work.

Before a specified "closing time", each participating institution publishes an encrypted basket of securities it wishes to liquidate. Before the closing time, the exchange may not decrypt the baskets; after that time, baskets may not be withdrawn or modified, and execution is guaranteed by the exchange.

The exchange then computes the remainder necessary for the exchange to reach equilibrium, i.e. the basket filling all trading interest not met by other parties. It reveals information about this remainder to various third-party "liquidity providers" who have agreed to liquidate large remainder baskets for the exchange; they in turn quote a price or liquidating the remainder.

The information provided might be direct risk analysis measurements on the remainder, or it might reveal the differences in risk incorporating the remainder would have on a sample portfolio provided by each third party. The liquidity providers then submit encrypted bids for liquidating the portfolio, and the exchange accepts the best price and issues a zero-knowledge style proof to all participating institutions and liquidity providers that it is optimal.

In practice today, liquidating these large basket trades takes hours or even days. Millisecond execution time is critical for high-frequency trading of single securities, but not for these relatively infrequent but high-value transactions that occur only several times a week and are based on liquidity, not price fluctuations. Thus, the cryptographic operations required to implement such an exchange are within reach of contemporary commodity computing hardware. See Appendix A for example calculations.

The exchange preserves the secrecy of the institutions' identities by acting as the middleman between all transactions. In our current setting, institutions may be known to participate in the exchange by virtue of their publishing encrypted baskets, but they can hide whether they are trading or not each day by submitting empty baskets on days they do not wish to trade. Where even further anonymity is desired (that is, the exchange never learns the institutions' identities), real-world entities, such as law or accounting firms, can be employed to represent the institutions; constructing a cryptographic protocol to preserve institutions' identities is beyond the scope of the present work. See [6] for one approach to the problem of privacy in securities exchanges.

This implies the following desiderata:

- The information in the baskets must remain secret, even from the exchange, until all baskets have been submitted.
- Once baskets have been submitted, they may not be modified or retracted.
- No party other than the exchange may learn anything about the direct composition of the baskets other than what is implied by any disclosures, including risk information sent to liquidity providers.
- The exchange must clear completely, that is, all orders are guaranteed to be filled.
- The exchange must clear efficiently: any computations must be completed within a few hours at reasonable cost.

- The cryptosystem employed can convince an independent verifier that the result of performing a computation on hidden inputs is either a particular value or lies in a range of values.

2.3   The Protocol

We consider n institutions P_i, where $i \in [1,n]$, each of which submits an integer vector (representing a basket) B_i, comprised of m integers (representing securities) S_j, where $j \in [1,m]$. Thus in a universe of 6 securities, B_3, P_3's basket, might be $\langle 0, -20000, 32000, 0, 45000, 0 \rangle$. We assume the exchange operates on a fixed universe of these m commonly traded and reasonably liquid securities, such as listed equities, standardized options, and government securities. The double subscript notation B_{ij} denotes the (unencrypted) quantity of security j in P_i's basket; in our example, $B_{35} = 45000$. $E(B_{ij})$ is the encrypted form of one such value. Zeroes are included to hide the number of distinct equities in the basket.

We assume a public price vector V of length m contains the values for the m securities at the time the exchange clears; V_j is the price for security j. This might be obtained from current market prices or the previous day's closing prices.

Since most underlying cryptosystems employ modular arithmetic, short positions can be easily represented as "negative numbers" (that is, very large numbers that are the additive inverses of the corresponding positive number). Alternatively, long and short positions may be represented by two encrypted vectors: one of the absolute values of the quantites and the other of 1 (long), -1 (short), or 0 (no position).

An encryption of a basket of equities is simply an integer vector one for each equity in the universe, including zeros. For visual comfort, we may write $E(B_i)$ as the encryption of an entire basket, which is in fact m separate encryptions: $\langle E(B_{i1}), E(B_{i2}), \ldots, E(B_{im}) \rangle$.

Step 1. The exchange announces clearing times, the universe of equities to be traded on the exchange, and any rules governing the composition of baskets participating in the exchange. If time-lapse cryptography (TLC) [17] or another technique used to enforce nonrepudiation requires posting of public information (for example, a public TLC encryption key), the exchange posts it.

Step 2. Before each clearing time, each institution P_i chooses which equities she wishes to trade and creates basket B_i and its encrypted form $E(B_i)$. She then creates a commitment to her basket, $\mathbf{Com}_i(E(B_i))$, and publishes that commitment where the exchange and other parties to the transaction can see them. The reason we add this pre-clearing commitment step is to prevent the exchange from observing the contents of any baskets and revealing that information before the "clearing time". This extra step ensures that the exchange cannot influence the outcome of the exchange even if it can somehow successfully leak data, because no baskes may be submitted or retracted after the auctioneer receives any material information.

Step 3. When the clearing time is reached, the institutions decommit: each institution P_i publishes $E(B_i)$, the encryption of its basket, and any additional information necessary to verify $\mathbf{Com}_i(E(B_i))$ matches. If a institution fails to decommit, and a nonrepudiation technique is employed, the commitment is forced open and the encryption of his basket is published.[5]

Step 4. Either the exchange, or each institution P_i, proves, using the now public $E(B_i)$, that B_i conforms to any announced basket composition requirements by proving a set of constraints on the encrypted number of shares of each security in the universe. These constraints can take the form of any equation or inequality representing a polynomial function of the encrypted baskets (security quantity vectors) B_i, public price vector V, and necessary constants. These constants might include minimum or maximum basket size, or a constant bound for what percentage of the basket is in a particular class (such as market sector or index member). Because P_i encrypted the basket itself, it is capable of proving its basket meets any such constraints (see Section 5) without the cooperation of the exchange, if necessary.

Step 5. Anyone can verify the "remainder" basket B_0 as above by computing its encrypted form from $E(B_i)$ (for all i). Table 1 illustrates an example of this on unencrypted values. Using our notation from Section 2.1, we write:

$$B_0 = \langle \bigoplus_{i=1}^{n} E(B_{i1}), \ldots, \bigoplus_{i=1}^{n} E(B_{im}) \rangle = \langle E(\sum_{i=1}^{n} B_{i1}), \ldots, E(\sum_{i=1}^{n} B_{im}) \rangle$$

Table 1. Example set of cross-clearing portfolios $B_1, \ldots, B_4$ with a "remainder" B_0

Security	B_1	B_2	B_3	B_4	B_0
ABC	+500	-200	0	0	+300
DEF	+300	-800	+300	+200	0
GHI	0	+100	-300	0	-200
JKL	+200	0	-400	+300	+100
MNO	-800	0	+500	0	-300

Step 6. The exchange privately decrypts the baskets, and obtains the unencrypted remainder basket.

Step 7. The exchange proves the constraints about the composition of the remainder basket B_0 to the third party liquidity providers, who individually or jointly determine transaction costs for the remainder basket and agree to provide liquidity to the pool.

Step 8. After the market-clearing liquidity has been secured, the exchange announces the protocol is complete and the market clears at prices fixed in accordance with a published standard procedure.

For example, the market might clear at the midpoint between the bid and ask quoted on the current primary market, or an agreement to trade at the volume-weighted average

---

[5] An alternative to the use of commitments is to employ distributed key generation for a public encryption key, then only reconstruct the private key after the clearing time is reached; this idea, formalized in TLC, still ensures that the exchange cannot decrypt the baskets prematurely.

price for a particular period of time. The mechanics of clearing securities trades are beyond the scope of this work; we assume that all parties trade with a trusted intermediary who accepts all securities sold and distributes those bought, clearing the market.

The exchange issues proofs that the procedures are followed, again by proving that a set of constraints are met over the institutions' encrypted baskets, the public price vector, necessary constants, and any (possibly encrypted) data provided by liquidity providers.

3 Secrecy-Preserving Proofs of Impact on Portfolio Risk

In the introduction, we describe how large basket orders are traded by revealing portfolio risk measurements of the baskets themselves, rather than the actual risk undertaken by the liquidity providers the baskets.

We propose a secure system that makes price discovery for basket trades more accurate by offering liquidity providers limited but more specific characteristics of their actual risks — how the risk of their inventory changes — not the characteristics of the incoming basket. In this section, we refer to an "institution" who is offering a basket and a "recipient" of that basket – a liquidity provider in our primary protocol. However, our protocol has more general applicability and may be used in any transaction in which a recipient wishes to estimate its risk in accepting a basket of equities. That basket may be the combination of many baskets (e.g. in a combinatorial exchange) or a single counterparty's basket.

Our protocol employs a server as a partially trusted third party, accepting encrypted forms of the institution's portfolio and the provider's book, and providing a set of risk characteristics of the recipient's resulting book after the integration of the equities in the portfolio. The protocol proves these characteristics correct in a zero-knowledge fashion based on the encrypted inputs, to assure the recipient that it received an accurate picture even if it does not win the bid. (Presently, only winners can verify the correctness of the submitted values because they are the only party who ever discovers the actual contents of the basket.)

Finally, we remark that wherever we refer to a recipient's "inventory", the recipient may use any representative portfolio in the protocol and compute the risk of accepting the basket on the basis of risk changes in this particular portfolio. This may be due to reluctance to reveal the exact portfolio to even a partially trusted third party, or to optimize price discovery by a specially tailored portfolio.

3.1 Mechanics of the Protocol

The protocol is comprised of a series of simple steps: the parameters of the transaction are agreed on; the transacting parties publish their encrypted information to all; the "institution" and "recipients" P_i for $i \in [1, n]$ send information to the partially trusted third party, the "exchange"; the exchange issues proofs to the recipient about its portfolio risk; and the recipients verify the proofs using the published information. When used in conjunction with the above protocol, the "institution's" basket is the remainder basket representing all unfilled orders.

Step 1. The institution and recipients agree on a set of risk characteristics to evaluate the portfolio resulting from each recipient's accepting the institution's portfolio. This protects the secrecy of the institution's information while providing enough information to the recipient to quote an accurate price. Each risk characteristic will be computed by performing a computation over the institution's encrypted portfolio and recipient's encrypted inventory. The institution may also require that certain outputs be reported as "bounds", where the results are only quoted accurately enough for the recipient to price the portfolio by proving they lie within a certain small range. This is of extreme importance to prevent any recipient from "backing out" private information from the encrypted data by carefully constructed queries. See also the more detailed discussion in the following section, 3.2.

Step 2. The institution prepares an encrypted basket B_0 as above in the combinatorial case. The encryptions are carried out in accordance with the underlying cryptographic protocol.[6] The institution submits the encrypted basket to the exchange.

Step 3. Each recipient prepares a similar basket B_i with its inventory, into which the basket would be integrated, and shares this encrypted portfolio with the exchange. It does *not* need to share it with the institution.

Step 4. The exchange and each recipient computes the encrypted result of incorporating the new basket B_0, $\hat{B}_i = B_i \oplus B_0$. The exchange then computes the risk characteristics of $\hat{B}_i$ and reveals them to recipient P_i with a correctness proof. Note that P_i never learns the exact composition of $\hat{B}_i$: only its risk profile.

Step 5. When the protocol is used to compute the cost of liquidating a basket of securities (for example, a remainder basket), the recipient examines the new risk characteristics of the resulting portfolio, estimates carrying and execution costs and submits a bid to the institution. (In practice, the computed characteristics might be sent to a portfolio management software system that compares the "before" and "after" portfolios to automatically estimate risk and hedging costs.)

3.2 What Information Should Be Revealed?

Presently, institutions submit the characteristics of their baskets to investment banks in spreadsheets with specific numbers in each category. This process "leaks" information, especially where the number of equities in a particular category is small. Occasionally, the information can create obvious implications: for example, if there is only one equity listed in the telecommunications sector, comprising 89,000 shares whose total value is $3,546,650, the bank probably has an excellent idea of the company's name. Institutions sometimes "white out" some information in their basket descriptions to prevent such information leakage, usually to eliminate obvious information leaks.

Yet even when such information is redacted, rigorous statistical analyses of the information submitted can still yield information about the composition of the baskets, and this is also possible in more complex situations where a large number of equities contribute to one line-item. Since values are often supplied to the penny, if the number of equities, total dollar amount as of a particular market close, and total number

---

[6] Providing the value quotation is a matter of convenience, as the encrypted value can be computed as the encrypted product of public previous close price and the encrypted number of shares.

of shares is known, it is possible that a computer could efficiently search the possible baskets created by equities in that sector and propose a small number of alternatives to the bank. While we have no reason to believe that the reports are being so exploited by the banks, eliminating any potential information leakage while still providing accurate risk assessments is an important benefit of our proposed protocol.

Because the cryptographic framework we describe supports interval proofs on encrypted values (or functions on encrypted values) the exchange can reveal approximate risk characteristics that are sufficient for price discovery but are more resistant to statistical analysis to back out the composition of the baskets. For instance, instead of reporting the sector breakdown exactly, the exchange can report values rounded to the nearest percentage point or thousands of dollars or shares. Although there is no reason that institutions can't submit baskets with such obfuscated data, they would not be able to prove it correct without cryptography. The ability to reveal "just enough" information (while still proving it correct) is an important feature of our proposal.[7]

3.3 How the Information Is Revealed

Rather than proving portfolio risk of a single portfolio, we are interested in revealing facts about a hypothetical portfolio that results from the combination of other portfolios.

Once our protocol is followed, the exchange privately knows the combined portfolio. To reveal a fact, the exchange obtains the result of the desired computation and sends the result to the verifiers, along with special verification data that allow them to verify the result.

3.4 Revealing Portfolio Value and Dividends

In most cases, the incoming basket order will involve long and short trades, and an important element of the risk is the "skew" — the difference between the total value of the short and long trades. Sometimes, when an institution is trading a basket with a significant skew (or even entirely one-sided) it may not wish the size of the skew to be known. In this case, the recipient might respond not with a specific cash price, but rather a discount quotation, an agreement to accept the equities in the basket at a particular volume-weighted average price, or other quotation based on the market prices of the equities after they are revealed. Because the recipient can accurately assess its risk profile in accepting these, it can offer more competitive discounts or execution quotes for less risky baskets, or, similarly, charge more for a riskier basket.

The institution and the recipient(s) may agree to reveal:

- The full value of the long and short sides of the portfolio:
  The exchange provides a proof that allows the recipient to decrypt the sum of all long positions and the sum of all short positions.[8]

---

[7] See Section 6 for a discussion of why this feature is best supported by protocols based on a partially trusted third party.

[8] While possible, the details of doing this without revealing *which* securities are long and short require great care and describing such a proof is beyond the scope of this paper.

- The value or range of the "skew" only:

  In this case, the exchange provides the recipient a proof of the sum of the portfolio's value: all long positions' values minus all short positions' values. Assuming that $\hat{B}_i$ holds signed quantities, the verifier simply computes the encrypted dot product of the portfolio and the price vector V: $E(W) \equiv \hat{B}_i \odot V$. The exchange might reveal the precise value W, or only that W lies within a particular interval.

- No information about the value of the incoming basket:

  In this case, the position values, quotes, and number of shares must all be kept secret; the risk profile of the resulting portfolio can still be evaluated by other means.

A similar approach can be applied to dividends, where the recipient receives aggregate calculations of historical and expected dividend payments, so that it can estimate any dividend payments it will make (for short sales) and receive (for long positions).

3.5   Portfolio Composition Statistics

For risk management and hedging calculations, the recipient may wish to know the composition of the combined portfolio based on various factors, including:

- Market sector (technology, health care, consumer goods, etc.)
- Market capitalization
- Index membership
- Dividend amount (as a percentage of share price)
- Average daily trading volume (possible in terms of both shares and notional value)
- Historical price volatility

Using our protocol, the institution need not reveal any information about the incoming basket's sector breakdown — for example, if there are balanced long and short trades in technology, and zero trades in utilities, this is indistinguishable to the recipient from a portfolio with zero technology and balanced utilities trades, provided that the balanced trades do not change the risk profile of the recipient's inventory. This provides additional secrecy to the institution while still meeting the needs of the recipient.

The exchange calculates the portfolio composition and proves it to the accepting recipient, who verifies the result using its own encrypted portfolio and the encrypted basket provided by the institution. Because the exchange can offer proofs that each sector's breakdown lies within a particular interval (say to the percentage point or 1/10 of 1%), the institution can reveal enough information for the recipient to offer an accurate price while making reconstruction of the portfolio infeasible.

Using the general cryptographic operations described above, the exchange can prove breakdowns for the various aspects of the portfolio as follows. We write that the portfolio B_0 is the sum of all n institutions' baskets B_i for all $i \in [1, n]$, each of which contains m securities. B_{i_j} is the jth security in basket i.

Step 1. Because the exchange knows the breakdown for each equity (e.g. market capitalization, market sector, etc.), it can compute encrypted sums of the number of shares and total value for each item in the breakdown by summing up the encrypted number of shares and total value from the combined portfolio and prove them correct. The recipient also recalls the encrypted total number of shares and encrypted total value of the basket. We recall that this is the *combined* portfolio, where any long and short trades in the incoming basket have already been incorporated into the recipient's inventory.

Step 2. The exchange first proves the sums are correct, namely, $E(B_{0j}) \equiv \bigoplus_{i=1}^{n}(B_{ij})$, for $j \in [1,m]$; and computes the encrypted total portfolio value $E(W) \equiv \bigoplus_{j=1}^{m} B_{0j} \cdot V_j$ from the encrypted combined portfolio and constant price vector.

Step 3. The exchange then prepares an encrypted "unit size" Z by computing Z and designating a public constant K such that $ZK \leq W$ and $(Z+1)K > W$. The exchange proves this by providing the recipient $E(Z)$ and a trivial encryption $E(K)$ and proving that $E(Z) \otimes E(K) \trianglelefteq E(W)$ and $(E(Z) \oplus E(1)) \otimes E(K) \triangleright E(W)$. Thus there are K "units" of size Z in the breakdown.[9]

Step 4. For each element of the breakdown, the exchange prepares an interval proof of how many "units" that element comprises. It begins by calculating and revealing two integer constants a_i, b_i and their "trivial" encryptions $E(a_i), E(b_i)$; the recipient can verify these are correct encryptions. For example, a_i might be 10 and b_i 12, to show the result is between 10 and 12 units.

Step 5. The exchange completes the interval proof, showing that $E(a_i) \otimes E(Z) \trianglelefteq E(v_i) \trianglelefteq E(b_i) \otimes E(Z)$. This proves that $a_i Z \leq v_i \leq b_i Z$. This bounds the value of the portfolio in bucket i without revealing any further information.

Step 6. Steps 4 and 5 are repeated for each "bucket" in the breakdown until the entire portfolio has been classified. The recipient might check that $\sum_i a_i \leq K \leq \sum_i b_i$ to be sure that the breakdown provided is appropriate.

3.6   Other Measurements of Risk

Because of the flexibility of the mathematical operations that can be performed on the recipient's basket and the incoming basket, other, more complicated risk measurements are possible. While the above examples are of linear functions, which permit the recipient to compute the incoming baskets' risk characteristics from the output risk characteristics and his own inputs, our protocol provides for computation of polynomial functions of modest degree by using repeated multiplications (including repeated squaring) of encrypted values to calculate exponents. This permits the computation of more complex risk analysis measurements whose definition under our framework we leave for future work.

4   Pricing and Payment

Two types of prices must be computed: the price at which each security is valued when the exchange clears, and the price that the third parties charge for providing the market-clearing liquidity. We treat these in turn, referring to the winning third party (which

---

[9] Care must be taken so that $W \bmod K$ is not too large, because this could skew the results. The exchange can even show the recipient that value by revealing the verifiable result $E(W) \ominus (E(K) \otimes E(Z))$, or proving that it is less than a small constant. Since K is public, the recipient can refuse a K that is too small.

might be a consortium) as the liquidity provider or recipient. We note that if our second protocol is used independently between a single institution and one or more liquidity providers for proving characteristics about a single basket trade, the institution's basket functions as the remainder.[10]

Because each of the securities in the exchange is presumed to be traded on a primary market, we adopt the common practice in block trading to allow the primary market to dictate a fair market price for the securities at the time of trading. The financial industry uses many reasonable methods for price determination in block trading, and we do not advocate a particular pricing model over another—provided that the trading prices are determined in a manner exogenous to the exchange. Examples of these methods include the closing or settlement price for the day of the transaction, average prices over time such as the volume-weighted average price (VWAP), or simply the midpoint of the best bid and offer at the time the market clears.

After the proofs are obtained, the third parties have learned enough information to calculate a price for the incoming basket. They can accurately assess the changes in risk on their own inventories if they accept the basket, and by measuring those changes, estimate hedging costs for equities it will carry and execution costs for unwinding the trades it does not wish to keep.

In Appendix B, we consider approaches to allocating the liquidation costs among the market participants; this can also be done in a provably correct fashion.

5   Keeping the Pool Safe

Although our methods are designed to provide transparency without revealing exploitable information, there remain ways in which unscrupulous traders might try to exploit the exchange we propose.

One misuse of our exchange might be for institutions to use its guaranteed liquidity to unload especially high-risk or illiquid securities. If the exchange becomes filled with undesirable assets, then liquidity providers will be less likely to want to participate. This is an important reason we advocate a pricing mechanism that charges institutions according to the amount of the remainder basket their trades represent—if the pricing mechanism is correctly defined, then institutions who submit less desirable portfolios will pay more for their liquidation costs.

Yet it might be desirable to make sure that the baskets the institutions submit to the exchange meet basic criteria for acceptability and portfolio risk. Using the same portfolio risk analysis techniques described above, institutions can issue zero-knowledge proofs about the baskets they submit so that all can be confident that their trades are acceptable. This should also reduce the third-party liquidation costs, because the third parties will be more confident that they won't receive a basket that has nice overall characteristics but might be comprised of less desirable individual securities.

As we mentioned in the introduction, other common exploits associated with dark pools are less of a concern because our protocol features guaranteed execution. Exploits such as probing for existing liquidity and baiting (where someone places an order and

---

[10] In fact, this is equivalent to operating our exchange with a single institutional participant.

then retracts it) are less of a problem, since once an order is placed, it cannot be re-tracted, and learning that your order was filled reveals nothing about existing opposite interest—every order is filled. Johnson [8] describes "toxic dark pools" that are known for being exploited.

6   Strengthening Secrecy

While our solutions offer an appropriate degree of secrecy and are practical to imple-ment, the exchange does learn private data that it could reveal to others after the fact. It learns the trades that took place, which may be undesirable to certain institutions (notably hedge funds), and could learn something about the recipient's inventory in the context of proving changes to the recipient's risk without revealing the incoming portfolio characteristics directly. While the trades must eventually be reported to the exchanges and become a matter of public record, and no such information could have any bearing on a particular round of the exchange, this information still has value. We thus consider how to mitigate the trust not to leak any information that we might place in the exchange operator.

The most compelling complement to our cryptographic solutions includes secure computing infrastructure such as Trusted Computing [18] hardware and network mon-itoring. We advance this idea in our previous work on cryptographic securities trading [21] and auctions protocols [14,16]. In this scheme, specially designed hardware and software are trusted not to leak information, and monitored for security. Moreover, the secrecy-preserving correctness proofs we advance in this work complement such "black boxes" extremely well, because we need not trust the black box to produce correct re-sults: we only use it to mitigate *ex post* disclosure. Thus, the actions of the exchange remain provably correct under all circumstances—even an undetected bug in the black box cannot result in incorrect behavior.

Even in these high-security settings, a determined adversary might be able to engi-neer steganographic leaks by "hiding" information in the protocol itself, often in prede-termined bits of "random" help values. Doing so would be a significant effort, because most trusted computing infrastructures will not run software that has not been verified and signed by a third party, but we mention that small risk nonetheless. Fair Zero-Knowledge, introduced by Lepinski et al. [10], describes a mechanism to combat such attacks and surveys related work.

Another approach is be to distribute trust among a group of entities who jointly act as the exchange. While this theoretically possible solution does eliminate any one single trusted third party, the architecture retains a functional entity of a trusted third party which happens to be comprised of several entities. Employing such a solution successfully in practice would require the cooperation of disparate, disinterested busi-ness entities to prevent collusion; moreover, the efficiency of such secure multiparty computation schemes may not be able to support the computations we require.

Finally, we observe that perfect security is never attainable in real life where hu-mans are involved: any dishonest party "in the know" can always pick up the phone to deliver an out-of-band information leak. And, even where there is no intentional disclo-sure, Brandt and Sandholm proved impossibility results for achieving complete secrecy in some auction settings [4]. These ideas lead to interesting security questions about modern markets where more and more trades are performed without human input: automated trading agents running on secure hardware could offer an unprecedented level of security against the human element.

7   Conclusions and Future Work

We have implemented a useful new mechanism for block trading of securities that meets two market requirements: institutions can trade directly with each other when liquidity is available, while still having guaranteed execution for their entire order to limit portfolio and carrying risk. We employ a combinatorial exchange model, but make it tractable through external price discovery and a third party who provides necessary liquidity to achieve market equilibrium so that all orders are filled.

We protect the secrecy of sensitive data while giving the third party information necessary to calculate a fair commission by combining two novel cryptographic protocols. They are efficient, straightforward to understand, and can be implemented using already accepted cryptographic primitives.

More general formulations of these protocols may be of independent interest. Consider an arbitrary function over a finite field with encrypted inputs and a prover who proves facts about the output of this function. Clearly, there are many functions for which a precise output reduces the space of possible inputs dramatically — an unintended consequence of revealing a single output. Our mechanisms can offer provably correct yet *approximate* outputs using interval proofs, where exact results would reveal too much information.

The protocol we describe to prove changes to a recipient's risk also generalizes into a new class of price discovery. We can construct a more general protocol that allows a buyer to evaluate a purchase on the basis of a change in a buyer's utility function, rather than calculating the utility of the good directly. This means that in many business settings, where direct revelation of the good in question might have negative consequences, a buyer can engage in "zero-knowledge due diligence" where the buyer can satisfy many concerns by learning about how her utility function changes based on incorporating the good into her possessions, without learning enough about the good to allow the information to be exploited. These settings might include the sale of a significant commercial building, a business unit of a large corporation, or, other methods of trading financial instruments.

We leave for future work a number of mechanism design questions. We believe it is possible to approach a true combinatorial exchange in which both institutions and liquidity providers post their desired baskets, where institutions post a maximum price they are willing to pay for liquidating their baskets, and whether and how their baskets are divisible; liquidity providers post "chunks" of liquidity associated with transaction costs for each chunk. The exchange then finds the optimal feasible allocation satisfying all possible atomic trades, and proves the outcome correct. Moreover, the use of such "chunks" could significantly reduce the size of any remainder basket, thereby reducing the size of any portfolio that needs to be traded blindly.

In addition to generalizing the protocols as described here, future work may also include a reference implementation of a prototype exchange or a more detailed technical specification based on a particular cryptosystem.

Acknowledgments

We thank Stephanie Borynack and Imad Labban, who brought our attention to an important class of large transations described in this work. We also thank Eric Budish, John Y. Campbell, and Luis Viceira for useful discussions about how this research might be used in practice, and ideas that improved the presentation of the work to readers with an economics background. We thank Aggelos Kiayias for suggesting a number of improvements we adopted in preparing our work for FC 2009. Finally, we thank the anonymous reviewers who evaluated various versions of this paper and offered many helpful suggestions we have incorporated into this work.

References

1. Bossaerts, P., Fine, L., Ledyard, J.: Inducing liquidity in thin financial markets through combined-value trading mechanisms. European Economic Review 46(9), 1671–1695 (2002)
2. Boudot, F.: Efficient proofs that a committed number lies in an interval. In: Preneel, B. (ed.) EUROCRYPT 2000. LNCS, vol. 1807, pp. 431–444. Springer, Heidelberg (2000)
3. Bradford, P.G., Park, S., Rothkopf, M.H.: Protocol completion incentive problems in cryptographic Vickrey auctions. Technical Report RRR 3-2004, Rutgers Center for Operations Research, RUTCOR (2004)
4. Brandt, F., Sandholm, T.: (Im)possibility of unconditionally privacy-preserving auctions. In: Proc. 3rd Int. Conf. on Autonomous Agents and Multi-Agent Systems, pp. 810–817 (2004)
5. Damgård, I., Jurik, M.: A generalisation, a simplification and some applications of Paillier's probabilistic public-key system. In: Proceedings of Public Key Cryptography 2001 (2001)
6. Di Crescenzo, G.: Privacy for the stock market. In: Syverson, P.F. (ed.) FC 2001. LNCS, vol. 2339, p. 259. Springer, Heidelberg (2002)
7. Fiat, A., Shamir, A.: How to prove yourself: Practical solutions to identification and signature problems. In: Odlyzko, A.M. (ed.) CRYPTO 1986. LNCS, vol. 263, pp. 186–194. Springer, Heidelberg (1987)
8. Johnson, J., Tabb, L.: Groping in the dark: Navigating crossing networks and other dark pools of liquidity, January 31 (2007)
9. Kiayias, A., Yung, M.: Efficient cryptographic protocols realizing e-markets with price discrimination. In: Financial Cryptography and Data Security, pp. 311–325 (2006)
10. Lepinski, M., Micali, S., Shelat, A.: Fair zero-knowledge. In: Proc. Theory of Cryptography Conference, pp. 245–263 (2005)
11. Paillier, P.: Public-key cryptosystems based on composite degree residuosity classes. In: Stern, J. (ed.) EUROCRYPT 1999. LNCS, vol. 1592, pp. 223–239. Springer, Heidelberg (1999)
12. Parkes, D.C., Cavallo, R., Elprin, N., Juda, A., Lahaie, S., Lubin, B., Michael, L., Shneidman, J., Sultan, H.: ICE: An iterative combinatorial exchange. In: ACM Conf. on Electronic Commerce, pp. 249–258 (2005)
13. Parkes, D.C., Kalagnanam, J.R., Eso, M.: Achieving budget-balance with Vickrey-based payment schemes in combinatorial exchanges. Technical report, IBM Research Report RC 22218 (2001)

14. Parkes, D.C., Rabin, M.O., Shieber, S.M., Thorpe, C.A.: Practical secrecy-preserving, verifiably correct and trustworthy auctions. In: ICEC 2006: Proceedings of the 8th international conference on Electronic commerce, pp. 70–81. ACM Press, New York (2006)
15. Parkes, D.C., Rabin, M.O., Shieber, S.M., Thorpe, C.A.: Practical secrecy-preserving, verifiably correct and trustworthy auctions. Electronic Commerce Research and Applications (to appear, 2008)
16. Rabin, M.O., Servedio, R.A., Thorpe, C.: Highly efficient secrecy-preserving proofs of correctness of computations and applications. In: Proc. IEEE Symposium on Logic in Computer Science (2007)
17. Rabin, M.O., Thorpe, C.: Time-lapse cryptography. Technical Report TR-22-06, Harvard University School of Engineering and Computer Science (2006)
18. Smith, S.W.: Trusted Computing Platforms: Design and Applications. Springer, New York (2005)
19. Smith, T., Sandholm, T., Simmons, R.: Constructing and clearing combinatorial exchanges using preference elicitation. In: AAAI 2002 workshop on Preferences in AI and CP: Symbolic Approaches (2002)
20. Szydlo, M.: Risk assurance for hedge funds using zero knowledge proofs. In: S. Patrick, A., Yung, M. (eds.) FC 2005. LNCS, vol. 3570, pp. 156–171. Springer, Heidelberg (2005)
21. Thorpe, C., Parkes, D.C.: Cryptographic securities exchanges. In: Dietrich, S., Dhamija, R. (eds.) FC 2007 and USEC 2007. LNCS, vol. 4886, pp. 163–178. Springer, Heidelberg (2007)

A   Efficiency of Our Protocols

While we have observed that any number of cryptographic systems might support our protocols, we have conducted empirical tests using Paillier cryptography libraries written in C++ with the GMP multi-precision library; we wrote these libraries to test the practicality of cryptographic auctions in [15].

Notably, these tests included interval proofs, additions, and multiplications, all of which are required to operate a cryptographic combinatorial securities exchange. Our empirical tests demonstrate that our efficiency claims are realistic, namely, that each step of the protocol can proceed in a reasonable amount of time on cost-effective commodity hardware. As noted above, we expect our combinatorial exchange to clear high value baskets within hours; our tests meet this goal.

We assumed a universe of 3,000 securities in each basket. We assumed that quantities of securities are 32-bit values (up to approximately 4 billion). We used a 1536-bit Paillier key, a composite of two 768-bit primes that offers expected security for at least a few years. We assume all four processors are running in a quad-core Intel Xeon 2.0GHz processor. Obviously, cryptographic computations can be parallelized across many machines; this can offer even greater speed at additional hardware cost.

- Encrypting a basket: 48 seconds
- Decrypting a basket: 15 seconds
- Computing/Verifying the encrypted remainder: ¡ 1 second
- Interval proof on a 32-bit value: 1.25 seconds of required server precomputation; 0.25 seconds of real-time server computation; 1.25 seconds of client verification
- Performing additions: negligible
- Multiplication with a constant: 0.001 seconds

- Multiplication (proving an encrypted value represents the product of two other encrypted values): 4.3 server seconds; ¡ 1 second of client verification
- Proving a basket of 3,000 securities is "well-formed": 1 hour of required server precomputation; 12 minutes of real-time server computation; 1 hour of client verification

Using these values, we anticipate a typical risk analysis measurement would assume a basket already proven to be well-formed, and perhaps 10 interval proofs and 10 multiplications. This means that for a particular basket (say, the remainder), a risk analysis measurement, such as a breakdown into 10 market sectors, could be performed in less than 1 minute of server and client time. This puts our protocol well within the realm of practicality.

The majority of time spent using a Paillier cryptosystem is in modular exponentiation of random help values. Using a specialized cryptographic coprocessor could significantly reduce computation time. Moreover, in many cases these computations can be precomputed before the exchange clears, and fully verified in the hours after it clears – clearly, if the exchange can be found out to have cheated within a day, that is a significant enough deterrent so that the verification operations need not be carried out in real time.

B   Allocating Liquidation Costs

The liquidity provider can be compensated in many ways; the simplest is for it to quote a brokerage commission that it accepts for executing the trades. A provider who perceives greater risk can charge a higher commission. Other pricing mechanisms are possible: if the cash value of the portfolio is revealed, the provider can quote a price based on that; if the skew is not revealed, then the provider can quote a price based on a discount factor or volume-weighted price after the transaction is agreed on. The institution can choose among the various providers' offers, and notify the winner. Once the transaction is complete, the liquidity provider accepting the basket will be able to verify that the information provided was correct when it receives the remainder portfolio — but we reiterate that an advantage of our protocol is that those that do not win still have convincing proof that the information was correct: the institution can't favor one bank over another.

Another interesting possibility is for the liquidity providers to publish deterministically verifiable valuation functions for their risk premium calculations. Using these, they can submit a representative portfolio to the exchange, obtain the changes in risk on their portfolio, then the exchange runs their calculations on the encrypted risk data and publishes a verifiable, encrypted result. These results would then be used to prove the payments correct, or could even be used in a verifiable sealed-bid auction to prove which of the liquidity providers' calculations yielded the most competitive bid for liquidating the remainder.

While total cost sharing is simple and convenient, we also consider a slightly more involved "pay for what you use" model: each institution pays its share of the commission based only on the benefit it derived from the securities provided by the liquidity providers. In this method, institutions that use more of the remainder (instead of the other institutions) to fill their trades pay a greater share of the commission. At the extremes, an institution that trades securities which do not appear in the remainder pays nothing, while an institution who is the only one trading a particular security pays the entire share of the commission for that security.

We illustrate this method with an example which refers back to Table 1. For simplicity, we will assume that each security trades at a price of $1, and the liquidity provider charged a commission of $9000. The notional values of the four institutions' baskets are $1800, $1100, $1500, and $500, respectively; the remainder basket's value is $900. The exchange operator then publishes the encrypted amounts of commission paid based on the pro rata notional value traded of each security: $3000 for ABC, $0 for DEF, $2000 for GHI, $1000 for JKL, and $3000 for MNO. The operator proves that their sum is the (public) total commission.

Next, the exchange operator proves the total trading interest for each security by publishing encrypted sums of the absolute notional value of the orders in each basket: 700 for ABC, 1600 for DEF, 400 for GHI, 900 for JKL, and 1300 for MNO. Then, using the above methods, the exchange operator can publish an encrypted breakdown of the commission to be paid per share.[11] In this case, the commissions work out to $429 per 100 shares of ABC, $0 per 100 shares of DEF, $500 per 100 shares of GHI, $112 per 100 shares of JKL, and $231 per 100 shares of MNO; this yields a total overcharge of $14 due to rounding error.[12] The exchange proves that these encrypted prorated commissions are correct given the encrypted values already computed.

The exchange finally uses these encrypted prorated commissions to give each institution a verifiable share of its commission without revealing the magnitude of the securities traded by other institutions or the composition of the remainder basket. For example, Institution 1 would pay
$$(5 \times 429) + (3 \times 0) + (0 \times 500) + (2 \times 112) + (8 \times 231) = 4217.$$
The others would pay $1358, $3103, and $336, respectively, for their share of the costs in liquidating the remainder.

We sketch a final, possibly fairer method inspired by the Vickrey auction, but we reserve a full treatment and analysis for later work. In this model, an institution's share of the commission would be based on its impact on the market versus the marginal economy without its basket. Thus, institutions who *improved* the market by submitting a basket with opposite interest from the remaining baskets would pay very little (or perhaps even be paid!). Institutions who made the market more unbalanced by submitting a basket with interest in the same direction the remaining baskets would pay a greater share of the commission, because its trades would only be filled by means of the liquidity providers.

---

[11] Since the numbers do not divide evenly, the exchange can simply round up to the nearest integer and prove that the result is within a small error, that is, the difference between the total commission and the reported commission is small.

[12] If verifiable operations over encrypted rationals are employed, even this rounding error can be (practically) eliminated at a constant factor of additional computation cost.

Cryptographic Combinatorial Clock-Proxy Auctions

David C. Parkes, Michael O. Rabin, and Christopher Thorpe

School of Engineering and Applied Sciences
Harvard University
parkes@eecs.harvard.edu, rabin@seas.harvard.edu, cat@eecs.harvard.edu

Abstract. We present a cryptographic protocol for conducting efficient, provably correct and secrecy-preserving combinatorial clock-proxy auctions. The "clock phase" functions as a trusted auction despite price discovery: bidders submit encrypted bids, and prove for themselves that they meet activity rules, and can compute total demand and thus verify price increases without revealing any information about individual demands. In the sealed-bid "proxy phase", all bids are revealed the auctioneer via time-lapse cryptography and a branch-and-bound algorithm is used to solve the winner-determination problem. Homomorphic encryption is used to prove the correctness of the solution, and establishes the correctness of the solution to any interested party. Still an NP-hard optimization problem, the use of homomorphic encryption imposes additional computational time on winner-determination that is linear in the size of the branch-and-bound search tree, and thus roughly linear in the original (search-based) computational time. The result is a solution that avoids, in the usual case, the exponential complexity of previous cryptographically-secure combinatorial auctions.

1 Introduction

While there now exist practical protocols for conducting cryptographic auctions of identical items, and practical methods of computing optimal outcomes in non-cryptographic combinatorial auctions, we know of no practical protocol for conducting a *cryptographic combinatorial auction*, in which a seller offers various quantities of distinct goods, bidders bid on bundles of these goods, and cryptography provides both secrecy and provable correctness. By secrecy, we mean that the auctioneer cannot exploit bid information to change the outcome of the auction. By provable correctness, we mean that the auctioneer is obligated to issue proofs of correctness to prove he did not deviate from the auction rules.

Indeed, the optimization problem associated with winner determination for combinatorial auctions is NP-hard and computing the outcome of such an auction in a secure manner is therefore a significant challenge. We describe a cryptographic auction protocol that meets our secrecy and provable correctness requirements, elicits accurate bids, and achieves a significant efficiency improvement over earlier solutions. Whereas all previous methods incur exponential computational cost, our solution avoids exponential cost in the usual case

R. Dingledine and P. Golle (Eds.): FC 2009, LNCS 5628, pp. 305–324, 2009.

because we can emply the use of branch-and-bound search, with additional cryptographic proofs whose complexity scales linearly in the size of the branch-and-bound search tree. Indded, one important contribution is to develop a *general framework for proving the correctness of a solution to mathematical optimization problems*, where the input and constraints are encrypted.

The particular combinatorial auction that we study is the *combinatorial clock-proxy auction* (CCP) [1], which is a simple and efficient protocol for conducting combinatorial auctions. It was originally developed for auctions of wireless spectrum but is applicable in many other domains such as those of airport landing slots and power generation rights. This auction combines a simple price discovery ("clock") phase with a sealed-bid round ("proxy") phase[1].

In the clock phase, the auctioneer creates a "clock" for each item for sale that represents the current price at which that item is to be sold, starting with low prices and increasing the price across rounds. In a sequence of rounds, bidders submit a bundle of the items they desire at the current clock prices. Whenever the demand exceeds the supply for a good, the clock price increases for that good in the next round. The clock phase ends when there is no excess demand for any good. At this point, bidders can submit additional bids, which, together with the clock bids, form the bids that define the input to the proxy phase. The proxy phase (or simply "proxy auction") is a second price, sealed-bid auction.

In our *cryptographic combinatorial clock-proxy* (CCCP) auction, all bid information is encrypted, and these encryptions are posted to the public. No party, including the auctioneer, can decrypt any values until all bids have been submitted in both phases. After all bids are in, only the auctioneer receives the decryption key. He computes the outcome in private, reveals individual outcomes to each bidder, and issues efficiently checkable proofs that the reported outcomes are correct given the public encrypted bids. This complete secrecy until the auction closes removes opportunities for collusion while assuring that the process remains trusted and verifiable by all participants, offering an unprecedented balance of efficiency, privacy, and transparency.

In non-cryptographic auctions, trust can be made possible at the cost of privacy via disclosure. Indeed, this is one path that Ausubel et al. [1], the designers of CCP, suggest. But this can be undesirable for a number of reasons: bidders may not want competitors to learn about the values of their bids even after the fact; it may be politically undesirable to reveal that the winning bidder was willing to pay much more that was charged via the auction rules, and revealing bids received during the clock phase may lead to new opportunities for collusion[2]. Ausubel et al. [1] also argue that the confidentiality of values is of primary importance in an implementation, and suggest that in some areas of the auction,

---

[1] Porter et al.[2] earlier described a combinatorial-clock auction, and Parkes and Ungar [3] and Ausubel and Milgrom [4] described variants on the proxy auction phase.

[2] In a recent FCC auction for the 700MHz spectrum the government has for the first time removed all feedback about the particular bids submitted in each round. Each bidder receives individualized feedback about its own bid activity. Clearly this higher degree of secrecy brings along the need for increased trust in the auctioneer.

some values should be hidden even from the auctioneer: "Only the computer need know." Our techniques complement such a "black box" system by guaranteeing the results are correct, not simply that the programs on the system are believed to be correct.

We advance several technical contributions in the present work. During the clock phase, we employ homomorphic cryptography to protect the secrecy of bids while allowing bidders to prove they satisfy "activity rules" and allowing everyone to compute the aggregate demand for goods that determines the next round's prices. As in our previous work on non-combinatorial sealed bid auctions [5], we employ time-lapse cryptography [6], to provide secrecy during the bidding process while enforcing *nonrepudiation*: guaranteed revelation of the bids to the auctioneer when the bidding is complete. This avoids protocol completion incentive problems [7] in which bidders who realizing they will lose or change their minds can refuse to complete a distributed commercial protocol.

In the primary technical contribution, *we demonstrate how to use our cryptographic framework to prove the correctness of solutions to general classes of integer linear optimization problems;* this is how we efficiently compute the auction outcome and prove it correct. Our auctioneer employs branch-and-bound, mixed-integer programming search techniques to compute the outcome in private, avoiding costly secure computation for the optimization task; he can then prove that the outcome is correct with efficiently checkable proofs. This seems to us to open up the possibility, for the first time, of large-scale, provably correct combinatorial auctions.

1.1   Related Work

A body of existing research considers the use of cryptographic methods to provide trust without compromising privacy; see Brandt [8] and Parkes et al. [5] for a recent discussion. Much of the previous work focuses on non-combinatorial sealed bid auctions with *complete privacy*, where no party learns anything except the outcome [9,10,11,12]. We previously advanced the security model adopted here, that of an auctioneer who must prove every action correct, and who learns bid information only after the auction closes—preventing meaningful disclosures [5].

We are only aware of one collection of research, by Yokoo and Suzuki [13], that considers cryptographic combinatorial auctions in depth. While their pioneering work offers a theoretical solution to an important problem, their solutions, which require exponential computations to prove the auction correct, can scale only to very small auctions in practice. One method they provide is based on dynamic programming using polynomial secret sharing to compute the optimal solution to the combinatorial optimization problem without revealing the inputs. Another method employs homomorphic encryption [14], but again fails to scale because computation is performed explicitly on each of the exponentially many possible allocations of goods. The same authors also extend their work to remove the need for a third-party auctioneer [15], but are again limited by the scalability of dynamic programming in this domain and also by additional process complexity implied by such a completely distributed solution. Naor et al. [11] have also proposed the use of garbled circuits to compute the outcome of a combinatorial auction. Though the work is important for its foresight and theoretical affirmative results, we know of no practical implementation of obfuscated circuits that has been applied to significant real-world problems on the scale of a commercial combinatorial auction.

2   Cryptographic Preliminaries

Several cryptographic systems support the secrecy-preserving, provably correct computation that we employ to conduct the auction. Because Paillier's cryptosystem [16] supports all of the operations we need and is widely accepted in secure protocols, we use it in our exposition. That said, there is nothing that necessitates the use of Paillier's system; in fact, other solutions can be constructed that are computationally more efficient, but may complicate the protocol. These include, among others, Pedersen commitments [17] and ElGamal encryption [18], based on the hardness of computing discrete logarithms modulo a prime, and the provably correct secure computation system described by Rabin et al. [19][3]. We reserve for future work a complete discussion of how these and other systems might also support our protocol.

Due to special mathematical properties Paillier encryption enjoys, it is possible for a *Prover* (in our application the Auctioneer) to create a random permutation S' of a set of encryptions S so that a verifier believes that S' encrypts precisely the same set of values that S does. In the spirit of our work, this can be done in a manner not revealing any information about the encrypted values.

In the Paillier cryptosystem, one can generate a new "random-looking" encryption of a particular element by multiplying it by a encryption of 0 — we call this a "re-encryption factor". The auctioneer can create many random permutations of the encrypted values and commit to the re-encryption factors in each permutation. The *Verifier* then asks the auctioneer to reveal the re-encryption factors for some of the permutations, and verifies that the factors are well-formed (that is, they are encryptions of zero) and that the permutation is correct. The remaining permutations, for which the factors remain unrevealed, are now verified correct with high probability. Cryptographers have formalized this idea as a "shuffle", or "mix network"[4,5].

---

[3] We have devised a similar protocol to the one we describe based on Pedersen commitments; while this protocol is computationally more efficient, it is mathematically more sophisticated, and we present the Paillier-based solution here because of the simplicity that a protocol with a single cryptosystem enjoys.

[4] We use "shuffle" as "mix network" also refers to hard-to-trace network communications protocols.

[5] See Abe et al. [20,21] for early work on such permutation networks, and Boneh and Golle [22] for an excellent formalization of shuffles, a brief survey of other solutions, and an interesting efficient protocol for proving a shuffle is correct with high (but not overwhelming) probability. Boneh and Golle's efficient solution should not be employed without using an additional mechanism to verify its correctness. See Boneh and Golle [22].

We will employ a shuffle to create a verifiable random permutation of the encrypted bids that are submitted to the proxy auction. This will allow the branching decisions of the branch-and-bound proof tree to be published without revealing any information about the actual underlying inputs to the linear optimization problems; bidders can thereby be satisfied they are given correct information without learning private bid information.

3 Combinatorial Auctions

We consider a multi-unit combinatorial allocation problem with goods $G = \{G_1, \ldots, G_m\}$ and bidders $B = \{B_1, \ldots, B_n\}$. There are C_j units of each good G_j available and each bidder B_i has a valuation function $v_i(s_i)$ on bundles $s_i \in \mathbb{Z}_{\geq 0}^m$, where $s_{ij} \leq C_j$ denotes the number of units of item G_j in the bundle.

An *efficient allocation* solves $V^* = \max_{s \in \mathbb{F}} \sum_i v_i(s_i)$ where $\mathbb{F} = \{s : \sum_i s_{ij} \leq C_j, \forall j \in G\}$ and $s = (s_1, \ldots, s_n)$ denotes the allocation of items to bidders.

We assume quasi-linear utility u_i (or *payoff* π_i), so that bidder B_i's utility for bundle s_i, given payment $y_i \in \mathbb{R}_{\geq 0}$, is $\pi_i = u_i(s_i, y_i) = v_i(s_i) - y_i$. We make the standard assumptions of *normalization*, with $v_i(s_i) = 0$ when $s_{ij} = 0$ for all items G_j, and *free disposal*, with $v_i(s_i) \geq v_i(s_i')$ for $s_i' \geq s_i$.

Table 1. A simple example of a combinatorial auction problem

Bidder	Bid	Items	Price
1	1	$\{A, B\}$	3
2	1	$\{B, C\}$	3
3	1	$\{A, C, D\}$	3
4	1	$\{C, D, E\}$	2
5	1	$\{E, F\}$	4.5
6	1	$\{F\}$	3
7	1	$\{D\}$	1

An example of a combinatorial auction problem is illustrated in Table 1. This example has 7 bids, each from a unique bidder, and 6 goods $G = \{A, B, \ldots, F\}$, all in unit supply. In this case each bidder is single-minded, and only interested in a single bundle of goods. The example is adapted from Sandholm et al. [23]. In the efficient allocation, two optimal outcomes exist, each with a total value of 8.5: $\{1, 5, 7\}$ and $\{2, 5, 7\}$ are the two sets of winning bidders in these outcomes.

The payments in the proxy auction are selected from the *bidder-optimal core*. Consider the payoff vector $\pi = \langle \pi_1, \ldots, \pi_n \rangle$ induced by an efficient allocation s^* and payment vector $y = \langle y_1, \ldots, y_n \rangle$, i.e. with $\pi_i = v_i(s_i^*) - y_i$. Let π_0 denote the payoff to the seller, which is the total revenue received by the seller, i.e. $\pi_0 = \sum_i y_i = V^* - \sum_i \pi_i$. A payoff profile $\langle \pi_0, \pi \rangle$ is in the *core* if $\pi_0 + \sum_{i \in K} \pi_i \geq V(K)$ for all $K \subseteq B$, where $V(K) = \max_{s \in \mathbb{F}} \sum_{k \in K} v_k(s_k)$. This states that no coalition of $K \subseteq B$ bidders and the seller can improve its total payoff by leaving the auction and allocating the items amongst itself, leaving all members weakly better off. Simple algebra shows that the core payoffs can be equivalently defined as:

$$Core = \{\pi : \sum_{i \in W \setminus K} \pi_i \leq V^* - V(K), \; \forall K \subseteq W, \pi_i \geq 0, \pi_i \leq v_i(s_i^*)\},$$

where W is the set of *winners* in the efficient allocation s^*. The *bidder-optimal core* defines a payoff vector that solves $\bar{\pi} \in \arg\max_{\pi \in Core} \sum_i \pi_i$.

The bidder-optimal core is related to the outcome of the Vickrey-Clarke-Groves (VCG) mechanism [24]. The VCG mechanism defines payments so that the payoff to bidder i is $\pi_i^{vcg} = V^* - V(B \setminus \{i\})$, i.e., each bidder's payoff is the marginal value it contributes by its presence. In general, $\sum_i \bar{\pi}_i < \sum_i \pi_i^{vcg}$ and the revenue to the seller is greater in a bidder-optimal core outcome than in the VCG mechanism. But when the VCG outcome is in the core then it coincides with the (unique) bidder-optimal core outcome. In the general case, the bidder-optimal core is not unique and the final payments in the proxy auction are selected to minimize the maximal difference to the VCG payoff across all bidder-optimal core outcomes[6].

In the example in Table 1, the payoff to winning bidders $\{1, 5\}$ and 7 in the VCG mechanism is $\{8.5 - 8.5 = 0, 8.5 - 8 = 0.5\}$ and $8.5 - 8 = 0.5$ respectively, with corresponding payments $\{\$3, \$4\}$ and $\$0.5$. It is easily checked that this outcome is in the core, and thus also the bidder-optimal core outcome.

4   Phase One: The Clock Auction

The presentation of our main results begins by considering the first phase of the CCP auction, which is the *clock-auction* phase. The clock phase proceeds in rounds until demand is weakly less than supply for every good. In each round t, a price vector $p^t = \langle p_1^t, \ldots, p_m^t \rangle$ associates prices with each good: p_j^t is the price for good G_j in round t. The price vector is initialized to low prices (although not necessarily uniformly across all goods) for the first round, $t = 1$, and is increased in each successive round based on the amount of excess demand. Bidders submit a bid $s_i^t \in \mathbb{Z}_{\geq 0}^m$ in each round. These bids are ultimately included within the proxy bids that form the input to the proxy phase.

We are interested in supporting this price discovery process, but without allowing any party—the auctioneer included—to learn anything about any bids not already implied by the public information. Following the description of Ausubel et al. [1], we allow the price increase on a good in a round to depend on the amount of excess demand on that good[7]. One requirement, then, is that any

---

[6] This particular choice follows the suggestion of *threshold payments* in Parkes et al. [25] in the context of a combinatorial exchange, and as refined in the context of the proxy auction by Day and Raghavan [26].

[7] Ausubel et al. [1] also discuss the idea of using *intra-round bids* in which the auction proceeds in a smaller number of discrete rounds and bidders express quantity demands in each round at all prices along a price trajectory that will be traced during the round. We save this extension for future work.

party (the auctioneer included) must be able to determine the excess demand on each good in the current round without learning anything else about the current bids. It will also be necessary to allow any party to verify that the bids meet an activity rule that restricts bidding strategies, in particular a *revealed preference activity rule*, and without revealing any information.

All bids made during the clock phase must also be submitted as proxy bids in the proxy phase. We ensure this and prevent non-repudiation through the use of a time-lapse cryptography (TLC) service [6]. At the start of the auction, the auctioneer in CCCP announces the initial price vector p^1 and the supply $C = \langle C_1, \ldots, C_m \rangle$ and designates a *public time-lapse cryptographic key* N. Because the secret key corresponding to N (and based on the factorization of N) is not revealed until after all bidder information has been submitted, the auctioneer cannot reveal private information that could affect the outcome. The forced reconstruction of N guarantees that the bids can be opened by the auctioneer when the auction is complete[8].

At the beginning of round t, the auctioneer publishes the current clock price vector $p^t = \langle p_1^t, \ldots, p_m^t \rangle$. Then, each bidder B_i publishes an encrypted version of her bid given the current prices: $E(s_i^t) = \langle E(s_{i1}^t, r_{i1}^t), \ldots, E(s_{im}^t, r_{im}^t) \rangle$. Bidders publish these encrypted bundles to all bidders, the auctioneer and any verifiers, either by broadcast or to a common "bulletin board" during a fixed period of time for round t. This encrypted bundle is represented as a vector of length m, in which each coefficient s_{ij}^t is an encryption of the quantity B_i wants for good G_j at price p_j^t. The values r_{ij}^t are independent, fresh *random help values* that each bidder selects in accordance with the probabilistic homomorphic encryption scheme, and kept secret. Encryptions of zero must be included for any undesired item to keep the number of items in the bundle secret.

Bid Validity and Activity Rules. Each bidder must now prove that the bid is valid and satisfies an *activity rule*[9]. The basic idea in a revealed-preference activity rule (RPAR) is to require bidders to follow a demand-revealing strategy that is consistent with some fixed valuation function across all clock rounds. Consider a current round t and some previous round $t' < t$, corresponding price vectors p^t and $p^{t'}$, and B_i's associated demands s_i^t and $s_i^{t'}$. A straightforward bidder with valuation v_i prefers s_i^t to $s_i^{t'}$ when prices are p^t, i.e. $v_i(s_i^t) - p^t \cdot s_i^t \geq v_i(s_i^{t'}) - p^t \cdot s_i^{t'}$, and prefers $s_i^{t'}$ to s_i^t when prices are $p^{t'}$, i.e. $v_i(s_i^{t'}) - p^{t'} \cdot s_i^{t'} \geq v_i(s_i^t) - p^{t'} \cdot s_i^t$. Adding these two inequalities (the values of the bundles cancel) yields the activity rule, i.e. $(p^t - p^{t'}) \cdot (s_i^t - s_i^{t'}) \leq 0$.

---

[8] The TLC service in Rabin et al. [6] creates a time-lock ElGamal key, but it can also create any cryptographic key for which a verifiable distributed key generation protocol exists, including Paillier keys (like RSA keys, the product of two large primes).

[9] While we talk about the "bidder" proving various facts about the bid history to the auctioneer and any other interested party, we of course intend the proofs to be generated by a computer program running on secure hardware controlled by the bidder, both to maintain the security of any private information and because the cryptographic computations should not be carried out by hand.

Before proving the RPAR, bidders must prove that their current demands are valid by using an interval proof: each B_i proves for the demand for good G_j, $0 \leq s_{ij}^t \leq C_j$. That is, the demand lies in the interval between 0 and the auction's capacity for that good[10].

Each bidder can now readily prove that she satisfies the activity rule using homomorphic cryptography via the clock prices and the published encrypted bids. This must be established in round t with respect to all previous rounds $t' < t$. The details of this are presented in Appendix A.1.

Computing Aggregate Demand. At the conclusion of each round, the aggregate demand for each item must be computed. The aggregate demand vector s^t for all goods at the end of round t is simply $s^t = \langle \sum_{i=1}^n s_{i1}^t, \ldots, \sum_{i=1}^n s_{im}^t \rangle$.

Given the encrypted demand vectors, we can compute use the homomorphic properties of the cryptosystem to compute an encryption of the aggregate demand vector s^t as follows:

$$E(s^t) = \langle \prod_{i=1}^n E(s_{i1}^t, r_{i1}^t), \ldots, \prod_{i=1}^n E(s_{im}^t, r_{im}^t) \rangle \qquad (1)$$

$$= \langle E(\sum_{i=1}^n s_{i1}^t, \prod_{i=1}^n r_{i1}^t), \ldots, E(\sum_{i=1}^n s_{im}^t, \prod_{i=1}^n r_{im}^t) \rangle \qquad (2)$$

By multiplying each bidder's encrypted demand for an item together, we obtain an encryption of the sum of all bidders' demands for that item; the random help value of this encryption is the product of the random help values from all bidders' encrypted demands. Since the secret decryption key does not yet exist, decryption can only be performed by unlocking the encrypted value with its random help value.

While the random help value could be directly constructed from the other values, such a direct computation would reveal too much, because each encrypted demand's random help value would unlock that particular demand. We thus employ another well-known cryptographic protocol, a simple, secure multi-party computation of a product of secret values, to compute the random help values needed to unlock the aggregate demand. We sketch the protocol but omit a more detailed description for reasons of space.

After each round t, we repeat the following process for each good G_j, obtaining the above aggregate demand vector (Eq. 2). B_i constructs shares of the random help value associated with the demand for good G_j, so that the product of these shares equals the random help value r_{ij}^t. B_i then distributes these shares among all bidders. Once all the shares are received, the bidders multiply their received shares together, yielding random factors of the help value $\prod i = 1^n r_{ij}^t$.

---

[10] We also require that the capacities C_j are less than half the modulus of the cryptosystem ($N/2$), but as the moduli are typically hundreds or thousands of bits, this poses no practical problems.

Then, bidders broadcast these random factors to all bidders, and multiply them together to yield the desired help value. This allows anyone to decrypt the encrypted sum of the aggregate demand for that good and verify the result. Recall that since the encrypted individual demands are public, one can compute an encryption of their sum by multiplying the encryptions.

We remark without proof that this sub-protocol to compute the random help values is information-theoretically secure and reveals no information other than the results. Furthermore, it requires only two broadcasts and scales linearly in the number of items for sale. Moreover, bidders who refuse to participate in this protocol to compute the aggregate demand can be disqualified, and the demand recomputed without them. If a bidder submits incorrect values during this protocol, then the computed values r_j^t will be discovered to be incorrect[11].

4.1 Transition to the Proxy Phase

Let T denote the number of rounds in the clock phase. Each bidder has submitted a bid on $\langle s_i^1, \ldots, s_i^T \rangle$ bundles at public prices $\langle p^1, \ldots, p^T \rangle$. A bidder can now:

(a) improve any bid submitted during the clock phase
(b) include bids on additional bundles

These additional bids are committed by each bidder, by encrypting with the key associated with the TLC service and then sharing them, for instance posting them to a public bulletin board. When the auctioneer receives the time-lapse decryption key he will then prove that each bidder meets the activity rules that constrain her ability to bid in this transition from clock to proxy.

For (a), we first require each bidder B_i to associate a bid price $b_i(s_i^t)$ with every bid. This bid price must satisfy:

$$b_i(s_i^t) \geq p^t \cdot s_i^t \tag{3}$$

For (b), each bidder can also submit additional bids, which we index $k > t$ to indicate that they are received after the close of the clock phase. Consider some bundle s_i^k, either one of the clock bundles or one of these additional bundles, and its associated bid price $b_i(s_i^k)$. Any such bid must satisfy the following constraints:

$$b_i(s_i^k) - p^t \cdot s_i^k \leq \alpha(b_i(s_i^t) - p^t \cdot s_i^t), \quad \forall t \in \{1, \ldots, T\} \tag{4}$$

This requires that the bidder would not have been much happier (by some relaxation parameter $\alpha \geq 1$) by bidding this bundle in any clock round than the bundle that it did bid in that round. We will also require each bidder to *pad* her bids (with zero bids), so that the total number of bundles that receive a bid is constant across all bidders. Let K denote the number of such bids.

---

[11] The auctioneer can always resort to a more complex *verifiable* multi-party computation (e.g. [27]) to identify and disqualify a bidder submitting bad data.

Once this transition round closes the auctioneer receives the time-lapse decryption key and will now generate a proof that all bids satisfy these activity rules (Eq. 3 and 4)[12]. If a bidder submits a non-compliant bid at this phase, the auctioneer can prove the bid is non-compliant and remove any such bids from the computation of the outcome.

5 Phase Two: The Proxy Auction

The proxy phase of the CCP auction is used to determine the final allocation of goods and the final payments. This requires solving a sequence of optimization problems. Given that the winner-determination problem for combinatorial auctions is NP-hard, it seems to us *essential* that bids must be revealed to the auctioneer in plain text in any efficient protocol. This enables the auctioneer to leverage efficient methods to determine the outcome, such as the branch-and-bound algorithm for integer programming we employ. We reiterate that the auctioneer is unable to submit or alter bids, or change the outcome of the auction in any way, once the bids are revealed. Moreover, until this point neither the auctioneer or any other party has received any exploitable information about the bids.

Our main technical innovation is to use cryptographic methods to prove that a solution to an integer program is optimal by establishing various linear constraints implied by a "fathomed" (or solved) *branch-and-bound* tree. An appealing aspect of our approach is that it is *completely agnostic to the particular heuristics by which a branch-and-bound proof tree is generated (e.g. depth-first, breadth-first, memory management, branch-selection heuristics, etc.).* Rather, the system works directly with the information that is established upon the conclusion of the search, i.e. from the final proof tree.

We confine our solution to what can be considered a standard, textbook treatment of branch-and-bound search (e.g., see Wolsey [28]). In doing so, we impose two main restrictions on the use of branch-and-bound algorithms: (a) no pre-processing, and (b) no cut-generation. While modern optimization solvers, such as ILOG's CPLEX, do make extensive use of both of these methods, good performance can be achieved on reasonably sized problems without either feature. Nevertheless, supporting such optimizations presents a appealing avenue for future work.

---

[12] To establish the activity rule, then for every bidder B_i and round $t \in \{1, \ldots, T\}$, the auctioneer computes provably correct encryptions of the dot products $p^t \cdot s_i^t$ for values bid during the clock phase. He further computes, for every bidder B_i, the $t(K - T)$ dot products $p^t \cdot s_i^k, \forall t \in \{1, \ldots, T\} \forall k \in \{T + 1, \ldots, K\}$. These dot products are computed in the same way encrypted dot products are computed at the end of Section 4. To prove Eq. 4, he shows that the bidder prefers each final proxy bid $\langle s_i^k, b_i(s_i^k)\rangle, T < k \leq K$, he computes the encrypted differences of these encrypted dot products and encrypted bid values $b_i(s_i^k)$ and $b_i(s_i^t)$ (respectively) and multiplies the second result by the public constant α; this allows him to use a simple interval proof to demonstrate the inequality.

5.1   Branch-and-Bound Search

To illustrate the principle of branch-and-bound search we will consider the winner-determination problem (WDP) in the proxy phase. In defining this, we index the proxy bids $s_i = \langle s_{i1}, \ldots, s_{iK} \rangle$ from each bidder i. Recall that K is the total number of bids received from each bidder (by padding if necessary.) Let $b_i = \langle b_{i1}, \ldots, b_{iK} \rangle$ denote the associated bid values. The integer programming (IP) formulation for the WDP is:

$$\max \left\{ \sum_i \sum_k x_{ik} b_{ik} \; : \; \text{s.t. } x \in \mathbb{F}, x_{ik} \in \{0, 1\}, \; \forall i, \forall k \right\} \tag{5}$$

$$\text{where } \mathbb{F} = \left\{ \begin{matrix} \sum_i \sum_k s_{ikj} x_{ik} \leq C_j, \; \forall j \in G, \\ \sum_k x_{ik} \qquad \leq 1, \; \forall i \in B \end{matrix} \right\}, \tag{6}$$

and these constraints ensure that no more units of a good are allocated than in the supply and that no more than one bid is accepted from any single bidder.

In describing branch-and-bound, let $\underline{z}$ denote the value of the best solution found so far (initialized to $-\infty$), and let $\underline{x}$ denote that solution (undefined when no solution has been found.) This is the *incumbent* solution. The first step in branch-and-bound is to solve the linear programming (LP) relaxation,

$$\max \left\{ \sum_i \sum_k x_{ik} b_{ik} \; : \; \text{s.t. } x \in \mathbb{F}, x_{ik} \geq 0, \; \forall i, \forall k \right\} \tag{7}$$

Let $L^0 = \{x : x \in \mathbb{F}, \; x_{ik} \geq 0, \forall i, \forall k\}$ denote the LP-relaxation of the solution space. Let $\overline{x}^0$ denote the solution on L^0 and $\overline{z}^0$ the value of this solution. If $\overline{x}^0$ is *integral* then branch-and-bound can stop with $\underline{x} := \overline{x}^0$ and $\underline{z} := \overline{z}^0$. The solution $\overline{x}^0$ will in general be *fractional*, meaning that one or more of the variables has a value that is neither 0 or 1.

To illustrate this, consider again the example in Table 1 and let x_{i1} denote the variable corresponding to the bid from each agent i. In the example, the solution to the LP relaxation is fractional, with an assignment $\langle 0.5, 0.5, 0.5, 0, 1, 0, 0.5 \rangle$ and total value of 9.5. When this occurs, a branching decision is made on one of the fractional variables. Continuing with the example, suppose that we branch on $x_{71} \leq 0$ and $x_{71} \geq 1$. This generates two new sub-problems, one defined on solution space $L^1 = \{x : x \in \mathbb{F}, x_{71} \leq 0, \; x_{ik} \geq 0, \; \forall i, \forall k\}$ and one defined on solution space $L^2 = \{x : x \in \mathbb{F}, x_{71} \geq 1, \; x_{ik} \geq 0, \; \forall i, \forall k\}$. Branch-and-bound continues by picking one of these and solving the associated linear program.

Let $(L^p, \overline{x}^p, \overline{z}^p)$ denote the associated LP and solution. In any one of the following three cases, this becomes a *"fathomed"* (or solved) leaf:

(a) the subproblem is infeasible
(b) the subproblem has an integral optimal solution; if $\underline{z} < \overline{z}^p$ then $\underline{z} := \overline{z}^p$ and $\underline{x} := \overline{x}^p$.
(c) the subproblem is feasible and the solution fractional, but $\beta \overline{z}^p \leq \underline{z}$ for some $\beta \leq 1$ that controls the optimality tolerance.

In our example, the solution to L^2 is integral and we would set $\underline{z} := \bar{z}^2 = 8.5$ and $\underline{x} := \bar{x}^2 = \langle 1, 0, 0, 0, 1, 0, 1 \rangle$. This leaf is now fathomed. But the solution to L^1 is fractional ($\bar{x}^1 = \langle 0.5, 0.5, 0.5, 0, 1, 0, 0 \rangle$) and has value $\bar{z}^1 = 9 \not\leq \underline{z} = 8.5$. In such a case, branch-and-bound search will generate two additional subproblems, typically by doing something like branching on the most fractional variable. The unsolved subproblems are stored on the "open list." Branch-and-bound finally terminates when the open list is empty, returning the incumbent as the solution. Finishing with the example, when we branch on $x_{11} \leq 0$ and $x_{11} \geq 1$ we obtain two leaves that are fathomed. The LP relaxations generate integral solutions and their value is less than that of the solution already found.

While there are many sophisticated strategies for managing the details of a branch-and-bound search, for our purposes all that is required is a *fathomed* branch-and-bound tree, i.e. one for which all leaves have been fathomed. An example of a so-called *proof tree* for the example is shown in Figure 1.

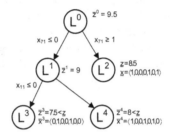

Fig. 1. Branch-and-Bound Proof Tree

5.2   Establishing Correctness of Integer Program Solutions

In this section we describe the general approach to establish the correctness of the solution to an integer program (IP). Along the way we also provide a method to establish the correctness of the solution to a linear program (LP). Recall that the *input* to the IP is published in encrypted form. In describing our approach we assume that the solution to the IP is revealed to all parties, but this is not necessary. All relevant steps can instead be performed using an encryption of the solution, if the solution itself is to remain private.

The cryptographic proof is constructed from a proof tree, as generated at the termination of a branch-and-bound search. To perform these steps on the encrypted inputs, we first note that IPs, LPs and their duals are all defined with linear inequalities and linear objective functions. Therefore, we can prove that a set of constraints are satisfied, or that a solution has a particular objective value, using the verifiable addition, subtraction and multiplication operations, and equality and inequality tests, on Paillier-encrypted values. All that is required are encryptions of all the private inputs (the bids in our case).

Because we have formulated all inputs as integers, it is theoretically possible to obtain LPs with rational coefficients at every point in the proof tree, which implies that they have rational solutions. Moreover, since any computation on rationals can be performed by an equivalent computation on integers (with at most a constant factor increase in the number of steps), we can employ established cryptographic techniques that prove integer computations correct for rational numbers as well. This allows us to calculate and prove correct exact solutions to rational LPs[13].

The proof of the correctness of a solution x^* to a IP proceeds with the following steps:

1. Any permutation-invariance in the class of problems being solved is leveraged for the purpose of secrecy by generating a random permutation using a shuffle as described in Section 2. This proves to verifiers that the set of encrypted values in the proof tree is the same as the set of inputs, but makes the correspondence between those sets is unknown.

2. The branching decisions that define the proof tree are revealed. (For instance, "at the root the left branch is $x_6 \leq 0$ and the right branch is $x_6 \geq 1$" and so on.) The amount of information that this reveals depends on the amount of permutation invariance in the class of problems. For example, if all inputs can be "mixed" with all other inputs then this reveals no information.

3. The solution x^* to the IP is revealed along with a claim $\beta \leq 1$ about its optimality (e.g., $\beta = 9999/10000$ would state that the solution quality is within multiplicative factor $9999/10000$ of the optimal solution.) The encrypted solution $E(x^*)$ is published and shown to be a valid encryption of x^*: this is because many of our operations only apply to two encrypted operands, and for those we need to use $E(x^*)$ rather than the unencrypted x^*.

4. Let q^* denote the leaf associated with the optimal solution. This is revealed by the prover. The prover then proceeds to:

   (a) Publish $E(V^*)$ and prove that its value is correct (i.e., the value is an encryption of the objective value of the IP given solution x^*).

   (b) Prove that x^* satisfies the constraints of the LP formulated at leaf L^{q^*} (i.e., prove inequalities defined in terms of the encrypted input to the IP and also the additional inequalities implied by the branching decisions.)

   (c) Prove that x^* is integral.

5. Consider every leaf q (including the optimal leaf) in turn. For every such leaf, the prover then proceeds to:

   (a) Let y^q denote the solution to the dual LP at leaf L^q and D^q the value of that dual solution. Publish the encrypted dual $E(y^q)$ solution and the encrypted dual value $E(D^q)$ at this leaf.

   (b) Prove that the dual solution satisfies the constraints of the dual LP formulated at leaf L^q.

---

[13] In practice, it is likely that the results will be computed using a computer program that yields a floating-point or real number as a result. We can instead convert this value to a rational number and prove that the constraints are satisfied with acceptably small error.

(c) Prove the correctness of the dual value $E(D^q)$ by reference to the dual formulation, and that $\beta E(D^q) \leq E(V^*)$.

This procedure encompasses both leaves that are fathomed by infeasibility and leaves that are fathomed by bound in the same way. Note that a leaf that is infeasible in its primal form has a dual solution with value $-\infty$ by the duality theory of LP. Therefore, the prover can always construct a feasible dual solution to prove that there is no better (primal) solution in the feasible solution space that corresponds to a particular leaf. It should be easy to see how to generalize the above approach to a mixed integer program[14].

5.3   Application: The Winner Determination Problem (WDP)

We now instantiate the general approach to the WDP for combinatorial auctions. Recall (s_{ik}, b_{ik}) denotes the kth proxy bid submitted by bidder i, where bundle s_{ik} contains s_{ikj} units of item $j \in G$. The IP formulation for the WDP is:

$$\max_{x_{ik}} \sum_{i \in B} \sum_{k} x_{ik} b_{ik} \qquad \text{WDP}(B)$$

$$\text{s.t.} \quad \sum_{i \in B} \sum_{k} s_{ikj}\, x_{ik} \leq C_j, \quad \forall j \in G \qquad (8)$$

$$\sum_{k} x_{ik} \leq 1, \quad \forall i \in B \qquad (9)$$

$$x_{ik} \in \{0, 1\}, \quad \forall i \in B, \forall k$$

where x_{ik} indicates whether the kth bid from bidder i is accepted. We label this formulation WDP(B) to make explicit that this is problem is defined for all bidders and to allow for variations WDP(L) defined on a subset $L \subseteq B$ of bidders. Constraints (8) ensure that the supply constraints are satisfied. Constraints (9) ensure that no bidder receives more than one bundle of items[15].

Once the solution x^* is published and associated with a leaf of the branch-and-bound tree, and once it has been shown to satisfy the constraints of the appropriate restricted-primal formulation for the leaf (see the Appendix) and also to be integral, the remaining work in proving the optimality is in terms of establishing properties for the dual of this restricted primal formulation for each leaf of the search tree. All the information required to complete these proofs is

---

[14] In the case that the original problem is an LP rather than a IP then there is no proof tree to deal with, and the procedure simplifies to: (a) publish $E(V^*)$ and prove this value is correct; (b) prove that x^* satisfies the constraints of the LP; (c) publish an encrypted dual solution $E(y^q)$ and associated dual value $E(D^q)$; (d) prove that the solution is dual feasible, and that $\beta E(D^q) \leq E(V^*)$.

[15] Details about the linear programming relaxation of WDP(B) and the corresponding dual DWDP(B), along with the restricted primal and dual formulations for the leaf of a winner-determination branch-and-bound tree are provided in Appendix A.2.

either available in the encrypted proxy bids (e.g. s_{ikj}, b_{ik}), publicly known (e.g. the capacity C_j), or defined by the branching decisions that are published by the mechanism.

5.4   Determining Payments and Announcing Results

The final step in the CCP auction is to find the bidder-optimal core point that minimizes the maximal deviation across all bidders from the payoff profile in the VCG mechanism, as discussed in Section 3. The details of this step are provided in Appendix A.3, and require solving and proving the correctness of sequence of optimization problems (each of which is a simple variant on the winner determination problem), and ultimately establishing the correctness of a solution to a linear program to determine the final payments.

Taken together, the above steps are sufficient to prove to any interested party that the allocation and payments are correct. But because we employed a shuffle to prevent bidders from learning the position of their bids in the proof tree, we still need to convince an individual bidder that the particular allocation announced for them is correct for them. This is easy to achieve by privately revealing to each bidder *only* the correspondence between their original proxy bid that was accepted and its position in the permutation generated by the shuffle. The bidder will then be satisfied that the outcome proven is correct from her perspective because she can verify that her bid was allocated in the optimal allocation. She will similarly believe that the payment corresponding to the bidder that submitted the bid, and hence her own payment, is correct[16].

6   Conclusions

We have described a cryptographic method to enable secret and provably correct combinatorial auctions. Whereas previous methods incur exponential cost in providing a secure solution to the NP-hard winner-determination problem, we can use branch-and-bound algorithms and generate a proof with overhead that is linear in the size of the ultimate branch-and-bound tree, and thus linear in the computational search time. In doing so, the solution presented here will avoid exponential time complexity with overwhelming probability. Our particular focus has been on the practically important combinatorial clock-proxy auction, which is used by governments in high-stakes settings. It bears additional emphasis that in striving for what we consider to be a practical solution, we require that the auctioneer is trusted not to reveal information about bids once an auction has closed. This is the same tradeoff that we made in our earlier work on non-combinatorial auctions [5]. In making this tradeoff, we achieve a system that is provably correct and trustworthy, and we believe can be implemented in a realistic business setting on cost-effective computing hardware.

---

[16] This does imply that a small amount of information that is leaked by our system, over and above that implied by the outcome of the auction: each bidder learns where in the various proof trees her own accepted bid was branched on. But this appears to us to disclose no useful information to a bidder.

References

1. Ausubel, L., Cramton, P., Milgrom, P.: The clock-proxy auction: A practical combinatorial auction design. In: Cramton, P., Shoham, Y., Steinberg, R. (eds.) Combinatorial Auctions. MIT Press, Cambridge (2006)
2. Porter, R., Shoham, Y.: On cheating in sealed bid auctions. In: Proc. ACM Conf. on Electronic Commerce (EC 2003) (2003)
3. Parkes, D.C., Ungar, L.H.: Iterative combinatorial auctions: Theory and practice. In: Proc. 17th Nat. Conf. on Artificial Intelligence (AAAI 2000), pp. 74–81 (2000)
4. Ausubel, L.M., Milgrom, P.: Ascending auctions with package bidding. Frontiers of Theoretical Economics 1, 1–42 (2002)
5. Parkes, D.C., Rabin, M.O., Shieber, S.M., Thorpe, C.A.: Practical secrecy-preserving, verifiably correct and trustworthy auctions. Electronic Commerce Research and Applications 7, 294–312 (2008)
6. Rabin, M.O., Thorpe, C.: Time-lapse cryptography. Technical Report TR-22-06, Harvard University School of Engineering and Computer Science (2006)
7. Bradford, P.G., Park, S., Rothkopf, M.H.: Protocol completion incentive problems in cryptographic Vickrey auctions. In: 7th Int. Conference on Electronic Comemrce Research (ICECR-7), pp. 55–64 (2004)
8. Brandt, F.: How to obtain full privacy in auctions. International Journal of Information Security, 201–216 (2006)
9. Franklin, M.K., Reiter, M.K.: The design and implementation of a secure auction server. IEEE Transactions on Software Engineering 22(5), 302–312 (1996)
10. Harkavy, M., Tygar, J.D., Kikuchi, H.: Electronic auctions with private bids. In: Proc. 3rd USENIX Workshop on Electronic Commerce (1998)
11. Naor, M., Pinkas, B., Sumner, R.: Privacy preserving auctions and mechanism design. In: Proc. First ACM Conf. on Elec. Commerce, pp. 129–139 (1999)
12. Lipmaa, H., Asokan, N., Niemi, V.: Secure Vickrey auctions without threshold trust. In: Blaze, M. (ed.) FC 2002. LNCS, vol. 2357, pp. 87–101. Springer, Heidelberg (2003)
13. Suzuki, K., Yokoo, M.: Secure combinatorial auctions by dynamic programming with polynomial secret sharing. In: Sixth International Financial Cryptography Conference (FC 2002), pp. 44–56 (2002)
14. Suzuki, K., Yokoo, M.: Secure generalized Vickrey auction using homomorphic encryption. In: Wright, R.N. (ed.) FC 2003. LNCS, vol. 2742, pp. 239–249. Springer, Heidelberg (2003)
15. Yokoo, M., Sakurai, Y., Matsubara, S.: The effect of false-name bids in combinatorial auctions: New Fraud in Internet Auctions. Games and Economic Behavior 46(1), 174–188 (2004)
16. Paillier, P.: Public-key cryptosystems based on composite degree residuosity classes. In: Stern, J. (ed.) EUROCRYPT 1999, vol. 1592, pp. 223–239. Springer, Heidelberg (1999)
17. Pedersen, T.P.: Non-interactive and information-theoretic secure verifiable secret sharing. In: Feigenbaum, J. (ed.) CRYPTO 1991. LNCS, vol. 576, pp. 129–140. Springer, Heidelberg (1992)
18. ElGamal, T.: A public key cryptosystem and a signature scheme based on discrete logarithms. IEEE Trans. Information Theory IT-31(4), 469–472 (1985)
19. Rabin, M.O., Servedio, R.A., Thorpe, C.: Highly efficient secrecy-preserving proofs of correctness of computations and applications. In: Proc. IEEE Symposium on Logic in Computer Science (2007)

20. Abe, M.: Mix-networks on permutation networks. In: Lam, K.-Y., Okamoto, E., Xing, C. (eds.) ASIACRYPT 1999. LNCS, vol. 1716, pp. 258–273. Springer, Heidelberg (1999)
21. Abe, M., Hoshino, F.: Remarks on mix-network based on permutation networks. In: Kim, K.-c. (ed.) PKC 2001. LNCS, vol. 1992, pp. 317–324. Springer, Heidelberg (2001)
22. Boneh, D., Golle, P.: Almost entirely correct mixing with applications to voting. In: CCS 2002: Proceedings of the 9th ACM conference on Computer and communications security, pp. 68–77. ACM, New York (2002)
23. Sandholm, T., Suri, S., Gilpin, A., Levine, D.: CABOB: A fast optimal algorithm for winner determination in combinatorial auctions. Management Science 51(3), 374–390 (2005)
24. Nisan, N.: Introduction to mechanism design (for computer scientists). Cambridge University Press, Cambridge (2007)
25. Parkes, D.C., Kalagnanam, J.R., Eso, M.: Achieving budget-balance with Vickrey-based payment schemes in exchanges. In: Proc. 17th International Joint Conference on Artificial Intelligence (IJCAI 2001), pp. 1161–1168 (2001)
26. Day, R.W., Raghavan, S.: Fair payments for efficient allocations in public sector combinatorial auctions. Management Science (2006)
27. Cramer, R., Damgård, I., Dziembowski, S., Hirt, M., Rabin, T.: Efficient multiparty computations secure against an adaptive adversary. In: Stern, J. (ed.) EUROCRYPT 1999. LNCS, vol. 1592, p. 311. Springer, Heidelberg (1999)
28. Wolsey, L.A.: Integer Programming. John Wiley, Chichester (1998)

A   Appendix: Further Details of the Auction Protocol

A.1 Establishing the Activity Rule: First, since the price vectors $p^{t'}$ and p^t are public, anyone can compute the price difference vector $\hat{p} = \langle \hat{p}_1, \ldots, \hat{p}_m \rangle = p^t - p^{t'}$. Second, using the encrypted demand vectors $E(s_i^t)$ and $E(s_i^{t'})$, the homomorphic properties of the cryptosystem allow computing B_i's encrypted demand difference vector $\hat{s}_i = \langle \hat{s}_{i1}, \ldots, \hat{s}_{im} \rangle = s_i^t - s_i^{t'}$:

$$E(s_i^t) = \langle E(s_{i1}^t, r_{i1}^t), \ldots, E(s_{im}^t, r_{im}^t) \rangle$$

$$E(s_i^{t'}) = \langle E(s_{i1}^{t'}, r_{i1}^{t'}), \ldots, E(s_{im}^{t'}, r_{im}^{t'}) \rangle$$

$$E(\hat{s}_i) = \langle \frac{E(s_{i1}^t, r_{i1}^t)}{E(s_{i1}^{t'}, r_{i1}^{t'})}, \ldots, \frac{E(s_{im}^t, r_{im}^t)}{E(s_{im}^{t'}, r_{im}^{t'})} \rangle$$

$$= \langle E(s_{i1}^t - s_{i1}^{t'}, r_{i1}^t/r_{i1}^{t'}), \ldots, E(s_{im}^t - s_{im}^{t'}, r_{im}^t/r_{im}^{t'}) \rangle$$

To compute the encrypted dot product of the price difference vector and the encrypted demand difference vector, $E(\hat{p} \cdot \hat{s}_i)$, we can again use the homomorphic properties of the cryptosystem:

$$E(\hat{p} \cdot \hat{s}_i) = E(\hat{s}_{i1}, r_{i1}^t/r_{i1'}^{t'})^{\hat{p}_1} \times \ldots \times E(\hat{s}_{im}, r_{im}^t/r_{im}^{t'})^{\hat{p}_m}$$

$$= E(\hat{p}_1 \times \hat{s}_{i1}, r_{i1}^t/r_{i1}^{t'}) \times \ldots \times E(\hat{p}_m \times \hat{s}_{im}, r_{im}^t/r_{im}^{t'})$$

$$= E(\hat{p}_1 \times \hat{s}_{i1} + \ldots + \hat{p}_m \times \hat{s}_{im}, r_{i1}^t/r_{i1}^{t'} \times \ldots \times r_{im}^t/r_{im}^{t'})$$

We adopt $\hat{r}_i$ to notate the random help value encrypting the dot product (the last formula above): $\hat{r}_i = r_{i1}^t/r_{i1}^{t'} \times \ldots \times r_{im}^t/r_{im}^{t'}$. We now have an encryption of this dot product—a single value that proves the activity rule when it is less than or equal to zero[17]. Consequently, each bidder now proves using another interval proof that this encrypted value is less than (but relatively close to) zero. Our example shows that B_i can compute the precise random help value corresponding to the encryption of a dot product of an encrypted vector with a public vector. This allows B_i to prove facts about the result like any other value it encrypted and even though the decryption key has not yet been constructed.

A.2 Detailing the LP Relaxations for Winner Determination: The linear programming relaxation of WDP(B) is defined by replacing $x_{ik} \in \{0, 1\}$ with $x_{ik} \geq 0$. In defining the dual (and overloading notation from the clock phase, which is no longer needed), we introduce variables p_j to denote the dual variable for constraints (8) and π_i to denote the dual variable for constraints (9). Given this, then the dual problem is:

$$\min_{p,\pi} \sum_j C_j p_j + \sum_i \pi_i \qquad \text{DWDP(B)}$$

$$\text{s.t.} \quad \sum_j s_{ikj}\, p_j + \pi_i \geq b_{ik}, \quad \forall i, k \qquad (10)$$

$$p_j \geq 0, \pi_i \geq 0$$

A sequence of branching decisions leading to a fathomed leaf in the search tree introduces additional constraints to WDP(B) and modifies the dual problem at the leaf. Let $(i, k) \in OUT$ indicate that branch $x_{ik} \leq 0$ has been taken and $(i, k) \in IN$ denote that branch $x_{ik} \geq 1$ has been taken. Given these constraints, the restricted primal and dual pair becomes:

$$\max_{x_{ik}} \sum_i \sum_k x_{ik} b_{ik} \qquad \text{RWDP(B)}$$

$$\text{s.t.} \quad \sum_i \sum_k s_{ikj}\, x_{ik} \leq C_j, \quad \forall j \in G \qquad (11)$$

$$\sum_k x_{ik} \leq 1, \quad \forall i \qquad (12)$$

$$x_{ik} \leq 0, \quad \forall (i, k) \in OUT \qquad (13)$$

$$x_{ik} \geq 1, \quad \forall (i, k) \in IN \qquad (14)$$

$$x_{ik} \geq 0, \quad \forall i, \forall k$$

---

[17] If the bidder does not prove the activity rule, then the bid is invalid and the auction rules should dictate whether the bidder must resubmit, or be disqualified for the round.

$$\min_{p,\pi,\delta} \sum_j C_j p_j + \sum_i \pi_i - \sum_{i|(i,k)\in W} \delta_i \qquad \text{DRWDP(B)}$$

$$\text{s.t.} \quad \sum_j s_{ikj}\, p_j + \pi_i \geq b_{ik}, \quad \forall(i,k) \notin (OUT \cup IN) \qquad (15)$$

$$\sum_j s_{ikj}\, p_j + \pi_i - \delta_i \geq b_{ik}, \quad \forall(i,k) \in IN \qquad (16)$$

$$p_j \geq 0, \pi_i \geq 0, \delta_i \geq 0$$

Dual variable δ_i corresponds to constraints (14) in RWDP(B). The variable that dualizes constraints (13) drops out of the dual formulation because it appears with coefficient zero in the objective and appears in a non-binding constraint.

A.3 Determining the Proxy Payments: To determine the payments we must determine the payoffs in the bidder-optimal core that minimize the maximal deviation across all bidders from the VCG payoff profile. Solving for this point requires the use of constraint generation, but the cryptographic proof can be constructed after-the-fact in terms of just the final set of constraints. By a slight reformulation of the method in Day and Raghavan [26], the payoffs to winning bidders $i \in W$ can be computed in the following LP:

$$\max_{\pi,m} \sum_{i \in W} \pi_i - \epsilon\, m \qquad \text{EBOP}$$

$$\text{s.t.} \quad \sum_{i \in W \setminus L} \pi_i \leq V^* - V(L), \quad \forall L \subseteq W \qquad (17)$$

$$\pi_i + m \geq \pi_i^{\text{vcg}}, \quad \forall i \in W \qquad (18)$$

$$0 \leq \pi_i, \quad \forall i \in W$$

$$0 \leq m,$$

with $\pi_i = 0$ for all $i \notin W$, and for some small $\epsilon > 0$. The objective is to maximize the total bidder payoff, but then for small ϵ to break ties in favor of minimizing the maximal deviation m from the VCG payoffs across all such bidders. Constraints (17) are the core constraints and constraints (18) force m to adopt the maximal difference to VCG payoffs. Given a solution π^* to EBOP, the payments collected from each winning bidder $i \in W$ are $b_i(s_i^*) - \pi_i^*$.

EBOP is an LP and has no integer variables. But notice that part of its input has required solving IPs (since constraints (17) are defined in terms of V^* and $V(L)$). More difficult, there are an exponential number of constraints (17). Day and Raghavan [26] suggest using *constraint generation* to construct a subset $\mathcal{L} \subseteq 2^W$ of coalitions, with constraints (17) reformulated as $\sum_{i \in W \setminus L} \pi_i \leq V^* - V(L)$, $\forall L \in \mathcal{L}$. Let EBOP($\mathcal{L}$) denote the relaxed form of EBOP in with just this subset of constraints. New constraints are introduced until it can be established that:

$$\max_{L \subseteq W} \sum_{i \in W \setminus L} \pi_i - (V^* - V(L)) \leq 0 \tag{19}$$

This establishes that none of the missing constraints is binding. (In practice, this is also the separation problem that is solved in generating a new constraint.) Given a solution π^* to EBOP($\mathcal{L}$), the separation problem can be formulated and solved via an IP as a simple variation on the regular WDP:

$$\max_{x_{ik}} \sum_{i \in W} \left(1 - \sum_k x_{ik}\right) \pi_i - V^* + \sum_{i \in W} \sum_k x_{ik} b_{ik} \qquad \text{SEP}(\pi^*)$$

$$\text{s.t.} \quad \sum_i \sum_k s_{ikj}\, x_{ik} \leq C_j, \quad \forall j \tag{20}$$

$$\sum_k x_{ik} \leq 1, \quad \forall i \in W \tag{21}$$

$$x_{ik} \in \{0,1\}$$

Putting this all together, the methodology for establishing the correctness of the final payments is as follows:

1. Publish the set $\mathcal{L}$ of coalitions of winners that are used to establish the correctness of payments. (Note that this does not reveal any information if a shuffle was used on the inputs.) Publish the parameter $\epsilon > 0$.

2. Publish the solution $E(\pi^*)$ and $E(m^*)$ to EBOP($\mathcal{L}$). Publish the vector of proxy payments $p^* = \langle p_1^*, \ldots, p_n^* \rangle$. Prove that $p_i^* = \sum_k x_{ik}^* b_{ik} - \pi_i^*$ for all bidders i.

3. Publish and establish the correctness of $E(\pi^{\mathrm{vcg}})$, for $\pi^{\mathrm{vcg}} = \langle \pi_1^{\mathrm{vcg}}, \ldots, p_n^{\mathrm{vcg}} \rangle$. Publish and establish the correctness of $E(V(L))$ for all $L \in \mathcal{L}$.

4. Publish and prove the solution to the separation problem $\text{SEP}(\pi^*)$.

5. Prove that the solution to EBOP is primal feasible.

6. Publish an encrypted solution to the dual problem and prove it is dual feasible. Prove the value $E(D^*) \leq \beta E(V^*)$ for some parameter $\beta \geq 1$, e.g. $\beta = 100001/100000$.

Step 3 requires proving facts about solutions to different winner determination problems. For the VCG payoff, $\pi_i^{\mathrm{vcg}} = V^* - V(B \setminus i)$ and thus this needs the value of $E(V(B \setminus i))$ to be proved correct. This can be done following the approach in the previous section for the WDP. Similarly, we need to prove the correctness of $E(V(L))$ for subsets $L \subseteq B$. Note that both kinds of proofs can be verified without revealing the solution to these subproblems, and that no useful information leaks from publishing branching decisions in the branch-and-bound search because of the use of a shuffle. Step 4 can be reduced to an instance of the WDP and proved analogously. In Step 6 we need the dual to the linear program EBOP($\mathcal{L}$).

Secure Multiparty Computation Goes Live[*]

Peter Bogetoft[3], Dan Lund Christensen[4], Ivan Damgård[2], Martin Geisler[2],
Thomas Jakobsen[4], Mikkel Krøigaard[2], Janus Dam Nielsen[2],
Jesper Buus Nielsen[2], Kurt Nielsen[1], Jakob Pagter[4], Michael Schwartzbach[2],
and Tomas Toft[5]

[1] Inst. of Food and Resource Economics, University of Copenhagen
[2] Department of Computer Science, University of Aarhus
[3] Dept. of Economics, Copenhagen Business School
[4] The Alexandra Institute
[5] CWI Amsterdam and TU/e

Abstract. In this note, we report on the first large-scale and practical application of secure multiparty computation, which took place in January 2008. We also report on the novel cryptographic protocols that were used.

1 Introduction

In this paper, we present the implementation of a secure system for trading quantities of a certain commodity among many buyers and sellers, a so-called double auction. In the particular case where our system has been deployed, it was used by Danish farmers to trade contracts for sugar beet production on a nation-wide market. The system was implemented using *secure multiparty computation* (MPC) This allowed us to ensure that each bid submitted to the auction was kept encrypted from the time it left the bidder's computer, no single party had access to the bids at any time. Nevertheless the system could efficiently compute the price at which contracts should be traded. This was, to the best of our knowledge, the first large-scale practical application of secure multiparty computation.

Below, we first explain the application scenario and the reasons why multiparty computation turned out to be a good solution. We then explain in detail the cryptographic protocols used and prove their security. In doing so, we propose a logarithmic-round comparison protocol that is much more practical than the one from [13] for numbers of realistic size. Finally, we describe the system that was implemented and report on how it performed.

---

[*] This work was supported by the Danish Strategic Research Council and the European Commision. Tomas Toft's work was partially performed at Aarhus University. In Holland, he was supported by the research program Sentinels, financed by Technology Foundation STW, the Netherlands Organization for Scientific Research (NWO), and the Dutch Ministry of Economic Affairs.

2   The Application Scenario

In this section we describe the practical case in which our system has been deployed. In [1], preliminary plans for this scenario and results from a small-scale demo were described.

In Denmark, several thousand farmers produce sugar beets, which are sold to the company Danisco, the only sugar beets processor on the Danish market. Farmers have contracts that give them rights and obligation to deliver a certain amount of beets to Danisco, who pay them according to a pricing scheme that is an integrated part of the contracts. These contracts can be traded between farmers, but trading has historically been very limited and has primarily been done via bilateral negotiations.

In recent years, however, the EU drastically reduced the support for sugar beet production. This and other factors meant that there was now an urgent need to reallocate contracts to farmers where productions pays off best. It was realized that this was best done via a nation-wide exchange, a double auction.

Market Clearing Price. Details of the particular business case can be found in [2]. Here, we briefly summarize the main points while more details on the actual computation to be done are given later. A double auction includes several buyers and sellers and the goal is to find the so called *market clearing price*, which is a price per unit of the commodity that is traded. What happens is that each buyer places a bid by specifying, for each potential price, how much he is willing to buy at that price. Similarly sellers say how much they are willing to sell at each price[1]. All bids go to an auctioneer, who computes, for each price, the total supply and demand in the market. Since we can assume that supply grows and demand decreases with increasing price, there is a price where total supply equals total demand, and this is the price we are looking for. Finally, all bidders who specified a non-zero amount to trade at the market clearing price get to sell/buy the amount at this price.

Ensuring Privacy of Bids. A satisfactory implementation of such an auction has to take some security concerns into account: Bids clearly reveal information, e.g., on a farmer's economic position and his productivity, and therefore farmers would be reluctant to accept Danisco acting as auctioneer, given its position in the market. This is because Danisco could potentially misuse knowledge of the bids in the ongoing renegotiations of the contracts (including the pricing scheme). And even if Danisco would never do so, the mere fear of this happening could affect the way farmers bid and lead to a suboptimal result of the auction. On the other hand, the entitled quantities in a given contract are administrated by Danisco (and adjusted frequently according to the EU administration) and in some cases the contracts act as security for debt that farmers have to Danisco. Hence running the auction independently of Danisco is not acceptable either.

---

[1] In real life, a bidder would only specify where the quantity he wants to trade changes, and by how much. The quantities to trade at other prices then follow from this.

Finally, the solution of delegating the legal and practical responsibility by paying e.g. a consultancy house to be the trusted auctioneer would have been a very expensive solution.

The solution decided on was to implement an electronic double auction, where the role of the auctioneer would be played by three parties, namely representatives for Danisco, DKS (the sugar beet growers' association) and the SIMAP research project (the project in which the authors of this paper participated). By interacting with each other, these three parties together could form a "virtual auctioneer", computing the market clearing price and quantities to trade, just as described above. This was implemented using secure multiparty computation technology: each bidder sends his bid in appropriately encrypted form to the three parties, who then compute on the data *while it is still in protected form*. Therefore, no single party ever has access to any bid in the clear. Still, by collaborating, the parties can produce the required output.

A three party solution was selected, partly because it was natural in the given scenario, but also because it allowed using very efficient cryptographic protocols to do the secure computation.

Motivation. It is interesting to ask what motivated DKS and Danisco to try using such a new and untested technology? One important factor was simply the obvious need for a nation-wide exchange for production rights, which had not existed before, so the opportunity to have a cheap electronic solution –secure or not– was certainly a major reason. We do believe, however, that security also played a role. An on-line survey carried out in connection with the auction showed that farmers do care about keeping their bids private (see table in Fig. 1). Also, in an interview with the involved decision markers from Danisco and DKS these confidentiality issues were well recognized.

Now, if Danisco and DKS would have tried to run the auction using conventional methods, one or more persons would have had to have access to the bids, or control over the system holding the bids in cleartext. As a result, some security policy would have had to be agreed, answering questions such as: who should have access to the data and when? who has responsibility if data leaks, and what are the consequences?

Since the parties have conflicting interests, this could have lead to very lengthy discussions, possibly bringing the whole project to a halt. Using a consultancy house as mediator would not have solved these problems: the parties would still have had to agree on whether the mediator's security policy was satisfactory. As it happened, there was no need for this kind of negotiation, since the multiparty computation ensured that no one needed to have access to bids at any point. In an interview with the decision makers, they recognized that this fact made it easy to communicate the security policy to the farmers.

Security and Risks. One must of course consider which attacks such a system might be subjected to. Attacks from external parties, hackers, etc. is of course an issue that must be considered in practice, but such attacks are not special to our system and are therefore less interesting for the discussion in this paper.

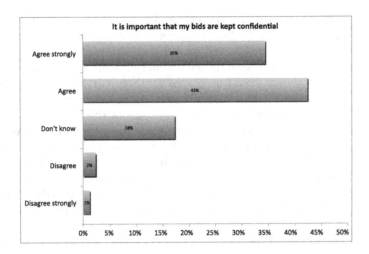

Fig. 1. Farmers' confidentiality expectations. (Numbers from survey based on questions asked to the farmers after they had submitted their bids.)

A more interesting question is whether the participants themselves might attack the system. With respect to the three parties doing the secure computation, the situation was as follows: none of the parties seriously suspected that any of the others would actively and maliciously attack the system. On the other hand, giving all the sensitive data in the clear to one party was not acceptable, and moreover, none of the parties wanted the responsibility of having to store the sensitive data – this would immediately lead to all the practical problems described above, with security policies and procedures.

A suitable solution was therefore a protocol where one assumes that all parties act as they are supposed to, but where no party ever gets access to any sensitive information. This is known as semi-honest security and this is the model we chose for our system. In a nutshell, semi-honest security can be described as a model where one can "choose not to know" any sensitive data and therefore does not have to assume sole responsibility for keeping them secret.

With respect to malicious attacks from bidders, we estimated that the risk of this happening in our particular case was not large enough to motivate the extra cost of protecting against it: Bidders have a clear interest in the auction working properly, and would anyway have to reverse engineer an applet supplied by the system to even start an attack. Still, in other scenarios, or perhaps in future instances of this auction, malicious attacks from the client side might be a valid concern, and we therefore show below protocols that protect against malicious bidders.

Alternative Cryptographic Solutions. One might also ask if the full power of multiparty computation was actually needed? Our solution ensures that no single player has any sensitive information, and it might seem that one could solve the problem more efficiently in a similar trust model using a trick often used in voting protocols: one party P_1 receives the bids in encrypted form from the bidders, however, the bids are encrypted with the public key of another party P_2. Then P_1 sends the encryptions, randomized and in permuted order to P_2 who decrypts the bids and computes the market clearing price. While this achieves some security because P2 does not know who placed which bids, we have to remember that bids contain much more information than what is conveyed by the result (the market clearing price), e.g., one can see the quantities people were willing to buy or sell at other prices than the clearing price. In principle, this type of information is highly valuable for a monopolist such as Danisco in order to exercise its market power, e.g., in terms of setting the price of an extension or a reduction of the total processing capacity. To what extend such a situation is relevant in practice is not easy to answer. Our conclusion was that using full-blown multiparty computation is a better solution because it frees us from even having to consider the question.

3   Introduction to Multiparty Computation

In the model of multiparty computation considered in this paper, we have a number of *input clients* $I_1, ..., I_m$ and a number of servers $P_1, ..., P_n$. The input clients each hold inputs $x_1, ..., x_m$, and we then want to securely compute some function f on these inputs, where $f(x_1, ..., x_n) = y$ becomes public, but we want to make sure that y is the only information on $x_1, ..., x_m$ that is revealed. This should hold, even if players exhibit some amount of adversarial behavior. The goal can be accomplished by an interactive protocol π that the players execute. Intuitively, we want that executing π is equivalent to having a trusted party T that receives privately x_i from I_i, computes the function, and returns y to everyone[2]. With such a protocol we can –in principle– solve virtually any cryptographic protocol problem. The general theory of MPC was founded in the late 80-ties [16,3,7]. The theory was later developed in several ways – see for instance [21,18,8]. An overview of the theoretical results known can be found in [6].

Despite the obvious potential that MPC has in solving a wide range of problems, we have seen virtually no practical applications of MPC in the past. This is probably in part due to the fact that direct implementation of the first general protocols would lead to very inefficient solutions. Another factor has been a general lack of understanding in the general public of the potential of the technology. A lot of research has gone into solving the efficiency problems, both for general protocols [11,17,9] and for special types of computations such as voting [4,12].

A different line of research has had explicit focus on a range of economic applications, which are particularly interesting for practical use. This approach was taken, for instance, by two research projects that the authors of this paper have been involved in: SCET (Secure Computing, Economy and Trust)[3] and SIMAP

---

[2] This "equivalence" can be formalized using, for instance, Canetti's Universal Composability framework[5].

[3] see http://sikkerhed.alexandra.dk/uk/projects/scet

(Secure Information Management and Processing)[4] which has been responsible for the practical application of MPC described in this paper. In the economic field of mechanism design the concept of a trusted third party has been a central assumption since the 70's [15,19,10]. Ever since the field was initiated it has grown in momentum and turned into a truly cross disciplinary field. Today, many practical mechanisms require a trusted third party and it is natural to consider the possibility of implementing such a party using MPC. In particular, we have considered:

- Various types of auctions that involves sealed bids for different reasons. The most well-known is probably the standard highest bid auction with sealed bids, however, in terms of turnover another common variant is the so called double auction with many sellers and buyers. This auction handles scenarios where one wants to find a fair market price for a commodity given the existing supply and demand in the market.
- Benchmarking, where several companies want to combine information on how their businesses are running, in order to compare themselves to best practice in the area. The benchmarking process is either used for learning, planning or motivation purposes. This of course has to be done while preserving confidentiality of companies' private data.

When looking at such applications, one finds that the computation needed is basically elementary arithmetic on integers of moderate size, say around 32 bits. More concretely, quite a wide range of the cases require only addition, multiplication and comparison of integers. As far as addition and multiplication is concerned, this can be handled quite efficiently by well-known generic MPC protocols. What they really do is actually operations modulo some prime p, because the protocols are based on secret sharing over $\mathbb{Z}_p$. But by choosing p large enough compared to the input numbers, we can avoid modular reductions and get efficient integer addition and multiplication.

This is efficient because each number is shared "in one piece" using a linear secret sharing scheme, so that secure addition, for instance, requires only one local addition by each player. Unfortunately, this also implies that comparison is much harder and cannot be done efficiently using generic methods. So instead one must develop special purpose techniques for comparison. One example of this is the constant-round comparison protocol from [13], which is improved on in this work.

In summary, this means that the protocols we developed for our auction system are in fact useful for a large range of applications, since they tend to use the same set of arithmetic operations as those needed for the auction.

4   The Cryptographic Protocols

Recall that the scenario we have includes input clients $I_1, \ldots, I_m$ who deliver inputs to a multiparty computation, that is to be executed by servers $P_1, \ldots, P_n$.

---

[4] see http://sikkerhed.alexandra.dk/uk/projects/simap

In the types of cases we are interested in, m is very large and variable while we think of n as a small constant. In our concrete case, we had $n = 3$ and m was about 1200.

The input from client I_i is an ordered list of non-negative integers $\{x_{ij}|\ j = 1, \ldots, P\}$, where index j refers to one of the P possible prices per unit, in increasing order. Such a list is called a *bid*. A bid can be a *sell* bid in which case the list is non-decreasing, or a *buy* bid in which case it is non-increasing. For a buy bid, x_{ij} is the quantity the bidder wants to buy at the i'th price per unit, similarly for sell bids, the elements of which we will denote by y_{ij}. Due to the practical constraints it must be possible to deliver these inputs non-interactively (and securely) to the servers.

The secure computation consists of computing the total demand and supply at each price, namely

$$d_j = \sum_i x_{ij}, \quad s_j = \sum_i y_{ij}, \quad j = 1, \ldots, P\,,$$

and to finally find the index j_0 for which $d_{j_0} - s_{j_0} = 0$, or rather an index where the difference is as close to 0 as possible. Since quantities are specified in units of fixed size, we cannot expect to find a price where supply exactly meets demand. This also means that there has to be agreed rules for how one handles cases where we must live with a price where supply is larger than demand or vice versa. Such rules were agreed for our concrete case, but the details of this are outside the scope of this paper.

In any case, since supply increases and demand decreases with increasing price, we can find the index we are looking for by binary search over the indices $1, \ldots, P$: We start by comparing $d_{P/2}$ to $s_{P/2}$. If the result is that $d_{P/2}$ was larger, then $j_0 \geq P/2$, else $j_0 < P/2$. Depending on the result, we do a similar comparison in the middle of the top or bottom half of the interval. Continuing in this way, we can find j_0 using secure comparisons between d_j and s_j for $\log P$ values of j.

Note that it is secure to make the comparison results public: we want j_0 to be public anyway, and from this, the result of the comparison between d_j and s_j already follows for any j. Finally j_0 is made public, as well as x_{ij_0}, y_{ij_0} for all i, i.e., the quantity each bidder said he would buy or sell at the market clearing price.

It will therefore be sufficient to design a protocol that (in the given scenario) implements the ideal functionality in Fig. 2.

We will assume a static and passive adversary who may corrupt any number of input clients and any minority of the servers. We show below that we can allow active corruption of the clients at the expense of some efficiency. In our concrete case, however, we have estimated that the risk of active attacks from clients was too small to motivate paying the loss in efficiency – see more details below. We assume secure point-to-point channels between the servers, this can be implemented with standard tools.

Our implementation will be based on standard Shamir secret sharing among the n servers, using a prime field $\mathbb{Z}_p$ where p is chosen such that its bit length

---

Functionality $\mathcal{F}$:

1. On input $\texttt{Input}(x_1, \ldots, x_P)$ from an input client I_j, where $x_1, \ldots, x_P$ is a list of integers where each number is at most ℓ bits long, for some fixed ℓ, and where the list is either increasing or decreasing. The ideal functionality $\mathcal{F}$ stores the numbers in uniquely named registers and notifies all players and the adversary that an input list has been received from I_j along with the names of the registers in which the numbers are stored.

2. On input $C = A + B$, where A, B, C are names of registers of $\mathcal{F}$, $\mathcal{F}$ adds the numbers in A and B and stores the result in C.

3. On input $C = A \times B$ where A, B, C are names of registers of $\mathcal{F}$, $\mathcal{F}$ multiplies the numbers in A and B and stores the result in C.

4. On input $\texttt{ConstantMult}(a, B)$ where $a \in \mathbb{Z}_p$ and B is a register, $\mathcal{F}$ multiplies the number in B by a and stores the result in B.

5. On input $\texttt{Compare}(A, B)$, $\mathcal{F}$ sends 1 to all servers if the number in A is larger than the number in B and 0 otherwise.

6. On input $\texttt{Open}(A)$, $\mathcal{F}$ sends the number stored in register A to all servers.

7. On input $\texttt{RandomBit}(A)$, $\mathcal{F}$ chooses a random 0/1 value and places it in register A.

Fig. 2. The ideal functionality $\mathcal{F}$ implemented by our protocols

is $\ell + \kappa$, where κ is a parameter that controls the statistical security of the comparison protocol. In our concrete case ℓ was 32 and p was 65 bits long).

We set $t = \lfloor (n-1)/2 \rfloor$, so a number is secret shared by choosing a random polynomial f of degree at most t with $f(0) = x$, and the shares of x are then $f(1), \ldots, f(n)$. By $[x]$ we denote a set of shares of the number x, suppressing for readability the random coins used in the sharing.

Let $\mathcal{F}'$ be the functionality that is the same as $\mathcal{F}$, but does not have the comparison command. In the following we will first describe how to implement $\mathcal{F}'$, and then show how to implement $\mathcal{F}$ based on $\mathcal{F}'$.

Setting up Public Keys. Our implementation assumes that public/secret key pairs have been set up by the servers before the computation starts, and that the public keys are available to the clients. More precisely, for every maximal unqualified set A of servers (i.e., $|A| = t$), we need that all servers not in A have a secret key sk_A, and the public key pk_A is available to all players (input clients I_j and servers P_i). This can be accomplished in our scenario by having one server in the complement of A generate pk_A, sk_A, send sk_A to all servers not in A and pk_A to all players.

Non-Interactive Input. The first issue is now how to implement the command where a client inputs numbers $x_1, \ldots, x_P$. The naive solution of simply secret sharing each x_i and encrypt each share under the corresponding server's public key has the problem that it would expand the data a client needs to send by a multiplicative factor of at least the number of servers.

Instead, we propose a variant of a non-interactive VSS technique from [14]. We describe it here for simplicity in our concrete case where $n = 3$. In this case the key set-up above becomes the following: we need 3 key pairs $(pk_i, sk_i), i = 1, 2, 3$, and server i has the two keys sk_j where $j \neq i$. Now let $f_i(x), i = 1, 2, 3$ denote polynomials of degree at most 1 satisfying that $f_i(0) = 1, f_i(i) = 0$. One can now communicate a list of numbers $x_1, \ldots, x_P$ in $\mathbb{Z}_p$ to the servers in encrypted form as follows:

1. Choose keys K_1, K_2, K_3 for a pseudorandom function (PRF) F that takes an index j as input and produces output in $\mathbb{Z}_p{}^5$.
2. Output encryptions $E_{pk_i}(K_i), i = 1, 2, 3$.
3. For $j = 1, \ldots, P$, compute and output

$$y_j = F_{K_1}(j) + F_{K_2}(j) + F_{K_3}(j) + x_j \bmod p .$$

Each server P_a can now process such an encryption and compute a Shamir share of each number:

1. Decrypt the two ciphertexts $E_{pk_i}(K_i)$ where $i \neq a$.
2. Compute your share $share_{a,j}$ of x_j as follows: $share_{a,j} =$

$$y_j - F_{K_1}(j)f_1(a) - F_{K_2}(j)f_2(a) - F_{K_3}(j)f_3(a)$$

bearing in mind that since $f_a(a) = 0$, it does not matter that you don't know K_a.

It is straightforward to see that if we define the polynomial g_j as $g_j = y_j - F_{K_1}(j)f_1 - F_{K_2}(j)f_2 - F_{K_3}(j)f_3$, then indeed $\deg(g) \leq 1$, $g_j(0) = x_j$ and $g_j(a) = share_{a,j}$ so that a valid set of shares has indeed been computed.

Generalizing this to an arbitrary number of servers and Shamir sharing with threshold t is straightforward: we use the general key set-up above with a key pair (pk_A, sk_A) for every set of servers of size t, and sk_A is given to all servers not in A. We then use the polynomials f_A of degree at most t where $f_A(0) = 1$ and $f_A(i) = 0$ for all $i \in A$. Of course, this does not scale well to large n, but we will not need this in our application.

This method has a number of advantages:

1. Except for an additive overhead depending on the number of servers, the encrypted list is the same size as the list itself.
2. Assuming the decryption algorithm of the public key system is deterministic, the decryption process always results in consistent shares of *some* list of values.
3. If a server loses its secret keys, they can be reconstructed with help from the other servers.
4. We only need communication from clients to servers. This is very convenient in a practical setting where we can control the configuration of the (relatively few) servers, but not the (many) clients – some might e.g. sit behind a firewall making it hard to send data from the servers to the clients.

---

[5] One can e.g. use a PRF F' with output in $\{0, 1\}^{\lceil \log p \rceil + \kappa}$, interpret the output as a number $y \in \{0, \ldots, 2^{\lceil \log p \rceil + \kappa} - 1\}$ and let $F(x) = F'(x) \bmod p$.

Addition and Multiplication. After the input phase, all values are shared using polynomials of degree $\leq t$. We thus can implement addition and multiplication using well known standard protocols and assuming as invariant that all numbers that $\mathcal{F}$ would store in a register are in the real protocol secret shared among the players. The addition command on input $[a], [b]$ is done by having servers locally add their shares of a and b, clearly $[a] + [b] = [a + b]$ since the sharing is linear. Likewise, multiplication by a constant is done by having each server multiply his share by the public constant. Multiplication is done by having server P_i multiply his shares of a, b: $d_i = a_i b_i$. He then forms shares $[d_i]$ and sends them to the servers. Finally, all servers compute $[ab] = \sum_i \lambda_i [d_i]$, where the λ_i are Lagrange interpolation coefficients that are chosen to reconstructing $g(0)$ from $g(1), \ldots, g(n)$ for a polynomial g of degree $\leq 2t$. Since $2t < n$ it is possible to compute such λ_i.

Random Bits. For the `RandomBit`, we borrow a trick from [13]: All servers secret share a random value, and add all shares locally, to form a sharing $[u]$ of a random unknown u. We then compute $[v] = [u^2 \bmod p]$ and open v. If $v = 0$ we start over, otherwise we publicly compute a square root w of v, say we choose the smallest one. We compute $w^{-1}[u] \bmod p$ which will be 1 with probability $1/2$ and -1 with probability $1/2$. Therefore, $[(w^{-1}u + 1)2^{-1} \bmod p]$ will produce the random shared binary value we wanted.

Lemma 1. *If the encryption used is semantically secure and the PRF used is secure, then the above protocol implements $\mathcal{F}'$ securely against a static, passive adversary corrupting any number of clients and at most t servers.*

Proof. We must provide a simulator that can, by only interacting with $\mathcal{F}'$, on behalf of the corrupted parties, simulate any adversary's view of the real life protocol. The simulator first generates key pairs (pk_A, sk_A) as described above, sends the public keys to the adversary as well as those secrets that are to be known by corrupt players.

We first show how to simulate the input operation. If the client sending input is corrupt then since he follows the protocol by assumption, the simulator can compute the input that is encrypted by monitoring the computing done by the client. The simulator sends these inputs to $\mathcal{F}'$. When $\mathcal{F}'$ says that inputs were received from an honest input client, the simulator generates an encrypted list of input numbers following the protocol, using 0 for all input numbers. It sends this as the simulated message from the client. The other commands are simulated in the standard way: when an honest server secret shares a value, the simulator generates (up to) t uniform field elements to simulate shares of corrupt players. When a sharing is opened, the simulator is given the value to open by $\mathcal{F}'$ and it completes the set of shares already known to the adversary to a complete set consistent with the value to open.

To argue that the simulation of the input command is indistinguishable from the real protocol, we note that it is clearly perfect for the case of a corrupt client, as we run $\mathcal{F}'$ on the input shared by the corrupted client. For simulation of an honest client, assume some set of t servers A is corrupt, let REAL denote the view of these corrupted parties in the real protocol, let SIM denote their view in the simulation, and consider a variant of the real process HYB$_1$ where all encryptions under pk_A are replaced by encryptions of zero. Likewise, we construct HYB$_2$ by replacing in the simulation all encryptions under pk_A by encryptions of zero. Assuming semantic security, HYB$_1$ is computationally indistinguishable from the real process, and HYB$_2$ is computationally indistinguishable from the simulation. In proving this we use, of course, that the adversary does not know sk_A. Namely, if there exists an environment and adversary for which one could distinguish, we could break semantic security: We get pk_A from an oracle as well as encryptions that are either encryptions of zeros or encryptions of the messages that would normally be used. A successful distinguisher now breaks semantic security. In both HYB$_1$ and HYB$_2$, the use to the PRF can be replaced by oracle access to the function without changing anything. We can then form two new processes HYB$_1'$, HYB$_2'$ by replacing the PRF oracle by a random oracle. This leads to indistinguishable processes by security of the PRF. Finally note that HYB$_1'$ = HYB$_2'$ because the only part that may now depend on the input is the number y_j. But this is in one case $x_j + r \bmod p$ where r is uniform in $\mathbb{Z}_p$ and independent of x_j and in the other case $0 + r \bmod p$. This gives, of course the same distribution, so our conclusion now follows from transitivity of indistinguishability.

Finally, the simulation of the commands other than input is perfect by standard arguments.

In the protocol above, we have assumed that the numbers in bids have the correct form, in particular they are significantly smaller than p. Assuming only passive attacks, one does not have to check for this, but one may still ask if we could protect efficiently against malicious clients?

Input without Trusting the Clients. The method described above produces consistently shared numbers no matter what the client does, but in principle allows a client to send numbers that are too large, possibly causing the computation to fail. We can protect against this as well, namely we would fix the size of the pseudorandom values $F_{K_i}(j)$ to be $\ell + \kappa$ bits, choose the length of p to be $2(\ell + \kappa + \log T)$ bits where T is the number of maximal unqualified sets A, and otherwise do the same protocol as above to send inputs.

Each y_j in the message sent by the client should be a sum of T pseudorandom values and the actual secret to be shared. By choice of the size of p, this sum will not involve any reduction modulo p, if y_j is correctly constructed. So we can demand that each y_j is at most a $\kappa + \ell + \log T$ bit number and reject the input otherwise. Even if a y_j is not correctly constructed, this guarantees that the secret we end up getting shares of will be of form $y_j - \sum_A F_{K_A}(j)$, and must therefore be numerically much smaller than p, in fact it must be in the interval $[-2^{\kappa+\ell+\log T}..2^{\kappa+\ell+\log T}]$. One can easily see that once we know such a constraint on the numbers we work with, the comparison protocol we show later can be used, indeed the only assumption it makes is that the numbers to compare are sufficiently smaller than p. The servers can therefore check that the input numbers are positive and increasing or decreasing as required.

Finally, the public-key encryption used must be chosen ciphertext secure in order to cope with malicious input clients, and each plaintext encrypted must include an identification of the intended receiver.

Changing the protocol as described here costs us an increase in size of p which implies a general loss of efficiency, an increase in size of data, and extra work to check the form of bids. On the other hand, to actually cheat, a bidder would have to write his own client program and convince the server side that the normal client was still used. For our concrete case, we estimated that the risk of bidders cheating in this way was too small to motivate the extra cost of protecting against it.

As an aside, we note that it can be shown that sending bids that are not increasing or decreasing cannot be to a bidders advantage and so this is in any case a minor concern.

4.1   Adding Secure Comparison

It remains to describe how to compare numbers securely. We show how to do this assuming access to the functionality $\mathcal{F}'$. Then this, the results from the previous section and the UC composition theorem gives us the desired implementation of $\mathcal{F}$. Recall that numbers to compare are assumed to be of length at most ℓ bits, and the prime used for secret sharing is $\ell + \kappa$ bits long.

In the description of the protocol below, we refer to arithmetic on objects written as $[d]$. In this protocol, where we assume access to $\mathcal{F}'$, this should be understood as referring to a register held by $\mathcal{F}'$, containing the number d. In the actual implementation $[d]$ would be a secret-sharing of d.

We will need an operator on bit-pairs, $\diamond$, defined as

$$\begin{pmatrix} x \\ X \end{pmatrix} \diamond \begin{pmatrix} y \\ Y \end{pmatrix} = \begin{pmatrix} x \wedge y \\ x \wedge (X \oplus Y) \oplus X \end{pmatrix},$$

where $\wedge$ denotes the Boolean AND operator. Note that if we have $[a], [b]$, where a, b are guaranteed to be $0/1$ values, then $[a \oplus b]$ can be computed using operations from $\mathcal{F}'$, as $[a] + [b] - 2[ab]$. So we can assume that $\oplus$ on binary values is available, as if it was an operation implemented in $\mathcal{F}'$, and so $\diamond$ can also be implemented. It is easy to verify that $\diamond$ is associative.

The comparison protocol is given in Fig. 3. Some intuition on the protocol: when comparing values d and s, it is easy to see that the comparison result follows from the ℓ'th bit of $2^\ell + d - s$ (counting the bits from zero). This bit is extracted in two steps: First the problem is transformed to one where the binary representation of involved numbers is available. This transformed instance can then be solved easily.

Lemma 2. *When given access to functionality $\mathcal{F}'$, the above comparison protocol implements the comparison operation with statistical security in $O(\log \ell)$ rounds.*

Proof. Once we note that none of the additions or subtractions we do can cause reductions modulo p because of the size for p that we have chosen, it should be

---

Comparison protocol:

Input: $[d], [s]$. Output: 1 if $d \geq s$, 0 otherwise

1. For $i = 0, \ldots, \ell + \kappa + 1$, call RandomBit to generate $[r_i]$ for random $r_i \in \{0, 1\}$. Compute $[r] = \sum_i 2^i [r_i]$.
2. Compute $[a] = 2^{\ell + \kappa + 1} - [r] + 2^\ell + [d] - [s]$. Open a, and compute the bits a_i of a.
3. Our goal is now to compute the ℓ'th bit of $a + r = 2^{\ell + \kappa + 1} + 2^\ell + d - s$. Note that we have a and $[r_i]$'s available. Compute

$$\begin{pmatrix} [z] \\ [Z] \end{pmatrix} = \begin{pmatrix} [a_{\ell-1} \oplus r_{\ell-1}] \\ [a_{\ell-1}] \end{pmatrix} \diamond \cdots \diamond \begin{pmatrix} [a_0 \oplus r_0] \\ [a_0] \end{pmatrix} \diamond \begin{pmatrix} 0 \\ 0 \end{pmatrix}.$$

Now Z is the carry bit at position ℓ when doing the addition $a + r$.
4. Compute $[res] = a_\ell \oplus [r_\ell] \oplus [Z]$, open and output res.

Fig. 3. The comparison protocol implementing the command Compare given $\mathcal{F}'$

straightforward that the protocol outputs the correct result, if indeed Z is the ℓ'th carry bit from the addition of a and r, as claimed. To see this, note that the computation of carry-bits can be perceived as follows. If $a_i \neq r_i$, then the present carry-bit c_i is propagated on up, $c_{i+1} = c_i$. However, if $a_i = r_i$, then the next carry-bit is set to their value, $c_{i+1} = a_i = r_i$. The goal is therefore to determine the value of a_i at the most significant (left most) bit-position $i < \ell$ where $a_i = r_i$. Now, looking at the definition of $\diamond$, one can verify that it outputs the y-pair when $x = 1$, otherwise the x-pair is output, and hence Z indeed ends up being the desired carry bit. Note that the $\begin{pmatrix} 0 \\ 0 \end{pmatrix}$ on the right is added to handle the case where $a_i \neq r_i$ for all i.

As for the round complexity, note that since $\diamond$ is associative, the expression in Step 3 can be evaluated in a standard tree-like fashion which will take $O(\log \ell)$ rounds since there are $\ell + 1$ operands and the $\diamond$ operation executes in constant-round.

Finally, note that an execution of the protocol can be simulated by choosing a uniform $\kappa + \ell + 2$ bit number r and outputting $2^{\kappa + \ell + 1} + 2^\ell - r$ to play the role of a. Note that this is the only actual communication in the protocol since everything else happens internally in $\mathcal{F}'$. Since d, s are only ℓ-bit numbers this simulation has statistical distance $2^{-\kappa}$ from the real distribution of a.

In [13] a (more complicated) constant-round comparison was proposed. However, our solution is much more practical for the size of numbers in question: The diamond operator executes in three rounds, so only $3 \log 32 = 15$ rounds are required for its repeated application. This implies less than 20 rounds overall. In comparison, the solution in [13] requires more than 100 rounds, and though more efficient constant-rounds solutions have been proposed, these are nowhere near as efficient as the present for the input sizes in question.

Lemmas 2 and 1 and the UC composition theorem now immediately imply

Theorem 1. *If the encryption used is semantically secure and the PRF used is secure, then the protocol for implementing $\mathcal{F}'$ together with the comparison protocol securely implement $\mathcal{F}$ against a static, passive adversary corrupting any number of clients and at most t servers.*

A Trick to Improve Efficiency. We can do the computation involving binary values in the comparison more efficiently by adding to $\mathcal{F}'$ a command that, given a register $[r_i]$ containing a binary value, produces a new register containing the same binary value, but now interpreted as an element in $GF(2^8)$, denoted $[r_i]_{256}$. The $\oplus$ operation is now simply addition in $GF(2^8)$. The idea behind this is of course that we will implement $[r_i]_{256}$ as sharing over the field $GF(2^8)$ so that secure $\oplus$ becomes only a local addition and so is much faster than before. This reduces the diamond operator to a single round implying only $\log 32 = 5$ rounds for the repeated application and less than 10 rounds overall.

This only leaves the question of how to do the conversion. We do this by having each server produce $[s_j], [b_j]_{256}$ for a random bit b_j, and random κ-bit number s_j, chosen such that its least significant bit is b_j. It is now (statistically) secure to open $r_i + \sum_j s_j$. The least significant bit of this number equals $r_i \oplus b_1 \oplus \cdots \oplus b_n$. Adding this bit to the shares of $[b_1 \oplus \cdots \oplus b_n]_{256}$ produces $[r_i]_{256}$.

We leave the (straightforward) formal proof that this is secure to the reader.

5   The Auction Implementation

In the system that was deployed, a web server was set up for receiving bids, and three servers were set up for doing the secure computation. Before the auction started, public/private key pairs were generated for the computation servers, and a representative for each involved organization stored the private key material on a USB stick, protected under a password.

Each bidder logged into the webserver and an applet was downloaded to his PC together with the public keys of the computation servers. After the user typed in his bid, the applet secret shared the bids, and encrypted the shares under the server public keys. Finally the entire set of ciphertexts were stored in a database by the webserver.

As for security precautions on the client side, we did not explicitly implement any security against cheating bidders, as mentioned and motivated in the previous section. Moreover, we considered security against third-party attacks on client machines as being the user's responsibility, and so did not explicitly handle this issue.

After the deadline for the auction had passed, the servers were connected to the database and each other, and the market clearing price was securely computed, as well as the quantity each bidder would buy/sell at that price. The representative for each of the involved parties triggered the computation by inserting his USB stick and entering his password on his own machine.

The system worked with a set of 4000 possible values for the price, meaning that the market clearing price could be found using about 12 secure comparisons.

The bidding phase ran smoothly, with very few technical questions asked by users. The only issue was that the applet on some PC's took up to a minute to complete the encryption of the bids. It is not surprising that the applet needed a non-trivial amount of time, since each bid consisted of 4000 numbers that had to be handled individually. A total of 1229 bidders participated in the auction, each of these had the option of submitting a bid for selling, for buying, or both.

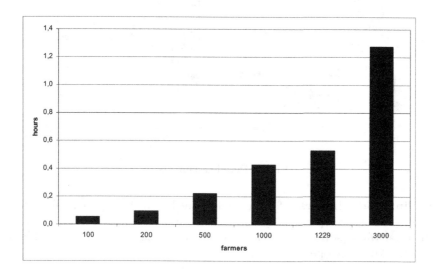

Fig. 4. Timings

The secure computation we implemented is slightly more complicated than the one we described in the previous theory section. This is because we have to take into account the possibility that there may not exist a price for which supply matches demand exactly. However, there must exists a maximal price for which demand is at least supply, and likewise a minimal price for which supply is at least demand. These will be an upper, respectively a lower bound on the market clearing price (MCP). The parties doing the computation are told these upper and lower bounds and must then decide what MCP should be based on these bounds, and rules that are agreed on in advance. The computation therefore involves the following steps:

decrypt to shares (buyers). the servers shares of buy bids are decrypted
decrypt to shares (sellers). the servers shares of sell bids are decrypted
first search. an upper bound on the MCP is located
second search. a lower bound on the MCP is located
marginal search. bids which may help resolve the MCP if the upper and lower bound do not match are located
open marginal bids. bids which may help resolve the MCP if the upper and lower bound do not match are opened

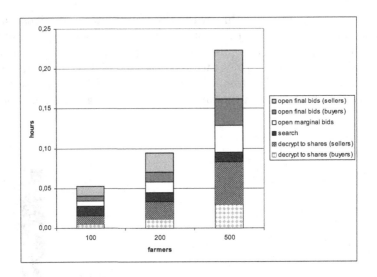

Fig. 5. Detailed Timings

open final bids (buyers). for each bidder the buying bids to be realised based on the MCP are opened

open final bids (sellers). for each bidder the selling bids to be realised based on the MCP are opened

Fig. 4 shows how much time is spent on the computation for different sizes of input (we did not time the real auction, as we did not find it appropriate to compute anything else than what was told to the participants. Timings where however performed in exactly the same setup, except that random bids where used). Both the timing runs as well as the actual auction used three Dell laptops (Latitude D630) with 4 GiB RAM (Java being allocated 1500 MiB on each machine), Intel Centrino Dual Core 2.2 GHz processor, running Windows XP Pro, and connected through an Ethernet LAN using a 100 Mbps switch.

In the figure, the number of prices is constant, but the number of bidders vary. Since the number of secure comparisons we need for the search steps only depend on the number of prices, we expect that the time needed to decrypt shares will dominate the time for searching when the number of bidders is large enough. Fig. 5 shows that this happens when the number of bidders reaches 500. This is not surprising, as the input to the computation, with e.g. 1229 bidders, consist of about 9 million individual numbers.

The lesson to learn here is that the optimized comparison protocol we have developed is efficient enough that it is not a limitation in our scenario, except perhaps in cases with a very small number of bidders. The potential for further optimization therefore lies in the procedure with which shares of bids are encrypted and decrypted. The low-level tools used for this (to do public-key crypto and PRF) were standard off-the-shelf, and there may therefore be faster solutions even without changing the protocols. It should be noted, however, that all this only holds for a double auction (where the number of comparisons does not depend on the number of bidders). For a standard first- or second-price auction, the number of comparisons grows with the number of bidders, and here the comparison time is very critical for a large auction.

The actual computation was done January 14, 2008. As a result of the auction, about 25 thousand tons of production rights changed owner. To the best of our knowledge, this was the first large-scale and genuinely practical application of multiparty computation.

6   Conclusion

How successful have we been with the auction system, and does the technology have further potential in practice?

Other than the fact that the system worked and produced correct results, it is noteworthy that about 80% of the respondents in an on-line survey said that it was important to them that the bids were kept confidential, and also that they were happy about the confidentiality that the system offered. Of course, one should not interpret this as support for the particular technical solution we chose, most farmers would not have any idea what multiparty computation is. But it is nevertheless interesting that confidentiality is seen as important. While it is sometimes claimed that ordinary people do not care about security, we believe our experience shows that they sometimes do care. Our impression is that this has to do with the fact that money is involved, and also that other parties are involved with interests that clearly conflict with yours. For instance, given the history of the sugar beet market, there is little doubt that "confidentiality" for the farmers include confidentiality against Danisco. Danisco and DKS have been satisfied with the system, and at the time of writing, the auction has already been run successfully a second time.

During the experiment we have therefore become convinced that the ability of multiparty computation to keep secret *everything* that is not intended to be public, really is useful in practice. As discussed earlier, it short-circuits discussions and concerns about which parts of the data are sensitive and what common security policy one should have for handling such data.

It is sometimes claimed that the same effect can be achieved by using secure hardware: just send all input data privately to the device which then does the computation internally, and outputs the result. Superficially, this may seem to be a very simple solution that also keeps all private data private. Taking a closer look, however, it is not hard to see that the hardware solution achieves something fundamentally different from what multiparty computation does, *even if one believes that the physical protection cannot be broken*: note that we are still in a situation where some component of our system –the hardware box– has access to *all* private data in cleartext. If we had been talking about an abstract ideal functionality, this would –by definition– not be a problem. But a real hardware box is a system component like any other: it must be securely installed, administrated, updated, backed up, etc. In this sense the hardware solution is not fundamentally different from a solution using an ordinary central server to receive the bids and do the computation. In both cases, the actual security level achieved depends on many factors, including whether the system is administrated according to appropriate procedures. Therefore, both solutions have all the practical problems we pointed out earlier with agreeing on common procedures and security policies if parties have conflicting interests. In addition, since both solutions have a component which becomes a single point of attack, they may be less robust than a distributed solution against outsider attacks.

We believe that a much more natural use of secure hardware is for each party in a multiparty computation to use it in order to improve *his own* security, i.e., to make sure that the protocol messages is the only data his system leaks.

Another standard alternative to MPC is to pay a trusted party such as a consultancy house to do the computation. We said earlier that the parties in our scenario decided against this because it would have been much more expensive. One could claim, of course, that this was only because the alternative was to have a research team do the whole thing for free – and that hence the experiment does not show that MPC is commercially viable. While the experiment has certainly not produced a business plan, we wish to point out that an MPC based solution only has to be developed once and costs can then be amortized over many applications. In some cases one may not even need to adapt the system – for instance, in the case of the sugar beet auction it is very likely that the same auction will be run once a year for some time to come.

In conclusion, we expect that multiparty computation will turn out to be useful in many practical scenarios in the future.

References

1. Bogetoft, P., Damgård, I., Jakobsen, T., Nielsen, K., Pagter, J., Toft, T.: A Practical Implementation of Secure Auctions based on Multiparty Integer Computation. In: Di Crescenzo, G., Rubin, A. (eds.) FC 2006. LNCS, vol. 4107, pp. 142–147. Springer, Heidelberg (2006)
2. Bogetoft, P., Boye, K., Neergaard-Petersen, H., Nielsen, K.: Reallocating sugar beet contracts: Can sugar production survive in Denmark? European Review of Agricultural Economics (34), 1–20 (2007)
3. Ben-Or, M., Goldwasser, S., Wigderson, A.: Completeness theorems for Non-Cryptographic Fault-Tolerant Distributed Computation. In: Proc. ACM STOC 1988, pp, pp. 1–10 (1988)
4. Cramer, R., Gennaro, R., Schoenmakers, B.: A Secure and Optimally Efficient Multi-Authority Election Scheme. In: Fumy, W. (ed.) EUROCRYPT 1997. LNCS, vol. 1233, pp. 103–118. Springer, Heidelberg (1997)
5. Canetti, R.: Universally Composable Security, The ePrint archive, www.iacr.org
6. Cramer, R., Damgård, I.: Multiparty Computation, an Introduction. In: Contemporary Cryptology, Advanced courses in Mathematics CRM Barcelona. Birkhäuser, Basel
7. Chaum, D., Crépeau, C., Damgård, I.: Multi-Party Unconditionally Secure Protocols. In: Proc. of ACM STOC 1998, pp. 11–19 (1988)

8. Cramer, R., Damgård, I., Maurer, U.: Multiparty Computations from Any Linear Secret Sharing Scheme. In: Preneel, B. (ed.) EUROCRYPT 2000. LNCS, vol. 1807, pp. 316–334. Springer, Heidelberg (2000)
9. Cramer, R., Damgård, I., Dziembowski, S., Hirt, M., Rabin, T.: Efficient Multiparty Computations With Dishonest Minority. In: Stern, J. (ed.) EUROCRYPT 1999. LNCS, vol. 1592, p. 311. Springer, Heidelberg (1999)
10. Dasgupta, P., Hammond, P., Maskin, E.: The Implementation of Social Choice Rules: Some General Results on Incentive Compatibility. Review of Economic Studies 46, 27–42 (1979)
11. Damgård, I.B., Nielsen, J.B.: Universally Composable Efficient Multiparty Computation from Threshold Homomorphic Encryption. In: Boneh, D. (ed.) CRYPTO 2003. LNCS, vol. 2729, pp. 247–264. Springer, Heidelberg (2003)
12. Damgård, I., Jurik, M.: A Generalisation, a Simplification and Some Applications of Paillier's Probabilistic Public-Key System. In: Public Key Cryptography 2001, pp. 119–136 (2001)
13. Damgård, I.B., Fitzi, M., Kiltz, E., Nielsen, J.B., Toft, T.: Unconditionally Secure Constant-Rounds Multi-party Computation for Equality, Comparison, Bits and Exponentiation. In: Halevi, S., Rabin, T. (eds.) TCC 2006. LNCS, vol. 3876, pp. 285–304. Springer, Heidelberg (2006)
14. Damgård, I., Thorbek, R.: Non-Interactive Proofs for Integer Multiplication. In: Naor, M. (ed.) EUROCRYPT 2007. LNCS, vol. 4515, pp. 412–429. Springer, Heidelberg (2007)
15. Gibbard, A.: Manipulation of Voting Schemes: A General Result. Econometrica 41, 587–601 (1973)
16. Goldreich, O., Micali, S., Wigderson, A.: How to Play Any Mental Game or a Completeness Theorem for Protocols with Honest Majority. In: Proc. of ACM STOC 1987, pp. 218–229 (1987)
17. Gennaro, R., Rabin, M., Rabin, T.: Simplified VSS and Fast-Track Multiparty Computations with Applications to Threshold Cryptography. In: Proc of ACM PODC 1998 (1998)
18. Hirt, M., Maurer, U.: Complete Characterization of Adversaries Tolerable in General Multiparty Computations. In: Proc. ACM PODC 1997, pp. 25–34 (1997)
19. Myerson, R.B.: Incentives Compatibility and the Bargaining Problem. Econometrica 47, 61–73 (1979)
20. Nielsen, J.D., Schwartzbach, M.I.: A domain-specific programming language for secure multipartycomputation. In: Proceedings of Programming Languages and Security (PLAS). ACM Press, New York (2007)
21. Rabin, T., Ben-Or, M.: Verifiable Secret Sharing and Multiparty Protocols with Honest majority. In: Proc. ACM STOC 1989, pp. 73–85 (1989)

Coercion Resistant End-to-end Voting*

Ryan W. Gardner, Sujata Garera, and Aviel D. Rubin

Johns Hopkins University, Baltimore MD 21218, USA

Abstract. End-to-end voting schemes have shown considerable promise for allowing voters to verify that tallies are accurate. At the same time, the threat of coercion has generally been considered only when voting devices are honest, and in many schemes, voters can be forced or incentivized to cast votes of an adversary's choice. In this paper, we examine the issue of voter coercion and identify one example method for coercing voters in a scheme by Benaloh. To address such attacks, we present a formal definition of coercion resistance for end-to-end voting. We then present a new scheme, extended from Benaloh's, that is provably coercion resistant. In addition to providing accuracy and coercion resistance, our scheme emphasizes ease-of-use for the voter.

Keywords: end-to-end voting, coercion, privacy, cryptography.

1 Introduction

Many parts of the world have been witnessing a rapid adoption of electronic voting systems to address the usability issues of the paper ballot and tally votes more conveniently. While these systems have offered many benefits, they have also generated a large number of new security concerns. Several studies have independently analyzed electronic voting systems and shown that they are vulnerable to a multitude of threats [1,2,3,4,5,6,7,8]. As these machines are added to an already unverifiable voting process, voters today are left with very few assurances of the integrity of their recorded votes or their tabulation.

To address these concerns, several researchers have explored the notion of end-to-end voting schemes [9,10,11,12,13,14]. These schemes are designed to allow each voter to publicly verify both that her vote is accurately recorded and that all recorded votes are correctly tallied in the final sums [15,16,17]. Specifically, end-to-end voting schemes aim to provide these properties without trusting the software that runs on the voting machines.

Although end-to-end voting schemes have potential to greatly increase the transparency and integrity of elections, strong privacy guarantees are generally secondary foci and have often been missed. For example, Moran and Naor [18] identify a vote buying attack in the Punchscan system as it is demonstrated [19]. Karlof *et al.* [17] identify possible means for revealing voter and vote information in schemes by Neff [9] and Chaum [10]. Other examples exist [20,21,22]. However, privacy is critical and not independent of integrity. Websites dedicated to the

---

* This work was supported by the National Science Foundation grant CNS-0524252.

R. Dingledine and P. Golle (Eds.): FC 2009, LNCS 5628, pp. 344–361, 2009.

sale of votes have been found on the Internet [23], and people have been caught selling votes on eBay [24,25]. Selling is simply a voluntary form of coercion.

In this paper, we explore the issue of coercion in end-to-end voting protocols. We examine a scheme by Benaloh [13,12] and describe a possible method for coercing voters in that scheme. We then present the first formal definition of coercion resistance we are aware of that encompasses a voter's actions at the polls and the final output from casting a ballot in the end-to-end voting setting. We construct a new end-to-end voting scheme that is provably coercion resistant. The scheme provides verifiability to the voter at a low cost. In order to achieve these guarantees, we assume at least one of each election's candidate parties is honest and rely on a private channel [21] between the voting device and the parties, which could be instantiated by an inexpensive smart card, for example.

In addition to security, our scheme's primary goal is to maintain the simplicity of the voting process for the voter. By building on the technique by Benaloh [13,12], our scheme requires a typical voter only to answer a single, simple question in addition to making her ballot selections. The assurances provided by the scheme are then probabilistic. We begin with related work, including a description of Benaloh's scheme, continue with our new definition and construction, and end with some brief practical considerations.

2   Related Work

Significant research has been conducted in cryptographic voting over the past 2 decades. The first voting schemes are pioneered independently by Yao [26], Benaloh [27], and Chaum [28] although they allow a voter to prove how she voted to a coercer. Benaloh and Tuinstra [21] introduce the notion of receipt freeness and describe a secret ballot election protocol that relies on private channels between some parties and utilizes a threshold scheme. Their scheme is later shown not to be receipt free by Hirt and Sako [22]. Sako et al. propose a receipt free system that uses mix networks [15]. In their scheme, however, a coercer can force a voter to vote randomly. A scheme by Magkos et al. relies on a tamper resistant smart card which collaborates with the voter to produce a valid encryption of her vote [29] but requires significant voter participation.

Chaum [10] and Neff [9] independently create the first electronic voting schemes that do not require the voter to possess any computational device to verify her vote. Chaum's scheme [10] relies on visual cryptography and provides the voter with a receipt that is a visual share of her cast ballot. Neff, on the other hand, introduces a scheme that encodes the voter's choice in an encrypted array of bits [9]. It further commits to the voter's choice by displaying a short string on the voting screen. Verification depends on the voter's ability to compare short strings. Karlof et al. analyze Chaum's and Neff's schemes [17] and discover a number of potential problems in them from a system's perspective, including possible methods for adversaries to leak information about voters' choices.

Riva et al. recently propose a voting scheme which requires the voter to prepare her ballot prior to arriving at the polls [11]. Unlike Neff's and Chaum's schemes, this scheme attempts to maintain vote secrecy even with respect to the voting booth.[1] Benaloh introduces the notion of auditing a completely marked ballot [12,13,30]. We discuss his scheme further in Section 4.

Prêt à Voter, introduced by Ryan et al., is a paper based scheme [31,32]. It is similar in concept to Chaum's scheme but does not rely on visual cryptography. Ryan et al. extend their scheme to use Pallier encryption [33] although Xia et al. examine the scheme and show that it can leak information about voters' intentions under several circumstances [34]. Rivest and Smith present 3 paper based voting protocols [14] that do not use any cryptography although the 2 schemes that allow the voter to verify her *own* vote require her to fill 3 separate ballots. Scantegrity II [35], introduced by Chaum et al., extends the original Scantegrity proposal [36] to avoid the need to locate physical ballots to resolve voter disputes. This paper based system relies on the use of invisible ink to allow each voter to verify the inclusion of her vote by looking up a confirmation code.

3   Notation

We consider a voting protocol to consist of interactions between several entities: a voter $\mathcal{V}$, a ballot marking machine $\mathcal{M}$, a public bulletin board $\mathcal{B}$,[2] and a receipt $\mathcal{R}$ (which is also often the physical ballot). We write $\mathcal{A} \xmapsto{x} \mathcal{B}$ to describe entity $\mathcal{A}$ sending datum x to entity $\mathcal{B}$. The notation $x \in_R A$ is used to denote a variable x drawn uniformly at random from set A. Further, we write $\mathsf{poly}(k)$ to denote any polynomial function of k and $\mathsf{negl}(k)$ to denote any function that is negligible in k.[3] Let v represent a voter's candidate vote or ballot.

In addition to the above notation, we assume the existence of 3 functions:

- $\mathsf{KeyGenEnc}(1^k, N_T)$: a key generation function that takes as input security parameter k and generates a public encryption key e and N_T shares of a corresponding distributed private key $\{d_1, \ldots, d_{N_T}\}$.
- $\mathsf{Enc}_{e,r}(p)$: an IND-CCA2 [37] secure encryption function that accepts a public key e, a random value r, and plaintext p. It gives ciphertext c as output.
- $\mathsf{EncVerify}(p, c, e, r)$: a ballot verification function that checks that encrypted ballot c is a valid encryption of plaintext vote p using public key e and randomness r. It returns SUCCESS if $c = \mathsf{Enc}_{e,r}(p)$ and FAILURE otherwise.

4   Benaloh's Scheme

We examine the recent cryptographic voting scheme of Benaloh [13,12] as an example for this paper. We focus on the scheme because it has a minimal impact on the traditional voting process while providing voters with guarantees of the tally's accuracy. At the same time, we find that, like several other schemes, its implicit use of probabilistic cryptographic operations enables possible coercion.

---

[1] An attack similar to one we describe on Benaloh's scheme is actually possible here since the scheme implicitly trusts the machine to produce truly random values.

[2] Generally this is thought of as a web-page on the Internet.

[3] A function $\mathsf{negl}(k)$ is negligible in k if $\forall d \geq 1 \; \exists \ell > 0 \; \forall k > \ell \; \mathsf{negl}(k) < \frac{1}{k^d}$.

4.1 Security Model

Benaloh states that we can never *guarantee* voter privacy, citing an example that one can never prove that hidden cameras are not installed at the voting booth [13]. He is correct in the absolute sense and considers strict privacy only in the setting where parties and machines are honest. Despite the impossibility of *unconditional* certainties in practice, however, it remains important to consider privacy in the face of dishonest machines. We can still reduce the types of attacks adversaries can perform and minimize threats of large scale coercion by applying a stronger theoretical model. Ideally, end-to-end voting schemes achieve the following properties:

Individual Verifiability- The voter should be able to verify that her intentions were accurately recorded in her cast ballot.
Universal Verifiability- Voters should be able to verify that all cast ballots were properly included in the final tallies and came from legitimate voters.
Mandatory Privacy- No one should be able to learn how another voter voted with certainty even if the voter would like that person to know.

4.2 Overview of the Scheme

We now present an overview of the steps involved in an election under the Benaloh scheme [13,12]. Since the original description of the scheme is informal, we necessarily make some assumptions about the details, particularly with respect to the encryption process. However, we believe our description is accurate with respect to the intentions of the scheme. We focus on the casting process and summarize the tallying and verification somewhat more informally since they are straightforward and less critically relevant to this study.

Initialization
Before the start of election day, a group of N_T trusties runs $\mathsf{KeyGenEnc}(1^k, N_T)$ with a k of their choice, distributes private key shares $d_1, \ldots, d_{N_T}$, and writes the public encryption key e to the ballot marking machine $\mathcal{M}$.

Ballot Marking

1. $\mathcal{V} \xmapsto{v} \mathcal{M}$: The voter enters her candidate selections v into the ballot marking machine.
2. $\mathcal{M} \xmapsto{c=\mathsf{Enc}_{e,r}(v)} \mathcal{R}$: The ballot marking machine generates a random r and prints a corresponding encryption of the voter's alleged ballot to a receipt.
3. $\mathcal{M} \xmapsto{\text{"Cast vote?"}} \mathcal{V}$: The machine asks the voter if she wants to cast her vote.

Option 1: Auditing

1. $\mathcal{V} \xmapsto{\text{"No"}} \mathcal{M}$: The voter optionally indicates that she would not like to cast this ballot. (Rather, she is choosing to audit the machine with it.)

2. $\mathcal{M} \overset{r,v}{\longmapsto} \mathcal{R}$: The ballot marking machine reveals the randomness r used for encryption and adds it to the receipt. It also prints the plaintext ballot. This marks the ballot invalid for casting. The voter can verify the plaintext and take the receipt home to test that $\mathsf{EncVerify}(v, c, e, r)$ returns SUCCESS.

The voter may choose to repeat the ballot marking and optional auditing steps on new ballots an unbounded number of times (even after she has cast her vote) to increase her certainty that the machine is behaving honestly. (See Section 7 for a brief discussion on the effectiveness of such auditing.)

Option 2: Casting

1. $\mathcal{V} \overset{\text{"Yes"}}{\longmapsto} \mathcal{M}$: The voter indicates that she would like to cast this ballot.
2. $\mathcal{R} \overset{c}{\longmapsto} \mathcal{B}$: The voter takes her valid receipt to a ballot casting station where it is used to cast her encrypted ballot, and it is posted to the public bulletin board. (She also presents any necessary identification.)

Tallying and Verification
When the voting period has ended, a group of trustees anonymizes the posted ballots through a mix-net [38,39,40]. Each trustee re-encrypts all the ballots and posts them back to the public bulletin board in random order along with a zero-knowledge proof [41] of correctness. Finally, a sufficiently large subset of the trustees uses a threshold scheme [42] to jointly decrypt the ballots, Again, a proof is provided with each decryption to allow public verification. Each voter can use her receipt $\mathcal{R}$ to verify that her vote has been cast and counted correctly.

4.3   Compromising Voter Privacy

The voting and verification processes of Benaloh's scheme are simple and, when described informally, seem to accomplish the goals of end-to-end voting clearly. However, the scheme's need to make random choices can be exploited to compromise voter privacy. One possible attack consists of an adversary replacing the code for obtaining the randomness used in the scheme's encryptions with a pseudorandom number generator, for which she exclusively knows the key. Such an attack effectively gives the adversary knowledge of the randomness r used in each encryption $\mathsf{Enc}_{e,r}(v)$ and allows her to determine the plaintext of each posted encrypted ballot since the message space is likely to be very small. As a result, such an adversary can also coerce voters into casting particular votes.

Another attack involves the adversary compromising the machine to actually encode information into the ciphertexts c themselves by trying new encryptions until a desired ciphertext is obtained. For example, in one naive approach, the parity of c could indicate a vote for republican or democrat. Similar observations were made by Karlof *et al.* [17] with respect to possible subliminal channels enabled by the randomness used in the cryptographic voting scheme of Andrew Neff [9]. Obviously, more sophisticated approaches could encode many more bits and information about the ballot in a more covert manner. Similar attacks are also possible against other proposed schemes [20,11].

5   Coercion Resistance

With nuanced attacks that compromise voter privacy such as those against Benaloh's scheme, the issue of coercion resistance needs to be treated rigorously. Several definitions for coercion resistance have been proposed in the literature. Juels *et al.* offer a definition centered around voters' potential use of fake keys to avoid coercion and is more specifically tailored for coercion resistance in a remote voting setting where machines are assumed uncompromised [43]. It also does not allow the adversary to adaptively interact with the voting system. Teague *et al.* offer a nice definition that considers the information content of the plaintext votes (but no other output from the protocol) [44]. For example, they consider attacks where an adversary requests that a voter fill out a specific permutation of votes on a portion of the ballot to identify it as belonging to that voter. Benaloh and Tuinstra introduce the notion of "receipt freeness" for end-to-end voting protocols although they do not give a formal definition [21]. Moran and Naor subsequently define receipt-freeness based on an ideal functionality of a voting protocol [20], extending from the work of Canetti and Gennaro [45]. However, their definition focuses on the adversary's view of a voter's interactions with a machine and allows privacy leaks in the final output of the protocol, such as the ones we describe.

We introduce a new definition of a coercion resistant vote casting protocol. Intuitively, it requires that an adversary who can adaptively interact with the protocol cannot distinguish between a vote cast using inputs of her choice and a vote cast using inputs of the voter's choice, including any possible vote. Alternatively, if the protocol is not functioning honestly, it can be detected by the voter (with probability varying by scheme).

Our definition is more direct than previous definitions, and by separating the vote casting from the entire voting protocol, we are able to address coercion enabled by examination of the protocol's final output. Note that our definition does not account for privacy leaks in the plaintext ballots themselves, such as information that would allow a coercer to identify ballots like specific permutations of votes or write-in candidate strings. This problem is independent of the one we examine, and we believe it is addressable by combining other approaches using disjoint definitions such as the one by Teague *et al.* [44][4].

We consider a vote casting protocol to consist of a series of interactions with a vote caster C^{*}[5] that takes a set of ordered inputs X, minimally including some ballot choice or vote v. The caster's output is an ordered set Ψ including some encoding of the voter's ballot c. We also introduce what we refer to as a unique seed $s \in \mathbb{S}$. The seed s is part of the vote casting input X. We refer to the set of all output that *could* be made available to an adversary from an interaction with C^{*} (if, for example, a voter were forced to reveal it) as $\Psi_{\mathcal{A}}$.[6] Let $\mathcal{P}$ represent a set of all public information.

---

[4] One trivial solution is to simply use separate logical ballots for each race.

[5] In practice, this might be one or several devices, poll workers, etc.

[6] This would minimally include data such as that available on voter receipts and posted to public bulletin boards.

For our end-to-end voting scenario, we let C^* also produce a proof of correctness π. To verify the correctness of a cast vote and to evade coercion, we refer to two functions respectively:

- BallotVerify($X, \Psi, \pi, \mathcal{P}$): takes the vote casting input X, the caster's output Ψ, the proof of correctness π, and public information $\mathcal{P}$. It returns SUCCESS if Ψ is a valid output for input X with proof π and FAILURE otherwise.
- GenerateInput($X_{\mathcal{A}}, s, v$): outputs a coercion resistant vote casting input $X_{\mathcal{V}}$ with vote v and seed s when an adversary demands that the voter use input $X_{\mathcal{A}}$ instead.

We write our definition in terms of a game between several algorithms (PTMs): an adversary $\mathcal{A}$, a challenger $\mathcal{G}$, a vote caster C^*, and a verifier $\mathcal{Z}$. The adversary's goal is to distinguish between the visible output of the vote casting protocol for 2 distinct votes. Formally:

Security Game: Indistinguishability of Encoded Votes (IEV)

1. An initialization phase establishes public data $\mathcal{P}$.
2. $\mathcal{A}$ adaptively sends inputs X to C^* and obtains corresponding outputs Ψ and π. $\mathcal{Z}$ is also given each (X, Ψ, π) tuple.
3. $\mathcal{A}$ selects an input X_0 including vote v_0, with the constraint that X_0's seed s' has not been the seed in any of $\mathcal{A}$'s previous queries to C^*. $\mathcal{A}$ also selects a second vote v_1[7] to be part of an input $X_1 = $ GenerateInput(X_0, s', v_1). $\mathcal{A}$ sends X_0 and X_1 to $\mathcal{G}$.
4. $\mathcal{G}$ chooses a random bit b and sends X_b to C^*. C^* gives $\mathcal{A}$ the visible output $\Psi_{b,\mathcal{A}}$ corresponding to the input X_b. It also gives the corresponding tuple (X_b, Ψ_b, π_b) to $\mathcal{Z}$.
5. $\mathcal{A}$ again adaptively sends inputs X to C^* under the constraint that s' is not the seed of any X and obtains corresponding outputs Ψ and π. $\mathcal{Z}$ receives each (X, Ψ, π).
6. $\mathcal{Z}$ runs BallotVerify($X, \Psi, \pi, \mathcal{P}$) with public $\mathcal{P}$ for each tuple (X, Ψ, π) it was given. If BallotVerify returns SUCCESS for each tuple, $\mathcal{Z}$ outputs $z = $ SUCCESS. Otherwise, it outputs $z = $ FAILURE.
7. $\mathcal{A}$ outputs b', its best guess of the value b.

The adversary's advantage in the game $\mathsf{adv}_{IEV}(\mathcal{A})$ is defined as:

$$\mathsf{adv}_{IEV}(\mathcal{A}) = Pr\left((b' = b) \cap (z = \text{SUCCESS})\right) - \frac{1}{2}.$$

Definition 1. *A vote casting protocol with security parameter k is coercion resistant if for all probabilistic poly(k) time algorithms $\mathcal{A}$ and all probabilistic vote casters C^*, $\mathsf{adv}_{IEV}(\mathcal{A}) < \mathsf{negl}(k)$.*

Notice that in this definition, the coercion resistance of a protocol depends entirely on the BallotVerify function and a correct GenerateInput. Although initially

---

[7] This is analogous to the voter's "desired vote".

it may seem counterintuitive to discard the entire vote encoding process, the threat model our definition aims to address is one where the caster C^* (such as a voting machine) may be completely corrupted by an adversary. In other words, the BallotVerify function of the scheme must lock C^* into a scheme where an adversary cannot distinguish the output from different votes. On the other hand, also note that our definition models the caster as something without any post-election communication with the adversary. Unfortunately, this is largely unavoidable since, for the most part, each voter must[8] divulge her vote to the caster. We may be able to approximate this model in practice by building voting machines with an exact, minimum amount of writable memory although this possibility requires more rigorous exploration. Nevertheless, our primary objective is to remove information that could be used to compromise a voter's privacy from the *public* domain. A significantly more powerful adversary is required to launch large scale coercion attacks by communicating with voting machines after they are used than an adversary who can determine votes by examining public information.

6   A Coercion Resistant End-to-end Voting Scheme

We now present a construction for a coercion resistant end-to-end voting scheme. It is an extension of Benaloh's [12,13] (Section 4) and roots the source of all entropy required of the scheme in a small number of keys distributed among parties with conflicting interests, which we assume to be all the candidate parties.[9] Voters can then verify uniquely correct outputs, and the scheme is secure as long as at least one candidate party behaves honestly. To utilize the key provided by each party, we rely on the existence of a private channel [21] between the voting machine and each party. In practice, this could be instantiated by inexpensive trusted hardware such as smart cards. Again, in addition to providing coercion resistance, our primary aim is to keep the voting process as simple as possible for the voter.

We begin with our assumptions and continue to a description of the vote casting protocol and a security proof.

6.1   Preliminaries

In addition to the variables and entities listed in Section 3, we also refer to N_C, the number of candidate parties, and T_i for $i = 1, \ldots, N_C$, an entity with a private channel to the voting machine and whose key, K_i, is written by candidate

---

[8] A scheme proposed by Riva and Ta-Shma [11] is one exception to this although it is arguably quite impractical in terms of complexity for the voter. The scheme is also susceptible to an attack very similar to the one we describe against Benaloh's.

[9] The entropy could be distributed among any variety of parties, but for the sake of concreteness, we assume it is distributed among each candidate's party in our descriptions.

party i. In practice, each entity $\mathcal{T}_i$ could be instantiated by an inexpensive smart card inserted into the ballot marking machine.[10] We write $\mathbb{S}$ to refer to the set of all valid ballot serial numbers s.

Our construction utilizes the verifiable random function of Dodis and Yampolskiy [46]. Its security relies on several assumptions. First, it requires an IND-CCA2 secure [37] public key encryption function $\mathsf{Enc}_{e,r} : \{0,1\}^* \rightarrow \{0,1\}^*$.[11] The construction also depends on the existence of groups $\mathbb{G}$ (of prime order $p > 2^k$) and $\mathbb{G}_1$ such that an (admissible) bilinear map exists between the groups and for which the the q-decisional bilinear Diffie-Hellman inversion assumption (q-DBDHI) [47] holds. We briefly review each of these below:

Definition 2. *An (admissible) bilinear map is a function* $e : \mathbb{G} \times \mathbb{G} \rightarrow \mathbb{G}_1$ *with the following 3 properties:*

1. *Bilinear:* $\forall g_1, g_2 \in \mathbb{G}$ *and* $x, y \in \mathbb{Z}$, $e(g_1^x, g_2^y) = e(g_1, g_2)^{xy}$.
2. *Non-degenerate:* $e(g, g) \neq 1$.
3. *Computable: There is an efficient (polynomial time) algorithm to compute* $e(g_1, g_2)$ $\forall g_1, g_2 \in \mathbb{G}$.

Suppose $\mathbb{G}$ and $\mathbb{G}_1$ are groups with an admissible bilinear map e and $|\mathbb{G}| = p$ with prime $p > 2^k$ and g a generator of $\mathbb{G}$. The q-DBDHI problem asks an algorithm $\mathcal{A}_D$ to distinguish $e(g, g)^{1/x}$ from random $\Gamma \in \mathbb{G}_1$ given $g, g^x, \ldots, g^{(x^q)}$. Formally, let $\beta_{0,D} = e(g, g)^{1/x}$ and $\beta_{1,D} = \Gamma$. If $b \in_R \{0, 1\}$, $\mathcal{A}_D$'s advantage $\mathsf{adv}_{DBDHI}(\mathcal{A}_D)$ is defined as

$$\mathsf{adv}_{DBDHI}(\mathcal{A}_D) = Pr\left(\mathcal{A}_D(g, g^x, \ldots, g^{(x^q)}, \beta_{b,D}) = b\right) - \frac{1}{2}$$

where the probability is over $\mathcal{A}_D$'s random tape and the choice of $x \in \mathbb{Z}_p^*$ and $\Gamma \in \mathbb{G}_1$.

Definition 3. *The* q-decisional bilinear Diffie-Hellman inversion assumption (q-DBDHI) [47] *for groups* $\mathbb{G}$ *and* $\mathbb{G}_1$ *with an admissible bilinear map* e *states that no algorithm* $\mathcal{A}_D$ *can win game* q-DBDHI *with advantage* $\mathsf{adv}_{DBDHI}(\mathcal{A}_D) > negl(k)$ *in time* $t_D \leq poly(k)$.

Certain groups over elliptic curves or abelian varieties are believed to satisfy these properties with bilinear maps that can be constructed from the Weil or Tate pairings [46,48,49,50].

We also constrain the valid ballot serial numbers $\mathbb{S}$ to a set $\mathbb{S} \subset \mathbb{Z}_p^*$, $|\mathbb{S}| \leq poly(k)$ for a protocol security parameter k.[12] Lastly, our scheme requires an

---

[10] Smart cards allow writing of keys such that they can never be read off the cards.

[11] For the complete voting process, the function must also allow publicly provable re-encryption or specific homomorphic operations to enable anonymous tallying although, in this paper, we go into depth on only the ballot casting phase.

[12] Although this size constraint has no practical effect on our scheme, it is necessary for our proof of security. Dodis and Yampolskiy show that an approximately 1000 bit $p = |\mathbb{G}|$ is sufficient for an $\mathbb{S}$ with $|\mathbb{S}| = 2^{160}$ as we use it [46].

efficiently computable mapping $\varphi : \mathbb{G}_1 \to \mathbb{H}$ where $\mathbb{H}$ is the partial domain of the encryption function $\mathsf{Enc}_{e,r}(v)$ that pertains to r, and φ has a uniform probability distribution over $\mathbb{H}$.[13]

6.2   Vote Casting Protocol

We now outline our scheme, presenting the steps required of an election. Again, we focus primarily on the ballot casting portion of the scheme.

Initialization

Prior to the election, a group of N_T trusties computes $\mathsf{KeyGenEnc}(1^k, N_T)$ with a k of their choice, distributes private key shares $d_1, \ldots, d_{N_T}$, and writes the public encryption key e to the ballot marking machine $\mathcal{M}$. Each of N_C candidate parties i also selects a $K_i \in \mathbb{Z}_p^*$ independently and uniformly at random, and writes secret key K_i to $\mathcal{T}_i$ (e.g. a smartcard, which is inserted into the machine for election day). The party sets the public key to $\lambda_i = g^{K_i}$. All public keys are made available on the public bulletin board $\mathcal{B}$. Physical ballots/receipts $\mathcal{R}$ are created and a unique serial number is printed to each.

Ballot Marking

1. $\mathcal{R} \overset{s}{\longmapsto} \mathcal{M}$: The ballot marking machine reads a serial number s off of the voter's receipt (i.e. a new, blank ballot with a printed serial number).
2. $\mathcal{V} \overset{v}{\longmapsto} \mathcal{M}$: The voter enters her candidate selections into the ballot marking machine.
3. $\mathcal{M} \overset{s}{\longmapsto} \mathcal{T}_i$: The ballot marking machine sends the serial number to each $\mathcal{T}_i$.
4. $\mathcal{T}_i \overset{\pi_i = g^{1/(s+K_i)}}{\longmapsto} \mathcal{M}$: Each $\mathcal{T}_i$ computes a pseudorandomness proof value $\pi_i = \mathsf{GenProof}_i(s)$ and sends it to the ballot marking machine where:
   - $\mathsf{GenProof}_i(s) = g^{1/(s+K_i)}$.
5. $\mathcal{M}$ computes $\mu = \prod_{i=1}^{N_C} \pi_i$ and pseudorandom value $r' = \varphi(e(g, \mu))$.
6. $\mathcal{M} \overset{c = \mathsf{Enc}_{e,r'}(v)}{\longmapsto} \mathcal{R}$: The ballot marking machine encrypts the voter's alleged ballot v using pseudorandom value r' and prints it to the receipt.
7. $\mathcal{M} \overset{\text{``Cast vote?''}}{\longmapsto} \mathcal{V}$: The ballot marking machine asks the voter if she would like to cast this ballot.

Option 1: Auditing

1. $\mathcal{V} \overset{\text{``No''}}{\longmapsto} \mathcal{M}$: The voter optionally indicates that she would not like to cast this ballot. (Rather, she is choosing to audit the machine with it.)
2. $\mathcal{M} \overset{s,v,c,\pi_1,\ldots,\pi_{N_C}}{\longmapsto} \mathcal{B}$: The ballot marking machine reveals proofs π_i for the pseudorandom values from each $\mathcal{T}_i$ to the public bulletin board. It also posts the encrypted and plaintext ballots c, v along with the serial number s.

---

[13] I.e. $\forall r_1, r_2 \in \mathbb{H}$ $Pr(\varphi(x) = r_1) = Pr(\varphi(x) = r_2)$ over the random choice of $x \in \mathbb{G}_1$. This property would likely be approximated in practice with a negligible error (varying inverse exponentially with $\log|\mathbb{G}_1|$) since achieving it exactly requires that $|\mathbb{G}_1| = N|\mathbb{H}|$ for some $N \in \mathbb{Z}$. For readability, however, we assume complete uniformity.

3. $\mathcal{M} \overset{v}{\longmapsto} \mathcal{R}$: The machine appends the plaintext ballot to the receipt, so the voter can verify its correctness. This marks the ballot invalid for casting.

4. $\mathcal{V}$ keeps her receipt $\mathcal{R}$ as evidence of her (uncastable) audit vote. To verify its correctness, she, herself needs only check that the printed plaintext accurately represents her vote and that the exact serial number s, plaintext v, and encryption c all appear together on the public bulletin board and that there is no additional information on the receipt.[14]

5. Any verifier, including $\mathcal{V}$, can read the posted data $s, v, c, \pi_1, \ldots, \pi_{N_C}$ off the bulletin board. That person then checks that BallotVerify($s, v, c, \pi_1, \ldots, \pi_{N_C}$, $e, \lambda_1, \ldots, \lambda_{N_C}$) outputs SUCCESS where it is defined as follows:

   - BallotVerify($s, v, c, \pi_1, \ldots, \pi_{N_C}, e, \lambda_1, \ldots, \lambda_{N_C}$): verifies that $e(g^s \lambda_i, \pi_i) = e(g, g)$ for each $i \in \{1, \ldots, N_c\}$. It computes $r' = \varphi\left(e\left(g, \prod_{i=1}^{N_C} \pi_i\right)\right)$ and $c'' = \mathsf{Enc}_{e,r'}(v)$, and checks that $c'' = c$. Lastly it verifies that $s \in \mathbb{S}$. It outputs SUCCESS if all of these checks hold and FAILURE otherwise.

   (Indeed for a correct π_i, $e(g^s \lambda_i, \pi_i) = e(g^s g^{K_i}, g^{1/(s+K_i)}) = e(g, g)$.)

Again, the voter may choose to repeat the ballot marking and optional auditing steps on new ballots an unbounded number of times, even after she has cast her vote. Section 7 discusses the effectiveness of such auditing.

Option 2: Casting

1. $\mathcal{V} \overset{\text{"Yes"}}{\longmapsto} \mathcal{M}$: The voter indicates that she would like to cast this ballot.

2. $\mathcal{R} \overset{c}{\longmapsto} \mathcal{B}$: The voter takes her receipt to a ballot casting station where it is used to cast her encrypted ballot, and it is posted to the bulletin board.

Tallying and Verification

Voters check that no serial number s appears on the bulletin board more than once. Then tallying and verification occur exactly as in Benaloh's scheme (Section 4.2) where encrypted votes are anonymously shuffled and decrypted with corresponding zero-knowledge proofs of correctness, which voters can verify.

6.3   Security

For readability, we first clarify the generic symbols of our definition with the elements of our specific scheme. The correlations are as follows:

- $\mathcal{P} = \{e, \lambda_1, \ldots, \lambda_{N_C}\}$: public information consists of all the public keys
- $X = \{s, v\}$: casting input consists of the ballot serial number and the vote
- $\Psi = \{c\}$: vote casting output consists of the encrypted ballot
- $\pi = \{\pi_1, \ldots, \pi_{N_C}\}$: proofs of correctness consist of the proofs of pseudorandomness from each $\mathcal{T}_i$
- $\Psi_{\mathcal{A}} = \{s, c\}$: adversary's visible output consists of the ballot serial number and the encrypted vote[15]

---

[14] "Helper organizations" may also be created to assist voters in this step, and the voter may go to a "helper organization" sponsored by a party she trusts.

[15] Implicitly, as we make this correlation, we are assuming the existence of a private channel [21] between $\mathcal{V}$ and $\mathcal{M}$, and between $\mathcal{M}$ and each $\mathcal{T}_i$.

- $s = s$: seed is the ballot serial number
- BallotVerify$(X, \Psi, \pi, \mathcal{P})$ = BallotVerify$(s, v, c, \pi_1, \ldots, \pi_{N_C}, e, \lambda_1, \ldots, \lambda_{N_C})$: verification function is directly represented by the one used in our scheme (where we slightly abuse the notation)
- GenerateInput$(X_{\mathcal{A}}, s, v) = \{s, v\}$: our coercion resistant inputs are generated by the trivial function giving the specified input vote and seed

Theorem 1. *For all inputs $X = \{s, v\}$ and public data $\mathcal{P}$, there do not exist two output value pairs $(\Psi, \pi) \neq (\Psi', \pi')$ such that BallotVerify$(X, \Psi, \pi, \mathcal{P})$ = SUCCESS and BallotVerify$(X, \Psi', \pi', \mathcal{P})$ = SUCCESS.*

Proof. Assume there exist $X = \{s, v\}, (\Psi, \pi), (\Psi', \pi')$ for which this does not hold. BallotVerify$(s, v, c, \pi_1, \ldots, \pi_{N_C}, e, \lambda_1, \ldots, \lambda_{N_C})$ recomputes c'' as a deterministic function of $s, v, \pi_1, \ldots, \pi_{N_C}$ and compares to the input c for equivalence. Hence, $\Psi \neq \Psi'$ implies $\pi \neq \pi'$.

Let $\pi = \{\pi_0, \ldots, \pi_{N_C}\}$ and $\pi' = \{\pi'_0, \ldots, \pi'_{N_C}\}$, and without loss of generality, assume $\pi_j \neq \pi'_j$. Because $\forall a, b \in \mathbb{G} \; e(a, b)^{|\mathbb{G}|} = e(a^{|\mathbb{G}|}, b) = e(a^0, b) = e(a, b)^0$, $|\mathbb{G}_1|$ divides $|\mathbb{G}|$. Since $e(g, g) \neq 1$, $|\mathbb{G}_1| = p$ prime. Let $\pi_j = g^x$ and $\pi'_j = g^y$. BallotVerify outputs SUCCESS implies $e(g^s \lambda_j, \pi_j) = e(g^s \lambda_j, \pi'_j) = e(g, g)$, so $e(g^s \lambda_j, g)^x = e(g^s \lambda_j, g)^y$. Thus, $x \equiv y \mod p$, and $\pi_j = \pi'_j$.

Theorem 2. *Suppose the $|\mathbb{S}|$-DBDHI assumption holds and $\mathbb{S}$, the input set of queries to GenProof$_i$, satisfies $|\mathbb{S}| \leq \mathsf{poly}(k)$. Then, if key $K_j, j \in \{1, \ldots, N_C\}$ is chosen independently at random from $\mathbb{Z}_p^*$,[16] and $\mathcal{K} = \{K_1, \ldots, K_{j-1}, K_{j+1}, \ldots, K_{N_C}\}$, for any $\mathsf{poly}(k)$ time algorithm $\mathcal{A}_R$:*

$$Pr\left[b = b'_R \middle| \begin{array}{l} (s, \mathsf{state}) \leftarrow \mathcal{A}_R^{\mathsf{GenProof}_j(\cdot)}(\lambda_j, \mathcal{K}); \\ \beta_{0,R} = \varphi\left(e(g, \prod_{i=1}^{N_C} \mathsf{GenProof}_i(s))\right); \beta_{1,R} \overset{R}{\leftarrow} \mathbb{H}; \\ b \overset{R}{\leftarrow} \{0, 1\}; b'_R \leftarrow \mathcal{A}_R^{\mathsf{GenProof}_j(\cdot)}(\beta_{b,R}, \lambda_j, \mathcal{K}, \mathsf{state}) \end{array}\right] \leq \frac{1}{2} + \mathsf{negl}(k)$$

with the constraint that $\mathcal{A}_R$ never queries GenProof on s.[17]

Proof. Dodis and Yampolskiy prove [46] that for any $\mathsf{poly}(k)$ time algorithm $\mathcal{A}_Y$:

$$Pr\left[b = b'_Y \middle| \begin{array}{l} (s, \mathsf{state}) \leftarrow \mathcal{A}_Y^{\mathsf{GenProof}_j(\cdot)}(\lambda_j); \\ \beta_{0,Y} = e(g, g)^{1/(s+K_j)}; \beta_{1,T} \overset{R}{\leftarrow} \mathbb{G}_1; \\ b \overset{R}{\leftarrow} \{0, 1\}; b'_Y \leftarrow \mathcal{A}_Y^{\mathsf{GenProof}_j(\cdot)}(\beta_{b,Y}, \lambda_j, \mathsf{state}) \end{array}\right] \leq \frac{1}{2} + \mathsf{negl}(k)$$

under the $|\mathbb{S}|$-DBDHI assumption and with the constraints that $\mathcal{A}_Y$ never queries GenProof on s and $|\mathbb{S}| \leq \mathsf{poly}(k)$. (We refer to this property as DY.) Our slightly modified theorem follows.

---

[16] I.e. at least one candidate party behaves honestly.

[17] Intuitively, no adversary with all but one of the party secret keys and the ability to adaptively query GenProof$_j$ with different seeds can efficiently distinguish the generated pseudorandom number r' from a random element in $\mathbb{H}$.

Assume there exists a $t_R \leq \mathsf{poly}(k)$ time algorithm $\mathcal{A}_R$ that contradicts our theorem. Then we can create a $\mathsf{poly}(k)$ time algorithm $\mathcal{A}_Y$ that interacts with $\mathcal{A}_R$ to contradict DY: Let K_i be any keys $K_i \in \mathbb{Z}_p^*$ $\forall i = 1,\ldots,N_C, i \neq j$ and known to $\mathcal{A}_Y$. Assume key K_j, unknown to $\mathcal{A}_Y$, is chosen independently and at random from $\mathbb{Z}_p^*$. $\mathcal{A}_Y$'s goal is to use $\mathcal{A}_R$ to distinguish $e(g,g)^{1/(s+K_j)}$ from a random element of $\mathbb{G}_1$ with non-negligible advantage.

$\mathcal{A}_Y$ responds to each of $\mathcal{A}_R$'s queries to $\mathsf{GenProof}_j$ by querying its own $\mathsf{GenProof}_j$ oracle and passing the response to $\mathcal{A}_R$. When $\mathcal{A}_R$ is ready for its challenge $\beta_{b,R}$, $\mathcal{A}_Y$ requests its challenge value $\beta_{b,Y}$ with $\mathcal{A}_R$'s query s. $\mathcal{A}_Y$ replies to $\mathcal{A}_R$ with $\beta_{b,R} = \varphi\Big(e(g,g)^{\sum_{i \neq j} 1/(s+K_i)} \beta_{b,Y}\Big)$. Because $\varphi(x)$ has a uniform probability distribution over x and $\beta_{1,Y}$ is chosen independently and randomly from $\mathbb{G}_1$, $\beta_{1,R}$ is a uniformly randomly chosen element of $\mathbb{H}$.

$$\beta_{0,R} = \varphi\left(e(g,g)^{\sum_{i \neq j} 1/(s+K_i)} e(g,g)^{1/(s+K_j)}\right)$$

$$= \varphi\left(e(g,g^{\sum_{i=1}^{N_C} 1/(s+K_i)})\right) = \varphi\left(e(g, \textstyle\prod_{i=1}^{N_C} \mathsf{GenProof}_i(s))\right)$$

Thus, $\mathcal{A}_R$'s bit b from the Theorem 2 simulation corresponds exactly to the challenger's bit b, and $\mathcal{A}_Y$, which replies to the challenger with $\mathcal{A}_R$'s output $b_Y' = b_R'$, is correct ($b_Y' = b$) exactly when $\mathcal{A}_R$ is. $\mathcal{A}_Y$'s work consists mainly of of responding to $\mathcal{A}_R$'s queries on $\mathsf{GenProof}_j$, so its run-time is bounded by $t_Y < n_1 t_R + n_2$ for some constants n_1, n_2, and therefore $t_Y \leq \mathsf{poly}(k)$.

Theorem 3. *Suppose at least one key K_j is selected independently at random from $\mathbb{Z}_p^*$ and is kept secret, $\mathsf{Enc}_{e,r}(\cdot)$ is an IND-CPA secure public key encryption function [51,52],[18] groups $\mathbb{G}$, $\mathbb{G}_1$ have an admissible bilinear map such that the $|\mathbb{S}|$-DBDHI assumption holds and $|\mathbb{G}| = p$, a function $\varphi : \mathbb{G}_1 \to \mathbb{H}$ exists as described above, and the set of possible seeds $\mathbb{S}$ satisfies $|\mathbb{S}| \leq \mathsf{poly}(k)$ (for security parameter k). Then the scheme presented in Section 6.2 is coercion resistant.*

Proof. We briefly review IND-CPA security for a public key encryption function (that uses a random number r as part of its input) below. It simply states that for any $\mathsf{poly}(k)$ time algorithm $\mathcal{A}_C$:

$$Pr\left[b = b_C' \middle| \begin{array}{l} (e,d) \leftarrow \mathsf{KeyGenEnc}(1^k, N_T); \\ (m_0, m_1, \mathsf{state}) \leftarrow \mathcal{A}_C(e); b \xleftarrow{R} \{0,1\}; r \xleftarrow{R} \mathbb{H} \\ \beta_C = \mathsf{Enc}_{e,r}(m_b); b_C' \leftarrow \mathcal{A}_C(e, \beta_C, \mathsf{state}) \end{array}\right] \leq \frac{1}{2} + \mathsf{negl}(k).$$

$\mathcal{A}$ cannot win IEV if $\mathsf{BallotVerify}$ outputs FAILURE. Hence, by Theorem 1, $\mathcal{A}$ wins IEV implies that $\mathcal{C}^*$ provides outputs $(\Psi, \pi) = (\{c = \mathsf{Enc}_{e,r'}(v)\}, \{\pi_i = \mathsf{GenProof}_i(s)\}_{i=1,\ldots,N_C})$ where $r' = \varphi\left(e(g, \textstyle\prod_{i=1}^{N_C} \pi_i)\right)$ for each input $X = \{s, v\}$.

---

[18] The use of an IND-CCA2 encryption scheme [37] for our construction is important for the decryption and tallying process of the scheme, which we separate from the ballot casting and do not analyze in depth in the paper. However, to be precise, coercion resistance of the ballot casting requires only IND-CPA security. Of course, IND-CCA2 security implies IND-CPA security.

From here we see that IEV closely models the CPA game where the random r is replaced by a pseudorandom r'. If we have a $t_{\mathcal{A}} < \mathsf{poly}(k)$ time algorithm $\mathcal{A}$ where $\mathsf{adv}_{IEV}(\mathcal{A}) > \mathsf{negl}(k)$, then we can either create an algorithm $\mathcal{A}_C$ that contradicts the IND-CPA security of Enc or an algorithm $\mathcal{A}_R$ that contradicts Theorem 2. Assume such an $\mathcal{A}$ exists. Let $K_i, i \neq j$ be any elements of $\mathbb{Z}_p^*$ known to $\mathcal{A}$, $\mathcal{A}_C$, and $\mathcal{A}_R$ and let $K_j \in_R \mathbb{Z}_p^*$ be known only to $\mathcal{A}_C$. $\lambda_j = g^{K_j}$ is public.

First we consider the possibility of an algorithm $\mathcal{A}_C$ running the IND-CPA security simulation whose goal is to distinguish 2 encrypted ciphertexts. For every query (s, v) made by $\mathcal{A}$ to $\mathcal{C}^*$, $\mathcal{A}_C$ replies to $\mathcal{A}$ with $c = \mathsf{Enc}_{e,r'}(v)$ and π_i values such that BallotVerify succeeds. When $\mathcal{A}$ submits its challenge votes $((s, v_0), (s, v_1))$, $\mathcal{A}_C$ passes (v_0, v_1) to its challenger, and receives β_C (computed as above), which it forwards to $\mathcal{A}$. $\mathcal{A}_C$ continues to reply to $\mathcal{A}$'s queries as before and finally submits $\mathcal{A}$'s value $b'_C = b'$. $\mathcal{A}_C$'s work consists mainly of computing values c and π_i in response to $\mathcal{A}$'s queries, so it's runtime is bounded by $t_C < n_1 t_{\mathcal{A}} + n_2$ for constants n_1, n_2. Let $Pr(b = b'_C) = \varepsilon_C$. If $\varepsilon_C > \frac{1}{2} + \mathsf{negl}(k)$, then we have contradicted that Enc is IND-CPA secure.

Suppose otherwise. Let $\mathcal{A}$ guess $b' = b$ in IEV with probability $\varepsilon > \frac{1}{2} + \mathsf{negl}(k)$ (when all verifications succeed) and $\mathcal{A}_C$ guess $b'_C = b$ in the IND-CPA simulation with probability $\varepsilon_C < \frac{1}{2} \pm \mathsf{negl}(k)$. We create a second algorithm $\mathcal{A}_R$ that contradicts Theorem 2. $\mathcal{A}_R$'s goal is to distinguish a truly random $r \in \mathbb{H}$ from an $r' = \varphi\left(e\left(g, \prod_{i=1}^{N_C} \pi_i\right)\right)$ following the simulation defined in Theorem 2. For each query (s, v) that $\mathcal{A}$ makes to $\mathcal{C}^*$, $\mathcal{A}_R$ computes $\mathsf{GenProof}_i$ for $i \neq j$ using K_i and queries its $\mathsf{GenProof}_j$ oracle to obtain each $\pi_i = \mathsf{GenProof}_i(s)$. It computes the corresponding r' and $c = \mathsf{Enc}_{e,r'}(v)$, with which it replies to $\mathcal{A}$. On the challenge $((s, v_0), (s, v_1))$, $\mathcal{A}_R$ submits s to its challenger and receives a value $r'' = \beta_{b,R}$, which it uses to compute $c = \mathsf{Enc}_{e,r''}(v_{b''})$ after choosing $b'' \in_R \{0, 1\}$. $\mathcal{A}_R$ answers $\mathcal{A}$'s queries as before until $\mathcal{A}$ outputs b'. If $b' = b''$, $\mathcal{A}_R$ outputs $b'_R = 0$. Otherwise, it outputs $b'_R = 1$. The probability of $\mathcal{A}_R$'s success is $Pr(b'_R = b) = Pr(b'_R = b | b = 0 \cap b = 0) + Pr(b'_R = b | b = 1 \cap b = 1) = \frac{1}{2}\varepsilon + \frac{1}{2}\varepsilon_C = \frac{1}{4} + \frac{1}{2}\varepsilon \pm \frac{1}{2}\mathsf{negl}'(k) > \frac{1}{2} + \mathsf{negl}(k)$. Since $\mathcal{A}_R$'s primary work is done computing responses to $\mathcal{A}$'s queries, its runtime is bounded by $t_R < n_1 t_{\mathcal{A}} + n_2$ for some constants n_1, n_2, so $t_R \leq \mathsf{poly}(k)$.

Although we focus on coercion resistance, lastly, we informally note that there is a guarantee that each output c is an encryption of the voter's vote v since BallotVerify explicitly recomputes the encryption of v and checks for equivalence (*individual verifiability*). Furthermore, each voter can compute and verify the tally using the public, decrypted ballots (*universal verifiability*).

7   Practical Considerations

To this point, we have focused largely on more rigorous coercion resistance, with minimal discussion of deployment. In this section, we briefly clarify a few of the more practical aspects of our protocol.

As mentioned, our protocol, adapted from Benaloh's technique [13,12], attempts to minimize impact on the voter. The typical voter in our scheme can simply walk into the voting booth, mark her ballot as she would normally vote on a common touchscreen system, choose to cast it, and take her receipt to a separate machine where it is scanned and cast. The choice not to cast a marked ballot and audit is completely optional. At the same time, recall that all a voter needs to do to successfully audit the machine with an uncastable receipt (marked ballot) is verify that the plaintext printed on it is correct and then check that the printed serial number, encrypted ballot, and plaintext all appear correctly on the bulletin board. Philanthropic or politically motivated organizations may also assist voters in this task. Lastly, as long as at least one honest voter verifies the cryptographic operations on the board, fallacious computation of the tally is detected, although anyone has the option of doing so.

This simplicity introduces several intricacies regarding verification. One result we notice, is that the scheme can directly prove nothing about the correctness of the content of ballots that are actually cast. Instead, it relies on the option for voters, officials, etc. to audit to provide probabilistic assurances. Because the ballot marking machine is separate from the receipt scanning, casting machine, the ballot marking machine does not need to know anything about the voter. With no voter information, the machine can do approximately no better than to cheat at random. As a result, only a small number of audits are necessary to achieve a relatively high guarantee of accuracy. An analysis by Neff [53], shows that in general, in an election with N_V voters, M_V compromised votes, and A_V audit votes, a very crude approximation of the probability of detection Pr_D when $N_V \gg M_V + A_V$ is $Pr_D \approx 1 - (1 - \frac{M_V}{N_V})^{A_V}$. More concretely (and using more precise calculations [53]), suppose there were an election with 100,000 voters and a machine attempted to dishonestly encrypt 500 ballots. If 1% of the created ballots were randomly audited, the cheating would be detected with greater than 99% probability.

As a final practical note, we notice from our definition that queried seeds s must be unique. To address this issue in practice, we suggest that each party supply a $\mathcal{T}_i$ that responds only to queries of strictly increasing seeds[19] and that ballots are provided to voters in sequence with respect to their serial numbers. Again, as long as at least one party behaves honestly, seed uniqueness and thus voter privacy are assured. To maintain usability, the ballot marking machine can check that each serial number is within an expected range prior to querying the $\mathcal{T}_i$s and provide a warning requesting poll worker assistance if not. Note that such functionality purely prevents accidental usage problems and does not place any trust on the machine with respect to vote integrity or privacy.

8   Conclusion

Coercion resistance is vital to election integrity. Because attacks are often subtle, it must be addressed rigorously. We formally define coercion resistance for end-to-end voting. We then construct an end-to-end voting scheme that is provably coercion resistant and minimally impacts the voting process for the typical voter.

---

[19] This only requires that $\mathcal{T}_i$ can store a single serial number and compute a comparison.

Acknowledgments

National Science Foundation grant CNS-0524252 supported this work. We thank Josh Benaloh, Ariel Feldman, and Susan Hohenberger for their insights.

References

1. Kohno, T., Stubblefield, A., Rubin, A.D., Wallach, D.S.: Analysis of an electronic voting system. In: IEEE Symposium on Security and Privacy (2004)
2. Feldman, A.J., Halderman, J.A., Felten, E.W.: Security analysis of the Diebold AccuVote-TS voting machine. In: EVT 2007:USENIX/ACCURATE Electronic Voting Technology Workshop (2007)
3. Hursti, H.: Diebold TSx evaluation: Critical security issues with Diebold TSx (May 2006), http://www.blackboxvoting.org/BBVreportIIunredacted.pdf
4. Proebstel, E., Riddle, S., Hsu, F., Cummins, J., Oakley, F., Stanionis, T., Bishop, M.: An analysis of the Hart Intercivic dau eslate. In: EVT 2007: USENIX/ACCURATE Electronic Voting Technology Workshop (2007)
5. Gardner, R., Yasinsac, A., Bishop, M., Kohno, T., Hartley, Z., Kerski, J., Gainey, D., Walega, R., Hollander, E., Gerke, M.: Software review and security analysis of the Diebold voting machine software. Technical report, Florida Department of State (July 2007)
6. Calandrino, J.A., Feldman, A.J., Halderman, J.A., Wagner, D., Yu, H., Zeller, W.P.: Source code review of the Diebold voting system. Technical report, California Secretary of State (July 2007)
7. Inguva, S., Rescorla, E., Shacham, H., Wallach, D.S.: Source code review of the Hart InterCivic voting system. Technical report, California Secretary of State (July 2007)
8. Blaze, M., Cordero, A., Engle, S., Karlof, C., Sastry, N., Sherr, M., Stegers, T., Yee, K.P.: Source code review of the Sequoia voting system. Technical report, California Secretary of State (July 2007)
9. Neff, A.: Practical high certainty intent verification for encrypted votes (2004), http://www.votehere.com/vhti/documentation
10. Chaum, D.: Secret-ballot receipts: True voter-verifiable elections. IEEE Security and Privacy 2(1), 38–47 (2004)
11. Riva, B., Ta-Shma, A.: Bare-handed electronic voting with pre-processing. In: EVT 2007:USENIX/ACCURATE Electronic Voting Technology Workshop (2007)
12. Benaloh, J.: Ballot casting assurance via voter-initiated poll station auditing. In: EVT 2007:USENIX/ACCURATE Electronic Voting Technology Workshop (2007)
13. Benaloh, J.: Simple verifiable elections. In: EVT 2006:USENIX/ACCURATE Electronic Voting Technology Workshop (2006)
14. Rivest, R.L., Smith, W.D.: Three voting protocols: Threeballot, VAV, and twin. In: EVT 2007: USENIX/ACCURATE Electronic Voting Technology Workshop (2007)
15. Sako, K., Kilian, J.: Receipt-free mix-type voting scheme. In: Guillou, L.C., Quisquater, J.-J. (eds.) EUROCRYPT 1995. LNCS, vol. 921, pp. 393–403. Springer, Heidelberg (1995)
16. Cranor, L.F., Cytron, R.K.: Sensus: A security-conscious electronic polling system for the internet. In: HICSS 1997: Hawaii International Conference on System Sciences (1997)

17. Karlof, C., Sastry, N., Wagner, D.: Cryptographic voting protocols: A systems perspective. In: USENIX Security Symposium (2005)
18. Moran, T., Naor, M.: Split-ballot voting: everlasting privacy with distributed trust. In: CCS 2007: ACM conference on Computer and Communications Security (2007)
19. Chaum, D.: Punch scan, http://www.punchscan.org/learnmore.php
20. Moran, T., Naor, M.: Receipt-free universally-verifiable voting with everlasting privacy. In: Dwork, C. (ed.) CRYPTO 2006. LNCS, vol. 4117, pp. 373–392. Springer, Heidelberg (2006)
21. Benaloh, J., Tuinstra, D.: Receipt-free secret-ballot elections (extended abstract). In: STOC 1994: ACM Symposium on Theory of Computing (1994)
22. Hirt, M., Sako, K.: Efficient receipt-free voting based on homomorphic encryption. In: Preneel, B. (ed.) EUROCRYPT 2000. LNCS, vol. 1807, p. 539. Springer, Heidelberg (2000)
23. Stenger, R.: Vote-selling web site to be revived, possibly offshore. CNN (August 2005),
    http://archives.cnn.com/2000/TECH/computing/08/24/
    internet.vote/index.html
24. Tribune, S.: U student who offered his vote on eBay gets community service. Star Tribune (2008), http://www.startribune.com/politics/state/26063069.html
25. Local 6, O.: Man accused of trying to sell vote (October 2004),
    http://www.local6.com/news/3834797/detail.html
26. Yao, A.C.: Protocols for secure computations. In: FOCS 1982: IEEE Symposium on Foundations of Computer Science (1982)
27. Benaloh, J.D.C.: Verifiable Secret-ballot Elections. PhD thesis, Yale University (1987)
28. Chaum, D.: Elections with unconditionally secret ballots and disruption equivalent to breaking RSA. In: Günther, C.G. (ed.) EUROCRYPT 1988. LNCS, vol. 330, pp. 177–182. Springer, Heidelberg (1988)
29. Magkos, E., Burmester, M., Chrissikopoulos, V.: Receipt-freeness in large-scale elections without untappable channels. In: I3E 2001: IFIP Conference on Towards The E-Society (2001)
30. Benaloh, J.: Administrative and public verifiablity: Can we have both? In: EVT 2008:USENIX/ACCURATE Electronic Voting Technology Workshop (2008)
31. Chaum, D., Ryan, P.Y., Schneider, S.: A practical voter-verifiable election scheme. In: di Vimercati, S.d.C., Syverson, P.F., Gollmann, D. (eds.) ESORICS 2005. LNCS, vol. 3679, pp. 118–139. Springer, Heidelberg (2005)
32. Ryan, P.Y., Peacock, T.: Prêt à voter: A systems perspective. Technical report, University of Newcastle (2005)
33. Ryan, P.: Prêt à Voter with Pallier encryption. Technical report (2006),
    http://www.cs.ncl.ac.uk/research/pubs/trs/papers/965.pdf
34. Xia, Z., Schneider, S.A., Heather, J., Traore, J.: Analysis, improvement and simplification of prêt à voter with pallier encryption. In: EVT 2008:USENIX/ACCURATE Electronic Voting Technology Workshop (2008)
35. Chaum, D., Carback, R., Clark, J., Essex, A., Popoveniuc, S., Rivest, R., Ryan, P., Shen, E., Sherman, A.T.: Scantegrity II: End-to-end verifiability for optical scan election systems using invisible ink confirmation codes. In: EVT 2008:USENIX/ACCURATE Electronic Voting Technology Workshop (2008)
36. Chaum, D., Essex, A., Carback, R., Clark, J., Popveniuc, S., Sherman, A.T., Vora, P.: Scantegrity: End-to-end voter verifiable optical scan voting. IEEE Security and Privacy 6 (2008)

37. Rackoff, C., Simon, D.R.: Non-interactive zero-knowledge proof of knowledge and chosen ciphertext attack. In: Feigenbaum, J. (ed.) CRYPTO 1991. LNCS, vol. 576, pp. 433–444. Springer, Heidelberg (1992)
38. Jakobsson, M., Juels, A.: Millimix: Mixing in small batches. Technical Report 99-33, DIMACS (1999)
39. Jakobsson, M., Juels, A., Rivest, R.L.: Making mix nets robust for electronic voting by randomized partial checking. In: USENIX Security Symposium (2002)
40. Golle, P., Jakobsson, M., Juels, A., Syverson, P.F.: Universal re-encryption for mixnets. In: Okamoto, T. (ed.) CT-RSA 2004. LNCS, vol. 2964, pp. 163–178. Springer, Heidelberg (2004)
41. Goldwasser, S., Micali, S., Rackoff, C.: The knowledge complexity of interactive proof systems. SIAM Journal on Computing 18(1) (1989)
42. Pedersen, T.P.: A threshold cryptosystem without a trusted party. In: Davies, D.W. (ed.) EUROCRYPT 1991. LNCS, vol. 547, pp. 522–526. Springer, Heidelberg (1991)
43. Juels, A., Catalano, D., Jakobsson, M.: Coercion-resistant electronic elections. In: WPES 2005:ACM Workshop on Privacy in the Electronic Society (2005)
44. Teague, V., Ramchen, K., Naish, L.: Coercion-resistant tallying for STV voting. In: EVT 2008:USENIX/ACCURATE Electronic Voting Technology Workshop (2008)
45. Canetti, R., Gennaro, R.: Incoercible multiparty computation (extended abstract). In: FOCS 1996: IEEE Symposium on Foundations of Computer Science (1996)
46. Dodis, Y., Yampolskiy, A.: A verifiable random function with short proofs and keys. In: Vaudenay, S. (ed.) PKC 2005. LNCS, vol. 3386, pp. 416–431. Springer, Heidelberg (2005)
47. Boneh, D., Boyen, X.: Efficient selective-ID secure identity-based encryption without random oracles. In: Cachin, C., Camenisch, J.L. (eds.) EUROCRYPT 2004. LNCS, vol. 3027, pp. 223–238. Springer, Heidelberg (2004)
48. Galbraith, S.D.: Supersingular curves in cryptography (2001)
49. Joux, A., Nguyen, K.: Separating decision diffie-hellman from computational diffie-hellman in cryptographic groups. Journal of Cryptography 16(4), 239–247 (2001)
50. Boneh, D., Franklin, M.K.: Identity-based encryption from the weil pairing. In: Kilian, J. (ed.) CRYPTO 2001. LNCS, vol. 2139, p. 213. Springer, Heidelberg (2001)
51. Goldwasser, S., Micali, S.: Probabalistic encryption. Journal of Computer and System Science 28(2) (1984)
52. Micali, S., Rackoff, C., Sloan, B.: The notion of security for probabilistic cryptosystems. SIAM Journal on Computing 17(2), 412–426 (1988)
53. Neff, A.: Election confidence: A comparison of methodologies and their relative effectiveness at achieving it (2003), http://www.votehere.com.

Relations Among Privacy Notions

Jens-Matthias Bohli and Andreas Pashalidis

NEC Laboratories Europe
Kurfürsten-Anlage 36
69115 Heidelberg, Germany

Abstract. This paper presents a hierarchy of privacy notions that covers multiple anonymity and unlinkability variants. The underlying definitions, which are based on the idea of indistinguishability between two worlds, provide new insights into the relation between, and the fundamental structure of, different privacy notions. We apply our definitions to group signatures and anonymous communication systems, and show how they relate to existing definitions.

1 Introduction

With the growing number of services and information offered in the digital world, the number of situations where there is a need to hide the correspondence between digital elements and the people that cause their appearance, is also increasing. A variety of privacy protecting systems address this need; anonymous communication systems, for example, hide how transmitted messages correspond to their senders (and their recipients); group signatures hide the identity of the signer of a given message, and secret voting schemes hide the identity of the voter who cast any given ballot. In general, a system is said to 'provide privacy' if it hides, perhaps to an extent, the correspondence between the elements it outputs, and its users.

What *exactly* it means for any given privacy protecting system to provide privacy naturally varies between system types. The privacy definition for group signatures [5], for example, differs from the one for anonymous credentials [8]. Similarly, privacy for voting schemes [1] is defined differently from privacy in the setting of anonymous communication [23]. Despite efforts for a consistent terminology [30], formal treatments *seem* to define privacy in an inconsistent and sometimes even contradictory manner; while, for example, some authors assert that 'anonymity and unlinkability are technically the same property' [5], others show that, although related, they are, in fact, distinct [23], and others insist that they are independent [24]. Unfortunately, it is not only the terminology that is used inconsistently; due to the discrepancies between the formal models, the resulting privacy notions themselves turn out to be incomparable. It remains unclear whether or not it is possible to construct a *single* formal framework in which privacy notions pertaining to *different* system types can be defined in a consistent and comparable manner.

R. Dingledine and P. Golle (Eds.): FC 2009, LNCS 5628, pp. 362–380, 2009.
© IFCA/Springer-Verlag Berlin Heidelberg 2009

Our Contributions: This work can be seen as first step towards a formal framework that aims to define multiple privacy notions in an application-agnostic manner. By so doing, it provides new insights into the inner structure of privacy notions. Starting from a generic system model that potentially hides the correspondence between digital elements and the users that cause their appearance, we systematically analyse different degrees to which this correspondence may be hidden, and place the resulting privacy notions into a well-characterised hierarchy. Furthermore, we examine the class of 'online' systems, and show why only some privacy notions apply to this class. Finally, we place existing definitions for group signature and anonymous communication systems in the context of our framework. This enables us, on the one hand, to understand the relationship between, and to compare, these traditionally disconnected privacy notions. On the other hand, it highlights a largely unexplored space of theoretically possible notions some of which may be of practical interest.

Related Work: The framework introduced in [23] has certain commonalities with the framework introduced in this paper; both define, for example, a hierarchy of privacy notions based on the principle that an adversary may break any privacy notion *except* the one of interest, and both follow the idea of left-or-right security introduced in [4]. However, the framework in [23] appears to be specific to anonymous communication systems. Moreover, the hierarchy of privacy notions defined in this paper is richer; when mapped to anonymous communication systems, notions beyond those considered in [23] arise. The framework in [24] also has certain commonalities with ours; both support, for example, the specification of privacy notions against adversaries with partial knowledge about a function. However, in contrast to the framework introduced in this paper, the one in [24] does not consider probabilistic adversaries, and is only applied to anonymous communication systems. Moreover, it is unclear how its privacy definitions map to existing and established application-specific ones.

Other related work includes the literature on *measuring* privacy (e.g. [3, 10, 11, 12, 13, 14, 15, 16, 19, 22, 27, 32, 33, 35]). The proposed metrics appear, however, to pertain to particular privacy notions, if not system types. Multiple, sometimes inconsistent metrics for the same notion have also been proposed. While, for example, the metric in [15], proposed for the anonymity in the setting of anonymous communication systems, focuses on the relationship between incoming and outgoing messages, the metric proposed in [20] focuses on the relationship between senders and receivers. Similarly, the metric for unlinkability proposed in [19, 34] does not take into account the skewness of the adversary's view on possible solutions, while the metric proposed in [18] does. The only work we are aware of that places multiple privacy notions into a single framework [29], does not relate the metrics it defines to privacy definitions from the cryptographic literature. It is important to note that most privacy metrics cited above are probabilistic. That is, they measure degree to which a system provides privacy. In contrast to this, the privacy definitions in this paper are 'all-or-nothing'; a system either provides or does not provide a given privacy notion.

While the most popular adversarial model in the anonymous communication literature is perhaps that of the 'global passive' adversary (see, for example, [25,28,31]), in this paper we consider an adaptive adversary that may corrupt users. This is in line with definitions from group signatures [5], anonymous credentials [8], and some of the literature on anonymous communication (e.g. [6,16]). Moreover, our privacy definitions classify systems as either succeeding, or failing to provide a given privacy notion; while this is in contrast with some works on anonymous communication that consider 'soft', probabilistic measures (see, for example, [16,22]), it, too, is in line with works on group signatures and some of the literature on anonymous communication systems (see, for example, [20]).

Outline: The rest of this paper is organised as follows. The next section introduces our notation and formal model, and Section 3 presents the hierarchy of privacy notions and examines its structure. Section 3.2 examines 'online' systems and shows why only some privacy notions apply in such systems. Section 4 examines group signature and anonymous communication systems in the context of the hierarchy. Section 5 concludes.

2 Preliminaries

This section introduces our notation and formal model. In particular, the next section introduces the class of systems that are considered in this paper, Section 2.2 introduces the different privacy notions considered, and Section 2.3 describes the adversarial model.

2.1 System Model

In this paper, we consider systems that may be *sequentially invoked* a finite number of times and that, for each invocation, produce an element $e \in \{0,1\}^*$. It is required that each invocation is uniquely associated with a user and with an input parameter $\alpha \in A$, where A is a system-specific parameter space, that may influence the behaviour of the system. It is furthermore required that each user is identified by means of a unique identifier from an identifier space; we use $\mathbb{N}$ for this purpose, but any large enough space can be used without loss of generality.

We assume that the system, denoted by Φ^A in the sequel, produces its output in batches of potentially varying sizes. That is, it is assumed that, on input a batch of invocations $(u_1, \alpha_1), (u_2, \alpha_2), \ldots, (u_c, \alpha_c) \in (\mathbb{N} \times A)^c$, Φ^A outputs a sequence $((e_1, \ldots, e_c), \beta)$, where the sequence $(e_1, \ldots, e_c)$ contains the elements that Φ^A produced as a result of the invocations. The order in which the elements appear in this sequence is determined by the system, and may differ from the order of the invocations. In particular, e_i is the element that Φ^A produces for the invocation $(u_{\pi(i)}, \alpha_{\pi(i)})$, for some potentially secret Φ^A-specific permutation π. Finally, $\beta \in \{0,1\}^*$ denotes some additional information that Φ^A outputs and that pertains to a batch as a whole, i.e. that is not associated with any specific invocation.

Remark 1. The system output being generated in batches models the behaviour of certain privacy-protecting systems that do not generate an output immediately after each invocation, but rather collect several inputs before producing some output. Mix networks [9] and secret voting schemes [1], for example, operate in this way: mix networks can provide privacy only if they forward multiple messages at a time, and secret voting schemes require multiple votes for different candidates to be cast before the tally is published in order to provide privacy. However, some privacy protecting systems, for example group signatures [5], do not exhibit this behaviour, i.e. have batch size 1. These systems are examined in Section 3.2.

2.2 Privacy Model

Let x denote the number of times the system is invoked during its lifetime. The correspondence between (the serial numbers of) the elements that occur during the lifetime of a system Φ^A and the set of its users is modelled as a function $f \in \mathfrak{F}$, where $\mathfrak{F} = \{f : \{1, 2, \ldots, x\} \to \mathbb{N}\}$ is the space of functions that map the serial number of each output element to the (identifier of the) user it corresponds to. The privacy notions considered in this paper describe potentially different degrees to which f remains hidden from an adversary. The adversary's goal is to identify f, or some 'interesting property' of f, possibly with respect to some subset of elements, through interaction with, or observation of, Φ^A. We consider the following properties of f with respect to a subset $I \subseteq \{1, 2, \ldots, x\}$ of element serial numbers, which may be of interest to an adversary.

$U_{f,I} = \{f(i) : i \in I\} \subset \mathbb{N}$ denotes the *participant set*, i.e. the set of user identifiers that are associated with the elements in I.

$Q_{f,I} = \{(u, \#u_{f,I}) : u \in U_{f,I}\}$, where $\#u_{f,I} = |\{i \in I : f(i) = u\}| \in \{1, 2, \ldots, |U_{f,I}|\}$, denotes *usage frequency set*, i.e. the collection of records that indicate how many elements correspond to each participant from I's participant set.

$P_{f,I} = \{I'_1, I'_2, \ldots, I'_{|U_{f,I}|}\} \vdash I$ denotes the *linking relation*, i.e. the partition of I that is induced by f. That is, $P_{f,I}$ denotes the partition that divides I into non-overlapping subsets such that, for all $i, i' \in I'_j$, $f(i) = f(i')$. Note that $\bigcup_j I'_j = I$.

In the sequel, omission of the modifier I implies that the property under consideration refers to the entire lifetime of the system, i.e. that $I = \{1, 2, \ldots, x\}$. Given the above properties, and based on the principle that the adversary should be allowed to break any privacy notion *except* the one of interest, we derive the following privacy notions. These notions are further formalised in Section 3.

- Strong anonymity, denoted SA: A system that provides SA does not enable the adversary to learn any information about how elements correspond to users, i.e., it does not leak any information about f.
- Participation hiding, denoted PH: A system that provides PH does not leak any information about f beyond the number of participants $|U_f|$. In particular, it does not enable the adversary to learn any information about the participant set U_f beyond its size.

- Strong unlinkability, denoted SU: A system that provides SU does not leak any information about f beyond the participant set U_f. In particular, it does not enable the adversary to link, or to unlink, different elements beyond the extent it can do so based on knowledge of U_f. In other words, a system that provides SU does not leak any information about the linking relation P_f beyond what is leaked by U_f.
- Weak unlinkability, denoted WU: A system that provides WU does not leak any information about f beyond the usage frequency set Q_f. In particular, it does not enable the adversary to link, or to unlink, different elements beyond the extent it can do so based on knowledge of Q_f. In other words, a system that provides WU does not leak any information about the linking relation P_f beyond what is leaked by Q_f.
- Pseudonymity, denoted PS: A system that provides PS does not leak any information about f beyond the linking relation P_f. In particular, it does not enable the adversary to learn any information about the participant set U_f beyond what it learns from P_f. This notion is called 'pseudonymity' because each equivalence class in P_f (which is assumed to be known) can be given a unique label, or 'pseudonym'.
- Anonymity, denoted AN: A system that provides AN does not leak any information about f beyond the linking relation P_f and the participation set U_f. Intuitively, a system that provides AN may enable the adversary divide all elements into non-overlapping groups, and also determine the set of participants they correspond to, but does not enable it to determine which group corresponds to which participant.
- Weak anonymity, denoted WA: A system that provides WA does not leak any information about f beyond the linking relation P_f and the usage frequency set Q_f. Similarly to AN, WA requires that the system hides the correspondence between element groups and participants. However, since knowledge of Q_f may enable the adversary to at least partially establish this correspondence, systems that provide WA (but not AN) hide less information about it that systems that provide AN (which do not reveal any information about it).

2.3   Adversarial Model

This section specifies the adversarial model considered in this paper. The adversary, denoted by $\mathcal{A}$ in the sequel, adaptively controls the usage of Φ^A, and is allowed to corrupt users, i.e. to obtain a copy of their private information and their internal state. Its interaction with Φ^A is modelled by means of an experiment that a challenger arranges for $\mathcal{A}$. At the beginning of this experiment, the user identifier space $\mathbb{N}$ and, if necessary, a security parameter $k \in \mathbb{N}$, are fixed and Φ^A is set up. The experiment, depicted in Figure 1, starts with the challenger selecting a bit $b \in \{0, 1\}$ uniformly at random, and by setting the initial value of the input counter c to zero. The challenger then offers the following interfaces to $\mathcal{A}$, through which the system can be controlled.

- input$((\cdot,\cdot),(\cdot,\cdot))$: on input $((u_0, \alpha_0), (u_1, \alpha_1)) \in (\mathbb{N} \times A)^2$, the challenger first increases the counter c by one and then remembers (u_b, α_b) as (u_c, α_c).

```
Experiment Exp^{priv−b}_{Φ^A,A}(k)
  b ← {0, 1};
  g ← A^{input((·,·),(·,·)),nextBatch(),corrupt(·)}
  return g == b
```

Fig. 1. Experiment $\mathbf{Exp}^{priv-b}_{\Phi^A,\mathcal{A}}(k)$

- nextBatch(): on reception of this query type, the challenger invokes Φ^A on input the 'remembered' values $(u_1, \alpha_1), (u_2, \alpha_2), \ldots, (u_c, \alpha_c)$ and outputs the system's output. We say that the challenger outputs a batch of size c in this case.[1] Subsequently, the input counter c is reset to zero.
- corrupt(·): on input $u \in \mathbb{N}$, the challenger outputs the internal state of the user identified by u. The specification of the information that is returned to $\mathcal{A}$ is specific to Φ^A.

$\mathcal{A}$ may issue a number of queries over these interfaces and, at some point in time, outputs a guess bit $g \in \{0, 1\}$. We say that $\mathcal{A}$ wins the experiment if and only if $g = b$, and its advantage is given by $\mathbf{Adv}_{\Phi^A,\mathcal{A}}(k) = \Pr(\mathbf{Exp}^{priv-0}_{\Phi^A,\mathcal{A}}(k)) - \Pr(\mathbf{Exp}^{priv-1}_{\Phi^A,\mathcal{A}}(k))$.

Some notation is in order. Let κ denote the number of nextBatch queries $\mathcal{A}$ has issued up to the point in time it outputs g in an $\mathbf{Exp}^{priv-b}_{\Phi^A,\mathcal{A}}(k)$ experiment. For all $1 \leq j \leq \kappa$, let c_j denote the size of the batch that the challenger output as a result of $\mathcal{A}$'s jth nextBatch query, and let π_j denote the permutation applied by Φ^A for the jth batch. Furthermore, let $x = \sum_{j=1}^{\kappa} c_j$ denote the total number of input$((·,·),(·,·))$ queries. For all $1 \leq i \leq x$, we denote by $u_{0,i}$ (resp. $u_{1,i}, \alpha_{0,i}, \alpha_{1,i}$) the value of u_0 (resp. u_1, α_0, α_1) in $\mathcal{A}$'s ith input$((u_0, \alpha_0), (u_1, \alpha_1))$ query. We further define the subsets of invocation serial numbers $I_1 = \{1, 2, \ldots, c_1\}, I_2 = \{c_1 + 1, c_1 + 2, \ldots, c_1 + c_2\}, \ldots, I_\kappa = \{c_1 + c_2 + \cdots + c_{\kappa-1} + 1, c_1 + c_2 + \cdots + c_{\kappa-1} + 2, \ldots, x\}$, and the 'global inverse permutation' Π as the permutation that maps the serial number of all elements that are output during the experiment to the serial number of their corresponding invocation. That is, Π permutes $(1, 2, \ldots, x)$ such that, for all $1 \leq i \leq x$, $\Pi(i) = \pi_j^{-1}(i - \sum_{j'=1}^{j-1} c_{j'}) + \sum_{j'=1}^{j-1} c_{j'}$, where $j \in \{1, 2, \ldots, \kappa\}$ is such that $i \in I_j$. Finally, the functions f_0, f_1 are defined such that, for all $i \in \{1, 2, \ldots, x\}$, $f_0(i) = u_{0,\Pi(i)}$ and $f_1(i) = u_{1,\Pi(i)}$.

3   Hierarchy of Privacy Notions

This section formalises the privacy notions introduced in Section 2.2 and shows how they relate to each other. We begin by defining the following seven notions of function distinguishability.

---

[1] The specification of β, π, and how α it influences the output of Φ^A, is specific to Φ^A. Moreover, if the adversary is polynomially bounded, then the length of $\alpha_0, \alpha_1, \beta$ and all e_i must be polynomial in the system's security parameter.

Definition 1. *Two functions* $f, f' \in \mathfrak{F}$, $f \neq f'$, *are said, with respect to a subset of invocations* $I \subseteq \{1, 2, \ldots, x\}$, *to be*

SA-distinguishable *in any case,*

PH-distinguishable *if and only if* $|U_{f,I}| = |U_{f',I}|$,

SU-distinguishable *if and only if* $U_{f,I} = U_{f',I}$,

WU-distinguishable *if and only if* $Q_{f,I} = Q_{f',I}$,

PS-distinguishable *if and only if* $P_{f,I} = P_{f',I}$,

AN-distinguishable *if and only if* $P_{f,I} = P_{f',I}$ *and* $U_{f,I} = U_{f',I}$, *and*

WA-distinguishable *if and only if* $P_{f,I} = P_{f',I}$ *and* $Q_{f,I} = Q_{f',I}$.

We are now ready to present our main privacy definitions.

Definition 2. *A privacy protecting system* Φ^A *is said to unconditionally (resp. statistically) provide privacy notion* X^* *for some* $X \in \{\mathsf{SA}, \mathsf{PH}, \mathsf{SU}, \mathsf{WU}, \mathsf{PS}, \mathsf{AN}, \mathsf{WA}\}$ *if and only if* f_0 *and* f_1 *are* X-*distinguishable with respect to all* $I \in 2^{\{I_1, \ldots, I_\kappa\}}$, *and, for all* $\mathcal{A}$, $\mathbf{Adv}_{\Phi^A, \mathcal{A}}(k) = 0$ *(resp.* $\mathbf{Adv}_{\Phi^A, \mathcal{A}}(k) \leq \epsilon(k)$ *for some negligible function* ϵ*). Moreover,* Φ^A *is said to computationally provide privacy notion* X^* *if and only if it statistically provides* X^* *and the running time of* $\mathcal{A}$ *is polynomial in* k.

The above privacy notions are very strong because they require that $\mathcal{A}$ does not obtain any advantage neither by corrupting users, nor on the basis of the parameter values that it passes in its **input** queries. We therefore require weaker notions that take corrupted users into account and that limit $\mathcal{A}$'s ability to distinguish between the two worlds on the basis of parameter values. The following notion of function indistinguishability is therefore necessary.

Definition 3. *Two functions* $f, f' \in \mathfrak{F}$ *are said to be* indistinguishable *with respect to a subset of (corrupted) users* $\hat{U} \subseteq \mathbb{N}$, *denoted by* $f \approx_{\hat{U}} f'$, *if and only if* $\{i : i \in \{1, 2, \ldots, x\}, f(i) \in \hat{U}\} = \{i : i \in \{1, 2, \ldots, x\}, f'(i) \in \hat{U}\}$, *i.e. if and only if the pre-image of* $\hat{U}$ *is identical in* f *and* f'.

Let $\hat{U} \subseteq \mathbb{N}$ denote the set of users that $\mathcal{A}$ has corrupted up to the point in time it outputs g, and let $A_0 = (\alpha_{0,1}, \alpha_{0,2}, \ldots, \alpha_{0,x})$ and $A_1 = (\alpha_{1,1}, \alpha_{1,2}, \ldots, \alpha_{1,x})$ denote the parameter sequences in the two worlds. We now present our weaker, more realistic notions.

Definition 4. *A privacy protecting system* Φ^A *is said to unconditionally (resp. statistically, computationally) provide privacy notions* X°, X^+ *and* X *for some* $X \in \{\mathsf{SA}, \mathsf{PH}, \mathsf{SU}, \mathsf{WU}, \mathsf{PS}, \mathsf{AN}, \mathsf{WA}\}$, *if and only if it provides* X^* *and* $\mathcal{A}$ *is restricted as shown below.*

Privacy notion	Restrictions
X°	$A_0 = A_1$
X^+	$f_0 \approx_{\hat{U}} f_1$
X	$A_0 = A_1$ and $f_0 \approx_{\hat{U}} f_1$

3.1   Relations between Notions

For all $X \in \{\mathsf{SA}, \mathsf{PH}, \mathsf{SU}, \mathsf{WU}, \mathsf{PS}, \mathsf{AN}, \mathsf{WA}\}$ it trivially holds that $X^* \Rightarrow X^+ \Rightarrow X$ and $X^* \Rightarrow X^\circ \Rightarrow X$ because $\mathcal{A}$ is more restricted in its choices in the context of X than it is in the contexts of X^+ and X°, and more restricted in the contexts of X^+ and X° than it is in the context of X^*.

The 'plain' privacy notions X are, perhaps, the most typical ones as they are concerned with the amount and type of information the system leaks *exclusively* on the basis of the identities of honest users. The notions X^+ are stronger, in the sense that a system providing some notion X^+ must not enable $\mathcal{A}$ to distinguish between system invocations on the basis of the parameters passed to the system; the system must ensure that the output corresponding to different users is indistinguishable, irrespective of the two users' potentially different input.

The privacy notions X° can be seen as a form of 'forward/backward privacy', analogous to notions of forward and backward security for encryption schemes. *Forward privacy* means that, even if a user is compromised via a `corrupt` query, the user's system interactions that occurred prior to this corruption remain private. Similarly, *backward privacy* means that system interactions of a user remain private, even if the user was corrupted prior to these interactions. Section 4.1 shows that the established privacy notion for group signatures a forward/backward privacy notion.

The privacy notions X^* are very strong, in the sense that a system providing X^* protects the privacy of *all* users, honest and corrupted alike, *and* does not enable $\mathcal{A}$ to distinguish between system invocations on the basis of the parameters passed to the system. That is, a system provides the notion X^* only if it provides X^+ and X° at the same time.

Figure 2 shows further relations between different privacy notions. These relations follow from the facts that knowledge of Q_f implies knowledge of U_f, and

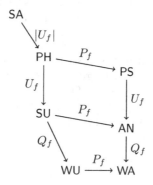

Fig. 2. Relations between privacy notions. The arrow labels indicate the property about f that the system may reveal. From left to right, more information about the linking relation P_f is revealed; from top to bottom, more information about the user involvement Q_f is revealed.

that knowledge of U_f or P_f implies knowledge of $|U_f|$. The same hierarchy also applies to the privacy notions X^+, X°, and X^*.

Remark 2. Intuitively, 'unobservability' is a privacy notion that ensures that $\mathcal{A}$ cannot determine whether or not a system invocation takes place. A system can only provide unobservability if it supports the notion of a 'void' invocation. That is, potentially unobservable systems must accept 'normal' invocations, i.e. invocations that are associated with some user/parameter pair from $\mathbb{N} \times A$, *and* void invocations, i.e. invocations that are not associated with anything. A system can only be unobservable if it produces an element for void invocations that is indistinguishable from the elements it produces as a result of normal invocations. Since our system model described in Section 2.1 does not support systems that that accept void invocations, our framework does not include an 'unobservability' privacy notion. However, this discussion demonstrates that extending the framework in this direction is straight-forward.

3.2   Online Systems

This section examines systems that process every input individually, i.e. systems that have a constant batch size equal to one. While such systems, which we call 'online' systems, enable $\mathcal{A}$ to trivially keep track of the mapping of input queries and the elements produced by the system, our definition still requires $\mathcal{A}$ to determine whether it is interacting in the left or the right world. Nevertheless, the mere fact that $\mathcal{A}$ can unambiguously determine which output elements correspond to which invocation serial numbers, has implications to the introduced hierarchy of privacy notions.

Lemma 1. *Consider two functions $f, f' \in \mathfrak{F}$. If $U_{f,I} = U_{f',I}$ for all $I \in \{\{1\}, \{2\}, \ldots, \{x\}\}$, then $f = f'$.*

Proof. Assume that $f \neq f'$, i.e. that there exists at least one $i \in \{1, 2, \ldots, x\}$ such that $f(i) \neq f'(i)$. Then $U_{f,\{i\}} \neq U_{f',\{i\}}$, contradicting the assumption. $\square$

The implication of Lemma 1 is that, for online systems, there exist no functions f_0 and f_1, $f_0 \neq f_1$, that are X-distinguishable for any $X \in \{\mathsf{SU}, \mathsf{WU}, \mathsf{AN}, \mathsf{WA}\}$; two functions that are PH-distinguishable are also PS-distinguishable. This can be seen easily, since, for all $I \in \{\{1\}, \{2\}, \ldots, \{x\}\}$, $|U_{f,I}| = |U_{f',I}| = 1$, and both P_{f_0} and P_{f_1} divide $\{1, 2, \ldots, x\}$ into partitions of singletons. Hence, $P_{f_0} = P_{f_1}$. The resulting collapsed hierarchy of privacy notions is sketched in Figure 3.

$$\mathsf{SA} \xrightarrow{\; P_f \;} \mathsf{PS}$$

Fig. 3. Privacy notions for online-systems

4 Applications

This section places the privacy definitions concerning group signature and anonymous communication systems into the hierarchy introduced in the previous section.

4.1 Group Signatures

Group signatures represent an important class of privacy protecting system. A group signature system consists of four algorithms (GKg, GSig, GVf, Open), as follows [5].

- The randomised *group key generation algorithm* GKg takes as input a security parameter $k \in \mathbb{N}$, and returns a tuple $(gpk, gmsk, gsk)$, where gpk is the *group public key*, $gmsk$ is the *group manager's secret key*, and gsk is an n-vector of keys where $gsk[u]$ is the *secret signing key* of user identified by $u \in \mathbb{N}$, and where $n \in \mathbb{N}$ is polynomially bounded in k.
- The randomised *group signing algorithm* GSig takes as input a secret signing key $gsk[u]$ and a message $m \in \mathcal{M}$, where $\mathcal{M}$ is the system's message space, to return a signature of m under $gsk[u](u \in \mathbb{N})$.
- The deterministic *group signature verification algorithm* GVf takes as input the group public key gpk, a message m, and a candidate signature σ for m to return either 1 or 0.
- The deterministic *opening algorithm* Open takes as input the group manager secret key $gmsk$, a message m, and a signature σ of m to return an identifier $u \in \mathbb{N}$ or the symbol $\bot$ to indicate failure.

Translated to the system model of Section 2.1, the parameter space of a group signature scheme is the its message space. That is, $A_{gs} = \mathcal{M}$. Since users compute and independently release signatures by themselves, the adversary is able to observe isolated system invocations. Thus, group signature schemes are online systems, and, hence, the only applicable privacy notions are SA and PS. The specification of the corrupt($\cdot$) query for group signatures systems is as follows.

- corrupt($\cdot$): on input $u \in \mathbb{N}$, the challenger outputs the secret key of the user identified by u, i.e. $gsk[u]$.

We now show why certain privacy notions do not apply to group signature systems, while others are equivalent.

Lemma 2. *No group signature system provides* SA*, PS*, SA$^+$, *or* PS$^+$. *Moreover, for group signature systems,* SA$^\circ$ *and* PS$^\circ$ *are equivalent, and* SA *and* PS *are distinct, privacy notions.*

The proof can be found in the appendix.

Full anonymity. Let us briefly revisit the definition of 'full anonymity' as defined in [5] and examine how it relates to the privacy notions that apply to online systems. Full anonymity is defined by means of an FA-experiment between an adversary $\mathcal{A}_{FA}$ and a challenger, which proceeds as follows. Initially, the adversary is given gsk and gpk, and access to an opening oracle $\mathsf{Open}(gmsk, \cdot, \cdot)$ that, on input a message/signature pair (m, σ), outputs $\mathsf{Open}(gmsk, m, \sigma)$. At some point in time, the adversary outputs a triple (u_0, u_1, m') and the challenger returns $\sigma' = \mathsf{GSig}(gsk[u_b], m')$, where $b \in \{0, 1\}$ is chosen uniformly at random. The adversary is then required to output a guess for b; before doing this, it may again query the $\mathsf{Open}(gmsk, \cdot, \cdot)$ oracle, albeit not on σ'. The adversary wins if its guess is correct, and the system is said to provide 'full anonymity', denoted FA, if no adversary can win the game with non-negligible advantage over random guessing.

Lemma 3. FA, *computational* SA°, *and computational* PS°, *are equivalent.*

The proof can be found in the appendix.

The fact that there exists only a single (computational) forward/backward privacy notion for group signatures, explains, perhaps, why [5] claims that 'anonymity and unlinkability are technically the same property'.

Remark 3. From our framework it is now obvious that weaker privacy notions for group signatures exist; it is possible to refrain from forward/backward privacy, and optionally in addition tolerate the group signatures of the same signer being linkable. Traceable group signature schemes were to our knowledge first considered in [26]. We modify a traceable scheme from [7] to construct an instance of a group signature scheme that provides PS but not SA. The required modification is minor, as it merely consists in setting a particular parameter of the scheme to one. We now briefly review the modified scheme; for a complete description see [7]. The scheme uses a bilinear group pair (G_1, G_2) consisting of cyclic groups G_1 and G_2 of prime order p with an efficiently computable isomorphism from G_2 to G_1, and an efficiently computable non-degenerate bilinear map $e : G_1 \times G_2 \to G_t$. For (G_1, G_2) the strong Diffie-Hellman assumption (see. [7]) has to hold. A public group key gpk is given by a triple of group elements (g_1, g_2, g_2^γ), where $g_1 \in G_1$, $g_2 \in G_2$ are randomly chosen from the respective groups and act as generators, and γ is secretly and uniformly at random chosen from $\mathbb{Z}_p$. Then a private signing key for a user U_i is given by $(A_i = g_1^{1/(\gamma+x_i)}, x_i)$ for a uniformly at random chosen element $x_i \in \mathbb{Z}_p$. Furthermore, a hash function $H : \{0, 1\}^* \to G_1 \times G_2$ is given. The signing procedure is as follows:

1. $(u, v) \leftarrow H(gpk)$
2. Choose $\alpha \leftarrow \mathbb{Z}_p$ uniformly at random and compute $T_1 \leftarrow u^\alpha$, $T_2 \leftarrow A_i v^\alpha$
3. Compute $c, s_\alpha, s_x, s_\delta$ as a witness indistinguishable proof of knowledge for correct computation of T_1, T_2 with respect to the private key A_i. This is done with Fiat-Shamir heuristic [17] and involves the message being signed.

The signature of a message is then given by $(T_1, T_2, c, s_\alpha, s_x, s_\delta)$. Now any two group signatures of the same signer can be linked by computing $e(A_i, u) =$

$e(T_2, u)/e(T_1, v)$ which is a value that, since the parameters u, v are common to the entire group, depends only on the signer's private key. Since this value cannot be traced back to any particular public key, some privacy remains.

Remark 4. We are not aware of any group signature scheme that provides SA but not FA at the same time, i.e. a scheme without forward-/backward privacy. The following example, however, demonstrates the existence of such a scheme. Consider a group signature scheme that provides FA. We modify this scheme as follows. Every signer is given a pseudorandom number generator whose seed is part of the user's secret key and, in order to sign a message, the user replaces all random choices by pseudo-randomness. As a result, every user behaves deterministically and, as long as the adversary does not know a user's seed, the produced signatures are computationally indistinguishable from those based on true randomness. Moreover, once the adversary calls `corrupt` on a user and learns his seed, all past and future signatures of this user become linkable; the modified scheme no longer provides forward-/backward privacy. In fact, it provides computational SA. Note that this scheme might well apply to smart-card group signature implementations where replacing randomness by pseudo-randomness is a common option.

4.2 Anonymous Communication

Anonymous communication systems are modelled as protocols that transmit messages from senders to receivers. The input to an anonymous communication system is a sequence of triples of the form $(\sigma, \rho, m) \in \mathbb{N} \times \mathbb{N} \times \mathcal{M}$, where $\sigma, \rho \in \mathbb{N}$ are identifiers of the sender and the intended recipient, respectively, $\mathcal{M}$ is the system's message space, and $m \in \mathcal{M}$ is the message that is to be transmitted from σ to ρ. The output that is associated to an input triple of this form, is the bitstring that the system produces as a result of this input, and that the adversary can observe.

For anonymous communication systems we define two variants of the base experiment $\mathbf{Exp}_{\Phi^A, \mathcal{A}}^{\mathrm{priv}-b}(k)$, depending on whether the experiment is intended to capture the privacy of senders or the privacy of recipients. In particular, the variant that captures sender privacy is denoted by $\mathbf{Exp}_{\Phi^A, \mathcal{A}}^{\mathrm{S-priv}-b}(k)$, and the variant that captures recipient privacy by $\mathbf{Exp}_{\Phi^A, \mathcal{A}}^{\mathrm{R-priv}-b}(k)$. In both variants, the parameter space is $A_{\mathrm{ac}} = \mathcal{M} \times \mathbb{N}$. The difference between the two variants is the way in which the challenger assigns the sender and receiver roles to the users indicated in an $\mathtt{input}((\cdot, \cdot), (\cdot, \cdot))$ query; in all other respects the two variants are identical to the base experiment.

Definition 5. *On reception of an* $\mathtt{input}((u_0, (m_0, u'_0)), (u_1, (m_1, u'_1)))$ *query in the context of an* $\mathbf{Exp}_{\Phi^A, \mathcal{A}}^{\mathrm{S-priv}-b}(k)$ *(resp.* $\mathbf{Exp}_{\Phi^A, \mathcal{A}}^{\mathrm{R-priv}-b}(k)$) *experiment, the challenger first increases the input counter* c *by one, and then remembers* $(u_b, (m_b, u'_b))$ *(resp* $(u'_b, (m_b, u_b))$) *as* (u_c, α_c).

In other words, the parameter $\alpha = (m, u) \in A_{\mathrm{ac}}$ either specifies a message together with (the identifier of) its intended recipient (in the context of an

$\mathbf{Exp}_{\varPhi^A,\mathcal{A}}^{\mathrm{S-priv-b}}(k)$ experiment), or a message together with (the identifier of) its sender (in the context of an $\mathbf{Exp}_{\varPhi^A,\mathcal{A}}^{\mathrm{R-priv-b}}(k)$ experiment). We now extend our generic definition for the context of anonymous communication.

Definition 6. *An anonymous communication system $\varPhi^{A_{ac}}$ is said to uncondition-ally (resp. statistically, computationally) provide 'sender-X', denoted S/X (resp. 'recipient-X', denoted R/X) for some privacy notion $X \in \{Y^*, Y^\circ, Y^+, Y\}$ where $Y \in \{\mathsf{SA}, \mathsf{PH}, \mathsf{SU}, \mathsf{WU}, \mathsf{PS}, \mathsf{AN}, \mathsf{WA}\}$, if and only if it unconditionally (resp. sta-tistically, computationally) provides X with respect to an $\mathbf{Exp}_{\varPhi^A,\mathcal{A}}^{\mathrm{S-priv-b}}(k)$ (resp. $\mathbf{Exp}_{\varPhi^A,\mathcal{A}}^{\mathrm{R-priv-b}}(k)$) experiment.*

It trivially follows from the definition that S/SA^+ and R/SA^+, as well as S/SA^* and R/SA^*, are equivalent notions. We define one more privacy notion, namely unlinkability, denoted UL. UL is specific to anonymous communication systems, and, like SA^*, its sender and recipient versions are equivalent. Unlinkability is the notion that ensures that $\mathcal{A}$ cannot learn anything about f beyond what follows from knowledge of how many messages each sender sent, and how many messages each receiver received. Let $A_0 = ((\cdot, u'_{0,1}), (\cdot, u'_{0,2}), \ldots, (\cdot, u'_{0,x}))$ and $A_1 = ((\cdot, u'_{1,1}), (\cdot, u'_{1,2}), \ldots, (\cdot, u'_{1,x}))$ denote parameter sequences issued by the adversary during an $\mathbf{Exp}_{\varPhi^A,\mathcal{A}}^{\mathrm{priv-b}}(k)$ experiment.

Definition 7. *An anonymous communication system $\varPhi^{A_{ac}}$ is said to uncondi-tionally (resp. statistically, computationally) provide privacy notion UL^* (resp. $\mathsf{UL}^\circ, \mathsf{UL}^+, \mathsf{UL}$), called unlinkability, if and only if it unconditionally (resp. sta-tistically, computationally) provides WU^* (resp. $\mathsf{WU}^\circ, \mathsf{WU}^+, \mathsf{WU}$) with respect to an $\mathbf{Exp}_{\varPhi^A,\mathcal{A}}^{\mathrm{S-priv-b}}(k)$ and an $\mathbf{Exp}_{\varPhi^A,\mathcal{A}}^{\mathrm{R-priv-b}}(k)$ experiment where, for all $i \in \{1, 2, \ldots, x\}$, $u'_{0,i} = u'_{1,i}$.*

Existing notions. We briefly revisit the privacy notions defined in [23] in order to examine how they relate to the ones defined above. [23] defines privacy by means of an experiment between an adversary and a challenger. The adversary specifies in advance two collections C^0 and C^1 of triples of the form $(\sigma, \rho, m) \in \mathbb{N}^2 \times \mathcal{M}$.[2] The two collections are then given to the challenger, which selects a bit $b \in \{0,1\}$ uniformly at random, and simulates $\varPhi^{A_{ac}}$ on input the triples in C^b. The adversary, given $\varPhi^{A_{ac}}$'s output, then produces a guess g for b and wins if and only if $g = b$; its advantage is defined in the usual way.

Let $S^b = \{\sigma \in \mathbb{N} : (\sigma, \cdot, \cdot) \in C^b\}$ and $R^b = \{\rho \in \mathbb{N} : (\cdot, \rho, \cdot) \in C^b\}$ de-note the set of senders and receivers according to C^b. For all $\sigma \in S^b$ (resp. $\rho \in R^b$), we denote by $\mathsf{sent}_\sigma^b = (\uplus m \in \mathcal{M} : (\sigma, \cdot, m) \in C^b)$ (resp. $\mathsf{rcvd}_\rho^b = (\uplus m \in \mathcal{M} : (\cdot, \rho, m) \in C^b))$ the multiset of messages sent by σ (resp. received by ρ) according to C^b. The different privacy notions defined in [23] arise due to restrictions imposed on the adversary in the construction of C^0 and C^1. In par-ticular, an anonymous communication system is said to provide privacy notion

---

[2] In [23] these collections are called 'message matrices', and are encoded as matrices.

Table 1. Conditions according to privacy definitions in [23]

Privacy notion	Label	Conditions
Sender Unlinkability	SUL	$S = S^0 = S^1$, $R = R^0 = R^1$, $\forall \sigma \in S$, $\lvert \mathsf{sent}_\sigma^0 \rvert = \lvert \mathsf{sent}_\sigma^1 \rvert$, and $\forall \rho \in R$, $\mathsf{rcvd}_\rho^0 = \mathsf{rcvd}_\rho^1$
Receiver Unlinkability	RUL	$S = S^0 = S^1$, $R = R^0 = R^1$, $\forall \sigma \in S$, $\mathsf{sent}_\sigma^0 = \mathsf{sent}_\sigma^1$, $\forall \rho \in R$, $\lvert \mathsf{rcvd}_\rho^0 \rvert = \lvert \mathsf{rcvd}_\rho^1 \rvert$, and
Unlinkability	UL	$S = S^0 = S^1$, $R = R^0 = R^1$, $\forall \sigma \in S$, $\lvert \mathsf{sent}_\sigma^0 \rvert = \lvert \mathsf{sent}_\sigma^1 \rvert$, and $\forall \rho \in R$, $\lvert \mathsf{rcvd}_\rho^0 \rvert = \lvert \mathsf{rcvd}_\rho^1 \rvert$
Sender Anonymity	SA	$R = R^0 = R^1$ and, $\forall \rho \in R$ $\mathsf{rcvd}_\rho^0 = \mathsf{rcvd}_\rho^1$
Receiver Anonymity	RA	$S = S^0 = S^1$ and, $\forall \sigma \in S$, $\mathsf{sent}_\sigma^0 = \mathsf{sent}_\sigma^1$
Strong Sender Anonymity	SA*	$R = R^0 = R^1$ and, $\forall \rho \in R$ $\lvert \mathsf{rcvd}_\rho^0 \rvert = \lvert \mathsf{rcvd}_\rho^1 \rvert$
Strong Receiver Anonymity	RA*	$S = S^0 = S^1$ and, $\forall \sigma \in S$, $\lvert \mathsf{sent}_\rho^0 \rvert = \lvert \mathsf{sent}_\rho^1 \rvert$
Sender-Receiver Anonymity	RA*	$\lvert C^0 \rvert = \lvert C^1 \rvert$
Unobservability	UO	none

$N \in \{\overline{\mathrm{SUL}}, \overline{\mathrm{RUL}}, \overline{\mathrm{UL}}, \overline{\mathrm{SA}}, \overline{\mathrm{RA}}, \overline{\mathrm{SA^*}}, \overline{\mathrm{RA^*}}, \overline{\mathrm{SRA}}, \overline{\mathrm{UO}}\}$ if no adversary, when restricted to choose C^0 and C^1 such that the conditions shown in Table 1 are satisfied, has a non-negligible advantage in the above experiment.

Comparison to existing notions. The adversarial model in [23] does not consider corrupted users, and does not consider adaptive adversaries. Translated to our system model, this amounts to the setting where $\mathcal{A}$ issues only a single nextBatch query, and no corrupt$(\cdot)$ queries. Due to this discrepancy of the adversarial models, the privacy notions defined in this paper are not directly comparable to the ones defined in [23]. If, however, $\mathcal{A}$ is restricted to observe only a single batch and is allowed no corruptions, then the following notions are equivalent.

Lemma 4. *If, during an* $\mathbf{Exp}_{\Phi^A, \mathcal{A}}^{\mathrm{S-priv-b}}(k)$ *or* $\mathbf{Exp}_{\Phi^A, \mathcal{A}}^{\mathrm{R-priv-b}}(k)$ *experiment,* $\mathcal{A}$ *does not issue any* corrupt$(\cdot)$ *queries and at most a single* nextBatch *query, then* $\overline{\mathrm{SUL}}$ *and* S/WU, $\overline{\mathrm{RUL}}$ *and* R/WU, $\overline{\mathrm{UL}}$ *and* UL, $\overline{\mathrm{SA}}$ *and* S/SA, $\overline{\mathrm{RA}}$ *and* R/SA, $\overline{\mathrm{SA^*}}$ *and* S/WU$^+$, $\overline{\mathrm{RA^*}}$ *and* R/WU$^+$, *and* $\overline{\mathrm{RA^*}}$ *and* (S/R)SA$^+$, *are equivalent privacy notions.*

The proof can be found in the appendix.

Remark 5. The above privacy notions form a hierarchy, described in [23], that is separate from the one described in Section 3. Moreover, [23] demonstrates that one can construct anonymous communication systems that offer a particular privacy notion by appropriately augmenting a system that provides a weaker notion, with encryption techniques and/or dummy traffic. Since, according to the model in [23], the adversary may observe only a single communication batch, these transformations do not necessarily suffice in the face an adversary that may adaptively influence the system over multiple communication batches, i.e. in the model considered in this paper.

Since in our model, $\mathcal{A}$ may issue multiple nextBatch queries, the notions S/WU, R/WU, UL, S/SA, R/SA, S/WU$^+$, R/WU$^+$, and (S/R)SA$^+$, are all strictly stronger than $\overline{\text{SUL}}$, $\overline{\text{RUL}}$, $\overline{\text{UL}}$, $\overline{\text{SA}}$, $\overline{\text{RA}}$,$\overline{\text{SA}^*}$,$\overline{\text{RA}^*}$, and $\overline{\text{RA}^*}$, respectively. Consider, for example, an anonymous communication system that provides notion $\overline{\text{RA}}$, i.e. a system where, for an adversarially chosen batch of communications (where certain conditions hold), the adversary may be able to determine which messages were received by which receivers, but no information beyond this. In contrast to this, the system would only provide notion S/SA if it does not leak any such information even for multiple, adversarially and adaptively chosen batches of communication (where certain conditions hold). This suggests that an anonymous communication system provides a privacy notion in {S/WU, R/WU, UL, S/SA, R/SA, S/WU$^+$, R/WU$^+$, (S/R)SA$^+$} only if it is, effectively immune to 'disclosure' (also known as 'hitting set') attacks [2, 25], while privacy notions in {$\overline{\text{SUL}}$, $\overline{\text{RUL}}$, $\overline{\text{UL}}$, $\overline{\text{SA}}$, $\overline{\text{RA}}$, $\overline{\text{SA}^*}$, $\overline{\text{RA}^*}$, $\overline{\text{SRA}}$} can be achieved without such immunity.

5   Conclusions and Open Questions

We presented an application-agnostic hierarchy of privacy notions that describe potentially different degrees to which the correspondence between digital elements and the users that cause their appearance remains hidden from an adversary. Previously isolated privacy notions pertaining to group signature and anonymous communication systems have been placed into this hierarchy, and thereby effectively made comparable. It is possible that privacy definitions pertaining to other system types, such as anonymous credentials, data anonymisation systems, and sensor information systems, can also be placed into our framework. Examining this possibility is subject of future research.

Our framework provides valuable insights into the relations and structure of different privacy notions, and highlights a largely unexplored space of such notions. Exemplarily, we identified two new notions for group signatures and pointed out how group signatures that match these definitions look like. Identifying useful schemes providing other 'new' notions, perhaps by trading off privacy against other features, is subject of future research. Of particular interest are techniques that transform systems achieving a given privacy notion into systems that provide another, perhaps stronger one in the adaptive adversarial model considered in this paper. We expect that the framework will also be useful in the construction and analysis of 'multi-layer' privacy protecting systems, i.e. systems that combine, for example, anonymous communication with group signing.

Finally, constructing 'soft', probabilistic privacy metrics for each of the notions in our framework is subject of current research. Such metrics will enable us to compare privacy protecting systems with considerably higher granularity than is possible with definitions that are based on asymptotic polynomial indistinguishability.

Acknowledgments

The authors would like to thank the anonymous reviewers for their insightful comments. This paper describes work undertaken partly in the context of the 'Integrating the Physical with the Digital World of the Network of the Future' (SENSEI) project (www.sensei-project.eu), and partly in the 'Secure Widespread Identities for Federated Telecommunications' (SWIFT) project (www.ist-swift.org). SENSEI and SWIFT are collaborative projects supported by the 7th European Framework Programme, with contract numbers 215923 and 215832, respectively.

References

1. Adida, B.: Advances in cryptographic voting systems. PhD thesis, Massachusetts Institute of Technology (2006)
2. Agrawal, D., Kesdogan, D.: Measuring anonymity: The disclosure attack. IEEE Security & Privacy 1(6), 27–34 (2003)
3. Andersson, C., Lundin, R.: On the fundamentals of anonymity metrics. In: The Future of Identity in the Information Society, IFIP International Federation for Information Processing. Springer Science & Business Media (2008)
4. Bellare, M., Desai, A., Jokipii, E., Rogaway, P.: A Concrete Security Treatment of Symmetric Encryption. In: Proceedings of the 38th Annual Symposium on Foundations of Computer Science (FOCS 1997), pp. 394–403 (1997)
5. Bellare, M., Micciancio, D., Warinschi, B.: Foundations of group signatures: Formal definitions, simplified requirements, and a construction based on general assumptions. In: Biham, E. (ed.) EUROCRYPT 2003. LNCS, vol. 2656, pp. 614–629. Springer, Heidelberg (2003)
6. Berman, R., Fiat, A., Ta-Shma, A.: Provable unlinkability against traffic analysis. In: Juels, A. (ed.) FC 2004. LNCS, vol. 3110, pp. 266–280. Springer, Heidelberg (2004)
7. Boneh, D., Shacham, H.: Group signatures with verifier-local revocation. In: ACM Conference on Computer and Communications Security, CCS 2004, pp. 168–177. ACM Press, New York (2004)
8. Camenisch, J., Lysyanskaya, A.: An efficient system for non-transferable anonymous credentials with optional anonymity revocation. In: Pfitzmann, B. (ed.) EUROCRYPT 2001. LNCS, vol. 2045, pp. 93–118. Springer, Heidelberg (2001)
9. Chaum, D.: Untraceable electronic mail, return addresses, and digital pseudonyms. Communications of the ACM 24(2), 84–90 (1981)
10. Clauß, S.: A framework for quantification of linkability within a privacy-enhancing identity management system. In: Müller, G. (ed.) ETRICS 2006. LNCS, vol. 3995, pp. 191–205. Springer, Heidelberg (2006)
11. Clauß, S., Schiffner, S.: Structuring anonymity metrics. In: DIM 2006: Proceedings of the second ACM workshop on Digital identity management, pp. 55–62. ACM Press, New York (2006)

12. Díaz, C.: Anonymity metrics revisited. In: Anonymous Communication and its Applications, number 05411 in Dagstuhl Seminar Proceedings (2005)
13. Díaz, C., Claessens, J., Seys, S., Preneel, B.: Information theory and anonymity. In: Macq, B., Quisquater, J. (eds.) Proceedings of the 23rd Symposium on Information Theory in the Benelux, pp. 179–186 (2002)
14. Díaz, C., Seys, S., Claessens, J., Preneel, B.: Towards measuring anonymity. In: Dingledine, R., Syverson, P.F. (eds.) PET 2002. LNCS, vol. 2482, pp. 54–68. Springer, Heidelberg (2003)
15. Edman, M., Sivrikaya, F., Yener, B.: A combinatorial approach to measuring anonymity. In: Proceedings of the 2007 IEEE International Conference on Intelligence and Security Informatics. IEEE, Los Alamitos (2007)
16. Feigenbaum, J., Johnson, A., Syverson, P.: Probabilistic analysis of onion routing in a black-box model. In: Proceedings of the 2007 ACM workshop on Privacy in electronic society, pp. 1–10. ACM Press, New York (2007)
17. Fiat, A., Shamir, A.: How to Prove Yourself: Practical Solutions to Identification and Signature Problems. In: Odlyzko, A.M. (ed.) CRYPTO 1986. LNCS, vol. 263, pp. 186–194. Springer, Heidelberg (1987)
18. Fischer, L., Katzenbeisser, S., Eckert, C.: Measuring unlinkability revisited. In: Winslett, M., R. H. to be published (ed.) Proceedings of the 2008 ACM Workshop on Privacy in the Electronic Society, WPES 2008, Alexandria, VA, USA, October 27. ACM, New York (2008)
19. Franz, M., Meyer, B., Pashalidis, A.: Attacking unlinkability: The importance of context. In: Borisov, N., Golle, P. (eds.) PET 2007. LNCS, vol. 4776, pp. 1–16. Springer, Heidelberg (2007)
20. Gierlichs, B., Troncoso, C., Díaz, C., Preneel, B., Verbauwhede, I.: Revisiting a combinatorial approach toward measuring anonymity. In: Proceedings of the 2008 ACM Workshop on Privacy in the Electronic Society, WPES 2008, Alexandria, VA, USA, October 27, pp. 111–116. ACM, New York (2008)
21. Goldwasser, S., Micali, S.: Probabilistic encryption. J. Comput. Syst. Sci. 28(2), 270–299 (1984)
22. Halpern, J.Y., O'Neill, K.R.: Anonymity and information hiding in multiagent systems. Journal of Computer Security 13(3), 483–514 (2005)
23. Hevia, A., Micciancio, D.: An Indistinguishability-Based Characterization of Anonymous Channels. In: Borisov, N., Goldberg, I. (eds.) PETS 2008. LNCS, vol. 5134, pp. 24–43. Springer, Heidelberg (2008)
24. Hughes, D., Shmatikov, V.: Information hiding, anonymity and privacy: a modular approach. Journal of Computer Security 12(1), 3–36 (2004)
25. Kesdogan, D., Agrawal, D., Penz, S.: Limits of anonymity in open environments. In: Petitcolas, F.A.P. (ed.) IH 2002. LNCS, vol. 2578, pp. 53–69. Springer, Heidelberg (2003)
26. Kiayias, A., Tsiounis, Y., Yung, M.: Traceable signatures. In: Cachin, C., Camenisch, J.L. (eds.) EUROCRYPT 2004. LNCS, vol. 3027, pp. 571–589. Springer, Heidelberg (2004)
27. Maitland, G., Reid, J., Foo, E., Boyd, C., Dawson, E.: Linkability in practical electronic cash design. In: Okamoto, E., Pieprzyk, J.P., Seberry, J. (eds.) ISW 2000. LNCS, vol. 1975, pp. 149–163. Springer, Heidelberg (2000)
28. Newman, R.E., Moskowitz, I.S., Syverson, P., Serjantov, A.: Metrics for traffic analysis prevention. In: Dingledine, R. (ed.) PET 2003. LNCS, vol. 2760, pp. 48–65. Springer, Heidelberg (2003)

29. Pashalidis, A.: Measuring the effectiveness and the fairness of relation hiding systems. In: Proceedings of the First International Workshop on Multimedia, Information Privacy and Intelligent Computing Systems. IEEE Computer Society Press, Los Alamitos (2008)
30. Pfitzmann, A., Köhntopp, M.: Anonymity, unobservability, and pseudonymity: A proposal for terminology. In: Federrath, H. (ed.) Designing Privacy Enhancing Technologies. LNCS, vol. 2009, pp. 1–9. Springer, Heidelberg (2001)
31. Serjantov, A.: On the Anonymity of Anonymity Systems. Phd thesis, University of Cambridge (2004)
32. Serjantov, A., Danezis, G.: Towards an information theoretic metric for anonymity. In: Dingledine, R., Syverson, P.F. (eds.) PET 2002. LNCS, vol. 2482, pp. 41–53. Springer, Heidelberg (2003)
33. Shmatikov, V., Wang, M.-H.: Measuring relationship anonymity in mix networks. In: WPES 2006: Proceedings of the 5th ACM workshop on Privacy in electronic society, pp. 59–62. ACM Press, New York (2006)
34. Steinbrecher, S., Köpsell, S.: Modelling unlinkability. In: Dingledine, R. (ed.) PET 2003. LNCS, vol. 2760, pp. 32–47. Springer, Heidelberg (2003)
35. Tóth, G., Hornák, Z., Vajda, F.: Measuring anonymity revisited. In: Liimatainen, S., Virtanen, T. (eds.) Proceedings of the Ninth Nordic Workshop on Secure IT Systems, Espoo, Finland, November 2004, pp. 85–90 (2004)

A   Proofs

A.1   Proof of Lemma 2

Proof. No group signature system can provide $\mathsf{SA}^*, \mathsf{PS}^*, \mathsf{SA}^+, \mathsf{PS}^+$ because the signed message is published along with its group signature; $\mathcal{A}$ can trivially win an $\mathbf{Exp}_{\Phi^A,\mathcal{A}}^{\mathrm{priv}-b}(k)$ experiment of providing different messages in the left and the right world. SA° and PS° are equivalent by Lemma 3, and SA and PS are distinct by Remark 3. $\qquad\square$

A.2   Proof of Lemma 3

Proof. We first show that PS° implies FA. An $\mathcal{A}_{\mathsf{PS}^\circ}$ adversary with access to an $\mathcal{A}_{\mathsf{FA}}$ adversary starts by corrupting all users, obtaining their secret keys, which it feeds into $\mathcal{A}_{\mathsf{FA}}$. $\mathcal{A}_{\mathsf{FA}}$ makes only one query which $\mathcal{A}_{\mathsf{PS}^\circ}$ passes on to the challenger and gives the response back to $\mathcal{A}_{\mathsf{FA}}$. The restriction $P_{f_0} = P_{f_1}$ is satisfied, since any two functions with a singleton domain induce the same partition on their domain. $\mathcal{A}_{\mathsf{PS}^\circ}$ answers in the same way as $\mathcal{A}_{\mathsf{FA}}$.

We show that FA also implies SA° by constructing an adversary $\mathcal{A}_{\mathsf{FA}}$ that has a non-negligible advantage in the FA-experiment, given black-box access to an adversary $\mathcal{A}_{\mathsf{SA}^\circ}$ with non-negligible advantage in a (computational) SA°-experiment. $\mathcal{A}_{\mathsf{FA}}$ proceeds as follows. It uniformly at random selects a value $i \in \mathbb{N}$ such that $1 \leq q(k)$, where $q(k)$ is the upper bound on the number of queries that $\mathcal{A}_{\mathsf{SA}^\circ}$ may issue. Using its knowledge of gsk, it answers $\mathcal{A}_{\mathsf{SA}^\circ}$'s first $i-1$ $\mathtt{input}((u_0,m),(u_1,m))$ queries with $\mathsf{GSig}(gsk[u_0],m)$. Before answering $\mathcal{A}_{\mathsf{SA}^\circ}$'s ith $\mathtt{input}((u_0,m'),(u_1,m'))$ query, it queries the challenger with the triple (u_0, u_1, m') with values taken from $\mathcal{A}_{\mathsf{SA}\circ}$'s query. $\mathcal{A}_{\mathsf{FA}}$ returns the challenger's answer σ' to $\mathcal{A}_{\mathsf{SA}\circ}$. Using its knowledge of gsk, it answers $\mathcal{A}_{\mathsf{SA}\circ}$'s remaining $\mathtt{input}((u_0, m), (u_1, m))$ queries with $\mathsf{GSig}(gsk[u_1], m)$, and finally outputs the same value as $\mathcal{A}_{\mathsf{SA}\circ}$. Using a standard hybrid argument [21], it can be shown that $\mathcal{A}_{\mathsf{FA}}$'s success probability is $(1/2) + \delta/q$, where q and δ are the number of queries issued by $\mathcal{A}_{\mathsf{SA}\circ}$ and $\mathcal{A}_{\mathsf{SA}\circ}$'s advantage, respectively. Since, as shown in Section 3.2, SA° implies PS°, a group signature system that provides FA also provides PS°.   □

A.3   Proof of Lemma 4

Proof. Consider an adversary $\mathcal{A}_{\overline{\mathsf{SUL}}}$. We construct an adversary $\mathcal{A}_{\mathsf{WU}}$ that wins an $\mathbf{Exp}_{\varPhi^A, \mathcal{A}}^{\mathsf{S}-\mathrm{priv}-b}(k)$ experiment if and only if $\mathcal{A}_{\overline{\mathsf{SUL}}}$ wins. Let C^0 and C^1 denote the collections output by $\mathcal{A}_{\overline{\mathsf{SUL}}}$. Due to the applicable restrictions $S = S^0 = S^1$, $R = R^0 = R^1$, $|\mathsf{sent}_\sigma^0| = |\mathsf{sent}_\sigma^1|$ for all $\sigma \in S$, and $\mathsf{rcvd}_\rho^0 = \mathsf{rcvd}_\rho^1$ for all $\rho \in R$ (see Table 1), for each triple $(\sigma_0, \rho_0, m_0) \in C^0$ there exists exactly one 'corresponding' triple in C^1, i.e. a triple (σ_1, ρ_1, m_1) such that $\rho_1 = \rho_0$ and $m_1 = m_0$. For each triple in $(\sigma_0, \rho_0, m_0) \in C_0$, $\mathcal{A}_{\mathsf{WU}}$ issues the query $\mathtt{input}((\sigma_0, (\rho_0, m_0)), (\sigma_1, (\rho_1, m_1)))$ where σ_1, ρ_1 and m_1 are the values from the corresponding triple in C^1. $\mathcal{A}_{\mathsf{WU}}$ then issues a $\mathtt{nextBatch}$ query, forwards the challenger's output to $\mathcal{A}_{\overline{\mathsf{SUL}}}$, and, finally outputs a guess that is identical to $\mathcal{A}_{\overline{\mathsf{SUL}}}$'s guess. Clearly, $\mathcal{A}_{\mathsf{WU}}$ wins if and only if $\mathcal{A}_{\overline{\mathsf{SUL}}}$ wins.

Consider adversary $\mathcal{A}_{\mathsf{WA}}$ of an $\mathbf{Exp}_{\varPhi^A, \mathcal{A}}^{\mathsf{S}-\mathrm{priv}-b}(k)$ experiment. We construct an adversary $\mathcal{A}_{\overline{\mathsf{SUL}}}$ who wins if and only if $\mathcal{A}_{\mathsf{WA}}$ wins. For every $\mathtt{input}((\sigma_0, (\rho_0, m_0)), (\sigma_1, (\rho_1, m_1)))$ query issued by $\mathcal{A}_{\mathsf{WA}}$, $\mathcal{A}_{\overline{\mathsf{SUL}}}$ adds the triple $(\sigma_0, (\rho_0, m_0))$ to C^0 and the triple $(\sigma_1, (\rho_1, m_1))$ to C^1. When $\mathcal{A}_{\mathsf{WA}}$ issues the $\mathtt{nextBatch}$ query, $\mathcal{A}_{\overline{\mathsf{SUL}}}$ starts its experiment with C^0 and C^1. Note that, due to the restrictions that apply in the experiment of $\mathcal{A}_{\mathsf{WA}}$, the collections C^0 and C^1, too, satisfy the required restrictions. $\mathcal{A}_{\overline{\mathsf{SUL}}}$ then forwards the challenger's output to $\mathcal{A}_{\mathsf{WA}}$, and, finally outputs a guess that is identical to $\mathcal{A}_{\mathsf{WA}}$'s guess. Clearly, $\mathcal{A}_{\overline{\mathsf{SUL}}}$ wins if and only if $\mathcal{A}_{\mathsf{WA}}$ wins. Thus, $\overline{\mathsf{SUL}}$ and $\mathsf{S/WU}$ are equivalent privacy notions. Showing the validity of the other equivalences is analogous.   □

Author Index